Henry B Davis, jr

GENERALS IN KHAKI

Henry Blaine Davis, jr.

GENERALS IN KHAKI

Henry Blaine Davis, jr.

Published by Pentland Press, Inc.
England • USA • Scotland

PUBLISHED BY PENTLAND PRESS, INC.
5122 Bur Oak Circle, Raleigh, North Carolina 27612
United States of America
919-782-0281

ISBN 1-57197-088-6
Library of Congress Catalog Card Number 97-069238

Printed in the United States of America

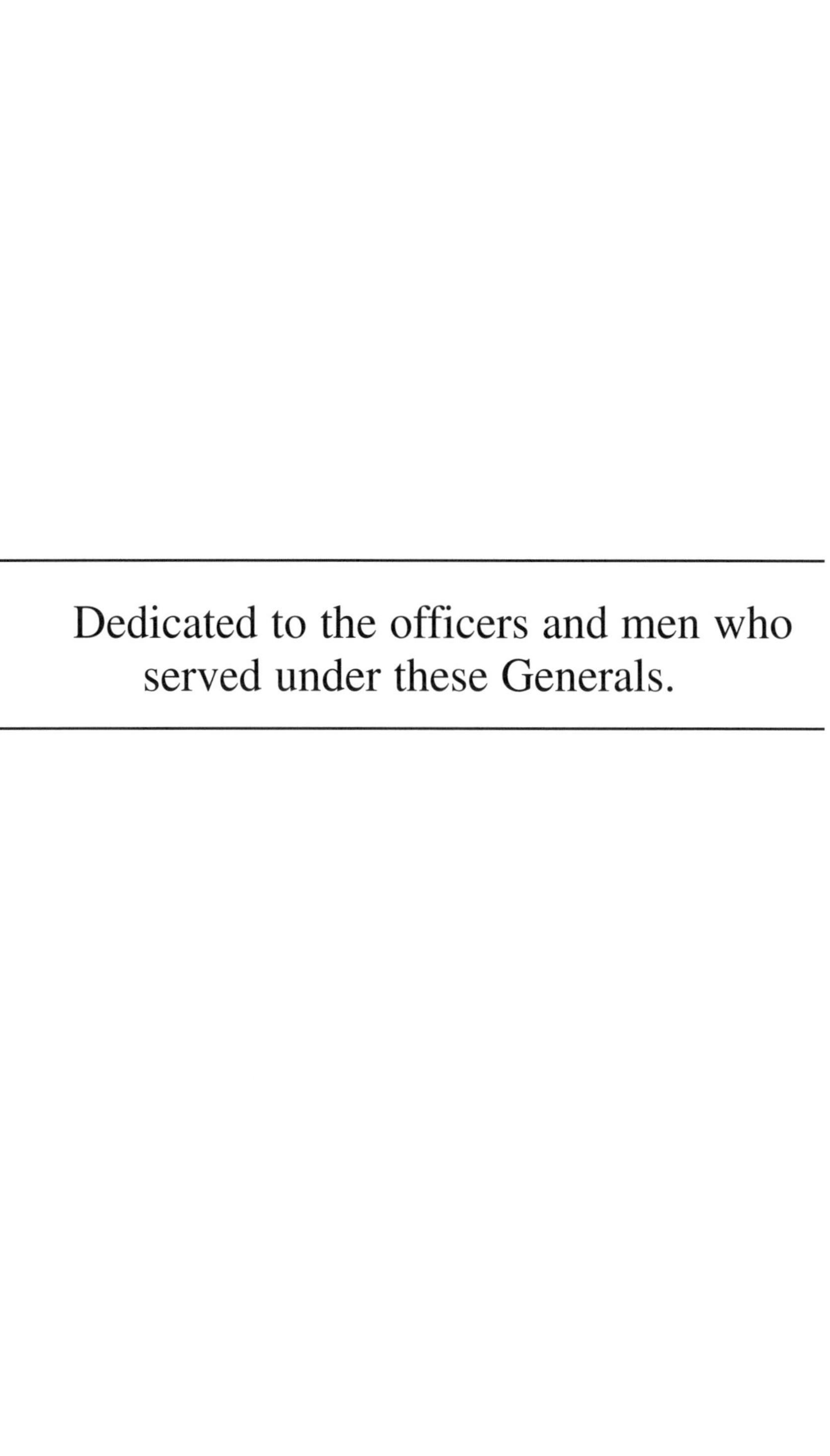

Dedicated to the officers and men who served under these Generals.

General Officers in World War I

Note to the reader: The Cullum numbers after the names are graduation numbers. An "x," given with the year of the class, designates a non-graduate who stayed most of the course.

Name Graduation Number Home State

1. Fredrick V. Abbott, 2760, Massachusetts
2. Frank H. Albright, 3237, Ohio
3. Robert Alexander, Maryland
4. William H. Allaire, Jr., 2964, Arkansas
5. Henry T. Allen, 2951, Kentucky
6. Hubert A. Allen, Iowa
7. George R. Allin, 4231, Iowa
8. Benjamin Alvord, Jr., 2948, Washington
9. Edward Anderson, 3267, Virginia
10. Edward D. Anderson, 3394, Tennessee
11. Avery D. Andrews, 3110, New York
12. Lincoln C. Andrews, 3524, Minnesota
13. Samuel T. Ansell, 3898, North Carolina
14. William H. Arthur, M.D., Pennsylvania
15. Thomas Q. Ashburn, 3802, Ohio
16. William W. Atterbury, Indiana
17. Dwight E. Aultman, 3576, Pennsylvania
18. Fred T. Austin, Vermont
19. Edwin Burr Babbitt, 3039, New York
20. Charles J. Bailey, 2834, Pennsylvania
21. Chauncey B. Baker, 3137, Ohio
22. Charles C. Ballou, 3159, New York
23. Frank E. Bamford, Wisconsin
24. Harry W. Bandholz, 3359, Michigan
25. Charles W. Barber, New Jersey
26. John W. Barker, 3611, New York
27. George C. Barnhardt, 3466, North Carolina

Name Graduation Number Home State

28. Malvern Hill Barnum, 3138, New York
29. John D. Barette, 3066, Louisiana
30. Thomas H. Barry, 2679, New York
31. Charles H. Barth, 2910, Iowa
32. George T. Bartlett, 2888, New Hampshire
33. William D. Beach, 2783, New York
34. George Bell, Jr., 2869, Maryland
35. James Franklin Bell, 2754, Kentucky
36. John B. Bennett, 3412, New Jersey
37. Lucian G. Berry, 3105, New York
38. Walter A. Bethel, 3295, Ohio
39. John Biddle, 2880, Michigan
40. Henry P. Birmingham, M.D., New York
41. Harry G. Bishop, 3796, Michigan
42. Percy P. Bishop, Tennessee
43. Alfred W. Bjornstad, Minnesota
44. William M. Black, 2641, Pennsylvania
45. Charles S. Blakely, 4243, Pennsylvania
46. George Blakely, 3453, Pennsylvania
47. Albert H. Blanding, Iowa
48. R. M. Blatchford, New York
49. Tasker H. Bliss, 2557, Pennsylvania
50. Augustus P. Blocksom, 2662, Ohio
51. Charles R. Boardman, Wisconsin
52. Ewing E. Booth, Missouri
53. Albert J. Bowley, 3754, California
54. Alfred E. Bradley, M.D., New York

55. John J. Bradley, 3437, Illinois
56. David L. Brainard, New York
57. Lloyd M. Brett, 2793, Maine
58. Andre W. Brewster, New Jersey
59. Raymond W. Briggs, Pennsylvania
60. Lytle Brown, 3812, Tennessee
61. Preston Brown, Kentucky
62. Robert A. Brown, 3068, Pennsylvania
63. Beverly F. Browne, 4025, Virginia
64. William Bryden, 4233, Connecticut
65. Beaumont B. Buck, 3087, Mississippi
66. Robert L. Bullard, 3084, Alabama
67. Omar Bundy, 3018, Indiana
68. William P. Burnham, x1881, Pennsylvania
69. Edward Burr, 2932, Missouri
70. George W. Burr, Jr., 3241, Illinois
71. Reynolds J. Burt, 3723, Nebraska
72. William H. Burt, Massachusetts
73. Wilson B. Burtt, 3906, Illinois
74. Henry W. Butner, 3826, North Carolina
75. DeRosey C. Cabell, 3028, Arkansas
76. Frank M. Caldwell, 3361, New York
77. Vernon A. Caldwell, 3384, Missouri
78. Robert E. Callan, 3672, Maryland
79. George H. Cameron, 2997, Illinois
80. Guy Carleton, 2895, Texas
81. John M. Carson, Jr., 3071, Pennsylvania
82. Jesse M. Carter, 3133, Missouri
83. Joseph C. Castner, New Jersey
84. J. L. Chamberlain, 2831, New York
85. William Chamberlaine, 3467, Virginia
86. Sherwood A. Cheney, 3246, Connecticut
87. Edward R. Chrisman, 3261, Indiana
88. Marlborough Churchill, Massachusetts
89. Harvey C. Clark, Missouri
90. Charles M. Clement, Pennsylvania
91. Frank S. Cocheu, 3590, New York
92. William B. Cochran, Virginia
93. Frank W. Coe, 3457, Kansas
94. Charles H. Cole, Massachusetts
95. William E. Cole, 3824, Utah
96. Fox Conner, 3825, Mississippi
97. William D. Connor, 3742, Wisconsin
98. Richard Coulter, Jr., Pennsylvania
99. Louis C. Covell, Michigan
100. Daniel F. Craig, Iowa
101. Malin Craig, 3841, Missouri
102. Charles Crawford, 3322, Ohio
103. George O. Cress, 3047, Illinois
104. Marcus D. Cronin, 3218, Massachusetts
105. Adelbert Cronkhite, New York
106. Enoch H. Crowder, 2909, Missouri
107. William Crozier, 2597, Ohio
108. William M. Cruikshank, Washington, D.C.
109. Thomas Cruse, 2785, Kentucky
110. Dennis H. Currie, 4024, Texas
111. Alexander L. Dade, 3219, Kentucky
112. Albert C. Dalton, Indiana
113. Robert M. Danford, 4247, Iowa
114. Thomas W. Darrah, 3637, Kansas
115. William R. Dashiell, 3275, Virginia
116. Richmond P. Davis, 3172, North Carolina
117. Robert C. Davis, 3844, Pennsylvania
118. Thomas F. Davis, 2585, New York
119. William C. Davis, 3345, New York
120. Peter W. Davison, 3494, Wisconsin
121. Charles G. Dawes, Ohio
122. Herbert Deakyne, 3333, Delaware
123. James T. Dean, 3225, Ohio
124. Edward H. DeArmond, 4040, Missouri

125. Charles I. DeBevoise, New York
126. Daniel B. DeVore, 3086, Ohio
127. Joseph T. Dickman, 2905, Ohio
128. Travey C. Dickson, 3455, Iowa
129. Brice P. Disque, Ohio
130. Arthur B. Donnelly, Missouri
131. Edward T. Donnelly, England
132. Charles B. Drake, 3696, Pennsylvania
133. Hugh A. Drum, Michigan
134. Thomas B. Dugan, 2962, Maryland
135. George B. Duncan, 3161, Kentucky
136. Lucius L. Durfee, 3163, Ohio
137. Clarence R. Edwards, 3020, Ohio
138. Oliver Edwards, 3602, Massachusetts
139. LeRoy Eltinge, 3678, New York
140. Hanson E. Ely, 3447, Iowa
141. William P. Ennis, 4013, California
142. James B. Erwin, 2848, Georgia
143. George H. Estes, Jr., 3599, Alabama
144. Fredric D. Evans, 3229, Illinois
145. Samuel L. Faison, 3009, North Carolina
146.Charles S. Farnsworth, 3220, Pennsylvania
147. William M. Fassett, 3782, New Hampshire
148. Harley B. Ferguson, 3248, North Carolina
149. Frank K. Fergusson, 3200, Tennessee
150. John M. T. Finney, Mississippi
151. Harold B. Fiske, 3766, Oregon
152. Clement A. F. Flagler, 3284, Georgia
153. Adrian S. Fleming, 3632, Kentucky
154. Fredric S. Foltz, 2774, Pennsylvania
155. Stephen M. Foote, 3030, Michigan
156. David Jack Foster, Illinois
157. Benjamin D. Foulois, Connecticut
158. Francis H. French, 2771, Indiana
159. Amos A. Fries, 3815, Wisconsin
160. Charles D. Gaither, Maryland
161. Ernest A. Garlington, South Carolina
162. Joseph A. Gaston, 2894, Pennsylvania
163. George W. Gatchell, 3186, Rhode Island
164. George G. Gatley, 3355, Maine
165. Charles Gerheart, 3221, Maryland
166. Robert N. Getty, 2750, New York
167. George S. Gibbs, Iowa
168. William. J. Glasgow, 3414, Missouri
169. Pelham D. Glassford, 4232, New Mexico
170. Edwin F. Glenn, 2699, North Carolina
171. James D. Glennan, M.D., New York
172. George W. Goethals, 2828, New York
173. Walter H. Gordon, 3148, Mississippi
174. William C. Gorgas, M.D., Alabama
175. William S. Graves, 3323, Texas
176. Edward Saint J. Greble, 2884, New York
177. Henry A. Greene, 2777, New York
178. William G. Haan, 3293, Indiana
179. Johnson Hagood, 3691, South Carolina
180. Harry C. Hale, 3004, Illinois
181. Herman Hall, 3215, Illinois
182. Daniel W. Hand, Minnesota
183. Thomas G. Hanson, 3209, California
184. James G. Harbord, Illinois
185. George H. Harries, Wales
186. Peter C. Harris, 3268, Georgia
187. Walter A. Harris, Georgia
188. John D. L. Hartman, 3257, Pennsylvania
189. William W. Harts, 3286, Illinois
190. William Edwin Harvey, Missouri
191. Everard E. Hatch, 3035, Maine
192. Henry J. Hatch, Michigan
193. William H. Hay, 3142, Florida
194. John L. Hayden, 3243, Illinois

195. Ira A. Haynes, 2983, Kentucky

196. John W. Heard, 3001, Mississippi

197. Clint C. Hearn, 3344, Texas

198. John W. Heavy, 3417, Illinois

199. Charles A. Hedekin, 3251, Indiana

200. Gordon G. Heiner, 3518, Washington, D.C.

201. Stuart Heintzelman, 3910, New York

202. Eli A. Helmick, 3276, Indiana

203. Guy V. Henry, Jr., 3853, Nebraska

204. Andrew Hero, Jr., 3392, Louisiana

205. Mark L. Hersey, 3232, Maine

206. H.R. Hickock, 3484, Missouri

207. Henry R. Hill, Illinois

208. Ernest Hinds, 3181, Alabama

209. Frank T. Hines, Utah

210. John L. Hines, 3432, West Virginia

211. Harry F. Hodges, 2882, Massachusetts

212. Henry C. Hodges, 2901, Washington

213. John N. Hodges, 4351, Maryland

214. Roy Hoffman, Kansas

215. Lucius R. Holbrook, 3703, Wisconsin

216. Willard A. Holbrook, 3024, Wisconsin

217. Tieman N. Horn, 3393, New York

218. James J. Hornbrook, 3363, Indiana

219. Odus C. Horney, 3380, Illinois

220. Harold P. Howard, 3407, Minnesota

221. Robert L. Howze, 3260, Texas

222. John A. Hulen, Missouri

223. Ora E. Hunt, 3591, California

224. George K. Hunter, 2707, Ohio

225. Grote Hutcheson, 3045, Ohio

226. Henry Hutchings, England

227. Meritte W. Ireland, M.D., Indiana

228. James A. Irons, 2808, Pennsylvania

229. George L. R. Irwine, 3305, Michigan

230. William P. Jackson, 3428, Missouri

231. Edgar Jadwin, 3331, Pennsylvania

232. George H. Jamerson, 3556, Virginia

233.Charles C. Jamieson, 3463, New Hampshire

234. Melville S. Jarvis, 3416, West Virginia

235. Henry Jervey, 3238, Virginia

236. Arthur Johnson, 3157, Minnesota

237. Evan M. Johnson, New York

238. Hugh S. Johnson, 4174, Kansas

239. William O. Johnson, 3336, Kentucky

240. John A. Johnston, 2782, Pennsylvania

241. William H. Johnston, Ohio

242. William V. Judson, 3240, Indiana

243. Jefferson R. Kean, M.D., Virginia

244. Charles Keller, 3332, New York

245. William L. Kenley, 3292, Maryland

246. Chase W. Kennedy, 2986, Ohio

247. Lyman W. V. Kennon, 2928, Rhode Island

248. Francis J. Kernan, 2896, Florida

249. James T. Kerr, 2906, West Virginia

250. Daniel W. Ketcham, 3351, Indiana

251. Charles Kilbourne, Virginia

252. John W. Kilbreth, New York

253. Campbell King, North Carolina

254. Edward L. King, 3717, Massachusetts

255. Albert D. Kniskern, 3121, Illinois

256. Francis J. Koester, 3252, Pennsylvania

257. Charles R. Krauthoff, Missouri

258. Edward A. Kreger, Iowa

259. Joseph E. Kuhn, 3058, Kansas

260. Charles W. Kutz, 3513, Pennsylvania

261. Eugene F. Ladd, 3032, Vermont

262. William C. Langfitt, 2970, Virginia

263. William Lassiter, 3304, Virginia

264. Howard L. Laubach, 3520, Pennsylvania

265. Laurin L. Lawson, Minnesota
266. Henry G. Learnard, 3362, Missouri
267. Joseph D. Leitch, 3325, Michigan
268. Michael J. Lenihan, 3230, Massachusetts
269. James W. Lester, New York
270. Edward M. Lewis, 3166, Indiana
271. Hunter Liggett, 2800, Pennsylvania
272. James R. Lindsay, 3346, New York
273. Julian R. Lindsey, 3481, Georgia
274. William Littebrant, 3278, California
275. Isaac W. Littell, 2996, New Jersey
276. P. D. Lochridge, 3194, Alabama
277. Albert J. Logan, Pennsylvania
278. Rufus E. Longan, 3228, Missouri
279. Herbert M. Lord, Maine
280. LeRoy S. Lyon, 3391, Pennsylvania
281. Theodore C. Lyster, M.D., Kansas
282. Douglas MacArthur, 4122, Arkansas
283. John F. Madden, California
284. John S. Mallory, 2815, Virginia
285. Paul B. Malone, 3579, New York
286. William A. Mann, 2574, Pennsylvania
287. Peyton C. March, 3247, Pennsylvania
288. Francis Marshall, 3349, Illinois
289. Richard C. Marshall, Virginia
290. Charles H. Martin, 3192, Indiana
291. Charles I. Martin, Illinois
292. William F. Martin, 3094, Ohio
293. Frank G. Mauldin, 3350, South Carolina
294. U. G. McAlexander, 3226, Minnesota
295. James W. McAndrew, 3249, Pennsylvania
296. Henry P. McCain, 3077, Mississippi
297. Walter D. McCaw, M.D., Virginia
298. Manus McClosky, 3816, Pennsylvania
299. Nathaniel F. McClure, 3196, Kentucky
300. Frank R. McCoy, 3775, Pennsylvania
301. John B. McDonald, 2930, Alabama
302. Munroe McFarland, 3269, Maryland
303. Edward F. McGlaghlin, 3301, Wisconsin
304. James F. McIndoe, 3388, Maryland
305. Augustine McIntyre, 3991, Tennessee
306. Frank McIntyre, 3106, Alabama
307. George W. McIver, 2950, North Carolina
308. Charles H. McKinstry, 3239, California
309. John E. McMahon, 3107, New York
310. William V. McMaken, Ohio
311. George H. McManus, 3520, Iowa
312. Leslie J. McNair, 4225, Minnesota
313. William S. McNair, 3353, Michigan
314. Clarence H. McNeil, 3679, New York
315. James H. McRae, 3144, Georgia
316. Samuel McRoberts, Missouri
317. Robert W. Mearns, 3510, Pennsylvania
318. Charles T. Menoher, 3112, Pennsylvania
319. Wilder S. Metcalf, Maine
320. Robert L. Michie, 3083, Virginia
321. Edward A. Millar, 2945, Pennsylvania
322. Samuel W. Miller, 2817, Pennsylvania
323. William L. Mitchell, France
324. George D. Moore, 3373, Pennsylvania
325. John F. Morrison, 2904, New York
326. Jay Johnson Morrow, 3389, Virginia
327. Benjamin C. Morse, 3054, Missouri
328. Charles G. Morton, 2986, Maine
329. George Van H. Moseley, 3904, Illinois
330. Andrew Moses, 3797, Texas
331. Charles H. Muir, 3065, Michigan
332. Edward L. Munson, M.D., Connecticut
333. Peter Murray, 3370, California
334. William K. Naylor, Illinois

335. Henry C. Newcomer, 3097, Pennsylvania
336. William J. Nicholson, Washington, D.C.
337. Robert E. Noble, M.D., Georgia
338. Robert H. Noble, 3052, Maryland
339. Dennis E. Nolan, 3719, New York
340. George A. Nugent, 3821, Michigan
341. Louis M. Nuttman, 3647, New Jersey
342. Joseph P. O'Neil, New York
343. Christopher O'Neill, Wales
344. John F. O'Ryan, New York
345. Francis L. Parker, 3524, South Carolina
346. Frank Parker, 3592, South Carolina
347. James Parker, 2623, New Jersey
348. Mason M. Patrick, 3098, West Virginia
349. William S. Peirce, 3245, Vermont
350. Julius A. Penn, 3165, Illinois
351. Frederick Perkins, 3017, Maine
352. John J. Pershing, 3126, Missouri
353. Charles Phillips, 2891, Illinois
354. Edward H. Plummer, 2660, Maryland
355. Benjamin A. Poore, 3129, Alabama
356. Guy H. Preston, 3262, Massachusetts
357. Harrison J. Price, West Virginia
358. William G. Price, Pennsylvania
359. William C. Rafferty, Indiana
360. George W. Read, 3008, Iowa
361. Robert I. Rees, Michigan
362. Thomas H. Rees, 3100, Michigan
363. Frederick E. Resche, Germany
364. Charles D. Rhodes, 3307, Ohio
365. John H. Rice, 3519, Missouri
366. Charles Richard, M.D., New York
367. Randolph A. Richards, Wisconsin
368. Wilds P. Richardson, Texas
369. Tyree R. Rivers, 2999, Mississippi
370. William C. Rivers, 3197, Tennessee
371. Samuel D. Rockenbach, Virginia
372. Harry L. Rogers, Washington, D.C.
373. William H. Rose, 4130, Pennsylvania
374. Otho B. Rosenbaum, 3598, Virginia
375. John W. Ruckman, 2979, Illinois
376. Colden H. Ruggles, 3335, Nebraska
377. Edgar Russell, Missouri
378. James A. Ryan, 3358, Connecticut
379. George C. Saffarans, 3425, Tennessee
380. William H. Sage, 2952, New York
381. Charles M. Saltzman, Iowa
382. William R. Sample, 3266, Tennessee
383. Ferrand Sayre, 3041, Missouri
384. S. J. G. Schindel, 3526, New Jersey
385. Hugh L. Scott, 2628, Kentucky
386. William S. Scott, 2852, Texas
387. George P. Scriven, 2721, Pennsylvania
388. David C. Shanks, 3053, Virginia
389. Henry G. Sharpe, 2872, New York
390. Frederick B. Shaw, New Jersey
391. George H. Shelton, 3704, Connecticut
392. John H. Sherburne, Massachusetts
393. James A. Shipton, 3464, Ohio
394. Walter Cowen Short, Ohio
395. William L. Sibert, 3027, Alabama
396. Edward Sigerfoos, Ohio
397. Benjamin T. Simmons, North Carolina
398. George S. Simonds, Iowa
399. Fred W. Sladen, 3357, Massachusetts
400. William R. Smedberg, Jr., 3257, California
401. Abiel L. Smith, 2756, Missouri
402. Harry A. Smith, 3423, Kansas
403. Matthew C. Smith, 3541, Alabama
404. William R. Smith, 3459, Tennessee

405. William J. Snow, 3354, New York
406. Oliver L. Spaulding, Michigan
407. John C. Speaks, Ohio
408. Marcellus G. Spinks, 3828, Mississippi
409. George O. Squier, 3180, Michigan
410. Sanford B. Stanbery, Ohio
411. Alfred E. Starbird, Maine
412. Robert E. Steiner, Alabama
413. John E. Stephens, 3817, Tennessee
414. Merch B. Stewart, 3715, Virginia
415. Frederick W. Stilwell, Pennsylvania
416. Frederick S. Strong, 2837, Michigan
417. Samuel D. Sturgis, Jr., 3033, Missouri
418. Henry D. Styer, 3049, Pennsylvania
419. Charles P. Sumerall, 3469, Florida
420. Archibald H. Sunderland, Illinois
421. E. Leroy Sweetzer, Massachusetts
422. Eben Swift, 2621, Texas
423. Harry Taylor, New Hampshire
424. William S. Thayer, M.D., Massachusetts
425. John T. Thompson, Kentucky
426. Henry Davis Todd, Jr., 2942, New York
427. Orval P. Townshend, Illinois
428. Clarence P. Townsley, 2892, New York
429. Peter E. Traub, 3127, New York
430. Charles G. Treat, 2944, Maine
431. Guy E. Tripp, Maine
432. Alexander M. Tuthill, M.D., New York
433. Lawrence D. Tyson, 3019, North Carolina
434. LaRoy S. Upton, 3422, Michigan
435. Cornelius Vanderbilt, New York
436. Robert C. VanVliet, Kansas
437. Cecil Vaughan, Jr., Virginia
438. Edward Vollrath, Ohio
439. Lutz Wahl, 3427, Wisconsin
440. Charles C. Walcutt, 3123, Ohio
441. Meriwether L. Walker, 3514, Virginia
442. Robert D. Walsh, 3005, California
443. Frank B. Watson, Virginia
444. Erasmus M. Weaver, 2563, Indiana
445. Edgar A. Wedgewood, Massachusetts
446. William Weigel, 3200, New Jersey
447. Briant H. Wells, 3610, Utah
448. William E. Welsh, 3606, Pennsylvania
449. William T. Westervelt, South Carolina
450. Charles B. Wheeler, 3127, Illinois
451. Henry H. Whitney, 3460, Pennsylvania
452. Pegram Whitworth, 3615, Louisiana
453. Wilber E. Wilder, 2672, Michigan
454. Harry E. Wilkins, 3187, Illinois
455. Clarence C. Williams, 3566, Georgia
456. Herbert O. Williams, 3440, Mississippi
457. Roger D. Williams, Kentucky
458. William Wilson, New York
459. Edwin B. Winans, 3403, Michigan
460. George A. Wingate, New York
461. Frank L. Winn, 3158, Kentucky
462. John S. Winn, 3246, Kentucky
463. E. E. Winslow, 3282, Washington, D.C.
464. Francis A. Winter, M.D., Louisiana
465. Edmund Wittenmyer, 3228, Ohio
466. Paul A. Wolf, 3371, Illinois
467. Leonard Wood, M.D., New Hampshire
468. Robert E. Wood, 3952, Missouri
469. William T. Wood, 2682, Illinois
470. John E. Woodward, 3500, Vermont
471. William M. Wright, x1886, New Jersey
472. Richard W. Young, 2946, Utah
473. Charles X. Zimmerman, Ohio
474. John Lincoln Clem, Ohio
475. Frederick Funston, Ohio
476. Andrew Summers Rowan, Virginia

Foreword

Henry Blaine Davis' new catalogue of World War I general officers, *Generals In Khaki*, duplicates nothing that has ever been compiled or published yet . . . It is a brand new contribution to the history of the United States in World War I. Considering the relatively brief length of our participation in this war, the number of general officers (473) might seem surprisingly large. It is a bit less than the number of Union Generals in the Civil War (583). Yet every general is there complete with picture. Additionally, there are numerous asides not found elsewhere. This book with its thoroughly researched biographical entries of each general is indispensable for libraries, historians, military researchers and war history buffs. Mr. Davis, a former horse cavalry officer and military museum director, brings to this work the thoroughness and honesty indispensible for the historian.

Joseph H. Ewing
Lt. Col., AUS-Ret
Staff Curator, Army Museums Ret
Author of *Sherman At War*

Preface

Why *Generals in Khaki*? Because khaki was the color of the service uniform of the United States Army at the time of the First World War and for a long time afterwards. It was eventually supplanted by olive drab, otherwise known as "OD." There were blue fatigues at that time, but they were worn only in the stables or during kitchen police or other dirty work, and were often worn over the uniform. When the British were fighting on the northwestern frontier of India in the last quarter of the nineteenth century, troops actually went into the field in white uniforms. The sometimes-hostile natives thought this was just great, as the Brits made much better targets and were killed by the score. However, the men weren't altogether foolish—they took handsful of mud and bedaubed themselves into a color that was more difficult to spot, i.e., dirt-colored, or khaki. This word may be pronounced "cocky" or "kaaky," depending on just how you choose to handle or mishandle the letter "a." Either way is acceptable and understood. By the time of the Boer War, the British army had gone to khaki so, of course, we promptly copied them.

In the American army, at the time of the First World War, there were 473 general officers in the National Army. Remember also that as of 6 April 1917, these 473 generals were of all ages; a few had graduated from West Point as recently as 1905, but others either were teetering on retirement or were a bit overripe. They came from almost all of the forty-eight contiguous states, and several were born abroad. One cannot talk of people who lived through this historic period without mentioning the terrible flu epidemic that raged from 1918 to 1920, both in the United States and in Europe. This epidemic took more human lives than all of our wars put together to the present time, both in the service and among the civilian population. There were neither miracle drugs nor antibiotics at that time, and few were the families that lost neither a friend nor a relative.

The generals described here are listed alphabetically, irrespective of rank. Among them were only three four-star generals and two three-star generals (i.e., lieutenant generals); there were also 108 major generals, and the rest were brigadier generals. There were at that time neither African American nor female general officers. Four generals had been appointed from civilian life because of extraordinary qualities needed by the government in the prosecution of the war—William W. Atterbury, Charles G. Dawes, Samuel McRoberts and Guy E. Tripp. For the sake of convenience,they are referred to here as "the civilian generals." Fifteen were medical officers, not including Leonard Wood and Alexander Tuthill (both doctors), who served as line officers. Approximately 352 were West Point graduates. Although we use the words interchangeably, West Point is actually a geographical location; the school itself is the United States Military Academy (USMA). The remaining generals were commissioned from the ranks, or were medical, civilian, National Guard or organized militia officers.

The USMA graduates are the easiest to track, through either the *Annual Report* (published up until World War II) or *The Assembly* (published since

World War II). Both are published by the Association of Graduates of the United States Military Academy. Of those in combat command in France, almost all were USMA graduates. William G. Price, Jr. of Pennsylvania and Roy Hoffman of Oklahoma were two of the rare exceptions. Many of these men achieved much more prominence after the war than during it, and some are more commonly known by their higher World War II rank. However, the rank used in this text is that of the World War I period. Many also fought against the American Indians; in fact, one of the officers present at the Battle of the Little Big Horn (Charles A. Varnum), while not a general officer, was still on duty during World War I.

This book makes no pretension of being a lengthy or detailed tome on any of its profiled subjects. Many of the more prominent have already been written up elsewhere, and many others were so obscure that they left almost no paper trail. The occasional carryover of Civil War or early American names is no accident; for example, see the entries on Cornelius Vanderbilt and Marlborough Churchill (USA).

Each name listed at the beginning of the book appears as the officer used it, and the full name of the officer appears with his biography. Some cases, e.g., P. D. Lochridge (whose initials, "P." and "D.," stand for nothing), remind us of Harry S. Truman (whose middle initial, "S.," represents nothing). Following the name is the army serial number (ASN); this number came into being in February 1918 for enlisted men and in 1921 for officers. Some died or were discharged prior to those dates and never had a serial number. Some, frankly, we just don't know.

Class standing in the graduating class was not only academic; it also helped to determine relative rank. Remember, a high percentage of these men entered USMA via very competitive examinations, so placing number forty-four of forty-five in a class does not attach any stigma to the individual as "standing behind the door." Standards were high, and the whole class was above average. Many top-ranking cadets fell into obscurity, not necessarily through any fault of their own. Not being famous does not mean that they were not good officers. Many anchor men (at the bottom of their class at graduation) had creditable careers.

There were considerable differences in commissions, which ranged from National Guard, Regular Army and Organized Reserve. National Army during World War I became Army of the United States during World War II. A regular commission is normally for life, and is no bar to holding a National Army or an AUS commission. It is through the federal government and is a full-time job. A National Guard commission can be from any one of the fifty states, is a voluntary affair, and is not under normal circumstances a full-time job. A guard officer may not serve under the federal government until he is federally recognized, i.e., approved by Uncle Sam. A reserve officer has no state connection, but when called to duty serves directly under the federal government. Any of these three categories may also hold a national army or AUS commission for the duration of any emergency. The holding of an NA or AUS commission in no way affects the regular commission, to which an officer reverts after the emergency is over. Also, an officer does not necessarily retire in the highest grade held. (This varies with the historical period.) He may be promoted on the retired list or posthumously.

Brevet rank, which no longer exists, was a recognition of some deed or feat (similar feats are now rewarded by a medal). It was an earlier and cheaper way for the government to give recognition, and it caused a great deal of confusion. The holder of brevet rank seldom served in that capacity. If he did, of course, then he wore the insignia, had an appropriate-sized command, and drew the pay. Otherwise, it was an empty and mostly social title. To the best of this writer's knowledge, there has been no brevet rank since Tasker H. Bliss was made a four-star general (by brevet) in 1918, for use at the Supreme War Council and the Paris Peace Conference.

Elbert Hubbard's great essay entitled "A Message to Garcia" is included herein because it sets the tone of action that typified many of these generals, and is a fine thing for any young soldier or officer to know well. Also, there are three biographical sketches that do not strictly fall into the category of this book: Johnny Clem, the drummer boy of Shiloh; Frederick Funston, who was headed for the command in Europe but quite unexpectedly died too soon (see the entry on Douglas MacArthur), and Andrew Summers Rowan, who never became a general at all, but whose performance of duty was the subject of the essay by Elbert Hubbard. His spirit and performance of duty earned him a place with the greatest.

Frontier duty was service at any of the small posts throughout the American West and was excellent training for the young officer, while not so desirable for the older ones. It came to an end in the 1890s.

The standing-collar blouse khaki uniform appeared at the turn of the last century, and it was no harder on the neck than the civilian starched collar of the period. For an example, see any photo of Presidents Woodrow Wilson or Herbert Hoover, or Vice President Charles G. Dawes. People were accustomed to it. While the roll-collar blouse (comparable to the coat of civilian business suits) became "regulation" on 1 January 1927, the standing collars were still used until World War II, when they were issued to many of the incoming draftees.

It was decided that all general officers in the United States should undergo a physical examination in Washington, D.C. before being declared eligible to go overseas, which was done from December 1917 to January 1918. Expectedly, many were eliminated, both National Guard and Regular. Those National Guard generals had to be traced through the various state archives, and they could be difficult to locate. Since some were discharged before 1921 they never had a serial number.

There is much variety in the clothing worn by the generals illustrated in this work. Some are in "civvies," and the word "mufti" was as unused as "tunic" in the American army. They wore blouses, and that was that. The civvies reflect the period as much as the uniforms do—hard collars, bow ties, et cetera. Among the uniforms, you will see some in cadet gray. (They are actually cadet photos.) Guy V. Henry, Jr. was quite proud of the fact that at his retirement dinner he could (and did) wear his cadet uniform. The greatest number by far are wearing the standing-collar blouse with either the garrison cap (with a flat, rounded top), which we copied from the British, or the overseas cap, copied from the French and Belgians.

The campaign hat (an American-style hat) was not used much with the blouse. It is still used by our drill sergeants and by the Canadian Mounties. At the time of World War I, all enlisted personnel wore a hat cord with the campaign hat. The color of the cord showed their arm of service: blue for infantry, red for artillery and yellow for cavalry. Only general officers wore gold hat cords. You will even see at least one American general wearing the American spiked dress helmet, which lasted well into the first decade of this century. Our version of the *Pickelhaube* was used with a spike for dismounted personnel, and a horsehair plume in a "bud vase" (yes, that is what they actually called it) for mounted personnel only.

We adopted the Sam Browne belt of the British army, which was worn only by overseas officers at first, then spread throughout the entire commissioned personnel of the army. It was normally worn with a single strap over the right shoulder to take the weight of the officer's saber, which, when worn, was on the left side. The Sam Browne was also used (with both shoulder straps) as the officer's field belt; the back straps were crossed, the front ones vertical. This was meant to carry the entire weight of the field equipment: pistol, pistol magazine pouch, canteen, first aid packet, compass and field glasses.

You will see quite a variety of dress uniforms, always dark blue and double-breasted with bright buttons and heavy, gold shoulder knots or epaulets. For field grade officers, the collar, cuffs and caps had a colored stripe indicating the branch of service of the wearer (similar to the colored cord on the hat): white and/or light blue for infantry, red for artillery and yellow for cavalry. General officers, by definition, did not wear the insignia or color of a particular arm or branch. The sole exception to this was the chief of an arm or branch, who wore both the collar insignia and the branch color.

Occasionally, you will see a roll-collar blouse, which is cut like a modern single-breasted business suit coat, and which became regulation on 1 January 1927. The photo of J. Franklin Bell is a good illustration of the old general officer's full dress uniform. The three-button spacing indicates a major general, while a brigadier would have had two-button spacing (see the photo of Christopher O'Neil). The coat had the cut and length of a frock coat and was decorated with heavy gold epaulets that were fringed at the end. A general officer's blouse also had black velvet on the cuffs and collar.

Long trousers were worn with the dress uniform, and with the service uniform everyone wore breeches and usually boots, regardless of the arm or service. Spurs were almost always worn, with the sole exception of the air service or air corps. The quality and cut of our boots and breeches improved considerably after contact with the British boot makers and tailors; after World War I both items were made with higher quality in the United States. Design and cut of breeches were important so they would not get horizontal tears above the knees from riding, bending or squatting. Stretch cloth was far off in the future. Infantry officers who were not mounted usually wore a combination of work shoes and puttees, minus the spurs, instead of riding boots. The men wore breeches and either canvas leggings or wrap puttees. In the last days of mounted troops, they had both three-buckle and laced full-height leather boots.

Fatigues (the army's term for work clothing) were made of blue denim; they were used for mechanical work, painting, stable work, horseshoeing and KP, but were never worn off post. To have done so would have incurred company punishment.

The officer's overcoat had a double row of plain horn (or composition) buttons, not brass. A general officer's overcoat cuffs had a black band with varying width, according to his rank and the appropriate number of stars to be placed on the band.

The shoulder patch (which was widely used during the Civil War and disappeared as the need for it disappeared) came back into use while the army was in France. During World War I, all blouse buttons were darkened, but by 1921 they were bright again.

So you thought the army used only horses, mules, dogs and camels way back when? See the entry on Daniel B. DeVore.

Edward Sigerfoos, born in Potsdam, Germany, did not live long enough to receive news of his promotion, as he was leading his brigade into action when he was killed. Another general made a round trip from major to brigadier to major again in nine months. See the entry on Archibald Sunderland. Henry R. Hill died with a captured smoking German pistol in his hand just after taking five German machine gun nests.

To avoid being mess officer, see the entry on Paul A. Wolf. The oldest living graduate (at age 104) was L. M. Nuttman. There were about ten or twelve officers on duty during World War I who still wore a beard. One was knighted by King George V of England. You find him!

When army officer serial numbers were assigned in July 1921, the first ten were as follows:

0-1, John J. Pershing; 0-2, Leonard Wood; 0-3, Hunter Liggett; 0-4, John F. Morrison; 0-5, C. G. Morton; 0-6, Peyton C. March; 0-7, Frank McIntyre; 0-8, George O. Squier; 0-9, John L. Chamberlain and 0-10, Enoch H. Crowder.

While conducting the research for this book, we encountered several stumbling blocks, of which I will mention only a few. We were aware of Brig. Gen. William D. Brach, but he was not on the list of World War I generals in the 1950 Army Almanac. We checked him out, determined that he should be included, and added him in. We tried every known source for Gen. William D. Brach—the Register of Graduates, Cullum, Heitman, the army list, the guard and militia lists, World War I insurance records, biographical references by the dozen, and the Mormon Church records. (We even tried the Brach candy company!) This work involved many letters and phone calls over a long period of time, but it was all to no avail. Then, a good researcher, Mike Winey of the United States Army Military History Institute at Carlisle Barracks, Pennsylvania, made the suggestion that the name "Brach" could have been a typographical error for "Beach." In both cases the Christian name is the same—William. The second letter of the surname and the middle initial are the only variances. The letters "e" and "r" are adjoining on any standard keyboard, and anyone is prone to make a mistake. The dates of rank are the same, so we just buried the nonexistent Brig. Gen. William L. Brach.

We also incurred a long search for Brig. Gen. James D. Gleman, after which (and with a little help from Mr. S. Paul Klein of the Walter Reed Army Research Institute) it turned out that "Gleman," too, was a typo. The name was James D. Glennan.

To the best of my knowledge and belief, the list used in this book is complete and correct. I am human and therefore subject to error, and if any errors exist I would be glad to hear about them. There have not been any deliberate omissions of the names of children, but the subjects themselves did not always mention their families. Many of the families and descendants (who have been most helpful) will have better photos than we sometimes used, but we had to use what was available. The photos were taken at many different periods and show quite a variety of uniforms and clothing.

In 1780, with orders from George Washington, both the one-star insignia of a brigadier general and the two-star insignia of a major general became regulation. There was no higher rank. Beginning in 1832, an eagle was worn on the shoulders of a colonel, and four years later, in 1836, lieutenant colonels and majors got their oak leaves (silver for the higher ranking). Also, captains got a double silver bar and first lieutenants got a single bar. There was no insignia of rank for second lieutenants until 1919, when they received a gold bar like that of a first lieutenant. Curiously, the silver insignia outranked the gold, both with oak leaves and bars. Ulysses S. Grant became a lieutenant general (with three stars) and later, a four-star general. Five-star rank did not occur until December 1944, when George C. Marshall, Douglas MacArthur, Dwight D. Eisenhower and Henry H. Arnold received that rank, in that order. While both four- and five-star generals are addressed merely as "General," the rank would have been titled "Field Marshal," except for the surname of our then-Chief of Staff. "Field Marshal Marshall" would have sounded a bit redundant (or ridiculous). No generals of that rank are still alive. The five stars were smaller than the usual size and were in a circle, rather than a straight line, on the shoulder strap.

If you have any valid corrections or interesting additions, I would be glad to hear from you.

Henry Blaine Davis, jr.
Los Lunas, New Mexico, April 1992

Acknowledgements

Very special thanks are due to each of the following for their valuable help in the preparation of this book:

Mrs. Laura P. Abbott, Vermont
Mr. J. Richard Abell, Head of History Department, Cincinnati and Hamilton County Public Library, Cincinnati, Ohio
Mr. Alan Aimone, Reference Librarian, USMA Library, West Point, New York
Maj. Gen. Richard C. Alexander, Adjutant General of Ohio
Col. George R. Allin, Alexandria, Virginia
Dr. Steven E. Anders, Quartermaster Historian, Fort Lee, Virginia
Mr. John E. Anderson, Austin, Texas
Brig. Gen. E. R. Andreotti, Adjutant General of Minnesota
Mr. Joseph L. Bair, Southwest National Bank, Greensburg, Pennsylvania
Miss Bette Barker, Archivist, Trenton, New Jersey
Mrs. Nancy Bartlett, Librarian, University of Michigan, Ann Arbor, Michigan
Mrs. Julia Boyd, Acting Director, State Veteran Affairs, Vermont
Mrs. Mary Ellen Calemmo, Scranton, Pennsylvania
Col. J. Duncan Campbell, Harrisburg, Pennsylvania
Col. Paul W. Child, Jr., Association of Graduates, USMA, West Point, New York
Miss Joan L. Clark, Head of Main Library, Cleveland, Ohio
Mrs. Rebecca Colestar, Librarian, Trenton, New Jersey
Mrs. Sidney Sayre Combs, Lexington, Kentucky
Mr. Edward Corson, Editor, Macon, Georgia
Mr. John Coulter, Greensburg, Pennsylvania
Mr. Clifford A. Cutchins, Norfolk, Virginia
Mrs. Jane Moore Davis, Los Lunas, New Mexico
Col. George A. Dawson, Adjutant General's Office, Alabama
Mrs. Carol Downey, Librarian, Phoenix, Arizona
Miss Vicky Jo Dutton, Register of Deeds, Sparta, Wisconsin
Mrs. Lauralee Ensign, Alumni Records, University of Michigan, Ann Arbor, Michigan
Lt. Col. Joseph Ewing, Chief Museum Curator, USA (Retired)
Mrs. Joan Eyer, HQ Twenty-eighth Infantry Division, Annville, Pennsylvania
Mr. James Fahey, Archivist, Natick, Massachusetts
Col. Calvin D. Fenton, NYMA, Cornwall-on-Hudson, New York
Mrs. Rita Flannery, Administrative Assistant, Scranton, Pennsylvania
Maj. Gen. Lawrence P. Flynn, Adjutant General of New York
Mr. Philip German, Quincy, Illinois
Maj. Gen. David Parker Gibbs, Chief Signal Officer (deceased)

Mr. Eric Gillespie, Archivist, Wheaton, Illinois
Mr. J. Edward Green, Researcher, Presidio (San Francisco) Army Museum
Mr. Michael R. Green, Photo Archivist, Austin, Texas
Mrs. Renee Hylton-Greene, Historical Services, National Guard Bureau, Alexandria, Virginia
Maj. Gen. Joseph W. Griffin, Adjutant General of Georgia
Capt. Dick Grube, Director, National Infantry Museum
Mrs. Maria Harmon, Promotion Assistant, San Francisco *Examiner*
Mrs. Patricia Harpole, Librarian, Saint Paul, Minnesota
Mrs. Mary Rogers Herr, Historian, Davenport, Iowa
Lt. Col. William Hickock, Pennsylvania National Guard, Dillsburg, Pennsylvania
Mr. Peter Hoffman, Oklahoma City, Oklahoma
Mr. David Holt, Librarian, Patton Museum, Fort Knox, Kentucky
Mrs. Sarah Huggins, Reference Librarian, Richmond, Virginia
Miss Madeline Hughes, Archival Assistant, Baltimore, Maryland
Miss May E. Jennison, State Veteran Affairs Officer, Vermont
Mr. David J. Johnson, Archivist, Fort Monroe, Virginia
Miss Susan M. Johnson, Alumni Coordinator, University of Michigan, Ann Arbor, Michigan
Mrs. Marie Holbrook Johnston, Las Cruces, New Mexico
Miss Margaret Kaiser, Reference Librarian, Bethesda, Maryland
Mr. John R. Kauffman, Jr., Librarian, Sunbury, Pennsylvania
Maj. Gen. Michael Kauffman (Retired), Fort Douglas, Utah
Mrs. Virginia E. Keene, Archivist, Frankfort, Kentucky
Mr. Homer W. Kiefer, Financial Consultant, Hilton Head, South Carolina
Mr. S. Paul Klein, Walter Reed Army Research Institute
Mr. Oliver A. Knapp, Mount Kisco, New York
Mr. Walter Kurth, Librarian, Portland, Oregon
Mrs. James T. Lawler, Ridgeway, Illinois
Mr. Xisoxiaong Li, Archivist, Johns Hopkins Medical Center, Baltimore, Maryland
Mr. George Lund, Executive Secretary, Wisconsin National Life Insurance Company, Oshkosh, Wisconsin
Mrs. Douglas MacArthur, New York
Maj. Gen. Alexander P. MacDonald, Adjutant General of North Dakota
Mr. David K. Marshall, Genealogist, Millersburg, Ohio
Mrs. Frederick W. Martin, Dedham, Massachusetts
Capt. Clyde B. Maryin, Jefferson City, Missouri
Mr. James V. T. McEnery, Special Collections, USMA Library, West Point, New York
Mr. Daniel McQuade, Archivist, Portland, Oregon
Mrs. Mary B. Monteith, Executive Secretary, Jefferson Medical College Alumni

Association, Philadelphia, Pennsylvania
Mrs. Mary G. Morris, Archivist, Front Royal, Virginia
Mr. Donald J. Morrison, Curator, 29th Division Museum Boalsburg, Pennsylvania
Mrs.Joy D. Moser, Director of Public Relations and Information, Kansas Adjutant General's Office, Topeka, Kansas
Col. Roger Nye, Librarian, USMA, West Point, New York
Dr. Jerry C. Oldshue, Archivist and Historian, Tuscaloosa, Alabama
Maj. Eugene Ott, National Guard Bureau, Alexandria, Virginia
Mrs. Dolores Padilla, Librarian, Belen, New Mexico
Mr. Fred Pernell, Director of Still Pictures, National Archives, Washington, D.C.
Miss Sigrid P. Perry, Library Archivist, Evanston, Illinois
Miss Becky Peterson, Archivist, Des Moines, Iowa
Mrs. Christine Peterson, Saint Peter, Minnesota
Mrs. Rosemary Phillips, Librarian, West Chester, Pennsylvania
SFC Samuel Pierce, Curator, 1st Cavalry division Museum, Fort Hood, Texas
Capt. Roger Pineau, USN (Retired), Washington, D.C. (deceased)
Mr. John Purdy, Director, Patton Museum, Fort Knox, Kentucky
Mr. Robin Rader, Librarian, Lexington, Kentucky
Miss Dorothy Rapp, Archivist, USMA, West Point, New York
Judge James W. Rice, Monroe County Circuit Court, Sparta, Wisconsin
Mr. Carlos J. Rios, Historian, Ft. McPherson, Augusta, Georgia
Mrs. Marion Holbrook Roberson, Washington, D.C.
Miss Judith A. Robins, Archivist, Philadelphia, Pennsylvania
Mr. Charles A. Ruch, Historian, Westinghouse, Pittsburgh, Pennsylvania
Mr. Richard D. Salmons, Jefferson City, Missouri
Col. John C. L. Scritner, Historian Texas AG Office, Austin, Texas
Mr. Bill Sharpe, Veterans Affairs, Des Moines, Iowa
Col. John Siemer, Ohio National Guard (Retired), Governor's Office of Veterans Affairs, Columbus, Ohio
Miss Bette L. Sigel, Reference Secretary, Boston, Massachusetts
Mr. John L. Slonager, Chief of Historical Reference Branch, United States Army Military History Institute, Carlisle Barracks, Pennsylvania
Miss JoAnn Smalley, Archivist-Historian, Atlanta, Georgia
Mrs. Gretchen L. Smith, Administrative Assistant, Wisconsin Adjutant General's Office
Mrs. Virginia H. Smith, Reference Librarian, Massachusetts
Mrs. Towanda D. Spivey, Director, Field Artillery Museum, Fort Sill, Oklahoma
Robert E. Steiner, III, Esq., Montgomery, Alabama
Mrs. Monica Sullivan, Obituary Editor, Association of Graduates, USMA, West Point, New York
Mrs. Ann L. Tressler, Office of the Mayor, Laurel, Maryland
Mr. William B. Tubbs, Reference Department, Springfield, Illinois

Col. Heath Twichell, Vineyard Haven, Massachusetts
Mr. Greg Vanney, Decorah, Iowa
Colonel John F. Votaw, First Infantry Division Museum, Cantisny, Wheaton, Illinois
Mr. Robert F. Wachs, Cemetery Manager, Louisville, Kentucky
Cdr. Don Walker, Public Affairs Officer, Utah National Guard
Maj. Thomas M. Weaver, D.C. National Guard, Researcher-Librarian, National Guard Association, Alexandria, Virginia
Col. William W. West lll, Cavalry (Retired), Warrenton, Virginia (deceased)
Mrs. Mary W. Williams, Bureau County Museum, Princeton, Illinois
Mr. Michael J. Winey, United States Army Military History Institute, Carlisle Barracks, Pennsylvania
Miss Nancy E. Wright, Research Assistant, Atlanta, Georgia
Miss Ella Gaines Yates, State Librarian, Richmond, Virginia

I sincerely thank all of you, PARTICULARLY Brig. Gen. James L. Collins, USA (Retired), formerly Chief of Military History, United States Army.

The following museums, historical societies, libraries and organizations have also been of great help:

Alan Mason Chesney Medical Archives, Johns Hopkins Medical Center, Baltimore, Maryland
Albuquerque, New Mexico Public Library
Archives, State of Arizona
Archives, State of Illinois
Archives, State of Maryland
Archives, State of Missouri
Archives, State of New Jersey
Archives, State of New Mexico
Archives, State of Virginia
Archives of the United States
Archives of the United States Military Academy
Arizona University Library, Tucson, Arizona
Army Signal Center, Fort Gordon, Georgia
Association of Graduates, USMA, West Point, New York
Atlanta, Georgia Historical Society
Belen, New Mexico Public Library
Bentley Historical Library, University of Michigan, Ann Arbor, Michigan
Bureau County Library, Princeton, Illinois
Burlington County, New Jersey Historical Society
Casemate Museum, Fort Monroe, Virginia

Cambridge Statistical Research Associates, Inc., Cambridge Massachussetts
Center of Military History, United States Army
Chester County, Pennsylvania Historical Society
Cincinnati and Hamilton County Public Library, Cincinnati, Ohio
Cleveland, Ohio Public Library
Commonwealth of Massachusetts Military Records, Natick, Massachusetts
Davenport, Iowa Public Library
Detroit, Michigan Free Press
Field Artillery Museum, Fort Sill, Oklahoma
First Cavalry Division Museum, Fort Hood, Texas
First Infantry Division Museum, Wheaton, Illinois
Georgia Department of Archives and History, Atlanta, Georgia
Illinois State Historical Library, Springfield, Illinois
Iowa Genealogical Society, Des Moines, Iowa
Iowa State Historical Society, Des Moines, Iowa
Iowa Veterans Affairs Office, Camp Dodge, Iowa
Lackawanna Historical Society, Scranton, Pennsylvania
Luther College, Decorah, Iowa
MacArthur Memorial, Norfolk, Virginia
Macon, Georgia *Telegraph and News*
Maryland State Library, Baltimore, Maryland
Massachusetts Historical Society, Boston, Massachusetts
Massachusetts State Library, Boston, Massachusetts
Matson Public Library, Princeton, Illinois
Michigan Technological University Archive, Houghton, Michigan
Minnesota Historical Society, Saint Paul, Minnesota
Missouri National Guard, 135th Military History Department
Mutnomah County Library, Portland, Oregon
National Guard Association of the United States
National Guard Bureau, Historical Services, Alexandria, Virginia
National Infantry Museum, Fort Benning, Georgia
National Library of Medicine, Bethesda, Maryland
National Portrait Gallery, London, England
National Portrait Gallery, Washington, D.C.
New Jersey Department of Military and Veterans Affairs, Trenton, New Jersey
New Jersey Historical Commission, Trenton, New Jersey
New Jersey State Library, Trenton, New Jersey
New Mexico State Library, Santa Fe, New Mexico
New York Education Department, Albany, New York
Quincy, Illinois Historical Society
Sierra Vista, Arizona Public Library
Social Security Death Index
Special Collections, USMA Library, West Point, New York
United States Naval Library, Washington, D.C.
University of Alabama Library, Tuscaloosa, Alabama

University of Michigan Alumni Records, Ann Arbor, Michigan
Vermont Historical Library, Mount Pelier, Vermont
Virginia State Library, Richmond, Virginia
Westinghouse, Pittsburgh, Pennsylvania

Also, the Offices of the Adjutants General of the following states:

Alabama, Arizona, California, Connecticut, Delaware, Florida, Georgia, Illinois, Iowa, Kansas, Kentucky, Maryland, Massachusetts, Minnesota, Missouri, New Jersey, New Mexico, New York, North Dakota, Ohio, Oregon, Pennsylvania, South Dakota, Utah and Vermont.

Abbreviations

Prior to the First World War, the United States Army was quite small. The typewriter had just come into use, and there were few lengthy titles that were constantly repeated, hence full words were still used in lieu of the later governmental acronyms. Terms like "AEF," "MP" (there were almost no military police previously), "AWOL," et cetera, came into use. A brief list of abbreviations is necessary for an understanding of that period. Relatively few acronyms were used:

ADC, Aide de Camp.

AEF, American Expeditionary Force—our troops in Europe between 6 April 1917 and 11 November 1918. This does not include any troops in the continental United States or elsewhere.

AFG, American Forces in Germany; i.e., the army of occupation in Germany, December 1918 to January 1923.

AGO, Adjutant General's Office.

ASN, Army Serial Number.

AUS, strictly a World War II designation for what was called the National Army during World War I. See below.

BSM, Bronze Star Medal.

CE, Corps of Engineers.

CG, Commanding General.

CO, Commanding Officer.

DSC, Distinguished Service Cross.

DSM, Distinguished Service Medal.

ETO, European Theater of Operations.

GAR, Grand Army of the Republic. (Civil War Northern Veterans)

JAG, Judge Advocate General. (the legal branch of the army)

KP, Kitchen Police

NA, National Army. This was the entire American army, the AEF in Europe, two different forces in Russia, and all troops still in the continental forty-eight states, of which there were many. NA was the World War I equivalent of AUS (Army of the United States), as used in World War II. Holding an NA commission in no way nullified a regular commission (RA or USA) of lesser rank, which was merely shelved for the moment.

NG, National Guard—state forces during wartime in the service of the United States government.

NGB, National Guard Bureau.

ORC, Officers' Reserve Corps.

OTC, Officers' Training Camp.

P.M.S.&T., Professor of Military Science and Tactics

q.v., quod vide (Latin for "which see").

RA, Regular Army, often used to mean USA, as below.

SATC, Student Army Training Corps (strictly World War I period).

SOS, Service of Supply.

"Star Rank," meaning a general officer.

USA, United States Army (a regular commission).

USMA, United States Military Academy.

USN, United States Navy.

USV, United States Volunteers.

Frederick Vaughan Abbott

Frederick Vaughan Abbott (0-13436), son of Brig. Gen. Henry L. Abbott and Mary Susan Everett Abbott of Beverly, Massachusetts, was born on 4 March 1858 in Cambridge, Massachusetts. Three of his great-great-grandfathers were officers during the American Revolution. He graduated from the Flushing Institute in Long Island, New York, then entered USMA; he graduated number one of sixty-seven in the class of 1879. Hunter Liggett, Fredric S. Foltz and William D. Beach (all *q.v.*) were three of his classmates. He was commissioned in the corps of engineers, in which he had a long and distinguished career, and surveyed the boundary line between Maryland and Virginia, from the mouth of the Potomac River to the Atlantic Ocean. On 15 October 1885, he married Sara Julie Dehon of Charleston, South Carolina, the daughter of Theodore Dehon, M.D. and granddaughter of Theodore Dehon, the Episcopal archbishop of South Carolina. The bishop was of Huguenot ancestry and had been born in Boston, Massachusetts in 1776. The young couple lived in Charleston for twelve years and took a lively interest in local affairs. Abbott was greatly loved by the people of that city and became their adopted citizen. The couple had three children: Marion B. Abbott, Elinor R. Abbott and Henry Dehon Abbott. From 1900 to 1910, Abbott was assistant to the Chief of Engineers in the United States Army. He also had extensive rivers and harbors duty, and was in charge of defensive works around New York Harbor. Later, he was simultaneously principal assistant to the Chief of Engineers, commandant of the Army Engineer School, and commandant of Washington Barracks. On 5 August 1917, he was promoted to brigadier general in the national army. During the absence of the Chief of Engineers to France, Abbott was acting Chief of Engineers and commanded thirty-five thousand engineer troops in the area of Washington, D.C. On 10 May 1920, Abbott retired as a colonel because of physical disabilities incurred in the line of duty. He died at age seventy at his summer home in Nonquitt, Massachusetts on 26 September 1928. In June 1930, he received a posthumous promotion to brigadier general, his wartime rank. Gen. Adolphus Greely wrote in a letter after Abbott's death, "He lived a spotless life." He was one of the few (about a dozen) bearded generals still on duty in 1918. Photo courtesy of the Annual Report, Association of Graduates, USMA.

Frank Herman Albright (0-13384), son of William I. Albright and Mary Shierlow Albright, was born on 2 August 1865 in Putnam County, Ohio, about forty-five miles west of Toledo. He entered USMA and graduated as the anchor man in the class of 1887. P. D. Lochridge, Thomas Q. Donaldson, Charles

Frank Herman Albright

Henry Martin and William Weigel (all *q.v.*) were four of his classmates. Albright was commissioned in the 12 th Infantry at Fort Sully, in the Dakota territory, and two months later was sent to Company G, Ninth Infantry, his permanent assignment at Camp Bowie, Arizona. A year later they marched to Fort Huachuca to take up station there. In March 1891 he married Minnie l. Scott, daughter of Winfield Scott, an army chaplain who had commanded a company from Syracuse, New York during the Civil War. Chaplain Scott was later chaplain-in-chief of the Grand Army of the Republic. (The GAR was an organization established by Union veterans, and for many years was a national, political force to be reckoned with.) When the Ninth Infantry moved to New York in the summer of 1891, Albright was stationed at Madison Barracks, then at Fort Ontario. In 1895 he was promoted and transferred to the 25th Infantry at Fort Buford, in the Dakota territory; he was later sent to Fort Assiniboine, Idaho. He became Professor of Military Science and Tactics at the University of North Dakota, and with the outbreak of the Spanish-American War he mustered in and inducted eight companies of the North Dakota National Guard, plus two troops of cavalry, into federal service. He took a large detachment of troops to Puerto Rico, but the war was over when he got there. On 5 September 1898, he left Puerto Rico for Montauk Point, New York, and took his company to Fort Grant, Arizona, where he was promoted to captain and again assigned to the 25th Infantry. From 1899 to 1902, he was in the Philippines; he then returned to Fort Reno, Oklahoma, just west of Oklahoma City (later to be one of the three remount depots). From 1902 to 1905, Albright was a Professor of Military Science and Tactics at Purdue University in Indiana, before returning to troop duty. He graduated from Army War College in 1915, and on 5 August 1917 he became a brigadier general in the national army. He commanded the 151st Infantry Brigade at Camp Devens, Massachusetts, and took it to France. In October 1918, Albright commanded the 55th Infantry Brigade, 28th Division (Pennsylvania troops), in combat and did quite well, receiving citations from Gen. Robert L. Bullard and Gen. Charles H. Muir (both *q.v.*). His aides were Lt. N. B. Paradise and Lt. William Hubbard. Shortly after the armistice, he reverted to the permanent rank of colonel and commanded a leave area at Bagneres, Haute Garonne, France. Upon his return to the States, Albright was sent to Fort George Wright, Washington. He had thirty-six years of service and requested retirement (as a colonel), which was granted on 23 July 1919. He lived in San Diego, California for twenty-one years; his rank of brigadier general was restored by act of Congress in June 1930. He was well-respected and had a good sense of humor. At the age of seventy-four, Albright died in San Diego on 21 July 1940, survived by his widow only, and was loyal, devoted and kindly. Photo courtesy of the Pennsylvania National Guard.

Robert Alexander (0-282), son of Judge and Mrs. William Alexander, was born on 17 October 1863 in Baltimore, Maryland. He enlisted in Company G, Fourth Infantry, in 1886 and by 1889 was first sergeant. He was commissioned a second lieutenant in the Seventh Infantry on 17 December 1889, and in 1892 he married Molly Augur Thomas, daughter of Brig. Gen. Earl D. Thomas. Their two sons were William Dennison Alexander and Robert Alexander, Jr. Alexander participated in the Great Sioux War of 1890 and 1891 and in the Spanish-American War, as well as in the Philippines, Cuba and Mexico. A distinguished graduate of the School of the Line's class of 1909, he also graduated from the Army Staff College in 1910. Promotion to brigadier general in the National Army came on 9 February 1918, and to major general (NA) on 26 August 1918. He was inspector general, Zone of Communications (AEF), from November 1917 to February 1918. His two principal commands in the AEF were the 41st Infantry Division (Oregon, Idaho and Montana Troops) and, after 27 August 1918, the 77th Infantry Division. His decorations included: from the United States, the Distinguished Service Cross, and from France, two citations for the Croix de Guerre and one as commander of the Legion of Honor. Saint John's College in Annapolis, Maryland gave him an LL.D. in 1920, as did the College of Puget Sound in Tacoma, Washington in 1931. He took command of the Third Field Artillery Brigade on 4 August 1921 and was made a major general (USA) on 26 August 1927; he retired on 17 October of that same year. After retirement he was elected to the Washington State Convention in 1933, was a thirty-third degree Mason, and lived in La Jolla, California. He died at the VA hospital in the Bronx, New York on 25 August 1941. Photo courtesy of the National Archives.

Robert Alexander

William Herbert Allaire, Jr. (0-121) was born on 1 January 1858 in Pocahontas, Arkansas. His father was a native New Yorker and his mother was from Nashville. He entered USMA and graduated number thirty-three of thirty-seven in the class of 1882. Henry T. Allen, Adelbert Cronkhite (both *q.v.*) and Frederick G. Bonfils were three of his classmates. Bonfils dropped out, did not graduate, and went on to found (together with H. H. Tammen) the *Denver Post*.

William Herbert Allaire, Jr.

Bonfils and Tammen were the subjects of a book by Gene Fowler entitled *Timberline*. Allaire was commissioned in the 23d Infantry and his first two years were on the southwestern frontier. He was sent to Fort Wayne, Indiana, then on to Texas from 1890 to 1893. From 1893 to 1897, he was an instructor at USMA, and after serving again with the 23d Infantry he was appointed Adjutant General of the District of Columbia National Guard. In February 1899, Allaire was sent to the Philippines, commanded a company there, earned a Silver Star commendation, and was sent back to the States again by July 1901. On 4 May 1902, twenty years after graduation, he married Florence Benton Whitehead. He served; at Fort McPherson, Georgia, and at Plattsburg Barracks until April 1903, when he returned to his regiment in the Philippines. After June 1903, Allaire served with Leonard Wood in his expeditions against the Moros, and stayed with the regiment until December 1904, when they were all brought back to the United States. He performed recruiting duty until 1907, when he became military attaché at the American Embassy in Vienna. On his return in 1911, he was in the office of the Chief of Staff in Washington for a short time; he then joined the Fourth Infantry at Fort Crook, Nebraska. From 1912 through 1915, Allaire was again in the Philippines. In October 1915, he commanded the 16th Infantry and took part in the Mexican Punitive Expedition. He took this unit to France in June 1917, and on 4 July 1917 one of his battalions was the first American unit to parade in Paris. On 5 August 1917, he became a brigadier general (NA) and provost-marshal general of the AEF. In June 1918, Allaire became Commanding General of the district of Paris. In July 1918, he was sent on special duty with Field Marshal Sir Douglas Haig at the headquarters of the British expeditionary force. From August until 17 November 1918, he commanded the 166th Infantry Brigade, then had special duty in Paris until June 1919, when he returned to the United States. Allaire was again on special duty at Governor's Island, New York until he retired as a colonel on 15 December 1921. After his retirement, he lived in southern California. In addition to receiving the Silver Star, he was decorated by the Austrian government and received the Legion of Honor from France. His rank of brigadier general was restored by act of Congress in June 1930. At the age of seventy-five, he died in his sleep in Santa Monica on 1 May 1933. Photo courtesy of the Annual Report, Association of Graduates, USMA.

Henry Tureman Allen (0-27) was born on 13 April 1859. He was the thirteenth child of Ruben Sanford Allen and Susannah Schumate Allen, who ran

Henry Tureman Allen

a dry goods store, owned land and ran cattle in Sharpsburg, Kentucky. Allen was a voracious reader of wide taste and had great facility for languages. After attending Georgetown (Kentucky) College, he entered USMA and graduated number twenty in a class of thirty-seven. He was commissioned and assigned to Troop E, Second Cavalry, which was stationed at Fort Keough, Montana, on the Yellowstone River. He volunteered to lead a mission to Ellesmere Island, well within the Arctic Circle, to rescue the Greely party, but did not get the assignment. As an aide to General Miles, Allen was sent in 1884 and 1885 to Alaska, where he did geographical exploration of great value. In 1887, he married Jennie Dora Johnson; they honeymooned in Europe. After duty in the Far West, he was sent to West Point to teach French. Later, in the Philippines, he headed the Philippine Constabulary. After this, at Yellowstone National Park, he commanded the cavalry troops stationed there before the National Park Service existed. He was made a major general on 5 August 1917 and was Commanding General of the 90th Division until 24 November 1918. On 8 May 1919, he commanded the Seventh Corps, and after the war, when Gen. John J. Pershing (*q.v.*) returned to the United States, he commanded the American forces in Germany (AFG), sometimes jokingly referred to as "Allen's Family in Germany." They were all first-class officers and men—fine specimens of the best American troops. Allen was always a great horseman, hunter, and polo player. On 12 April 1932, he retired after forty-one years of service. He was civically active on a national scale, and died of a stroke at Buena Vista Springs, Maryland (now Camp David) on 30 August 1930. Photo courtesy of Col. Heath Twichell, the author of an excellent biography of Gen. Henry Tureman Allen.

Hubert Allison Allen (0-672), son of Joel M. Allen and Mary Jane McGary Allen, was born on 4 April 1872 in Independence, Buchanan County, Iowa (between Waterloo and Dubuque). He was a descendant of Ethan Allen, who took Fort Ticonderoga from the British during the American Revolution. His grandparents moved from Ticonderoga, New York to Buchanan County, Iowa in 1855. Allen graduated from Iowa State College at Ames in 1892. On 2 October 1892 he married Jessie Mainus and they had two children: Herbert M. Allen and Angela Odette Allen (later Mrs. Arthur E. Warson). On 26 April 1898 he enlisted with the 49th Iowa Volunteer Infantry, and his permanent career was started. He served in Havana, Cuba from 19 December 1898 to 8 April 1899 and took the surrender of and occupied the forts guarding Havana. Twice, in Cuba, he was provost-marshal of the Seventh Army Corps. In Savannah, Georgia he was honorably discharged as a captain on 13 May 1899. In civil life, Allen served as the

Hubert Allison Allen

manager of the Iowa Telephone Company, and was for twenty-five years actively identified with the Iowa National Guard. On 26 June 1915, he was made brigadier general, Iowa National Guard, for service on the Mexican border. On 4 August 1917, Allen was promoted to brigadier general (NA) and given command of the 67th Infantry Brigade, 34th Division, at Camp Cody, in New Mexico. This was in Deming, on I-10 in the southwestern part of the state. He was in France from 15 September 1918 until 30 April 1919, and graduated from the general officer school in Langres, France. He also commanded the 56th Infantry Brigade, 28th Infantry Division, Pennsylvania National Guard troops in France. He was discharged as a brigadier general (NA) on 15 May 1919, but was promptly commissioned a colonel (USA), the only one so honored. He then had two years of duty in the Philippines commanding a regiment of Philippine Scouts and was sent to Panama to command the 14th Infantry there. After two years in the Canal Zone he was sent to Oregon as senior instructor to the National Guard there. When his four-year tour in this post was completed, the state of Oregon requested his continuance three consecutive times, and it was always granted. He stayed there until his retirement, a record never equalled by any other regular officer. On 30 September 1935, Allen retired, living in Portland, Oregon. He belonged to the United Spanish War Veterans, the Knights of Pythias, the Masons, and was a republican. When he died at age seventy-two on 15 May 1942, the governor of Oregon and a number of general officers were his pallbearers. Photo courtesy of the Iowa State Historical Society.

George R. Allin (0-1898) was the son of Thomas Banbury Allin and Catherine Jane Detwiler Allin. (His middle initial, "R.," stands for nothing, just as Harry S. Truman's middle initial, "S.," stood for nothing.) He was born on 15 January 1880 with a Dr. Houser in attendance—the same man who had delivered little Herbert to Mrs. Hoover in West Branch six years earlier. Allin was born on the family farm in Scott township, Johnson County, Iowa (about six miles southeast of Iowa City). He entered USMA with the first contingent of senatorial appointments. He was a cadet first

George R. Allin

sergeant and later a cadet captain, when there were only six companies. He graduated number seventeen of one hundred twenty-four in the notable class of 1904. Leslie J. McNair, Pelham D. Glassford (both *q.v.*), Robert C. Richardson, Joseph W. Stilwell, Edmund L. Gruber (who wrote the song *Caisson*), Stanley Koch, Innis P. Swift (this author's division commander) and Arthur H. Wilson were some of his classmates. Allin was commissioned in the artillery, and his success at USMA proved that he was no flash in the pan. Throughout his long and distinguished service, he was a sought-after man, one for whom an important job was always waiting. Among those jobs were instructor at the academy; executive officer for the first Chief of Artillery (which in 1918 earned him both the Distinguished Service Medal and the Legion of Merit); brigadier (commanding a brigade during World War I); member of the War Department General Staff, the service schools and the inspector general's department; Chief of Staff of a corps area; again a general, during World War II, and his last active duty—the most prized of all—commandant of the Field Artillery School from 20 January 1941 to 30 June 1942. In all of these posts, his duty was performed with an ability and tact that rated superior. While he was a student at the University of Iowa before entering USMA, Allin met Jessie Cooper Pontius. They were later married in Omaha, and their first home was in Texas City, Texas. They had two children: Elizabeth Allin (later Mrs. Edwin R. Clarke of Lake Forest, Illinois) and George R. Allin, Jr., who followed his father into field artillery and is at the time of this writing retired in Alexandria, Virginia. Allin was an accomplished horseman and one of the outstanding army polo players of his time. In 1916, at the open championship tournament of the Manila Polo Club, the team of which he was captain and back (second artillery team), won the big cup in a field that included two cavalry regimental teams, two Manila teams, and a British team. After his retirement in 1942, Allin became superintendent of the Sewanee Military Academy in Sewanee, Tennessee. Around 1948, he retired a second time, left Sewanee, and lived in Carmel, California. At the age of seventy-six, he died at Fort Ord, California on 2 June 1956. Photo courtesy of Col. George R. Allin, Jr.

Benjamin Alvord, Jr. (0-110), son of Brig. Gen. and Mrs. Benjamin Alvord (USA), was born on 15 May 1860 in Vancouver, Washington. His boyhood was spent at various army posts—his father's stations. He entered USMA and graduated number seventeen of thirty-seven in the class of 1882. Henry T. Allen, Adelbert Cronkhite (both *q.v.*) and Frederick G. Bonfils were classmates. Alvord was commissioned in the 20th Infantry and married Margaret McCleery, the daughter of an army chaplain, in 1886. They had two daughters, who became Mrs. R. Rutherford of Washington, D.C. and Mrs. O. L. Spiller, and a son, Benjamin Alvord, III, of San Francisco, California. Except for a tour at USMA (from 1887 to 1892), where he taught modern languages, Alvord spent his time with the 20th Infantry until the Spanish-American War; for the majority of this war, he was a major in the Adjutant General's department. During the Philippine insurrection, he commanded the 20th Infantry, then became Adjutant General of

Benjamin Alvord, Jr.

the Department of Northern Luzon. He was first secretary of the General Staff when it was organized in 1901 and in 1905 he was permanently transferred to the Adjutant General's department. In 1914, Alvord was the Chief of Staff for Gen. Frederick Funston (*q.v.*) on the Vera Cruz Expedition. In May 1917, he went to France with Gen. John J. Pershing (*q.v.*) as Adjutant General of the AEF; he remained in that assignment until he was relieved due to poor health in May 1918. In 1922, Alvord became a brigadier general (USA) and assistant to the Adjutant General; he served in this capacity until he retired on 15 June 1924. He received the Distinguished Service Medal for services in France. Aside from his profession, Alvord's major interests were athletics and music. He was a pioneer of golf in the army, and played tennis and baseball as well. He was also a patron of the opera and symphony concerts. He died in Washington, D.C. on 13 April 1927, and was survived by his widow and three children. Photo courtesy of the Annual Report, Association of Graduates, USMA.

Edward Anderson (0-210) was born on 31 May 1864 in Virginia. He graduated USMA number thirty of forty-four in the class of 1888. He was a classmate of Peyton C. March and Guy H. Preston (both *q.v.*). Originally commissioned a second lieutenant of infantry, Anderson quickly switched to cavalry, and performed frontier duty from graduation until 1895. He was in the Great Sioux War of 1890 and 1891 and served in the Santiago campaign in Cuba, where he was briefly in the sanitary corps, receiving three Silver Star commendations for that service. He was also in the Puerto Rican campaign in 1898. From 1917 to 1920, Anderson commanded many camps and units in the United States; he received a promotion to brigadier on 1 October 1918. After World War I, he commanded the 13th Cavalry and the post of Fort Clark, Texas, from 19 March 1919 to 23 February 1921. From 3 April 1921 to 11 October 1922, he commanded the Ninth Cavalry at Camp Stotsenberg, in the Philippines, then from October 1922 until 6 January 1923, he organized and commanded the 26th Cavalry of Philippine Scouts. This unit in World War II was

Edward Anderson

the last American horse cavalry in combat, and it gave a credible performance indeed. On 28 April 1923, Anderson requested retirement as a colonel after thirty-eight years of service, and his brigadier general's star was restored by act of Congress on 21 June 1930. At the age of seventy-two, he died in Florida on 2 November 1937. Photo courtesy of the Annual Report, Association of Graduates, USMA.

Edward D. Anderson

Edward D. Anderson (0-319), son of Milton Ward Anderson and Elizabeth Miller Anderson, was born on 22 January 1868 in Jasper, Marion County, Tennessee (just above the northeast corner of Alabama). After completing elementary school in Jasper, he attended high school in Winchester, and before entering USMA attended Lieutenant Braden's school in Highland Falls, New York. He was described as having a definite southern manner and accent. He graduated number ten of sixty-five in the class of 1891. Odus C. Horney, William J. Glasgow and John L. Hines (all *q.v.*) were four of his classmates. He was commissioned in the Fourth Cavalry and joined his troop at Fort Walla Walla, Washington. While there, he married Adelaide Ewen in 1893, and they had two sons. In 1897, Anderson was transferred to the Tenth Cavalry and commanded Troop C during the Spanish-American War. He also served as topographical officer of the Second Cavalry Brigade. During the action at San Juan Hill on 1 July 1898, Anderson was wounded; this earned him a Silver Star citation. From September 1898 to June 1899, he was an instructor of chemistry, geology and mineralogy at USMA. His promotion to major came in July 1899 and he served with the 26th United States Volunteer Infantry, one of the organizations raised by the federal government to replace state volunteers returning from the Philippines. He was with this unit until muster-out in 1901, when he reverted to his permanent rank of captain with the 12th Cavalry in south Texas. From 1903 to 1905, the 12th was in the Philippines, and once back in the States he became regimental quartermaster. On 31 May 1908, Anderson was given a four-year detail as paymaster which took him to Atlanta, the Philippines (again) and New York. After this he was sent to the Sixth Cavalry at Fort Des Moines, Iowa; to Texas City, Texas, and to Mexico with the Punitive Expedition. He attended the Mounted Service School at Fort Riley, Kansas, in 1914 and the Army Service School special course in 1915, where he was retained as an instructor. From May through July 1917, Anderson was an observer with the British and French troops, and from 22 August 1917 to 21 August 1921, he was detailed with the General Staff. During this period, from 8 August 1918 to 31 October 1919, he was a brigadier general (NA). He was chairman of the equipment committee of the General Staff until 6 May 1918 and chief of the operations branch (GS) until 21 August 1921. On 21 December 1921, he retired after more than thirty-four years of service and became a brigadier general (USA) on the retired list by operation of 1930. His service was characterized by quiet efficiency in all of the duties which fell his lot. At the age of seventy-two, Anderson died in Washington, D.C. on 23 May 1940; he was survived by his widow and both sons. Photo courtesy of the Association of Graduates.

Avery Delano Andrews (ASN unknown), son of Hannibal Andrews and Harriet Delano Andrews, was born on 4 April 1864 in Massena, New York. He attended Williston Seminary from 1881 to 1882 before entering USMA. There, he was a classmate of John J. Pershing and Mason M. Patrick (both *q.v.*). In September 1888, Andrews married Mary Schofield, and they had two sons: Schofield and Delano. He received an LL.B. from Columbia in 1891, and from 1889 to 1892 he was an aide to Gen. John McAllister Schofield. He graduated from New York Law School in 1892 and resigned from the army the following year. Beginning in 1891, he practiced law in New York City. Andrews was an officer and director of many corporations. These positions included: general counsel for Barber Asphalt Paving Company, 1897; vice president of Barber Asphalt Paving Company, 1902; American representative, Royal Dutch Shell Petroleum Company; Director of Irving Trust Company, New York City; Director of Central National Bank, Philadelphia, and Police Commissioner of New York City, from 1895 to 1898. During the Spanish-American War, he served as Adjutant General of New York, Chief of Staff to Gov. Theodore Roosevelt, and commanding officer of Squadron A, New York Cavalry. At the beginning of World War I, he returned to the Regular Army as a colonel of engineers with the AEF. He became a brigadier general on the General Staff in 1918 and received the Distinguished Service Medal from the United States, commander of the Legion of Honor from France and Order of the Crown from Italy. He remained a brigadier general in the Officers' Reserve Corps after 7 April 1921. He belonged to many clubs, societies and fraternities, and was president of the Association of Graduates, USMA, from 1928 to 1931. His literary effort was *My Friend and Classmate John J. Pershing* and he was the last surviving member of his 1886 USMA class. He died in Winter Park, Florida on 19 April 1959. Photo courtesy of the National Archives.

Avery Delano Andrews

Lincoln Clark Andrews

Lincoln Clark Andrews (0-13624), son of Charles T. Andrews and Mary Clark Andrews, was born on 21 November 1867 in Owatonna, Minnesota. He studied at Cornell from 1888 to 1889; he then went to USMA and graduated number thirteen of fifty-one in the class of 1893. Howard L. Lauback and Herbert B. Crosby (later the Chief of Cavalry) were two of his classmates. He was commissioned in the Third Cavalry, and during the Spanish-American War was an aide to Gen. Edwin Vose Sumner, the Commanding General of the cavalry division at Santiago in 1898. In 1899, Andrews was briefly an instructor of physics at USMA; he then served in the Philippines from 1899 to 1903. He married Charlotte Graves on 5 October 1899 and they had one son, John G. Andrews. Andrews was governor of the island of Leyte and participated in the campaign against the Moros. From 1903 to 1906, he was again an instructor at USMA, this time in cavalry tactics. From 1908 to 1909, Andrews was back in Cuba. Next, he was instructor and inspector of cavalry to the New York National Guard from 1911 to 1915; he ended that year in charge of the cavalry instructors at the first Plattsburg training camp. From 1916 to 1917, Andrews was back in the Philippines as inspector general and in charge of training the Philippine National Guard Division. Returning stateside, he organized the third Officers' Training Camp at Fort Dix, New Jersey, in December 1917. From there, he went to Leon Springs, Texas, where he organized the 304th Cavalry in February 1918. Then, he was sent to Camp Grant, Illinois. There, as a brigadier general (NA), he commanded the 172d Infantry Brigade, 86th Division, which he took to France in August 1918. After the armistice, he became assistant provost marshal at general headquarters until it was disbanded. He retired at his own request, after thirty years of service, on 30 September 1919. After retirement, Andrews was first in charge of the New York State Universal Training Commission until May 1921, then Chief Executive of the New York Transit Commission until January 1923. He was receiver for the New York and Queens County Railway until 1 April 1925, when he became Assistant Secretary of the Treasury of the United States. In November 1927, he became President of the Guardian Investment Trust in Hartford, Connecticut, and in June 1928 was President of the Rubber Institute. In 1930, Andrews became Chairman of the Board of International Development Corporation. He wrote five books: *Basic Course for Cavalry*, 1914; *Fundamentals of Military Service*, 1916; *Leadership and Military Training*, 1918; *Man Power*, 1921, and *Military Man Power*, also 1921. He lived in Grand Isle, Vermont (on Lake Champlain, near Plattsburg). His rank of brigadier general was restored by act of Congress in June 1930. Andrews died at age eighty-four in Northampton, Massachusetts on 27 November 1950. Photo courtesy of *The Assembly*, USMA.

Samuel Tilden Ansell (no ASN assigned), son of Henry B. Ansell and Lydia S. Ansell, was born on 1 January 1875 in Coinjock, North Carolina. He graduated USMA number thirty-one of seventy-two in the class of 1899, and was a classmate of Leon B. Kromer (later Chief of Cavalry), George Van Horn Mosley and Stuart Heintzelman. Originally commissioned in the 11th Infantry, Ansell later transferred to the Judge Advocate General's Department. From 1902 to 1904, and again from 1906 to 1910, he was an instructor of law at USMA. The University of North Carolina gave him an LL.B. in 1904, and on 16 February of that year he married Emelda Tracy. They had four children: Emelda (who died), Burr Tracy, Samuel Tilden, and Nancy Lydia. As a prosecuting attorney, Ansell was part of the civil government of the Philippines; during World War I he became acting Judge Advocate General of the army. He started the movement to reform the court-martial system and to rewrite the Articles of War. On 21 July 1919, Ansell resigned to resume the practice of law. His service as judge advocate earned him the Distinguished Service Medal. The first Mrs. Ansell (Emelda) died in 1944, and he remarried on 8 November 1948 to the former Mrs. Annie Clay. While he lived and worked in Washington, he also kept a home in Rehoboth Beach, Delaware. At the age of seventy-nine, Ansell died on 27 May 1954. Photo courtesy of the National Archives.

Samuel Tilden Ansell

☆

William Hemple Arthur, M.D. (0-13348), son of Robert Arthur and Mary Hemple Arthur, was born on 1 April 1856 in Philadelphia, Pennsylvania. He received an M.D. from the University of Maryland in 1877 and was appointed assistant surgeon in the United States Army in 1881. He married Laura Bouvier on 26 September of the same year. On 18 February 1886, Arthur was promoted to captain-assistant surgeon; he commanded a hospital ship from 1899 to 1900, during the Spanish-American War. He was with the China Relief Expedition of 1900, then was in the Philippines from 1900 to 1902. His next assignments took him to the Soldiers Home and Walter Reed Army Medical Center, both in Washington, D.C., until 1915. He was the third commandant of

William Hemple Arthur, M.D.

the Army Medical Department Research and Graduate School from 1 October 1915 until he retired on 3 December 1918. On 2 October 1917, Arthur was promoted to brigadier general (NA), with date of rank from 7 August 1917. After his retirement he became the medical director of Georgetown University Hospital. His home was in Washington, D.C., where he died on 19 April 1936. Photo courtesy of the Walter Reed Army Research Institute.

Thomas Quinn Ashburn

Thomas Quinn Ashburn (0-575), son of Dr. Allen Wright and Julia Kennedy Ashburn, was born on 17 November 1874 in Batavia, Ohio (east of Cincinnati). Both of his parents were Ohio natives of distinguished Revolutionary War ancestry. He attended local public schools before entering USMA, from which he graduated number sixty-one of sixty-seven in the class of 1897. Harley B. Ferguson, Harold B. Fiske and Frank R. McCoy (all *q.v.*) were three of his classmates. Ashburn's first duty was with the 25th Infantry at Fort Missoula, Montana, but the following year, just before the Spanish-American War, he transferred to the artillery. On 12 January 1898, he married Frances Marshall Fee of Louisville, Kentucky; they had one son, who was named for his father and graduated from USMA in 1925. Ashburn was commissioned a captain in the 34th United States Volunteer Infantry and was shipped to the Philippines. He was in General Wheaton's expedition to Lingayen Gulf, and as a major of volunteers he fought at Badooc. In May 1900, he commanded one column of the pursuit of Emilio Aguinaldo. He was made a brevet major for gallantry in action at San Jacinto on 11 November 1899. Ashburn was both civil and military governor of the province of Abra on Luzon and organized and commanded the department of police in Manila. In April 1901, he was mustered out of the volunteer service and reverted to his regular rank of first lieutenant before being promoted to captain and resuming his duties in the artillery. From 1901 to 1902, he was aide to Gen. Arthur MacArthur, but in 1902 he sailed for Cuba in command of the 18th, 19th and 24th Companies of Coast Artillery. He returned from Cuba in 1903 and his duties were routine, except that he graduated from the School of Submarine Defense in 1907 and served a second tour in the Philippines. Ashburn organized and commanded the 324th Field Artillery Brigade and the 158th Field Artillery Brigade (NA), and took those units to France in 1918. He participated in the Meuse-Argonne; after the armistice, until 24 April 1919, he was with the army of occupation in Germany. After May 1919, back in the States, he had much to do with demobilization and repatriation of prisoners of war. He reverted to colonel and was assistant and later chief of the inland waterway service in Washington, D.C. Ashburn became a brigadier general (USA) in 1924 and chairman of the advisory board of the Inland Waterways Corporation, which he created and made a going and paying concern. In 1927, Ashburn became a major general (USA). In 1938, he retired from the army, but he remained with Inland Waterways and Warrior River Terminal Company until late 1939. He earned a Silver Star and was commended publicly and personally by Gen. John J. Pershing (*q.v.*). He also received both the Croix de Guerre and Legion of Honor from France, as well as the Mexican Order of Military Merit and the Distinguished Service Medal from the United States. He was the author of *A History of the 324th Field Artillery* and numerous articles dealing with military matters, river transportation, forest fires, et cetera. At the age of sixty-six, he died at Walter Reed Army Medical Center on 2 May 1941; thirteen of his classmates were honorary pallbearers, and he was buried at Arlington National Cemetery. Photo courtesy of *The Assembly*, USMA.

William Wallace Atterbury

William Wallace Atterbury (no ASN assigned) was born on 31 January 1866 in New Albany, Indiana. He graduated from Yale with a Ph.D. in 1886. He began his business life as an apprentice in the Altoona shops of the Pennsylvania Railroad after graduation. He was road foreman of various divisions from 1889 to 1892 and assistant engineer of Motive Power Pennsylvania Lines (Northwest System) in 1892 and 1893. From 1893 to 1896, Atterbury was master mechanic of the Pennsylvania Company, at Fort Wayne, Indiana. He was later general superintendent and general manager of Motive Power Lines (east of Pittsburgh and Erie), fifth vice president in charge of transportation of Pennsylvania Railroad from 24 March 1909 to 3 March 1911, and vice president in charge of operations in 1912. He was granted a leave of absence and commissioned a brigadier general (NA) on 6 August 1917 in order to direct construction and operation of the United States military railway system in France. After a successful military career, Atterbury returned to civilian life on 31 May 1919, and returned to the roles of vice president in charge of operations of the Pennsylvania Railroad, vice president without designation, and president of PRR effective 1 October 1925. He also served as a director at Chicago Union Station, Washington Terminal Company, Pennsylvania Road Corporation, Norfolk and Western Railway Company, and Philadelphia National Bank and Guaranty Trust Company of New York, and as a trustee of the Pennsylvania Mutual Life Insurance Company. His decorations, honors, and degrees are innumerable; they included: from the United States, the Distinguished Service Medal; from France, the commander of the Legion of Honor; from Britain, Order of the Bath; from Belgium, the commander of the Order of the Crown; from Serbia, the Royal Order of the White Eagle, and from Romania, the grand officer of the Order of the Crown. He received the following degrees from American colleges: from Yale, an A.M. in 1911; from the University of Pennsylvania, an LL.D. in 1919; the same from Yale in 1926, Villanova in 1927 and Temple University in 1929, and from Pennsylvania Military College, an E.D. in 1932. He married the former Mrs. A. R. MacLend; he lived in Philadelphia, Pennsylvania and died there on 20 September 1935. Photo courtesy of the National Archives.

Dwight Edward Aultman

Dwight Edward Aultman (0-81), son of Mathias W. Aultman and Mary Beach Aultman, was born on 2 February 1872 in Allegheny, Pennsylvania. He entered USMA and graduated number fourteen of fifty-four in the class of 1894. Paul B. Malone, George H. Estes, Jr. (both *q.v.*) and Hamilton S. Hawkins were three of his classmates. He was commissioned a second lieutenant in the Fourth Cavalry. On 5 January 1898, he married Alma Y. Hickock, and they had three children: Edith H. (later Mrs. Mark H. Doty), Dwight W., and Anita B. During the Spanish-American War, Aultman took part in the Battle of San Juan Hill in July 1898, and the siege of Santiago in Cuba, as well. From December 1898 to January 1899, he was aide to Gen. Lloyd Wheaton and later to Gen. Joseph Warren Keifer. During 1901 and after, he organized and commanded the Cuban artillery and was their instructor from 1903 to 1906. He was an instructor at the department of languages of the service schools from 1907 to 1911, and during 1914 and 1915 he was on special mission to Germany. After graduation from the Army War College in 1916, Aultman was retained as an instructor until 1917, when he wrote a book entitled *Military Strength and Resources of the United States*. From October 1917 to May 1918, he commanded the Fifth Field Artillery Brigade, First Infantry Division (AEF). On 18 April 1918, he was promoted to brigadier general (NA), and he later commanded the 51st Field Artillery Brigade, 26th Division (AEF). He was appointed Chief of Artillery, Fifth Corps, in October 1918, and had the same assignment for the Second Army in December 1918. He hardly missed a World War I battle involving American troops in Europe. In 1920, he graduated from the Army War College, and on 27 April 1921 he was made a brigadier general (USA). He was decorated by the United States with the Distinguished Service Medal and by France with the Croix de Guerre and commander of the Legion of Honor. At the age of fifty-seven, Aultman died on 12 December 1929. Photo courtesy of the National Archives.

Fred Thaddeus Austin

Fred Thaddeus Austin (0-888), son of Julius Tilden Austin and Manora Keith Austin, was born on 28 December 1866 in Hancock, Vermont. He graduated from Norwich University with a B.S. in 1888, and received an M.S. from them in 1894, plus a C.E. in 1896. He worked as an architect in Brockton and Boston, Massachusetts from 1889 to 1898. He then entered the army as a first lieutenant and adjutant, Fifth Massachusetts Volunteer Infantry, on 1 July 1898. On 17 August 1899, he became a first lieutenant, 46th United States Volunteer Infantry, and on 22 August 1901, he transferred in grade to the Artillery Corps, where he served the rest of his career. He married Lenora Harrison on 21 October 1909. On 12 April 1918, he was promoted to brigadier general in theNational Army. After World War I, Austin was director of the Field Artillery School at Fort Sill, Oklahoma, then served for a while in the Inspector General's Department. He became a major general (USA), and was the Chief of Field Artillery from 20 December 1927 until 15 February 1938. Photo courtesy of the Field Artillery Museum, Fort Sill, Oklahoma.

Edwin Burr Babbitt (0-48), son of Col. and Mrs. Lawrence Sprague Babbitt, was born on 26 July 1862 at Watervliet Arsenal on the Hudson River, just south of West Point. He was a third generation West Point graduate. At USMA he was a classmate of Isaac Newton Lewis, who made the Lewis machine gun for the Allies during World War 1. He graduated number nineteen of thirty-seven in the class of 1884, and was commissioned in the artillery but later transferred to ordnance. On 5 November 1884, he married Emily A. Fenno of Boston. They had no children, and she died in 1918. After graduation from the artillery school in 1889, Babbitt was an instructor in ordnance and gunnery

Edwin Burr Babbitt

at USMA from 1890 to 1896. His promotion to brigadier general (NA) came on 5 August 1917, and he was promoted to brigadier general (USA) on 12 February 1918. He commanded the Fourth Field Artillery Brigade (AEF) during the Marne, Argonne and Saint Mihiel offensives, for which he received the Distinguished Service Medal. He was part of the American Forces in Germany (AFG), irreverently referred to as "Allen's Family in Germany," which speaks well for him, as they were the cream of the American army. He was promoted to major general (USA) in 1923. His decorations included: the Distinguished Service Medal from the United States, officer of the Legion of Honor from France, Commandetor Order of El Sol de Peru, and Abdon Calderon First-Class from Ecuador. On 23 February 1924, he married a second time to Maud Ainsworth, and he retired on 19 September of that same year. There were no children from the second marriage either. Babbitt lived in Santa Barbara, where he died at age seventy-seven on 9 December 1939. Photo courtesy of the Association of Graduates, USMA.

Charles Justin Bailey

Charles Justin Bailey (0-37), son of Mr. and Mrs. Milton Bailey, was born on 21 June 1859 in Tamaqua, Pennsylvania. At USMA he was a classmate of George W. Goethals, who built the Panama Canal. They graduated in 1880, and Bailey was commissioned in the artillery. On 4 November 1885, he married Mary M. Dodge; they had two daughters, who became Mrs. Omira Chilton and Mrs. Mary Alden Gandy. In 1888, he graduated from the Artillery School. The University of Vermont granted him a master's degree in 1898, and on 2 March 1899 he was promoted to captain. From 1906 to 1909, he was a major in the War Department General Staff, and by 11 March 1911 he was a colonel of Coast Artillery. He was promoted to brigadier general (USA) on 10 October 1913 and major general (NA) on 15 August 1917. Bailey was Commanding General of the Philippine Department from 15 April until 15 August 1918. He also served as Commanding General of the 81st Infantry Division (NA) during the war in Europe, from August 1918 until the war ended; he then brought the troops back and the unit was disbanded. He became Commanding General of the Middle Atlantic Coast Artillery District in July 1919, and on 16 August 1921 he became Commanding General of the Third Corps Area. Shortly after getting his last command he was promoted to major general (USA) on 5 October 1921. From the United States, he received the Distinguished Service Medal; from Belgium, commander of the Order of Leopold, and from France, the Croix de Guerre with palms and officer of the

Legion of Honor. In December 1922 he received an LL.D. from Saint John's College in Annapolis, Maryland, and on 1 December of that year he retired. The following May, Mrs. Bailey died. On 27 December 1924, Bailey remarried, to the former Mrs. Elizabeth Hegeman. He was a trustee of the Chatnuqua Institution, a member of the Army and Navy Club in Washington, and resided at 153 South Main Street, Jamestown, New York. He died at age eighty-seven on 21 September 1946. Photo courtesy of *The Assembly*, USMA.

Chauncey Brooke Baker (0-137), son of Emanuel R. P. Baker and Eliza Stoneberger Baker, was born on 26 August 1860 in Lancaster, Ohio. At USMA, he was a classmate of John J. Pershing and Mason M. Patrick (both *q.v.*); he graduated number forty-one of seventy-seven in the class of 1886, and was commissioned in the infantry. He graduated with honor from the Infantry and Cavalry School at Fort Leavenworth, in Kansas, in 1889, and on 19 June of that year he married Lucy McCook, daughter of Gen. Alexander D. McCook. From 1890 to 1895, Baker was aide to General McCook. From 1886 to 1898, his entire service was on frontier duty. He was a depot quartermaster in Havana from August 1900 to May 1902, with various quartermaster assignments until 1914. He then served in the office of the Quartermaster General from 1914 to 1916. He was senior member of the military commission to France in July 1917 and was promoted to brigadier general (NA). Two days later, he became Chief of Embarkation Service for the office of the Chief of Staff in the War Department; he served in this capacity until February 1918. On 21 April 1921 he retired as a colonel. Lucy McCook Baker, his first wife, died in 1923, and in 1924 he married Ella Turner, who died in 1932. He married a third (and last) time to Emily Burr, who survived him. Baker was an officer of many major corporations, as well as being the author of at least four books: *Notes on Fire Tactics*, 1889; *Transportation of Troops and Materiel,* 1905; *Handbook of Transportation* by Rail and Commercial Vessels, 1916, and *Coordination Between Transportation Companies and the Military Service*, 1916. After retirement he made his home in Bexley, Ohio. He died at age seventy-six in Washington, D.C. on 18 October 1936. Photo courtesy of the Association of Graduates, USMA.

Chauncey Brooke Baker

Charles Clarendon Ballou (0-178), son of William H. Ballou and Julia A. Ballou, was born on 13 June 1862 in Orange township, New York. He

Charles Clarendon Ballou

graduated USMA number sixty-three of seventy-seven in the class of 1886. John J. Pershing and Mason M. Patrick (both *q.v.*) were two of his classmates. Upon graduation, Ballou was commissioned in the Sixteenth Infantry and immediately went on frontier duty in the Far West. He took part in the Sioux Campaign of 1890 and 1891, where one of the interesting things he did was to pass through the camp of five thousand hostile Sioux with one other man right after the Battle of Wounded Knee. From 1891 to 1893, Ballou was Professor of Military Science and Tactics at Florida State Agriculture College. During 1897 and 1898, he went to the Infantry and Cavalry School. From 8 July to 20 October 1898, he was a major in the Seventh Illinois Volunteer Infantry. He was regimental quartermaster in the Philippines in 1899, participating in the battle of Zapote River and several other minor engagements. He attended the Field Officers School in 1916 and the Army War College in 1916 and 1917, and was promoted to brigadier general (NA) on August 1917. On 28 November 1917, he was made a major general (NA); he then commanded the 92d (Colored) Infantry Division from 27 October to 18 November 1918. From 19 November to 1 February 1919, Ballou commanded the 89th Division. He was in the Argonne, Moselle, and Saint Die sectors. His decorations included a Silver Star presented by President Calvin Coolidge and the Croix de Guerre with palm and the Legion of Honor from France. He retired in 1926 as a colonel with forty years of service; he lived in Spokane, Washington, and died there at age sixty-six on 23 July 1928. His rank of major general was restored by act of Congress (posthumously) in June 1930. Photo courtesy of the Annual Report, Association of Graduates, USMA.

Frank Ellis Bamford (0-435) was born in Milwaukee, Wisconsin. In 1883, he entered the University of Wisconsin; during the first month of his freshman year he had a memorable experience when he sailed with two other students from a landing on Lake Mendota, and apparently none of them knew anything about sailing. The boat capsized and they spent three hours on the lake, clinging to the hull before being rescued—not too much the worse for wear, but definitely a bit wiser for the experience. He graduated with a degree in mechanical engineering in 1887. On 14 July 1891, Bamford enlisted in the Second Infantry and progressed rapidly from corporal sergeant to sergeant major of the regiment; on 7 October 1893 he was commissioned a second lieutenant in the Fifth Infantry. On 26 April 1898, Bamford was promoted to first lieutenant and transferred to the 15th Infantry. After the Spanish-American War, on 2 February 1901, he became a captain and went to the 28th Infantry. During World War I, he successively commanded a battalion, regiment and brigade, and then the First Infantry Division in France. He organized and conducted the Second Corps School, participating in all battles from Cantigny to the Meuse-Argonne. He was awarded the Distinguished Service Medal, was promoted to brigadier general (NA) on 8 August 1918, and from 12 to 17 October commanded the First Infantry Division. He also commanded the army school in Langres, France. In 1919 he lived in Omaha, Nebraska, but during the 1920s he retired and lived in Summit Point, West Virginia, where he died at age sixty-six on 27 June 1932. Photo courtesy of the National Archives.

Frank Ellis Bamford

Harry Hill Bandholz

Harry Hill Bandholz (0-79), son of Christopher John Bandholz and Elizabeth Ann Hill Bandholz, was born on 18 December 1864 in Constantine, Michigan. He graduated USMA number twenty-nine of fifty-four in the class of 1890; he was a classmate of Edgar Jadwin, Herbert Deakyne and Fred W. Sladen (all *q.v.*). He was commissioned in the Sixth Infantry, and a month later married May Cleveland of Chicago, Illinois. He was Professor of Military Science and Tactics at Michigan Agricultural College in 1896. During the Spanish-American War, Bandholz served in the Seventh Infantry and the Sanitary Corps. During the Philippine insurrection, he served with the Second Infantry. He was Chief of the Philippine Constabulary as a brigadier general (PC) from 1907 to 1913. While in the Philippines, he was governor of Tabayas province during 1902 and 1903; he was the only regular officer elected to such a position. He commanded the district of southern Luzon and conducted the campaign against Simeon Ola at Albay, resulting in the destruction of Ola's forces. In October 1905, he was transferred to the command of central Luzon, where he forced the surrender of Montalan Sakay and accomplished the destruction of Felizardo. In 1915 he was promoted to major (USA) and assigned to the 30th Infantry. He received the rank of brigadier general (NA) on 17 December 1917 and was Commanding General of the 58th Infantry Brigade (AEF). In

France he was Provost Marshal (AEF) and Chief of Staff of the 27th Infantry Division. His promotion to brigadier general (USA) came in 1920, and on 19 April 1922 he married Inez G. Gorman. For a while he was commander of the Spanish-American War Veterans. He was retired due to a disability in 1923 and died at age sixty in Michigan on 7 May 1925. Photo courtesy of the New Jersey State Archives.

Charles Williams Barber

Charles Williams Barber (0-13857), son of George W. Barber and Ellen Taggart Barber, was born on 21 September 1872 in Gloucester County, New Jersey. He went to public schools, then attended Pierce Business College in Philadelphia before studying law in the office of H. S. Grey, former attorney general of New Jersey. He had a brother named Alfred, of Woodbury, New Jersey, and married Katherine Runge; they had one son, Russell G. Barber. Commissioned a second lieutenant in the Fourth New Jersey Infantry for the Spanish-American War on 16 July 1898, Barber was made a first lieutenant on 27 September of that year. On 3 March 1899 he was made captain, but he was mustered out on 6 April 1899. He was made a first lieutenant of the 28th United States Volunteer Infantry on 5 July 1899, and was again mustered out of the volunteer service on 1 May 1901. On 2 February 1901, he was commissioned a second lieutenant, Second Infantry (USA), and was back to first lieutenant by 11 November of that same year. However, he remained a first lieutenant for almost ten years, serving in the Philippines from 1899 to 1901, 1902 to 1903 and 1906 to 1908. From 1908 to 1915, Barber was with the Panama Canal Commission and retired as a major, Third Infantry, on 1 September 1916. Service on the Mexican border followed, and he was Adjutant General of New Jersey from 5 December 1916 to 24 July 1917; he was made a brigadier general (NA) on 15 July 1917. He had been in charge of the organization of state troops for war and the registration and selection of drafted men. From July to August, he commanded the 29th Infantry Division, and on 11 September 1917 he took command of the 57th Infantry Brigade at Camp McClellan, Alabama. Barber took his brigade to France and commanded it in front line sectors. He was a General Staff officer (AEF) and also commanded Base Section Number 2 in Bordeaux until July 1919. Upon his return to the States, he retired again (as a colonel). His rank of brigadier general was restored by act of Congress, on the retired list, in June 1930. For the remainder of his life, he was busy both commercially and financially, as a representative of the Atlantic Refining Company in Mexico, his own investment banking company, and as director on the boards of several corporations.

The United States awarded him the Distinguished Service Medal, as did New Jersey. France awarded him the Legion of Honor, and he also received the Military Order of the Carabao. His home was in Short Hills, New Jersey and his office was in New York City. Several months after his seventieth birthday, he died at the home of his son Russell in Charlotte, North Carolina on 7 January 1943. The funeral was in Washington, D.C. and was followed by burial at Arlington National Cemetery. Photo courtesy of the New Jersey State Archives.

John William Barker

John William Barker (0-13457), son of Fredrick William Barker and Adelaine Ring Barker, was born on 25 December 1872 in Syracuse, New York. Both sides of his family were of pioneer stock, and he prepared for USMA at Syracuse High School. He won a competitive examination there, got the appointment, and was one of the youngest in his class. He graduated number forty-nine of fifty-four in the class of 1894, with Paul B. Malone, George H. Estes, Jr. (both *q.v.*). and Hamilton S. Hawkins. Barker was commissioned in the Ninth Infantry, then stationed at Sackett's Harbor, New York, about ninety miles from Syracuse. While just starting to enjoy his graduation leave, the great Pullman strike began in Chicago, and Barker learned that the Ninth Infantry was ordered to go to Chicago and would be passing through Syracuse on its way west. He went to the railroad station to greet his prospective regiment and to meet his brother officers, and begged to be taken along. His wish was granted, while provision was made en route to uniform and equip him, and he had his first taste of regular army duties within three weeks of graduation. Later, he was transferred to the Third Infantry at Fort Snelling, Minnesota; he was with them for sixteen years. During the Spanish-American War, he was in El Caney and Santiago; he contracted yellow fever and was sent home as an invalid. He then did recruiting duty in Norfolk, Virginia before going to the Philippines with his regiment. He earned a Silver Star commendation in both Cuba and the Philippines. Upon his return to the United States, Barker spent several years at Fort Thomas, Kentucky, then went to Fort Seward, Alaska, and Fort Lewis, Washington. In 1907, he married Mathilde Fritchie, a native of Dun-sur-Meuse, France. From Fort Lawton, they went to the Philippines at the time of the Moro uprisings. On Christmas Eve 1907, in Zamboanga (where the monkeys have no tails), he was severely wounded and spent six weeks in the hospital. Next, he went to the school of the Line at Fort Leavenworth, Kansas, where he graduated with honor, then back to his old regiment at Sackett's Harbor, N.Y. Early in 1914 he was signally honored with an invitation by the French Government to study French Infantry Tactics for a year with the option of remaining a second year if he so desired. They left in June, presented their credentials, were assigned to a regiment in Normandy, and given orders to report there in September for the Fall Maneuvers. With two months to spare, they visited her old home at Dan-sur-Meuse, and ancient village that would shortly be erased from the map by the WWI. They were also sightseeing in Rhiems when the war broke out. He reported at once to Myron T. Herrick, the American Ambassador in Paris, and was made an Attache, for a while this kept him extremely busy, at the center of everything. President Wilson designated him a Neutral Observer: with the permission of the French Ministry of War he was to follow the movements of the French Army at the Front. This interesting and valuable detail gave him and unusual opportunity to study the war and the movements of troops on an unsurpassed scale. When General Pershing and his party arrived in the Spring of 1917 Capt. Barker was on the Official Reception Committee to meet him! Very quickly he was on General Pershing's staff at Chaumont, as a Lt. Colonel, and commanded the 165th Infantry, which included the "Fighting 69th" of New York. He became a Colonel and served with distinction. In the Spring of 1918 he was promoted to Brigadier General (NA). After the war he served in the Adjutant General's Office until ill health forced him to retire. Including his time at West Point, he had served thirty-two years. He was decorated by our own government and by that of the French. For a year he resided in New York and at the age of 51 he died there, on 14 May 1924. His widow returned to France to live. He was also survived by a son, Robert Barker. His rank as a Brigadier General was restored later by Act of Congress in June 1930. Photo courtesy of the Association of Graduates, USMA.

George Columbus Barnhardt (0-400), son of Marshal L. Barnhardt and Sarah Dunlap Barnhardt, was born on 28 December 1868 in Gold Hill, North Carolina. He graduated USMA number seventeen of sixty-two in the class of 1892; he was a classmate of Charles P. Sumerall (*q.v.*). Commissioned a second lieutenant in the Sixth Cavalry, he served two years at Fort McKinney, New York from 30 September 1892 to 2 October 1894. On 19 December 1895, Barnhardt married Floy Rice. During the Spanish-American War, he commanded a cavalry troop in the Santiago campaign. Two years of duty at Fort Leavenworth, in Kansas, followed; he next participated in the China Relief Expedition, followed by four years in the Philippines. From 1907 to 1909, he was back in Cuba and from 1909 to 1912 was adjutant of the 15th Cavalry. Next, he

George Columbus Barnhardt

did General Staff duty from 1913 to 1916 and was on the Mexican border. Also in 1916, he was serving with the Quartermaster Corps. He commanded the 329th Infantry at Camp Sherman, in Ohio, and was in France with the AEF; later, he commanded the 28th Infantry. This was a part of the First Infantry Division during the Saint Mihiel and Meuse-Argonne operations, from July to October 1918. His promotion to brigadier general (NA) came on 1 August 1918. After the armistice, he was assigned the 178th Infantry Brigade in France and Germany, returning with it to the States on 31 May 1919. From 1921 to 1925, Barnhardt was a General Staff colonel, and from 1925 to 1927 he commanded his old unit, the Sixth Cavalry. From July to September 1927, he commanded the Military District of Washington, and his last assignment was command of the 22d Infantry Brigade in Hawaii. The United States awarded him the Distinguished Service Medal and France gave him both the Croix de Guerre with palm and the Legion of Honor. Barnhardt died at age sixty-one in Texas on 10 December 1930. Photo courtesy of the Annual Report, Association of Graduates, USMA.

Malvern Hill Barnum

Malvern Hill Barnum (0-161), son of Gen. Henry A. Barnum and Lavina King Barnum, was born on 3 September 1863 in Syracuse, New York. He graduated USMA number forty-two of seventy-seven in the class of 1886, and was a classmate of John J. Pershing (*q.v.*). He was commissioned in the Third Cavalry, and on 24 October 1889 he married Martha Maginnes. They had a daughter, Martha Barnum, and a son, Malvern Hill Barnum, Jr. In 1893 Barnum became a distinguished graduate of the Infantry and Cavalry School, and he was on duty at Rock Island Arsenal from 1893 to 1894. In the Santiago campaign he was adjutant of the Tenth Cavalry, and he was wounded at San Juan Hill on 2 July 1898; he was cited for bravery after this event. From 1899 to 1902, Barnum was assistant quartermaster at USMA. For four years, he was aide to Gen. J. Weston in the Philippines, and from 1910 to 1911 he was adjutant of the Eighth Cavalry. In 1915 he graduated from Army War College and was on General Staff duty until 1917. On 31 October 1917, he was made a brigadier general (NA) and took command of the 183rd Infantry Brigade,92d Division (AEF). From December 1918 to July 1919, he was chief of the American section of the Inter-Allied Armistice Commission. From 1920 to 1923, Barnum commanded the Disciplinary Barracks at Fort Leavenworth, Kansas. On 9 February 1923, he became a brigadier general (USA) and given command of the 18th Infantry Brigade. His rank of major general (USA) came on 12 June 1927, and the following September he retired, making his home in Brookline, Massachusetts. For his services he was decorated with: the Distinguished Service Medal and the Purple Heart from the United States, commander of the Legion of Honor from France, commander of the Order of the Bath from Britain, commander of the Order of Leopold and Croix de Guerre from Belgium, and the Order of Saints Maurice and Lazarus from Italy. He was also commander of the Massachusetts and national commander of the Loyal Legion. He was an Episcopalian, a golfer, and belonged to many nationally known clubs. He died at age seventy-eight in Massachusetts on 18 February 1942. Photo courtesy of the National Archives.

John Davenport Barette (0-49), son of John Dunsworth Barette and Margaret Elizabeth Maybanks Barette, was born on 14 May 1862 in Thibideauville, La Fourche Parish, Louisiana. When he was a small child, his family moved to Illinois and then to Davenport, Iowa, where he grew up and received his early education. He graduated from Davenport High School and attended Iowa State University for a year, then entered USMA. He graduated from there number nine of thirty-nine in the class of 1885 with Joseph Kuhn, Charles Henry Muir, Willard Holbrook and Robert L. Bullard (all *q.v.*). Upon graduation his commission was as a second lieutenant in the Third Artillery Brigade. From 1885 to 1890, his first station was Washington Barracks in the District of Columbia. On 13 June 1894 he married Katherine Biddle, and they had five daughters. From 1903 to 1907, Barette instructed at the Artillery School, and from 1907 to 1909 he was director of the department of artillery and gun defense at the Artillery School at Fort Monroe, Virginia. He commanded Fort McKinney in 1910. In 1911 he commanded the artillery district at Charleston, South Carolina; he was also lieutenant colonel of the First Provisional Coast Artillery Regiment and Coast Defense Officer of the Eastern Department. In 1912, Barette commanded the coast defenses of Baltimore, and during 1913 and 1914 he did the same for Long Island Sound. He was Adjutant General of the Western Department in 1915, and in 1916 he went to the Philippine Department, where he became a brigadier general (NA) on 5 August 1917. From December 1917 to May 1918, Barette was acting Chief of Coast Artillery. With the AEF he commanded the Artillery School in Saumur (the former French Cavalry School) from June to November 1918. After World War I he commanded various Coast Artillery districts. His last assignment was as Commanding General of the First Corps Area, headquartered in Boston, Massachusetts. He retired in 1926, and at age seventy-two he died in Missouri on 16 July 1934. He was among the last of the few bearded general offi-

John Davenport Barette

cers on duty in the United States Army. Photo courtesy of the Annual Report, Association of Graduates, USMA.

Thomas Henry Barry

Thomas Henry Barry (no ASN assigned), son of David Barry and Margaret Dimond Barry, was born on 13 October 1855 in New York City. He attended public schools, then went to the College of the City of New York. He graduated USMA number thirty-nine of seventy-six in the class of 1877. Also in his class was Henry Ossian Flipper, the first African American ever to graduate from USMA. Barry was commissioned in the Seventh Cavalry and went straight to frontier duty, later serving in the infantry. On 23 January 1884 he married Ellen Bestor. He participated in the Sioux Campaign from 1890 to 1891. During the Spanish-American War, Barry served as a lieutenant colonel of volunteers; he received a Silver Star commendation for service during the Philippine insurrection. From 8 August 1898 to February 1900, he was Adjutant General of the Eighth Army Corps and Chief of Staff of the Division of the Philippines. Promotion to brigadier general (USV) came on 13 June 1900; then, he was on the China Relief Expedition, and was made a brigadier general (USA) in 1903. During the Russian-Japanese War in 1905 he was an observer with the Russian army. In 1908 he was promoted to major general (USA), and from 31 August 1910 to the same date in 1912 he was superintendent of USMA. From 15 February to 20 March 1918, he commanded the 86th Infantry Division (AEF); he then became Commanding General of the Central Department. He died at age sixty-four in Washington, D.C. on 30 December 1919. Photo courtesy of the Annual Report, Association of Graduates, USMA.

Charles Henry Barth (0-116), son of George Fredrick Barth and Christine Barth, was born on 28 December 1858 in Sheridan, Iowa. He was the oldest of six children. He entered USMA, where he was seriously handicapped by recurring malaria in a time when sick leave for cadets was unknown. He graduated number thirty-two of fifty-three in the class of 1881. Joseph T. Dickman, Harry and Henry Hodges, Edward Saint J. Greble and Andrew S. Rowan (all *q.v.*) were classmates of his. Barth was commissioned in the 12th Infantry and joined them just in time to take part in the campaign against Geronimo, the notorious Apache. He had frontier duty from 1881 to 1882 and again from 1887 until 1889. As a junior officer at Fort Leavenworth, Kansas, his company commander, Capt.

Charles Henry Barth

Hugh G. Brown, got him interested in the study of military art. This became a lifelong interest for Barth; he was a student, participant and instructor. On 5 December 1893, Barth married Harriet Bittman. They had three children: a daughter who died quite early and two sons, George Bittman Barth, who went into field artillery, and Charles Henry Barth, Jr., who went into engineering. In 1899 he went to the Philippines with his regiment, was in several engagements and was cited for gallantry in action, receiving a Silver Star commendation. From September 1903 to December 1905, he was an instructor in military art at the Infantry and Cavalry School at Fort Leavenworth. During this time, at the instigation of Gen. J. Franklin Bell and Gen. Eben Swift (at that time, respectively, commandant and assistant commandant of the Infantry and Cavalry School), he did a translation of the German general Griepenkerl's *Letters on Applied Tactics*. This book had considerable influence on the study of tactics and became the text at Leavenworth and the Army War College. In 1908, Barth graduated from Army War College and was retained as an instructor. He became a thirty-third degree Mason on 20 October 1909. In the fall of 1910 he had a second tour of duty in the Philippines, then was at the Presidio in Monterey until October 1912, when he was promoted to lieutenant colonel after thirty-one years in the 12th Infantry. He became Adjutant General in Atlanta, Georgia. From there he went to Laredo, Texas, then for a third tour to the Philippines, where he commanded in Manila. On 5 August 1917, Barth was promoted to brigadier general (NA), and from 28 August 1917 to 7 October 1917 he commanded Camp Jackson, in South Carolina, where he organized and trained the 81st Infantry Division. From 1 January 1918 to 23 October 1918, he completed the organization and training of the Seventh Infantry Division at Camp MacArthur, Texas; he took it to France and commanded it in action at Metz shortly before the armistice. He received the Distinguished Service Medal twice, and the French awarded him the Croix de Guerre and Officer of the Legion of Honor. Back in the States, Barth commanded Camp Grant, Illinois, and on 5 February 1919, he reverted to his permanent rank of colonel. He commanded the 62d Infantry Regiment at Camp Lee, Virginia, and later commanded the entire camp as well. When 62d was mustered out, he went back to the Philippines for his fourth and last tour of duty there. He had four different commands, and when returning to the States (by sea, of course) he received his promotion to brigadier general (USA). He retired on 28 December 1922, after which he was appointed governor of the National Military Home at Fort Leavenworth. He continued to serve there until he died at age sixty-seven on 5 December 1926. Barth was by nature a student and teacher, rather than a man of action, but he also had the gift of leadership, so both could and did sink the student in leadership of men. He had great natural charm, and his care for his officers and men and his fair dealing earned him great respect and admiration. Photo courtesy of the Annual Report, Association of Graduates, USMA.

George True Bartlett

George True Bartlett (0-13119), son of Thomas Bartlett and Elizabeth W. T. Bartlett, was born on 29 April 1856 in New Hampshire. He graduated USMA number ten of fifty-three in the class of 1881. Harry Hodges, Joseph T. Dickman, Enoch H. Crowder and Andrew S. Rowan (all *q.v.*) were four of his classmates. Bartlett was commissioned in the Third Artillery Brigade upon graduation, and on 18 September he married Cornelia Terrell, with whom he had two sons: Charles and Geoffrey. He was Professor of Military Science and Tactics at Pennsylvania Military College from 1885 to 1888. Cornelia died on 14 February 1888. In 1889 Bartlett was promoted to first lieutenant, and in 1890 he graduated from the Artillery School. He married a second time to Helen Walton on 28 November 1893. From 1894 to 1898, he was again Professor of Military Science and Tactics, this time at the Agricultural and Mechanical College of Texas (Texas A & M). When the Spanish-American War started, Bartlett became a major of United States Volunteers and chief commissary of the Department of Santiago in Cuba, was promoted to captain of artillery (USA) in 1899, and was the adjutant of the Artillery School at Fort Monroe, in Virginia, from 1903 to 1906. During this time he was also a member of the board to revise the Coast Artillery drill regulations. On 26 March 1906, Bartlett was promoted to major, Coast Artillery (USA), and on 4 December 1909 he became lieutenant colonel. He became colonel of the Coast Artillery in December 1911 and a brigadier general (NA) in August 1917, serving two long tours of duty with the General Staff. With the AEF in France, he commanded a brigade of railroad artillery, and from 7 October 1917 to 22 March 1918 he commanded Base Section Number 3. Next, he became a member of the Inter-Allied Military Commission in Greece, as well as being our military attaché in Athens. On 25 September 1918, Bartlett retired at his own request as a brigadier general with over forty years of service. In 1930, while on the retired list, his second star (major general) was restored by act of Congress. He was the oldest living graduate of USMA; he lived in San Antonio, Texas from February 1948 until he died at age ninety-two on 11 March 1949. Photo courtesy of *The Assembly*, USMA.

William Dorrance Beach

William Dorrance Beach (0-13443), son of Joshua Munson Beach and Sarah Ford Beach, was born on 18 June 1856 in Brooklyn, New York. His family was originally British and had immigrated to the United States in the eighteenth century. After attending a private school in New Jersey, Beach went to public schools in New York before entering USMA. There he was a classmate of Fredric S. Foltz and Hunter Liggett (both *q.v.*); he graduated number twenty-four of sixty-four in the class of 1879. He was commissioned in the Third Cavalry and performed frontier duty until 1883. He participated in the Ute Expedition in 1879, and on 27 April 1882 he married Katherine C. Bullens of Missouri. They had one son, Edwin Ray Beach. In 1882 and 1883, Beach was on the Apache Expedition. From 1884 to 1888, he was an assistant professor at USMA, after which he was on the Mexican border with troops in 1891 and 1892. From 1892 to 1898, Beach was an instructor at the Infantry and Cavalry School at Fort Leavenworth, Kansas. During the Spanish-American War, he was a major and Chief Engineer of the cavalry division in the Fifth Corps in Cuba; he received two Silver Star commendations for his services. From 1900 to 1902, he was in the Philippines, suppressing the insurrection there, and from 1903 to 1906 he was on duty with the War Department General Staff as chief of the military information division. Later, he returned to Cuba and was governor of Santa Clara province. From 1910 to 1912, Beach was again in the Philippines as Chief of Staff of the Philippine Division. In 1916 he commanded the Eighth Cavalry on the Mexican border, and in 1917 he became a brigadier general (NA) commanding the 176th Infantry Brigade (AEF), for which he received the Distinguished Service Medal. From 24 May to 10 September 1918, Beach commanded the 88th Infantry Division. Upon his return to the States, he performed as executive officer of Camp Jackson, South Carolina, until his retirement in 1920. He retired as a colonel, but was promoted on the retired list to brigadier general in 1927. In addition to the DSM and the Silver Stars referred to above, he received from France the Croix de Guerre with palms and officer of the Legion of Honor. He lived in San Diego, California and wrote several books on military engineering. Beach died on his seventy-sixth birthday in Pelham, New York on 18 June 1932. Photo courtesy of *The Assembly*, USMA.

George Bell, Jr. (0-38), son of George Bell and Isabella McCormick Bell, was born on 23 January 1859 at Fort McHenry, in Maryland. He graduated USMA number forty-three of fifty-two in the class of 1880, with James Walker Benét (a relative of the poet Stephen Vincent Benét, who wrote the epic poem on the Civil War entitled *John Brown's Body*), George W. Goethals (*q.v.*) and David

George Bell, Jr.

J. Rumbough. Bell was commissioned in the infantry, and remained a lifelong friend of Goethals. From 1880 to 1891, he did frontier duty. On 5 January 1885 he married Elizabeth Hunt, daughter of Confederate Maj. Gen. Robert Ransom. They had a daughter, Fannie M. G. Bell, later Mrs. William S. Wood. Bell became a Professor of Military Science and Tactics at Cornell University in 1892 and received a law degree while there; subsequently, he was admitted to the bar in New York. During the Spanish-American War, Bell went to Cuba with his regiment in 1898; he also served in the Sanitary Corps in the Philippines in 1900. While there he captured Vicente Lukban, an insurrectionist on Leyte and Samar, thus ending the insurrection in those localities. In 1903 he was promoted to major; he then commanded Fort Porter, New York. In 1906, Bell was again sent to the Philippines, where he captured the leader of a collection of religious fanatics who were causing trouble. In 1907 he went to the Inspector General's Department, and after that he headed a newly organized Maneuver Department. He also headed an American military mission attending the French and Swiss maneuvers. In 1913 he was made a colonel and commanded the 16th Infantry at the Presidio in San Francisco, California. In 1914 he was promoted to brigadier general (USA) and was sent to the Mexican border. There he commanded a brigade in Arizona; he was also commander of the El Paso district, with fifty thousand troops. On 5 August 1917, he was again promoted to major general (NA); he then commanded the 33d Division (AEF), for which he received the Distinguished Service Medal. On 20 December 1918 Bell took command of the Sixth Corps until 12 January 1919, when he was relieved by Gen. Adelbert Cronkhite (*q.v.*). After his return stateside he commanded the 86th Infantry Division, then the Sixth Corps Area, headquartered in Chicago. He retired on 30 November 1922. In addition to the DSM referred to above, he received from Britain the Order of Saint Michael and Saint George, and from France the Croix de Guerre with palm and commander of the Legion of Honor. In honor of his retirement, the *Chicago Citizen* presented him with thirty thousand dollars. He died at age sixty-seven in Chicago, Illinois on 28 October 1926. He was one of the last bearded general officers in the American army. Photo courtesy of the Annual Report, Association of Graduates, USMA.

James Franklin Bell (0-1687), son of John Wilson Bell and Sarah Margaret Venable Allen Bell, was born on 9 January 1856 in Shelbyville, Kentucky. He graduated USMA number thirty-eight of forty-three in the class of 1878. He was commissioned as an "additional" lieutenant in the Ninth Cavalry, but was soon transferred to the Seventh Cavalry. On 5 January 1881, he married Sarah Buford, and they had a son, James Franklin Bell, who also became a major general. From 1878 to 1894, Bell was on frontier duty with the Seventh, capturing a band of half-breed Cree Indians near Fort Buford, Dakota Territory, in 1883. He also participated in the Great Sioux War of 1890 and 1891; he then acted as adjutant of the Seventh Cavalry and secretary of the Cavalry and Light Artillery School at Fort Riley, Kansas, from 1891 to 1894. In the Philippines he served as aide to Gen. John W. Forsythe, and on 9 September 1899 he won a Medal of Honor. He was promoted to brigadier general (USV) on 5 December 1899 and to brigadier general (USA) on 19 February 1901. He was both a brigade commander and district commander in the Philippines, and became the provost marshal in Manila. In 1903 he returned to the States and was commandant of the Infantry and Cavalry School, the Signal School and the Staff College (all at Fort Leavenworth, Kansas). From April 1906 to April 1910, Bell was Chief of Staff (USA); in 1911 he was made commander of the Philippine Division, and in 1914 he commanded the Second Infantry Division in Texas. In 1915 he commanded the Western Division in San Francisco, California; in 1917 he got the same assignment, but with the Eastern Division. His last post was the 77th Infantry Division. He died on 8 January 1919, one day short of his sixty-third birthday. Photo courtesy of the Association of Graduates, USMA.

James Franklin Bell

☆

John Bradbury Bennett

John Bradbury Bennett (0-324), son of Hiram Pitt Bennett and Sarah McCabe Bennett, was born on 6 December 1865 in New Brunswick, New Jersey. His forebears had come to the United States from England in the eighteenth century. He graduated USMA number twenty-eight of sixty-five in the class of 1891, and was commissioned in the Seventh Infantry, which was then stationed at Fort Lupton, Colorado. He married Nelly Sharp in Leavenworth, Kansas on 12 August 1891; they had three sons: John B., Hiram W. and Alexander S. During the Spanish-American War, Bennett was aide to Gen. Henry Merriam, and during the Philippine insurrection he commanded a company of the 16th Infantry. Later, he was assistant commandant and inspector of the Philippine Constabulary under Gen. Henry T. Allen (*q.v.*). He organized a school for the constabulary in Baguio. In 1917 he was assistant chief of the Aviation Section of the Signal Corps, as a lieutenant colonel. He was in command of embarkation at Camp Merritt, New Jersey; in France, he commanded the 11th Infantry. On 1 October 1918 he became a brigadier general (NA); after the Saint Mihiel and Meuse-Argonne, he commanded a casual officers' detachment and Base Section Number 4 at LeHarve. The French made him an officer of the Legion of Honor. After the war, Bennett operated the demobilization camp at Camp Meade, Maryland, then served on the War Department General Staff. He graduated in 1921 from the Army War College and in 1930 from the General Staff School at Fort Leavenworth, Kansas. In 1925, Bennett retired as a colonel; he was again promoted to brigadier general on the retired list in 1930. He was able, energetic, sincere and loyal. He died at age sixty-four in Washington on 2 September 1930. Photo courtesy of the Annual Report, Association of Graduates, USMA.

Lucian Grant Berry

Lucian Grant Berry (0-107), son of Samuel Spicer Berry and Olive Elizabeth Read Berry, was born on 29 November 1863 in Caton, New York. He entered USMA and graduated number nine of seventy-seven in the class of 1886; his classmates included Mason M. Patrick, Charles T. Menoher and John J. Pershing (all *q.v.*). On 28 October 1886, Berry married Emily Ross, and they had six children: Marilla S. (later Mrs. Thomas Watson Brown), Olive E. (later Mrs. John Wesley Sherwood), Emily Minier Berry, Lucian S. S. Berry; Lucy (later Mrs. Thomas Warren Fox) and Helen Margaret. Berry was quite proud of the fact that his son and all but one of his sons-in-law were United States Army officers. He was commissioned in the Fourth Artillery Brigade and served at Fort Preble, Maine; Fort Snelling, Minnesota, and Fort McPherson, Georgia. After graduating from the Artillery School at Fort Monroe, Virginia, in 1892, he spent four years as an instructor at USMA, then rejoined his regiment at Fort McHenry, Baltimore. He was in the Puerto Rican Expedition in 1898, then was sent to Fort Slocum, New York, and Fort Adams, Rhode Island. In 1900 he was on the China Relief Expedition; he became a captain and was sent to the Philippines. After his return to the States, Berry commanded the 21st Battery, Field Artillery, at Fort Sheridan, Illinois; from there he was sent to the School of Fire at Fort Sill, Oklahoma, and in 1907 was promoted to major. For three years he commanded a battalion of the Third Field Artillery Brigade at Fort Sam

Houston, Texas. In late 1910 and early 1911 he commanded another battalion of the same regiment at Fort Myer, Virginia. On 11 March 1911 he was promoted to lieutenant colonel and went to the Army War College, graduating in 1912. Then, he commanded the Third Field Artillery Brigade at Fort D. A. Russel, Wyoming (later called Fort Francis E. Warren and now known as Warren Air Force Base), until 1913, when he was promoted to colonel and given command of the Fourth (Mountain) Field Artillery Brigade. He took this brigade to Vera Cruz, Mexico in 1914; he also took it into Mexico with Gen. John J. Pershing (*q.v.*) on the Mexican Punitive Expedition in 1916 and 1917. On 5 August 1917, he was promoted to brigadier general (NA); he then commanded the 60th Field Artillery Brigade in Oklahoma. In May 1918, he took this brigade to France and joined the 35th Infantry Division in the Vosges Mountains. He was the 35th Division's Chief of Artillery; for a while, he also supported the First Infantry Division in battle. He returned with this unit to the States in April 1919, and on 5 June 1919 he reverted to his permanent rank of colonel. He commanded the 78th Field Artillery Brigade and later, the Sixth Field Artillery Brigade until 19 June 1921, when he retired as a colonel. After his retirement he lived in Corning, New York. He was conscientious in the training of new officers, and was quite successful at it. He was promoted to brigadier general in 1930 while retired. At the age of seventy-four, Berry died in Corning on 30 December 1937. Photo courtesy of the Annual Report, Association of Graduates, USMA.

Walter Augustus Bethel

Walter Augustus Bethel (0-316) was born on 25 November 1866 in Freeport, Ohio. During his public school education he was a better-than-average student, so he was offered and accepted a job as an elementary school teacher. He read in the local newspaper of an examination to be held to fill a vacancy USMA. He took this exam and entered the academy, graduating number fourteen in the class of 1889. His classmates included E. E. Winslow, William W. Harts, Charles Crawford, William G. Haan and William Lassiter (all *q.v.*). He was commissioned in the artillery but later switched to the Judge Advocate General's Department. During 1884 and 1885 he was an instructor of chemistry at USMA, and from 1895 to 1899 he instructed law. This latter detail was interrupted by his service on the Puerto Rican Expedition from January to November 1898. In 1904 he married Elizabeth Strong of Portland, Oregon, and they had three daughters, including a set of twins. Bethel was a good athlete and played tennis, winning the 1903 Pacific Northwest tennis championship and a high national tennis rank. He gave the sport up at age sixty because of his eyesight.

On 5 August 1917, he was promoted to brigadier general (NA); he was the Judge Advocate General (AEF) from 1917 to 1920, for which he received the Distinguished Service Medal. He had gone to France on the *Baltic* with Gen. John J. Pershing (*q.v.*) in April 1917, and after the war he served in the JAG headquarters in Washington. When Gen. Enoch H. Crowder (*q.v.*) retired in 1923, Bethel became the Judge Advocate General of the army, with the rank of major general. He still considered his service as JAG of the AEF as the high point of his career. In 1924 he retired due to poor eyesight, and from 1926 to 1947 he engaged in the practice of international law. At the age of eighty-seven, he died at Walter Reed Army Medical Center on 11 January 1954. Photo courtesy of the Association of Graduates, USMA.

John Biddle

John Biddle (0-13130), son of William S. Biddle and Susan Ogden Biddle, was born on 2 February 1859 in Detroit, Michigan. After early education in Detroit, he had further education in Geneva as well as in Heidelberg and at the University of Michigan. He entered USMA and was a distinguished cadet for all four years; he graduated number two of fifty-three in the class of 1881. Harry and Henry Hodges, Joseph T. Dickman and Andrew S. Rowan (all *q.v.*) were four of his classmates. Biddle's commission was in the corps of engineers, and he served in the late Indian Wars. He was in charge of rivers and harbors work in Nashville, Tennessee from 1891 to 1898, then was a lieutenant colonel as the Chief Engineer of the United States Volunteers during the Spanish-American War. First he went to Puerto Rico, then to Cuba, then to the Philippines. From 1901 to 1907 he was Commissioner (engineer) for the District of Columbia, and in 1911 he was in charge of rivers and harbors work in San Francisco, California. After that, he spent three years on the War Department General Staff, followed by three months of rivers and harbors duty in Savannah, Georgia. From December 1914 to June 1915, Bethel was an American observer with the Austro-Hungarian army in Austria and Poland. Upon his return to the States, he did rivers and harbors duty in Baltimore during the winter of 1915 and 1916. He was appointed superintendent of USMA in 1916 and 1917, then commanded the Sixth Engineering Regiment in 1917. He was also promoted to brigadier general (USA) and became a major general (NA) in 1917. From July to October 1917, Bethel commanded the United States railway regiments in France (AEF). From November 1917 to March 1918, he was assistant Chief of Staff (AEF). For the next fifteen months, he commanded all American troops in Britain, then Camp Travis, Texas, from August 1919 to January 1920 and Camp

Custer from February to September 1920. He retired on 1 December 1920 as a brigadier general and was promoted to major general on the retired list in 1930. He then went to Texas, where he died at age seventy-six on 18 January 1936, still a bachelor. Photo courtesy of the Association of Graduates, USMA.

Henry Patrick Birmingham, M.D.

Henry Patrick Birmingham, M.D. (0-13346) was born on 15 March 1854 in Brooklyn, New York. He received his medical degree from the University of Michigan in 1876, and on 18 February 1881 he entered the army as an assistant surgeon (first lieutenant) of the Medical Corps. His first tours of duty were with the Fourth Cavalry in actions against the Apaches in the far southwest. Promotion to assistant surgeon (captain) came on 18 February 1886. During the Spanish-American War, Birmingham served first in Puerto Rico and then in the Philippines. On 4 June 1898 he was promoted to major, brigade surgeon of volunteers, and on 23 April 1908 he was promoted to lieutenant colonel, Medical Corps. At one time he commanded Walter Reed Army Medical Center, and in 1914 he was the chief surgeon of the Vera Cruz Expedition under Gen. Frederick Funston (*q.v.*). On 2 October 1917, Birmingham was promoted to brigadier general (NA); that same year, he received an honorary master's degree from the University of Michigan. During World War I, Birmingham was in charge of the ambulance service of the army, and also of the gas defense service of the medical department. In 1918 he retired as a colonel, then went right back to active duty. In 1930, he was retired by operation of law as a brigadier general. He never married; he lived briefly in Washington, and then at the United States Soldiers Home. A high school in Van Nuys, California is named for him, as is Birmingham General Hospital in San Fernando, California. At the age of seventy-eight, he died of arteriosclerosis in Washington on 4 May 1932. He was buried in Arlington National Cemetery. Photo courtesy of the National Archives.

Harry Gore Bishop (0-254), son of Louis Haswell Bishop and Jeanette Atwater Bishop, was born on 22 November 1874 in Grand Rapids, Michigan. One of his ancestors had come from England and settled in New York City in 1765. After graduating from high school in Goshen, Indiana, he worked for a year helping the county surveyor and city engineer. Bishop entered USMA and graduated number fifty-four of sixty-seven in the class of 1897 with Harley B.

Harry Gore Bishop

Ferguson and Frank R. McCoy (both *q.v.*). Originally commissioned in the infantry, he later changed to the artillery corps, then went with the field artillery after 1907. After serving at five different posts in the States, he was sent to the Philippines to help meet the insurrection, and served mainly in Luzon and Cebu. For eighteen months he ran the licenses and collected the taxes for the city of Manila. In September 1901, he was sent to Fort Adams, in Rhode Island, to command a battery of Coast Artillery. From there he was sent to Fort Totten, New York, as adjutant of the School of Submarine Defense until 1906, when he was sent to Oregon as artillery engineer for the District of Columbia (river basin). In 1907, when the field artillery became a separate arm, he was transferred to Fort Sam Houston, Texas, as a captain; he commanded a battery of field artillery there. In 1910 he was sent to Fort Leavenworth, Kansas, first as a student officer, then as an instructor of military art. While stationed there, he had a number of interesting side assignments with the Ohio National Guard at Camp Perry (the small arms firing center) and with the Pennsylvania National Guard at Mount Gretna (just north of Lancaster and south of Indiantown Gap). His next station was Fort Sill, Oklahoma; then, he went to the Mexican border, where he commanded the field artillery at El Paso, Texas. In 1917, he was detailed to the General Staff in Washington and headed the War Plans Division. On 26 June 1918, Bishop was promoted to brigadier general (NA) and placed in command of the 159th Field Artillery Brigade, 84th Infantry Division Artillery, but shortly after his arrival in France he was transferred to the Third Field Artillery Brigade. He commanded this unit in the Meuse-Argonne and during the advance to Germany. He was especially praised by Gen. Hanson E. Ely and Gen. John J. Pershing (both *q.v.*), and upon his return to the States he became commandant of the Artillery School at Fort Sill. He was later director of the Army War College, then went back to the War Plans Division. After reverting to his permanent rank of colonel, he commanded the Fifteenth, Sixth and Eighth Field Artillery Regiments. From 10 March 1930 to 9 March 1934, he was Chief of Field Artillery; this duty carried with it the temporary rank of major general. He received the Distinguished Service Medal from Pershing and was also an officer of the French Legion of Honor. His was an innovative type of mind: he made a miniature field gun to save money for artillery practice during the Great Depression. He also wrote a number of books, manuals and pamphlets as well as magazine articles. His first marriage was to Agnes Watkins, the summer he graduated, and apparently she later died. On 15 December 1928, he remarried, to Mrs. Ella Van Horn Foulois, former wife of Gen. Benjamin D. Foulois (*q.v.*) of the Army Air Corps. At the age of fifty-nine, Bishop died in Washington on 31

August 1934. Apparently there were no children. Photo courtesy of the Association of Graduates, USMA.

Percy Poe Bishop

Percy Poe Bishop (0-655), son of John McElroy Bishop and Margaret Wood Bishop, was born on 27 May 1877 in Powell, Tennessee. In 1898 he graduated from the University of Tennessee with a B.S.; he was commissioned a second lieutenant in the Fourth Artillery Brigade on 9 July of that year. He was an honor graduate of the Artillery School in 1902 and an instructor there through 1903. He served as assistant to the Chief of Coast Artillery from 1907 to 1911, and in 1911 he married Grace Waldron Calvert. From 1914 to 1917, he was again assistant to the Chief of Coast Artillery, and he was transferred to the General Staff Corps on 16 October 1917. On that date he became assistant to the secretary of the General Staff, and on 6 February 1918 he was promoted to colonel. On 21 March 1918, Bishop himself became secretary of the General Staff, and for that performance of duty he received the Distinguished Service Medal. He was promoted to brigadier general (NA) on 1 October 1918 and held that rank until 1 November 1919, when he reverted to his peacetime rank. From September 1918 until October 1921, he was chief of the Personnel Branch of the General Staff. In 1926, he graduated from the Army War College. During his military career he served in the Philippines, on both coasts of the United States, as both assistant commandant and later commandant of the Coast Artillery School, as commander of the Fourth Coast Artillery District, as commander of the harbor defenses of Manila and Subic Bays, and as Commanding General of the Seventh Corps Area. He became a brigadier general (USA) in 1934 and a major general (USA) in 1938; he retired in 1941. In Washington, Bishop belonged to both the Army and Navy Club and the Chevy Chase Club; in Omaha, Nebraska, he belonged to the Omaha Club. His home was in Portland, Maine; he died at age eighty-nine on 8 April 1967. Photo courtesy of the National Archives.

Alfred William Bjornstad (0-615), son of Mr. and Mrs. Julius Bjornstad, was born on 13 October 1874 in Saint Paul, Minnesota. He attended Luther College (in Decorah, Iowa) in 1891 and 1892, then attended the University of Minnesota. He spoke five languages and was a great athlete. He received his original commission as first lieutenant in the 13th Minnesota Infantry on 7 May 1898. He was a captain, 42d United States Volunteer Infantry, by 17 August 1899, and a first lieutenant (USA), 29th Infantry, by February 1901. He was engaged in thirty-four actions and battles in the Philippines between 1898 and 1904. He married Pearl Ladd Sabin on 3 October 1905, but they had no children. In 1909 he was an honor graduate of the Army School of the Line, and in 1910 he graduated from the Army Staff College. General Staff duty came during 1911 and 1912, and in 1912 and 1913 he was the United States military attaché in Berlin. This was followed by duty as an instructor at the Army Staff College in 1915 and 1916. Late 1916 saw him as Professor of Military Science and Tactics at Harvard University. After this he returned to the General Staff, organizing and directing the sixteen training camps which produced the original 25,341 officers of the National Army. In 1917, Bjornstad was the first Chief of Staff of the 30th Infantry Division, and later that year he organized and directed the army's General Staff college in France. He became a brigadier general (NA) on 12 July 1918, with date of rank from 26 January 1918. His next assignment was as Chief of Staff, Third Corps (AEF), followed by duty as Commanding General, 13th Infantry Brigade, in 1918 and 1919. He participated in all the major engagements in France. During 1919 he was on duty at the General Staff college, and from 1920 to 1923 he commanded Fort Snelling, Minnesota. He was decorated with: from the United States, the Distinguished Service Cross, the Distinguished Service Medal and the Purple Heart; from Britain, the Order of Saints Michael and George, and from France, the Croix de Guerre and Legion of Honor. He belonged to the Masons, and retired in 1928, maintaining homes in both Santa Barbara and San Francisco, California. At the age of sixty, he died at Letterman General Hospital on 4 November 1934. Photo courtesy of the National Archives.

Alfred William Bjornstad

William Murray Black (0-12992), son of James Black and Eliza M. Black, was born on 8 December 1855 in Lancaster, Pennsylvania. After graduating from Lancaster High School, he entered Franklin and Marshall College (also in Lancaster); during his junior year he won an appointment to USMA by competitive examination. He graduated number one of seventy-six in the class of 1877, and was commissioned in the corps of engineers. In 1912, he received a doctor of science degree from Franklin and Marshall College and a doctorate in engineering from Pennsylvania Military College. He married Daisy Peyton, daughter of Capt. George H. Derby (USA). After she died, he married Gertrude Totten, daughter of Cdr. William M. Gamble (USN). Black was promoted to lieutenant colonel and Chief Engineer, United States Volunteers, on 25 May 1898.

William Murray Black

Long tours of duty followed in rivers and harbors work, after which he became an instructor of practical military engineering at USMA and instructor in civil engineering at the United States Engineer School in Willett's Point, New York. Next, he was the assistant in charge of fortifications work in the office of the Chief of Engineers (USA) in Washington, D.C. from 1895 to 1897. In 1897 and 1898, Black was a commissioner of the District of Columbia. He was Chief Engineer in Puerto Rico in 1898, in the Department of Havana from 2 January 1899 to 3 April 1900, and in the division of Cuba from January 1900 to April 1901, on the staff of Gen. Leonard Wood (*q.v.*). He was senior member of the board charged with raising the wreck of the *Maine* from Havana Harbor between 1910 and 1913. He was brigadier general, Chief of Engineers and major general. After serving as Chief Engineer of the Eastern Department, Black retired on 31 October 1919. He received the Distinguished Service Medal and was author of several engineering books, as well as inventor of a method of purifying sewage by aeration. From 1920 until 1929, he worked as a consulting engineer. Black died at age seventy-seven in Washington on 24 September 1933. Photo courtesy of the National Archives.

Charles School Blakely

Charles School Blakely (0-1909), younger brother of Brig. Gen. George Blakely, was born on 6 November 1880 in Pennsylvania. After completing his early education, Blakely entered USMA and graduated number twenty-nine of one hundred twenty-four in the class of 1904. George R. Allin, Leslie J. McNair, Pelham D. Glassford (all *q.v.*), Edmund L. Gruber and Joseph W. Stilwell were classmates of his. He was an artilleryman, and was promoted to brigadier general (NA) on 1 October 1918, commanding an artillery brigade in France. After this, he was the Commanding General of the brigade fire center. From 1922 to 1925, he was executive officer for the Chief of Field Artillery in Washington. During 1926 and 1927, Blakely studied at the Naval War College in Newport, Rhode Island. From 1934 to 1937, he was assistant commandant of the Field Artillery School at Fort

Sill, Oklahoma. In 1938, after thirty-four years of service, he retired due to disabilities. He lived in Louisville, Kentucky and died there at age ninety-four on 11 January 1975. Photo courtesy of Special Collections, USMA Library.

George Blakely

George Blakely (0-232) was born on 5 July 1870 in Pennsylvania. He graduated USMA number four of sixty-two in the class of 1892. Charles P. Sumerall, William Chamberlaine, James A. Shipton (all *q.v.*) and Kirby Walker were four of his classmates. He was commissioned in the Second Artillery Brigade and graduated from the Artillery School in 1896. From 1898 until 1901 and again from 1903 to 1908, he was an assistant professor of mathematics at USMA. He served in the Coast Artillery, but was later detailed to the Inspector General's Department. On 3 August 1917, Blakely was promoted to brigadier general (NA), in command of the 61st Field Artillery Brigade at Fort Worth, Texas. From 18 September 1917 until 5 December 1917, he temporarily commanded the 36th Infantry Division. From July to October 1918, he commanded the South Atlantic Coast Artillery District; he was then sent to France as Commanding General of the 38th Artillery Brigade (AEF) from October 1918 to February 1919. After the war, he commanded the North Pacific Coast Artillery District. He retired in 1924 as a colonel, but his rank of brigadier general was restored by act of Congress in June 1930. He lived in San Francisco, California and died there at age ninety-five on 16 November 1965. Photo courtesy of the National Archives.

Albert Hazen Blanding (0-222742), son of Abram O. Blanding and Sarah Ann Nattinger Blanding, was born on 9 November 1876 in Lyons, Iowa. He graduated from East Florida Seminary in 1894. From 1898 to 1910, he was a mine superintendent and assistant manager of the Dutton Phosphate Company; in 1899 he entered the Florida National Guard. On 1 June 1908, he married Mildred M. Hale, and they had three children: Sarah E., Mildred L., and William N. He operated a lumber and naval store business from 1910 to 1916, and was a Florida National Guard colonel when he went on active duty to the Mexican border in 1916 and 1917. Shortly after this, when the National Guard was mustered into federal service for World War I, Blanding became a brigadier general (NA) on 5 August 1917. He commanded the 185th Infantry Brigade, of which the 370th (Colored) Infantry of Illinois was a part, and served in France during 1918 and 1919, for which he received the Distinguished Service Medal, the Florida

Active Service Medal and the Florida Cross. He was also one of the original incorporators of the American Legion. After World War I, he was with the Consolidated Lumber Company from 1919 to 1922, and then the Florida Citrus Exchange from 1922 to 1933. It was during this period, in 1924, that the state of Florida appointed Blanding a National Guard major general. From 1 February 1936 to 31 January 1940, he was the chief of the National Guard Bureau in Washington. After that he was promoted to lieutenant general of the Florida National Guard; he retired on 9 November 1940. During World War II, Blanding was busy with the civil defense of Florida, and served on a number of Florida state boards. He was a Democrat, an Elk, a Kiwanian and a Mason. His retirement home was in Tallahassee; he died there at age ninety-four in December 1970. Photo courtesy of the Adjutant General of Florida.

Albert Hazen Blanding

Richard Milford Blatchford

Richard Milford Blatchford (0-46), son of Samuel T. Blatchford and Agnes Leadbeater Blatchford, was born on 17 August 1859 at Fort Hamilton, New York. His ancestors had come from Devonshire, England in the eighteenth century. He was educated at Williston Seminary in Massachusetts and Claverack College in New York; he graduated from Rensselaer Polytechnic Institute with the class of 1882. He was commissioned a second lieutenant in the 11th Infantry on 10 October 1883 by President Chester A. Arthur. On 27 July 1887 Blatchford married Natalie Cary Green of New Jersey. He also graduated from the Infantry and Cavalry School at Fort Leavenworth, Kansas, in 1887, and on 7 December of that year he was promoted to first lieutenant. From 1893 to 1895, he was an American Indian Agent at Fort Apache, Arizona. During the Spanish-American War, Blatchford took part in the Puerto Rican campaign and was the first American military mayor of San Juan, Puerto Rico. He received his captaincy on 26 April 1898, and his next duty was in the Philippines with the 28th, 11th and 6th Infantry Regiments. After a brief tour as a recruiter in New York, he was an instructor and inspector for the Missouri National Guard. In 1913, Mrs. Blatchford died. On 30 April 1913, Blatchford became a colonel and given command of the 12th Infantry in Nogales, Arizona. Nogales was the site of a peace conference between Mexico's General Obregon and his adversary, Pancho Villa. Gen. John J. Pershing (*q.v.*) was present on this occasion; with him was his aide, Lieutenant James L. Collins, who became the father of both Brig. Gen. James L. Collins (the chief of military history) and Michael Collins (the astronaut). There is now a photo of General Pershing and Lieutenant Collins in Nogales, and unfortunately Lieutenant Collins gets identified as Lt. G. S. Patton. On 15 May 1917, Blatchford was promoted to brigadier general (NA); he was in charge of supply in the AEF from 25 July to 1 November 1917. On 5 August 1917, he was again promoted to major general (NA), and in November he was assigned to the command of the Panama Canal Zone. With the coming of peace he reverted to brigadier general but continued in the same command. On 6 January 1921, he married a second time to Elinor Hall, who, like his first wife, was from New Jersey. There were no children in either marriage. In his last three years of service, Blatchford commanded the 158th Depot Brigade at Camp Sherman, Ohio; the Presidio in San Francisco, California; the Eighth Infantry Brigade at Camp Lewis, Washington; the post of Vancouver Barracks, Washington, and the Fifth Infantry Brigade. On 1 December 1922, he retired as a brigadier general, and his rank of major general was restored on the retired list, by act of Congress, in 1930. He lived in San Francisco, and died there at age seventy-five on 31 August 1934. Photo courtesy of the National Archives.

Tasker Howard Bliss

Tasker Howard Bliss (0-12990) was born on 31 December 1853 in Lewisburg, Pennsylvania. He entered Bucknell University in 1870 and joined the Phi Kappa Psi fraternity before entering USMA. He graduated number eight of forty-three in the class of 1875 and was one of the oldest general officers on duty during World War I. (Three of them were born in 1853.) He graduated from the Artillery School in 1884 and served in both the artillery and the commissary. From 1876 to 1880 he was an assistant professor at USMA. In 1884 he was appointed recorder on a presidential board to report on the military value of the inland waterways of the United States. He was a scholarly person and served on many projects where technical capacity beyond mere tactics and strategy were needed. He was a professor of military science at the Naval War College from 1885 to 1888. Bliss was both an aide to Gen. John McAllister Schofield and inspector of rifle practice from 1888 to 1895. He was on special duty with the Secretary of War and was military attaché in Madrid from 1895 to 1897. From 1898 to 1899, Bliss was a lieutenant colonel of United States

Volunteers and served in Puerto Rico and Cuba as chief of Cuban customs. In 1902, he was promoted to brigadier general (USA), and in 1909 he became assistant Chief of Staff. In 1915 he became a major general (USA), and as of 22 September 1917 he was Chief of Staff of the United States Army. He actually retired in 1917 but was required to be on active duty as a brevet four-star general in order to be the American representative on the Supreme War Council from 1917 to 1919; he received the Distinguished Service Medal for this. He was at the Paris Peace Conference in 1918 and 1919, and from 1920 to 1927 was governor of the Soldiers Home in Washington, D.C. Bliss was again made a four-star general on the retired list in 1930, and he received numerous honors, decorations and degrees. He was one of only three four-star American generals in World War I, and to the best of the author's knowledge he received the last brevet commission given by the army. He died at age seventy-six in Washington, D.C. on 9 December 1930. Photo courtesy of USMA Library. Notice the two-button spacing, indicating that he was a brigadier general at the time the photo was taken.

Augustus Perry Blocksom

Augustus Perry Blocksom (0-13120) was born on 7 November 1854 in Ohio. He graduated USMA number twenty-two of seventy-six in the class of 1877. William M. Black, Thomas H. Barry (both *q.v.*) and Henry Ossian Flipper (the first African-American graduate of USMA) were classmates. On 15 June 1877, Blocksom was commissioned a second lieutenant of cavalry and sent on frontier duty. He was brevetted a first lieutenant on 27 July 1890 for gallant services against the American Indians at Ash Creek, Arizona on 7 May 1880. (Thirteen years after being commissioned and ten years after the event—there's nothing like a grateful and appreciative government!) Blocksom served in many campaigns against the Apaches in Arizona, then participated in the Sioux Campaign of 1890 and 1891. He was wounded during the attack on San Juan Hill in Cuba in 1898, and received a Silver Star citation for his performance there. During the China Relief Expedition, he commanded a squadron of the Sixth Cavalry, again earning a Silver Star citation. From 1900 to 1902, he served during the Philippine insurrection. He was made a major general (NA) on 5 August 1917 and commanded Camp Cody, in New Mexico (near Deming), until 18 April 1918. He commanded the 34th Infantry Division from 25 August 1917 until 17 September 1917. He was honorably discharged from the national army and reverted to his permanent rank of brigadier general on 18 April 1918. He commanded the Hawaiian Department until 7 November 1918, when he retired. After his retirement he lived in Miami, Florida; he died there at age seventy-six on 26 July 1931. Photo courtesy of the Annual Report, Association of Graduates, USMA. Major general, retired list, 1930.

Charles R. Boardman

Charles R. Boardman (no ASN assigned), son of Napoleon Boardman (a Wisconsin Civil War veteran) and Mary Louise Tallmadge Boardman, was born on 28 October 1860 in Empire, Fond du Lac County, Wisconsin. An ancestor on his father's side was a Norman soldier who went to England with William the Conqueror, and an ancestor on his mother's side was the Major Tallmadge who had charge of the unfortunate Major Andre during the American Revolution. His maternal grandfather was a United States senator from New York and the third territorial governor of Wisconsin. Boardman's education began in the local public schools, and he graduated from Fond du Lac High School in 1878. He received a B.A. from the University of Wisconsin, went into business and steadily progressed. In 1884, Boardman was city editor of the *Daily Northwestern* (of Oshkosh) and was business manager from 1884 to 1897. In 1940 he was still vice president of the paper. He also organized and headed the Globe Printing Company. At the age of nineteen, he had enlisted in the Wisconsin National Guard; he was a captain by 1885 and a major by 1889. On 4 January 1897, he was appointed Adjutant General of Wisconsin; he was reappointed through the terms of succeeding governors. Having served thirty-three years, he retired on 1 October 1913. He transferred to the National Guard Reserve on 1 May 1917 and was given command of the First Wisconsin Infantry Brigade. In France he commanded the 64th Infantry Brigade, 32d Infantry Division. He was married and had one son, Robert, who also was an army officer during World War I. Boardman served in France from 13 January to 11 August 1918, when he was relieved by Gen. John A. Lejeune (USMC). On 13 August he received an honorable discharge after thirty-eight years of service. He was one of the oldest American general officers in command of American combat troops in France. An extremely active man in civil as well as military life, he was also president of the Wisconsin National Life Insurance Company, president of the Globe Printing Company, a director of the *Daily Northwestern* and a bank director. He died at age eighty-nine on 5 April 1950. Photo courtesy of the Wisconsin National Life Insurance Company, Oshkosh. This photo was obviously taken some time after the war, in a "blank" uniform: no hat cord, collar brass, et cetera.

Ewing E. Booth

Ewing E. Booth (0-614), son of Nathaniel Booth and Martha Bower Booth, was born on 2 February 1870 in Bower's Mill, located in the Vineyard Township of northern Lawrence County, Missouri, just north of Mount Vernon and west of Springfield. He married and had one daughter, Gladys (later Mrs. P. L. Thomas). Booth served as a captain in the First Colorado Volunteer Infantry during the Spanish-American War and was honorably discharged on 14 July 1899. On 5 July 1899 he was commissioned a captain in the 36th United States Volunteer Infantry, and he was honorably mustered out of that unit on 16 March 1901. On 2 February 1901 he was commissioned a first lieutenant in the Seventh Cavalry. It is interesting how he landed on the next safe place before jumping off the first, but we have seen this often during this period in American history; he was by no means the only one. On 22 August 1904, Booth became captain in the Tenth Cavalry, but he transferred back to the Seventh on 11 May 1905. From 1912 to 1915, he was an aide to Maj. Gen. J. Franklin Bell (*q.v.*). On 5 October 1915, he was assigned to the First Cavalry Regiment, and by 15 May 1917 he was a major. On 5 August 1917, he was made a lieutenant colonel (NA), and from June to August 1917 he served as Chief of Staff of the Eastern Department. As of 5 August 1917 (when he became a lieutenant colonel), he became Chief of Staff of the 77th Infantry Division. By 3 February 1918 he was a colonel (NA), and on 25 June 1918 he became a brigadier general (NA). He commanded the Eighth Infantry Brigade, Fourth Infantry Division (AEF). He participated in the French sector activities during May, June and July 1918. That same year, he also took part in the second Battle of the Marne in July and August, the Saint Mihiel offensive in September, and the Meuse-Argonne in September and October. From 18 November to 10 January 1919, he was with the army of occupation in Germany. Then, until 20 June 1919, he was assistant Chief of Staff, G-1, of the Service of Supply (SOS). On that date he was made Chief of Staff, and the following day he became Chief of Staff of all American Forces in France. On 8 January 1920, Booth was made deputy allied high commander in Armenia; he served in this capacity until 30 June 1920. On 1 July 1920 he reverted to colonel of cavalry (USA) and became assistant commandant of the General Service School. From 1921 to 1923, he was director of the General Service School. He served as an instructor at the Army War College in 1923 and 1924. He then commanded the Fourth Cavalry on the Mexican border, followed by command of the First Cavalry Brigade. From 1 July 1925 to 1 May 1927 (this note dates the photos taken with Will Rogers), he was commandant of the Cavalry School at Fort Riley, Kansas. From 1 May 1927 to 11 October 1930, he was assistant Chief of Staff, G-4, at the War Department. On 21 December 1930, he was promoted to deputy Chief of Staff, and on 27 April 1931 he was given command of the First Cavalry Division at Fort Bliss, Texas. His next assignment was in the Philippines, from 31 January 1932 until 28 February 1934; he then retired and lived in Chevy Chase, Maryland, just outside Washington, D.C. Booth was commended for the action on the Vesle (1918) and cited with the Seventh and Eighth Brigades for service in the Bois de Fays. He also received the Distinguished Service Medal, Croix de Guerre, Legion of Honor, Philippine Congressional Medal and Spanish-American War Medal. He died at age seventy-nine on 19 February 1949, and is buried in Arlington National Cemetary. Photos from *The Rasp*, an annual publication of the Cavalry School at Fort Riley, Kansas.

Albert Jesse Bowley (0-256), son of Freeman S. Bowley and Flora Pepper Bowley, was born on 24 November 1875 in Westminster, California, near Los Angeles. He graduated USMA number thirteen of sixty-seven in the class of 1897 and was commissioned in the Fourth Artillery Brigade. He was at the siege of Santiago, Cuba in 1898 and also served in the Sanitary Corps there. Then, he was in the Philippines until 1901, when he returned to USMA as an instructor of four sciences and senior instructor of artillery tactics. This lasted until 1905, when he became aide to Gen. Fredrick Dent Grant (son of Ulysses S. Grant) at Governor's Island and in Chicago. During 1910 and 1911, Bowley was back in the Philippines for a second time; then, from 1911 to 1914, he was military attaché in China. He was on duty at Fort Sill, Oklahoma, and on the Mexican border from 1915 until 1917, when he organized the 17th Field Artillery Brigade. He took this brigade to France for World War I, and on 26 June 1918 he was promoted to brigadier general (NA). He also commanded the Second Field Artillery Brigade, Second Infantry Division (AEF); he received the Distinguished Service Medal for this performance of duty. He became Chief of Artillery of the Sixth Corps on 6 November 1918. In 1919 and 1920, he attended General Staff College, and during 1920 and 1921 he served as a member of the General Staff. In July 1921, Bowley commanded Fort Bragg, in North Carolina; after this he commanded the Eighth Corps Area, Second Infantry Division, Fourth Army. From 1929 to 1931, he was assistant Chief of Staff, G-1, in Washington, and in 1931 he became a major general (USA). That year he married Elsie Ball Wright. For the next three years he commanded the Hawaiian Division, and during 1934 and 1935 he commanded the Fifth Corps Area. His promotion to lieutenant general came in 1939, but on 30 November of that year he was retired as a major general. His list of medals and decorations

Albert Jesse Bowley

was considerable: the Spanish-American War Medal; medals for involvement with the Cuban occupation, Philippine insurrection, Mexican border and World War I victory; from the United States, the General Staff Medal (USA) and the Distinguished Service Medal; from France, the Croix de Guerre and Legion of Honor; from China, the Order of Plentiful Rice; from Panama, the Order of Solidad, and from Siam, the Order of the White Elephant. Bowley died at age sixty-nine in Northumberland County, Virginia on 22 May 1945. Photo courtesy of the Association of Graduates, USMA.

Alfred Eugene Bradley, M.D.

Alfred Eugene Bradley, M.D. (0-13408), son of Arthur A. Bradley and Jane Parsons Bradley, was born on 25 November 1864 in Jamestown, New York. He graduated from Frewsburg Union School before entering Jefferson Medical College in Philadelphia. Dr. T. J. Whitney was his preceptor. He gave his address as Frewsburg, Chautanqua County, New York. Upon his graduation in 1887 he received the faculty prize; he interned at Philadelphia Hospital during 1887 and 1888. On 4 October 1887, Bradley married Letitia Follett. On 29 October 1888 he was appointed assistant surgeon, United States Army; he then took part in the Pine Ridge campaign of 1890 and 1891. He was promoted to captain, assistant surgeon, on 29 October 1893. During the Spanish-American War, Bradley served as a major and was a brigade surgeon of volunteers. During 1898 and 1899 he commanded the hospital ship *Relief*, which he took from New York to San Francisco, California via Marseille, the Suez Canal, Japan and the Hawaiian Islands (learning how to do things the government way!) He was honorably discharged from the volunteer service on 10 November 1899; on 1 January 1902 he was promoted to major, medical corps. From 1911 to 1913, Bradley commanded the division hospital in Manila, and on 1 July 1916 he was promoted to colonel, Medical Corps. From May 1916 to July 1917 he was an observer with the British, stationed at the American embassy in London. He was promoted to brigadier general (NA) on 5 August 1917; he acted as Chief Surgeon at General Headquarters (AEF) in Chaumont, France, for which he received the Distinguished Service Medal. Bradley developed lung trouble, was found physically incapacitated, and was relieved by Gen. Meritte W. Ireland (*q.v.*). On 28 June 1918 he was discharged from the national army and invalided back to the United States. He had an operation at the army hospital at Fort Totten, in New York, but did not fully recover; he was retired from the United States Army on 13 March 1920. He wrote for medical journals from his home in Highland Park, Illinois, just outside of Chicago. Bradley died at age fifty-eight in Montgomery,

Alabama on 17 December 1922; he was buried at Arlington National Cemetery. Photo courtesy of Mr. S. Paul Klein of the Walter Reed Army Research Institute.

John Jewsbury Bradley (0-342), son of Timothy M. Bradley and Emma Cookson Bradley, was born on 20 April 1869 in Chicago, Illinois. He graduated USMA number fifty-three of sixty-five in the class of 1891 and was commissioned in the Fourteenth Infantry. On 14 September 1893, he married Caroline Staden, and they had three children: Frances Bradley (later Mrs. William E. Chickering), John J. Bradley, Jr., and Joseph S. Bradley. He served in the Philippines during the insurrection, for which he received both a Silver Star commendation and a Purple Heart. He graduated in 1912 from the Army School of the Line, and in 1913 from the Army Staff College. He served on the War Department General Staff in 1917 and 1918, earning a Distinguished Service Medal. On 26 June 1918, he was promoted to brigadier general (NA), and with the AEF in France he commanded a brigade of the 82d Infantry Division. In November 1918 he commanded the Eighth Infantry Division. In 1927 he was retired as a colonel due to disabilities; he was admitted to the bar in New York and practiced law there. His rank of brigadier general (USA) was restored on the retired list, by act of Congress, in June 1930. In addition to the previously mentioned decorations, he received the following: from France, an Officer of the Legion of Honor; from Britain, the Companion of the Order of Saint Michael and Saint George, and from Italy, Commander of the Order of the Crown. He was a trustee of the Disabled American Veterans Service Foundation. He also belonged to the Military Order of the World War, the Guards Club in London and the Army and Navy Club in Washington. He died at age seventy-nine in Detroit, Michigan on 21 May 1948, and was buried in West Point, New York. Photo courtesy of the Association of Graduates, USMA.

John Jewsbury Bradley

David Legge Brainard (0-13116), son of Alanson Brainard and Maria Brainard, was born on 21 December 1856 in Norway, New York. He was educated at the State Normal School in Cortland, New York. He enlisted in the Seventh Cavalry and was a private, corporal and sergeant in Troop L from 18 September 1876 to 31 July 1884. He served in the signal corps from 1 August 1884 to 21 October 1886, when he was discharged to accept a commission. He participated in the Sioux, Nez Percé and Bannock campaigns of 1877 and 1878,

David Legge Brainard

and was wounded in the face and right hand. He was detailed for duty with the Howgate Arctic Exploring Expedition in 1880 and with the Lady Franklin Bay Arctic Exploring Expedition under Lieutenant Greely from 1881 to 1884. He served with James Booth Lockwood while exploring the interior of Grinnell Land and the northwestern coast of Greenland, and on 13 May 1882 he reached the highest point ever attained in the north to that date: 83°, 24′, 30″. He was one of the seven survivors rescued by Cdr. W. S. Schley in June 1884. He was commissioned a second lieutenant, Second Cavalry, on 22 October 1886 for "distinguished and meritorious service in connection with the Arctic Expedition of 1881 [to] 1884." He was awarded the Back Grant of the Royal Geographical Society in 1885 for special services in connection with his work of exploration in Arctic regions. In June 1917, Brainard married Sara H. Guthrie; they had no children. On 25 July 1918, he was promoted to brigadier general (USA), and he retired that same day. He received the Charles P. Daly Gold Medal in 1926 from the American Geographical Society for Arctic Explorations and the Explorer's Medal from the Explorer's Club in New York City in 1929; he also received a Purple Heart in 1933. He was a Fellow of the American Geographical Society and a member of the National Geographic Society. He belonged to the Explorer's Club in New York and the Army and Navy Club in Washington, where he lived in his last days. He wrote several books, including *Outpost of the Lost* (1929) and *Six Came Back* (1946). He was the last survivor of the Greely Arctic Expedition, and died at age eighty-nine on 22 March 1946; he is buried at Arlington National Cemetery. Photo courtesy of the National Archives.

Lloyd Milton Brett (0-13420), son of John Brett and Elizabeth Brown Brett, was born on 22 February 1856 in Dead River, Maine. He graduated USMA number thirty-four of sixty-seven in the class of 1879, and was commissioned a second lieutenant in the Second Cavalry. Brett performed frontier duty from 1879 to 1898, and during this time he married Elma Wallace. While still a second lieutenant, he won a Medal of Honor for most distinguished gallantry in action against the hostile Sioux Indians in the last of the Indian wars. He served as a major in the United States Volunteers during the Philippine insurrection, and from 1903 to 1908 was Adjutant General of the District of Columbia Militia. From 1910 to 1916, he was assigned as Superintendent of Yellowstone Park (then under the direction of the War Department), which was garrisoned by cavalry troops to prevent poaching and generally keep good order. With the entry of the United States into World War I, Brett received his star as a brigadier general

(NA) on 5 August 1917 and took command of the 160th Infantry Brigade at Camp (now Fort) Lee, in Virginia. He took them to France with the AEF and received a Distinguished Service Medal for his performance. Also, from 26 November 1917 to 28 December 1917, he commanded the 80th Infantry Division. Upon his return to the United States at the end of the war, he was dropped back to colonel and given command of the Third Cavalry at Fort Myer, Virginia. This regiment became the United States' household cavalry in its day. It turned out for all major government functions; the president's own horses were kept there (after the White House stable closed), and the family, as well as the president himself, rode there. In 1920 Brett retired as a colonel. From 23 November 1923 to 23 September 1927 he was Adjutant General of the District of Columbia; he held this assignment until his death. In 1927 he was promoted to brigadier general (USA) on the retired list. In addition to the decorations previously mentioned, he was an officer of the Legion of Honor and also received the Croix de Guerre. He died at age seventy-one in Washington on 23 September 1927. Photo courtesy of the National Archives.

Lloyd Milton Brett

Andre Walker Brewster

Andre Walker Brewster (0-54) was born on 9 December 1862 in Hoboken, New Jersey. He was commissioned a second lieutenant (directly from civil life) on 19 January 1885 into the Tenth Infantry. On 17 December 1891, he was promoted to first lieutenant in the 22d Infantry; he was transferred to the Ninth Infantry on 9 February 1892. With the coming of the Spanish-American War, he was promoted to captain, acting quartermaster of volunteers, on 15 October 1898. On 2 March 1899, he received his captaincy (USA), and he was discharged from the volunteers on 12 May 1899. In 1907 he graduated from the Army War College. He transferred to the 25th Infantry on 29 January 1908 and was promoted to major, 19th Infantry, on 15 March 1908. He served in the Inspector General's Department from 1909 to 1913, then was promoted to lieutenant colonel. In 1916 he was made a colonel of infantry; he became a brigadier general (NA) on 28 November 1917. He organized and administered the Inspector General's Department of the American Expeditionary Force, and received both the Medal of

Honor and the Distinguished Service Medal. After the war, on 1 December 1922, he became a major general (USA), and on 9 December 1925 he retired. He died at age seventy-nine in Washington, D.C. on 27 March 1942. Photo courtesy of the National Archives.

Raymond Westcott Briggs (0-1233), son of Joseph S. Briggs and Clara J. Donehoo Briggs, was born on 19 July 1878 in Beaver, Pennsylvania, just northwest of Pittsburgh on the Ohio River and just east of the Ohio state line. He attended elementary school in Beaver, then transferred to Norristown, northwest of Philadelphia. For two or three years he went to the University of Pennsylvania in Philadelphia; he played on the earliest all-American football team there. He enlisted in the army for the Spanish-American War on 20 July 1898. On 31 August 1900, Briggs was commissioned a second lieutenant of infantry, and on 18 April 1901 he transferred to the artillery corps. During 1901 and 1902 he was in the Philippines; he was a sort of custodian of Emilio Aguinaldo, who was treated by the United States more as a political leader than a rebel in order to slow the resistance movement. In 1904 Briggs returned to Fort Miley, in California (now part of the Presidio in San Francisco). At the time of the great San Francisco earthquake and fire in 1906, he was credited with saving much property when he dynamited numerous buildings to stop the progress of the fire. On 16 April 1956 the mayor of San Francisco declared a holiday to honor Briggs. From 1912 to 1914, Briggs was the American representative in Japan. By 16 August 1917, he was a colonel and was on the staff of Gen. John J. Pershing (*q.v.*). He commanded the 304th and 311th Field Artillery Regiments in France until 8 August 1918, when he was promoted to brigadier general (NA). When appointed at age forty, he was the next-to-youngest brigadier in the AEF. He became Commanding General of the Eighth and Eighteenth Field Artillery Brigades. He was also chief of the Remount Service of the AEF; for these services he received the Distinguished Service Medal. After the war, Briggs dropped back to his permanent rank. He enjoyed long service again with MacArthur as his Chief of Staff in the Philippines between the wars, and on 30 June 1942 he retired from active service. He was almost immediately recalled to active duty as Commanding General, Seventh Corps Area, headquartered in Omaha, Nebraska. He retired again on 20 February 1944, making him a World War I and World War II man, as well as having a record of two years of enlisted service and forty-four years of commissioned ser-

Raymond Westcott Briggs

vice. At the age of eighty-one, Briggs died from a heart ailment in San Francisco on 24 December 1959. He was survived by his widow, Mrs. Helen Briggs, a son, Rear Admiral Cameron Briggs (USN), and a daughter, the wife of Maj. Gen. Garrison E. Coverdale (USA). Photo courtesy of the *San Diego Tribune*.

Lytle Brown

Lytle Brown (0-588), son of James Trimble Brown and Jane Nichol Brown, was born on 22 November 1872 in Nashville, Tennessee. He graduated from Vanderbilt University with a B.E. in 1893 and earned a C.E. in 1894. He also entered USMA and graduated number four of fifty-nine in the class of 1898; he was then commissioned in the Corps of Engineers. Malin Craig and Guy V. Henry, Jr. (both *q.v.*) were two of his classmates. After participating in the Santiago campaign and the San Juan battle in Cuba during 1898, he went to the Philippines. There, he first served as the city engineer of Manila, and until 1902 he was engineer officer of the Department of Northern Luzon. On 23 December 1902 he married Louise Lewis, and they had six children: Lytle Brown, Jr., Eugene L. Brown, Pauline Lewis Brown, Neill Smith Brown, James Trimble Brown and Lewis Castner Brown. From 1903 to 1907, Brown was an instructor and assistant professor of civil and military engineering at USMA. He then commanded Company E, Second Engineer Battalion, during 1907 and 1908. From 1908 to 1912, he was in charge of the United States engineering district in Louisville, Kentucky, and from 1912 until the Pancho Villa Raid he commanded the Second Engineer Battalion. He was the Engineer Officer for the Mexican Punitive Expedition under Gen. John J. Pershing (*q.v.*) in 1916 and 1917, before returning to Nashville to take charge of the engineering district in 1917 and 1918. He commanded the 106th Engineer Regiment and was Engineer Officer for the 31st Infantry Division. In 1918, Brown was promoted to brigadier general (NA); he received the same commission in the USA ten years later. With his promotion to brigadier general (NA), he was also appointed director of the War Plans Division and president of the Army War College. He was a member of the War Department General Staff during 1918 and 1919. After World War I he was in charge of the United States engineer districts in Florence, Alabama and Chattanooga, Tennessee. He was in charge of construction of the Wilson Dam in Muscle Shoals, Alabama; then, in 1920 and 1921, he commanded the Second Engineer Regiment. Next, he was senior instructor of engineering at the General Service School at Fort Leavenworth, Kansas. He served as director and assistant commandant of the General Staff School (USA) in 1924 and 1925. After a brief tour as commander of the Second Engineer Regiment, Brown was Assistant commandant of the Army War College during 1926 and 1928; he then commanded the Nineteenth Brigade at the Canal Zone. From 1929 to 1933, he was at the peak of his career as Chief of Engineers, United States Army, with the temporary rank of major general. Afterwards, as a brigadier, he was Commanding General, Atlantic Sector, Panama Canal. He was made a major general (USA) and commanded the entire Panama Canal Department in 1935 and 1936. Brown retired in 1936 and lived on his farm near Franklin, Tennessee. His decorations included: from the United States, the Distinguished Service Medal; from Britain, Order of the Bath, and from France, Officer of the Legion of Honor. After his retirement, he was quite active as a member of the National Capitol Park and Planning Commission, the engineers advisory board for the Reconstruction Finance Corporation, and many Tennessee state boards. Brown died at age seventy-eight on 3 May 1951. Photo courtesy of *The Assembly*, USMA.

Preston Brown (0-574), son of Col. John Mason Brown, was born on 2 January 1872 in Lexington, Kentucky. He graduated from Yale with an A.B. in 1892. He enlisted in the army in September 1894, and was a private and corporal in Battery A, Fifth Field Artillery Brigade, until 26 March 1897. On 2 March 1897, he was commissioned a second lieutenant in the infantry. He married Susan Ford Dorrance on 8 February 1905, and they had one son, Dorrance. Brown was an honor graduate of the Army School of the Line in 1913 and graduated from the Army Staff College in 1914. He was Chief of Staff of the Second Infantry Division (AEF) at Verdun, Chateau Thierry, Soissons Saint Mihiel in 1918. He was Commanding General, Third Infantry Division, in the Meuse-Argonne and assistant Chief of Staff (AEF) at the advanced headquarters in Germany in November 1918. From 1919 through 1921, Brown was director and acting commandant of the Army War College; during this period he received the Distinguished Service Medal. In 1920 he received a master's degree from Yale; also that year, he was commandant of the Army War College. In 1921 he was Commanding General, Third Brigade. This was followed by service as commander of the Second and then the First Infantry Division in 1924 and 1925. From 1926 to 1930 he was Commanding General, First Corps Area, and from 9 March to 10 October 1930 he was Deputy Chief of Staff of the United States Army. Brown commanded the Panama Canal Department from 24 November 1930 to 14 November 1933. His last assignment was as Commanding General of the Second Corps Area, from 1933 until his retirement on 30 November 1934. In addition to the DSM referred to above, Brown was made a Commander of the

Preston Brown

Legion of Honor (France) and Commander of the Order of the Crown (Belgium). He belonged to the Order of the Cincinnati, the University Club in New York, the Graduate Club in New Haven, Connecticut and the University Club in Denver, Colorado. His home was in Vineyard Haven, Massachusetts, and he died at age seventy-six on 30 June 1948. Photo courtesy of the National Archives.

Robert Alexander Brown

Robert Alexander Brown (0-148), son of James Brown and Ann Stewart Brown, was born on 7 November 1859 on a farm near Cheney, Delaware County, Pennsylvania (just southwest of Philadelphia). His early education was typical; he attended a one-room schoolhouse, then the West Chester State Normal School, i.e., a teachers college. He graduated USMA number eleven of thirty-nine in the class of 1885, and was a classmate of Willard Holbrook and Robert L. Bullard (both *q.v.*). His commission was in the Fourth Cavalry, and he pulled frontier duty from 1885 to 1887. In 1886 Brown led the American Indian Scouts of Henry Lawton's command; they secured the surrender of Geronimo that year. In 1889 he graduated from the Infantry and Cavalry School at Fort Leavenworth, Kansas. From 1891 to 1893, he served as a tactical officer at USMA, and on 8 November 1893 he married Virginia Long. During 1898 and 1899, Brown served as a major, inspector general, with the United States Volunteers in Cuba. During 1901 and 1902, he was an aide to Gen. Arthur MacArthur (the "boy colonel" of the Civil War) in the Philippines. From 1910 to 1913, he instructed at the Army War College. He served on the General Staff and acted as Chief of Staff of the Southern Department in 1913 and 1914. When he received his promotion to brigadier general (NA) on 5 August 1917, he was given command of the 84th Infantry Brigade at Camp Mills, New York. By 14 November 1917 he was with the AEF in France, and he stayed after World War I to serve with the American Forces in Germany. He retired in 1923 as a colonel, but his rank of brigadier general was restored in 1930 on the retired list, by act of Congress. Brown died at age seventy-seven in San Francisco, California on 30 September 1937. Photo courtesy of the Annual Report, Association of Graduates, USMA.

Beverly Fielding Browne (0-1339), son of Thomas Bayly Browne and Anna Fletcher Browne, was born on 24 March 1880 in Accomac, Virginia. He entered USMA and graduated number thirty-two of seventy-four in the class

Beverly Fielding Browne

of 1901. One of his classmates was Frank P. Lahm, who won the balloon race in Paris in 1906 and was one of the first two military pilots trained by Wilbur Wright in October 1909. Browne was commissioned in artillery; because his class graduated in February rather than in June (due to the Philippine insurrection), he was commissioned more than a month before his twenty-first birthday. There was an advantage to being the youngest of his class; he was also its last survivor! He had three tours of duty with the Coast Artillery before the Coast and Field Artillery became two separate arms. At that time, he was sent to a battery of the Sixth Field Artillery Brigade at Fort Riley, Kansas; he served under Capt. Peyton C. March (*q.v.*), who he greatly respected and saw as a role model. Two more important things in his life happened at Fort Riley: in 1907 he married Louise Adams, daughter of an artillery colonel stationed there, and he was introduced to another lifelong love affair, the game of polo. Like many other officers, he firmly believed in the value of polo for training young officers to make quick and decisive actions under stress. He was one of the top polo players in the United States during the early 1900s, with a ten-goal rating. He was captain of the Sixth Field Artillery team in 1909; he won against Kansas City, then won the middle-western polo tournament at Fort Riley. He went on to Denver, Colorado in the fall, and again topped off the year by winning the Army Championship in Washington. In 1911, as a captain, Browne was transferred to the Fifth Field Artillery Brigade at Fort Sill, Oklahoma; he went from there to the Philippines. He played polo at both Fort Stotsenberg and Manila, where there were international competitions. Also in 1911, he was on a six-month detail with the French artillery and lived in a private home for two months in order to get a better working knowledge of the native language. While in the Philippines, he took leave and made a long tour through China. In 1915 he returned to the United States and was stationed at Front Royal, Virginia, one of the three remount depots of the United States Army. The other two were Fort Robinson, Nebraska, and Fort Reno, Oklahoma. Early in 1917, Browne bought a home in Front Royal; in May he went to France with the first contingent of American troops as commander of a battalion of the Fifth Field Artillery Brigade. Since no horses had been shipped from the United States and since he had just come from the remount depot, he spent some time buying horses from the French. In October 1917, he was on the staff of Gen. Peyton C. March (*q.v.*) as chief of artillery information service. This was a great opportunity, allowing Browne access to the British and French and allowing him to make policy for the American information services. On 8 August 1918, he was promoted to brigadier general (NA) in command of the 166th Field Artillery Brigade. After the armistice, this became part of the American Forces in Germany, and when it was demobilized in April

1919, Browne was temporarily the acting Chief of Field Artillery. In August 1919, he reverted to his permanent rank of major of Field Artillery, stationed at Fort Myer, Virginia. He spent the summer as aide to General March on the western front and in Germany. By 1921, he was back up to lieutenant colonel; he was sent to Hawaii and commanded the Eleventh Field Artillery Brigade, his first motorized unit. In 1925 he returned to the United States and was detailed to the inspector general's department for his terminal assignment at headquarters, Third Corps Area, in Baltimore, Maryland. In 1928, Browne requested retirement as a lieutenant colonel and returned to his home in Front Royal; he then ran an oyster and clam farm in nearby Accomac. This area of Virginia had many apple orchards, and Browne became president of the Blue Ridge Distilleries, a brandy distilling operation. He was president and general manager from 1935 to 1943; he quit working in 1942 due to lack of help (because of the war), but he paid out his stockholders completely. Browne traveled in Europe a bit, but he basically stayed in Front Royal until he died at age ninety-four on 22 April 1974. His rank of brigadier general was restored by act of Congress in June 1930. He was survived by his widow, Louise, and a nephew, Dr. Bayly Turlington of Sewanee, Tennessee. He was buried in West Point, New York. Photo courtesy of *The Assembly*, USMA.

William Bryden

William Bryden (0-1900), son of George Bryden and Florence Bliss Bryden, was born on 3 February 1880 in Hartford, Connecticut. He graduated USMA number nineteen of one hundred twenty-four in the class of 1904. He was a classmate of Leslie J. McNair, Pelham D. Glassford (both *q.v.*), Robert C. Richardson, Jr., Joseph W. Stilwell, Edmund L. Gruber, Innis P. Swift and Arthur H. Wilson (the author's one-time unit instructor). Bryden was commissioned in Field Artillery and was an instructor of mathematics at USMA from 1908 to 1912. On 26 October 1912, he married Ellen Barry; they had two children: Ellen, later Mrs. Alexander D. Surles, and Marian, later Mrs. F. W. Moorman. Both of their husbands served in the army. During 1917 and 1918, Bryden was director of the Field Artillery School, for which he received his first Distinguished Service Medal. His promotion to brigadier general (NA) came on 1 October 1918. He was made a major general (USA) in 1941, and was deputy Chief of Staff (USA) from 1940 through 1942; he again received the Distinguished Service Medal for this service. From 1942 to 1944, he was Commanding General, Fourth Service Command; for this service he received his third Distinguished Service Medal. He retired in 1944 but was immediately returned to active duty as president of the Secretary of War's Separation Board. He held this position until 1946, when he again retired, this time due to disabilities. He belonged to the American Legion, the Newcomer Society and the Army and Navy Club in Washington, D.C. He died at age ninety-two in 1972. Photo courtesy of the National Archives.

Beaumont Bonaparte Buck (0-151), son of J. G. H. Buck and Martha Garner Buck, was born on 16 January 1860 in Mayhew, Mississippi. He graduated USMA number thirty of thirty-nine in the class of 1885. Willard A. Holbrook and Robert L. Bullard (both *q.v.*) were two of his classmates. He was commissioned in the Sixteenth Infantry and pulled frontier duty from 1885 to 1889. After a brief tour of duty in the Philippines during the insurrection, he was commandant of cadets at Baylor University in Waco, Texas from 1893 to 1894. During the Spanish-American War, he was a major in the Second Texas Volunteer Infantry. In 1898 he was mustered out of the volunteers; he was made a captain (USA) on 1 March 1899. He was Commandant of Cadets at the University of Missouri from 1899 to 1902. On 30 December 1908, Buck married Susanne Long. He had three separate tours of duty in the Philippines between 1899 and 1914, when he was sent to the Mexican border. From 1915 to 1917, he was on duty with the Massachusetts National Guard, after which he commanded the 28th Infantry, First Infantry Division (AEF). On 5 August 1917, he was promoted to brigadier general (NA) and given command of the Second Infantry Brigade, First Infantry Division, at Cantigny; he received the Distinguished Service Cross for this service. This was the first all-American offensive in World War I. On 8 August 1918, Buck was promoted to major general (NA); he then commanded the Third Infantry Division and the 34th Division. Returning to the States in November 1918, he commanded Camp MacArthur, California, then Camp Meade, Maryland, before going back to the Mexican border. He had a brief tour of duty at Fort Crook, Nebraska, then went back again to Texas, where he retired in 1924 as a colonel. His decorations included (in addition to the Distinguished Service Cross referred to above): from France, chevalier and commander of the Legion of Honor and the Croix de Guerre with palms, and from Italy, the Italian War Cross. After his retirement he lived in San Antonio, Texas. His rank of major general was restored by act of Congress in June 1930. He died at age seventy on 10 February 1950. Photo courtesy of the National Archives.

Beaumont Bonaparte Buck

Robert Lee Bullard

Robert Lee Bullard (0-16) was born on 15 January 1861 in Youngsborough, Alabama. After attending local schools, he studied at the Alabama Agricultural and Mechanical College. He entered USMA and graduated number twenty-seven of thirty-nine in the class of 1885; classmates included Willard Holbrook, Joseph E. Kuhn, and Charles H. Muir (all *q.v.*). Bullard was commissioned in the infantry and did frontier duty (fighting Apaches) from 1885 to 1889. From 1895 to 1897 he was Professor of Military Science and Tactics at North Georgia Agricultural College, and from 1898 to 1899 he was a colonel of the Alabama Colored Volunteers. During the Philippine insurrection, Bullard was colonel of the 39th United States Volunteer Infantry. By 1917 he was a major general (NA) and in command of the First Infantry Division (AEF); he received the Distinguished Service Medal for this service. As of 14 July 1918 he was Commanding General of the Third Corps, and on 16 October 1918 he was promoted to lieutenant general. Also in 1918, he was promoted to major general (USA) and was given command of the Eastern Department (with headquarters at Governor's Island, New York). He served there as a two-star general until his retirement in 1925. In June 1930, he was promoted to lieutenant general on the retired list. He earned numerous honors, degrees, and decorations, including the Distinguished Service Medal for his command of the Second Army (AEF). Together with Earl Reeves, he wrote *American Soldiers Also Fought* in 1936. He and Hunter Liggett were the only two United States lieutenant generals of World War I, and both had the same date of rank: 16 October 1918. Bullard died at age eighty-six at Governor's Island on 11 September 1947. Photo courtesy of the National Archives.

Omar Bundy (0-31), son of Martin Bundy and Amanda Elliott Bundy, was born on 17 June 1861 in Newcastle, Indiana. He graduated USMA number fifty of fifty-two in the class of 1883. He was commissioned in the Second Infantry and did frontier duty from 1883 to 1885. In 1887 he graduated from the Infantry and Cavalry School at Fort Leavenworth, Kansas; he then went back to frontier duty until 1891. During that period, on 27 November 1889, he married a Miss Harden. He participated in the Great Sioux War of 1890 and 1891. During the Spanish-American War, he was at El Caney and the siege of Santiago in Cuba. Sent next to the Philippines, he operated against insurgents and ladrones during 1899 and 1900. From July 1900 until 1901, he was inspector general of the Department of Visayas; he then served as provost-marshal of Iloilo until 1902. From 1902 to 1905, Bundy was on duty with the general service and staff college; he then went back to the Philippines for a two-year period. He commanded one of the columns in the assault on the Moro stronghold at Mount Dajo in 1906. He was made a brigadier general (NA) on 15 May 1917 and a major general (NA) on 5 August 1917. He commanded the Second Infantry Division (AEF) in France from October 1917 to July 1918. Interestingly, this division had one army brigade and one marine brigade; to the best of the author's knowledge, this is the only time such a thing happened in the American military. After that, Bundy commanded the Sixth and Seventh Corps until October 1918. After the war, in 1922, he commanded the Philippine Division, and his last assignment was as Commanding General, Fifth Corps Area, in 1924 and 1925. On 17 June 1925 he retired from active service. He died at age seventy-eight in Washington, D.C. on 2 January 1940. Photo courtesy of the National Archives.

Omar Bundy

William Power Burnham

William Power Burnham (0-132), son of Maj. David Roe Burnham and Olive Power Burnham, was born on 10 January 1860 in Scranton, Pennsylvania. He attended Kansas State Agricultural College in Manhattan, Kansas. He then entered USMA; he was in the class of 1881 but did not graduate. Harry and Henry Hodges, Joseph T. Dickman and Andrew S. Rowan (all *q.v.*) were four of his classmates. After he left USMA, Burnham enlisted in the 14th Infantry. He rose rapidly through the enlisted grades, and in July 1883 he was commissioned in the Sixth Infantry. He graduated from the Infantry and Cavalry School at Fort Leavenworth, Kansas, in 1889, and on 18 February 1890 he married Grace F. Meacham. They had one son, Edward M. Burnham. During the Spanish-American War, he was a lieutenant colonel in the Fourth Missouri Volunteer Infantry; he was mustered out of the volunteers in 1899. He served during the Philippine insurrection from 1902 to 1903; during this period he became a captain of the 20th Infantry. His promotion to major (USA) came on 20 August 1906, and from 1907 to 1911 he served on the General Staff. From 1912 to 1914, he was a lieutenant colonel and commandant of the Army Service School at Fort Leavenworth. From 1914 to 1917, he was the colonel commanding the Puerto Rican Regiment and the District of Puerto Rico. This was followed by a brief tour of duty in the Canal Zone. On 5 August 1917, Burnham was promoted to brigadier general (NA) and given command of the 164th Infantry Brigade of the 82d Infantry Division (AEF). On 12 April 1918 he was made a major general; he commanded the82d Division through many battles in France. From 20 October 1918 to 9 June 1919, he was military attaché and American delegate to the Inter-Allied Military Commission in Athens, Greece. In July 1919 Burnham reverted to his permanent rank of colonel of infantry. He then commanded Fort McDowell, California on Angel Island, and the Presidio in San Francisco, California until 1924, when he retired as a brigadier general. He wrote two books: *Two Roads to a Commission in the United States Army* and *Duties of Outposts, Advance Guards, Etc.* His decorations included: Order of the Bath from Britain, the Croix de Guerre and officer of the Legion of Honor from France, and the Medal of Military Merit, First-Class, from Greece. Burnham died at age seventy at Letterman General Hospital. Photo courtesy of the National Archives.

Edward Burr (0-98), son of William E. Burr and Harriet Brand Burr, was born on 19 May 1859 in Booneville, Missouri. He attended Washington University from 1874 to 1878; he then entered USMA and graduated number one of thirty-seven in the class of 1882. Some of his classmates were Adelbert Cronkhite, Henry T. Allen (both *q.v.*) and Fredrick G. Bonfils of the *Denver Post*. Burr was commissioned in the Corps of Engineers. He served as a lieutenant colonel of volunteers during the Spanish-American War, and was mustered out of the volunteer service in 1899. In 1903 he was made a major (USA) and served in the Sanitary Corps in Cuba. From 1903 to 1906, he was commandant of the Army Engineer School at Washington Barracks in the District of Columbia. On 5 August 1917, he was promoted to brigadier general (NA) and given command of the 166th Field Artillery Brigade, 91st Infantry Division. He later commanded the 62d Field Artillery Brigade (AEF). After World War I, Burr reverted to his peacetime rank of colonel, and in 1923 he retired. He then worked as a consulting engineer in New York until 1928. He died at age ninety-two at Walter Reed Army Medical Center on 15 April 1952; he was the last surviving member of his class. The instrument shown in the photograph is a range finder. Photo courtesy of the National Archives.

Edward Burr

George Washington Burr, Jr.

George Washington Burr, Jr. (0-66), son of George Washington Burr and Nancy Scott Burr, was born on 3 December 1865 in Tolono, Illinois. He graduated USMA number four of forty-four in the class of 1888, was commissioned in the First Artillery Regiment, and married Lydia Kent. He was a classmate of Peyton C. March and Guy H. Preston (both *q.v.*). He was stationed at the Presidio in San Francisco, California until 1890; then, he was sent to Fort Hamilton, in New York, until 1893. From 1893 to 1894, he was Professor of Military Science and Tactics at Mississippi Agricultural and Mechanical College. From 1907 to 1910, he was Chief Ordnance Officer in the Philippines, and in 1910 and 1911 he commanded the arsenal in Augusta, Georgia. From 1911 to 1918, Burr was Chief Ordnance Officer of the central district at the Rock Island Arsenal in Illinois. In 1918 he was Chief Ordnance Officer of American forces in Britain. On 8 August 1918 he was made a brigadier general (NA). In October 1918, Burr was appointed Chief of the Engineering division, Ordnance Department. On 29 November 1918, he was made Assistant Chief of Staff and director of purchase, storage and traffic, General Staff. His promotion to major general (NA) quickly followed on 5 March 1919. During 1919 and 1920 he was on the War Department General Staff. From September to December 1920, Burr was special representative of the Secretary of War, settling business with the British and other foreign governments. From January 1921 until his death, he was assistant to the Chief of Ordnance. His decorations included: from the United States, the Distinguished Service Medal, and from Britain, Order of the Bath. He died at age fifty-seven in Washington, D.C. on 4 March 1923. His rank of major general was restored posthumously by act of Congress. Photo courtesy of the Association of Graduates, USMA.

Reynolds J. Burt (0-520), son of Col. and Mrs. Andrew S. Burt (USA), was born on 2 August 1874 in Nebraska. His father, a Civil War veteran from Ohio, stayed in the army until his retirement in 1902. Burt entered USMA and graduated number fifty-five of seventy-three in the class of 1896; after graduation he married Lillian Stewart of Cincinnati, Ohio. They had two children: a son who also served in the army and a daughter who married Lt. H. W. Kiefer. Originally commissioned in the infantry, Burt served in Logan, Colorado until being sent to the Philippines in 1899. He served during the insurrection in the provinces of Rizal, Pampanga and Zamboanga until 1901. On 23 July 1901 he was promoted to captain in the Ninth Infantry. In 1902, he returned to the United States and was stationed at Madison Barracks, New York. In 1908, he graduated

Reynolds J. Burt

from the Army School of the Line at Fort Leavenworth, Kansas, where he was a distinguished graduate. Next came Army Staff College, where he was again a distinguished graduate. In 1910 he was detailed to the Signal Corps, serving at Fort Leavenworth, Nebraska and in the office of the Chief Signal Officer in Washington. During 1912, he was relieved from the signal corps detail and commanded a company of the 27th Infantry at Fort Sheridan, Illinois (just north of Chicago). He took this company to Texas City and stayed with them until 1 July 1915, when he transferred to the 15th Infantry and was sent to Tiensin, China. On 11 November 1915, Burt was detailed to the quartermaster; he then served in Shanghai, Hong Kong, and Manila. His promotion to major came on 1 July 1916 and he was sent to the office of the depot quartermaster in Charleston, South Carolina. One interesting event in his life occurred on 5 August 1917, when he received two promotions: one to lieutenant colonel and the other to colonel (NA). He was sent to the office of the Quartermaster General, where he was in charge of water transportation. Following this, he was in the office of the Chief of Staff in charge of the Training Instruction branch (G-3). On 1 October 1918, Burt was promoted to brigadier general (NA) and given command of the 22d Infantry Brigade, a part of the 11th Division, until 4 February 1919. He was the author and composer of the official USMA marching chorus, *West Point Thy Sons Salute Thee*, and retired due to disabilities in 1937, as a brigadier general. He died on the Swiss-French border in April 1970, and was buried in Arlington National Cemetery. Photo courtesy of Homer Kiefer, Jr., a grandson.

William Henry Burt (0-1253) was born on 22 February 1876 in Provincetown, Massachusetts, on the tip of Cape Cod. He received an A.B. from the University of Vermont in 1898; in May of that year he enlisted as a corporal in Company M, First Vermont Infantry, for the Spanish-American War. He served with that unit until 7 November 1898, and was commissioned a second lieutenant in the 43d United States Volunteer Infantry in September 1899. On 1 July 1901 he received a regular commission in the artillery corps. He graduated from the Artillery School in 1904. When the artillery was divided into Field and Coast Artillery in 1907, he was assigned to the 21st Field Artillery Brigade. Burt stayed with this unit until 1918, when he was transferred to the Fourth Field Artillery Brigade. He remained there until his promotion to brigadier general (NA) on 8 August 1918. During the war, he served for eighteen months in France. When he was discharged as a brigadier general (NA) on 10 March 1919, he transferred to the Finance Department; then he transferred to Field Artillery, and became a colonel all in the same month (July 1920). In 1920, he was a dis-

William Henry Burt

tinguished graduate of the School of the Line, and the following year he graduated from the General Staff School. In 1924 he graduated from the Army War College, and in 1932 he was on duty as field artillery officer in the Seventh Corps Area's headquarters in Chicago, Illinois. The remainder of his active service was with the Inspector General's Department, and he served in San Francisco, California; at Camp Shelby, Mississippi; at Camp Funston, Kansas; at Camp Jackson, South Carolina, and at Camps Logan and Stanley, Texas. On 30 September 1934, he retired as a brigadier general due to disabilities incurred in the line of duty. Burt died at the age of sixty-four in Westwood, Massachusetts, just southwest of Boston, on 21 November 1940. Photo courtesy of the National Archives.

Wilson Bryant Burtt, son of George H. Burtt and Ellen Keyes Burtt, was born on 1 January 1875 in Hinsdale, Illinois. He graduated USMA number thirty-nine of seventy-two in the class of 1899; he was commissioned in the infantry and sent straight to Cuba. From 1900 to 1910, he was in the Philippines, except from 1904 to 1907, when he was Professor of Military Science and Tactics at Kentucky State University. During 1913 and 1914, Burtt instructed the California National Guard. He was an observer with the German armies in the field during 1915 and 1916. He went to Mexico with the Punitive Expedition under Gen. John J. Pershing (*q.v.*), and then to France as Assistant Chief of the Air Service and Chief of Staff, Fifth Army Corps. He served in most of the major actions, and after the war he was an instructor at the General Staff College. He resigned in 1920 as a major and was reappointed the same year. He retired as a brigadier general in 1938, and was made a major general on the retired list in 1942. His decorations included: the Distinguished Service Medal from the United States, the Legion of Honor and Croix de Guerre from France, the Order of Saint Michael and Saint George from Britain, and the Order of the Crown from Italy. He died at age eighty-one in Chelsea, Massachusetts on 21 March 1957. Photo courtesy of USMA Library.

Wilson Bryant Burtt

Henry Wolfe Butner

Henry Wolfe Butner (0-332), second son of Francis A. Butner and Sarah Wolfe Butner, was born on 6 April 1875. His parents were from old German families who had settled in North Carolina in the 1760s. After attending public schools, Butner entered USMA. He graduated number eighteen of fifty-nine in the class of 1898, and was commissioned in the artillery. Classmates included Malin Craig, Fox Conner and Guy V. Henry, Jr. (all *q.v.*). Butner graduated from the General Staff College in 1906, and was promoted to brigadier general in the National Army on 1 October 1918. He commanded the First Field Artillery Brigade (AEF), for which he received the Distinguished Service Medal. After the war he reverted to colonel, but his rank of brigadier general was restored by act of Congress on 7 March 1930. He was commandant of the Field Artillery School at Fort Sill, Oklahoma, from 17 September 1934 until 10 May 1936. He was promoted to major general on 1 February 1936. To the best of the author's knowledge, he never married. At the age of sixty-two, Butner died in Washington, D.C. on 13 March 1937. Photo courtesy of the Annual Report, Association of Graduates, USMA.

DeRosey Caroll Cabell (0-4453) was born on 7 July 1861 in Charleston, Arkansas. He graduated USMA number eighteen of thirty-seven in the class of 1884, and was commissioned in the Eighth Cavalry. Two of his classmates were William L. Sibert (*q.v.*) and Isaac Newton Lewis, the inventor of the Lewis machine gun. Cabell was on frontier duty from 1884 to 1886; he participated in the Geronimo campaign and was wounded. He also participated in the Great Sioux War of 1890 and 1891. During the Spanish-American War, he was a lieutenant in the Second Arkansas Infantry, but he was mustered out of the volunteers in 1899. Returning to federal service, he was in the China Relief Expedition in 1900 and in the Philippines from 1900 to 1902. He was Gen. John J. Pershing's Chief of Staff on the Mexican Punitive Expedition in 1916 and 1917; for this duty he received the Distinguished Service Medal. On 17

DeRosey Caroll Cabell

December 1917, Cabell was promoted to brigadier general (NA); he was Commanding General of the Mexican border command until 1919. He received his promotion to major general (NA) on 1 October 1918, while on that assignment. In 1919, he retired and moved to San Diego, California. He died there at age sixty-two on 15 March 1924. Photo courtesy of the National Archives. On Pershing's left is John L. Hines; on Cabell's right is Pershing's aide, Lieutenant Collins, father of both the astronaut Michael Collins and Brig. Gen. James L. Collins, the chief of military history.

Frank Merrill Caldwell

Frank Merrill Caldwell (0-293), son of Walter L Caldwell and Jane Carter Caldwell, was born on 8 November 1866 in Rochester, New York. He graduated USMA number thirty-one of fifty-four in the class of 1890, and was commissioned in the Third Cavalry. Classmates included Edgar Jadwin, James R. Lindsay and Fred W. Sladen (all *q.v.*). On 6 June 1894, Caldwell married Mary Hay, and they had three daughters: Dorothy (later Mrs. C. F. Beach), Jane C. (later Mrs. Harrison Lobdell) and Mary (later Mrs. David Bath). During the Spanish-American War, Caldwell served as lieutenant colonel of the Fourth Wisconsin Volunteer Infantry; he was mustered out of the volunteer service in 1899. He was a distinguished graduate of the Army School of the Line in 1909, and he graduated from the Army Staff College in 1910. He served in the Inspector General's Department from 1916 until 12 April 1918, when he was promoted to brigadier general (NA). He commanded the 75th Infantry Brigade, 38th Infantry Division (AEF), from May to October 1918. This was followed by command of the 83d Infantry Brigade, 42d Infantry Division, until 1919. During 1920 and 1921 he was with the Inspector General's Department again, and from 1921 to 1924 he was Chief of Staff of the Sixth Corps Area. From 1926 to 1927, Caldwell commanded the harbor defenses of the Philippines. As his last assignment, he commanded the harbor defenses of the Pacific coast until 30 November 1931, when he retired. He died at age seventy in San Francisco, California on 8 March 1937. Photo courtesy of the National Archives.

Vernon Avondale Caldwell (ASN unknown), son of William Wesley Caldwell and Hannah Snorf Caldwell, was born on 3 July 1866 in Holden, Johnson County, Missouri. The family moved to Marion, Indiana, where Caldwell received his appointment. He entered USMA and graduated number fifty-four of fifty-four in the class of 1890. Edgar Jadwin, Fred W. Sladen and James A. Ryan (all *q.v.*) were three of his classmates. Caldwell was commissioned in the 25th Infantry, then stationed at Fort Missoula, Montana. In 1897 he graduated from the Infantry and Cavalry School at Fort Leavenworth, Kansas. On 23 November 1898, he married Luella E. Noble of Saint Marys, Ohio, and they had no children. During the Spanish-American War, Caldwell served with his regiment in Cuba throughout the Santiago campaign, participating at El Caney and San Juan. He was in the Philippines during the insurrection, and took part in a number of engagements; he served two tours of duty there and received a Silver Star commendation. He was Professor of Military Science and Tactics at the New Hampshire College of Agricultural and Mechanical Arts, as well as at Oregon Agricultural College. He served in Alaska, Hawaii, France and Belgium. He commanded the 365th Infantry Regiment in the Saint Die defensive sector and was promoted to brigadier general (NA) on 1 October 1918. He then commanded the 58th Infantry Brigade during the Meuse-Argonne and the 182nd Infantry Brigade in the Ypres-Lys major operation. He returned to the United States on 1 April 1919 and retired that same year. He was recalled to active duty and served as Professor of Military Science and Tactics at Montana State College of Agriculture and Mechanical Arts. In addition to the Silver Star for gallantry in action at El Caney, he was awarded the Belgian Croix de Guerre and the Italian Croce de Guerra. While he retired as a colonel, his rank of brigadier general was restored by act of Congress in June 1930. He died at age sixty-five in Ohio on 15 November 1931. Photo courtesy of the New Jersey State Archives.

Vernon Avondale Caldwell

Robert Emmet Callan (0-384), son of Frank J. Callan and Sarah Riley Callan, was born on 24 March 1874 in Baltimore, Maryland. He graduated USMA number four of seventy-three in the class of 1896. Classmates included Lucius R. Holbrook, Edward L. King and Dennis E. Nolan (all *q.v.*), and he was commissioned in the Fifth Artillery. During the Spanish-American War, Callan was in the field in Puerto Rico; he taught mathematics at USMA from 1899 to 1903. He was a member of the Torpedo Board at Fort Totten, in New York, from 1904 until 1907. After that service, he was an assistant to the Chief of Coast Artillery until 1912. On 10 October 1912, Callan married Margaret Valentine Kelly. He commanded Fort Andrews, Massachusetts, from 1912 to 1914. In 1914 and 1915, he was president of the Coast Artillery Board at Fort Monroe, Virginia. He was on the General Staff from 1915 to 1917. Callan organized the 65th Heavy Artillery Brigade and arrived with it in France on 8 April 1918; on that date, he received his promotion to brigadier general (NA). He was Chief of Staff of Army

Robert Emmet Callan

Artillery, First Army, and Commanding General, Coast Artillery Brigade (AEF), for which he received the Distinguished Service Medal. After graduating from the Army War College in 1921, he commanded the Second Coast Artillery District, with headquarters at Fort Totten. Next, he commanded the Panama Coast Artillery District until 1924. From 1924 to 1929 he commanded the Third Coast Artillery District and the Seacoast branch of the Artillery School. He served in this capacity until 1931, when he became a major general. He was assistant Chief of Staff (G-4) of the army from 19 January 1931 until 18 January 1935. In addition to the Distinguished Service Medal, France made him an officer of the Legion of Honor, and Italy gave him the Order of the Crown of Italy. He retired due to disabilities in 1936; he died at age sixty-two in Washington, D.C. on 20 November of that same year. Photo courtesy of the Association of Graduates, USMA.

George Hamilton Cameron (ASN unknown), son of Dwight Foster Cameron and Fanny Norris Cameron, was born on 8 January 1861 in Ottawa, Illinois. He studied at Northwestern University for two years, then entered USMA. He graduated number twenty-nine of fifty-two in the class of 1883. William C. Langfitt and Tyree R. Rivers (both *q.v.*) were two of his classmates. He was commissioned in the Seventh Cavalry and had frontier duty from 1883 to 1887 in Kansas and the Dakotas. On 27 May 1888, he married Nina D. Tilford, an army daughter, and they had three children: Douglas T., Nina T. (later Mrs. John B. Thompson), and Margaret (later Mrs. Buckner M. Creel). Cameron was assistant professor of drawing at USMA from 1888 to 1895; he taught in Washington and California from 1895 to 1898. He equipped the first United States horse transport, and went to Manila in 1898. There, he was in both the northern and southern Luzon campaigns. From 1907 to 1910, Cameron was secretary and assistant commandant of the Mounted Service School at Fort Riley, Kansas. From 1910 to 1912, he was at Fort Stotsenberg, in the Philippines, and

George Hamilton Cameron

in 1913 he briefly commanded the Big Bend district on the border of Texas. From 1913 to 1917, he was a student, instructor and director of the Army War College. In 1917 he was promoted to major general (NA). He was, in succession, Commanding General, 40th Infantry Division (AEF), from 18 September to 19 November 1917; Commanding General, Fourth Infantry Division (AEF), from 3 December to 14 August 1918, and Commanding General, Fifth Corps (AEF), from 21 August to 12 October 1918. Upon his return to the United States, Cameron commanded Camp Gordon, in Georgia. He then went back to Fort Riley, where he was both post commander and commandant of the Cavalry School. While he retired as a colonel, his two-star rank (major general) was restored by act of Congress in June 1930. At the age of eighty-three, Cameron died in Staunton, Virginia on 28 January 1944. Photo courtesy of USMA Library.

Guy Carleton

Guy Carleton (0-128), son of William Carleton and Elizabeth Carleton, was born on 9 September 1857 in Austin, Texas. He entered USMA and graduated number seven of fifty-three in the class of 1881. Harry and Henry Hodges and Andrew S. Rowan (all *q.v.*) were three of his classmates. Upon graduation, Carleton was commissioned in the Second Cavalry; he did frontier duty from 1881 to 1886 in Montana, Idaho and Washington. During that time, on 20 June 1883, he married Cora B. Arthur. From 1886 to 1889, he was Professor of Military Science and Tactics at Texas Agricultural College. From 1895 to 1898, he had recruiting duty at Fort Riley, Kansas. During the Spanish-American War, Carleton commanded troops at Montauk Point, New York; Huntsville, Alabama, and San Antonio, Texas. In 1899 he commanded the districts of Campechuela, Manzanillo and Baymo, Cuba. From 1901 to 1907, he was in the Philippines, and from 1909 to 1912 he was on the General Staff and served as director of the Army War College. During 1916 and 1917, he was inspector general of the Philippine Department. Promotion to brigadier general (NA) came in 1917 and to major general (NA) on 1 October 1918. He commanded the 159th Depot Brigade at Camp Taylor, Kentucky. Then, he was appointed Commanding General of the Provisional Depot for corps and army troops at Camp Wadsworth, South Carolina; he received the Distinguished Service Medal for this service. While he retired as a colonel in 1921, his two-star rank (major general) was restored by act of Congress in June 1930. He died at age eighty-eight at Fort Sam Houston, Texas, on 8 January 1946. Photo courtesy of the National Archives.

John Miller Carson, Jr.

John Miller Carson, Jr. (0-64), son of Capt. John Miller Carson and Annie Miller Carson, was born on 26 June 1864 in Philadelphia, Pennsylvania. He entered USMA and graduated number fourteen of thirty-nine in the class of 1885. He was a classmate of Joseph E. Kuhn, Charles H. Muir, Willard Holbrook and Robert L. Bullard. Upon graduation, Carson was commissioned in the Fifth Cavalry; on 14 December 1887 he married Margaret Forster Sumner. They had one daughter, Margaret, who became Mrs. Henry C. Holt. From 1890 to 1895, he was adjutant of USMA; he served as adjutant of the Fifth Cavalry from 1895 to 1897. During the Spanish-American War, he was Quartermaster at the headquarters of United States troops in Puerto Rico. He acted as assistant to the chief quartermaster of Puerto Rico in 1898 and 1899, before going to the Philippines. From 1900 to 1903, Carson was on duty in the office of the Quartermaster General. Afterwards, he had a long tour of duty at USMA again from 1903 to 1911. He was both disbursing officer and officer in charge of construction. From 1911 to 1914, Carson was constructing quartermaster at Corregidor in the Philippines. During 1915 and 1916, he was assistant to the Depot Quartermaster in New York, and in 1916 and 1917 he himself was the Depot Quartermaster of New York. He was also the General Superintendent of the Army Transportation Service in New York. He then went to France, where he was Chief Quartermaster of the Zone of Communications and Deputy Quartermaster for the AEF. For his performance of this duty, Carson received the Distinguished Service Medal. Promotion to brigadier general (NA) came on 1 October 1918. He became Assistant Quartermaster, United States Army, from 1920 to 1922; he then retired as a brigadier general. In addition to the DSM referred to above, he received the Spanish-American War Medal, the Puerto Rican Occupation Medal, the Philippine Insurrection Medal, commander of the Legion of Honor of France, and the Polonia Restituta from Poland. After his retirement, Carson lived on his farm in Connecticut. He died at age ninety-one at Fort Jackson, in South Carolina, on 18 January 1956. Photo courtesy of the National Archives.

Jesse McIlvane Carter (0-59) was born on 23 April 1863 in Saint Francois County, Missouri (south of St. Louis). He graduated USMA number thirty-seven of seventy-seven in the famous class of 1886. Mason M. Patrick, John J. Pershing, Charles T. Menoher and Peter E. Traub (all *q.v.*) were some of his classmates. This class had so many general officers that it was called "the class the stars fell on." Upon graduation, Carter was commissioned in the Third

Jesse McIlvane Carter

Cavalry. He did frontier duty from 1886 to 1890, then was Professor of Military Science and Tactics at Norwich University in 1891. During the Spanish-American War, Carter served as captain of Puerto Rican volunteers from 1899 to 1901. From 1909 to 1913, he was on duty with the General Staff, and from 26 June 1912 to 10 June 1913 he was Secretary of the General Staff. In 1916, Carter was assigned to the Militia Bureau, and in 1917 he became chief of the bureau. He organized and commanded the Eleventh Infantry Division from August 1918 to February 1919; he received the Distinguished Service Medal for this service. In 1921, Carter retired as a brigadier general, and in 1930 he was promoted to major general on the retired list. After his retirement, he lived and managed properties in Magnet, Texas. He died there at age sixty-seven on 23 June 1930. Photo courtesy of USMA Archives.

Joseph Compton Castner (0-360) was born on 18 November 1869 in New Brunswick, New Jersey. He attended Rutgers College in New Jersey and graduated in 1891 with a B.S. He was commissioned in the Fourth Infantry on 1 August 1891 and graduated from the Infantry and Cavalry School at Fort Leavenworth, in Kansas. On 26 April 1898, he was promoted to first lieutenant. He was in the Philippines in 1900 as a captain of the Philippine Volunteer Cavalry, and was honorably mustered out of the volunteer service on 30 June 1901. He was commissioned a captain (USA) on 2 February 1901; on 26 February 1908 he was detailed to the Quartermaster Corps. He graduated from Army War College in 1915, and was Adjutant General of the District of Columbia from 1 April 1915 to 2 October 1917. In 1916, Rutgers awarded him an M.S., and the army gave him three Silver Star citations and a Distinguished Service Medal. Promotion to brigadier general (NA) came on 12 April 1918. He went to the General Staff College in 1920 and to Army War College again in 1921. On 14 November 1921, Castner received his promotion to brigadier general (USA), and on 30 November 1933 he retired as a brigadier general. Later, he was advanced to major general on the retired list. Castner Range at Fort Bliss, in

Joseph Compton Castner

Texas, was named for him. He was a Phi Beta Kappa. His home after retirement was in Oakland, California; he died there on 8 July 1946. Photo courtesy of the Adjutant General of the District of Columbia.

John Loomis Chamberlain

John Loomis Chamberlain (0-9), son of Jabez L. Chamberlain and Charity Hart Chamberlain, was born on 20 January 1858 in South Livonia, New York (south of Rochester). He attended the Geneseo State Normal School for four years; he then entered USMA and graduated number five of fifty-two in the class of 1880. Some of his classmates were George W. Goethals (*q.v.*), David J. Rumbough and James Walker Benét. Chamberlain was commissioned in the First Artillery, then switched to ordnance. From 1884 to 1888 he was an instructor at USMA. He graduated from the Artillery School in 1890, and participated in the Great Sioux War of 1890 and 1891—the last gasp of the late Indian Wars. He was Chief Ordnance Officer for the Department of the Missouri from 1891 to 1893. In 1895 and 1896, he was Professor of Military Science and Tactics at Peekskill Military Academy in the Hudson River Valley of New York. On 9 September 1896, Chamberlain married Carolyn Morrow, and they had two children: John L. Chamberlain, Jr. and Mary Carolyn Chamberlain. During 1897 and 1898, he was the United States military attaché in Vienna; he then served in the Spanish-American War. He served with the United States Volunteers both in the Siege Train, in Cuba, and with the Seventh Army Corps, as a major of volunteers. He took part in the campaign against the Moros in 1903, and was an Inspector General in the Philippines and California from 1901 through 1905. After this, Chamberlain had the following tours of duty, all as inspector general: Pacific Division, December 1906 to June 1907; Department of the East, 13 August 1907 to 30 June 1909; Philippine Division, 1 September 1909 to 15 September 1911; Western Division, 11 November 1911 to 15 August 1912; Western Department, 1 August 1913 to September 1914, and Eastern Department, 1914 to February 1917. On 21 February 1917, he was promoted to brigadier general (USA) and appointed Inspector General (USA). This was followed on 6 October 1917 by promotion to major general, then Inspector General. He did an inspection of the American Expeditionary Force from 10 July to 20 September 1918, and from July through September 1920 he did an inspection of all activities under the War Department in Europe. From July to November 1921, Chamberlain completed a four-month tour of Europe, the Near East and Africa, and was awarded the Distinguished Service Medal for "exceptionally meritorious service to the United States government." He died well beyond the age of eighty-nine in Washington, D.C. on 14 November 1948, and was buried at Arlington National Cemetery. Photo courtesy of USMA Archives.

William Chamberlaine (0-309) was born on 1 March 1871 in Norfolk, Virginia. He entered USMA and graduated number eighteen of sixty-two in the class of 1892. Charles P. Sumerall, William R. Smith and Peter W. Davison (all *q.v.*) were three of his classmates. Upon his graduation, Chamberlaine was commissioned in the Second Artillery Brigade. From 1899 to 1901, he was on duty in West Point, New York, and from May 1901 to October 1903 he was assistant to the Chief of Artillery in Washington. From 1903 to 1906, he was a member of the Coast Artillery Board; he was a member of the General Staff from 1906 to 1910. After that he served as assistant Chief of Staff in the Philippines and director of the Coast Artillery School until 1913. He was Adjutant General at Fort Totten, in New York, in 1917, and on 17 December of that year he was promoted to brigadier general (NA). He organized and took to France the Sixth Provisional Coast Artillery Regiment, and he served as Chief of Artillery of the Second Division in May and June 1918 at Belleau Woods. He was the Commanding General of Railway Artillery (AEF) and commanded the railway artillery during the Saint Mihiel and Meuse-Argonne. In 1919 he was detailed to the General Staff Corps and was Chief of Staff of the Hawaiian Department. He received from the United States the Distinguished Service Medal, and from France the Croix de Guerre with palms and officer of the Legion of Honor. He retired in 1922 as a colonel, and he died at age fifty-four in Paris on 8 June 1925. His rank of brigadier general was restored posthumously by act of Congress in 1930. Photo courtesy of USMA.

William Chamberlaine

Sherwood Alfred Cheney (0-539), son of Mr. and Mrs. John S. Cheney, was born on 24 August 1873 in South Manchester, Connecticut. He frequently visited Europe and studied French methods of silk culture. He went to Yale for a year while waiting to enter USMA, where he ranked in the first section of his class for all four years. He graduated number five of sixty-seven in the class of 1897 and was commissioned in the Corp of Engineers; he was a classmate of Frank R. McCoy (*q.v.*). Cheney served in the field in Cuba in 1898 with Company C of the Battalion of Engineers and in the Philippines from 1899 to 1901. He was Chief Engineer of the Department of Southern Luzon, then from

Sherwood Alfred Cheney

1903 to 1905 was aide to Gen. J. C. Bates in Chicago, Illinois and Saint Louis, Missouri. From 1907 to 1911, he was on duty with the General Staff. In the fall of 1911, after some "behind-the-curtains" negotiations with regard to an alternative canal route to Panama, it was determined that somebody should go over the route rather than depend on the study of former expeditions in the Atrato Valley. The question was stirred up by a Chilean engineer who sought a concession for an easy canal route from the Atlantic to the Pacific, promoting a plan fathered by Colombia in delayed hostilities resulting from the earlier Panama affair. The State Department was considering making a large payment to Colombia for this supposedly easy route; in fact, the sum of twenty-five million dollars had been proposed as a settlement, and it was then being considered by the Senate Foreign Relations Committee. Leonard Wood, Chief of Staff, directed a writer to go over the route and to take someone with him. A telegram was sent to Cheney, who was then on duty in San Francisco, California. The telegram read, "Are you up to a hard and dangerous tropical trip of some months under secret orders of the Chief of Staff? If so, meet me at the Saint Charles Hotel, New Orleans, 27 December." Without knowing any more than the bare outline of where he was going or why, Cheney promptly replied, "Will meet you on December 27th." After his return, his brief and conclusive report was sufficient to have the twenty-five-million-dollar appropriation struck from the Senate plan. Cheney served in 1914 as Director of the Army Field Engineering School, then went to the Mexican border. In June 1917 he was sent to France, and in 1918 he commanded the 110th Engineer Regiment. He was promoted to brigadier general on 1 October 1918; he was also assistant to the Chief Engineer (AEF) and Director of the Army Transport Service, for which he received the Distinguished Service Medal. He received the French Croix de Guerre and the Legion of Honor as well. In 1919 and 1920, he was a member of the Inter-Allied Mission to the Baltic States and Germany, and from 1921 to 1924 he was the United States military attaché in China. Before going to China he married Louise Delano, and his first daughter, Matilda Delano Cheney, was born. His wife died only a few years after their marriage. From 5 November 1924 to 7 April 1925, he was commandant of the Engineer School at Fort Humphreys (now Fort Belvoir), in Virginia. In April 1925, he succeeded Col. Clarence O. Sherrill as military aide to President Coolidge; later, he requested reassignment and was succeeded by Col. Blanton Winship. He had been junior aide to Theodore Roosevelt and senior aide to Coolidge. In 1933, Cheney was promoted to brigadier general (USA). In 1937 he lived in Manchester, Connecticut. He died at age seventy-five on 13 March 1949. Survivors were his second wife, Mrs. Charlotte D. Cheney; Miss Emily V. Cheney, and two sisters, Mrs. Clifford D. Cheney and Miss Emily Grace Cheney.

He died peacefully at home, within sight of the house where he was born. Photo courtesy of Special Collections, USMA Library.

Edward Robert Chrisman

Edward Robert Chrisman (0-13518), son of Mr. and Mrs. Jesse A. Chrisman, was born on 13 August 1866 in Connersville, Indiana. He graduated USMA number twenty-four of forty-four in the class of 1888 and was commissioned in the infantry. He was a classmate of Peyton C. March and Guy H. Preston (both *q.v.*). The years 1888 to 1891 were spent on frontier duty and participating in the Sioux Campaign. The year 1892 was a busy one; Chrisman graduated from the School of Submarine Mining at Willet's Point, New York, and on 28 March 1892 he married Florence Ryan. They had two children: Catherine V. and Ord Gariche. Chrisman was Professor of Military Science and Tactics at the University of Idaho from 1894 to 1898. He was in Cuba during the Spanish-American War, and was cited for gallantry in action. He also served in the Sanitary Corps while in Cuba; he was awarded a Silver Star commendation for his performance of that duty. From 1899 to 1902, he was in the Philippines; he returned to the teaching assignment in Idaho from 1902 to 1905. From 1905 to 1907, he again served in the Philippines, in the Leyte campaign and also at the Pulujan Outbreak. From 1909 to 1911, Chrisman was Professor of Military Science and Tactics at South Dakota State College. On 26 June 1918, he was promoted to brigadier general (NA). During World War I, he was Commanding General of the tactical brigade in the Panama Canal Zone; he was later Commanding General of the United States forces in Puerto Rico. In 1921, he retired as a colonel; however, he was still on active duty as Professor of Military Science and Tactics at the University in Moscow, Idaho from 1919 to 1936. He was also Commandant of Cadets from 1932 to 1935. He was approved by the local university regents by special act of Congress. He was also named Professor of Military Science and Tactics emeritus for life; this was a most unusual honor and a vote of confidence and approval. He died at age seventy-two in Moscow, Idaho on 15 January 1939. Cadet photo courtesy of USMA Archives. World War I photo courtesy of the National Archives.

Marlborough Churchill (0-1646), son of John Wesley Churchill and Mary Donald Churchill, was born on 11 August 1878 in Andover, Massachusetts. In 1900, he graduated from Harvard with an A.B., and on 7

Marlborough Churchill

October 1904 he married Mary Smith. He was commissioned a second lieutenant in the artillery corps on 16 July 1901 and first lieutenant on 25 January 1907. (This was the year the artillery corps was divided into Field Artillery and Coast Artillery, separate arms of the service.) Churchill transferred to the Third Field Artillery the following June and to the First Field Artillery on 2 August 1910. On 13 April 1911, he was promoted to captain, and on 8 January 1912 he was transferred to the Fifth Field Artillery. He was promoted to major on 15 May 1917, and on 5 August that same year he was again promoted to lieutenant colonel (NA). On 12 June 1918, he was again promoted to colonel (NA), and on 8 August 1918 he was promoted to brigadier general (NA). He was an instructor at the School of Fire for Field Artillery from 1912 to 1914. From 1914 to 1916, he was both inspector and instructor of field artillery for the organized militia of Virginia, the District of Columbia, and Pennsylvania. During the same period, he was editor of the Field Artillery Journal and managed to get some interesting assignments—from January 1916 to April 1917, he was military observer with the French armies in the field. He then served as executive officer of the American Military Mission in Paris from April through June 1917. He was on the General Staff (AEF) from August 1917 through January 1918, and was acting Chief of Staff, Army Artillery, First Army (AEF), from January through May 1918. He was returned to the United States by June 1918 (as were many others who had gone over early and gained much experience there). He then served on the General Staff, United States Army, as Chief of the Military Intelligence Branch. From June to August 1918, Churchill was assistant Chief of Staff and Director of Military Intelligence. He was a Special Deputy of the American commission to negotiate peace from December 1918 through April 1919. He continued as head of military intelligence until 25 August 1920. His decorations included: from the United States, the Distinguished Service Medal; from Britain, Order of the Bath; from France, officer of the Legion of Honor; from Italy, commander of the Order of the Crown, and from Belgium, commander of the Order of Leopold. He belonged to the Army and Navy Clubs in Washington and Manila, the Harvard Club in New York City and the Metropolitan and Racquet Clubs. He lived at 2301 Connecticut Avenue NW in Washington, D.C. and died there on 9 July 1947. Photo courtesy of the National Archives.

Harvey Cyrus Clark (no ASN assigned), son of James C. Clark and Melissa Myers Clark, was born on 17 September 1869 in Morgan County, Missouri. He was educated first at Wentworth Military Academy in Lexington,

Missouri from 1877 to 1888. He then earned an A.B. from Scarrett College in Neosho, Missouri in 1891. He was admitted to the Missouri bar in 1893, and was prosecuting attorney of Bates County from 1896 to 1901. On 7 December 1909, he married Sudye C. Berry. He was a partner of Graves and Clark until Graves was elected chief justice of Missouri. Clark was appointed District Attorney for the Missouri Pacific Railway in 1910, and was also attorney for the Kansas City Southern Railway and Western Coal Mining Company. In 1888, he was commissioned a captain in the Second Missouri Infantry; he was promoted to major on 1 July 1897. On 20 July 1898, he was made lieutenant colonel of the Sixth Missouri Infantry; he then served during the Spanish-American War. He became a brigadier general of the Missouri National Guard on 2 February 1899. After the Villa raid on Columbus, New Mexico, he was Commanding General of Missouri troops on the Mexican border from 19 June to 31 December 1916. On 5 August 1917, he became a brigadier general (NA) and was appointed Commanding General, 60th Depot Brigade, at Camp Doniphan, Oklahoma. He was honorably discharged due to a physical disability on 26 December 1917, and was appointed Adjutant General of Missouri on 1 January 1918. He was a Democrat, a Presbyterian, and belonged to the Masonic lodge. His home was in Nevada, Missouri, and he died there on 1 April 1921. Photo courtesy of the National Archives.

Harvey Cyrus Clark

Charles Maxwell Clement (no ASN assigned), son of John K. Clement and Mary S. Zeigler Clement, was born on 28 October 1855 in Sunbury, Pennsylvania, near the Susquehanna River and north of Harrisburg. He was the son of a Civil War veteran, grandson of a War of 1812 veteran, and descendant of Gregory Clement, member of Parliament (Regicide) in 1646. Gregory's son James found life healthier in America after the restoration of 1660. Clement was educated at private academies in Sunbury and Burlington, New Jersey, then worked for six years in the prothonotary's office in Sunbury. (A prothonotary is a chief clerk of various courts of law.) After this, he read law in his father's office and was admitted to the bar on 11 March 1878. He basically performed as a trial lawyer in cases affecting corporate interests. On 19 November 1879, Clement married Alice V. Withington, and they had four sons: John K., a regular army colonel; Charles F.; Martin W., president of the Pennsylvania Railroad and Theron B. Just after the completion of his legal education, Clement organized Company E, 12th Pennsylvania Infantry, in Sunbury, with himself as a private. He remained in the Pennsylvania National Guard (PNG) for the rest of his life

Charles Maxwell Clement

and was elected up to and including the grade of colonel. At the time of the Spanish-American War, he was a lieutenant colonel, and in 1899 he became a colonel. In 1910, Clement became a brigadier general (PNG), commanding the Third Pennsylvania Brigade. On 22 December 1915, he became a major general (PNG), commanding the 28th Division. He was sent to France in 1917 to observe trench warfare. Always a popular officer with the division, he was retired just before the 28th sailed for France in May 1918. Clement had many interests in civil life other than the law. He was a school director, member of the Sunbury Council and assistant burgess; he also held many other offices. He was both a Mason and a Shriner, secretary of the Episcopal Diocese of Harrisburg, and member of the Sons of the American Revolution and of the Military and Naval Order of the Spanish War. He died at age seventy-eight on 9 September 1934 in Sunbury, and he is buried there. Photo, obviously taken long after his retirement from the military, courtesy of the Pennsylvania National Guard.

Frank Sherwood Cocheu (0-449), son of Mr. and Mrs. Theodore Cocheu, was born on 22 November 1871 in Brooklyn, New York. He graduated USMA number twenty-eight of fifty-four in the class of 1894, a classmate of Paul B. Malone, George H. Estes, Jr. (both *q.v.*) and Hamilton S. Hawkins. He was commissioned in the infantry, and on 4 August 1897 he married Kathleen Lacy. During the Spanish-American War, Cocheu participated in the Santiago campaign in Cuba; he was sent to the Philippines from 1899 to 1902, during the insurrection. He graduated from the Army War College in 1908, and was an assistant director from 1908 to 1911. From 1914 to 1917, he had one of his many tours of duty with the General Staff. During World War I he commanded both infantry regiments and brigades in the American Expeditionary Force; he was awarded the Distinguished Service Medal for this service. He was promoted to brigadier general (NA) on 1 October 1918, and he participated in the Saint Mihiel and Meuse-Argonne. After the war, he graduated from the General Staff school in 1919. From 1925 to 1927, he was assistant commandant of the

Frank Sherwood Cocheu

Infantry School at Fort Benning, Georgia. He was promoted to brigadier general (USA) in 1927, and during the Mexican revolution of 1929 he was Commanding General of American troops in Arizona. His second star (major general) came in 1934, and he retired in 1935. In addition to the DSM mentioned above, he received the Conspicuous Service Medal from the state of New York. After his retirement, Cocheu lived in Washington, D.C. He died at age eighty-seven at Walter Reed Army Medical Center on 28 May 1959. Photo courtesy of the New Jersey State Archives.

William Burr Cochran

William Burr Cochran (0-499), son of John Henry Cochran and Charlotte Carr Cochran, was born on 9 July 1863 in Middleburg, Virginia. He graduated from Virginia Military Institute (VMI) in 1888; he then taught school, and enlisted in the Fifth Infantry on 11 September 1892. He rose rapidly, and on 28 March 1896 he was commissioned a second lieutenant in the 25th Infantry. He served during the Spanish-American War, and on 16 April 1901 he became a captain in the 24th Infantry. During the insurrection in the Philippines, he met Colonel Kessler, commanding the First Montana Volunteers. They became good friends, and after returning to the United States, Cochran was stationed at Fort Harrison, in Montana. It seems that the colonel had a most attractive daughter, named Mathilde but called "Tillie." Three years earlier, while attending Miss Ely's Seminary in New York, she had fallen in love with a fellow Montanan—a man named Albert Raleigh, a wealthy socialite and VMI graduate then working on the old *New York World* as a cartoonist. They became engaged and returned to Montana, where the trouble began. Colonel Kessler, a millionaire brewer, fell ill. Just before he died, he wrote a will that would leave everything to Tillie in the event she married Captain Cochran, but would cut her off without a cent if she married Raleigh. The captain readily fell in with the colonel's suggestion that he make a match with the daughter, and a fierce rivalry between the two men was started. Raleigh traveled east by train, swearing he would never return to Montana; he did return in two months, but by then Tillie was engaged to Cochran. Friends of the family had been invited to a dinner at which the engagement was to be announced. That morning Miss Kessler met Raleigh downtown, and on the spur of the moment she married him in a photo studio. Arriving that night, the guests were curtly told that the newly-wed Mrs. Raleigh could not see them. Raleigh appeared and was chased away by the bride's brother. From that moment on, the Raleighs never spoke to each other again. Cochran challenged Raleigh to a duel, which was accepted, but friends of both parties intervened and stopped it. Mrs. Raleigh secured an annulment on grounds of temporary insanity and resumed her maiden name. Raleigh left the area, and Tillie and Captain Cochran got married and had two daughters: Louise Kessler and Marian Lee. From August 1917 to 30 September 1918, Cochran was a colonel (NA), and on 1 October 1918 he was promoted to brigadier general (NA). He was sent to Camp Bowie, in Texas, to organize the 100th Infantry Division. In February 1919, he reverted to major of infantry; he was promoted to lieutenant colonel on 7 January 1920 and colonel (USA) on 1 July 1920. On 30 November 1922, he retired after thirty years of service; he lived at Happy Hollow Farm in Princess Anne, Maryland. One week short of his sixty-third birthday, he was killed in an automobile accident on the Eastern Shore of Maryland. Photo courtesy of the National Archives.

Frank Winston Coe (0-11) was born on 27 November 1870 in Manhattan, Kansas (fifteen miles east of Fort Riley). He graduated USMA number eight of sixty-two in the class of 1892. He was a classmate of Charles P. Sumerall and Julian R. Lindsay (both *q.v.*). After his graduation he was commissioned in the First Artillery Brigade, but after the artillery corps split in 1907 into field and Coast Artillery, he stayed with the latter. In 1895, he married Anne Chamberlaine, and they had one son, William Chamberlaine Coe. In 1896, Coe graduated from the Artillery School at Fort Monroe, Virginia. From 1898 to 1902, he taught mathematics at USMA and from 1903 to 1907 he was adjutant there. His next assignment was as assistant to the Chief of Coast Artillery in Washington from 1908 to 1919. In 1909, he was appointed director of the Coast Artillery School at Fort Monroe. In 1916 he was made Chief of Staff of the Western Department at the Presidio in San Francisco, California. He was promoted to brigadier general in 1917 and was the Chief of Staff of the First Infantry Division (AEF) from June to August 1917. After this he commanded the 30th Heavy Artillery Brigade (AEF). He was Commanding General of the Railroad Artillery Reserve, First Army (AEF); for the performance of this duty he was awarded the Distinguished Service Medal. He was made Chief of Coast Artillery on 24 May 1918, and was promoted to major general five days later. He retained this assignment until 19 March 1926, when he retired at age seventy-six. He died at Walter Reed Army Medical Center on 25 May 1947. Photo courtesy of the National Archives.

Frank Winston Coe

Charles Henry Cole

Charles Henry Cole (no ASN assigned), son of Charles Henry Cole and Mary Ball Cole, was born on 30 October 1871 in Boston, Massachusetts. He graduated from English High School in Boston in 1888 and enlisted in the Massachusetts National Guard in 1890. In his civil life, he was a clerk and cashier with several mining companies. In the National Guard, he was rapidly commissioned and advanced; by 1905 he was a colonel and in charge of rifle practice for the state. He resigned in 1906 and enlisted as a private. In 1910 he married Grace Fletcher Blanchard of Brookline, Massachusetts. He was a National Guard brigadier and Adjutant General of the state from 27 May 1914 to 5 August 1916. In 1916 he again resigned, enlisting as a private in 1917. He shortly became a captain, and on 5 August 1917 he became a brigadier general (NA). In France from 1917 to 1919, Cole was in a half dozen major battles, and from 22 October 1917 to 31 October 1917 he was Commanding General of the 26th Infantry Division. After returning to the United States, he went into politics; he was a delegate at large from Massachusetts to the Democratic National Conventions of 1924 and 1928. In 1928, he also ran for governor of Massachusetts. He was a delegate at large again to the 1932 Democratic Convention, and from 1934 to 1935 he was chairman of the Massachusetts State Racing Commission. From 7 January 1937 to 5 January 1939, he was again Adjutant General of the state. He was also, at the same time, Chief of Staff of the state—this double duty was quite a rarity. His basic civilian occupation was as a corporation executive—other than politics, that is! He belonged to many clubs and fraternal organizations. Both his office and residence were in Boston. Cole died at age eighty-one at the Chelsea (Massachusetts) Soldiers Home on 13 November 1952. He was buried at the Woodlawn Cemetery in Everett, Massachusetts. Photo courtesy of the Massachusetts Military Archives.

William Edward Cole (0-593) was born on 22 September 1874 in Utah. After attending public schools, he entered USMA and graduated number sixteen of fifty-nine in the class of 1898. Classmates included Robert C. Davis, Malin Craig and Guy V. Henry, Jr. (all *q.v.*). Cole was commissioned in the artillery corps, and when that arm was divided in 1907 into Field and Coast Artillery, he went into the Coast Artillery. He was an honor graduate of the Coast Artillery School in 1911 and of the advanced course of the Coast Artillery School in 1912. During World War I, Cole commanded several field artillery regiments; he was promoted to brigadier general (NA) on 8 August 1918. After this he commanded several field artillery brigades. For his performance of this duty, Cole received the Distinguished Service Medal. After the war, he reverted to colonel, but he was promoted to brigadier general (USA) in 1930. On 8 February 1938 he was promoted to major general (USA), and that same year he retired. However, he was returned to duty for World War II in 1941 and served until a second retirement due to physical disability in 1944. At the age of seventy-eight, he died at Walter Reed Army Medical Center on 18 May 1953. Photo courtesy of the National Archives.

William Edward Cole

Fox Conner

Fox Conner (0-85), son of Robert H. Conner and Nannie Fox Conner, was born on 2 November 1874 in Slate Springs, Mississippi. After attending a local elementary school, he entered USMA and graduated number seventeen of fifty-nine in the class of 1898. He was a classmate of Malin Craig and Guy V. Henry, Jr. (both *q.v.*). Originally commissioned in the Second Artillery, his first station was Fort Adams, in Rhode Island, but soon after he went to Cuba for the Spanish-American War. On his return, he commanded the 123rd Coast Artillery Company at Fort Hamilton, New York, from 1901 to 1905. He married Virginia Brandreth on 4 June 1902 and they had three children: Betty V., Fox B., and Florence S. In 1906 Conner graduated from the Army Staff College and in 1907 he was detailed to the General Staff. In 1908 he graduated from the Army War College. During 1911 and 1912, he served with the French field artillery. Arriving in France in 1917, Conner served with the Inspector General's Department. On 8 August 1918, he received his promotion to brigadier general (NA), and was G-3 (Operations) at General Headquarters (AEF); for this service he received both the Distinguished Service Medal and a Purple Heart. He was assistant Chief of Staff (USA) and later G-4 (SOS) from 1 December 1924 until 8 March 1926; on 20 October 1925 he was promoted to major general (USA). From January to December 1927 he was deputy Chief of Staff (USA). From 1928 to 1930, he commanded the Hawaiian Department, and his final assignment (from 1930 to 1938) was as Commanding General, First Corps Area. He then retired due to disabilities and died at Walter Reed Army Medical Center, just short of his seventy-seventh birthday, on 13 October 1951. Photo courtesy of the National Archives.

William Durward Connor (0-84), son of Edward D. Connor and Adeline Powers Connor, was born on 22 February 1874 near Beloit, Wisconsin. He entered USMA, graduated number one of sixty-seven in the class of 1897, and was commissioned in the corps of engineers. He was a classmate of Frank R. McCoy (*q.v.*). His first tours of duty were in the Philippine campaign and in the suppression of the insurrection, which followed shortly afterwards. Next, he was city engineer of Manila; he received a Silver Star commendation for his performance of that duty. From Manila he was sent to New London, Connecticut for fortifications work there, and after that he was sent to do improvements on the Mississippi River. On 6 June 1907, Connor married Elsie Van Vleet. From 1910 to 1912, he taught civil engineering. During the four years preceding our entry into World War I, Connor was on the General Staff, and from July to November 1916 he was assistant Chief of Staff of the Southern Department. From December 1916 to May 1917 he was department engineer in the Philippines; then, he was sent to duty with the General Staff of the AEF. He was assistant Chief of Staff (G-4) of the Service of Supply (SOS), and was later Chief of Staff of the 32d Infantry Division (AEF); these were National Guard troops from Michigan and Wisconsin. On 26 June 1918, he was promoted to brigadier general (NA) and given command of the 63d Infantry Brigade, 32d Division. Later, he commanded Base Section Number 2 at Bordeaux. Following that he became Chief of Staff of the Service of Supply; he then commanded the Service of Supply until 1 September 1919. Beginning on 7 January 1920, he commanded all American forces remaining in France. He served there until he returned to the States, where he commanded the Engineer School at Fort Belvoir, Virginia. He became assistant Chief of Staff, United States Army, after which (from 1923 to 1926) he commanded American forces in China (where and when the above photo was taken). Returning again to the United States, he commanded the Second Infantry Division, then the Army War College, from 1927 to 1932. He served as superintendent at USMA from May 1932 until his retirement in 1938. On 7 May 1941, Connor was called to active duty as chairman of the construction advisory committee; he reverted to retired status again on 21 March 1942. His decorations included: the Distinguished Service Medal and the Silver Star from the United States, Order of the Bath from Britain, and

William Durward Connor

the Croix de Guerre and Commander of the Legion of Honor from France. At the age of eighty-six, he died at Walter Reed Army Medical Center.

Richard Coulter, Jr.

Richard Coulter, Jr. (no ASN assigned) There were four men named Richard Coulter in Greensburg, Pennsylvania. These men were Justice Richard Coulter of the Pennsylvania Supreme Court (who lived from 1788 to 1852), Maj. Gen. Richard Coulter of the Pennsylvania Militia (who fought in the Mexican War and the Civil War), Brig. Gen. Richard Coulter, Jr. of the Pennsylvania National Guard (who lived from 3 October 1870 to 26 September 1955) and his nephew Richard Coulter (who lived from 4 November 1906 to 20 July 1938). The subject of this biography is Brig. Gen. Richard Coulter, Jr. His father had enlisted in the Pennsylvania Militia during the Mexican War, and by the close of the Civil War a few years later he was a brevet major general of those troops. Richard Coulter, Jr. graduated from Princeton; he was a lawyer with banking, mining and manufacturing interests. He married Matilda Bowman of Uniontown, Pennsylvania, and they had one daughter, Emma (later Mrs. Emma Coulter Ware of St. Louis, Missouri). His long association with the Pennsylvania National Guard included service during the Spanish-American War, the Philippine insurrection and the First World War. As of 1907, he commanded the old Tenth Pennsylvania Infantry. In 1908 he was elected president of the First National Bank in Greensburg, succeeding his father in that office. He was interested in the welfare of his community, and used the bank and other means to promote the financial and physical growth of the city. On 5 August 1917 he was promoted to brigadier general (NA) and given command of the 81st Infantry Brigade, a part of the 41st Infantry Division. This greatly upset him, as his life, like his father's, was spent in and for the Pennsylvania National Guard. The 41st Infantry Division troops were from Washington, Idaho and Oregon. As a brigadier general, Coulter was also ad interim commander of the 41st Infantry Division from 23 January to 13 February 1918. After 14 January, he commanded Base Section Number 4, headquartered at Le Havre, France. On 4 January 1919 he was discharged from the national army; after returning to Pennsylvania, he became the Commanding General of the 55th Infantry Brigade, 28th Division, Pennsylvania National Guard. He died at his home and is buried in the family plot there. Photo courtesy of the Pennsylvania National Guard.

Louis Chapin Covell

Louis Chapin Covell (ASN unknown), son of Elliott Franklin Covell and Laura Chapin Covell, was born on 22 June 1875 in Grand Rapids, Michigan. His grandfather had been a pioneer of Grand Rapids in the 1830s. He enlisted in the Michigan National Guard on 6 April 1892 at age seventeen, while still in high school. The following year, he graduated from high school; he was then employed by Macey and Company for twelve years as advertising and sales manager. On 12 June 1906, he married Florence Davidson and they had three sons: George Covell, Louis Covell, Jr. and Robert Covell. The elder Covell was commissioned a second lieutenant on 26 June 1895. During the Spanish-American War, Covell served as a captain; he was a major by 1900 and a lieutenant colonel by 1911. In 1915 he was organizer and president of Covell-Hensen Company, doing advertising and printing. On 7 February 1917, he became a brigadier general , and on 5 August 1917 he became a brigadier general (NA). He commanded the 63d Infantry Brigade, which was composed of the 125th and 126th Infantry Regiments, in combat with the AEF. He received the French Croix de Guerre with palms, and was discharged from the national army on 17 February 1919. Next, he managed the Reynolds Chrysler Company in Flint, and later he was an executive in the sales department of General Motors in Detroit. After retiring from General Motors he lived in Maryland; Mount Vernon, New York, and Falls Church, Virginia. He belonged to the American Legion, the Sons of the American Revolution, and the Military Order of Foreign Wars; he was a Mason, a Republican and a Congregationalist. He died at age seventy-six on 26 February 1952, while on a trip through Vermont. Photo courtesy of the National Archives.

Daniel Frank Craig (0-1242), son of Mr. and Mrs. Samuel Craig, was born on 3 October 1875 near Oskaloosa in Makaska County, Iowa. He was originally commissioned a first lieutenant in the 20th Kansas Infantry on 18 May 1898 and was a captain by 9 May 1899. Honorably discharged as a captain from the Kansas Infantry on 12 June 1899, he was recommissioned a captain in the 36th United States Volunteer Infantry on 5 July of the same year. On 16 March 1901, he was mustered out of the volunteers after having served in the Philippines. On 8 May 1901 he received a regular commission as a second lieutenant, artillery. By 28 July 1903 he was promoted to first lieutenant (USA), and he served in the Philippines from 1904 to 1907. He married Florence Elizabeth Burt on 19 May 1906, and on 25 January 1907 he was again promoted to captain. The following June he was assigned to the Fourth Field Artillery Brigade,

Daniel Frank Craig

and in 1910 he graduated from the Mounted Service School at Fort Riley, Kansas. In 1912 he was a distinguished graduate of the School of the Line. From 26 April to 26 November 1914, Craig was on the Vera Cruz Expedition. Early in 1916 he graduated from the Army Staff College; he then went on the Mexican Punitive Expedition from 21 May to 1 December 1916. He was transferred to the General Staff Corps on 25 November 1916. He acted as Chief of Staff of the 12th Infantry Division until 24 March 1917, when he became assistant Chief of Staff of the Southern Department. Promotion to major came on 15 May 1917. He remained with the Southern Department until the day war was declared (6 April 1917); he then served in the War College Division (GS) until August 1917. In August he was sent to France as a colonel (NA). He commanded the 302nd Field Artillery Regiment, 76th Division, there until October 1918, when he became a brigadier general (NA). He became Commanding General of the 157th Field Artillery Brigade on 21 October 1918, of the Second Field Artillery Brigade on 24 January 1919, and of the 158th Field Artillery Brigade on 11 March 1919. For this service he received the Distinguished Service Medal from the United States, and he was awarded a Silver Plaque from France. In private life, he was a Mason, a Shriner, and an Episcopalian, not necessarily in that order. His permanent home was in Garnett, Kansas. He died on 17 April 1929. Photo courtesy of the National Archives.

Malin Craig (0-86), son of Louis Aleck Craig and Georgie Malin Craig, was born on 5 August 1875 in Saint Joseph, Missouri, the town from which the Pony Express had started its runs to California just a few years previously. He went to Georgetown University before entering the class of 1898 at USMA; he was a classmate of Fox Conner and Guy V. Henry, Jr. (both *q.v.*). He graduated number thirty-three of fifty-nine and was commissioned in the infantry. However, during the Spanish-American War—immediately after his graduation—he served in the Sixth Cavalry during the Santiago campaign. By June of that year he transferred to the Fourth Cavalry at Fort Yellowstone, Wyoming,

Malin Craig

then administered by the army; it is now known as "Yellowstone National Park." After taking part in the China Relief Expedition, he came back to the Philippines, where he was aide to Gen. Thomas H. Barry and later to Gen. J. Franklin Bell (both *q.v.*). From 1910 to 1912, Craig had duty with the General Staff as an instructor at the War College, then as Chief of Staff of the Maneuver Division in San Antonio, Texas. Next, he became an assistant to the Chief of Staff of the Western Division in San Francisco, California. During 1916 and 1917, he was an instructor at the Army Service Schools at Fort Leavenworth, Kansas. After this he was sent to the Adjutant General's Office in Washington. On 15 July 1917, Craig was promoted to brigadier general (NA) and became Chief of Staff, Fourth Infantry Division (AEF); he received the Distinguished Service Medal for this service. Next, he became Chief of Staff of the First Army Corps, which included the battles of Marne and Saint Mihiel and the Meuse-Argonne. He then served as Chief of Staff, Third Army (AFG). This lasted until the fall of 1919, when he was sent back to Washington as the director of the Army War College. In 1921 he received a promotion to brigadier general (USA). After a brief tour in Arizona he became commandant of the Cavalry School at Fort Riley, Kansas, from 1 September 1921 until 30 June 1923. He was Chief of Cavalry from 24 July 1924 to 21 March 1926; this assignment carried with it the temporary rank of major general. In 1926, Craig was promoted to major general (USA), and served as assistant Chief of Staff (USA). From 1930 to 1935 he was Commanding General, Ninth Corps Area. He filled this position until 2 October 1935; he was then made Chief of Staff (USA), with temporary four-star rank. For this he received another Distinguished Service Medal. He retired in 1939, but was recalled to active duty on 26 September 1941. At the age of sixty-nine, Craig died in Washington, D.C., while still on duty, on 25 July 1945. He shrank from publicity and was little known to the general public. At his own request he was buried at Arlington National Cemetery, but without military honors. Photo courtesy of the National Archives.

Charles Crawford (0-13373), son of Thomas Crawford and Margaret Parkhill Crawford, was born in Coshockton, Ohio (northeast of Columbus). He entered USMA and graduated number forty-one of forty-nine in the class of 1889. Charles D. Rhodes and William Lassiter (both *q.v.*) were two of his classmates. Crawford married a woman named E. M. Miller, and they apparently had no children. He was commissioned in the Tenth Infantry and did frontier duty from 1889 to 1895; this included military police duty in Oklahoma City during 1889 and 1890. He organized an Apache Indian Company in the Tenth Infantry in 1891 and 1892. During the Spanish-American War, Crawford was at the Battle of San Juan Hill; his courage there drew official written attention. From 1900 to 1902 he was in the Philippines; afterwards, he was an instructor at the Infantry and Cavalry School and at the Army Staff College, both at Fort Leavenworth, Kansas. From 1913 to 1916 he was on the General Staff and from 1916 to 1917 he was in the Panama Canal Zone. On 17 December 1917 he was promoted to

Charles Crawford

brigadier general (NA); he was also given command of the Sixth Infantry Brigade, Third Infantry Division, at the second Battle of the Marne and on the Vesle. From 19 March to 12 April 1918, he commanded the Third Infantry Division (AEF). He retired as a colonel in 1919 due to disabilities, and his wife died that same year. He wrote two books: *Six Months with the Sixth Brigade* and *Restarting Economic Theory*. He was a Presbyterian and made his home in Paola, Kansas; he was killed in an automobile accident in Kansas on 28 December 1945. Photo courtesy of the National Archives.

George Oscar Cress (0-143), son of Mr. and Mrs. George Cress, was born in Warsaw, Illinois (at the junction of the Des Moines and Mississippi Rivers, on the western edge of Illinois). He graduated USMA number twenty-seven of thirty-seven in the class of 1884. Classmates included DeRosey Cabell (also in this photo), William L. Sibert (both *q.v.*) and Isaac Newton Lewis. Cress was commissioned in the Second Cavalry and did frontier duty from 1884 to 1889. During this period, on 26 May 1886, he married Donna Scott Dean. From 1889 to 1893 he was Professor of Military Science and Tactics at Knox College in Galesburg, Illinois. In 1897 and 1898, he was stationed at Yellowstone National Park, and during 1899 and 1900 he was in the Philippines with Gen. Henry Lawton. From 1900 to 1904 Cress was constructing quartermaster at the Cavalry School at Fort Riley, Kansas. This was followed by a second tour as Professor of Military Science and Tactics, this time at Michigan Military Academy from 1904 to 1908. In 1916 and 1917, he was on Gen. John J. Pershing's staff on the Mexican Punitive Expedition. He then served with the Inspector General's Department until 1918, when he organized the 49th Field Artillery Brigade. On 1 October 1918 he was promoted to brigadier general (NA). After the war he was put in charge of militia affairs in the Southern Department; he then commanded Columbus Barracks. He retired in 1926 as a colonel, but his rank of brigadier general was restored by act of Congress in 1930, on the retired list. Well beyond his ninety-first birthday,

George Oscar Cress

Cress died in Oakland, California on 8 May 1954. Photo courtesy of the National Archives.

Marcus Daniel Cronin

Marcus Daniel Cronin (0-196) was born on 9 January 1865 in Worcester, Massachusetts. He graduated USMA number forty-five of sixty-four in the class of 1887. Richmond P. Davis, George O. Squier and P. D. Lochridge (all *q.v.*) were three of his classmates. He was a class behind John J. Pershing and a class ahead of Peyton C. March (both *q.v.*). He was commissioned in the infantry and did frontier duty from 1887 to 1893. On 2 August 1893, he married Helen Hannay. From 1893 to 1897, he was an instructor at USMA. During the Spanish-American War he was regimental adjutant of the 25th Infantry during the Santiago campaign, as well as serving in the Sanitary Corps. During the Philippine insurrection he was a colonel of United States Volunteers, and he was later assistant chief of the Philippine Constabulary. On 5 August 1917 he was promoted to brigadier general (NA). He then commanded the 163rd Infantry Brigade at Camp (now Fort) Gordon, Georgia, and took them to France with the AEF. In 1925 he retired with his peacetime rank of colonel, but in 1930 his rank of brigadier general was restored by act of Congress on the retired list. He lived in La Jolla, California, just north of San Diego. At the age of seventy-one, Cronin died in New York on 12 August 1936. Photo courtesy of USMA Archives.

Adelbert Cronkhite (0-29) was born on 5 January 1861 at Lietchfield Center, New York. He graduated USMA number ten of thirty-seven in the class of 1882; classmates included Henry T. Allen (*q.v.*) and Frederick G. Bonfils, who did not graduate. Cronkhite was commissioned in the Fourth Artillery and graduated from the Artillery School in 1886. He was in the Sioux Campaign of 1890 and 1891, the last of the late Indian Wars. He then worked as Professor of Military Science and Tactics at Michigan Military Academy in 1891 and 1892. In the Spanish-American War, he served as a quartermaster and commissary of a field artillery brigade, both in Cuba and with the Puerto Rican Expedition. He served as quarter-

Adelbert Cronkhite

master from 1904 to 1907, then had four years as an inspector general. From 1911 to 1914, Cronkhite commanded the coast defenses of eastern New York, and from 1914 to 1917 he had the same assignment in the Panama Canal Zone. From there he was sent to Camp (now Fort) Lee, in Petersburg, Virginia (about twenty miles south of Richmond). There he commanded the 80th Infantry Division; he also took this unit to France with the AEF, and he received the Distinguished Service Medal for this service. Later, he commanded the Sixth and the Ninth Army Corps. In 1920 he became a major general (USA), and on 1 February 1923 he retired. At the age of seventy-six, he died in Florida on 15 June 1937. Photo courtesy of the Quartermaster Center, Fort Lee, Virginia.

Enoch Herbert Crowder

Enoch Herbert Crowder (0-10) was born in 1859 in Grundy County, Missouri (northeast of Saint Joseph). He was both a regular army officer and a statesman. He graduated USMA number thirty-one of fifty-three in the class of 1881. He was a classmate of Harry and Henry Hodges, Edward Saint J. Greble and Joseph T. Dickman (all *q.v.*). Crowder was commissioned in the cavalry. He served during the late Indian Wars against both Sitting Bull and Geronimo. From 1885 to 1889, he was Professor of Military Science and Tactics at the University of Missouri. While there, in 1886, he received a law degree, and after 1891 he transferred to the Judge Advocate General's (JAG) Department. He was the JAG of the Eighth Army Corps in 1898 and 1899, and from 1899 to 1901 he was an associate justice of the Philippine Supreme Court. In 1901 he was made a brigadier general of United States Volunteers, and in 1904 and 1905 he was an observer with the Japanese army during the Russo-Japanese War. From 1906 to 1909, Crowder was Secretary of State and Justice in Cuba. In 1911 he was promoted to brigadier general and became Judge Advocate General (USA); he held this post until 1923—something of a record! He helped frame and administer the Selective Service Act, and was responsible for eliminating many of the draft mistakes of the Civil War period by the use of the (BG) James Oakes Report of 1866. He is best known as the Provost-Marshal, United States Army, of the World War I period. At the invitation of the Cuban government, Crowder visited in 1919 to help with electoral reforms. He wrote *The Spirit of Selective Service* in 1920. He became the personal representative of President Warren G. Harding in 1921 and was the first United States Ambassador to Cuba, serving from 1923 to 1927. He retired from the army in 1923 with substantial honors and degrees. He died in Washington, D.C. on 7 May 1932. Camp Crowder, in Missouri (in the southwest corner of the state, near Joplin), was named for him. Photo courtesy of the Annual Report, Association of Graduates, USMA.

William Crozier (0-12991), son of Robert Crozier and Margaret Atkinson Crozier, was born on 19 February 1855 in Carrollton, Ohio. His ancestors had left France in 1698, and his grandfather had come to the United States from Ireland early in the nineteenth century. His father founded the newspaper in Leavenworth, Kansas, practiced law, and represented Kansas in the United States Senate. The younger Crozier entered USMA and graduated number five of forty-eight in the class of 1876. James Parker, Hugh L. Scott and Eben Swift (all *q.v.*) were three of his classmates. Crozier was commissioned in the Fourth Artillery and did frontier duty from 1876 to 1879. He served in campaigns against the Sioux and the Bannocks. From 1879 to 1884 he was Assistant Professor of Mathematics at USMA; in 1881 he transferred from artillery to ordnance. His first station as an ordnance officer was at the Watertown, Massachusetts arsenal; he served there from 1884 to 1887. From 1887 to 1888 and again from 1889 to 1892, he was in the office of the Chief of Ordnance, involved in the invention and design of heavy guns. In 1899 he was a military delegate to the first International Peace Conference at the Hague. From there he was sent to the Philippines, then to China as Chief Ordnance Officer of the China Relief Expedition, under Gen. Adna Chaffee. In 1901 President Theodore Roosevelt made Crozier the Chief of Ordnance of the United States Army; he held this post for seventeen years, creating a long and distinguished record. In 1905 he was invited to the grand maneuvers of the French army. In 1912 and 1913 he was president of the Army War College, and was co-inventor of a disappearing gun carriage, one of his many contributions to ordnance engineering. On 31 October 1913, in London, England, he married Mary Hoyt Williams of New London, Connecticut. He became a major general on 6 October 1917 and retired at his own request on 1 January 1919. Until the end of his life, he retained a great interest in military and international affairs. He was the last surviving member of the class of 1876, and died at age eighty-seven in Washington on 10 November 1942. Photo courtesy of the Ordnance Museum, Aberdeen, Maryland.

William Crozier

William Mackey Cruikshank (0-238), son of Mr. and Mrs. John C. Cruikshank, was born on 7 November 1870 in Washington, D.C. He entered

William Mackey Cruikshank

USMA and graduated number six of fifty in the class of 1893; he was a classmate of Herbert Ball Crosby, later the Chief of Cavalry. Upon graduation Cruikshank was commissioned in the Second Artillery. From 1895 to 1898, he was instructor of mathematics at USMA, but he managed to get into the Santiago campaign of 1898. He graduated from the School of Submarine Defense at Willet's Point, New York in 1903, and on 30 April 1904 he married Cornelia B. Holabird. They had one daughter, Mary Holabird Cruikshank. From 1904 to 1907, Cruikshank was stationed at Fort Howard, Maryland, and from 1907 to 1909 he was adjutant of the Fifth Field Artillery in the Philippines. In France he commanded a field artillery regiment of the First Infantry Division, until his promotion to brigadier general (NA) on 26 June 1918. Then, he commanded the Third Field Artillery, Third Infantry Division. He also served as Chief of Artillery for the Fourth Corps (AEF), for which he received the Distinguished Service Medal. He was with the American Forces in Germany until 5 August 1919, then had four years with the General Staff back in the United States. From 1930 until his retirement in 1934 he was commandant of the Field Artillery School at Fort Sill, Oklahoma. At the age of seventy-two, he died in Washington, D.C. on 23 February 1943. Photo courtesy of the National Archives.

Thomas Cruse (0-13113), son of James Barnhill Cruse and Mildred Davis King Cruse, was born on 29 December 1857 in Owensboro, Kentucky. He studied at Center College, Kentucky, then entered USMA. He graduated number twenty-six of sixty-seven in the class of 1879; classmates included Fredrick S. Foltz, William D. Beach and Hunter Liggett (all *q.v.*). Cruse was commissioned in the Sixth Cavalry, then stationed in Arizona. On 4 February 1882, he married Beatrice Cottrell, and they had two sons: Fred T. and James T. The elder Cruse's behavior in action against hostile American Indians in 1882 earned him a Congressional Medal of Honor as well as the Indian Campaign Medal. On 28 September 1887, he was promoted to first lieutenant. He did frontier duty from 1879 to 1890, and in 1891 he graduated from the

Thomas Cruse

Infantry and Cavalry School at Fort Leavenworth, Kansas. During the Spanish-American War, he was a major and quartermaster of the United States Volunteers in 1898 and 1899; he then took part in the Philippine campaign. On 1 February 1913, he was made a colonel, Quartermaster Corps, and on 9 January 1917 he was again promoted to brigadier general (USA). He retired in 1918; he was a Baptist, a Democrat, and a Mason. After his retirement he lived in Longport, New Jersey, and he died at age eighty-five in Texas on 8 June 1943. Photo courtesy of USMA Archives.

Dennis Hadley Currie

Dennis Hadley Currie (0-1338), son of Mr. and Mrs. Angus Currie, was born on 22 July 1874 in Glen Rose, Texas. His boyhood was spent on the family farm there. He was educated at Glen Rose High School and a small nearby college; he then taught school for a year. He entered USMA and graduated number thirty-one of seventy-four in the class of 1901, a classmate of Beverly F. Browne (*q.v.*). Currie was commissioned in the artillery corps; when it was reorganized, he went with the field artillery. With the exception of a brief detail in the signal corps and two details with the General Staff, he served with the field artillery until he retired. In 1907, he was a distinguished graduate of the Infantry and Cavalry School at Fort Leavenworth, Kansas, and in 1908 he graduated from the Army Staff College. He was on the original General Staff Corps eligible list. He served in many parts of the United States, as well as in the Philippines against the Moros. He was a man of sterling qualities: sharp, loyal, a devoted father and a faithful friend. He had been handicapped by illness in his second year; this delayed his graduation and active service, and eventually caused his early retirement and untimely death. On 1 October 1918, Currie was promoted to brigadier general (NA), but on 10 June 1919 he reverted to his permanent rank of major of field artillery. On 11 July 1920 he was promoted to lieutenant colonel, and on 31 December 1922 he was retired for disability incident to the service. He was in ill health for nearly seventeen years and suffered continual discomfort for the last two years of his life. At the age of fifty-three, he died in Piedmont, California on 26 March 1928. He was survived by his widow, a son, Lt. William Ross Currie, and a daughter, Annie Virginia Currie. His rank of brigadier general was restored posthumously by act of Congress in June 1930. Photo courtesy of the Association of Graduates, USMA.

Alexander Lucian Dade

Alexander Lucian Dade (0-13451) was born on 18 July 1863 in Hopkinsville, Kentucky, where he spent his boyhood. He entered USMA and graduated number forty-six of sixty-four in the class of 1887. P. D. Lochridge, Charles H. Martin, William Weigel, George O. Squier (all *q.v.*) and Thomas Q. Donaldson were some of his classmates. Upon graduation, Dade was commissioned in the 13th Infantry, but in 1888 he transferred to the Tenth Cavalry and was involved with the Apaches in southern Arizona. He was a studious person, and when he got the chance he went to the Infantry and Cavalry School, graduating in 1893. He was transferred to the Third Cavalry and sailed with it to Cuba in 1898. He was cited for gallantry in the Santiago campaign; then, he was invalided home and rejoined his regiment at Fort Ethan Allen, Vermont. On 9 September 1899 he was promoted to major of volunteers and joined the 38th United States Volunteer Infantry in the Philippines. There, he served as an inspector on the staff of Gen. S. B. M. Young during the expedition into northern Luzon. He was promoted to captain in the regular army, and returned to that grade on 30 June 1901. From 1902 to 1905, Dade was inspector of the Philippine Constabulary, and when he returned to the United States he was assigned to the Ninth Cavalry. He graduated from the Army War College in 1910 and became a major in 1911. In 1913 he became the base port inspector at Galveston, Texas, and was later inspector of the Second Division when that unit went to Vera Cruz. He married Josephine Worth, granddaughter of the General Worth who entered Mexico City in 1848. They had a daughter, Margaret Dade (later Mrs. J. M. Hutchinson of Chicago), and a son, Alexander L. Dade, Jr., a businessman in Tulsa, Oklahoma. After the Vera Cruz Expedition, Dade again served with the Ninth Cavalry. He then served with the Seventh Cavalry, which included going on the Mexican Punitive Expedition with Gen. John J. Pershing (*q.v.*) in 1916 and 1917. At this time, Dade was promoted to colonel. On 11 April 1917, a week after the declaration of war with Germany, he was assigned to organize and head the Aviation Section of the Signal Corps. On 27 October 1917, Dade was promoted to brigadier general (NA). He was grossly overworked and returned to the grade of colonel as Inspector General in Chicago, Illinois. He was quite sick and never regained his health, although he remained an Inspector General until he retired, because of a disability, on 25 June 1920. In October 1918, General Pershing, who had twice cited Dade for gallantry in Mexico, discovered Dade was available for service abroad and requested that he be appointed brigadier general and sent to France to join him. Arrangements were made to do so; Dade had received his orders and his kit was on the train when the War Department wired to him that he had failed to pass the physical exam. So, his reappointment to brigadier general and his foreign travel orders were cancelled. He lingered on until he died at age sixty-three in Hopkinsville, Kentucky on 8 January 1927. Photo courtesy of the Association of Graduates, USMA.

Albert Clayton Dalton

Albert Clayton Dalton (0-357) was born on 2 October 1867 in Thornton, Indiana. He enlisted in Company A, 22nd Infantry, on 18 January 1889 and was discharged two years later to accept a commission as a second lieutenant in the same regiment. He participated in the Cheyenne campaign in 1890 and in the Sioux Campaign of 1890 and 1891. He graduated from the Infantry and Cavalry School at Fort Leavenworth, Kansas, in 1895. During the Spanish-American War, Dalton was in the Santiago campaign in Cuba in 1898; he was in the Philippine campaign from 1899 to 1902. In 1907 he married Caro Gordon, and from 1907 to 1909 he was with the army of Cuban occupation. In 1914, he was in Vera Cruz, Mexico, and in 1916 and 1917 he was on the Mexican border. The day that war was declared in 1917, he was a major on duty in Gen. John J. Pershing's headquarters. The expeditionary depot in Philadelphia was organized by Dalton in the early fall of 1917; he then served as General Superintendent of the Army Transport Service in New York until 5 November 1918. On 1 October 1918 he was made a brigadier general (NA). As of 6 November, he commanded the 18th Infantry Brigade, Ninth Infantry Division, in France; this duty lasted until August 1919. His final assignment was as assistant quartermaster General in Washington, D.C. He retired on 7 July 1926; the following day, he was appointed to the United States Shipping Board Merchant Fleet Corporation. He received a Silver Star commendation for gallantry in action in Cuba, the Distinguished Service Medal for his World War I service, and Grand Officer of the Crown of Romania. His last days were spent in Washington, D.C., where he lived at 2540 Massachusetts Avenue, NW. He died at age eighty-nine on 24 March 1957. He had been remarried in 1948 to Mary Ellen Garner, who survived him. He was buried at Arlington National Cemetery. Photo courtesy of the National Archives.

Robert Melville Danford (0-1913) was born on 7 July 1879 in New Boston, Iowa (on the Mississippi River, between Rock Island and Burlington). He entered USMA and graduated number thirty-three of one hundred twenty-four in the class of 1904. George R. Allin, Leslie J. McNair, Pelham D. Glassford (all *q.v.*) and Edmund L. Gruber were four of his classmates.

Originally commissioned in the artillery corps, Danford changed permanently to field artillery when the artillery corps was divided. He served in the Philippines with the Fifth Field Artillery, and from 10 June 1907 to 15 August 1907 he was on detached service with the Coast Artillery at the Presidio at San Francisco, California. From 10 March 1908 to 30 June 1912, he was secretary of the Mounted Service School at Fort Riley, Kansas. During this period, from 1 July to 4 December 1910, he was an aide to Brig. Gen. F. R. Ward, conductiong a special study on horses and horse breeding. From 3 October 1912 to 24 January 1915, he was with his battery both at Fort Sill, Oklahoma, and in Naco, Arizona (on the border, near Douglas). Then, he spent sixteen months as instructor at the School of Fire for Field Artillery in Fort Sill. After that service he was sent to Connecticut as instructor-inspector to the ConnecticutField Artillery. Four of these six batteries were composed entirely of Yale University students. He was Professor of Military Science and Tactics at Yale from February until July 1917, and was awarded an honorary M.A. by Yale during this period. He mustered into federal service as part of the Pennsylvania National Guard in Allentown. Returning to Fort Sill, he was assigned to the 42nd Division. By this time he was a lieutenant colonel, field artillery, and senior instructor at the Second Officers' Training Camp at Plattsburg, New York, commanding the 302nd Field Artillery Brigade. Back at Fort Sill, he commanded the 129th Field Artillery Brigade before being sent to the office of the Chief of Field Artillery from 14 March to 23 April 1918. Next, he organized and commanded the Field Artillery Replacement Depot at Camp Jackson, South Carolina. On 8 August 1918 he was promoted to brigadier general (NA) and again sent back to the office of the Chief of Field Artillery. He stayed there until 19 March 1919, when he reverted to his permanent rank of major. He also found time for two and a half months with the AEF before going to West Point as Commandant of Cadets. He died at age ninety-five in Stamford, Connecticut on 12 September 1974. Photo courtesy of *The Assembly*, USMA.

Robert Melville Danford

Thomas Walter Darrah (0-476) was born on 11 July 1873 in Marquette, McPherson County, Kansas. After attending the local public schools, he entered USMA. He graduated number twenty-one of fifty-one in the class of 1895. One of his classmates was Joe Wheeler, Jr., son of the famous Confederate cavalry general who, many years later, returned to duty in the United States Army as a major general during the Spanish-American War. Darrah was commissioned a second lieutenant in 1895 and married Rose Wood in 1899. They had two daugh-

Thomas Walter Darrah

ters: Marion M. (later Mrs. Warren D. Brewer) and Jean West (later Mrs. Woodlief Thomas). Darrah was in the sanitary corps in Cuba (where he received a Silver Star citation) and in the Moro Expedition in the Philippines from 1903 to 1905. He advanced steadily through the ranks until he became a brigadier general. From 1901 to 1905 he was in the Subsistence Department, and he was an instructor of chemistry at USMA from 1907 to 1911. He was senior instructor at the Officers' Training Camp at Fort Benjamin Harrison, Indianapolis, in 1917. Arriving in France, he participated in the Champagne-Marne, Aisne Marne, Oise-Aine and Meuse-Argonne. He went to the Army School of the Line in 1920, the Army Staff College in 1921, and the Army War College in 1923. From 1924 to 1926 he was Chief of Staff, Fourth Corps Area; from 1926 to 1928 he commanded the 34th Infantry at Fort Meade, Maryland. After that he became Chief of Staff at the Third Corps Area headquarters in Baltimore; he served there until 1931. He commanded the Pacific sector of the Panama Canal Department from 1932 to 1934, and he retired to his home in New York City in 1937. With the American entry into World War II, Darrah became Deputy Director of Civilian Defense for the state of New York. He received two Silver Star commendations in the Spanish-American War: one for action in Cuba and one for action in the Philippines. Darrah died at age eighty-one on 21 January 1955, and is buried at Arlington National Cemetery. Photo courtesy of the Pennsylvania National Guard.

William Robert Dashiell (0-212) was born on 3 April 1863 in Mecklenburg County, Virginia. When he was six years old his parents moved to Norfolk, and he lived there until he entered USMA on 15 June 1884. He graduated number thirty-eight of forty-four in the class of 1888. Peyton C. March and Guy H. Preston (both *q.v.*) were two of his classmates. He was commissioned in the 17th Infantry and joined his unit at Fort D. A. Russel, Wyoming (now Warren Air Force Base). He later served with the 24th, 27th, 2nd, 43d and 35th Infantry Regiments. He participated in the Sioux Campaign of 1890

William Robert Dashiell

and 1891 and again fought against hostile American Indians in southeastern Arizona in August 1896. This was followed by two tours of duty in the Philippines and two in Hawaii. He graduated in 1909 from the Army School of the Line and in 1915 from the Army War College. During the Spanish-American War, Dashiell received the unwelcome duty of post commander of Fort Douglas, Utah, while his regiment was in Cuba. During the Philippine insurrection he commanded Company C, 24th Infantry, in advance of Gen. Henry Lawton's column through San Isidro and San Jose; these troops were sent to gain the left and rear of Emilio Aguinaldo's forces. Dashiell participated in the capture of Arayat on 12 October 1899 and in a night attack at Cabanatuan on 31 December 1899. In November 1899, he married Ida Pearson of Cave Spring, Georgia; they had no children. On his second tour of duty in the Philippines, Dashiell commanded Camp Downes, on Leyte, for eighteen months. During a Pulajane uprising, he commanded the Third District, the whole west side of the island, from August 1906 to February 1907. For this service he was most highly commended by his department commander, Gen. Jesse M. Lee. On 12 April 1918, Dashiell was promoted to brigadier general (NA). He then commanded the 11th Infantry Brigade, Sixth Infantry Division, until it was demobilized in June 1919. For his service in France he received a Silver Star. He was interested in youth and had a number of tours of duty (even after his so-called retirement) in his later years. These included stints as Professor of Military Science and Tactics at North Georgia Agricultural College, from 1892 to 1895; at Virginia Polytechnic Institute, from 1909 to 1911, and at the Atlanta and Fulton County schools in Georgia, from 1925 to 1932. He bought a home, called "Maplewood," on Peachtree Road in Atlanta in 1909. After over forty-eight years of service, Dashiell died at age seventy-five in Atlanta on 16 March 1939. Photo courtesy of the Association of Graduates, USMA.

Richmond Pearson Davis

Richmond Pearson Davis (0-111) was born on 23 June 1866 in Statesville, North Carolina. He entered USMA on 1 September 1883; he graduated number six of sixty-four in the class of 1887. P. D. Lochridge, Charles H. Martin and George O. Squier (all *q.v.*) were three of his classmates. Davis was commissioned in the Second Artillery and sent to Jackson Barracks, Louisiana. On 19 June 1889 he married Bertha M. Bouvier of Washington, D.C.; they had no surviving children. After leaving Jackson Barracks, Davis served at Fort Wadsworth, at New York Harbor, until May 1890. He then reported to USMA as an instructor in the department of chemistry, mineralogy and geology. He served there for seven years, the last four as assistant professor of the department. In 1897 he rejoined the Second Artillery. He found himself back at the same assistant professorship at USMA (over his protest) on 20 August 1898. Early in 1904 he was sent to Fort Totten, New York; he commanded the artillery there, as well as the School of Submarine Defense. In 1906, he was returned to West Point, promoted to major and transferred to the Coast Artillery. Next, he was director of the Coast Artillery School and President of the Coast Artillery Board, both at Fort Monroe, Virginia, on the lower end of the Chesapeake Bay. On 10 March 1911 he was promoted to lieutenant colonel and given command of the Second Provisional Coast Artillery Regiment in Galveston, Texas. In 1911 he took a special course at the Army War College; after graduation, he was detailed as General Staff in the office of the Chief of Coast Artillery. After asking to be relieved from this service, he commanded Fort H. G. Wright and the New London, Connecticut Coast Artillery District. A little more than a year later he was sent to command Fort Winfield Scott, California and the coast defenses of San Francisco, California. He served in this capacity until 5 August 1917, when he was promoted to brigadier general (NA). Then, he took command of and trained the 162nd Field Artillery Brigade at Camp Pike, in Arkansas. They were also at Camp Dix, New Jersey, for several months, but got to France in time to participate in the Saint Mihiel offensive. He was transferred to the 151st Field Artillery Brigade on 20 September 1918, and participated in the Meuse-Argonne and other offensives. In January 1919 he was relieved of this duty and sent back to the United States to become commander of coast defenses of Manila. When Davis reverted to his permanent grade of colonel in 1920, he was sent to Fort Monroe to command the Coast Artillery School. On 1 December 1922, he was promoted to brigadier general (USA). He commanded the coast defenses of Hawaii for three years; after this he had the same assignment in San Francisco. Following that service, he commanded a field artillery brigade at Fort Lewis, Washington, for a short time. He was promoted to major general (USA) and commanded the Fourth Corps Area in Atlanta, Georgia. After two years in that position, and with more than forty years of service to his credit, he retired on 22 December 1929. After his retirement, Davis was active almost to the day of his death. He worked as Vice President of the investment firm of Fenner Bean and Company, in Washington, D.C., and president of Harriman and Keech, another investment company. At the age of seventy-one, he became ill; he died two days later on 15 September 1937. By his own request (as with Malin Craig), there were no military formalities. Only his widow survived. Photo courtesy of the Association of Graduates, USMA.

Robert C. Davis (0-87), son of Thomas Jefferson Davis and Lydia Lemon Davis, was born on 12 October 1876 in Lancaster, Pennsylvania. His father practiced law there at 15 North Duke Street, across from the courthouse. The family's home was about two blocks away, at 39 South Prince Street, near the Stevens House (a hotel). Davis attended public schools and finished his freshman year at

Robert C. Davis

Franklin and Marshall College before entering USMA. He graduated number thirty-six of fifty-nine in the class of 1898, and was commissioned in the Seventeenth Infantry. Three of his classmates were Malin Craig, Fox Conner, and Guy V. Henry, Jr. (all *q.v.*). During the Spanish-American War, Davis was at both the El Caney and San Juan battles, and collected his first Silver Star commendation. He then went to the Philippines and earned a second. From 1901 to 1905, he was in the tactics department at USMA, and during this period, on 12 November 1902, he married Ruby C. Hale of Reading, Pennsylvania. They had no children. From 1906 to 1909, Davis took part in the Cuban Pacification, but during the summers, from 1907 to 1909, he was on duty with the Massachusetts National Guard. From 1909 to 1911, he was an aide to Gen. Thomas H. Barry (*q.v.*). In 1912 he was adjutant of USMA; he then served as adjutant of the 17th Infantry until 1914, when he returned to the Philippines. There, he was instructor-inspector of the Philippine Scouts. Upon his return to the States in 1916, he was stationed at the Adjutant General's Office in Washington. He went to France in 1917 as assistant to the Adjutant General of the AEF, and from November 1917 to January 1918 he was acting Adjutant General. In May 1918, he became Adjutant General of the AEF. After the war, he commanded the Sixth Infantry Brigade at Camp Pike, in Arkansas. From July to November 1921, Davis served on a board to improve the organization of the War Department General Staff. Afterwards, he was sent to Plattsburg, New York, both as post commander and commander of the 64th Infantry. In 1922, he was promoted to Adjutant General (USA); at his own request, he retired from that post and from the army in 1927. The Secretary of War, John W. Weeks, put Davis in charge of the World War Adjusted Compensation Act, the largest single clerical operation of the United States government up to that time. Through this act, Davis distributed more than four billion dollars in bonuses to veterans of World War I. In civil life, he went into the manufacture of photo-processing machinery (black and white, of course). From 1932 to 1944, he was an executive of the American Red Cross. He had numerous decorations, including: the Distinguished Service Medal from the United States, Order of the Bath from Britain, commander of the Order of the Crown from Belgium, commander of the Legion of Honor from France, commander of the Order of the Crown from Italy, grand officer of the Order of Prince Danilo of Montenegro, and the Order of La Solidaridad from Panama. He was an Episcopalian and a great golfer, and belonged to many clubs and associations. He died shortly before his sixty-eighth birthday in New York City on 2 September 1944. Photo courtesy of USMA Library.

Thomas Francis Davis

Thomas Francis Davis (0-13111), son of James Davis and Mary Hennon Davis, was born on 8 March 1853 in New York. (He was one of the three oldest World War I generals, all born that year.) He entered USMA and graduated number thirty-six of forty-three in the class of 1875. Tasker H. Bliss (*q.v.*) and Robert P. P. Wainwright, father of the World War II general, were two of his classmates. Upon graduation Davis was commissioned in the 15th Infantry. He did frontier duty until 1890, participating in many of the late Indian Wars. He was also on the Ute Expedition in 1879, and went into Mexico after the Apaches in September and October 1880. He married Paulina Hart, daughter of a prominent miller in El Paso, Texas. During the Spanish-American War, he commanded a battalion of the 15th Infantry in Cuba, then was collector of customs in Santiago. He had three tours of duty in the Philippines; during his last tour he commanded the 18th Infantry in action against the Moros. He was in charge of general recruiting in the Saint Louis, Missouri area, then was military secretary at the headquarters of Department of the Colorado. He also had troop duty at Fort Roots, Arkansas; Fort Leavenworth, Kansas, and Fort McKenzie, Wyoming. On 16 May 1913, he was promoted to brigadier general (USA) and given command of the Fifth Infantry Brigade at Galveston, Texas. In February 1914, Davis commanded the Sixth Infantry Brigade at Texas City, Texas. Afterwards, he served in Waco, Texas and Douglas, Arizona (in Cochise County, just southeast of Fort Huachuca). From May 1916 to May 1917, he commanded the Arizona district. He had sound judgment, ability, and high personal character, winning the confidence and esteem of all with whom he served. In May 1917 Davis retired. He lived in El Paso at the old home of his wife's family, on the banks of the Rio Grande, where his father-in-law had run a flour mill years before. Mrs. Davis preceded him in death, as did his son, Capt. Thomas H. Davis, who was killed in action in France with the 12th Field Artillery Brigade. At the age of eighty-two, Davis died in El Paso on 10 December 1935. He was survived by his son, James H. Davis of California, and a daughter, who married Col. Joseph M. Cummins. Photo courtesy of the Annual Report, Association of Graduates, USMA.

William Church Davis (0-13519) was born on 11 May 1866 in McGraw, New York (between Syracuse and Binghamton). His parents, Samuel Davis and Roxana Brown Davis, were of Welsh and British descent. After graduating from Spencer Academy in New York, Davis entered USMA; he graduated number fifteen of fifty-four in the class of 1890. Edgar Jadwin, Fred

W. Sladen and James A. Ryan (all *q.v.*) were three of his classmates. Davis was commissioned in the Fifth Artillery, and after one year of service he became Professor of Military Science and Tactics at Colorado State Agricultural College in Fort Collins. He graduated from the Artillery School at Fort Monroe, Virginia, in 1896, and on 9 September of that year he married Margaret Turner Schenk of Boston, Massachusetts. They had three children: Margaret B., William S., and Samuel. During the Spanish-American War, Davis was depot quartermaster at Fort McHenry, Baltimore, Maryland, purchasing, inspecting and shipping to American troops in the field. He was then sent to Manila and was what we would currently call a "transportation officer." In 1903 he graduated from the School of Submarine Defense at Fort Totten, New York. From 1904 to 1907, he was stationed at the Presidio in San Francisco, California as the district artillery engineer. While serving in that position, he installed a fire-control system for the guns defending San Francisco and the Bay area; he also conducted mine-laying operations outside the mouth of the harbor. He did extensive work on the subject of portable searchlights, with application to all major American ports. On 17 December 1917, Davis was promoted to brigadier general (NA) and given command of the 32nd Heavy Artillery Brigade, which he took to Limoges, France. At the time of the Saint Mihiel operation he had a quite unusual command: his own three-regiment brigade, two battalions of French artillery and a separate French heavy artillery battalion, plus four separate batteries. His work during the Saint Mihiel and Meuse-Argonne and elsewhere was most impressive; Gen. John J. Pershing (*q.v.*) not only gave him the Distinguished Service Medal, but also nominated him for promotion to major general. However, it was too late in the game, and the War Department was getting tight with promotions. On 1 February 1919, Davis was ordered back to the States and sent to Camp Lewis, in Washington. In July 1920, he reverted to his permanent rank of colonel, and on 31 January 1921, after nearly thirty-five years of service, he retired. In November of that year, President Warren G. Harding nominated him for promotion to brigadier general (ORC). He received his brigadier general (USA) (Retired) in 1942 and died at age ninety-two in Berkeley, California on 23 September 1958. Photo courtesy of the National Archives.

William Church Davis

Peter Weimer Davison (ASN unknown), son of James Davison and Sarah Weimer Davison, was born on 15 May 1869 on his parent's farm, just south of Waupun, Wisconsin (southwest of Fond du Lac and Oshkosh). He was

Peter Weimer Davison

Scotch-Irish on his father's side and French-German on his mother's, and was one of their ten children. After attending public schools near the farm and in Waupun, he entered the University of Wisconsin at age sixteen. He left to enter USMA, and graduated from there number forty-five of sixty-two in the class of 1892. Charles P. Sumerall (*q.v.*) and Kirby Walker were classmates of his. Much interested in all sports, Davison was one of the founders of the football team at USMA. He played halfback on the famous team of 1891, and was one of the most successful and brilliant players on the first military academy team to beat the navy team. He was assigned to the 22d Infantry at Fort Keough, Montana, and had duty at the Lame Deer Indian Agency. In 1896 the 22d Infantry was sent to Fort Crook, Nebraska, and while there he married Mary Adele Casey, daughter of his regimental commander. In 1898 the regiment was sent to Cuba and Davison was on detached service as Commissary in Gen. William Ludlow's brigade. He returned from Cuba to Montauk Point, Long Island, New York, and almost died there. Shortly after his recovery, on 11 November 1898, his wife died in New York City. In 1899 he went with his regiment to the Philippines, where he did outstanding work. Gen. S. B. M. Young said Davison's battalion was the finest he had ever seen in the army. Upon their return to the States they were again stationed at Fort Crook, and he was appointed quartermaster. From 1903 to 1905, he had a second tour of duty in the Philippines. When his 22d Infantry returned to the States again, they were assigned to island stations in San Francisco Bay, which made possible the excellent work they did during the terrible earthquake and fire there in 1906. After that he was in Alaska until 1910, when he was detailed to the General Staff; he served with it until his third tour in the Philippines, as aide to Gen. J. Franklin Bell (*q.v.*). Davison briefly returned to the States, married Esther Fleming on 10 April 1913, and immediately returned to Tien Tsin, China. Later in 1913, he was transferred to the Philippines again for a fourth tour and was in command at Baguio, where he stayed for two years. He returned to the States as a major in the 26th Infantry at Texas City, Texas. Next, he was appointed disbursing officer of the Alaska Road Commission at Valdez, Alaska. He made many friends there and was held with great respect. When the United States entered World War I, Davison was sent to Camp Lewis, in Washington, where he organized and trained the 166th Depot Brigade. In June 1918 he took command of the Eighth Infantry, and on 8 August 1918 he was promoted to brigadier general (NA) and given command of the 16th Infantry Division. In February 1919 he became post commander of Fort D. A. Russel, Wyoming (now Warren Air Force Base), and from there he was ordered to duty as executive officer and second in command of the port of embarkation at Hoboken, New Jersey. He received the Navy Cross for his performance of duty there. His work at this station made him feel stressed, broke down his health, and finished him. In November 1919 he began to feel slight but increasing heart pains, and he was sent to Fox Hills Hospital in Staten Island for a complete rest. There, at age fifty, he suffered a severe stroke and died within eight minutes on 12 February 1920. He was survived by his widow. Photo courtesy of the Annual Report, Association of Graduates, USMA.

Charles Gates Dawes (no ASN assigned) was born 27 August 1865 in Marietta, Ohio where he grew up and graduated from Marietta College. He then went to Cincinnati Law School and received his second degree. He practiced law in Lincoln, Nebraska where he met and became permanent friends with William Jennings Bryan and a young army officer (Captain Pershing) teaching military science as well as a mathematics course at the University of Nebraska. He almost persuaded the young army officer to leave the army for the practice of law. On 24 January 1889, he married Carolyn Blymer, and they had two children Rufus and Carolyn. Rufus died in a boating accident in 1912. They later adopted two more children, Dana and Virginia. Between his law practice and his business, Dawes prospered. In 1894, he left Lincoln for Evanston, Illinois where he purchased a gas, light and coke company. In 1896, he headed William McKinley's presidential campaign in Illinois, and afterwards was given the post of Comptroller of the Currency. He later ran for the Senate. He did not get elected, and concentrated instead on his business interests in Illinois. With the coming of World War I, Dawes was selected by his old Lincoln friend, now General Pershing, to head military procurement for the AEF, and he was quickly promoted from major to brigadier general on 1 October 1918. He did an excellent job, but resigned from the military in 1919. He declined the post of Secretary of the Treasury under President Harding, but did accept the job of first Director of the Budget. In 1923, he was chairman of the Allied Reparations Commission and originated the Dawes Plan for German reparations. When Calvin Coolidge ran for president in 1924, Dawes was his running mate, and they were elected. He was a man of very firm opinions, not one to be easily shaken or turned aside, and not exactly the diplomat. In 1925, he received the Nobel Peace Prize for his work on German reparations and the restoration of the German economy. Herbert Hoover talked him into accepting the post of Ambassador to England as a necessary prelude to the London Five-Power Naval Conference, and he was most cordially received by King George V at Windsor Castle. He returned to the States in 1932 to take charge of the Reconstruction Finance Corporation, and four

Charles Gates Dawes

months later returned to his bank in Chicago to enjoy a few years of life at home. Retaining lifetime use, he donated his home and papers to Northwestern University. At age eighty-five, he died in his home, on 23 April 1951. His trademark was the underslung pipe he habitually smoked, the bowl of which was below the level of the straight stem. He was one of the four civilian generals at the time; see also Atterbury, McRoberts and Tripp. Picture courtesy of Northwestern University.

Herbert Deakyne

Herbert Deakyne (0-344), the son of Napoleon Bonaparte Deakyne and Mary Ann David Deakyne, was born 29 December 1967 in Deakyneville, Delaware. His forebears arrived there circa 1700. He attended Delaware College (now the University of Delaware) for two years before entering USMA. After four years he graduated number three of fifty-four in the class of 1890. Edgar Jadwin, Fred W. Sladen and James A. Ryan (all *q.v.*) were three of his classmates. After being commissioned in the Corps of Engineers, he spent his first three years at the Engineering School of Application in Willet's Point, New York. From 1893 to 1900, he did fortifications, rivers and harbors work in California. It was during this period, on 15 June 1899, that he married Sadie McKinnon Nickerson in Eureka, California. They had two daughters Ramona (Mrs. John Bell Hughes) and Rosalind (Mrs. George Washington Waldron). From 1897 to 1901, he was on the California Debris Commission (after the great earthquake and fire). From 1901 to 1903, he did rivers and harbors work in Florida. Next he spent two years at Fort Leavenworth, Kansas and then two years in the Philippines. From 1908 to 1912, he worked in the Philadelphia area and from 1912 to 1916, he worked on the Missouri River and its tributaries. In 1916, he was in the Office of the Chief of Engineers in Washington, and in 1917 he graduated from the Army War College. He organized the Tenth Railway Engineers. in Philadelphia, took them to France in August and commanded them at St. Nazaire until January 1918. He was up north on the British front commanding the 11th Railway Engineers from January to May 1918. He became Director of Railways and Roads at GHQ (AEF) in Chaumont. On return to the United States, he was first the division engineer at New Orleans, then did fortifications, rivers and harbors work in San Francisco from 1920 to 1925. From 1926 to 1929, he was assistant Chief of Engineers (USA). From 7 August to 1 October1929, he was Chief of Engineers (USA). In 1931, he retired as a brigadier general and lived in California. At the age of seventy-seven, he died there, on 28 May 1945. Photo from the National Archives.

James Theodore Dean (0-198), the son of Ezra VanNess Dean and Charlotte Weaver Dean, was born 12 May 1965 in Ironton, Ohio on the Ohio River. He entered USMA and graduated number fifty-two of sixty-four in the class of 1887. P. D. Lochridge, Thomas Q. Donaldson, Charles Henry Martin and William Weigel (all *q.v.*) were four of his classmates. He was commissioned in the Third Infantry, and had much ordnance duty. He never married. From 1893 to 1895 and from 1899 to 1902, he was aide to Maj. Gen. John Rutter Brooke. As a major, he was Chief Ordnance Officer in Cuba and Puerto Rico during the Spanish-American War. From 1906 to 1908, he was in Alaska, and in 1911 he graduated from the Army War College. The years 1912 to 1915 found him in the Philippines, and on 5 August 1917, he was promoted to brigadier general (NA) and placed in command of the 156th Infantry Brigade, which he took to France. From 16 March to 20 April 1918, he commanded the 78th Infantry Division (AEF). He participated in both the St. Mihiel and Meuse-Argonne offensives. With the war past, he reverted to his permanent rank of colonel and commanded the 20th Infantry. On 23 August 1920, he was detailed to the Adjutant General's Department and served two years as adjutant of the Philippine Department in Manila. The next two years he commanded the 11th Infantry, and on 23 April 1924, he was put in charge of recruiting in the New York area. His terminal assignment was as Chief of Staff of the 77th Infantry Division (Organized Reserve). On 3 September 1928, he retired. At the age of seventy-four, he died while in Canada, on 15 June 1939. The photo, from the National Archives, was taken as he was boarding for shipment back to the United States in 1919.

James Theodore Dean

☆

Edward Harrison DeArmond (0-1351) was born in Greenfield, in Dade County, Missouri. After attending local schools he entered USMA and graduated number forty-seven of seventy-four in the class of 1901. Beverly F. Browne (*q.v.*) and Frank P. Lahm (qualified by Wilbur Wright in 1909 as one of the first two military pilots) were two of his classmates. He was commissioned in the Artillery Corps, and when that corps split into Coast and Field Artillery, he chose the latter. He served during the Moro Expedition in 1904 in the Philippines, and from 1909 to1912, he was in the Tactics

Edward Harrison DeArmond

Department at USMA. During the World War I he served as Chief of Staff of the 32d Infantry Division (Wisconsin and Michigan National Guard troops) both during the period of its training and also in France from 26 August 1917 to 1 May 1918. Next he became Chief of Artillery for the AEF, and on 8 August 1918, he was promoted to brigadier general (NA). For his performance as brigadier general he received the Distinguished Service Medal. From 1924 to 1928, he was in the Office of the Chief of Field Artillery, and during 1941 and 1942 he was artillery officer of the Second Army. He retired in 1942 as a brigadier general. At the age of seventy, he died in Lexington, Virginia, on 21 October 1948. The photo, from the National Archives, shows him at a balloon ascension on the Polo Grounds at Fort Myer, Virginia.

Charles I. DeBevoise

Charles I. DeBevoise (ASN unknown) was born in Brooklyn, New York on 17 October 1872. He was a New York National Guard officer who commanded the trains (sanitary, ammunition, quartermaster, military police, etc.). He also later commanded the 107th Infantry Regiment. From 1918 to 1919, he commanded the 53d Infantry Brigade of the 27th Division. He received the Distinguished Service Medal, and after the war, from 1954 to 1958, he was a member of the board of the National Horse Show Foundation, among other activities. His home address was 802 Carroll Street, Brooklyn, New York. He died on 10 December 1958. The photo, from the National Archives, taken on 26 October 1918, shows him talking with Capt. T. J. Brady of the 27th Division, on the morning of the return from the Hindenburg Line and St. Souplet battles in the Amiens District, Somme, France.

Daniel Bradford Devore (0-150), born 14 May 1860 in Monroe County Ohio, was the son of John Wesley DeVore and Mary Gray DeVore. He entered USMA and graduated number twenty-nine of thirty-nine in the class of 1885. Robert Lee Bullard, Willard Holbrook, Joseph E. Kuhn and Charles H. Muir (all *q.v.*) were four of his classmates. He was commissioned in the 23d Infantry and married Helen Gray Stewart of Washington, D.C. From 1891 to 1892, he was an aide to Gen. D. S. Stanley, and from 1892 to 1897, he was an Assistant Professor of Mathematics at USMA. During 1897 and 1898, he was on special duty for the Secretary of War; he purchased 538 reindeer (caribou) in Norway and delivered all but one to Seattle for use in Alaska that winter. From 1899 to 1901, and again

Daniel Bradford Devore

from 1903 to 1906, he was in the Philippines. From 1906 to 1907, he was constructing quartermaster at Madison Barracks in New York, and in 1907, he was with his regiment at the Jamestown exposition and the dedication of the McKinley Monument in Canton, Ohio. From 1908 to 1909, he commanded a small post in Cuba. From 1911 to 1914, he was on the General Staff, and during 1916 and early 1917, he commanded the Tenth Infantry in the Canal Zone. As the U.S. became involved in World War I, he organized both the 45th and 46th Infantry Regiments with troops from the Tenth Infantry. He was promoted to a brigadier general (NA) on 5 August 1917, mustered into federal service the Illinois National Guard, and commanded the 167th Infantry Brigade in France from September to December 1918. Returning to the States, he reverted to his permanent rank of colonel and commanded Camp Logan at Houston, Texas, after which he was on duty at headquarters in Chicago, commanded the Tenth Infantry in Ohio, and took his terminal assignment as Adjutant General, Second Corps Area, with headquarters in New York Harbor on Governor's Island, ten minutes by ferry from lower Manhattan. He retired in 1922 as a colonel, and his rank of brigadier general was restored by act of Congress in June 1930. He was past his ninety-fifth birthday, when he died in Washington, D.C., on 10 March 1956. Photo from the National Archives.

Joseph Theodore Dickman

Joseph Theodore Dickman (0-17) was born in Dayton, Ohio on 6 October 1857. He entered USMA and graduated number twenty-seven of fifty-three in the class of 1881. Harry and Henry Hodges, Edwin St. John Greble and Andrew Summers Rowan were among his classmates. Upon graduating he was commissioned in the cavalry, and on 26 September 1882, he married Mary Rector at Fort Smith, Arkansas. From 1883 to 1890, he had frontier duty and served in the late Indian Wars. During the Spanish-American War he was a lieutenant colonel of United States volunteers, and also served in the Sanitary Corps in Cuba. He then served in the Philippines during the insurrection, and he was Chief of Staff of the China Relief Expedition under Gen.

Adna Chaffee. He became one of the original members of the War Department General Staff when it was founded in 1903, and remained a member until 1906. Between 1909 and 1911, he was again in the Philippines. On 5 August 1917, he was promoted to major general (NA), and he commanded the 85th Infantry Division from 25 August to 25 November 1917. He was Commanding General of the Third Infantry Division from 12 April 1918 to 18 August 1918, and a corps commander, Fourth Corps, from 18 August 1918 to 12 October 1918. On 7 November 1918, the Third Army was activated with Dickman as Commanding General and was designated the Army of Occupation in Germany. In 1919, he was promoted to major general (USA) and he had many decorations from the United States, Britain, France, Belgium, Italy and Panama. He wrote only one book, *The Great Crusade*, published in 1927. At the age of seventy, he died in Washington, D.C., on 23 October 1927. Photo courtesy of the Pennsylvania National Guard.

Tracy Campbell Dickson (0-359), son of Campbell Dickson and Lucy Ellen Tracy Dickson, was born 17 September1868 in Independence, Iowa. His family had come from Londonderry, Ireland in the mid-eighteenth century to settle in Londonderry, New Hampshire. His father was a Civil War veteran from the Ninth New York Cavalry. After elementary and secondary education, he entered USMA and graduated number six of sixty-two in the class of 1892. William Chamberlaine, James A. Shipton, Charles P. Sumerall and Kirby Walker were among his classmates. He was commissioned in the Second Artillery but as a first lieutenant was transferred to ordnance. On 7 November 1894, he married Isabella Kendrick Abbott of Atlanta, and they had two sons Tracy Campbell Dickson, Jr. and Benjamin Abbott Dickson, both of whom graduated from USMA and became regular officers during World War I. He spent five years as assistant to the commanding officer of the Springfield (Massachusetts) Armory, and was simultaneously an inspector for a number of major small arms manufacturers. In 1898, he was on a Joint Army-Navy-Marine Board to make uniform the small arms calibers used by the three services. From 1899 to 1902, he was assistant to the commanding officer at Rock Island Arsenal. From July 1902 to 1906, he was assistant to the Chief of Ordnance. He served on the board that adopted of the M-1903 Springfield rifle. For four years starting in June 1906, he was assistant to the commander at Sandy Hook (New Jersey) Proving Ground. From 1907 to 1910, he was on the Isthmian Canal Commission and was in charge of repair work and designing permanent repair and mainte-

Tracy Campbell Dickson

nance shops. From 1910 to 1914, he worked on the construction of the Panama Canal, holding the job of inspector of shops. In April 1914, he chose to retire, as a colonel. On 17 September 1916, he was returned to active duty at the Watertown, New York Arsenal and served on the board that adopted the Browning machine guns, of which there were three a water-cooled .30, a lightweight air-cooled .30, and a heavy air-cooled .50. At the beginning of World War I, he was Assistant Chief of Ordnance in the War Department, but he was transferred in June 1917 to Bethlehem Steel Company, and was put in charge of production there. In the fall of 1917, he was transferred to Watertown, New York, where he built and put into operation the modern arsenal there. During his years at Watertown he, together with Dr. Frederick C. Landenberg, perfected many steps in gun manufacturing as well as the autofrottage system of manufacture. Beginning 17 March 1917, he commanded the Watertown Arsenal, and on 10 January 1918, he was promoted to brigadier general (NA). In 1920, the ordnance schools were consolidated under his command at Watertown. In 1933, he retired as a brigadier general and lived with his son, Benjamin Abbott Dickson, in Haverford, Pennsylvania. At the age of sixty-seven, he died there while taking a walk, on 17 May 1936. In addition to his two brothers he was survived by two sisters, Mrs. Thompson and Mrs. Abernethy, and another son, T. C. Dickson, Jr. of Bridgeport, Connecticut. Photo courtesy of Special Collections, USMA Library.

Brice Purcell Disque

Brice Purcell Disque (ASN unknown), business executive and soldier, was born 17 July 1879 in California, Ohio, just southeast of Cincinatti on the Clermont-Hamilton County line. The town no longer exists. His parents were Jacob Disque and Ella Purcell Disque. He attended public schools in Cincinatti and the Walnut Hill School. Commissioned a second lieutenant in 1899, he served during the Philippine insurrection and captured Emilio Aguinaldo's southern commander, Ermetario Funes and his troops on 21 January 1901. He married Mary Florence Coulter on 22 October of the same year, and they had two sons Brice P. Disque, Jr. and Gordon Coulter Disque. He was a distinguished graduate of Infantry and Cavalry School in 1906, and graduated from the Army Staff College in 1907. As manager of the Michigan State Prison he developed a system of providing gainful employment for all inmates and operated the prison at a profit without financial aid from the state from 1916 to 1917. He became a brigadier general (NA) on 1 October 1918, and was Commanding General and organizer of the Spruce

Division, U.S. Army, and president of the U.S. Spruce Corporation from 1917 to 1919. He was organizer and president of the Loyal Legion Loggers and Lumbermen for the lumber industry in the Pacific Northwest in 1918, working as a coordinator to establish peaceful relations between employers and employees. He was a brigadier general (ORC) from 1919 to 1949. He was president and/or senior executive of many companies between the two world wars, and was back on duty between 1941 and 1942. From 1943 to 1946, he was chairman of the Area Advisory Committee on Local Distribution of the Solid Fuels Administration for the war. He belonged to the Sons of the American Revolution, and had the Distinguished Service Medal for his service during World War I. He was also a commander of the Order of Saints Maurice and Lazarus in Italy and had commendations from both Great Britain and France. He belonged to the Disciples of Christ Church, the Army and Navy Clubs in Washington and Manila, and the Metropolitan and Uptown Clubs in New York. His residence was at Spuyten Duyvl, New York. He died in March 1960. Photo from the National Archives.

Arthur Barrett Donnelly

Arthur Barrett Donnelly (ASN unknown) was born in St. Louis, Missouri on 31 May 1875, the son of James J. Donnelly and Elizabeth Taafe Donnelly. He married Anna Pike Renick on 10 May 1898. He was a factory department manager from 1901 to 1906 and an assistant factory superintendent and buyer from 1906 to 1908 at the Hamilton-Brown Shoe Company in St. Louis. He became president of Arthur B. Donnelly and Company, Interstate Mercantile Company and Missouri Paint Varnish Company. On 7 December 1892, he enlisted in Company F, First Missouri Infantry and served during the Spanish-American War as captain of his original company. By the time of the Mexican border duty (18 June to 25 September 1916), he commanded the regiment. He was promoted through all grades to Adjutant General of Missouri with the rank of brigadier general on 8 January 1917, but was granted an indefinite leave of absence by the governor on 25 March 1917 in order to assume command of the First Missouri Infantry. He was appointed brigadier general (NA) on 5 August 1917 and commanded the 69th Infantry Brigade at Camp Doniphan, Oklahoma, the present site of Fort Sill. He was a Republican and a Roman Catholic. His home was at 5076 Cates Avenue in St. Louis. At only forty-four years of age, he died on 29 July 1919, one of the youngest World War I generals at the time of his death. Photo courtesy of the Missouri National Guard.

Edward Terence Donnelly

Edward Terence Donnelly (0-911) was born in London, England on 22 August 1871, son of Edward C. Donnelly of New York City. He was educated at Manhattan College, Columbia University and New York Law School, where he received an LL.B. On 17 May 1898, he was commissioned a captain in the Eighth New York Infantry, and was honorably mustered out of the volunteer service on 3 November 1898. Next he was commissioned a first lieutenant in the 43d U.S. Volunteer Infantry on 17 August 1899, and was again honorably mustered out of the U.S. Volunteers on 5 July 1901. He didn't stay a civilian very long; he was commissioned a first lieutenant, artillery (USA), on 1 August 1901. In 1905, he graduated from the School of Application for Cavalry and Field Artillery, and on 25 January 1907 he was promoted to captain and was transferred to the First Field Artillery on 6 June. He married Flora Fitten Berwick on 22 November 1909, and later served with the Sixth, Third and Fifth Field Artillery Regiments. Promotion to major came on 1 July 1916, and to colonel (NA) on 5 August 1916. On 12 April 1918, he was made a brigadier general (NA). His served in the Spanish-American War, the Philippine insurrection and at the Mexican border before going to France. He was Commanding General, 164th Field Artiliery Brigade, 89th Infantry Division (AEF) from July 1918 to May 1919. He received the French Croix de Guerre. He was a Roman Catholic. At the age of fifty-seven, he died on 8 February1929. Photo from the National Archives.

Charles Bryant Drake (0-507), son of Mr. and Mrs. Thomas Drake, was born 14 September 1872 in Old Forge, Pennsylvania, near Scranton, on his parents' farm. His family had been in this country since before the Revolution. He went to public schools then attended the Wyoming Seminary in Pennsylvania, from which he graduated. Like many of his peers, he took and won a competitive examination for his appointment, and entered USMA as a cadet on 15 June 1892. One of the Scranton newspapers published a very complimentary article about his success in the examination, which unfortunately fell into the hands of a member of the yearling class. He was made to commit it to memory and had to recite it on demand of upper classmen. He was able to accept this duty with good humor. He graduated number twenty-eight of seventy-three in the class of 1896. Lucius R. Holbrook, Edward L. King and Dennis Nolan (all *q.v.*) were three of his classmates. He was commissioned in the Fifth Cavalry stationed at Fort Sam Houston, Texas. While stationed there he met Hilda E. Jacobs, daughter of Barron Jacobs of Tucson. They were married on 17 March 1898. He was later,

Charles Bryant Drake

with his troop, at Forts McIntosh and Brown in Texas, then in camp in Huntsville, Alabama. In January 1899 his unit sailed to Bayamon, Puerto Rico. In February 1900, he was promoted to first lieutenant and transferred to the First Cavalry at Fort Yates, North Dakota and Fort Yellowstone, Wyoming. In June 1902, he became a captain, was again transferred, and spent a year with the 14th Cavalry at Fort Grant in southeastern Arizona. In October 1903, he sailed with his unit to Jolo in the southern Philippines. He was in the Second Sulu Expedition and won a Silver Star Commendation. He was also in the Third Sulu Expedition and won another Silver Star. He was mentioned in orders from headquarters in Mindinao and was recommended for a brevet to major. In October and November 1905, the regiment returned to the United States and he was fortunate to have a post of his own in Boise Barracks, Idaho, a very desirable one-troop post. From August 1906 to January 1909, he was on recruiting duty at Fort Slocum, New York. He returned to his regiment and served as quartermaster at Camp Stotsenberg in the Phillipine Islands until March 1912. He and the regiment returned to the United States and served at border posts until 1915. Later he had a detail at the Quartermaster Depot in Philadelphia, and then took part in the Mexican Punitive Expedition where he commanded one of the motor supply trains. In August 1918, he was selected to organize the Motor Transport Corps and was made a brigadier general (NA) on 1 October 1918. He was the chief until July 1920, when the Motor Transport Corps became a part of the Quartermaster Corps. For this position he received the Distinguished Service Medal. From July to September 1919, he was assistant to the Quartermaster General, and he acted then assistant to the Chief of Finance until February 1921. His last assignment was Director of Cavalry in the Militia Bureau. After thirty years of service he chose to retire on 31 October 1922, as a colonel. He was appointed brigadier general, retired list, on 21 June 1940. At the age of eighty-three, he finally died of cancer of the throat in Rehoboth, Delaware, on 14 August 1956. Picture from *The Assembly*, Association of Graduates, USMA.

Hugh Aloysius Drum (0-89), son of Captain John Drum (KIA, San Juan, Cuba) and Margaret Desmond Drum, was born 19 September 1879 in Fort Brady, Michigan. He did not attend USMA, but was commissioned in the 12th Infantry on 9 September 1898 and served in the Philippines during the insurrection until 1901. He was also aide to Gen. Theodore A. Baldwin. On 14 October he married Mary Reaume. They had one daughter, Anna Carroll Drum (Mrs.

Thomas H. Johnson). He was Adjutant General of the Southwestern (USA) Division until 1906, and returned to the Philippines for the years 1908 and 1910. In 1911, he was an honor graduate of the Army School of the Line, and graduated from the staff school in 1912. From 1912 to 1914, he was in rapid succession an instructor, a director and an assistant commandant of the Command and General Staff School. In 1914, he was on the Mexican border and on the Vera Cruz Expedition. That year he was an assistant Chief of Staff to Gen. Fredrick Funston. After this he was an assistant instructor in military art at the service schools, then was aide to General Funston until the general's sudden and tragic death at the St. Anthony Hotel in San Antonio, Texas, on the evening of 19 February 1917 (see the MacArthur biography). After General Funston's death, he became assistant to the Chief of Staff under General Pershing and accompanied him to France in the spring of 1917. He became Chief of Staff, First U.S. Army (AEF), and was promoted to brigadier general (NA) on 1 October 1918. He remained Chief of Staff until April 1919. From April to July 1919 he was Chief of Staff for Service of Supply. With the coming of peace he reverted to his permanent rank of major of infantry and became director of the Army School of the Line. He was made a temporary brigadier general on 21 September 1920 and was commandant of the Command and General Staff College. In 1922, he was assigned to command the coastal and air defenses of the Second Corps Area, and from 4 December 1923 to 8 April 1926, he was Assistant Chief of Staff (G-3, operations and training) of the army. From 15 October to 15 November 1927, he commanded the First Infantry Brigade of the First Infantry Division, and then was given command of the division. On 29 January 1930, he was appointed Inspector General of the army as a major general. In June 1933, he was made Deputy Chief of Staff of the Army, until April 1935. From 1935 to 1937, he commanded the Hawaiian Department, and during 1937 and 1938, he commanded the Second Army and Sixth Corps Area headquartered in Chicago. On 5 November 1938, he was appointed commander of the First Army and Second Corps Area headquartered on Governor's Island in New York. On 5 August 1939, he was promoted to lieutenant general (USA), and until 15 October 1943, he commanded the First Army and Eastern Defense Command. He was not lacking for honorary degrees and decorations. Boston College gave him an A.B. in 1921; Manhattan College made him a doctor of science in 1940; then he received honors from Boston College again, as well as from St. Lawrence University, Fordham, Loyola, Columbia, Rutgers, New York University, Pennsylvania Military College, Georgetown University and the University of Delaware. As for decorations, he held the Silver Star, a Medal of Merit, and the Distinguished Service Medal with cluster (most unusual) from the United States,

Hugh Aloysius Drum

was a Commander of the Legion of Honor and received a Croix de Guerre with two palms from France; was a commander of the Order of the Crown in Belgium and Italy; was commander of the Order of Olaf in Norway and received campaign and theater ribbons from many countries. He lived in New York City, where he belonged to a number of clubs and associations. At the age of seventy-two, he died in New York ,on 3 October 1951. Photo courtesy of the National Archives.

Thomas Buchanan Dugan

Thomas Buchanan Dugan (0-130), the son of Cumberland Dugan and Harriet Buchanan Dugan, was born 27 July 1858 in Baltimore, Maryland. He entered USMA and graduated number thirty-one of thirty-seven in the class of 1882. Henry T. Allen, Adelbert Cronkhite (both *q.v.*) and Fredrick Bonfils (of the *Denver Post*) were three of his classmates. He was commissioned in the Tenth Cavalry and did frontier duty from 1882 to 1890. From 1884 to 1885, he commanded a company of Apache Indian scouts. He served at various posts in Arizona, New Mexico, Texas, Oklahoma and Missouri until 1898. On 24 November 1897 he married Geraldine Wessels, daughter of Gen. Henry Walton Wessels (USA). They had three children Cumberland Dugan, Thomas B. Dugan, Jr. and Eliza Lane Dugan. During the Spanish-American War, he was in the Santiago Campaign and the Battle of San Juan. He was briefly in the Sanitary Corps and earned a Silver Star Commendation. He was in the Philippines in 1905 and again in 1916. On 5 August 1917, he was promoted to a brigadier general (NA) and conducted a brigade and field officers' school from December 1917 to May 1918. During the war, he commanded brigades in the 86th, 85th, 53d and Fifth Infantry Divisions. From 25 November to December 1918 and again from 27 December 1918 to inactivation in April 1919, he commanded the 35th Infantry Division. He retired 27 July 1922 as a colonel. In addition to the Silver Star he was given the Distinguished Service Medal. On 28 February 1927, his rank of brigadier general was restored. He was a Roman Catholic. At the age of eighty-one, he died in Washington, D.C., on 27 April 1940. Photo courtesy of the USMA Archives.

George Brand Duncan (0-60), son of Henry T. Duncan and Lily Brand Duncan, was born 10 October 1861 in Lexington, Kentucky. He entered USMA and graduated number sixty-five of seventy-seven in the class of 1886. Edward W. McCaskey, Charles T. Menoher, Mason M. Patrick and John J. Pershing (all *q.v.*) were four of his classmates. He was commissioned in the Ninth Infantry and did frontier duty from 1886 to 1892. He was on the staff of Maj. Gen. John M. Schofield from 1892 to 1894, and was adjutant of the Fourth Infantry from 1894 to 1898. During this latter period, on 23 October 1895, he married Mary Kercheval. In July 1898 he was Adjutant General of the Provisional Division in Santiago, Cuba, and from August to October had the same assignment in Puerto Rico. From 1899 to 1909, he was in the Philippines, the last five years of which he commanded a battalion of Philippine Scouts. In 1912, he graduated from the Army War College, and from 1914 to 1917, was on the General Staff. He was promoted to brigadier general (NA) in 1917, and went to France in June. He was the first American general officer to command a sector on the battle front. On 12 April 1918, he was again promoted to major general (NA), and from 8 May to 20 July, he commanded the 77th Infantry Division in combat. From 4 October to 11 November 1918, he commanded the 82d Infantry Division during the Meuse-Argonne, and for this he received the Distinguished Service Medal. From 1922 until his retirement in 1925, he commanded the Seventh Corps Area headquartered in Omaha. Aside from the decorations aforementioned, Britain awarded him Companion of the Bath, and France made him a Commander of the Legion of Honor and gave him the Croix de Guerre. He was an Episcopalian, and in retirement lived in Lexington, Kentucky. At the age of eighty-eight, he died, on 15 March 1950. Photo from the Signal Corps collection (number 106704). He is in the blue shirt, center, facing the camera. Notice also the solar topees on the two other officers, and the old campaign hats.

George Brand Duncan

Lucius Loyd Durfee (0-13432), son of Lucius E. Durfee and Sophia C. Durfee, was born 3 March 1881 in Chardon, Ohio. His father was an attorney. He spent his boyhood years in Chardon and attended school there, after which he taught school for a year or two. When he saw the notice of the competitive examination for USMA, he decided to take the test, and he won the appointment. From the day he entered the military academy until he retired in the 1920s, his life was dedicated to wholehearted and loyal service to his government and his country. He was a very firm believer in duty and honor. He graduated number sixty-seven of seventy-seven in the class of 1886. Edward W. McCaskey, Charles T. Menoher, Mason Patrick and John Pershing (all *q.v.*) were four of his classmates. He was commissioned in the 17th Infantry, and joined them at Fort D. A. Russel (now Warren Air Force Base) in Wyoming, performing frontier duty until 1893.

Lucius Loyd Durfee

Naturally, he was in the Sioux War of 1890 to 1891. In 1891, he married Fannie Morris Van Home, daughter of Colonel William M. Van Home, a Civil War veteran. They had five children Gordon, Loyd V. H., Francis M., Dorothy and Donald L. Durfee. As a first lieutenant he served with distinction in the Santiago Campaign and was awarded a Silver Star Commendation for his part in the action at El Caney. Between 1899 and 1905, he made three trips to and from the Philippines, serving as a captain in the Third Sulu Expedition and several minor operations against the Moros. Until 1914, he served at Fort McPherson, Georgia, Forts Brady and Wayne in Michigan, and also on the Mexican border. He was then detailed as a student at the Army War College. After graduation, he was retained as an instructor. In 1918, as a colonel, he was detailed to the General Staff and became Chief of Staff of the Southern Department stationed at San Antonio, Texas. On 26 June 1918, he was promoted to a brigadier general (NA), and he took his brigade to France the same year. The French government gave him the Croix de Guerre and Legion of Honor. Returning stateside in June 1919, he reverted to his wartime rank and was put in command of the Sixth Infantry Division at Camp Grant, Illinois. That November he contracted flu and pneumonia, from which he never recovered sufficiently to continue in active service. (Few people today realize there were more deaths from flu and pneumonia in 1918 to 1920 than in all the wars of the United States prior to 1991.) On 14 April 1920, he was retired. His own son, Loyd Van Horn Durfee, tells a very nice story which reflects the best of both father and son. Loyd, while serving as a first lieutenant in command of a company, was presented to a major just joining the regiment who would be his battalion commander. On hearing his name, the major asked if he was General Durfee's son. Learning he was, the major replied, "Well, you start off all right with me, young man. I served under your father, and a finer officer and gentleman I've never met." After retirement, General Durfee lived five years in Zanesville, Ohio, then moved to Los Angeles, and after two years moved to Riverside. At the age of seventy-two, he died there, on 19 March 1933. His widow and all five children survived him. Photo courtesy of the Annual Report, Association of Graduates, USMA.

Clarence R. Edwards (0-36) was born 1 January 1859 in Cleveland, Ohio. Four years after entering USMA in West Point, he graduated number fifty-two of fifty-two in the class of 1883. Chase W. Kennedy, George Cameron and Tyree Rhodes Rivers (all *q.v.*) were three of his classmates. He was commissioned in the infantry and served at Fort Porter, New York until 10 May 1890. He was Professor of Military Science and Tactics at St. John's College, Fordham, New York from 1890 to 1893. During this time, on 25 February 1891, he was promoted to first lieutenant. From 1 November 1893 to 1 November 1895, he served in the Information Division, Office of the Adjutant General in Washington, D.C. After this he did garrison duty at Fort Clark, Texas, on the Rio Grande River, with the 23rd Infantry until 12 April 1898, when he served a month in New Orleans, Louisiana. On 12 May 1898, he was promoted to major and assistant Adjutant General, U.S. Volunteers. From 25 May to 15 September 1898, he was Adjutant General, Fourth Army Corps at Mobile and Huntsville, Alabama. He received his promotion to captain of infantry (USA) on 30 July 1898, and was assigned to the First Infantry. While en route to Cuba, he was reassigned to the staff of Gen. Henry Lawton in the Philippines as his Adjutant General. When General Lawton was killed on 19 December 1899, Colonel Edwards accompanied the general's body back to the United States. He received three Silver Star Citations for his services in the Phillipine Islands during the insurrection. From 1900 to 1913, he was Chief of the Bureau of Insular Affairs at the War Department. In 1906, he received a promotion to brigadier general (USA), and on 5 August 1917, he received a promotion to major general (NA). After serving in Texas, Hawaii and the Canal Zone, he organized the 20th Division, took it to France and commanded it there for ten months. From1921 to 1922 he commanded the First Corps Area headquartered in Boston. In 1922, he was made a major general (USA). He retired that year. He died in Boston, on 14 February 1931. He had many degrees and decorations, and had been president of the Infantry Association, the predecessor of the Association of the United States Army (AUSA). Photo from the National Archives, taken on Boston Common on 24 December 1918 at the presentation of the Congressional Medal of Honor to Lt. Col. Whittlesley, heroic commander of the Lost Battalion during the Meuse-Argonne.

Clarence R. Edwards

Oliver Edwards (no ASN assigned), was born in Massachusetts on 2 December 1871. He entered USMA in June 1890. He graduated number forty of fifty-four in the class of 1894. Paul B. Malone, Hamilton S. Hawkins and George H. Estes, Jr. (all *q.v.*) were three of his classmates. He was commissioned in the 11th Infantry, and later served in the 6th, 28th, 23d and 5th Regiments, in that order. He was on the Puerto Rican Expedition at the time of the Spanish-American War, and was an aide to Gen. J. F. Smith during the Philippine insurrection. He also served in the Cuban Pacification from 1906 to 1909. In 1910, he

Oliver Edwards

was a distinguished graduate of the Army School of the Line, and in 1911 he graduated from the Army Staff College. There he was retained as an instructor until 1912, when he accepted a detail with the French Army for a course of instruction. On his return he did troop duty and went to Panama, where he was an intelligence officer and later Chief of Staff. On 8 August 1918, he was promoted to brigadier general (NA) and organized and commanded the Machine Gun Training Center in France, for which he received the Distinguished Service Medal. After the war, back in the United States, he reverted to his permanent rank of colonel and entered the General Staff College as a student. He was retained as a member of the War Department General Staff in the Intelligence Division. He had great devotion to duty, an eagerness to perform, and a very alert and superior mind. At the age of forty-nine, while on that assignment, he became ill, and he died on 25 February 1921. Picture courtesy of the Annual Report, Association of Graduates, USMA.

LeRoy Eltinge (0-502), son of Lamont and Arvelia Lake Eltinge, was born 17 September 1872 in South Woodstock, New York. After four years at USMA he graduated number ten of seventy-three in the class of 1896. Lucius R. Holbrook, Edward King and Dennis E. Nolan (all *q.v.*) were three of his classmates. He was commissioned in the Fourth Cavalry, and on 3 December 1897, he married Effee B. Trotter. They had one daughter, Margaret (Mrs. James L. Bolt). He served in the Philippines during 1898 and 1899 and also from 1901 o 1903. In the Philippine insurrection he was wounded, and he won a Silver Star Commendation. The years 1906 and 1907 found him with the Army of Pacification in Cuba, and in 1908, he was an honor graduate of the Army School of the Line at Fort Leavenworth, Kansas. In 1909, he graduated from the Army Staff College, and from 1909 to 1912 he was an instructor there. In 1914, he was on the Mexican border, and in 1916, he went into Mexico with Pershing and the Punitive Expedition. By the end of 1917, he was in France in the G-3 Operations Section of the General Staff. He became Deputy Chief of Staff on 1

LeRoy Eltinge

May 1918, and was promoted to brigadier general (NA) on 1 August 1918. His assignment lasted until 30 June 1919. He received the Distinguished Service Medal for his work. After the war, from 1921 to 1923, he was Assistant Chief of Staff of the Philippine Department. From 2 July 1924 to 19 April 1925, he was Commanding General of the Operations and Training Division of the U.S. Army (G-3). In addition to the American decorations previously mentioned, he was a commander of the Legion of Honor and received the Croix de Guerre from France, was a commander of the Order of the Crown in Belgium and Italy and was a Companion of the Bath in Britain, as well as in the Order of La Solidaridad in Panama. At the age of fifty-eight, he died at Fort Omaha, Nebraska, on 13 May 1931. Photo from West Point Archives.

Hanson Edward Ely

Hanson Edward Ely (0-80), son of Eugene Hanson Ely and Julia Lamb Ely, was born 23 November 1867 in Independence Iowa, east of Waterloo. After attending local schools he entered USMA, and graduated number sixty-three of sixty-five in the class of 1891. William J. Glasgow, John L. Hines, Andrew Hero, Jr. and Odus C. Homey (all *q.v.*) were four of his classmates. After graduation, he was commissioned in the 22nd Infantry, and he served in Montana, North Dakota and Nebraska before becoming Professor of Military Science and Tactics at the University of Iowa in 1897 and 1898. At the time of the Spanish-American War he reported to his regiment at Fort Wikoff, New York, and was in the Philippines from 1899 to 1901, where he received his first Silver Star Commendation. He commanded General Funston's mounted scouts, and was a regimental and district adjutant in Luzon. In 1906, he was an observer at the German Army Maneuvers, and from 1907 to 1912, he was back in the Philippines. During that period, on 6 July 1910, he married Eleanor Boyle. In 1914, he was again with General Funston, this time on the Vera Cruz Expedition to Mexico. As a lieutenant colonel, he was Provost-Marshal of the AEF in France from 20 July to 24 August 1917. In France, he commanded the 20th Infantry Regiment until he was promoted to brigadier general in 1918. He was again promoted, on 1 October 1918, to major general—this, while his permanent rank was lieutenant colonel! From 18 November 1918 on, he commanded the Second and then the Fifth Infantry Divisions, for which he received the Distinguished Service Cross, the Distinguished Service Medal and another Silver Star. When the war was over, he was commandant of the Command and General Staff School from August 1921 to June 1923. In 1923, he was promoted to major general (USA), and became commandant of the Army War College until 1927.

His next command was Second Corps Area headquartered on Governor's Island in New York. This was his terminal assignment; he retired in 1931. In addition to the aforementioned decorations, France made him an officer of the Legion of Honor and gave him five Croix de Guerre. He was past his ninetieth birthday, when he died at Atlantic Beach, Florida, on 28 April 1958. Picture courtesy of Special Collections, USMA Library.

William Pierce Ennis

William Pierce Ennis (0-1331), son of Lieutenant and Mrs. William Ennis of the Fourth Artillery, was born at the Presidio in San Francisco on 30 January 1878. His mother was Andrine L. Pierce of Boston. His father graduated from USMA in 1864, was brevetted twice for gallantry in action before the year was out and was for five years (1933 to 1938) the oldest living graduate of USMA. The family lived for years at Newport, Rhode Island, where young William developed a love for the water, light artillery and horses. He entered USMA and graduated number twenty of seventy-four in the class of 1901. Beverly F. Browne (*q.v.*) was one of his classmates. He was commissioned in the Artillery Corps, and on 25 April 1903 married Eda Totten, not only an army girl, but an artillery daughter. She had the reputation of being one of the most beloved women in the army, always ready to comfort the stricken and help the overburdened. They had only one child William P. Ennis, Jr., who retired as a lieutenant general. His first three years of duty were in a light artillery battery at Fort Hamilton, followed by four years in West Point, then three years at the Remount Depot at Fort Reno, Oklahoma, just west of Oklahoma City. He had the reputation of being the best trainer of artillery horses in the army. In 1912, he went with the First Battalion, First Field Artillery to the Philippines. They rejoined the rest of the regiment in Hawaii in 1913, and in 1915, he was ordered back to West Point to command the artillery detachment there. He was known as "Roaring Bill," and was admired in the corps as a man who ran his business without a hitch and always knew exactly how much to demand from his horses and his men (including cadets). At the end of 1917, he was sent to Fort Sill as senior instructor in the Department of Materiel, School of Fire. He became a colonel (NA) in May 1918, and received the Distinguished Service Medal for his work as director of the Department of Materiel. On 8 August 1918, he was promoted to brigadier general (NA) and commanded the 13th Field Artillery Brigade at Camp Lewis, Washington. Armistice came and everyone reverted to their permanent ranks, so he again became a major. He spent the next six years in school at Fort Leavenworth, Kansas at the Army War College, and on General Staff assignments. His energy and curiosity spread in all directions. While G-4 in Panama (1922 to 1925), he, with a collection of fellow fishing enthusiasts, purchased an old sub-chaser named *Papagallo*, and he became the engineer. He personally patched the hull, tore down and rebuilt the engines, installed new prop shafts and happily cruised the Gulf of Panama for a long time. He studied navigation, and took the exam for and received ship's captain's papers. When the skipper was rotated home, he became the captain. He habitually rose at 0500 to supervise before office hours the training of a carload of green horses, supposedly polo ponies. He received the greatest compliment the Chief of Artillery could then offer—the position of assistant commandant of the Field Artillery School. The field artillery was being reorganized into battalions and regiments. During his term he surrounded himself with very able men, including Devers, Honeycutt, Swing, Brooks and Sibert, to name just a few. People were proud of the training they got from him, and were proud of him, also. He left Sill in 1929, commanded the Second Battalion of the 16th Field Artillery for the next two years, then had General Staff duty with his old friend Fox Conner in Boston. For three years he commanded the Sixth Field Artillery at Fort Hoyle, Maryland. Most of the time he was in command of the First Field Artillery Brigade and the post as well. He retired in 1941, and his family went to Martha's Vineyard, Massachusetts to live. They had twenty-seven peaceful and happy years there. At the age of ninety, he died, on 28 July 1968, survived by his widow and son. His one-time brigade chaplain, Rt. Rev. Herman R. Page, conducted the service. Picture courtesy of *The Assembly*, Association of Graduates, USMA.

James Brailsford Erwin

James Brailsford Erwin (0-13478), the son of Robert and Mary Ann Galludet Erwin, was born 11 July 1856 in Savannah, Georgia. He graduated from Trinity College in Connecticut (B.S.) before entering USMA, from which he graduated number twenty-two of fifty-two in the class of 1880. George W. Goethals (builder of the Panama Canal), David J. Rumbough and James W. Benet (son of the author of *John Brown's Body*, the best one-volume poem on the Civil War) were three of his classmates. He was commissioned in the Fourth Cavalry and did frontier duty from 1880 to 1881. He was an honor graduate of the Infantry and Cavalry School at Fort Leavenworth, Kansas in 1893, and on 27 June of that year, he married Isabel Doan. He was on frontier duty from 1883 to 1896. During 1897 and 1898, he was superintendent of Yellowstone National Park. He was in the Philippines during the insurrection, and in 1906 was in Oakland, California, in charge of relief work after the San Francisco earthquake and fire. From 19 August to 27 December 1916, he commanded the Ninth Cavalry, and from 27 December 1916 to August 1917, he commanded the Seventh Cavalry during the Mexican Punitive Expedition, for which he received a Silver Star Commendation. On 5 August 1917, was promoted to brigadier general (NA). He was placed in command of the 157th Depot Brigade at Camp (now Fort) Gordon, Georgia. From 17 November to 27 December 1917, he commanded the 82d Infantry Division. From 29 December 1917 to August 1918, he commanded the Sixth Infantry Division, and from 16 December 1918 to its inactivation in February 1919, he commanded the 92d Infantry Division. From March to September 1919, he commanded the El Paso District, where in mid-June he ordered troops across the border to protect the lives and property of American citizens in El Paso, Texas. On 7 September 1919, he reverted to his permanent rank of colonel, and commanded the Sixth Cavalry. He retired in 1920, and lived in California, At the age of sixty-eight, he died in California, on 10 July 1924. His rank of brigadier general was restored posthumously by act of Congress in June 1930. Photo from the USMA Archives.

George Henson Estes, Jr. (0-456) was the son of George H. Estes and Anna Thornton Estes. He was born 30 January 1873 in Eufala, Alabama, on the Chattahoochee River. He was a student at the University of Georgia before entering USMA. He graduated number thirty-seven of fifty-four in the class of 1894. Paul B. Malone and Hamilton Hawkins (both *q.v.*) were two of his classmates. Commissioned in the infantry, he also served in the Sanitary Corps in Cuba, where he earned a Silver Star Commendation. On 4 January 1899, he married Frances Farrell, and they had a boy and a girl Henson F. Estes and Frances Estes (Mrs. Claude D. Collins). He was in the Philippines during the insurrection, and was treasurer and quartermaster in USMA from 1914 to 1917. He was then transferred to the Inspector General's Department, and on 8 August 1918, he was promoted to brigadier general (NA). He stayed on the War Department General Staff. In 1920, after the war, he graduated from the General Staff School, and in 1921, from the Army War College. He served under General Helmick in the Inspector General's Department from 1921 to 1925. On 2 January 1929, he was promoted to brigadier general (USA), and from 4 May 1929 to 31 May 1937, he was commandant of the Infantry School at Fort Benning, Georgia. On 1 January 1937, he retired due to disabilities, and lived in Clearwater, Florida. He died there at the age of ninety-six, on 2 July 1969. Photo courtesy of the West Point Library.

George Henson Estes, Jr.

Fredric Dahl Evans

Fredric Dahl Evans (0-202) was born 29 June 1866 in Illinois. Four years after entering USMA he graduated number fifty-six of sixty-four in the class of 1887. Thomas Q. Donaldson, P. D. Lochridge, Charles Henry Martin and William Weigel (all *q.v.*) were four of his classmates. Originally commissioned in the 22d Infantry, he did frontier duty from 1887 to 1889. Later he served in the 20th, 18th, 17th and 4th Infantry Regiments. He commanded the Seminole Indian Scouts and was at Fort Bliss, Texas from 1893 to 1898, when his regiment was sent to the Philippines. He participated in the Battles of Manila, Jaro and the Jaro River. On Colonel Carpenter's expedition from Iloilo to Panay Island in 1899, he was the adjutant. He came back to the States, but returned to the Islands from 1903 to 1905. In 1906, he graduated from the Army War College. During 1906 and 1907, he was a member of the Infantry Examining Board at Fort Leavenworth, Kansas. On 5 August 1917, he was promoted to a brigadier general (NA) and commanded the 152nd Infantry Brigade at Camp Devens, Massachusetts. In France, with the AEF, he commanded the 156th Infantry Brigade (a part of the 76th Division). His classmate, William Weigel, was for a time his division commander. On 27 November 1918 (after the Armistice), he reverted to his permanent rank of colonel, and retired in 1924. His rank of brigadier general was restored by act of Congress in June 1930. At the age of eighty-six, he died in Walter Reed Army Medical Center in Washington, on 1 May 1953. Photo from USMA Archives.

Samson Lane Faison (0-127) was born 29 November 1860 in Faison, in Duplin County, North Carolina. Faison town is still very small (population 650), and that the town shares his surname is no accident. He entered USMA and graduated number forty-one of fifty-two in the class of 1883. Omar Bundy, George Cameron and Tyree Rhodes Rivers (all *q.v.*) were three of his classmates. On graduation he was commissioned in the First Infantry and did frontier duty from 1883 to 1886. From 1896 to 1899 he was in the Tactics Department at USMA, and during the Philippine insurrection he commanded a company at Guadaloupe Ridge on 10 June 1899, where he saw considerable action. He served both as a judge on a provost court and as a Judge-Advocate of

Samson Lane Faison

the Military Commission in Manila, where he was a member of the general court-martial. During 1907 and 1908, he commanded Camp Downs on Leyte. In 1911, he graduated from the Army War College. He was at Schofield Barracks in 1916, and on 5 August 1917, he was promoted to brigadier general (NA). He commanded the 60th Infantry Brigade, which was a part of the 30th Infantry Division (AEF).This was a National Guard unit with troops from the Carolinas, Georgia and Tennessee. He commanded the 30th Infantry Division six different times, from 1 December 1917 to 6 December 1917; from 17 December 1917 to 22 December 1917; from 1 January 1918 to 30 March 1918; from 7 April 1918 to 3 May 1918; from 15 June 1918 to 18 July 1919; from 23 December 1918 to April 1919, which was when the division was inactivated. On 15 July 1919, he reverted to his permanent rank of colonel and commanded the 43d Infantry Regiment at Camp (now Fort) Lee, Virginia, in Petersburg. He was promoted to a brigadier general (USA) in 1922, and retired due to disabilities the same year. His received the Distinguished Service Medal, was an Officer of the Legion of Honor in France, and received a Croix de Guerre with palm. At the age of seventy-nine, he died in Maryland, on 17 October 1940. Photo from the National Archives.

☆

Charles Stewart Farnsworth

Charles Stewart Farnsworth (0-26) was born 28 October 1862 in Lycoming County, north of Williamsport, Pennsylvania. After attending local schools he entered USMA, where he graduated number forty-seven of seventy-four in the class of 1887. Thomas Q. Donaldson, P. D. Lochridge, Charles Henry Martin, William Weigel and George Owen Squier (all *q.v.*) were five of his classmates. He was commissioned in the infantry and sent to the Dakota Territory for the last of the Late Indian Wars. During the Santiago Campaign in Cuba he served both as a quartermaster and aide to Gen. Adna R. Chaffee. From 1903 to 1907 he was Professor of Military Science and Tactics at the University of North Dakota. He was sent to Alaska, where he headed construction of and commanded Fort Gibbon. He also went to the Philippines, where he headed construction of Fort McKinley, and then to San Francisco, where he headed construction of the Presidio Cantonments, and went on to Montana, Michigan and Kansas. He married Helen B. and they had one son, Robert J. Farnsworth of Altadena, California. In 1909, he was a distinguished graduate of the Army School of the Line at Fort Leavenworth, Kansas, and also of the staff college there. In 1916, he graduated from the Army War College in Washington. During the Mexican Punitive Expedition he served both as a battalion commander and supply base commander. Shortly after the declaration of war in April 1917, he was commandant of the Infantry School of Arms at Fort Sill, Oklahoma, after which he commanded the 159th Infantry Brigade at Camp (now Fort) Lee, Virginia. By 16 April 1918, he was a major general (NA). He trained and commanded the 37th Infantry Division, (Ohio National Guard) took it to France, and kept it busy in combat there. In 1925, he received an official thanks from the state of Ohio. For his services in France he received the Distinguished Service Cross and Silver Star Commendation from the United States. He also received the Croix de Guerre with palm, and Officer of the Legion of Honor from France and Commander of the Order of Leopold from Belgium. On his return to the States he briefly commanded Camp Bowie, Texas, then organized and constructed the Infantry School at Fort Benning, Georgia, and was its first commandant. From 1 July 1920 until his retirement after forty years service on 27 March 1925, he was Chief of Infantry. In retirement he lived with his family at 430 East Flores Drive, Altadena, California. He was quite active, and led the Tournament of Roses Parade in 1931 riding Rudolph Valentino's Arabian Stallion (Jadaan, AHC number 196). His wife died in 1951. At age ninety-three, he died in Corona, California, on 19 December 1955. Photo from the National Archives.

William Mason Fasset (0-563), son of James B. Fasset and Elien Morrill Fasset, was born 28 January 1876 in Nashua, New Hampshire. He entered USMA and graduated number forty-one of sixty-seven in the class of 1897. Harley B. Ferguson and Frank R. McCoy (both *q.v.*) were two of his classmates. He was commissioned in the infantry and served in Santiago, Cuba during the Spanish-American War, where he won a Silver Star Commendation. He served during the Philippine insurrection before returning to the United States. He was Chief of Staff of the 31st Infantry Division which was made up of National Guard troops from Florida, Alabama and Georgia. On 1 October 1918, he was promoted to a brigadier general (NA) and commanded the 73d Infantry Brigade (AEF). For his performance of this duty he received the Distinguished Service Medal. He retired in 1924 as a colonel, his permanent rank. In addition to the decorations previously mentioned, he received the Croix de Guerre from Belgium and was an Officer of the Legion of Honor in France. During retirement he raised citrus fruits in Florida, and by act of Congress in June 1930, his rank of brigadier general was restored. At the age of eighty-two, he died in Orlando, Florida , on 23 March 1958. He never married. Photo from the National Archives.

William Mason Fasset

Harley Bascom Ferguson

Harley Bascom Ferguson (0-540), son of William Burder Ferguson and Laura Adelaide Reeves Ferguson, was born 14 August 1875 in Waynesville, North Carolina. After his elementary education he entered USMA, graduating number seven of sixty-seven in the class of 1897. Frank R. McCoy(*q.v.*) and Francis Pope were two of his classmates. He was commissioned in the Corps of Engineers, served in Cuba during the Spanish-American War, and was then sent to the Philippines in 1899. On the China Relief Expedition of 1900 he was the Chief Engineer. In 1904, he graduated from the Army Staff School at Fort Leavenworth, Kansas. On 3 January 1907, he married Mary Virginia McCormack of St. Paul, Minnesota. They had three children Adele, Virginia and Harley B. Ferguson, Jr. From 1907 to 1909 he was the district engineer in Montgomery, Alabama, and during 1910 and 1911 he was the executive officer in charge of raising the battleship Maine. He was district engineer again in Milwaukee, Wisconsin from 1913 to 1916. He commanded the 105th Engineers from 12 September 1917 to 16 June 1918, and was Second Corps Engineer from 17 June 1918 to 3 October 1918. Promotion to a brigadier general (NA) came on 8 August 1918, and he received the Distinguished Service Medal for his work as Chief Engineer of the Second Corps. After the war he reverted to permanent rank, and was district engineer in Pittsburgh in 1920. From 1921 to 1926 he served in the Office of the Assistant Secretary of War establishing the Army Industrial College. From 1927 to 1929 he was district engineer in Cincinnati, Ohio, and also served in New Orleans, Vicksburg and Norfolk. As of 1930, he was a member of the Rivers and Harbors Board and a member of the St. Lawrence Waterway Board. From 1932 on, he was president of the Mississippi River Commission as a brigadier general. On 3 December 1934, he was promoted to major general (USA). He retired in 1939, but was recalled to active duty in 1942. In retirement he lived in Vicksburg, Mississippi. At the age of ninety-three, he died in Lafayette, Louisiana, on 29 August 1968. Photo from the National Archives.

Frank Kerby Fergusson (0-394), son of William W. Fergusson and Medora C. K. Fergusson, was born 28 February 1874 in Riddletown, Tennessee. He went to local public schools before entering USMA, from which he graduated number thirty-two of seventy-three in the class of 1896. Lucius R. Holbrook, Edward King and Dennis E. Nolan were three of his classmates. Originally commissioned in the Third Artillery, he was stationed at Fort Monroe, Virginia. This was a short assignment; by October he was at Fort Canby, Washington, and in

December 1897, he was sent to Battery K, First Artillery. With this unit he traveled more than he ever had before, to Camp Wickoff, Fort Sam Houston, Galveston, Fort McIntosh and Fort Brown, all in Texas. From February to August 1901, he commanded Fort Brown as a first lieutenant. He received his promotion to captain on 1 August 1901, and until 20 November 1902, he commanded the 111th Company, Coast Artillery at Fort Dade, Florida. Then he was transferred to the 73d Company, Coast Artillery at Fort Monroe, Virginia. In August 1905, he was ordered to the School of Submarine Defense at Fort Totten, New York. After completing a course in July 1906, he was put in command of the *Armistead*, an army mine planter. He fitted out for sea four mine planters and took them from Fort Monroe to San Francisco around the Horn, a four-and-a-half-month trip. After his arrival there, he spent sixteen months as an aide to Gen. Thomas H. Barry (*q.v.*), during which time he was also coast defense officer of California. From 1911 to 1912, he attended the Army War College, after which he was Adjutant General of the maneuver camp at Mount Gretna, just north of Lancaster, in Pennsylvania. From 1912 to 1914, he was on the Ordnance Board, and until December 1916, he was in the Philippines. While commanding the Sixth Coast Artillery as a lieutenant colonel, he declined promotion to colonel in field artillery to stay in his own arm of the service. In August 1917, he took the Eighth Coast Artillery to France. In February 1918, he was returned to the United States by War Department order to command the Artillery Training Center at Fort Monroe. On 8 August 1918, he was promoted to brigadier general (NA) and simultaneously Commanded the Coast Artillery School, the coastal defenses of the Chesapeake Bay, the artillery firing range at Mulberry Island and the Coast Artillery Training and Concentration Camp at Fort Eustis, Virginia. He commanded these with great credit and distinction until the Armistice. He then spent a year as Coast Artillery district commander in San Francisco, and in August 1919, he returned to Washington, to the General Staff College (now the Army War College). He was briefly at Fort DuPont, Delaware, and then was Chief of Staff of the Third Corps Area in Baltimore. Returning to the Philippines in March 1922, he became Chief of Staff of the Philippine Division. When he returned to the States in September 1924, he commanded the harbor defenses of the Long Island Sound and the 11th Coast Artillery Regiment. the years 1919 to 1930 found him in the Canal Zone. He then returned to the States and became Chief of Staff of the Organized Reserve Second Corps Area until September 1924. His last assignment was as commanding officer of the 62d Coast Artillery, the harbor defenses of eastern New York and the Eighth Corps District. At the age of sixty-three, he died on duty, on 17 July 1937. His widow and stepdaughter survived. Photo from the Annual Report, Association of Graduates, USMA.

Frank Kerby Fergusson

John Miller Turpin Finney, M.D.

John Miller Turpin Finney, M.D. (ASN unknown), was the son of a Presbyterian minister, Ebenezer Dickey Finney, and his wife, Annie Parker Finney. He was born on a plantation near Natchez, Mississippi on 20 June 1863. His mother did not long survive his birth; however, he had several solicitous foster mothers and a grandmother. Foul speech never came from his lips, as during his childhood, his grandmother had cured that tendency with her own brand of mouthwash, a mixture of pepper, salt, vinegar and ashes. He went to Princeton, was a star on the football team and graduated on his twenty-first birthday. Then he went to medical school at Harvard, and in his first year there he played on the football team. After graduation he interned at Massachusetts General Hospital and joined the surgical staff of Johns-Hopkins in Baltimore. He was on duty there the day the hospital opened. He ranked next to Dr. Halstead and worked with that brilliant surgeon for thirty-three years. When his chief died, he was offered the professorship of surgery at Johns-Hopkins. He started the dispensary there, and his fine surgical work led to a very extensive practice, including patients from all over the country and house calls to the White House. In 1892, he married Mary Elizabeth Gross of Harrisburg, Pennsylvania. She was a registered nurse and a member of the first class of the Johns-Hopkins Training School. They had three sons and a daughter Dr. John M. T. Finney, Jr, Dr. George Gross Finney, Eben Dickey Finney, a Baltimore architect, and Mrs. James S. McDonnel, Jr., whose husband was head of the McDonnel Aircraft Corporation in St. Louis. When Woodrow Wilson resigned as president of Princeton to become governor of New Jersey, the trustees unanimously chose Dr. Finney for his post. He declined, saying his work in Baltimore was incomplete, and that he was better fitted for it than to be president of Princeton. For three years he was the president of the American College of Surgeons. In 1898, he was commissioned a major in the Maryland National Guard, and during World War I he commanded Base Hospital Number Eighteen, the Johns-Hopkins Medical Unit, as a colonel. Dr. Finney, the Canadian soldier-poet, Dr. John McRae (*In Flander's Fields*) and Dr. William Thayer (*q.v.*) all knew each other at John-Hopkins. On 1 October 1918, he was promoted to a brigadier general (NA) and became chief consultant in surgery for the American Expeditionary Force. While skilled in all types of operations, he specialized in gastric surgery; his procedure for the relief of duodenal ulcers remains the standard. He was also quite sincerely interested in the Presbyterian Church, and was at one time vice moderator. He was admired, respected and loved by all who knew him. He was a life member of the Princeton Trustees, and wrote a book, *A Surgeon's Life*, published by G. P. Putnam's Sons in 1940. At the age of seventy-eight , he died in his home in Baltimore, on 30 May 1942. Photo courtesy of Johns-Hopkins Medical Center Archives.

Harold Benjamin Fiske

Harold Benjamin Fiske (0-551), son of Rufus Eugene and Charlotte Grubbe Fiske, was born 6 November 1871 in Salem, Oregon. He entered USMA and graduated number twenty-five of sixty-seven in the class of 1897. Harley B. Ferguson, William D. Connor and Frank R. McCoy (all *q.v.*) were three of his classmates. His original commission was in the Eighteenth Infantry. On 17 April 1898 he married Lucy Brooks, and they had two children Bernice and Virginia. After the Spanish-American War he served in the Philippines, where he won a Silver Star Commendation, and served both during the insurrection and the Moro Expedition. In 1910, he became an honor graduate of the Army School of the Line, and in 1911 he graduated from the Army Staff College. The year 1914 saw him on the Vera Cruz Expedition. On 26 June 1918 he was promoted to a brigadier general (NA) and was assistant Chief of Staff for training at GHQ (AEF) in Chaumont, where he earned the Distinguished Service Medal. He participated in the battles of St. Mihiel, Aisne-Marne and Meuse-Argonne. In addition to the honors already mentioned, he received Commander of the Legion of Honor from France, Commander of the Order of the Crown from Italy, and Commander of the Order of Leopold from Belgium. After the war he reverted to his permanent rank, but received his brigadier general (USA) in 1922 and became a major general (USA) in 1933. Retiring in 1933, he lived in San Diego, California. At the age of eighty-eight he died there, on 1 May 1960. Photo from the Special Collections, USMA Library.

Clement Alexander Finley Flagler (0-216) was born 17 August 1867 in Georgia. After graduating from Griswold College in Iowa with a B.S. degree, he entered USMA and graduated number three of forty-nine in the class of 1889. William Lassiter, E. E. Winslow, William G. Hahn, Charles Crawford and William W. Harts (all *q.v.*) were five of his classmates. Originally commissioned in the Corps of Engineers, he graduated in 1892 from the Engineer School of Application, and during 1894 and 1895 he taught the subject at USMA. At the time of the Spanish-American War he served as a major of U.S. Volunteers and was on the staff of Gen. James H. Wilson in Chickamauga Park, Georgia, Charleston, South Carolina and Puerto Rico. From 1900 to 1902, he was engineer officer of the Department of the East, and in 1906, he was on the Delaware and Chesapeake Canal Commission. At the time of the 1914 Vera Cruz Expedition under General Funston, he was Chief Engineer. The next two years he spent at the Army War College. On 4 January 1918 he was promoted to

Clement Alexander Finley Flagler

brigadier general (NA) and commanded the artillery of the Fifth Infantry Division at St. Mihiel. On 1 October 1918, he was again promoted, this time to major general (NA), and commanded the 42d (Rainbow) Division after General MacArthur in Germany until 6 April 1919. He was also a corps commander in the Meuse-Argonne. After returning to the States and reverting to his permanent rank of colonel, he was commandant of the Engineer School at Fort Humphreys, Virginia. In 1920, he was the department engineer in Honolulu, then was brought back to be division engineer in Baltimore. At the age of fifty-four, still on duty, he died in Baltimore, on 7 May 1922. The photo, courtesy of the National Archives, was taken at the headquarters of the 42d Division during the war.

Adrian Sebastian Fleming (0-244), son of William Boyer Fleming and Susan Harris Fleming, was born 6 December 1872 in Midway, Kentucky, northwest of Lexington. His family were Scots who had come to the colonies in the mid-eighteenth century and had fought on the American side during the Revolutionary War. Fleming entered USMA and graduated number sixteen of fifty-one in the class of 1895. Joseph Wheeler, Jr. (son of the Confederate cavalryman) was one of his classmates. (Incidentally, Joseph Wheeler, Sr. came back to duty in the United States Army during the Spanish-American War, and Joe, Jr. was his aide.) On graduation he was commissioned in the Fifth Artillery, transferred to the Sixth Artillery, and went with them to the Philippines. He did quite well there, collecting two Silver Star Commendations. He was wounded, sent back to the United States and put on recruiting duty in Louisville, Kentucky. In 1901, he was promoted to captain and served in California. In 1905, he attended the School of Submarine Defense at Fort Totten, New York, then commanded the 15th Field Artillery Battery. From 26 September 1917 until 11 May 1918, he was commandant of the Artillery School. On 12 April 1918, he was promoted to brigadier general (NA) and commanded the

Adrian Sebastian Fleming

158th Field Artillery Brigade at Camp Sherman, Ohio. This unit he took to France, commanded it in combat during the Meuse-Argonne, and for this received the Distinguished Service Medal. In October 1918, he temporarily commanded all of the 32d Infantry Division Artillery. Then he returned to his own brigade and supported the 17th French Army in Verdun, after which they returned to the 32d Division. They marched to the Rhine as a part of the American Forces in Germany until July 1919, when they returned to the States. Then he reverted to his permanent rank of colonel, graduated from the Army War College, and did staff work in Washington for a short time. On 17 June 1921 he retired as a colonel due to physical disability after thirty years of service. He was a treasurer and director of large paper companies in the Pacific Northwest. His rank of brigadier general was restored by act of Congress in 1930, and At the age of sixty-seven, he died in Oregon, on 1 December 1940. The photo, courtesy of the National Archives, shows him with his graduating class at the Army War College.

Fredrick Steinman Foltz

Fredrick Steinman Foltz (0-122), son of Johnathan M. Foltz, Surgeon General, U.S. Navy and Rebecca Steinman Foltz, was born in Lancaster, Pennsylvania on 15 December 1857. He was sent to the Episcopal Academy, a private school in Philadelphia, before entering USMA. He graduated number fifteen of sixty-seven in the class of 1879. Hunter Liggett (*q.v.*), fellow Pennsylvanian from adjoining Lebanon County, was one of his classmates. He was commissioned in the First Cavalry Regiment, then did frontier duty in the far Northwest. On 11 July 1883, he married Mary F. Keefer, but they had no children. From 1884 to 1888 he was an assistant professor at USMA, and then from 1888 to 1891, he went back to frontier duty, again in the Northwest, guarding the Canadian border to prevent hostile Indians from escaping to Canada and exploring and mapping in the area that later became Glacier National Park. During the Spanish-American War he served both in Cuba and Puerto Rico, originally as quartermaster, Second Cavalry Brigade, then as intelligence officer under Gen. Nelson A. Miles. He was in the action at San Juan Hill, and in Puerto Rico served again with the First Cavalry. Later he was a customs collector and inspector general of several different departments in Cuba. Assignments followed as chief of police, chief of secret police, provost-marshal and captain of the Port of Havana. In 1902, he returned to the states, to Washington, D.C., Fort

Ethan Allen, Vermont and Fort Myer, Virginia. In Washington, he was a member of the board that caused the adoption of the M-1903 Springfield rifle. At both Fort Ethan Allen and Fort Myer, he had a keen interest in the army remount program, improving the quality of army horses. He was also instrumental in causing the adoption of the English-type officer's saddle by the army. From 1903 to 1906, he was in the Philippines, and in 1908, he was made governor of the Province of Havana in Cuba. At the coronation of King George V in 1911 he was in charge of the American Army team at the huge coronation horse show. The following year, he occupied the same position with the American Army horse show team at the Olympics in Stockholm. Much of his military horse equipment he gave to the museum at the Rock Island arsenal in Illinois. On 27 September 1914, he was promoted to colonel and put in command of the First Cavalry Regiment. As of 5 August 1917, he was made a brigadier general (NA) and commanded the 182d Infantry Brigade (AEF). From 25 December 1917 to 19 June 1918, he commanded the 91st Infantry Division. When the war was over, he reverted to his permanent rank of colonel, and in 1921, he retired. His rank of brigadier general was restored by act of Congress in June 1930. Among his other talents he was a landscape artist of some ability, and exhibited his work at Corcoran Art Gallery in Washington, D.C. He was the last surviving member of his class, and from 30 January to 28 August 1952, was the oldest living graduate of West Point. At the age of ninety-four, he died in Washington, D.C., on 28 August 1952. Photo courtesy of his granddaughter, Mrs. Fredrick W. Martin of Dedham, Massachusetts.

Stephen Miller Foote (no ASN assigned), son of Henry William Foote and Rebecca Dunlap Foote, was born 19 February 1859 in LaSalle, in Monroe County, Michigan. He entered USMA and graduated number ten of thirty-seven in the class of 1884. William L. Sibert, DeRosey Cabell and Samuel D. Sturgis (all *q.v.*) were three of his classmates. While his first commission was in the Fourth Artillery, he later served in the Sixth Artillery. In 1888, he graduated from the Artillery School at Fort Monroe, and was retained as an instructor until 1891. During that period he married Sara Brooke of Radnor, Pennsylvania, on 24 April 1889. From 1892 to 1894 he was with the Intercontinental Railway Commission in Central America. From 1895 to 1897 he was commandant of cadets at the Vermont Military Academy, and he had the same duty at the New York Military Academy on the Hudson River, below West Point during 1897 and 1898. During the Spanish-American War he served as a major of U.S. Volunteer Engineers and as an aide during the Santiago Campaign.

Stephen Miller Foote

In the Philippines, from 1899 to 1901, he commanded an artillery battery acting as infantry. In April 1906, he participated in the march of a field artillery battalion from Salt Lake to Cheyenne, Wyoming—500 miles. From 1907 to 1911, he commanded coastal defenses on both coasts and the Gulf of Mexico. In 1913, he graduated from the Army War College and was sent to command the South Atlantic Coast Artillery District. From 1916 to 1917 he was in command of the Coast Artillery School and the coastal defenses of the Chesapeake Bay, and also ran a reserve officers' training camp. On 5 August 1917, he was promoted to brigadier general (NA). He then organized, took to France and commanded the 163rd Field Artillery Brigade in combat in the Meuse-Argonne until it was demobilized in February 1919. From September to December he also commanded a training center for 155mm field guns in France. At only sixty years of age, he died in Massachusetts, on 30 October 1919. He had retired as a colonel, but his rank of brigadier general was restored by act of Congress in June 1930. The photo, from the National Archives, was taken at Camp Dodge, Iowa.

David Jack Foster

David Jack Foster (no ASN assigned), son of Reuben Foster and Sarah Zearing Foster, was born 2 November 1859 in Princeton, in Bureau County, Illinois. When he was quite young his father died, so after attending local public schools he left to look for better opportunities in Chicago. His mother and sister Lue soon followed, while his brother, R. B. Foster, went to Florida, and was one of the early producers of pink grapefruit. In Chicago, he sold insurance, then worked for the post office in Chicago, and when he retired at seventy-two, he was the superintendent of mail there. On 17 July 1877, he enlisted in the Sixth Illinois Infantry, and about a year later he was commissioned a second lieutenant in that regiment. On 11 February 1879, he was made a first lieutenant, and on 27 July 1880, with a promotion to captain, he was transferred to the command of Company B, Fourth Illinois Infantry. He skipped the grade of major somehow. As a lieutenant colonel, he still gave Princeton as his home address. When he became a colonel on 6 January 1893 and commanded the Sixth Illinois Infantry, he used his address in Chicago. At six feet, four-and-a-half inches, he was the largest officer in the regiment, had blue eyes, and dark hair and complexion. On 11 May 1898, he and his regiment were mustered into federal service for the Spanish-American War. They were shipped by rail to Camp Alger, Virginia, then on to Charleston, South Carolina, Guantanamo Bay, Cuba, and Ponce, Puerto Rico. On 7 September1898, they embarked on the Manitoba for Weehawken, New Jersey. On 13 September 1898, they landed and traveled by rail to Springfield,

Illinois, where they were mustered out on 25 November. On 3 August 1903, he was promoted to brigadier general (Illinois National Guard) and commanded the 32d Infantry Brigade, headquartered at 90 LaSalle Street, Chicago. In 1907, he was assigned command of the First Infantry Brigade. In 1910, he married Caroline Horton, also of Princeton, Illinois. They had no children. From June to October 1916, he had the First Infantry Brigade on the Mexican border, and on 25 July 1917, they were back in federal service for World War I. On 5 August 1917, he was commissioned a brigadier general (NA) and commanded the 64th Infantry Brigade, which became the 66th Brigade, a part of the 33d (Illinois) Infantry Division. In the latter half of December 1917, he failed the physical examination for general officers in Washington, and on 8 January 1918, he was succeeded in command by Brig. Gen. Paul A Wolf (*q.v.*). He received an honorable discharge on that date. Mrs. Foster died in 1928, and for the last twenty years of his life he lived at the Gladstone Hotel in Chicago. He died on 10 September 1948 after a three-week illness, in the Illinois Central Hospital. His closest living family were two nieces, Doris Philip of Chicago and Mrs. George Clark of Effingham, and cousins, Judge L. A. Zearing and Elmer Zearing. Photo courtesy of the Bureau County, Illinois Historical Society.

Benjamin Delahauf Foulois (0-1590), "Father of the Air Force," was born 9 December 1879 in Washington, Connecticut. In 1898, he enlisted in the Army Engineers as a private, but served as an infantryman in the Philippines. After twenty-two engagements, he was commissioned a second lieutenant. He became interested in aviation while at the Signal School at Fort Leavenworth, Kansas. Alongside piloting dirigibles, he took a mail-order course from the Wright Brothers. After one flight with Orville Wright he soloed, but crash-landed. A week later he flew again. As a first lieutenant, he ran the final flight test of the first U.S. Army airplane, which had been built by the Wright Brothers to meet military specifications. Due to the speed it attained, the brothers earned $500 over the contract price of $25,000. With eight pilots and U.S. Military Aircraft Number One, he established the U.S. Army Air Service at Fort Sam Houston, Texas. In 1916, as a captain, he commanded the First Aero Squadron on the Mexican Punitive Expedition, which began operations out of Columbus, New Mexico. He had the satisfaction of hearing a remark from General Pershing, himself a cavalryman, that one airplane was worth a regiment of cavalry. On 24 July 1917, he was promoted to brigadier general (NA) and went to France, became Chief of Air Service (AEF) and led the first all-

Benjamin Delahauf Foulois

American squadron against the Germans. He became the assistant chief of the Army Air Corps in 1927, and was promoted to chief in 1931. He was largely responsible for the adoption of the B-17 bomber of World War II. He retired in 1935, and continued to further aviation causes until his death at the age of eighty-seven, in Maryland, 25 July 1967. The photo, from the National Archives, shows him on a return trip from one of the flights in Mexico.

Francis Henry French

Francis Henry French (no ASN assigned) was born 27 September 1857 in Indiana. He entered USMA and graduated number twelve of sixty-seven in the class of 1879. Fredrick S. Foltz, William D. Beach and Hunter Liggett (all *q.v.*) were three of his classmates. He was commissioned in the infantry and did frontier duty from 1879 to 1889. During his career he served in or commanded the 2d, 11th, 12th, 16th, 21st and 28th Infantry Regiments. He was on the Puerto Rican Expedition, and also served in the Philippines during the insurrection. From 1916 to 1917, he was on the Mexican border, and it was during this time, on 30 September 1916, that he was promoted to brigadier general (USA). On 5 August 1917, he was promoted to major general (NA) and commanded Camp Jackson, South Carolina. From 15 March to 28 September 1918, he commanded the 31st Infantry Division (AEF)—Alabama, Florida and Georgia National Guard troops. He retired in 1920 as a brigadier general. At the age of sixty-three, he died in the District of Columbia, on 10 March 1921. His two-star rank was restored posthumously in June 1930. The photo, from the National Archives, was taken 25 February 1903, when he was a major in the 16th Infantry.

Amos Alfred Fries (0-62), the son of Christian May Fries and Mary Ellen Shreve Fries, was born 17 March 1873 in Debello, in Vernon County, Wisconsin. After primary and secondary education he entered USMA and graduated number seven of fifty-nine in the class of 1898. Fox Conner, Malin Craig and Guy V. Henry, Jr. (all *q.v.*) were three of his classmates. Commissioned in the Corps of Engineers, he later transferred to the Chemical Warfare Service. He assisted in the building of fortifications at the mouth of the Columbia River in 1899, and on 16 August of that year, he married Elizabeth Christine Wait. They had four children Elizabeth Christine, Gilbert Stuart, Barbara Hyacinth and Carol Stephanie. From 1901 to 1903, he was in the Philippines, and from 1906 to 1909, he worked in the Los Angeles River and Harbor District. In 1912, he graduated from Army

Engineer School and became director of military engineering there. From 1914 to 1917 he was in charge of road and bridge construction at Yellowstone National Park. On 16 August 1918, he was promoted to brigadier general (NA) and became chief of the Chemical Warfare Service (AEF). He received his promotion to brigadier general (USA) on 1 July 1920, and became Chief of the Chemical Warfare Service, (USA) which assignment he held until 1929. On 16 May 1929, he retired, but was a writer and editor, and kept extremely busy. He wrote about many subjects, including communism, and edited a bulletin called "Friends of the Public School." His medals included the Distinguished Service Medal, Companion of St. Michael and St. George of Great Britain and Commander of the Legion of Honor from France. He was a life member of the American Society of Civil Engineers, the American Association of Engineers, the American Legion, Veterans of Foreign Wars, the Military Order of the World War and the Engineers and Architects Association of Southern California. He was a Republican, a Mason and an Episcopalian. He was promoted to major general (USA) on 24 February 1925. At the age of ninety, he died in Washington, D.C. on 30 December 1963. Photo from the National Archives.

Amos Alfred Fries

Charles D. Gaither

Charles D. Gaither (ASN unknown), the son of Mr. and Mrs. Charles Riggs Gaither, was born 27 November 1860 on an 1800-acre farm called Oakland Manor, two miles south of Ellicott City, in Howard County, Maryland. During the Civil War his father had raised a troop of cavalry to serve under Jeb Stuart, the famous Confederate cavalryman, after the Civil War, he helped to raise the Fifth Maryland Infantry and was its lieutenant colonel until he retired in 1877. There were very serious and destructive riots in Maryland when Charles was a young man, and the police were completely routed. The Fifth and Sixth Infantry regiments were called into service. The Sixth Infantry acted in squads, platoons and companies, and received the same treatment as the civilian police. The Fifth Infantry operated as a unit, and was adequate to every occasion, never being overwhelmed, and carrying its point with the bayonet when necessary. Gaither never forgot this, and when in later years he headed the police, he never sent out any details inadequate to handle the situation. Baltimore and Maryland both benefited from his experience. In 1890, he retired for the first of three times. In1896, he was back in the Maryland Guard as a captain, and went with the regiment to Tampa, Florida during the Spanish-American War. He went to Cuba as an officer of the Ninth (colored) U.S. Volunteer Infantry. There they fell victim to typhoid, and were mustered out and shipped home. Back in Baltimore he became colonel of the Fifth Maryland Veterans Corps, succeeding his father, who had died that year. In 1912, he became a brigadier general, and commanded the First Maryland Brigade. Also, he headed the American rifle team that won the International match in Buenos Aires in 1912. In 1917, he was on the Mexican border, and commanded Camp McClellan, Alabama until the arrival of General Barber in October, then commanded the 58th Infantry Brigade. It was discovered that he had a heart murmur, so he was retired, having served for over forty-three years. Governor Richie named him head of the state police, and he performed in a most exemplary manner. In 1937, a New York prosecutor made the statement, "There is only one decent police force in the United States, and that's in Baltimore." He was three times married—to Alice Stockton Williams, whom he divorced; to his brother John's previous wife, who later died; and to Marie L. Towson. He had two daughters. His city home was at the Walbert Apartments in Baltimore, and his country home was near Columbia, in Howard County. At the age of eighty-six, he died after several weeks in the hospital, on 29 March 1947. Photo from the National Archives.

Ernest Albert Garlington

Ernest Albert Garlington (0-13110), son of Albert Creswell Garlington, former officer of the Confederate States Army, and Sally Moon Garlington, was born 20 February 1853 in Newberry, South Carolina. His family had come from England in the seventeenth century. Of the four World War I American general officers born during 1853, was the oldest to serve during the war. He attended the University of Georgia from 1869 to 1872 before entering USMA. He graduated number thirty of forty-eight in the class of 1876. Eben Swift, Jr., James Parker and Hugh L. Scott (all *q.v.*) were three of his classmates. He was commissioned in the Seventh Cavalry, which was short-handed, having lost two squadrons and the Regimental Second in command at Little Big Horn. He obtained permission from General Sherman to surrender his graduation leave in order to join the regiment immediately, and commanded Company H, Seventh Cavalry, for the remainder of the campaign. From 6 June

1877 to 30 November 1881, he was regimental adjutant, and took part in many well known Indian battles. Next he commanded Company L of the Seventh Cavalry, traditionally called the Indian Troop. These were not Indian scouts, but Indians enlisted as regular soldiers. In 1882, he was in the field protecting the construction of the Northern Pacific Railroad when he answered a War Department call for volunteers to rescue the Greely Arctic Expedition. He was selected and went north, but his ship was crushed by the ice. The officers escaped in lifeboats and were picked up in northern Greenland by the crew of the USS *Yantic* in September 1883. On 17 August 1886, he married Anna Bowers Buford of Rock Island, Illinois, and they had three children: Creswell, who became an officer in the Corps of Engineer, Buford, who died young, and Sally, who married Harry D. Chamberlain, the great army horseman of the 1920s and 1930s. He returned to the Seventh Cavalry in the Dakotas, Fort Riley and Oklahoma. He was in action against hostile Sioux at Wounded Knee on 29 December 1890, was severely wounded and won a Congressional Medal of Honor. He rejoined the regiment in the fall of 1892, and was later on a board to revise the cavalry drill regulations. On 2 July 1895, he was promoted to major, Inspector General's Department, and became an assistant to the inspector general of the army. He was the inspector general of the Cavalry Division in Cuba in 1898, and was present at the surrender of Santiago. He continued serving with the inspector general in Washington until he was sent to the Philippines as inspector general of the Eighth Army Corps. He spent the rest of his career was as an inspector general in Chicago, California, Governor's Island and the Philippines. On 1 October 1906, President Theodore Roosevelt made him Inspector General of the Army. Presidents Taft and Wilson both later reappointed him. In 1911, he was an observer at the German Army Maneuvers. While he was retired due to his age on 20 February 1917, he served in the office of the Chief of Staff from 30 April to 21 September 1917 (which qualifies him for inclusion in this book). He wrote a number of short articles, all on cavalry subjects, was a great horseman, a voracious reader, and quite social. At the age of eighty-one, he died in Coronado, California , on 16 October1934. He was truly bound to duty, honor and his country. Photo from the Annual Report, Association of Graduates, USMA.

Joseph Alfred Gaston (0-13494), son of Joseph Gaston, M.D. and Agnes Greenback Gaston, was born 2 September 1856 in Honeybrook, in Chester County, Pennsylvania. He studied at Wyoming Seminary and at Commercial College in Pennsylvania before entering USMA from which he graduated number sixteen of fifty-three in the class of 1881. Joseph T. Dickman, Henry and John Hodges, Edward St. John Greble and Andrew S. Rowan (deliverer of the message to Garcia) (all *q.v.*) were among his classmates. Originally commissioned in the Eighth Cavalry, he did frontier duty from 1881 to 1891, principally chasing the Sioux. During the Spanish-American War, he served in Cuba from 1899 to 1902, then was sent to the Philippines. In 1906, after the great earthquake and fire in San Francisco, he commanded permanent relief camps. He later

Joseph Alfred Gaston

returned to the Islands, but from November 1913 to April 1914 he was a colonel commanding the Cavalry School at Fort Riley, Kansas. Commanding the Sixth Cavalry, he was both on the Mexican border and in the Mexican Punitive Expedition under General Pershing. On 5 August 1917, he was promoted to a brigadier general (NA) and commanded the 165th Depot Brigade at Camp Travis, Texas. From 23 November to 27 December, he commanded the 19th Infantry Division (Texas and Oklahoma troops), and from 25 April to 8 May 1918, he commanded the 37th Infantry Division (National Guard division from Ohio). From June 1918 to 5 February 1919, he commanded Camp (now Fort) Meade, Maryland; then he reverted to his permanent rank of colonel of cavalry, and was put on recruiting duty in Philadelphia until 2 September 1920, when he retired. His rank of brigadier general was restored by act of Congress in June 1930. At the age of eighty, he died on 31 March 1937. Photo courtesy of the National Archives.

George Washington Gatchell

George Washington Gatchell (0-13406), son of James Lawrence Gatchell and Mary Jones Gatchell, was born 22 February 1865 in Rhode Island. After attending local schools, he entered USMA and graduated number thirteen of sixty-four in the class of 1887. Charles Henry Martin, P. D. Lochridge, William Weigel (all *q.v.*), Thomas Q. Donaldson and John Hanks Alexander (the second African-American ever to graduate) were among his classmates. He was commissioned in the Fifth Artillery, and was later transferred to the Coast Artillery. After serving in the Sioux War (1890 to1891), he became Professor of Military Science and Tactics at the Vermont Academy (1891 to 1895). In the Spanish-American War, during the summer of 1898, he was with the Siege Artillery in Ybor City, Florida. From 1901 to 1902, he conducted mortar-firing tests in Portland, Maine. In 1902, he was sent to Cuba. There were few long marches in the continental United States then, because of the coming of the railroads, but Gatchell was on one such march from Fort Riley, Kansas to Fort Sam Houston, Texas, in the winter of 1905 to 1906. In 1907, he commanded Fort Rosecrans and the San Diego District, and in 1910, he commanded Fort Strong, Massachusetts. From 1911 to 1915, he was inspector and instructor of the Rhode Island National Guard. Between 1915 and January 1918, he commanded Fort Williams, Maine and the defenses of Portland, and within this period, on 17 August 1917, he was promoted to brigadier general (NA). As such he commanded the 31st Heavy Artillery Brigade (AEF) until August 1918, when he became Chief of Artillery, Third Corps. He participated in the Aisne-Marne, Oise-Aisne and Meuse-Argonne battles. After the Armistice he reverted to his permanent rank of colonel and commanded the embarkation camp in Pauillac, France, and then he was transferred to the Washington, D.C. area. He commanded Fort Howard and the harbor defenses of Baltimore, and on 6 December 1919, he retired. His rank of brigadier general was restored by act of Congress in June 1930. At the age of seventy-three, he died in San Diego, on 4 February 1939. Photo courtesy of Special Collections, USMA Library.

George Grant Gatley

George Grant Gatley (0-223) was born 10 September 1868 in Portland, Maine. After attending local public schools he entered USMA and graduated number twenty-five of fifty-four in the class of 1890, Edgar Jadwin, Fred W. Sladen and James A. Ryan were three of his classmates. Originally commissioned in the Fifth Artillery, he also later served in the Second and Third Artillery Regiments. On 10 February 1896, he married Bessie W. Crabb in the summer of 1898. During the Spanish-American War, he served with Siege Battery K, Fifth Artillery at Tampa, Florida. He organized the 17th Battery and commanded it in the Philippines from 1903 to 1905 under both Pershing and Leonard Wood on the Moro Expedition. During the second intervention in Cuba (1906 to 1909) and from 1909 to 1913, he organized and instructed the Cuban Artillery. From 1913 to 1915, he was on the Mexican border, then spent two years on the Ordnance Board. On 5 May 1917, he was promoted to a brigadier general (NA) and commanded the 55th Field Artillery (30th Division) in South Carolina. In September 1917, he was transferred to the 42d (Rainbow) Infantry Division and commanded their Sixth Field Artillery (AEF). While commanding the Sixth Field Artillery, he participated in the Champagne-Marne, Aisne-Marne, St. Mihiel and Meuse-Argonne battles. From 28 December 1917 to 1 January 1918, he commanded the 30th Infantry Division (National Guard troops from the Carolinas, Georgia and Tennessee), and served with the American forces in

Germany. During May, June and July 1919, he was on demobilization duty. In 1921, he graduated from the Army War College. His last command was the Eighth Field Artillery Brigade at Camp (now Fort) Knox, Kentucky. He retired in his permanent rank of colonel, but on 7 June 1930, his rank of brigadier general was restored by act of Congress. On 8 January 1931, he died in California. Photo from the USMA Library.

Charles Gerhardt

Charles Gerhardt (0-197), son of Henry Gerhardt and Emily Jane Carter Gerhardt, was born in Baltimore, Maryland on 19 March 1863. His forebears had come from Hesse, Germany in the early nineteenth century. He attended Baltimore public schools, then entered USMA, from which he graduated number forty-eight of sixty-four in the class of 1887, one class behind that of John J. Pershing. Richard P. Davis, George O. Squier and P. D. Lochridge (all *q.v.*) were three of his classmates. He was commissioned in the 20th Infantry, stationed in Montana. He married Kate Watkins of Richmond, Virginia, and they had two children Virginia (Mrs. John H. Stutesman) and Charles. He was in the Sioux Campaign of 1890 to 1891. From 1894 to 1897, he was Professor of Military Science and Tactics at Cumberland University in Lebanon, Tennessee. While attending the university he was secretary of the U.S. Military Wheelmen, a civilian organization promoting the military use of bicycles (see Frederic Remington's book *Pony Tracks*, still in print). He was in Cuba from 1899 to 1900, and then returned to Minnesota and Montana. In 1902, he took an infantry company to Fort Gibbon, Alaska for two years. When he returned, he was stationed in Baltimore briefly and was then sent to Columbus, Ohio. From 1906 to 1908, he was in the Philippines, and was in command at Iloilo for a year. In 1913, he graduated from the Army War College, then was detailed as an instructor at the student camp at Gettysburg in 1913. From there he was sent to the Canal Zone for eighteen months, and then to the Militia Bureau in Washington. He took the Fourth Infantry from Camp Geene, North Carolina to Camp Stuart, Virginia, then to France for World Was I. He commanded the Intermediate Section, Service of Supply, and Base Section Number Seven. On 12 April 1918, he was made a brigadier general, and he served at the front with the 35th Infantry Division (Kansas, Missouri and Nebraska National Guard troops) on the Somme. He later commanded a brigade of the 92d Infantry Division. On returning to the States, he commanded the 161st Depot Brigade at Camp Grant, Illinois, where he was doing demobilization work. It is hard to find an American army post where this officer didn't serve at one time or another. He retired in 1927 as a colonel, but his rank of brigadier general was restored in June 1930. He had an active mind and was a very prolific writer who wrote about a great variety of subjects. At the age of ninety-four, he died in Mendham, New Jersey, on 7 June 1957. Photo courtesy of the National Archives.

Robert Nelson Getty

Robert Nelson Getty (0-13361), son of Maj. George Washington Getty, West Point Graduate and artilleryman who served in both the Mexican and Civil Wars, and Elizabeth Stevenson Getty, was born 17 January 1855 at Fort Hamilton, New York. He entered USMA and graduated number thirty-four of forty-three in the class of 1878. John Fulton Reynolds Landis and J. Franklin Bell were two of his classmates. Originally commissioned in the 22d Infantry, he did frontier duty from 1878 to 1896, during which time he took part in the Ute War of 1884 and the Sioux Campaign of 1890 to 1891. On 14 October 1885, he married Cornelia T. Colegate. During the Spanish-American War he participated in the Battles of El Caney and San Juan, and in the Siege of Santiago. While in the Sanitary Corps he won a Silver Star Commendation. He served in the Philippines from 1900 to 1911. From 1914 to1917, he commanded the Recruit Depot at Fort Logan, Colorado, and on 5 August 1917, he was made a brigadier general (NA) and commanded the 175th Infantry Brigade at Camp Dodge, Iowa. From 27 November to 19 February 1918 and from 15 March to 24 May 1918, he commanded the 88th Infantry Division, which did not operate as a division in combat. He retired in 1919 as a colonel (his permanent rank), but his rank of brigadier general was restored by act of Congress in June 1930. Though he lived in Warrenton, Virginia, he died at the age of eighty-six in California, on 15 April 1941. Photo courtesy of the National Archives, Washington.

George Sabin Gibbs (0-746), of old New England stock, was born in Harlan, Iowa on 14 December 1875. After attending public schools he went to the University of Iowa, where he graduated with a B.S. in electrical engineering in 1897. While in college he enlisted in the 51st Iowa Infantry (National Guard). He continued his studies in electrical engineering towards a master's degree, but the Spanish-American War interrupted his plans, and he was sent to the Philippines. Soon transferred to the First U.S. Volunteer Signal Company, he won a battlefield commission, and the Signal Corps became his life. He was first over the wall in Manila, and captured a Spanish flag which is still in the Army Collection. He was recommended for a Medal of Honor. In Manila on 6 January 1899, he married Ruth Hobby, a fellow student from the University of Iowa who had traveled overseas to marry him. They had five children, four of whom lived. The oldest was a daughter, and the youngest was a son, David Parker Gibbs, who years later, like his father, commanded the Signal Corps. During World War I he was deputy chief signal (AEF), his actual assignment being Chief Signal Officer of Advance Section. He was promoted to brigadier general (NA) on 1 October 1918, and had the Distinguished Service Medal and many decorations from the British, French and Italian governments. On his return to the States, he reverted to his permanent rank of lieutenant colonel and became a student at the Army War College, studying under officers who had neither been dropped in grade nor even been abroad in combat. He soon regained his wartime rank and exceeded it, becoming a major general, and from 9 January 1928 to 30 June 1931, he was Chief Signal Officer (USA). He was a friend and, while at Fort Sam, neighbor of Gen. Billy Mitchell. He was a very capable horseman and polo player, as well as a great fisherman. Retiring in 1932, he lived on his property in Connecticut. In June 1940, Mrs. Gibbs died. He became executive vice president of AT&T, and later, president of Mackay Radio after the founder, Clarence Mackay. He also had a house in Florida where he fished, and he caught an eight-foot sailfish. He died within a week of the day, on 7 January 1947. He was the senior of the only father-son pair of Chief Signal Officers. This is probably the only instance when father and son, each in his own time, commanded a branch of the service. The above photo was from Gen. David P. Gibbs, son of the officer on the right in the picture. This unusual photo shows six of the Chief Signal Officers of the United States Army on 9 January 1928, at the swearing-in ceremony. In order from left to right Gen. Adolphus Greely, Gen. James Allen, General Scriven, General Squier, Gen. Charles M. Saltzman (outgoing) and Gen. George Sabin Gibbs (incoming).

George Sabin Gibbs (far right)

William Jefferson Glasgow (0-381), son of Edward J. Glasgow and Harriet Clark Glasgow, was born 18 May 1866 in St. Louis, Missouri. After attending local schools he entered USMA and graduated number thirty of sixty-five in the class of 1891. Odus C. Horney, Andrew Hero, Jr. and John L. Hines (all *q.v.*) were three of his classmates. He was commissioned in the First Cavalry

William Jefferson Glasgow

(Regiment). On 29 October1896, he married Josephine Richardson Magoffin, member of a noted, early El Paso family who sold their original property for the first Fort Bliss. This was also the Magoffin family that had been very prominent in the Santa Fe Trade in the early nineteenth century. Glasgow served during the Spanish-American War and the Cuban Occupation following the Mexican Punitive Expedition and World War I. On 8 August 1918, he was promoted to brigadier general (NA) and was Commanding General of the 20th Infantry Brigade at Camp Funston, Kansas, under General Leonard Wood. After the war he reverted to his permanent rank of colonel, but he got his star back in 1927, then retired. His home was in El Paso, Texas, and for a time he was personnel director of a copper refinery there. As of 25 March 1964, he was oldest living graduate of USMA. He died at the age of 101, on 4 August 1967. His burial was at the Fort Bliss National Cemetery. Photo courtesy of *The Assembly*, Association of Graduates, USMA.

Pelham Davis Glassford (0-1899), son of William Alexander Glassford and Allie Seymour Glassford, was born 8 August 1883 in Las Vegas, New Mexico. His father was Chief of Air Service in the Signal Corps during the early part of World War I. He entered USMA and graduated number eighteen of one hundred twenty-four in the class of 1904. George R. Allin, Leslie J. McNair and Edmund L. Gruber (all *q.v.*) were three of his classmates. Originally commissioned in the artillery, he was stationed at Fort Riley, Kansas, and graduated from the Mounted Service School there in 1907. On 25 December 1907, he married Cora Arthur Carleton, an army girl, and they had four children Guy Carleton Glassford, Cora Elizabeth Glassford (Mrs. Lee Parke), Pelham Davis Glassford, Jr. and Dorothy Seymour Glassford (Mrs. William Graham). From 1907 to 1912, he served as an instructor at USMA in topography and graphic arts. From 1912 to 1916, he served with the First Field Artillery in the Philippines, Hawaii and on the Mexican border. When the United States entered World War I, he was sent to France with the Fifth Field Artillery.

Pelham Davis Glassford

He was secretary of the Artillery School in Saumur (the former French Cavalry school) very briefly, then both organized and directed the United States Artillery School in Grondecourt, France. For the first half of 1918 he was commandant of the Artillery School; then he commanded the 103rd Field Artillery (of the 26th, (Yankee) Infantry Division in the Marne, Second Marne, St. Mihiel and Meuse-Argonne battles. He was wounded near St. Mihiel, and was promoted to brigadier general (NA) on 1 October 1918, which made him the youngest brigadier general in the U.S. Army (thirty-five years, one month and twenty-two days) at the time. After recovery he commanded the 55th Field Artillery Brigade of the 26th Division, and early in 1919 he commanded the 152nd Field Artillery Brigade of the 77th Infantry Division. He received the Distinguished Service Medal, the Silver Star, and much later, the Purple Heart. When the war was over, he reverted to his permanent rank, returned to the United States, and for four years instructed at Fort Leavenworth, Kansas. During 1923 and 1924, he attended the Army War College, and was retained there as an instructor. In 1927 and 1928, he commanded the First Field Artillery at Fort Sill, then spent 1928 and 1929 in the Inspector General's Office in Washington. His terminal assignment was as Chief of the Mobilization Branch of G-3. When he retired he was again advanced to brigadier general (USA), and in 1931 and 1932 he served for one year as superintendent of the Metropolitan Police in Washington. During this time the Glassfords were divorced. In the midst of the Great Depression, the remnants of the "Bonus Army," i.e., a replay of "Coxey's Army" of the nineteenth century, were still in Washington. There had already been a major distribution of bonus money to veterans of World War I in the 1920s, and there was still more to be paid to them that was not yet due. Twenty-two thousand men came to the capitol to pressure politicians to pass of legislation favorable to them. The government offered to pay their way home, and all but four thousand took advantage of this offer. Glassford, still superintendent, did not believe these men were dangerous, and gathered money to help feed and shelter them, including $600 of his own money. On 28 July 1932, the Treasury Department issued an order to evict them, provoking a riot which Glassford stopped with immediate action. A second riot started in the afternoon, and federal troops were brought in, completing the exodus with dispatch and violence. Glassford believed the police could have handled the situation, and resented outside interference in his department's duty, for which reason he resigned not long afterwards. There is a famous photo of General MacArthur (then the Chief of Staff) and his aide, Major D. D. Eisenhower, standing on the street talking to the colonel and the sergeant major of the Third Cavalry from this time. Glassford studied the subject of unemployment, and it was largely because of him that a bill was introduced to start camps for unemployed youths. These camps were the forerunners of the Civilian Conservation Corps. He retired a second time and lived near Phoenix, where he farmed, wrote and painted. He became good at painting and wrote several text books; he also wrote for the newspapers and *American Mercury* magazine. His paintings, which he sold, were exhibited in five different countries and won prizes. On 5 September 1934, he married Lucille Kathryn Painter of St. Louis.

Hugh Johnson, at Love Field in Dallas after making his 1st Flight

Gen. Henry T. Allen

Munson Last Shoe (issue)

Brig Gen FARRAND SAYRE,O-141

Commanding Brownsville District of the Mexican Border

Frederick Perkins. Unusual in that it shows a Mounted Officer wearing the Spiked rather than the Plumed helmet

The day after his seventy-sixth birthday, he died in Laguna Beach, California, on 9 August 1959. Photo courtesy of the National Archives.

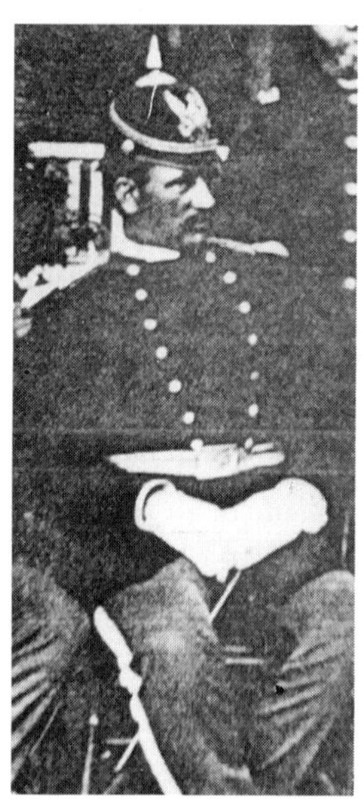

Edwin Forbes Glenn

Edwin Forbes Glenn (0-13126), son of Dr. Robert Washington Glenn and Julia Gilmer Glenn, was born 10 January 1857 near Greensboro, North Carolina. After attending a private boys school in North Carolina and a preparatory school in New York, he entered USMA and graduated number fifty-eight of seventy-six in the class of 1877. Augustus P. Blocksom, William M. Black and Thomas Henry Barry (all *q.v.*) were three of his classmates. Originally commissioned in the 25th Infantry, he did frontier duty from 1877 to 1888, during which period he married Louise Smythe of St. Paul, Minnesota. In 1888, he became the first Professor of Military Science and Tactics at the University of Minnesota, and also taught mathematics there. In addition, he studied law, got a degree, and was admitted to the Minnesota Bar. He became judge advocate of the Department of Dakota, and later of the Department of the Columbia (River). From 1898 to 1899, he commanded both exploration and rescue operations in Alaska before being a judge advocate in the Philippines in 1900. From 1905 to 1907, he commanded the Columbus (Ohio) Barracks, and then returned to the Philippines with the 32d Infantry until 1913, when he attended the Army War College. After graduating he became Chief of Staff of the Department of the East. During 1916 and 1917, he commanded the 18th Infantry and First Separate Brigade at Camp Cody, Deming, New Mexico. On 5 August 1917, he was promoted to brigadier general (NA), then organized and commanded the 83d Infantry Division. This was a depot division, i.e., a replacement division, so while certain of its units were in action, the division, as such, was not in combat during World War I. He commanded this division from 25 August 1917 to 13 January 1918. He was one of the earlier presidents of the Infantry Association (predecessor of AUSA). Later, and throughout the demobilization in 1919, he commanded Camp Sherman, Ohio, and retired in December of that year. He was a Commander of the French Legion of Honor, and wrote at least two books *Glenn's International Law* (1895) and *Rules of Land Warfare* (1914). Retiring as a brigadier general, he lived in Glendon, North Carolina. At the age of seventy, he died there, on 5 August 1926. His two-star rank was restored posthumously by act of Congress in June 1930. In the photo, from the National Archives, he is the center seated figure wearing the American "pickelhaube" or spiked helmet, worn well into the first decade of the twentieth century.

James Denver Glennan

James Denver Glennan (0-170), son of Dr. and Mrs. Patrick Glennan, was born in New York on 2 March 1862. His father had come from Ireland and had served as surgeon in the Union Army during the American Civil War. He received his medical degree from Columbian University (later called George Washington University) in 1886, and was appointed assistant surgeon in the regular army on 29 October 1888. He was promoted to major (surgeon) of the 38th U.S. Volunteer Infantry on 17 August 1899, and on 1 January 1910 he was promoted to lieutenant colonel in the Medical Corps. During World War I, on 1 October 1918, he was made a brigadier general (NA), and was discharged from the National Army on 15 March 1919. He reverted to the rank of colonel, but was promoted to brigadier general (USA) on 9 February 1925 and served as assistant to the Surgeon General. On 2 March 1926, he retired and lived in Washington, D. C. At the age of sixty-five he died, on 24 December 1927. Photo courtesy of J. Paul Klein of the Walter Reed Army Medical Center, Washington, D.C. The lady with him in the photo is Mrs. Walter Reed.

☆

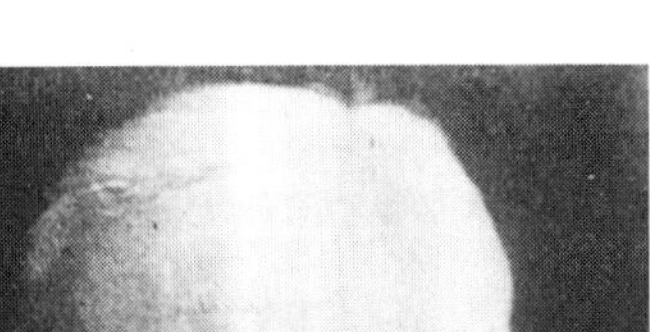
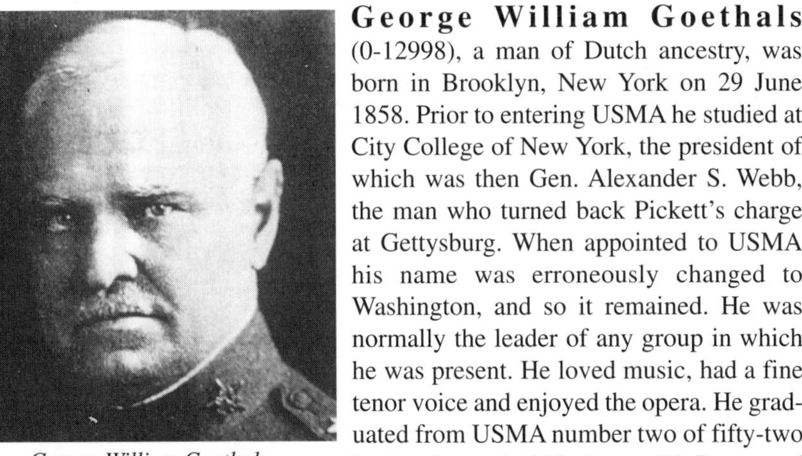
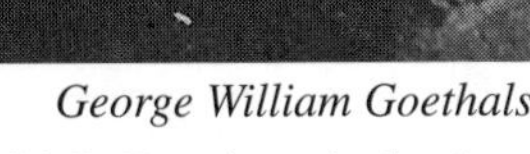
George William Goethals

George William Goethals (0-12998), a man of Dutch ancestry, was born in Brooklyn, New York on 29 June 1858. Prior to entering USMA he studied at City College of New York, the president of which was then Gen. Alexander S. Webb, the man who turned back Pickett's charge at Gettysburg. When appointed to USMA his name was erroneously changed to Washington, and so it remained. He was normally the leader of any group in which he was present. He loved music, had a fine tenor voice and enjoyed the opera. He graduated from USMA number two of fifty-two in the class of 1880. James W. Benet and David J. Rumbough (both *q.v.*) were two of his classmates. He was originally commissioned in the Corps of Engineers, was sent to Washington, and escorted William T. Sherman, then Commanding General of the Army, on an inspection trip through the Northwest. Sherman was quite interested in him because of his resemblance to a friend (also an engineer), Gen. James B. McPherson, who was killed in Atlanta during the Civil War. Sherman predicted a brilliant future for

Goethals, and he was right. In September 1884, he worked under Major William E. Merrill, the greatest authority in the country on lock and dam construction. On 3 December 1884, he married Effie Rodman of New Bedford, Massachusetts, and they had two sons George R. Goethals (USMA 1908, C of E) and Thomas R. Goethals, a surgeon, of Boston, Massachusetts. After this he taught civil and military engineering at USMA for four years. After 1889, he worked on the Tennessee River designing a lock, eighty by three hundred fifty feet, with a lift of twenty-five feet. From the outbreak of the Spanish-American War, he was in the Washington office of the Chief of Engineers, and became a lieutenant colonel, Chief Engineer of the U.S. Volunteers. From Cuba and Puerto Rico he went back to West Point and became a major in 1900. He attended the Army War College in 1905, and did a great amount of canals, rivers and harbors work. His most meaningful post of this period was as secretary of the National Coast Defense Board, of which William Howard Taft was president. Goethals was soon the Chairman and Chief Engineer of the Panama Canal construction, the War Department's most important assignment at the time. In 1907 he was appointed by President Theodore Roosevelt to be in charge of the work, and the canal was opened in 1914. In 1915, he was promoted from colonel to major general (USA) and was made governor of the Canal Zone. He retired 15 November 1916, but by December 1917 was recalled to active duty as acting Quartermaster General, then headed the Division of Storage and Traffic on the General Staff. In March 1919, he again retired, headed his own engineering firm and became consulting engineer to the city of New York. This man successfully completed one of the great engineering feats of modern times. Following an eight-month illness, at the age of sixty-nine, he died in his home in New York, on 21 January 1928. Photo from the Association of Graduates, USMA.

Walter Henry Gordon

Walter Henry Gordon (0-73) was born in Artonish, Mississippi on 24 June 1863. His father was a native of Georgia and his mother was from New York. Shortly after his birth his father bought a plantation in Louisiana, where he was raised. He was attending school in Virginia when he received his appointment to USMA from Louisiana. After graduating number fifty-two of seventy-seven in the class of 1886, he was commissioned in the 12th Infantry, then serving at Fort Yates, Montana. Charles T. Menoher, Edward W. McCaskey, Mason M. Patrick and John J. Pershing (all *q.v.*) were four of his classmates. From 1887 to 1890, he did frontier duty, then had a year at the army School of Submarine Mining. He was promoted to first lieutenant soon after. In

1892, he commanded a picked detachment at the Columbian Exposition in Chicago then performed garrison duty at Forts Bliss and Sam Houston, both in Texas. Twice he was detailed as Professor of Military Science and Tactics, first at Louisiana State University, then at Delaware College. He married Laura Doan of St. Louis. During the Spanish-American War he became a major of the First Delaware Infantry and was soon promoted to colonel, commanding it. When they were mustered out in November 1898, he reverted to first lieutenant, 18th Infantry, and joined them in the Philippines. There he was promoted to captain and organized a group of mounted scouts known as "Gordon's Scouts." He was extremely successful, annihilating the forces of Quinton Salas, an insurrection leader. Twice he was recommended for promotion to lieutenant colonel. From November 1907 to April 1909, he served on the General Staff, then had four years with the Inspector General's Department. From August 1913 to June 1914, he studied at the Army War College. In July 1916, as a full colonel, he organized and commanded the 31st Infantry. When war was declared with Germany, he was in the Philippines, and was sent to command the American forces in Tiensin, China. On 31 August 1917, he was promoted to brigadier general (NA) and sent to command the 154th Depot Brigade at Camp Meade, Maryland. In December, he was sent to Camp Forrest, Georgia, to command the Tenth Infantry Brigade of the Fifth Infantry Division. In August 1918, he took this unit to France, and planned and led the first attack of the Fifth Division at Frapelle. This attack was so successful that it gained him a promotion to major general and assignment to the Sixth Division, which he commanded in Vosges, Meuse-Argonne and the army of occupation in Germany. He brought his division home in June 1919 and reverted to his permanent rank of colonel. Next he commanded the 21st Infantry at Fort George Wright, Washington. On 3 July 1920, he was again promoted to brigadier general (USA), and was commandant of the Infantry School at Camp (later Fort) Benning, Georgia from 11 September 1920 to 8 November 1923. Its present success owes much to what he accomplished there. He was at the same time Commanding General of the Fourth Corps Area. On 7 November 1923, he was promoted to major general (USA), and reported to the office of the Chief of Staff. After more than forty years service he retired on 18 January 1924. While stepping down from a street car on 26 April 1924, died from heart disease at aged sixty. He was buried in Arlington National Cemetery. Photo from the Annual Report, Association of Graduates, USMA.

William Crawford Gorgas (no ASN assigned), the son of a former U.S. ordnance officer who became the Chief of Ordnance (CSA), was born 3 October 1854 in Toulminville, near Mobile, Alabama. He was a child living in Richmond throughout the Civil War. During the evacuation of Richmond, his father accompanied President Jefferson Davis. He attended the University of the South at Sewanee, Tennessee, where he received his B.A. degree. Later he studied at Bellevue Hospital Medical College where he received his M.D. degree in 1879. In June 1880, he received an appointment in the Army Medical Corps,

William Crawford Gorgas

which became his life. Service followed in the Dakotas and later, in Fort Brown, Texas, where he contracted yellow fever. In 1898, he was the Chief Sanitary Officer of Havana, and traced the origins of yellow fever to the Stegomyia mosquito. His success in Havana earned him an international reputation. He headed the cleanup that permitted the successful completion of the Panama Canal, and by 1913, he was generally regarded as the foremost sanitary expert in the world. In 1915, he became a major general (USA). He was sent to Johannesburg, South Africa, to study sanitary conditions in that country. From 16 January 1914 to 3 October 1918, he was both surgeon general and Chief of the Army Medical Service. He published *Sanitation in Panama* in 1915. During his terminal illness, in a London hospital, he was visited and knighted by King George V. He died in London of apoplexy on 3 July 1920. His widow was Marie Cook Doughty of Cincinnati. Photo courtesy of J. Paul Klein, Walter Reed Army Medical Center, Washington, D. C.

William Sidney Graves (0-53), son of Andrew C. Graves and Evelyn Bennett Graves, was born 27 March 1865 in Mount Calm, Texas. He entered USMA and graduated number forty-two of forty-nine in the class of 1889. William W. Harts, E. E. Winslow, William Lassiter, William G. Hahn and Charles Crawford (all *q.v.*) were five of his classmates. Originally commissioned in the Seventh Infantry, he did frontier duty from 1889 to 1897. On 9 February 1891, he married Katherine Boyd, and they had two children Sidney and Dorothy (Mrs. William R. Orton). From 1897 to 1899, he was the instructor in small arms in the Department of the Columbia (River). He was sent to the Philippines and earned the special thanks of Gen. J. Franklin Bell for gallantry in action. In 1906, he was sent to San Francisco at the time of the great fire and earthquake. From 1909 to 1918, he was on the War Department General Staff, acting as secretary from 3 September 1914 until 22 March 1918. Having been promoted brigadier general (NA) in 1917, he was further promoted to major general (NA) on 26 June 1918. From 18 July to 4 August 1918, he was Commanding General, Eighth Infantry Division. From 1918 to 1920, he commanded the American Expeditionary Forces in Siberia, for which he received the

William Sidney Graves

Distinguished Service Medal. From the end of 1920, he commanded the First Infantry Brigade until 1 April 1925, when he commanded the First Infantry Division until July of that year. The following year, he commanded the Sixth Corps Area, headquartered in Chicago. On 14 December 1926, he was sent to command the Panama Canal Division and later, the department. He retired in 1928 and lived in Shrewsbury, New Jersey. In addition to the honors already mentioned, he was awarded the Order of the Rising Sun (Japan), the Order of the Striped Tiger (China), the War Cross (Czechoslovakia) and the Order of the Crown (Italy). He wrote *America's Siberian Adventure 1918-20*, published in New York by Johnathan Carr and Harrison Smith. At age seventy-four, he died in New Jersey, on 27 February 1940. Picture from the Association of Graduates, USMA.

Edwin St. John Greble

Edwin St. John Greble (0-13118), son of John Trout Greble and Sarah Bradley French Greble, was born at West Point on 24 June 1859. Just after his second birthday his father was killed in Big Bethel, Virginia, in the Civil War. He was born in West Point because his father had been teaching English and Ethics on the faculty of the academy. Young Greble entered USMA and graduated number six of fifty-three in the class of 1881. Joseph T. Dickman, Harry and Henry Hodges (all *q.v.*) and Andrew Summers Rowan, who delivered the message to Garcia for President McKinley, were four of his classmates. He was commissioned in the Second Artillery, and was later in field artillery. In 1884, he graduated from the Infantry and Cavalry School at Fort Leavenworth, Kansas. On 24 June 1885, he married Gertrude Poland, daughter of Gen. John Scroggs Poland. In 1892, he graduated from the Coast Artillery School at Fort Monroe, Virginia. From 1885 to 1889, he was aide to Gen. O. O. Howard. During the Spanish-American War, he was in Cuba from 1898 to 1900, first as Adjutant General of the Second Division, then as assistant Adjutant General of the Department of Havana under General Ludlow. He was in charge of public buildings being evacuated by the Spanish, and under Gen. Leonard Wood organized the Department of Charities. He was supervisor of the secretary of the Interior during the second intervention in Cuba. From 1901 to 1904, he taught in the Tactics Department at West Point, and from 1906 to 1909, he was back in Cuba. In 1910, he was on the General Staff, and from 13 September 1914 to 22 August 1917, he was on the Mexican border, serving in Naco and Douglas, Arizona (in southern Cochise County, just southeast of Fort Huachuca) and in El Paso, Texas. On 13 October 1916, he was promoted to brigadier general (USA) and on 5 August 1917, to major general (NA). From 25 August to 18 September 1917 and from 6 December 1917 to 8 July 1918, he was commanding general of the 36th Infantry Division (Texas and Oklahoma troops). He was retired in October 1918 due to disabilities incurred in line of duty, and he lived in Washington, D.C. At the age of seventy-two, he died in New Jersey, on 30 September 1931. Photo from the Association of Graduates, USMA.

Henry Alexander Greene (ASN unknown), son of Edgar G. Greene and Margaret Scott Greene, was born 5 August 1856 in Matteawan, New York. He entered USMA and graduated number eighteen of sixty-seven in the class of 1879. Fredrick S. Foltz, William D. Beach and Hunter Liggett (all *q.v.*) were three of his classmates. Originally commissioned in the 20th Infantry, he was assigned frontier duty from 1879 to 1894. On 21 December 1881, he married Augusta B. Barlow. He organized and commanded a company of Sioux Indian scouts, serving in Montana and Texas. In Cuba and again in the Philippines, he commanded a company of infantry. Also, he was an aide to Major General E. S. Otis. In 1903, he was a member of the board to select the first General Staff of the army. During 1903 to 1904, he was a member of the War College Board, and was secretary of the General Staff from 15 August 1903 to 30 June 1904. Following this he was Chief of Staff, Southwest Division, stationed in Oklahoma City, Oklahoma Territory From 1905 to 1907, he was Chief of Staff, Northern Division, stationed in St. Louis. During 1907 to 1908, he commanded the Tenth Infantry in Alaska, then was sent to Fort Benjamin Harrison in Indianapolis, Indiana from 1908 to 1911. During this period he was President of the Infantry Equipment Board at the Rock Island Arsenal. In 1914, he was promoted to brigadier general (USA), and from September 1914 to August 1916, he was commandant of the Command and General Staff School at Fort Leavenworth, Kansas. On 5 August 1917, he became a major general (NA), and from 26 August to 24 November 1917 and 3 March to June 1918, he commanded the 91st Infantry Division. On 29 November 1918, he retired and lived in Berkeley, California. At the age of sixty-five, he died in California, on 19 August 1921. His rank of major general was restored posthumously in June 1930. Photo courtesy of the Association of Graduates, USMA.

Henry Alexander Greene

William George Haan

William George Haan (0-35), son of Nicholas Haan and Anna M. Haan, was born 4 October 1863 near Crown Point, Indiana. He entered USMA and graduated number twelve of forty-nine, class of 1889. Charles D. Rhodes, E. E Winslow and William Lassiter (all *q.v.*) were three of his classmates. Originally commissioned in the First Artillery, he transferred to the Fifth Artillery in 1891. On 29 August 1896, he was promoted to first lieutenant, and from 1897 to 1899, he was Professor of Military Science and Tactics at Illinois Normal School. During the Spanish-American War, he served as a captain of quartermaster volunteers, beginning 17 October 1898. From 1898 to 1901, he served in Cuba and the Philippines. On 17 October 1901, he was promoted to captain, Artillery Corps (USA). On 16 August 1905, he married a women named Margaret and also graduated from the Army War College. From 1903 to 1906 and from 1912 to 1914, he was on the General Staff. His promotion to major came on 9 April 1907; to lieutenant colonel, Coast Artillery, 6 December 1911; and to colonel, 1 July 1916. On 5 August 1917, he was made a brigadier general (NA). He must have been a good officer, having been recommended three times for brevets during the Spanish-American War. He was also cited for conspicuous conduct in action. He became Chief of Staff of the Eastern Department, and later became a member of the Panama Fortification Board and the National Land Defense Board. He was commanding general of the 57th Field Artillery Brigade at Camp MacArthur in Texas in 1917, and was commanding general of the 32d Infantry Division (AEF) (Michigan and Wisconsin National Guard troops). From 21 November 1918 to 23 April 1919, he was commanding general, Seventh Corps, for which duty he received the Distinguished Service Medal. He was also cited by the president of France. In 1920, after the Armistice with the American forces in Germany, he became a major general (USA). He retired in 1922. At the age of sixty-one, he died in the District of Columbia, on 26 October 1924. Photo courtesy of the Association of Graduates, USMA.

Johnson Hagood (0-82), son of Lee Hagood and nephew of Brig. Gen. Johnson Hagood (CSA), governor of South Carolina, was born 16 June 1873 in Orangeburg, South Carolina. A student at the University of South Carolina from 1888 to 1891, he entered USMA and graduated number twenty-three of seventy-three in the class of 1896. On 14 December 1899, he married Jean Gordon Small, and they had three children Jean Gordon Hagood, wife of Admiral J. L. Holloway (USN), Johnson Hagood, Jr. (USA) and Francesca Hagood, wife of A. B. Packard (USA). He was commissioned in the Second Artillery on 12 June

Johnson Hagood

1896, and performed garrison duty in Rhode Island, Connecticut and South Carolina from 1896 to 1901. From 1901 to 1904, he was an instructor in the Department of Philosophy, USMA, and from 1905 to 1907 he was assistant to the Chief of Artillery in Washington. In 1908, he went to the General Staff Corps, and from 1908 to 1910, he was aide to the Chief of Staff, Gen. J. Franklin Bell. From 1910 to 1912, he was an assistant to Leonard Wood, after which he was commander of Fort Flagler, Washington, from 1912 to 1913. The years 1913 to 1915 found him in the Philippines, but from 1915 to 1917, he was back in the coastal defense command. In July 1917, he commanded the Seventh Coast Artillery Regiment. He arrived in France 11 September 1917, and was in battles near Soissons during September and October. He organized and commanded the Advance Section, Line of Communications (AEF), and was in command at Neufchateau from 1 November to 1 December 1917. As of 10 January 1918, he was on the General Staff of the AEF. He was president of the board that reorganized the AEF and created the SOS (Service of Supply). Until the Armistice, he was Chief of Staff of the SOS, and he received the Distinguished Service Medal for his performance of this duty. He represented the American army in replying to the address of Marshal Joffre in Paris on 12 May 1918. On 20 October 1918, he was promoted to major general (NA). He was commanding general of the 30th Coast Artillery Brigade, and on 10 November 1918, he was transferred to the 66th Field Artillery Brigade. He crossed the Rhine and established headquarters in Hohr, Germany. Until 10 April 1919, he was in command of the artillery of the Third Army and Third Corps, and he received another Distinguished Service Medal. In 1920, he was made a brigadier general (USA), and in 1925, he was promoted to major general (USA). He was commanding general of the Seventh Corps Area, headquartered in Omaha, Nebraska, beginning 15 August 1932, and was Commanding General of the Fourth Army as well. In 1936, he retired and drafted army legislation. He was a prolific writer, and a very good one. In addition to the decorations already mentioned, he was made a Commander of the Legion of Honor (France); a Commander of the Order of the Crown (Italy); and a Grand Officer of the Order of the Sacred Treasure (Japan). He belonged to the United Confederate Veterans, the Society of the Cincinnati and the American Legion. He was an Episcopalian, a Rotarian and a member of the Army and Navy Clubs in Washington and Manila. Among his inventions were the Hagood tripod mount, the mortar deflection board, and other apparatus connected with seacoast defense. His books included *The Services of Supply, a Memoir of the Great War* (1927), *We Can Defend America* (1937), *Soldier's Handbook, Meet Your Grandfather* (1946), *General Wood As I Knew Him* and *Closing the Gap in National Defense*. His work "I Had A Talk With the President" ran in the Saturday Evening Post. He maintained homes in Charleston, South Carolina and San Antonio, Texas. He hated governmental red tape and verbosity; fame came to him for one of his annual reports to the Secretary of War, "Nothing to report." At the age of seventy-five, he died on 22 December 1948. Photo courtesy of the National Archives.

Harry Clay Hale

Harry Clay Hale (0-45), son of Thomas Judson Hale and Sarah Pierce Hale, was born in Knoxville, Illinois on 10 July 1861. He attended Knox College in Illinois, then entered USMA and graduated number thirty-six of fifty-two in the class of 1883. George H. Cameron and Tyree Rhodes Rivers (both *q.v.*) were two of his classmates. Commissioned in the 12th Infantry, he was stationed at Fort Niagara, New York. On 2 December 1886, he married Elizabeth C. Smith. They had no children. In 1886, his regiment went west to Fort Bennett, South Dakota, and he participated in the Sioux Campaign. He was recommended for the Congressional Medal of Honor, but did not get it since there was no firing in the accomplishment of his work. In 1891, he was in charge of Sioux Indian prisoners at Fort Sully, South Dakota. From 1893 to 1899, he was an aide to Gen. Wesley Merritt, and was therefore in the Philippines during the Spanish-American War. He was also briefly an aide to Gen. Arthur MacArthur, then commanded a battalion of the 44th U.S. Volunteer Infantry during the Philippine insurrection. In 1902, he commanded Bilbid Prison in Manila, and was acting commander of the 20th Infantry during the Luzon Campaign. From 1903 to 1906, he was on the General Staff in Washington, then spent three more years in the Philippines. During 1910 and 1911, he was Adjutant-General of the Department of the Lakes and the Department of the Missouri (River). In Texas in 1914, he commanded the 17th Infantry on the Mexican border, and in 1915, he commanded the 20th Infantry. That same year he was sent to China to command the 15th Infantry at Hensin, but was soon returned to the States to organize the 84th Infantry Division at Camp Zachary Taylor, Kentucky. After a 1917 tour of duty in France as a combat observer, he returned to the 84th Infantry and took it to France. Being composed of troops from Kentucky, Illinois and Indiana, he called it the "Lincoln Division." On 5 August 1917, he was promoted to a major general (NA) and received the Distinguished Service Medal for his command of the 84th Infantry. After the war was over, he commanded the 26th Division in France and brought them back to the United States, then commanded the First Infantry Division and finally was commanding general of the Sixth Corps Area, headquartered in Chicago. Knox College gave him an LL.D. in 1923, and he was retired due to his age in 1925. He lived in Palo Alto, California, where at the age of eighty-four he died, on 21 March 1946. Photo courtesy of the Association of Graduates, USMA.

Herman Hall

Herman Hall (0-195), son of Dr. George Hall and Mary McQuary Hall, was born on 6 June 1864 in Carthage, Illinois. He entered USMA and graduated number forty-two of sixty-four in the class of 1887. Charles Henry Martin, P. D. Lochridge, William Weigel (all *q.v.*) and Thomas Q. Donaldson were four of his classmates. After graduating he was commissioned in the Fourth Infantry. On 18 October 1893, he married Anna Grace Jack. After the usual stint of frontier duty, he was sent to Cuba during the Spanish-American War, and also served there in the Sanitary Corps. Next he was sent to the Philippines, where he won a Silver Star Commendation during the insurrection. From 1915 to 1917, he was chief of the Philippine Constabulary. On 5 August 1917, he was promoted to brigadier general (NA), and from 27 August to 9 September, he was temporary commanding general of the 80th Infantry Division. He also commanded several infantry brigades in France with the AEF and served with the American Forces in Germany. On 23 October 1923, he retired as a colonel, and lived in Santa Barbara, California. At the age of sixty-four he died, on 6 September 1928. His rank of brigadier general was restored posthumously by act of Congress in June 1930. Photo from the Association of Graduates, USMA.

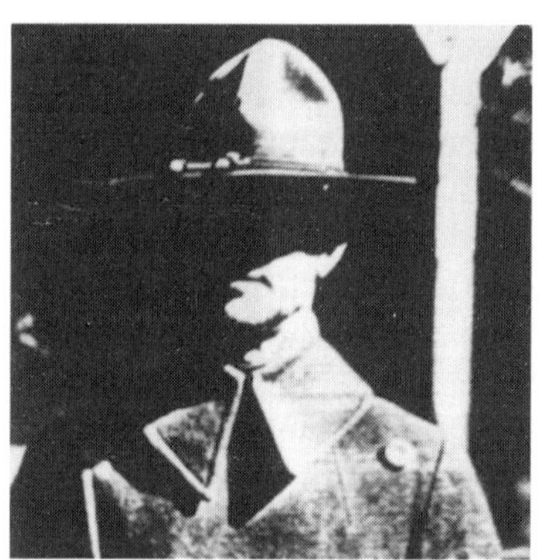

Daniel Whilldin Hand

Daniel Whilldin Hand (0-908) was born in St. Paul, Minnesota. During the Spanish-American War, he served as a major in the 15th Minnesota Infantry, from 2 July 1898 until he was honorably mustered out on 27 March 1899. On 27 August 1899, he was made captain of the 45th United States Volunteer Infantry, after which he got a regular commission as a first lieutenant in the Artillery Corps on 22 August 1901. During World War I, he was promoted to a brigadier general (NA) on 1 October 1918, and served as assistant director, then Director of the School of Fire for Field Artillery at Fort Sill, Oklahoma. For his performance of duty he received the Distinguished Service Medal. After the war, he reverted to his permanent rank of colonel and was stationed at Oakmont, Pennsylvania. He was instructor of Field Artillery of the National Guard stationed at headquarters, Ninth Corps Area, Presidio of San Francisco in 1932. He died there on 28 September 1945. Photo courtesy of the National Archives, Washington.

Thomas Grafon Hanson (0-13357), son of Thomas Hawkins Hanson and Carlotta Milewater Hanson, was born on 1 May 1865 in San Rafael, California. He graduated from USMA number thirty-six of sixty-four in the class of 1887. George Washington Patrick, great grand-nephew of George Washington, who was killed in a railroad accident in Mexico at the age of twenty-five and John Hanks Alexander, the second African-American to graduate from USMA, were two of his classmates. He was commissioned in the Nineteenth Infantry and performed frontier duty from 1887 to 1890. He graduated from Infantry and Cavalry School in 1891. On 1 September 1893, he married Pauline DeForest. They had two children Thomas Grafton Hanson, Jr. and Elizabeth Hanson (Mrs. B. R. Alexander). He served both in Cuba and in Puerto Rico during the Spanish-American War before going to the Philippines. From 1901 to 1905, he was assistant professor of modern languages at USMA. Between 1910 and 1912, he graduated from the Army School of the Line and the Army Staff College, both at Fort Leavenworth, Kansas. On 5 August 1917, he was made a brigadier general (NA), and he led the 178th Infantry Brigade, part of the 89th Infantry Division, at Camp Funston, Kansas, on the east side of Fort Riley. He took this brigade to France and commanded it in many battles there. From 24 to 27 December 1917, he commanded the 89th Division. In 1919, he retired as a colonel and lived in San Francisco. At the age of eighty, he died in Oakland, California, on 23 May 1945. Photo from the National Archives.

Thomas Grafon Hanson

James Guthrie Harbord (0-18), son of George W. Harbord and Effie Gault Harbord, was born on 21 March 1866 in Bloomington, Illinois. He graduated with a B.S. from Kansas State Agricultural College in Manhattan, Kansas (northeast of Fort Riley) in 1886. After enlisting in the Fourth Infantry in 1889, he went through the noncommissioned grades in a hurry, and was soon commissioned in the Fifth Cavalry on 31 July 1891. On 21 January 1899, he married

James Guthrie Harbord

Emma Yateman Ovenshine. Service followed in Cuba and in the Philippines, and he rose through the ranks until he was made a brigadier general (NA) on 5 August 1917. As a colonel he had served as Assistant Chief of the Philippine Constabulary under Gen. Henry T. Allen (*q.v.*), and he performed General Staff duty immediately before America's entry into World War I. From May 1917 until May 1919, with very little interruption, he was Chief of Staff (AEF). In June 1918, he commanded the Marine Brigade of the Second Infantry Division near Chateau Thierry, and in July of the same year he commanded the Second Infantry Division at Soissons. After being Chief of Staff, he commanded the SOS (Service of Supply). During 1921 to 1922, he was Deputy Chief of Staff (USA), under his old commanding officer, General Pershing. He retired in 1922 as a lieutenant general and became a business executive, serving first as president and later as chairman of the board of the Radio Corporation of America. His books include *Leaves from a War Diary* (1925) and *The American Expeditionary Force* (1929). He was a magnificent officer, a great scholar, an erudite gentleman, and a great credit to the uniform he wore. At the age of eighty-one, he died at Dogwood Lane in Rye, New York, on 20 August 1947. Photo courtesy of the National Archives.

George Herbert Harries (ASN unknown), son of John Harries and Sarah Davies Harries, was born on 19 September 1860 in Haverfordwest, South Wales. He received his early education at Haverfordwest Grammar School. He was given an honorary A.M. at Howard University in Washington, D.C. in recognition of his lectures on colonial history, and also received an LL.D. from Kentucky State University. On 23 April 1883, he married Elizabeth Langley, and they had two children Lt. Col. Herbert Langley Harries and 1st Lt. Warren Goodwin Harries, killed in France in 1918. Mrs. Harries died 29 May 1925, and the general married Alice Loveland on 11 January 1927. He was a printer, newspaper reporter, and syndicated writer, member of the staff and later associate editor of the *Washington Evening Star* (Washington, D.C.), president of the

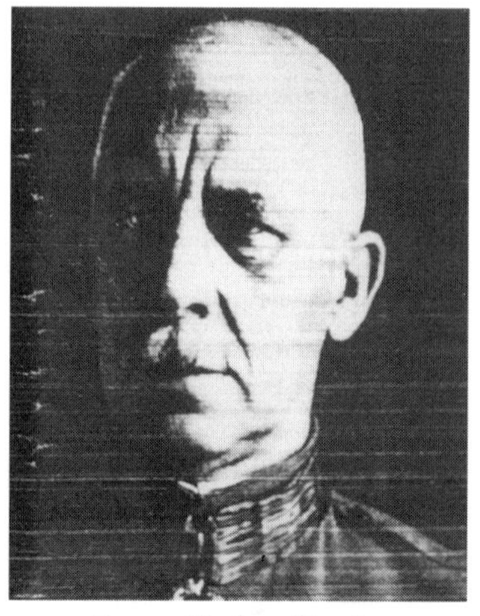

George Herbert Harries

Metropolitan Railroad Company and vice president of the Washington Railway and Electric Company from 1900 to 1911. He was a volunteer aide to Gen. Nelson A. Miles of the Sioux Commission, which established the boundary line between the Pine Ridge and Rosebud Indian Reservations and removed the Northern Cheyennes, returning them to their old home in Lame Deer, Montana. From 30 November 1897 to 1898 May 1915, he was a brigadier general commanding both the Military and Naval Militia of Washington, D.C. On 18 May 1915, he was promoted to major general and on 26 May of the same year, he retired. He had been colonel of the First D.C. Volunteer Infantry during the Spanish-American War, and served both at Santiago and with the army of occupation in Cuba. He was on the War Department board for the promotion of rifle practice as a brigadier general (NA) from 5 August 1917 to 30 September 1919. He commanded, successively, the 59th Depot Brigade, Base Section Number Five (AEF), and the 173d Infantry Brigade. He was chief of the military mission to Berlin, Germany, from 3 December 1918 to 30 September 1919. He was made a brigadier general (ORC) on 28 December 1920, and was made a major general (ORC) on 16 September 1924. He was awarded the Distinguished Service Medal by both the army and navy, and was made a commander of the Legion of Honor (France) for construction and operation of the Port of Brest. Eight other foreign governments awarded him decorations. He was a Republican, belonged to the Methodist Church, and had homes both in Washington, D.C. and Los Angeles, California. At the age of sixty-four he died, on 28 September 1924. Photo from the National Archives.

Peter Charles Harris

Peter Charles Harris (0-13), son of Charles Hooks Harris and Margaret Monk Harris, was born on 10 November 1865 in Kingston, Georgia, northwest of Atlanta. He entered USMA and graduated number thirty-one of forty-four in the class of 1888. Peyton C. March and Guy Henry Preston (both *q.v.*) were two of his classmates. Commissioned in the Thirteenth Infantry, he performed frontier duty from 1888 to 1893. On 30 September 1894, he married Mary Guthrie. He was transferred to the Ninth Infantry, then to the Tenth, Twenty-fourth, Fifth and Thirteenth Infantry Regiments, in that order. In 1895, he was an honor graduate of the Infantry and Cavalry School at Fort Leavenworth, Kansas, and he graduated from the Army War College in 1908. During the Spanish-American War, he was in the Battle of San Juan Hill and the Siege of Santiago de Cuba. From 1899 to 1900, he was in the Philippines, fighting the insurgents. He returned to the Phillipine Islands for the years 1905 to

1907, and from 21 May 1907 to 13 April 1908, he was a member of the War College Committee, WDGS (War Department General Staff). He served on the General Staff from 1907 to 1911, then returned to the Philippines for the years 1912 through 1915. In 1916, he began duty in the Adjutant General's Office, and remained there for the rest of his career. On 17 December 1917, he was promoted to brigadier general (NA), and on 1 September 1918, he was made both a major general (NA) and Adjutant General (USA). For this latter duty he received the Distinguished Service Medal. France made him a Commander of the Legion of Honor, and Italy made him a Commander of the Order of the Crown. On 31 August 1922, he retired after over thirty years of service. His retirement home was in Washington, D.C., and at the age of eighty-five he died there in Walter Reed Army Medical Center, on 18 March 1951. The photo, taken 1 June 1920, is from the National Archives.

Walter Alexander Harris (no ASN assigned), son of Nathaniel Edwin Harris and Fannie Burke Harris, was born on 17 November 1875 in Macon, Georgia. In 1895, he graduated from the University of Georgia with an A.B. degree, he received an LL.B. in 1896 as well as an LL.D. in 1928. On 9 January 1901, he married Emily Williamson. Admitted to the Georgia Bar in 1896, he practiced law in Macon as a member of the legal firm of Harris, Russel, Weaver and Watkins. From 1905 to 1912, he was a member of the Bibb County Board of Education. On 1 May 1898, he enlisted in the Third Georgia Volunteer Infantry as a private, and by 22 April 1899, he was a captain. He served in Cuba with the army of occupation. In 1916 and 1917, he commanded the Georgia National Guard on the Mexican border. He was commanding general of the 61st Infantry Brigade of the 31st Infantry Division, and returned from France as commanding general of the 174th Infantry Brigade of the 87th Division on 10 January 1919. Honorably discharged from the National Army on 10 January 1919, he became a major general of the Georgia National Guard, retired. He belonged to the Macon, Georgia and American Bar Associations, was president of the Macon Historical Association and a member of the Society for Georgia Archaeology, was commander of the Georgia Department of the American Legion, and was a Phi Beta Kappa and trustee of Wesleyan College. He also found time to write two books *Emperor Brim* and *Here the Creeks Sat Down*. In June 1936, his wife died. He was an avid student and researcher of the Creek Indian tribe, a Democrat, an Episcopalian, and also a Kiwanian. At the age of eighty-two, he died in his home on 644 College Street in Macon, survived by a

Walter Alexander Harris

sister, a brother, and some nieces and nephews. Photo courtesy of the *Macon Telegraph and News.*

John Daniel Leinbach Hartman

John Daniel Leinbach Hartman (0-207) was born on 9 August 1865 in Pennsylvania. He entered USMA and graduated number twenty of forty-four in the class of 1888. Peyton March and Guy Henry Preston (both *q.v.*) were two of his classmates. After graduating, he was commissioned in the First Cavalry and sent to Fort Assiniboine, Montana territory, where he performed frontier duty from 1888 to 1895. During that time he married Helen Canby Ward, daughter of Captain and Mrs. F. K. Ward, also of the First Cavalry. They had two sons John Hartman, who died in 1932, and George F. Hartman, who died 1945. He was there when the Sioux trouble broke out in 1890, and he was in the Battle of Wounded Knee that followed. From 1892 to 1895, he served in Arizona and New Mexico. During the Spanish-American War, he was sent to Cuba with his regiment and participated in the Santiago Campaign. In August 1900, he went to the Philippines, took part in suppressing the insurrection, and was promoted to captain on 2 February 1901. Upon his return to the States, he was an instructor at Fort Leavenworth, Kansas for three years, spent a year at Fort Riley, then returned to the Philippines for two years as regimental adjutant at Camp Stotsenberg. Returning to the States via India and the Suez Canal, he took leave there and in Europe along the way. On 11 September 1911, he was promoted to major, Fourth Cavalry, and served at Fort Bliss, Texas until 1912. He was quartermaster of the Blue Army at the 1912 Connecticut Maneuvers, and was also officer in charge of manufacturing at the Schuykill Arsenal in Philadelphia. In 1915, he was sent to the Third Cavalry on the Mexican border. When he was promoted to lieutenant colonel on 1 July 1916, he was placed in command of the First Provisional Cavalry Regiment, composed of National Guard cavalry troops already on the border. On 5 May 1917, he became a colonel commanding the Sixth Cavalry in Marfa, Texas. For a while he ran an officers training camp in Leon Springs, Texas. Then he commanded the 17th Cavalry in Douglas, Arizona, until he was promoted to brigadier general (NA) on 1 October 1918. He commanded a training camp in Waco, Texas, and when it closed after the Armistice, he reverted to his permanent rank of colonel and was reassigned to the 17th Cavalry in Douglas, Arizona. They were moved to Schofield Barracks, Hawaii, where he commanded the cavalry until 1 July 1922, when he was detailed to the Signal Corps. He remained on duty until 9 August 1929, when he was retired due to his age. His rank of brigadier general was restored on 21 June

1930. His family made their home at 5502 Sixteenth Avenue Northeast, Seattle, Washington. At the age of eighty-seven he died there, on 29 July 1953. Photo from *The Assembly*, Association of Graduates, USMA.

William Wright Harts (0-279), son of Peter Wilde Harts and Harriet Bates Harts, was born on 29 August 1866 in Springfield, Illinois. He attended Princeton University from 1884 to 1885. He entered USMA and graduated number five of forty-nine in the class of 1889. Charles Young, the third African-American to graduate from USMA and the first one to have a successful career in the army and retire as a colonel, was one of his classmates. In 1892 Harts graduated from the Engineer School of Application, and on 27 October 1898, he married Martha Davis Hale. They had four children Mary, Clement, William and Cynthia. He served in nearly every capacity available to an engineer officer, in many locations. In 1912, he graduated from the Army War College, and also taught there. In 1913, he graduated from the Naval War College. He served during the Philippine insurrection, and was in the Phillipine Islands from 1903 to 1907. Later, from 1913 to 1917, he was construction engineer of the Lincoln Memorial. In 1917, he was commandant of the engineer school in Washington. From 1913 to 1918, he was military aide to President Wilson. In France, he commanded the Sixth Engineer Regiment, and on 17 December 1917, he was promoted to brigadier general (NA). He was the commanding general of a provisional brigade with the British Fifth Army. During 1918 and 1919, he commanded the District of Paris and received the Distinguished Service Medal. From 1919 to 1920, he was Chief of Staff of the American forces in Germany under Gen. Henry T. Allen (*q.v.*). He was made a brigadier general (USA) in 1924, and commanded the artillery defense of the Panama Canal from 1924 to 1926. From 1926 until his retirement in 1930, he was the American military attache in Paris. He held a number of decorations, both from the United States and Europe. He was given the K. C. M. G. (Great Britain) and was made a commander of the Legion of Honor (France) and an officer of the Ordre de la Couronne (Belgium), just to mention a few. His membership in professional societies and fraternal and social organizations was extensive. During his retirement, his family lived in Madison, Connecticut where, at the age of ninety-four, he died on 21 April 1961. The photo, from the National Archives, is of a painting by Mrs. Leslie Cotton of Paris.

William Wright Harts

William Edwin Harvey

William Edwin Harvey (no ASN assigned), son of William Egbert Harvey and Martha Bates Beach Harvey, was born in Kirkwood, Missouri. He enlisted in the Washington, D.C. National Guard in 1890 and served in all grades. Columbia University gave him an LL.B. in 1893 and an LL.M. in 1894. On 12 February 1896, he married Katherine E. Heydrick, and from 1893 to 1919, he practiced law in Washington, D.C. as a member of King and King and Associates. He was appointed brigadier general commanding the district militia on 4 June 1915, and on 22 August 1917, he was made brigadier general (NA) and commanded the 75th Infantry Brigade at Camp Shelby, Mississippi. He was transferred to commanding general, First Provisional Brigade Army Troops, and was honorably discharged on 9 May 1918. He was an Episcopalian, and lived in Chevy Chase. He died on 18 January 1922. Photo courtesy of the adjutant general of Washington, D.C.

Everard Enos Hatch (0-119), son of Enos M. Hatch, a Civil War veteran who lost his right arm while serving under General Hancock in the Wilderness, and Kate Newham Hatch, was born on 18 July 1859 on his father's farm in Mountville, Waldo County, Maine. He went to public schools in Maine from 1865 to 1877, then spent 1878 working in a general store and teaching. He attended the Eastern State Normal School in 1879, and in 1880, he entered USMA. He graduated number fifteen of thirty-seven in the class of 1884. William L. Sibert (*q.v.*) and Isaac Newton Lewis, inventor of the Lewis machine gun, were two of his classmates. He was commissioned to the 18th Infantry in the far west, and performed frontier duty from 1884 to 1888. On 7 August 1888, he married Mellie S. Rowe. He was sent to the Maine Agricultural College as Professor of Military Science and Tactics, and he remained there until 1891. Then he was sent to Fort Ringgold, Texas, 100 miles upriver from Fort Brown, near present Rio Grande City. During 1894 to 1895, he was on duty at the Clinton Liberal Institute at Fort Plain, New York. He served both in the Spanish-American War and during the Philippine insurrection, as well as on the Vera Cruz Expedition in

Everard Enos Hatch

1914. On 5 August 1917, he was promoted to a brigadier general (NA) and both organized and trained the 158th Infantry Brigade (315th and 316th Infantry Regiments). After the war, he reverted to his permanent rank of colonel and commanded Fort Benjamin Harrison in Indianapolis, Indiana. He was again with the AEF from June through August 1919. In 1921, he retired as a colonel, but his rank of brigadier general was restored in June 1930. From 1936 to 1940, he was the mayor of Laurel, Maryland, right next to Fort Meade. An Episcopalian, he died at the age of eighty, in Washington, D.C., on 14 May 1940. Photo courtesy of Mrs. Ann L. Tressler of Laurel, Maryland.

Henry James Hatch

Henry James Hatch (0-659), son of F. J. Hatch and Sarah Hatch, was born on 28 April 1869 in Charlottesville, Michigan. He received a B.S. in civil engineering in 1891 from the University of Michigan. He married Alice E. Hill in 1893, and they had two children Walter A. Hatch and Melton A. Hatch. From 1891 to 1897, he was cashier of the Arkansas City National Bank. On 9 July 1898, he was commissioned a second lieutenant, Artillery Corps, and graduated from the artillery school. On 6 February 1918, he became a colonel, and he was made a brigadier general (NA) on 26 June 1918. He was chief of the Heavy Artillery section on the staff of the Chief of Artillery (AEF). From 1918 to 1919, he commanded the Railway Artillery, Second Army. On 1 July 1920, he was made a colonel in the Coast Artillery (USA), and on 5 September 1927, he was promoted to brigadier general (USA). Later assignments were as commander of coast defenses, Los Angeles, California, commander of harbor defenses, Manila and Subic Bays and commander, Second Coast Artillery District. The United States awarded him the Distinguished Service Medal, and France gave him the Legion of Honor. His home was in Washington, D.C. At age 62 , he died, in Washington, D.C., on 31 December 1931. Photo courtesy of the Casemate Museum, Fort Monroe, Virginia.

William Henry Hay (0-162) was born on 16 July 1860 in Monticello, Florida, just below the Georgia state line. He graduated from USMA number forty-six of seventy-seven in the class of 1886. Mason M. Patrick, Avery D. Andrews, Charles T. Menoher and John J. Pershing (all *q.v.*) were four of his classmates. After graduation, he was commissioned in the Third Cavalry and performed frontier duty during 1886 and 1887. He took the Infantry and Cavalry

William Henry Hay

School course in 1891. From 1899 to 1902, he was in Cuba as a captain, assistant quartermaster of volunteers. His commission as a regular captain came on 2 February 1901, and he was Professor of Military Science and Tactics at the Pennsylvania State College from 1905 to 1909. He graduated from the Army War College in 1913. He was married and had four sons Thomas, William, Edward and Richard. By 1916, he was a colonel commanding the 15th Cavalry in the Philippines. He was promoted to brigadier general (NA) on 31 October 1917, and became commanding general of the 184th Infantry Brigade, 92d Infantry Division from 5 November 1917 to 24 October 1918. From 25 October 1918 until 17 April 1919, he commanded the 28th Division, Pennsylvania National Guard (AEF). On 15 March 1920, he reverted to his permanent rank of colonel (USA) and served as an inspector general. From 9 May 1921 until 25 April 1922, he was Chief of Staff of the American forces in Germany. On 11 April 1922, he became a brigadier general (USA) and commanded the First Cavalry Brigade from 18 August until 17 November 1922 on the Mexican border. He retired 6 November of that year due to physical problems. Three years later he became superintendent of construction at Camp Peekskill (New York National Guard) until 1939. At the age of eighty-six, he died in New York City, on 17 December 1946. His decorations included the Distinguished Service Medal (USA) and the Croix de Guerre with two palms (France), and he was made a Commander of the Legion of Honor (France) and a Commander of the Order of Leopold (Belgium). Photo courtesy of the Pennsylvania National Guard.

John Louis Hayden (0-169), son of James Hayden, a Civil War veteran from the 19th Illinois Volunteer Infantry, and Amelia Daul Hayden, was born on 2 November 1866 in Chicago, Illinois. He entered USMA and graduated number six of forty-four in the class of 1888. Henry Jervey, Peyton C. March and Guy Henry Preston (all *q.v.*) were three of his classmates. He was commissioned in the First Artillery, and served at the Presidio of San Francisco at Fort Mason, California, at Fort Canby, Washington, at Fort Columbus, New York and at Fort Riley, Kansas. From Fort Riley, he was detached in command of the Hotchkiss revolving cannon in the Sioux Campaign in South Dakota from November 1890 to 28 January 1891. On Christmas Eve, with his command, he joined a battalion of the Ninth Cavalry under Maj. Guy V. Henry. This mixed command made a march of ninety miles, followed by one of one hundred two miles, in thirty hours. It was in action at Wounded Knee on 29 December and near Catholic Mission on White Clay Creek the following day. For gallantry in the latter fight he was

John Louis Hayden

recommended for a brevet promotion by Major Henry, who wrote "It was owing to the fire of your guns and prompt action that the Indians were drawn off." General Miles fully concurred "I was aware of the very gallant and conspicuous conduct of Lieutenant Hayden." From 1892 to 1896, he was Professor of Military Science and Tactics at the University of Washington. During that period, on 6 June 1894, he married Myra Lord, daughter of a quartermaster major. They had two children Major James Lord Hayden (CAC) and Captain Fredrick Lord Hayden (CAC), both stationed in West Point at the time of their father's death. He was promoted to brigadier general (NA) on 5 August 1917, and commanded the 56th Field Artillery Brigade in September 1917. On 18 September 1917, he became commanding general, 31st Infantry Division, a position he held until 15 March 1918. Mrs. Hayden died in New York on 11 December 1918. The first general strike occurred in Seattle in February 1919, and, faced with an unprecedented situation, he commanded the forces in Seattle with notable strength of character and showed such discretion and tact in handling city, state and national interests that he received the praise of radicals and conservatives alike. Because of his efforts, the general strike was localized and led to no catastrophic results. He retired in 1922, and lived at Port Townsend in order to be as near as possible to the life he had known and loved. He fished and hunted until his eyesight failed, and visited old friends. In 1930, his two-star rank was restored. At the age of sixty-nine, on 22 February 1936, he died quietly at home, with both his sons present. Photo courtesy of *The Assembly*, Association of Graduates, USMA.

Ira Allen Haynes (0-99) was born on 10 September 1859 in Kentucky. He graduated from USMA number fifteen of fifty-two in the class of 1883. George H. Cameron and Tyree Rhodes Rivers (both *q.v.*) were two of his classmates. He was first commissioned in the Third Artillery, but later changed to Coast Artillery. After graduating from the Artillery School in 1888, he served with the Virginia State Militia in 1893, then was stationed at Washington Barracks from 1893 to 1895. From 1899 to 1900, he was in Honolulu, and he was in the Philippines from 1907 to 1909. From 1913 to 1916, he was com-

Ira Allen Haynes

mandant of the Seacoast Branch of the Artillery School. On 5 August 1917, he was promoted to brigadier general (NA) and commanded the 64th Field Artillery Brigade at Camp Beauregarde, Louisiana. He was in France with the AEF until April 1919, and he commanded the Ninth Coast Artillery District in San Francisco. He was made a brigadier general (USA) and retired in 1923. At the age of ninety-five, he died in Menlo Park, just south of San Francisco, California, on 24 February 1955. He was the last survivor of his USMA class. Photo courtesy of the Casemate Museum, Fort Monroe, Virginia.

John William Heard

John William Heard (ASN unknown) was born on 27 March 1860 on Woodstock Plantation in Senatobia, Mississippi. His father had come a few years before his birth from Heard County, Georgia. He attended Vanderbilt University before entering USMA. He graduated number thirty-three of fifty-two in the class of 1883. Omar Bundy, George H. Cameron and Tyree Rhodes Rivers (all *q.v.*) were three of his classmates. After graduating, he was assigned to the Third Cavalry and performed frontier duty until 1890. During this period, on 3 June 1886, he married Mildred Townsend of New York City. They had five sons, all of whom went into the army. From the days of his youth he was known for his daring and bravery. On 23 July 1898, he was in charge of troops on the steamer *Wanderer*, landing ammunition and provisions for the insurgents in Cuba. When they were overwhelmingly attacked he saved the day, at great personal risk, and was given the Medal of Honor. He was one of the better revolver shots in the army, and won many competitions. He served as Adjutant General of the Southern Department under Tasker H. Bliss, who had nothing but the highest praise for him. He was in command of the Fourth Cavalry at Schofield Barracks when war with Germany was declared. On 1 October 1918, he was promoted to a brigadier general (NA) and commanded the Hawaiian Department. When he left he was given a most unusual honor the legislature of Hawaii gave him a special resolution of thanks for his services. Once back in the States, he reverted to his permanent rank of colonel of cavalry. At the age of sixty-one, he died after an operation in Louisiana on 4 February 1922. His widow and all five sons survived him. Photo from the Annual Report, Association of Graduates, USMA.

Clint Calvin Hearn (0-222), son of Levi A. Hearn and Margaret Routh Hearn, was born on 29 March 1866 in Weston, Texas. He graduated from USMA number fourteen of fifty-four in the class of 1890. Edgar Jadwin (*q.v.*), later the

Chief of Engineers, was number one in his class. He was commissioned in the Fourth Artillery, and in 1894, he graduated from the Artillery School. On 2 December 1897, he married Laura Wright Ovaker. He graduated from the School of Submarine Defense in 1898 and from the Army War College in 1912. On 5 August 1917, he was commissioned a brigadier general (NA), a position he held until 15 June 1919, when he reverted to colonel. During World War I, he was commanding general, 153rd Field Artillery Brigade, 78th Infantry Division (AEF), for which he received the Distinguished Service Medal. After the war he served in Harrisburg, Pennsylvania, as Chief of Staff, Non-Divisional Group, Reserve Units. In 1927, he retired as a colonel due to disabilities. At the age of sixty-one, he died in Georgia, on 11 February 1928. His rank of brigadier general was restored posthumously in June 1930. Photo from the Annual Report, Association of Graduates, USMA.

Clint Calvin Hearn

John William Heavey

John William Heavey (0-326), son of Patrick Heavey and Susan Mahan Heavey, was born on 19 February 1867 in Vandalia, Illinois. He graduated from USMA number thirty-three of sixty-five in the class of 1891. Odus C. Horney, Andrew Hero, Jr., William J. Glasgow and John l. Hines (all *q.v.*) were four of his classmates. He was commissioned in the infantry, and on 19 April 1894, he married Julia Bagette. They had no children. He was in the Puerto Rican Expedition, and later the Moro Expedition in 1902 in the Philippines. From 1906 to 1908, he was involved in the pacification of Cuba. In 1912, he graduated from the General Staff school, and in 1913, from the Army War College. From 1917 until 1922, he served with the Militia Bureau in Washington, during which time, on 9 August 1918, he was promoted to brigadier general (NA). During this period, he remarried to Katherine Theresa Sullivan, and they had three sons William Francis, Thomas Jackson, and Wade Hampton. On 28 February 1931, he retired as a brigadier general (USA), and his family lived in the Washington area. At the age of seventy-four, he died there, on 18 November 1941. Photo from the Annual Report, Association of Graduates, USMA.

Charles Aloysius Hedekin

Charles Aloysius Hedekin (0-13487) was born on 9 December 1865 at Fort Wayne, Indiana. He entered USMA and graduated number fourteen of forty-four in the class of 1888. Peyton C. March and Guy Henry Preston (both *q.v.*) were two of his classmates. He was an outstanding gymnast and the only cadet who could do a chin-up using one hand. He was the best boxer at the academy. Prior to the John I. Sullivan/James A. Corbett match, he was one of the people with whom Corbett loved to practice. When the fight occurred, in 1892, Hedekin was in a ringside seat cheering for the new champion. On graduation he was commissioned in the Third Cavalry, in which he spent twenty-three years. From 1888 to 1895, he performed frontier duty. From March 1891 to May 1892, he was on detached service with the Intercontinental Railway Commission, which took him through the Central American states and was one of his most instructive, interesting and professionally satisfactory details of his long career. He served on the Mexican border during the Garza Revolution of 1892 to 1893, covering thousands of miles on patrol of the Mexican border with the Third Cavalry. In December 1898, he married Adelaide Drew at her brother's home in Brooklyn. They had two sons: Tom, who was a colonel during World War II, and David, a great athlete killed in a polo accident at Fort Oglethorpe in 1930. He spent three years at Jefferson Barracks in St. Louis, Missouri, then went on to Fort Ethan Allen, Vermont, Fort Sheridan Illinois and Fort Myer, Virginia. He served two years in the Philippines, and returned to the States in 1902, when he was sent to Fort Apache, Arizona. From 1906 to 1908, he was back in the Philippines at Camp Stotsenberg. When the Third Cavalry came back from the Philippines, they were stationed at Fort Clark and Fort Sam Houston, Texas. Promoted to major on 3 September 1911, he was transferred to command the Second Squadron, 15th Cavalry at Fort Leavenworth, Kansas. After completing the special field officers course there, he went to Fort Riley and graduated from the Mounted Service School, then from the Army War College in 1912. In two short years, he had completed all three schools open to field officers. He was stationed with the Militia Division of the War Department, and from August to October 1914 he rescued stranded American tourists from Europe. In 1916, he accompanied the Fourth Cavalry to Schofield Barracks, then returned in July 1917 and commanded the 13th Cavalry at Fort Riley. He took them to the Mexican border, but was personally recalled to Washington. He was promoted on 26 June 1918 to brigadier general (NA), and commanded replacements and the 155th Depot Brigade at Camp Lee, Virginia, near Petersburg. In October 1919, he commanded the 15th Cavalry, and in February 1920, he commanded the Seventh Cavalry at Fort Bliss. On 5 August 1920, he retired with over thirty years of service. His family bought a home in Bethesda, Maryland and lived there for seven years. In 1930, they sold the house and went on an extended trip through Europe. He became sick, and late in 1931 returned home and was admitted to Walter Reed Army Medical Center, where he was a patient for four months. The family again left for Europe and spent ten months overseas. They returned in October 1933. At the age of seventy-eight, he died in Washington, on 30 January 1944. Photo courtesy of *The Assembly*, Association of Graduates, USMA.

Gordon Graham Heiner

Gordon Graham Heiner (0-315), son of Robert Gland Heiner and Helen Slemaker Heiner, was born on 2 November 1869 in Washington, D.C. His family had been soldiers since the American Revolution. At sixteen he entered West Virginia University, and he graduated with an A.B. in 1889. He entered USMA and graduated number seven of fifty-one in the class of 1893. Lincoln C. Andrews and Herbert B. Crosby (both *q.v.*) were two of his classmates. He was commissioned a second lieutenant in the Second Artillery and later served in the Fourth Artillery. On 12 November 1895, he married Elizabeth C. Kent, and they had two sons and two daughters. His namesake went into the Field Artillery. He participated in the Cuban and Puerto Rican Campaigns under Gen. Oswald H. Ernst. From 1900 to 1904, he served in West Point as an instructor in ordnance and gunnery. He was an honor graduate of the Artillery School, and served as secretary, adjutant and Chief of Staff of the Coast Artillery School at Fort Monroe, Virginia. He commanded the coastal defenses in Savannah, Georgia and Balboa in the Canal Zone. He served a four-year detail with the Department of the Inspector General, and he was Chief of Staff of the Coast Artillery, Organized Reserve, Third Corps Area Headquarters in Baltimore. During the Mexican border struggles before World War I, he commanded a provisional regiment organized from the Coast Artillery. On 5 August 1917, he was promoted to brigadier general (NA) and commanded the 155th Field Artillery Brigade. He trained his men at Camp Lee, Virginia, then took them to France on 11 May 1918. He was in the Meuse-Argonne offensive during September and October 1918. After the Armistice, he reverted to his permanent rank of lieutenant colonel and was retained at Bordeaux as Assistant Chief of Staff at the port of embarkation until the following June. On 21 March 1919, he was promoted to colonel, in which grade he served until retirement. On 10 September 1929, he retired as a colonel, and the following June was restored to his rank of brigadier general. After his retirement, he devoted much time to the Society of the Cincinnati of Pennsylvania, of which he was treasurer and later president. On 19 June 1937, Mrs. Heiner died. Several years later at the age of seventy-four, he died in Baltimore, on 23 December 1943, survived by all four of his children. Photo courtesy of the West Point Library.

Stuart Heintzelman

Stuart Heintzelman (0-774), son of C. S. Heintzelman (USA) and grandson of S. P. Heintzelman (USA), was born on 19 November 1876 in New York City. His grandfather was one of four Union generals known to have gone aloft in Lowe's balloon during the Civil War. He entered USMA and graduated number forty-three of seventy-two in the class of 1899. Leon B. Kromer and Stanley D. Embrick (both *q.v.*) were two of his classmates. He was commissioned in the cavalry. After being on the China Relief Expedition, he was an honor graduate of the Infantry and Cavalry School in 1905, and of the Army Staff College in 1906. He served during the Philippine insurrection, and was an instructor in the Army Service Schools from 1909 to 1912, and again from 1914 to 1916. In 1916 and 1917, he was an instructor at Princeton University, and was given an honorary M.A. from there. He was promoted from lieutenant colonel to brigadier general (NA). Arriving in France in July 1917, he ran the operations section at General Headquarters (AEF) until January 1918, and was the Chief of Operations, First Corps until June 1918. From June to September of that year, he was Chief of Operations, Fourth Corps, and was Chief of Staff, Second U.S. Army until it was demobilized in April 1919. He went to the Army War College in 1920, and was director there until 1921, when he became Assistant Chief of Staff (USA) until 1924. From 1929 to 1935, he was commandant of the Command and General Staff School at Fort Leavenworth, Kansas. His final assignment was as commanding general, Seventh Corps Area. He was given many U.S. and foreign decorations. At the age of fifty-eight, he died in Hot Springs, Arkansas on 6 July 1935. Photo courtesy of the National Archives.

Eli Alva Helmick (0-213), son of Hiram T. Helmick and Matilda Ann Helmick, was born on 23 September 1863 in Point, Indiana. He entered USMA and graduated thirty-nine of forty-four in the class of 1888. Peyton C. March and Guy Henry Preston (both *q.v.*) were two of his classmates. He was commissioned and assigned to the 11th Infantry. On 20 November 1889, he married Elizabeth Allen Clarke. They had three children Charles Gardiner, Florence (Mrs. John Macaulay), and George Randall. He performed frontier duty from 1888 to 1892, and was on duty in Idaho during the Coeur d'Alene riots of September through

Eli Alva Helmick

November 1892. In 1893, he was on duty at the Chicago Exposition, and from 1894 through 1896, he was Professor of Military Science and Tactics at Hillsdale College, Michigan. During 1898 and 1899, he commanded Fort Reno, just west of Oklahoma City, later the Quartermaster Remount Depot. He was provost marshal and inspector of the Rural Guard of Cuba from 1899 to 1901, for which he received a Silver Star Commendation. He went from Cuba to the Philippines, where he commanded a battalion in action against the Moros on Mindinao in 1902. He then performed recruiting duty in Springfield, Massachusetts from 1903 to 1906, after which he commanded Fort Liscum, Alaska, in 1906 and 1907. From there he was sent to the Mexican border until the Punitive Expedition and World War I. On 8 August 1918, he was promoted to major general (NA), and from September to November 1918, he commanded the Eighth Infantry Division, after which he commanded Base Section Number Five Service of Supply in Brest, France. After 24 August 1919, he was detailed to the General Staff and was Chief of Staff, Central Department (USA) from 23 August 1919 to 10 May 1921. Then he became Inspector General (USA), and was reappointed to that office. On 27 September 1927, he retired and lived in Honolulu. At the age of eighty-one he died, on 13 January 1945, and was buried in Arlington National Cemetery. Photo courtesy of the National Archives, Washington, D.C.

Guy Vernor Henry, Jr. (0-605), son of Guy Venor Henry, famous Indian-fighting cavalryman and medal of honor recipient, and Julia McNair Henry, was born on 28 January 1875 at Fort Robinson, Nebraska which later became one of the three remount depots of the army. He entered USMA and graduated forty-five of fifty-nine in the class of 1898. Fox Conner, Malin Craig and Richard C. Davis (all *q.v.*) were three of his classmates. He was commissioned in the infantry but immediately switched to cavalry where he spent the rest of his long, successful career. In the Spanish-American War, he served as a major of U.S. Volunteers. During the

Guy Vernor Henry, Jr.

Philippine insurrection, he received a Silver Star Commendation, after which he graduated from the United States Cavalry School at Fort Riley, Kansas, in 1904. During 1906 and 1907, he attended and graduated from the French Cavalry School at Saumur. On 29 October 1910, he married Mary Ingraham Rogers, and they had two daughters Mary Ingraham Henry and Patricia Vernor Henry. In July 1912, he was in Stockholm as head of the United States Olympic Equestrian Team (of which Ben Lear was a first lieutenant). From 1916 to 1918, he was commandant of cadets in West Point. On 8 August 1918, he received his promotion to brigadier general (NA) and went to France. From 22 March 1930 to 21 Mar 1934, he was Chief of Cavalry, with the temporary rank of major general. Reverting to brigadier general after that assignment, he was commandant of the Cavalry School at Fort Riley in its great days—from 25 July 1935 to 31 January 1938. He retired as a major general in 1939, but returned to active duty from 1941 to 1947, for which he received the Distinguished Service Medal. He was chairman of the U.S. section of the Permanent Joint Defense Board with Canada from 1948 to 1954, for which he was given another Distnguished Service Medal. After retiring, he went to the home of his son-in-law, Colonel Williams, on a ranch in Wenatchee, Washington. During this period he visited Fort Riley. His decorations, in addition to those referred to above, were from the British, French, Swedish, German and Mexican governments. He was quite proud of the fact that at his retirement dinner he could, and did, wear his cadet jacket from USMA. The depiction of General Henry, Sr. by Fredrick Remington can be seen in his work Pony Tracks published by the University of Oklahoma Press. Photo from *The Rasp*, annual publication of the Cavalry School.

Andrew Hero, Jr.

Andrew Hero, Jr. (0-224), son of Andrew Hero and Otweana Pugh Hero, was born on 13 December 1868 in New Orleans, Louisiana. He attended Tulane University for three years and spent a year at Columbia University, then entered USMA in West Point and graduated number eight of sixty-five in the class of 1891. Odus C. Homey, John W. Furlong, William J. Glassow and John Hines (all *q.v.*) were four of his classmates. Commissioned a second lieutenant and assigned to the 12th Infantry, he soon transferred to the Artillery, then to the Coast Artillery. In 1896, he graduated from the Coast Artillery School. On 14 July 1897, he married Fanny C. Davis, daughter of an army captain. They had four children Jacklyn (Mrs. H. W. Brimmer), Prentice, Elinor (Mrs. T. G. Murrell) and Andrew. From 1896 to 1898, he did research in electricity at the Artillery School. During the Spanish-American War, he was with the

Third Division at Chickamauga Park, then served in Cuba from January to May 1899. From 1899 to 1902, he was an instructor at USMA, and went on to edit the *Artillery Journal* for five years. From 1901 to 1911, he was assistant to the Chief of Coast Artillery from 1911 to 1915, he was adjutant of the First Separate Brigade at Galveston, Texas, after which he was adjutant of the South Atlantic Coast Artillery District in Charleston, South Carolina. He was promoted to brigadier general (NA) on 5 August 1917, and commanded the 154th Field Artillery Brigade, 79th Infantry Division (AEF) during the Meuse-Argonne offensive in November 1918, then served at headquarters (AEF) from December 1918 through January 1919. He was at the Army Center of Artillery Studies in Treves, Germany from February through April 1919. Back in the states, he commanded the 39th Coast Artillery Brigade, then was Chief of Staff of the Second Coast Artillery District. From January 1923 to March 1925, he commanded the coast defenses of Subic Bay in the Philippines. From June to December 1925, he commanded the Fourth Coast Artillery District, and from 20 March 1926 to 21 March 1930 he was the Chief of Coast Artillery with the rank of major general. He retired in May 1930, and his family lived in Washington, D.C. He was a Republican and an Episcopalian. At the age of seventy-three, he died in Washington, D.C., on 7 February 1942. Photo courtesy of the National Archives.

Mark Leslie Hersey (0-224), son of George L. Hersey and Olive Hodson Hersey, was born on 1 December 1863 in Stetson, Maine. After graduating from Bates College in Maine with an A.B. degree, he entered USMA and graduated number fifty-three of sixty-four in the class of 1887. Richmond P. Davis, George O. Squier, Edgar Russel, P. D Lochridge (all *q.v.*) and John Hanks Alexander, the second African-American ever to graduate from USMA were five of his classmates. He was commissioned and assigned to the 19th Infantry. On 16 September 1887, he married Elizabeth Noyes. They had three children Mark Leslie Hersey, Jr., Dorothy Hersey, and Alice Elizabeth Hersey. From 1887 to 1891, he performed frontier duty, then went to the University of Maine as a Professor of Military Science and Tactics from 1891 to 1905. He was with the Philippine Constabulary from 1905 to 1914, was on the China Relief Expedition, and also served with the Mexican Punitive Expedition in 1916 and 1917. On 28 August 1917, he was promoted to brigadier general (NA) and took command of the 155th Infantry Brigade at Camp Dix, New Jersey. He took this brigade to France with the AEF, commanded it in many

Mark Leslie Hersey

battles, and was promoted to major general on 15 October 1918. He was assigned command of the Fourth Infantry Division, which he took to Germany as a part of the army of occupation, and returned with it to the States on 31 July 1919. He was awarded the Distinguished Service Medal and the Croix de Guerre with palms and was made an officer of the Legion of Honor (France). In 1924, he retired as a major general and lived in Washington, D.C. At the age of seventy, he died on 22 January 1934. Photo from the National Archives.

Howard Russell Hickock

Howard Russell Hickock (0-407) was born on 26 November 1870 in Florida, Monroe County, Missouri. He entered USMA and graduated number thirty-five of sixty-two in the class of 1892. William Chamberlain, James A. Shipton, Chas P. Sumerall and Kirby Walker (all *q.v.*) were four of his classmates. He was commissioned and served with the Ninth Cavalry, both in the Northwest and in Arizona and New Mexico. He married Anna Elizabeth Whitbread of Syracuse, New York. During 1904, he was on duty with the National Guard, both in Pennsylvania and in Washington, D.C. He served in Alaska and in the Philippines during the insurrection, and also served during the Moro Uprising of 1903. In 1906, he was an honor graduate of the Infantry and Cavalry School, and during 1906 and 1907, he was on duty with the provisional government of Cuba. In 1908, he graduated from the Army Staff College, and he was on duty at various times with the National Guards of Indiana, Georgia, Florida, Mississippi and West Virginia. On 5 August 1917, he was promoted to colonel (NA), and was Chief of Staff of the Fifth Infantry Division (AEF). On 26 June 1918, he was again promoted to brigadier general (NA), and returned to the States to command the 19th Infantry Brigade of the 10th Infantry Division at Camp Funston, Kansas, just east of Fort Riley. Following the war, he commanded the Arizona District, headquartered in Douglas, Cochise County, southeast Arizona. After that, he served with the Seventh Cavalry at Fort Bliss until attending the War College in 1920. He commanded of the Fourth Cavalry at Fort Brown in Brownsville, Texas, at the mouth of the Rio Grande, and also at Laredo, Texas, farther upriver. His last assignment was as Sixth Corps Area inspector in Chicago. He was hospitalized for six months, first at the Army-Navy General Hospital in Hot Springs, Arkansas, then at Walter Reed Army Medical Center in Washington. At the age of fifty-five, he died On 7 July 1926, as a colonel. His rank as brigadier general was restored posthumously in June 1930. Photo courtesy of the Annual Report, Association of Graduates, USMA.

Henry Root Hill

Henry Root Hill (ASN unknown), son of Fredrick Terrence Hill and Cecelia Root Hill, was born on 20 June 1876 in Quincy, Illinois. After public school he worked for his father at F.T. Hill Company, a very successful dealership in furniture and carpeting. When his father died in 1905, he succeeded him as owner and operator of the business. His military career started when he enlisted in the Illinois National Guard as a private, Company F, Fifth Illinois Infantry in 1894. By the time of the Spanish-American War, he was First sergeant of his company, but the regiment was sent to Georgia and did not get to serve. He was commissioned in 1899 and rose rapidly through the ranks, becoming a National Guard brigadier general in 1914. When the National Guard was mobilized at the time of the Pancho Villa trouble in 1916, he took his brigade to the Mexican border. They were back home only a very short time before after they were remobilized for World War I. He was one of the very few National Guard brigadiers who were kept in command of his unit; his performance was well respected. In 1917, there were race riots in east St. Louis, Illinois, which were quelled by the Illinois National Guard, and he was president of the board called to investigate the handling of this matter. On 25 July 1917, he was promoted to brigadier general (NA) and commanded the 65th Infantry Brigade. He trained it and took it to France, and was then supplanted and offered his choice of a discharge or a colonel's commission in the Service of Supply. He declined, saying he went to France to serve and preferred to be at the front in any capacity. Four years after he was promoted to a guard brigadier, and after almost fourteen months as a successful National Army brigadier, he was commissioned a Major on 29 August 1918 and posted to the 128th Infantry Regiment, headed for the front. Six weeks later, during the Meuse-Argonne battle, he was leading his battalion in action near Romagne-sous-Mont faucon when he was shot and killed. He had led his command through a maze of machine-gun nests, and had reached his objective. Another group of four machine gunners were about to open fire on his flank, so he charged them, took three prisoners, and was killed by the fourth. He was posthumously awarded the Distinguished Service Cross for this act. General Hill had never married. At the age of forty-two, he died on 16 October 1918. Photo from the Quincy Historical Society, Illinois.

Ernest Hinds (0-74), son of Dr. Byram W. Hinds, a Confederate veteran, and Margaret Rebecca Pickett Hinds, was born on 18 August 1864 in Red Hill, Alabama. His family had come from England to New Jersey, North Carolina and Alabama. He graduated from USMA number eight of sixty-four in the class of

Ernest Hinds

1887. Richmond P. Davis, George O. Squier, Thomas Donaldson and P. D. Lochridge (all *q.v.*) were four of his classmates. He was commissioned in the artillery. His early stations were in Little Rock, New Orleans and at Fort Preble, Maine. On 24 January 1889, he married Minnie Hatton in Little Rock, Arkansas, and they had two children Marjorie Hamilton Hinds (Mrs. Fred Taylor Cruse) and John Hamilton Hinds. From 1892 to 1895, he was in the Mounted Service School at Fort Riley, Kansas and in the Field Artillery School at Fort Sill, Oklahoma. He also graduated with honors from the Seacoast Artillery School at Fort Monroe, Virginia. He commanded a light battery during the Santiago Campaign in Cuba, for which he was officially commended and given the brevet rank of major. As a temporary major, he served in the 49th U.S. Volunteer Infantry in Cuba, and was sent with them to the Philippines. In northern Luzon, he was in charge of a subdistrict and captured Manuel Vieta, one of the insurgent leaders. In 1901, he was discharged from the U.S. Volunteers and given command of the Second Field Artillery Battery at Fort Sam Houston, Texas. From 1903 to 1905, he served on a board writing regulations for the new three-inch artillery piece (one of which is now at the southeast corner of the old parade ground at Fort Huachuca, Ariz) at Fort Riley, Kansas. During 1906 and 1907, he was a member of the Field Artillery Board. He served in the Adjutant General's Department for two years as assistant to the Adjutant General of the Philippine Division, then attended the service schools at Fort Sill, Fort Riley and Fort Leavenworth. From 1914 to 1917, he had his third tour of duty in the Philippines as Chief of Staff of the department. He received his promotion to brigadier general (NA) in 1917, and was sent to Camp Taylor in Louisville, Kentucky to command the 159th Field Artillery Brigade. In October of that year, he was sent to France to command the Artillery School at Saumur, the old French Cavalry School. He commanded the I Corps Artillery and later the First Army Artillery. His last World War I duty was as Chief of Artillery (AEF). Returning to the States after the war, he commanded the Field Artillery School at Fort Sill, Oklahoma, and then the Second Infantry Division at Fort Sam Houston, Texas. His final command was the Eighth Corps Area, headquartered at Fort Sam Houston, and in 1928, he retired as a major general. He was very interested in the United Services Automobile Association, and served there in a variety of offices, including that of general manager. His decorations included the Distinguished Service Medal, the Croix de Guerre with palms, and he was made a Commander of the Order of Leopold (Belgium), a Commander of the Legion of Honor (France) and a member of the Order of Saints Maurice and Lazarus (Italy).

At the age of seventy-six, he died at Fort Sam Houston, Texas, on 17 June 1941. Photo courtesy of the National Archives.

Frank Thomas Hines

Frank Thomas Hines (ASN unknown), son of Frank L. Hines and Martha J. Hines, was born on 11 April 1879, in Salt Lake City, Utah. His military service started with the Spanish-American War, during which he served as a sergeant and first sergeant of Battery B, Utah Light Artillery, from 9 May 1898 to 22 March 1899. He was commissioned a second lieutenant in the Utah Light Artillery in 1899, but was mustered out of the U.S. Volunteers on 16 August of the same year. He married Nellie M. Vier on 4 October 1900, and they had two children Mrs. Viera H. Kennedy and Frank T. Hines, Jr. On 20 September 1901, he was commissioned a second lieutenant, Artillery (USA), and from this point his career really began. He was in twenty-four engagements in the Philippines, and was recommended for the Congressional Medal of Honor. In Europe at the outbreak of World War I, he assisted in the return of 3,100 American citizens to the United States. Upon his return to the States, he was in the Chief of Staff's office as assistant in the Embarkation Service. On 26 January 1918, he was appointed Chief of Embarkation, and on 18 April he became a brigadier general (NA). In 1919, he was appointed Chief of Transportation Service (USA). He went to London in September 1918 with Secretary of War Newton D. Baker to attend the Inter-Allied Transport Council. In January 1919, he again went to England and France to work with the Allied Nations. On 7 January 1920, he received his promotion to brigadier general (USA), but he resigned on 31 August of that year, and was appointed a brigadier general (ORC) a week later. He directed the Veterans Bureau from 1923 to 1930, and was administrator of veterans affairs from 1930 to 1944, when he retired as a brigadier general. He was made Ambassador to Panama and stayed there until 1948. He was a member of the American Society of Mechanical Engineers. His decorations included the Distinguished Service Medal from both the army and the navy and the War Cross from Czechoslovakia, and he was made a Companion of the Order of the Bath (Great Britain), a Grand Officer of the Order of Leopold (Belgium), an Officer of the Legion of Honor (France) and a member of the Order of the Sacred Treasure, Second Class (Japan). In retirement his family lived in Washington, D.C., where he died a week before his eighty-first birthday, on 3 April 1960. Photo from the National Archives, Washington.

John Leonard Hines

John Leonard Hines (0-23), son of Edward Hines and Mary Leopard Hines, was born on 21 May 1868 in White Sulphur Springs, West Virginia. He graduated from USMA number forty-eight of sixty-five in the class of 1891. William J. Glasgow, whom he succeeded as the oldest living graduate of the academy was one of his classmates. He was commissioned a second lieutenant of infantry, and served from 1891 to 1896 at Fort Omaha, Nebraska. In 1898, he was acting quartermaster of the Second Infantry in Tampa, Florida and Santiago de Cuba. On 19 December 1898, he married Rita S. Wherry, daughter of Gen. William H. Wherry (USA), and they had two children Alice G. Hines (Mrs. J. R. D. Cleland) and Col. John L. Hines, Jr. (USA). From 1899 to 1900, he was in Cienfuegos, Cuba, and on four occasions afterwards he was stationed in the Philippines (1900 to 1901, 1903 to 1905, 1911 to 1912 and 1930 to 1932). He was chief quartermaster of U.S. troops at the Jamestown Exposition in 1907, and was assistant chief quartermaster of the Department of the Missouri River, from 1908 to 1909. He was in Nagasaki, Japan, during 1910 and 1911, and he served as adjutant on the Mexican Punitive Expedition in 1916 and 1917. He arrived in France with General Pershing on 13 June 1917, and was assistant Adjutant General (AEF) from May to October 1917. He commanded regiments, brigades, divisions and corps in the AEF, for which he received both the Distinguished Service Cross and the Distinguished Service Medal. On 6 August 1918, he was promoted to brigadier general (NA), and he became a major general (USA) in1920. From January 1923 to January 1925, he was Deputy Chief of Staff (USA). After General Pershing was relieved of all assignment but not retired he succeeded him as Chief of Staff (USA), with the temporary rank of general (four-star), from 1924 to 1926. He retired in 1932 as a major general and lived in Chevy Chase, Maryland. By special act of Congress in 1940, he was promoted to four-star rank on the retired list. He died in Washington, D.C. on 13 August 1968, not only the last survivor of his class, but as of 4 August 1967, the longest-lived graduate. Photo courtesy of the National Archives.

Harry Foote Hodges (0-39), son of Edward Fuller Hodges and Anne Frances Hamatt Hodges, was born on 25 February 1860 in Boston, Massachusetts. He attended the Boston Latin School and Adams Academy in Quincy, Massachusetts, then entered USMA and graduated number four of fifty-three in the class of 1881. He was commissioned in the Corps of Engineers. On 8 December1887, he married Alma L'Hommedieu Raynolds, and they had four children Antoinette, Frances (widow of Col. A.H. Archer), Alma Louise (Mrs. G.

L. Dickson), and Duncan. He was a lieutenant colonel, First U.S. Volunteer Engineers, beginning 10 June 1898. He performed rivers, harbors and fortifications duty, and also served in Cuba, Puerto Rico and the Panama Canal Zone. During 1901 and 1902, he was Chief Engineer, Department of Cuba, and from 1902 to 1907, he was in the office of the Chief of Engineers in Washington. From 1907 to 1914, he was General Purchasing Officer, assistant Chief Engineer and a member of the Isthmian Canal Commission. During 1914 and 1915, he was in charge of the design of locks, dams and regulation works in the Panama Canal, as well as engineer of maintenance, for which he received the thanks of Congress and a promotion to brigadier general (USA) on 4 March 1915. From 1915 to 1917, he was commanding general, North and Middle Atlantic Coast Artillery Districts. From 25 August 1917 to 1 January 1919, he was commanding general, 76th Infantry Division, both at Camp Devens, Massachusetts, and in France, for which he received the Distinguished Service Medal. From 1 January to 1 July 1919, he was commanding general of the 20th Infantry Division at Camp Sevier, South Carolina and at Camp Travis, Texas. His final assignment was as commanding general, North Pacific and Third Coast Artillery Districts. On 21 December 1921, he was promoted to major general (USA), and the following day he retired. He was an Episcopalian, and made his retirement home in Lake Forest, Illinois. At age sixty-nine, he died in Chicago, on 24 September 1929. Photo from the National Archives.

Harry Foote Hodges

☆

Henry Clay Hodges, Jr. (0-13131), son of Henry Clay Hodges, a USMA graduate of 1851, and Annie Abernethy, daughter of the first elected governor of the Oregon Territory, was born on 20 April 1860 at Fort Vancouver, Washington Territory. He became the longest lived graduate. He attended public schools prior to entering USMA. He received his appointment from his father's very good friend, Ulysses S. Grant, who had served with him in the Fourth Infantry in Oregon before Henry was born. At USMA in West Point, he was second youngest in his class, and went by the nickname "Cap." He graduated number twenty-

Henry Clay Hodges, Jr.

three of fifty-three in the class of 1881. Joseph T. Dickman, Harry F. Hodges, Edward St. John Greble and Andrew S. Rowan (all *q.v.*) were four of his classmates. He was commissioned, to the 22d Infantry and first served at Fort Clark, Texas, on the Rio Grande River. There he helped to round up Comanches who had jumped their reservation near the Pecos River. He continued performing frontier duty, and was aide to General Augur in 1884 and 1885. In 1886, he was sent to USMA as assistant professor of mathematics. On 24 December 1891, he married Netta Haines in Poughkeepsie, New York, daughter of Thomas Jefferson Haines, USMA, class of 1849. They had three children Evelyn of Stamford, Connecticut, Mrs. James L. Crenshaw of Bryn Mawr, Pennsylvania and a son, Parke, of New York City. He returned briefly to frontier duty at Fort Keough, Montana, then was assigned as an instructor at the Groton School in Massachusetts, after which he was Professor of Military Science and Tactics at what is now the University of New Hampshire. In 1896, he returned to Fort Crook, Nebraska, but was soon sent to the Philippines and participated in eleven battles during the Moro insurrection. From there he went to Boston, Newport and back to the Philippines. He was Secretary of the General Staff from 11 June 1913 to 31 August 1914, then was sent to the 17h Infantry in EaGle Pass, Texas, to help suppress Mexican raids across the border. He was promoted to major general (NA) on 5 August 1917, and was commanding general, 39th (AEF). When he left Camp Beauregarde with the 39th Division, the citizens of Alexandria, Louisiana presented him with a chest of 200 pieces of silver engraved with his name. After the war, he was again sent to Camp Beauregarde, and commanded the 17th Infantry Division until it was deactivated. He reverted to the rank of brigadier general and was sent to Hawaii. Mrs. Hodges died in 1919. With over forty years of service, he retired on 1 December 1920. In retirement he lived in Connecticut. On 27 December 1920 he married Carrie Jones and they lived in Norton, Connecticut. After her death in 1949, he lived in Stamford with his older daughter. The Corps of Cadets was his principal interest. At the age of 103, he died in Stamford, on 15 July 1963. Photo from *The Assembly*, Association of Graduates, USMA.

John Neal Hodges

John Neal Hodges (0-2029) was born on 13 February 1884 in Baltimore, Maryland. He entered USMA and graduated number thirteen of one hundred fourteen in the class of 1905.This may have been the last graduating class to include World War I general officers in its ranks. He was commissioned in the Corps of Engineers, and during World War I, he commanded the Sixth Engineer Regiment, serving with the British and constructing heavy bridges on the Somme River. For this he received the Distinguished Service Medal, and he was promoted to brigadier general (NA) on 26 June 1918. After the war, he served in the office of the Chief of Engineers in

Washington. From 1929 to 1931, the was editor of the *Military Engineer*. He received a Legion of Merit for World War II service, and from 1943 to 1944, was Chief Engineer of the North Atlantic Division. He retired in 1944, and died at the age of eighty-one, in Brooks Army Hospital, on 18 January 1965. The photo, from National Archives, was taken in France.

Roy Hoffman

Roy Hoffman (ASN unknown), son of Peter Hoffman and Julia Hakins Hoffman, was born on 13 June 1869 in Neosho County, Kansas. He was a newspaper man, an attorney, a judge and a banker, as well as a soldier. After completing his education at the Kansas State Normal School at Fort Scott, he founded the Guthrie, Oklahoma *Daily Leader* in 1889. The same year, he married Estelle Conklin, and they had four children Dorothy, Margaret, Roy and Edgar. From 1903 to 1907, he was the United States Attorney for Oklahoma. From 1908 to 1912, he was judge of the Tenth District of Oklahoma. Volunteering for service as a private at the time of the Spanish-American War, he was soon made a captain of Company K, First Oklahoma Volunteer Infantry, and was colonel of the regiment from 1901 to 1916, serving in part on the Mexican border. On 5 August 1917, he was made a brigadier general (NA) and commanded Fort Sill, Oklahoma. Later he commanded the 61st Depot Brigade at Camp Bowie, Texas, and helped to organize the 36th Infantry Division. On 3 December 1917, he organized and commanded the 93d (Colored) Infantry Division in Newport News, Virginia, and was in continuous front line service under the French, until the division was attached to the First U.S. Infantry Division at Cantigny. (Racially integrated units did not exist until mid-World War II). His last active command was at Camp Shelby in Mississippi, where he was honorably discharged from the National Army in March 1919. He was recomissioned a brigadier general in the Organized Reserve the next year, and later retired as commanding general, 45th Infantry Division (Oklahoma National Guard). He was decorated by many foreign governments. He was made a Commander of the Legion of Honor (France) and a Commander of the Order of the Crown (Belgium, Italy and Roumania), and was given the Distinguished Service Medal from both the United States and the State of Oklahoma. In retirement he lived in Oklahoma City, where at the age of eighty-four he died, on 18 June 1953. Photo courtesy of the National Archives.

Lucius Roy Holbrook

Lucius Roy Holbrook (0-352), son of Willard Francis Holbrook and Mary Ames Holbrook, was born on 30 April 1875 in Arkansaw, Wisconsin. He was younger brother of Willard Holbrook (*q.v.*). After attending public schools he entered USMA and graduated number thirty-five of seventy-three in the class of 1896. Edward L. King and Dennis E. Nolan (both *q.v.*) were two of his classmates. After being commissioned, he was sent to the Fourth Cavalry at Boise Barracks, Idaho, until 1898. On 7 June 1899, he married Henrietta Coffin, and they had three sons Frank, John and Lucius Roy Holbrook, Jr. He was in the Philippines from 1899 to 1903, and won a Silver Star Commendation there. He was on the China Relief Expedition before returning to the States. In 1905, he was a distinguished graduate of the Infantry and Cavalry School at Fort Leavenworth. In 1906, he graduated from the Staff College. From 1907 to 1911, he organized and operated the Cooks and Bakers School at Fort Riley, Kansas, where he developed new army field baking and cooking equipment. From 1911 to 1913, he attended a French school of supply in Paris. On 15 July 1917, he returned to France as a lieutenant colonel with the First Field Artillery Brigade, and on 18 August 1918, he was made a brigadier general (NA). Commanding the First, then the 54th Field Artillery Brigade won him both the Distinguished Service Medal and another Silver Star. Returning from France in May 1919, he became senior artillery instructor at the Command and General Staff School at Fort Leavenworth, Kansas, until 1920. He then served with the General Staff, and in 1925, he served with the Inspector General's Department. During 1925 and 1926, he commanded Fort Douglas, Utah, a very beautiful post just uphill from Salt Lake City. From 1926 to 1929, he commanded Fort Stotsenberg in the Philippines, after which he commanded Fort Bragg, North Carolina. From 1936 to 1939, he commanded the First Infantry Division, and in 1933, he received his second-star promotion to major general (USA). Next he commanded the Philippine Department and troops in China from 1936 to 1938, and on 31 January 1939, he retired due to disabilities. In addition to the decorations previously mentioned, he received the Croix de Guerre, was made an Officer of the Legion of Honor (France), and he was given the Silver Medal for Bravery and Cross of Prince Danilo of Montenegro. At the age of seventy-seven, he died in Letterman General Hospital, on 19 October 1952. Photo courtesy of Mrs. Marjorie Holbrook Johnston.

Willard Ames Holbrook (0-24), son of Willard F. Holbrook and Mary Ames Holbrook, was born on 23 July 1860 in Arkansaw, Wisconsin. He entered

USMA and graduated number seventeen of thirty-nine in the class of 1885. He was sent to the First Cavalry as soon as he was commissioned, and performed frontier duty from 1885 to 1891. He participated in both the Crow Indian War of 1887 and the Sioux Campaign of 1890 to 1891. Being an honor graduate of the Infantry and Cavalry School at Fort Leavenworth, Kansas, he was appointed aide to Gen. D. S. Stanley, his future father-in-law. From 1892 to 1896, he was a tactical officer at USMA. He also served as a second lieutenant in the Seventh Cavalry in 1891. During the Spanish-American War, he was a captain, assistant Adjutant General of volunteers and later, in Cuba, acting quartermaster. As of 17 August 1899, he was a major, 38th U.S. Volunteer Infantry in the Philippines, helping to subdue the insurrection. In 1901 he became involved in the civil government of one of the Philippine provinces. After discharge from the Volunteer Service, he became a captain (USA) in the Fifth Cavalry. From 1905 to 1909, he was on duty at the Pennsylvania Military Academy in Chester, Pennsylvania. On 6 October 1909, he married Josephine Stanley, daughter of General D. S. Stanley, commanding general of the 1874 Black Hills Expedition. On 3 March 1911, he became a major, Eighth Cavalry, and during that period performed brief service as a quartermaster. In 1912, he was director of the Army Staff College and School of the Line at Fort Leavenworth, Kansas, and also commanded a squadron of regular cavalry at the beginning of the coal miner's strike in Trinidad, Colorado. On 5 August 1917, he was made a brigadier general (NA) and commanded the 165th Infantry Brigade at Camp Sherman, Ohio. On 16 April 1918, he received his promotion to major general (NA) and was sent to command the Southern Department. He was in charge of the Mexican border from 3 May to 26 September 1918, after which he commanded the Ninth Infantry Division at Camp Sheridan, Alabama until its demobilization in February 1919. He commanded the Camp Grant Demobilization Center from February until May 1919. He went to Europe, then served as Chief of Staff of the Southern Department. He became the first Chief of Cavalry with the establishment of that office on 1 July 1920, as a major general. He was a large well built man with a very distinguished and impressive appearance. He retired on 23 July 1924, and died five days short of his seventy-second birthday, on 18 July 1932. Photo from the Association of Graduates, USMA.

Willard Ames Holbrook

Tiemann Newell Horn (0-225), son of Daniel Heman Horn and Frances Capron Horn, was born on 18 January 1868 in Brooklyn, New York. He entered USMA and graduated number nine of sixty-five in the class of 1891. He

Tiemann Newell Horn

was commissioned in the Third Cavalry, transferred to the Second Artillery. On 28 November 1894, he married Myra Rivers. In 1903, he graduated from the School of Submarine Defense. He was district ordnance officer and artillery engineer for the Southern Artillery District of New York from 1903 to 1906. He served in the Jamestown Exposition in 1907. He was an honor graduate of the Army School of the Line in 1911, and graduated from the Army Staff College in 1912. From 1913 to 1915, he was in the Philippines, and from 1915 to 1918, he was in Hawaii. He was made a brigadier general (NA) on 6 February 1918, and commanded the Seventh Field Artillery Brigade (AEF), part of the Seventh Infantry Division, during World War I. From 17 February 1918 to 21 June 1918, he commanded the Seventh Infantry Division. He was an Episcopalian and a Mason, and made his retirement home in Plainfield, New Jersey. At the age of fifty-five, he died in Hawaii, On 5 May 1923, as a colonel. His rank of brigadier general was restored posthumously. Photo from the National Archives.

James Joseph Hornbrook (0-294), son of Mr. and Mrs. Richard Saunders Hornbrook, was born in Evansville, Indiana in 1868. His father had been a captain in the 65th Indiana Volunteer Infantry during the Civil War. After attending Evansville public schools and a private German language school, he entered USMA and graduated number thirty-three of fifty-four in the class of 1890. Edgar Jadwin, James A. Ryan and Fred W. Sladen (all *q.v.*) were three of his classmates. He was commissioned and sent to the Second Cavalry at Fort Bowie, Arizona Territory, and continued frontier duty at Forts Huachuca, McIntosh, and Wingate (New Mexico) until the Spanish-American War. In 1898, he was stationed in Tampa and Huntsville, Alabama, principally fighting typhoid and malaria. He married Mary Worth Shanno, daughter of Gen. James J. Shanno, a Civil War veteran and old Indian fighter. They were happy to be sent to Puerto Rico. He graduated from the Infantry and Cavalry School at Fort Leavenworth, Kansas and the Army War College. Between the Spanish-American War and the World War I, he had two tours of

James Joseph Hornbrook

duty in the Philippines and served at Fort Oglethorpe, Omaha and Fort Des Moines. In 1916 and 1917, he was in Mexico with the Punitive Expedition. At Camp Greene, North Carolina, he organized and trained the Fourth Infantry Division and took it to France. On 16 June 1918, he was promoted to brigadier general (NA) and was returned to the States, where he commanded the important El Paso (Texas) District. Here he handled a difficult international situation with great discretion and tact. After the war, when he reverted to the rank of colonel, he commanded the Fifth Cavalry and the Big Bend District in Texas until 1921, when he was detailed to the Army War College. After graduating and until his retirement, his duty was primarily with the Organized Reserve. With forty-three years of service, he retired at his own request on 2 September 1929, and lived for a year in Palo Alto, California. His family then moved to Hollywood, where he spent the remainder of his days. At age seventy-four, he died in his home, on 1 October 1942. Photo from *The Assembly*, Associaton of Graduates, USMA.

Odus Creamer Horney

Odus Creamer Horney (0-434), son of James W. Horney and Josephine Creamer Horney, was born on 18 September 1866 in Lexington, Illinois. He entered USMA and graduated number six of sixty-five in the class of 1891. Andrew Hero, Jr. James W. Furlong, William J. Glasgow and John L. Hines (all *q.v.*) were four of his classmates. He was commissioned in the infantry, and within a month he married Rezia Bryan, on 29 July 1891. They had four children Ruth, Grace, Esther and Odus C. Horney, Jr. He stayed in the infantry until 1894, when he transferred to ordnance, in which branch he stayed until his retirement in 1930. He designed and developed the M-1903 U.S. rifle, caliber thirty (the Springfield, as it was commonly called), and pioneered the sixteen-inch rifle in the United States. He built and operated the first USA smokeless-powder plant. He resigned in 1916 as a lieutenant colonel, but he was soon back on duty for World War I, and in August 1918, he was made a brigadier general (NA). In 1919, he was reappointed lieutenant colonel (USA), and was ordnance officer of the Philippine Department from 1927 to 1929. In 1930, he retired as a brigadier general and lived in San Mateo, California. At the age of eighty-nine, he died at the Presidio of San Francisco California, on 16 February 1957. Photo from the Association of Graduates, USMA.

Harold Palmer Howard

Harold Palmer Howard (0-13442), son of John Reed Palmer Howard, an officer veteran of the Civil War, was born on 24 November 1866 in Sauk Center, Minnesota. He entered USMA and graduated number twenty-three of sixty-five in the class of 1891. William J. Glasgow, John L. Hines, Andrew Hero, Jr. and Odus C. Horney (all *q.v.*) were four of his classmates. After graduating, he was commissioned, sent to the Sixth Cavalry, and performed frontier duty until the onset of the Spanish-American War. He married Jessie Angst, and they had two sons and two daughters, all of whom survived him. During the Spanish-American War and the Philippine insurrection, he was an aide to General S. B. M. Young, and he received two Silver Star Citations. He was a regimental quartermaster, had two details with the Quartermaster Corps, was an instructor in philosophy at USMA and had charge of the observatory there as well. During the First World War I, he commanded the 82d Field Artillery Regiment until he was promoted to brigadier general on 1 October 1918, when he was given command of the 17th Field Artillery Brigade. He later graduated from the Command and General Staff School, Fort Leavenworth, Kansas. A classmate commented in his obituary notice "Both as a cadet and as an officer he was marked by great calmness, dignity and sedateness. I do not know of anyone who ever saw him exhibit anger, excitement or haste. He possessed a quiet, unruffled serenity which enabled him to master his studies and discharge his responsibilities with assured efficiency and without the explosiveness sometimes exhibited by others." His judgment and common sense were of the best. He loved the outdoors, hunting, travel, riding, fishing, boating and visiting unusual places. He searched for wildflowers, gardened, studied the Sioux and Chippewa dialects and became quite proficient in them. He retired as a colonel in 1920, but his rank of brigadier general was restored by act of Congress in June 1930. He was the Professor of Military Science and Tactics at St. Thomas College in St. Paul, Minnesota from 1921 to 1923, and later worked with the Federal Reserve Bank in Minneapolis. At the age of eighty-four, he died in Minneapolis, on 1 March 1951, survived by his widow and four children. Photo from *The Assembly*, Association of Graduates, USMA.

Robert Lee Howze (0-77), son of James Augustus Howze and Amanda Hamilton Brown Howze, was born on 22 August 1864 in Rusk County, southeast of Tyler, Texas. After graduating from Hubbard College in Texas with an A.B. in 1883, he entered USMA and graduated number twenty-three of forty-four in the class of 1888. Peyton C. March and Guy Henry Preston (both *q.v.*) were two

Robert Lee Howze

of his classmates. After graduating, he was commissioned, sent to the Sixth Cavalry, and performed frontier duty until 1891. He won a Medal of Honor for his service during the Sioux Indian Uprising. On 24 February 1897 he married Anne Chiffele Hawkins, daughter of Hamilton Hawkins (USA). They had three children Harriot Howze, Robert L. Howze and Hamilton Hawkins Howze. During the Spanish-American War he served as a major in the Puerto Rican Provisional Infantry Regiment. During the Philippine insurrection, he commanded a detachment of the 34th Volunteer Infantry in the rescue of Lieutenant Commander Gilmore (USN) and other American prisoners of the insurgents. From 1905 to 1909, he was Commandant of Cadets with the temporary rank of lieutenant colonel. Next he commanded the Puerto Rican Regiment and Military District of Puerto Rico. He was promoted to a major in the Fourth Cavalry in 1911, and in December of that year, he was transferred to the 11th Cavalry, commanding one of their squadrons and entering Mexico with General Pershing in 1916. He was detailed to the General Staff, and on 15 May 1917, he was made a colonel of cavalry and Chief of Staff of the very short-lived Tenth Provisional Cavalry Division. He was again transferred to the Northeastern Department as Chief of Staff, and in December 1917, he was made a brigadier general (NA). His command was the Second Cavalry Brigade at Fort Bliss, Texas. On 8 August 1918, he was promoted to major general (NA) commanding the 38th Infantry Division serving in France. He commanded the Third Infantry Division on the Meuse, marched to the Rhine and was with the American Forces in Germany until 14 August 1919. He brought the Third Division back to the United States, then commanded the District of El Paso and the First Cavalry Division. In December 1922, he was promoted to major general (USA). In addition to the decorations mentioned above, he was awarded the Distinguished Service Medal and the Croix de Guerre with palm, and was made an Officer of the Legion of Honor. Although his home was in Washington, D.C., he died in Ohio at the age of 62, on 19 December 1926. Photo from the National Archives.

John Augustus Hulen (0-204374), son of Harvey Hulen and Fanny Morter Hulen, was born in Centralia, Missouri. He graduated from Marmaduke Military Academy in Sweet Springs, Missouri in 1891. On 14 February 1903, he married Frankie L. Rice. He worked in the real estate and insurance business in Gainesville, Texas from 1891 to 1898. He became a lieutenant in the Texas National Guard and advanced through all grades to lieutenant general, and retired, by 1935. He served during the Philippine Insurrection from 1898 to 1901, and was awarded a Silver Star Citation. He was twice recommended for a brevet promotion to major, and also to receive the Medal of Honor. During 1907 and 1908, he was city passenger agent for the Frisco railway lines in Houston, Texas. Later, he was general agent for both the Frisco and Rock Island lines. He was appointed general freight and passenger agent for the Trinity and Brazos Valley Railroad Company in 1910. At the time of the Mexican Punitive Expedition, he was commanding general, Sixth Separate Brigade, on the Texas-Mexico border. On 5 August 1917, he became a brigadier general (NA), and he commanded the 36th Infantry Division from 8 to 13 July 1918, for which he received the Distinguished Service Medal. He also received the Croix de Guerre from France. On 1 May 1919, he reverted to his permanent rank of colonel in the Texas National Guard. By 2 May 1923, he was commanding general, 36th Infantry Division (Texas National Guard). After the war, he became president and Receiver of the Trinity and Brazos Valley Railroad, and President of the Galveston Terminal Railway Company. He was appointed traffic manager of the Fort Worth and Denver City Railway Company and of the Wichita Valley Railway Company in 1920, and was vice president of both until 1942. He retired in 1941 and lived in Palacios, Texas. He died 13 September 1957. Photo from the Texas State Library, Archives Division.

John Augustus Hulen

Ora Elmer Hunt (0-450), son of Frank Martin Hunt and Mary E. Southard Hunt, was born on 26 June 1872 near Napa, California. He entered USMA and graduated number twenty-nine of fifty-four in the class of 1894. He was commissioned in the infantry and was assigned to Vancouver Barracks, Washington. Paul B. Malone and Hamilton Hawkins (both *q.v.*) were two of his classmates. On 1 January 1896, he married Eva B. Smith, and they had three children Ora L. Hunt; Edna V. Hunt (Mrs. Colin T. Penn) and Margaret Hunt (Mrs. M. H. Pringle). In 1898, he left Vancouver Barracks for the Philippines, and took part in the suppression of the Insurrection. Following this, he had a long tour of duty in West Point. He was a distinguished graduate of the Infantry and Cavalry

Ora Elmer Hunt

School at Fort Leavenworth, Kansas in 1906, and also graduated from the Army Staff College in 1907. From 1908 to 1910, he was an instructor in English, history and modern languages at USMA. From 1912 to 1914, he was with troops in Texas City, Texas, then went back to USMA as associate professor of modern languages until 1917. In 1917, he was the first senior instructor in infantry tactics at the Officers Training Camp at Fort Myer, Virginia. As a colonel, he commanded the 320th Infantry, 80th Division at Camp Lee, Virginia. until his promotion to brigadier general (NA) on 12 April 1918. His next command was the 165th Infantry Brigade, 83d Division, and he also commanded the Sixth Infantry Brigade, Third Division (AEF) during the St. Mihiel and Meuse-Argonne battles, for which he received the Distinguished Service Medal and the Silver Star. For a while he stayed with the American Forces in Germany, and was then sent to command the Third Division at Pike, Arkansas in 1919. The last four years of his service was with the Inspector General's Department. In 1923, he retired as a colonel. He and his wife were divorced 18 August 1927. In 1928, he was a member of the U.S. mission to Nicaragua, supervising presidential elections. In addition to the decorations previously mentioned, he received the Marine Corps Medal for service in the second Nicaraguan campaign. On 16 March 1929, he married Josephine W. Guion, and they had one daughter, Katherine Guion Hunt. He was a Presbyterian and a Republican. He belonged to the West Point Alumni Association, and served as editor of volume five of the *Photographic History of the Civil War* published in 1911. In retirement his family lived in Berkeley, California, where at the age of ninety-seven he died, on 20 August 1969. Photo from *The Assembly*, Association of Graduates, USMA.

George Ring Hunter (0-13334), son of Henry B. Hunter and Josephine Ring Hunter, was born on 6 April 1855 in Lancaster, Ohio. He entered USMA and graduated number sixty-seven of seventy-six in the class of 1877. William M. Black, A. P. Blocksom and Thomas H. Barry (all *q.v.*) were three of his classmates. He was commissioned and sent to the Fourth Cavalry, performing frontier duty from 1877 to 1894. He participated in many Indian campaigns. On 17 December 1878, he married Mary E. Hinman. During the Spanish-American War, he was wounded at San Juan Hill. From Cuba he was sent to the Philippines until 1903, to help suppress the Insurrection. He was in the Philippines again from 1911 to 1914. He was promoted to brigadier general (NA) on 5 August 1917, and he served at Camp Funston, Kansas, just east of Fort Riley. He retired on 1 February 1918, and was immediately returned to duty as

George Ring Hunter

commander of Jefferson Barracks, southwest of St. Louis, Missouri, from 22 February 1918 until 28 July 1919, when he again retired, as a colonel. His rank as brigadier general was restored by act of Congress in June 1930, while he was on the retired list. He was an Episcopalian, and his family's home was in Cleveland, Ohio. He died at the age of eighty-four at the Fifth Avenue Hotel in New York City. He was survived by his wife and children Russell H. Hunter, Col. George B. Hunter, Mrs. Robert Sterett and Mrs. Fredrick D. Griffith, Jr. Photo courtesy of the USMA Library.

Grote Hutcheson

Grote Hutcheson (0-72), son of Ebenezer E. Hutcheson and Therese Turpin Hutcheson, was born on 1 April 1862 in Cincinnati, Ohio. He entered USMA and graduated number twenty-five of thirty-seven in the class of 1884. William Seibert (Panama Canal) and Isaac Newton Lewis (Inventor of the Lewis machine gun) were two of his class mates. He was commissioned was sent to the Ninth Cavalry, performed frontier duty in Oklahoma, and also took part in the Sioux Indian Campaign of 1890 to 1891. In 1894, he performed railway strike duty, and he fought against the Bannock Indians in 1885. He was Adjutant General of the Puerto Rican Expedition of 1898, for which he received a Silver Star. He was both adjutant and judge advocate general of the Department of the Missouri River from 1899 to 1900. On 16 January 1900, he married Rosalie St. George. He also participated in the China Relief Expedition that year, for which he received two more Silver Star Commendations. During 1901 and 1902, he was secretary to the military governor of the Philippines. From 1903 to 1904, he was Judge Advocate, Department of the East, on Governor's Island, New York. From 1904 to 1908, he was on the General Staff, serving in the office of the Chief of Staff. In 1905, he was a member of a special mission to witness the French Army Maneuvers. Three times he served in the Philippines from 1901 to 1902, from 1908 to 1910 and from 1915 to 1916. He was on the Mexican border, from 1911 to 1912 and from 1916 to 1917. He created, organized and commanded the Port of Embarkation in Newport News and Norfolk between 1917 and 1918, for which he was awarded both the Army and Navy Distinguished Service Medals. He was promoted to major general (NA) on 8 August 1918. At Camp Custer, Michigan he commanded the Fourteenth Infantry Division and took it to Camp Meade, Maryland. He was promoted to brigadier general (USA) in 1920, and he commanded the New York General Intermediate Depot, reducing war activities and supplies in the New York area, from 1921 to 1923. He was then sent to command the Eleventh Field Artillery Brigade at Schofield Barracks, Hawaii. In

1924, he retired due to disabilities, as a major general. In retirement he lived in Saratoga, California. He was a member of the Order of the Dragon, the Order of the Carabao, the VFW, the Army and Navy Club in Washington and the Union League Club in San Francisco. He was an Episcopalian. At the age of eighty-six he died, on 14 December 1948. He was buried in Arlington National Cemetery. Photo from *The Assembly*, Association of Graduates, USMA.

Henry Hutchings

Henry Hutchings (0-204354) was born on 17 August 1865 in Somersetshire, England and came to the states with his parents the following year. They moved to Iowa, and in 1882 he joined the Iowa National Guard. Soon afterwards they moved to Texas, and in 1885, he joined the Texas National Guard. He married Whittie Brown in 1886, and they had four boys and three girls. In 1890, he founded and published the *Austin Evening News*, and for a time he also published the *Austin Statesman*. He was the Adjutant General of Texas from 23 January 1911 to 28 September 1917. His promotion to brigadier general (NA) was on 5 August 1917. He resigned as Adjutant General to organize and command the 71st Infantry Brigade, which he commanded in France with the AEF. In 1923, he became the Texas Secretary of State under Governor Patrick M. Neff, and on 18 January 1933, he again became the Texas Adjutant General, until 14 January 1935. He had forty-two years of military service to Texas and the United States. On 9 March 1935, he married Hallie White of Dallas. An Episcopalian, he was vestryman of St. David's Church in Austin for twenty years. At the age of seventy-three, he died in his home in Austin, survived by his widow and six of his children. One of his sons, Henry Hutchings, Jr., became an officer in the Corps of Engineers. Photo courtesy of the Texas State Library, Archives Division.

Merritte Weber Ireland, M.D. (0-15), son of Martin Ireland and Sarah Ireland, was born 31 May 1867 in Columbia City, Indiana. He was given his degree from the Detroit College of Medicine in 1890. He was appointed an assistant surgeon (USA) in 1901. On 8 November 1893, he married Elizabeth Liggetton and they had one son, Paul Miller Ireland. In 1896, he was promoted to captain, assistant surgeon. During the Spanish-American War, he was in the Santiago Campaign in Cuba, and also in the Philippines. He was made a major surgeon, with the 45th U.S. Volunteer Infantry in 1899, and was honorably dis-

Merritte Weber Ireland, M.D.

charged from the U.S. Volunteers in 1901. In 1903, he was commissioned a major surgeon, Medical Corps (USA). He was made a lieutenant colonel, Medical Corps on 1 May 1911, and a colonel on 15 May 1917. He was Chief Surgeon of the American Expeditionary Force until 12 October 1918, for which he received the Distinguished Service Medal. On 16 May 1918, he was promoted to brigadier general (NA), and in August he was detailed as Assistant Surgeon General (USA) with the rank of major general (NA). From 4 October 1918 to 31 May 1931, he was Surgeon General (USA), which was his last assignment before he retired. Jefferson Medical College in Philadelphia gave him an honorary LL.D. award in 1919, the University of Michigan gave him an A.M. in 1920, Gettysburg College awarded him another LL.D. in 1922 and Wayne University gave him his third LL.D. in 1939. He belonged to both the Army and Navy Club in Washington, and the Army and Navy Country Club. He was a Lutheran. He died 5 July 1952. The Army General Hospital at Fort Riley, Kansas, is named in his honor. Photo courtesy of the National Archives.

James Anderson Irons (no ASN assigned), son of James R. Irons and Sarah Anderson Irons, was born on 21 February 1857 in Philadelphia, Pennsylvania. After graduating from Central High School in 1875, he entered USMA in West Point and graduated number forty-nine of sixty-seven in the class of 1879. Hunter Liggett and Fredrick S. Foltz (both *q.v.*) were two of his classmates. Commissioned a second lieutenant, he was assigned to the 20th Infantry, Fort Brown, Texas, and performed frontier duty from 1879 to 1883. He graduated from the Infantry and Cavalry School at Fort Leavenworth, Kansas in 1885, then went back to frontier duty until 1887. He served with the 16th, 14th, 20th, 2nd and 49th Infantry Regiments. In 1887, he was promoted to first lieutenant. On 7 June 1888, he married Florence Farrell. During the Spanish-American War he was in El Caney, San Juan Hill and the Siege of Santiago. In 1899, he sailed with his regiment to the Philippines. From 1901 to 1903, he was Inspector General of the Department of Colorado. From 1903 to 1905, he served on the General Staff. He

James Anderson Irons

served as military attache in Tokyo from 1907 to 1910. From 1914 to 1917, he went on a tour of duty in China and returned to Tokyo. He was an observer the Japanese Army at the siege and capture of Tsingtao from the Germans in 1914, and was military attache to the Imperial Japanese War Mission (under Viscount Ishii) which came to the United States in 1917. He was promoted to brigadier general (NA) on 5 August 1917, and he commanded the 166th Depot Brigade at Camp Lewis, Washington, in September 1917. In February and March 1918, he commanded the Third Infantry Division. He retired as a colonel in 1920. At the age of sixty-four he died in Sant Agnello di Sorrento, Italy, on 20 July 1921. He was cited posthumously for excellent performance of duty in the Sanitary Corps in Cuba and for action during the Philippine Insurrection. He was a gentleman of great character and very high standards, and a fine officer, very highly regarded by all. Photo courtesy of Special Collections, USMA Library.

George LeRoy Irwin

George LeRoy Irwin (0-173), son of Brigadier General Bernard John Dowling Irwin, was born on 26 August 1868 at Fort Wayne, Michigan. He entered USMA and graduated number twenty-four of forty-nine of the class of 1889. William G. Haan, E. E. Winslow, William Lassiter and Charles D. Rhodes (all *q.v.*) were four of his classmates. He was assigned to the Fifth Artillery. On 30 April 1892, he married Elizabeth Barker. In 1894, he was sent to the Coast Artillery School, and in 1910, he went to the Army War College. He served in the Philippines from 1899 to 1901, in Cuba from 1906 to 1909 and later, in the Panama Canal Zone. He was promoted to brigadier general (NA) on 5 August 1917, and he commanded the 57th Field Artillery Brigade (AEF), for which he was awarded the Distinguished Service Medal. From 12 December 1917, he commanded the 41st Infantry Division. From November 1918 to February 1919, he commanded the Saumur Artillery School. He served at Verdun, Alsace and Aisne-Marne, and returned to the United States in May 1919. He was commandant of the Artillery School at Fort Sill, Oklahoma. In addition to the Distinguished Service Medal, he was made a member of the Legion of Honor (France). He was promoted to major general (USA) in 1928. He died at the age of sixty-two, in Trinidad, British West Indies, on 19 February 1931. Photo from Special Collections, USMA Library.

William Payne Jackson (0-341), son of William James Jackson and Russelle Clagett Jackson, was born on 9 January 1868 in Palmyra, northwest of

Hannibal, Missouri. He entered USMA and graduated number forty-four of sixty-five in the class of 1891. William J. Glasgow, John L. Hines, Andrew Hero, Jr. and Odus C. Horney (all *q.v.*) were four of his classmates. He was commissioned and sent to the 24th Infantry and performed frontier duty until 1892, after which he spent two years on the International Boundary Commission in Arizona. In 1895, he went to an electrical and mining school in Willet's Point, New York, after which he returned west to his unit. During the Spanish-American War, he was an aide to Gen. Jacob F. Kent, commanding general of the First Division. He served in the Sanitary Corps and received a Silver Star Commendation. In the Philippines, from 1899 on, he was a battalion adjutant in the 20th Infantry, for which he received another Silver Star Commendation. From 1902 to 1904, he was with the Third Infantry at Fort Thomas, Kentucky, serving as quartermaster. During this period, on 20 October 1903, he married Julia Crosby Carr, and they had one daughter, Margaret (Mrs. Eugene V. Slattery). Next he spent three years in Alaska, after which he returned to the Philippines and served in the 1911 Moro Expedition. From 1913 to 1917, he was in the office of the Inspector General in Washington. He organized and trained the 368th Infantry Regiment and took it to France. On 26 June 1918, he was promoted to brigadier general (NA) and commanded the 74th Infantry Brigade (part of the 37th Division). For his performance of this duty he received the Distinguished Service Medal. He had participated in the Meuse-Argonne, Ypres-Lys and St. Mihiel battles. When he returned to the States, he reverted to his permanent rank of colonel and attended the General Staff College at Fort Leavenworth, Kansas, after which he went back to the Inspector General's office until 1926. He commanded the First Citizen's Military Training Camp in 1921. From 1926 to 1929, he commanded the First Coast Artillery District in Boston, and then the Second Infantry Brigade, which was his terminal assignment. He also commanded the 90th Infantry Division (Organized Reserve). In addition to the decorations previously mentioned, he received the (Belgium) Croix de Guerre, was made an Officer of the Legion of Honor (France) and was given a Meritorious Military Service Medal from the State of Missouri. He was a Democrat, and also a golfer. Shortly after his Seventy-seventh birthday, he died in San Francisco, on 13 January 1945. Photo from the National Archives.

William Payne Jackson

Edgar Jadwin (0-330) was born on 7 August 1865 in Honesdale, Pennsylvania. He first studied at Lafayette College, then went on to USMA, from which he graduated number one of fifty-four in the class of 1890. Herbert

Edgar Jadwin

Deakyne, Henry Davis Todd, Jr. and Fred W. Sladen were three of his classmates. He was commissioned in the Corps of Engineers and was an assistant in government engineering from 1890 to 1891. By 1898, he was a lieutenant colonel of the Third U.S. Volunteer Engineers, and commanded a battalion of this regiment in the sanitation of Matanzas, Cuba. He became a captain, Corps of Engineers (USA) in 1900. He was in the Canal Zone from 1907 to 1911, and on 17 December 1917, he was promoted to brigadier general (NA) and performed various construction projects in the AEF, for which he received the Distinguished Service Medal. In 1924, he was made brigadier general (USA). From 27 June 1926 to 7 August 1929, he was the Chief of Engineers as a major general. He died at the age of sixty-five, in Panama, on 2 March 1931. Photo courtesy of the U.S. Army Military History Institute, Carlisle Barracks, Pennsylvania.

George Hairston Jamerson

George Hairston Jamerson (0-432), son of Thomas J. Jamerson and Louisa Salmons Jamerson, was born on 8 November 1869 in Martinsville, Virginia. He was a student at both the Ruffner Institute in Martinsville from 1882 to 1887 and at the Virginia A and M College in Blacksburg from 1888 to 1889. He entered USMA and graduated number forty-five of fifty-one in the class of 1893. Gordon G. Heiner, Lincoln C. Andrews, Howard Laubach (all *q.v.*) and Herbert B. Crosby were four of his classmates. He was commissioned in the infantry. On 20 October 1897, he married Elsie T. Barbour, and they had one son, Osmund T. Jamerson. During the Spanish-American War, he served in both Cuba and the Philippines, for which he received two Silver Star Commendations. From 1906 to 1909, he was Professor of Military Science and Tactics at the Virginia Polytechnic Institute, and in 1916 to 1917, he was on the Mexican border. On 12 April 1918, he was promoted to brigadier general (NA) and commanded the 159th Infantry Brigade of the 80th Infantry Division (AEF), for which he received the Distinguished Service Medal. In addition to the decorations already mentioned, he was given the World War I Victory Medal with four clasps, the Spanish-American War Medal, the Cuban Occupation Medal, the Philippine Insurrection Medal and the Mexican Border Medal. He graduated from the Army War College both in 1910 and in 1922. He was a Presbyterian. In retirement, he lived in Richmond, Virginia. There, at the age of ninety, he died, on 31 August 1960. Photo courtesy of the U.S. Army Military History Institute, Carlisle Barracks, Pennsylvania.

Charles Clark Jamieson

Charles Clark Jamieson (0-13823), son of William S. Jamieson of Stewartstown, New Hampshire and Isabella McDowell Jamieson of Scotland, was born on 3 November 1866 in Glover, Vermont. He entered USMA and graduated number fourteen of sixty-two in the class of 1892. Charles P. Sumerall, later Chief of Staff (USA), was one of his classmates. He was commissioned and was sent to the 15th Infantry, and was on duty at Fort Sheridan, north of Chicago, from 1892 to 1895. While there, on 12 June 1894, he married Frances P. Floyd, and they had two children Floyd M. Jamieson and Eleanor Jamieson. In 1895, he was promoted to first lieutenant, ordnance, and from 1897 to 1900, he was on duty at Sandy Hook Proving Ground. From 1900 to 1903, he was an instructor at USMA, after which he was sent to Rock Island Arsenal where he stayed until 1905. By 25 June 1906, he was a major of ordnance, and until 1910, he served at Watervliet Arsenal on the Hudson River, near West Point. On 12 October 1910, he was retired due to disabilities incurred in the line of duty. In civilian life, he worked as an engineer. He was recalled to active duty for World War I in 1917, and was promoted to colonel (NA) on 11 January 1918. On 1 October 1918, he was promoted to brigadier general (NA), and was assistant to the chief of production and special assistant to the Chief of Ordnance until December 1918, when he was made director of sales of War Department property acquired for World War I. On 3 January 1919, at his own request, he again retired. He was vice president of the George W. Goethals (Engineering) Company. He was both a consulting engineer and president of an engineering company in Jacksonville, Florida. His wife died on 24 July 1924, and he married Anne Uezzel on 12 July 1930. He was a Presbyterian, and lived in retirement in Ocala, Florida. There, at the age of sixty-eight, he died, on 21 August 1935. Photo courtesy of Special Collections, USMA Library.

Melville Shinn Jarvis (0-325) was born on 15 June 1868 in Harrison County, West Virginia. He entered USMA in West Point and graduated number thirty-two of sixty-five in the class of 1891. William J. Glasgow, John L. Hines, Andrew Hero, Jr. and Odus C. Horney (all *q.v.*) were four of his classmates. He was commissioned and assigned to the Fourth Infantry. In 1895, he married Mary Hamond, who had been a friend since childhood. They were both from Clarksburg, West Virginia. He stayed with the Fourth Infantry in Santiago, Cuba, and from 1900 to 1902, he was with the First Infantry Regiment before going to the Philippines. From 1 June 1902 to 11 August 1908, he was back with the Fourth Infantry at Fort Sam Houston, Texas. After three months of leave (12 September-12 December 1908), he was quartermaster and commissary on the U.S. transport *Sumner* for four months. He also served in the Pay Department in New York from 11 April 1909 to 10 October 1911, when he was promoted to major and sent back to the Philippines, first stationed in Stotsenberg and Corrigedor, then detailed to the Inspector General's Department. In 1914 and 1915, he was with the 26th Infantry in both Galveston and Texas City, Texas. He was acting Chief of Staff of the Eagle Pass (Texas) District until February 1917, when he joined the 30th Infantry. On 5 August 1917, he was promoted to colonel (NA) and assigned to command the 45th Infantry Regiment, which he commanded until October 1918. On 1 October, he was promoted to brigadier general (NA) and assigned to the 98th Division at Camp McClellan, Alabama. Because of the Armistice, the 98th Division was not organized, so he commanded the 157th Depot Brigade until 30 April 1919. Reverting to his permanent rank of colonel, he commanded the 65th Infantry and the post of San Juan, Puerto Rico, until July 1922. He was then the officer in charge of National Guard affairs in the Fourth Corps Area, headquartered in Atlanta and at Fort McPherson, Georgia, until 1928. His final assignment was as senior unit instructor of the Organized Reserve in Washington, D.C. until 30 June 1932, when he retired. His family lived in Washington. He was a man of unfailing good nature and kindness and was a cheerful companion. His wife died a few months before he did. At the age seventy-four, he died in Fitsimmons Army Hospital in Denver, on 4 June 1943. Photo from *The Assembly,* Association of Graduates, USMA.

Melville Shinn Jarvis

Henry Jervey, Jr. (0-58), son of Dr. and Mrs. Henry Jervey, was born on 5 June 1866 in Dublin, Virginia. After graduating from the University of the South in 1884, he entered USMA, and graduated number one in the class of 1888. Peyton C. March and Guy Henry Preston (both *q.v.*) were two of his classmates. He graduated from the Army Engineering School of Application in 1891. On 14 November 1895, he married Katherine Irwin, and they had one son,

Henry Jervey, Jr.

William Jesson Jervey. He was in charge of improvement of the Mississippi River in the Fourth District from 1898 to 1899, and during 1899 to 1900, he was in charge of the rivers and harbors on the west coast of Florida, as well as the defenses of Tampa Bay. From 1901 to 1903, he served in the Philippines, and from 1903 to 1905, he was an instructor in West Point. From 1905 to 1910, he was in charge of rivers, harbors and defenses of the Mobile District, after which he had five years of river duty in Cincinatti. From 1915 to 1917, he was an instructor at the Army War College, and was then made a brigadier general and placed in command of the 66th Field Artillery Brigade at Camp Greene in Charlotte, North Carolina. Next he was sent to Washington Barracks in Washington, D.C. as commandant of the Engineer School until February 1918, when he was made G-3 (director of operations) of the War Department General Staff. For his performance of this duty he received the Distinguished Service Medal. He commanded the 41st Infantry Division (NA) at Camp Greene and Camp Mills from 20 September 1917 to 8 January 1918. On 1 October 1918, he was promoted to major general (NA). After the war, he reverted to his permanent rank of brigadier general, and commanded the 11th Field Artillery Brigade in Hawaii until his retirement on 10 April 1922. In 1929, his wife died, and on 19 March 1930 he married Henriette Postell. In addition to the honor already mentioned, he received Companion of the Bath (Great Britain), Commander of the Legion of Honor (France), Grand Officer of the Order of Leopold (Belgium) and a Member of the Order of the Crown (Italy). He wrote one book, *Warfare of the Future*, in 1917. His two-star rank was restored in 1930. At the age of seventy, he died in South Carolina, on 30 September 1942. Photo courtesy of the U.S. Army Military History Institute, Carlisle Barracks, Pennsylvania.

Arthur Johnson (0-189), son of Swan Johnson and Margaret Elizabeth Nelson Johnson, was born in 1862 on a farm near Swan Lake, Minnesota. He had a brother, Franklin Oliver Johnson, who graduated from USMA in 1881, but never reached star rank. He entered USMA and graduated number sixty-one of seventy-seven in the class of 1886. Mason M. Patrick, Charles T. Menoher and John J. Pershing (all *q.v.*) were three of his classmates. He was commissioned in the infantry and performed frontier duty from 1891 to 1894, serving in the 11th and 17th Infantry Regiments in Arizona. He commanded the 12th Infantry in the siege and surrender of Santiago, Cuba. After this he went to the Philippines where he served during the Insurrection, for which he received a Silver Star

Commendation. During 1901 to 1902, he was on leave and detached service. During 1902 and 1903, he was on recruiting duty in Evansville, Indiana. From November 1903 to October 1904, he commanded a company on Alcatraz Island, California, then served in Point Bonita. He was sent back to the Philippines to command a company at Camp Eldridge from 1905 to 1906. In 1908 and 1909, he went to Fort Leavenworth Kansas, to the Army Service Schools, and to the Army War College in Washington. On 1 November 1909, he was promoted to major and commanded a battalion of the Nineteenth Infantry in the Philippines. Following this he became instructor and inspector of the Minnesota Militia until 2 September 1913, when he was sent to Texas City, Texas, to command a battalion. His wife's name was Edith, and they had one daughter, Mrs. Robert Ogden Annin, wife of the commanding officer at Camp Maxey, Texas (1946), and three sons Franklin Oliver, the oldest, who went into the Navy, Major William Oliver Johnson, who retired to Wilmette, Illinois and Arthur A. Johnson, who lived in Madison, Wisconsin. From Texas he returned to Minnesota until 11 August 1916, when he was assigned to the 36th Infantry in Brownsville, Texas. On 15 May 1917, he became a colonel of infantry and commanded the 36th Infantry at Fort Snelling, Minnesota. He was sent to Paris in November 1917, and was placed in command of the intermediate section, Service of Supply. He very successfully utilized female labor in the Quartermaster Corps in Nevers, France. For his performance of this duty, he was awarded the Distinguished Service Medal. He was also made an Officer of the Legion of Honor (France). On 12 April 1918, he was promoted to brigadier general (NA). On 15 March 1920, he reverted to his permanent rank of colonel and was retired on 9 July 1925. His rank as a brigadier general was restored by act of Congress in June 1930. In retirement his family lived in Wilmette, Illinois, where at the age of eighty-four he died, on 3 February 1946. Photo from the National Archives.

Arthur Johnson

Evan Malbone Johnson, Jr. (0-153) , son of Captain Evan M. Johnson (USV) and Amy Grant Johnson, was born on 26 September 1861 in Brooklyn, New York. He attended the Alexander Military Institute in White Plains, the Polytechnic Institute in Brooklyn and Mount Union College. He enlisted as a private in Company F, Tenth Infantry on 12 June 1882, was commissioned a second lieutenant 15 August 1885 and campaigned against the Apaches from 1885 to 1886. He was Professor of Military Science and Tactics at Mount Union College from 1891 to 1894. He married Bessie Seaman on 12 February 1896. On 2 March 1889, he was promoted to captain, and that same year he graduated from the

Evan Malbone Johnson, Jr.

Infantry and Cavalry School at Fort Leavenworth, Kansas. He served both in Cuba and Puerto Rico during the Spanish-American War, and was a major, 29th U.S. Volunteer Infantry from 1899 to 1901. He was honorably discharged from the volunteer service on 10 May 1901. On 9 April 1904, he transferred to the Eighth Infantry, and also received an M.S. degree from Mount Union College. Two years later, he was promoted to a major in the Sixth Infantry, and had duty on the Island of Lotte in the Philippines in 1907. That same year he went to the Army War College. He was instructor and inspector of the New Jersey Militia from 1911 to 1912. From 1912 to 1914, he was in the Division of Military Affairs, office of the Chief of Staff, Washington, D.C. On 20 August 1914, he was promoted to lieutenant colonel. Pennsylvania Military College gave him an honorary M.M.S. in 1914. That same year he was on the Vera Cruz Expedition, was secretary of the Infantry Association and was also editor of the Infantry Journal. On 5 August 1917, he was promoted to Brigadier General (NA) and placed in command of the 154th Infantry Brigadier at Camp Upton on Long Island, New York. He commanded the 77th Infantry Division from 4 December 1917 to 6 May 1918, and again from 20 July to 19 August 1918. He was the United States military attache in Rome as of 15 September 1919. At the age of sixty-two, he died in the United States, on 13 October 1923. Photo courtesy of the National Archives.

Hugh Samuel Johnson (no ASN assigned) was born at Fort Scott in southeastern Kansas in 1882. He entered USMA and graduated number fifty-three of ninety-three in the class of 1903. Douglas MacArthur (*q.v.*), Ulysses Grant III, Thomas E. Selfridge (first person in the world to die in an air crash) and Dorsey R. Rodney (Second Cavalry) were four of his classmates. Commissioned in the cavalry, he rose rapidly and served in the Mexican Punitive Expedition under General Pershing in 1916 and 1917. In 1917, he worked with General Crowder, making plans for the Selective Service Act. As Deputy Provost Marshal, he was

Hugh Samuel Johnson

given the Distinguished Service Medal. He resigned as a brigadier general in 1919 to go into business, and in 1927, he joined the staff of Bernard Baruch, a great man and longtime friend. Baruch was the advisor of most of the Presidents from Wilson to Eisenhower: an unselfish great help to all of them, and friend of both Gen. Pershing and Will Rogers, one of the great men of his era. In 1933, Johnson was summoned to Washington to help write, and later to administer, the National Industrial Recovery Act. In 1935, he became the WPA (Works Progress Administration) Administrator for New York City, after which he worked as a newspaper columnist and popular radio commentator. He died at the age of fifty-nine in Washington, D.C. on 15 April 1942. The photo, courtesy of the National Archives, was taken at Love Field in Dallas after his first flight, during which he was accompanied by Lt. William T. Campbell.

William Orlando Johnson

William Orlando Johnson (0-292) was born in 1865 in Louisa, Kentucky, where he taught school until entering USMA in West Point in 1886. As a cadet, he was editor of the original edition of the *Howitzer*, the academy yearbook. He graduated number six of fifty-four in the class of 1890. Edgar Jadwin, Fred W. Sladen and James A. Ryan (all *q.v.*) were three of his classmates. He was commissioned in the infantry and stationed at Fort Brady, Michigan, where he met and married May Norton of Sault Sainte Marie, Michigan. They had one daughter, Mrs. Dorothy Johnson McWary. In 1896, he returned to West Point as assistant professor of mathematics, after which he was sent to Fort Thomas, Kentucky with the 19th Infantry, then on to Anniston, Alabama. He was stationed at Fort Sheridan, Illinois, at the time of the Philippine Insurrection, and he left for the Islands in 1900, arriving there in time to participate in the last of the fighting. After two years there with the Fourth Infantry, he returned first to Fort Sheridan, then to Fort Slocum, New York. Over the next three years he recruited in Chillicothe and had a short tour in Cuba. By 1908, he was sent back to the Philippines, but later was assigned to the Eighth Infantry at the Presidio of Monterey. During 1910 to 1911, he was a student at both the School of the Line and the Staff School at Fort Leavenworth, and became a noted graduate of both. In 1912, he was back in the Philippines, commanding a battalion of the Eleventh Infantry at Jolo, then commanding the battalion post of Camp Ward Cheney in Baccor. His final year there was as Inspector General, stationed in Manila. He compiled both a Moro dictionary and a Tagalog grammar, which he turned over to, and which was widely used by the War Department. Again he returned to Fort Sheridan, this time as Inspector General. When the United States entered World

War I, he served at several mobilization centers, then went to Waco, Texas where the Seventh Division was forming, and commanded the 56th Infantry Regiment. When in August 1918 the Seventh sailed for France, he was in temporary command of the division. On 1 October 1918, he was made a brigadier general (NA), and served with the Seventh overseas until after the Armistice. Next he was a president of a general court-martial, which traveled widely over France and cleaned up a number of important cases. His court was finally disbanded in San Diego, and he returned to Camp Meade, Maryland, for demobilization. Reverting to the rank of colonel of infantry, he served in Douglas, Arizona and at Camp Furlong, New Mexico, until September 1920. He was then sent to Panama, and for three years he commanded the 33d Infantry Regiment. He returned to the States and was Chief of Staff of the Organized Reserve in the Eighth Corps Area, stationed in Oklahoma City. There, on 13 September 1926, at the age of sixty and still on duty, he died. His wife and daughter survived him. He was a great student and was devoted to duty and his family, and people enjoyed serving with him. Photo courtesy of *The Assembly*, Association of Graduates, USMA.

John Alexander Johnston (no ASN assigned), son of Alexander Johnston and Sarah R. Johnston, was born on 22 February 1858 in Allegheny, Pennsylvania. He entered USMA and graduated number twenty-three of sixty-seven in the class of 1879. Fredrick S. Foltz, William D. Beach and Hunter Liggett (all *q.v.*) were three of his classmates. After being commissioned in the cavalry, he was sent to Texas, where he performed frontier duty from 1879 to 1982. In 1883, he was an honor graduate of the Infantry and Cavalry School at Fort Leavenworth, Kansas. In 1888, he married Henrietta V. Vandergrift. From 1883 to 1885, he was an instructor at the Infantry and Cavalry School. He was promoted to first lieutenant on 20 January 1886. He continued performing frontier duty in South Dakota from 1886 to 1887, and also served in that capacity from 1891 to 1893 and from 1895 to 1897. From 1891 to 1897, he was an instructor at West Point. From 1893 to 1895, he instructed in horsemanship at Jefferson Barracks Cavalry Depot, southwest near St. Louis, Missouri. The latter part of his career was spent in the Adjutant General's Department in Washington, D.C., in charge of muster in and mustering out all Spanish-American War Volunteers. He performed the same duty for volunteers in the Philippine Insurrection. He was promoted to a brigadier general and resigned in 1903. From 1910 to 1913, he was a commissioner in Washington, D.C. On 5 August 1917, he was appointed brigadier general (NA) and com-

John Alexander Johnston

manded the Northeastern Department, headquartered in Boston. From October 1918, he commanded the 34th Division, for which service he received the Distinguished Service Medal. In 1919, he was honorably discharged. At the age of eighty-one, he died in Washington, D.C., on 5 January 1940. Photo courtesy of Special Collections, USMA Library.

William Hartshorne Johnston, Jr.

William Hartshorne Johnston, Jr. (0-133), son of William Hartshorne Johnston and Mary Neele Johnston, was born on 19 October 1861 in Cincinnati, Ohio. He attended Washington University in St. Louis, Missouri from 1876 to 1897, and received his LL.B. in 1897. He enlisted in the Lafayette Guard in St. Louis and was promoted to corporal and then to sergeant. During 1881 and 1882, he was a first lieutenant in the Arizona Territorial Militia in Prescott. On 10 October 1883, he was commissioned in the 16th Infantry (USA). In 1887, he was an honor graduate of the Infantry and Cavalry School at Fort Leavenworth, Kansas. On 27 June 1888, he married Lucille Barat Wilkinson. During the Spanish-American War, he served as a major in the 46th U.S. Volunteer Infantry, and when mustered out of the volunteer service, he became governor of Isabella Province in the Philippines from 1901 to 1902. From April 1904 to October 1906, he was a major commanding the First Battalion of Philippine scouts. In 1907 and 1908, he was at the Army War College. From 1914 to 1917, he was on the General Staff serving at the Army War College. In 1917, his wife died. On 5 August 1917, he was promoted to a brigadier general (NA). From 25 August 1917 to 27 August 1918, he organized, trained and took to France the 180th (Texas) Infantry Brigade (AEF).They served in the Toul Sector. On 8 August 1918, he was promoted to major general (NA), and commanded the 91st Infantry Division during the St. Mihiel and Meuse-Argonne offensives. He was with the French Army under the command of the King of Belgium during the Ypres-Lys Campaign from 19 October 1918 until the Armistice. He returned to the States and was stationed at Camp Lewis, Washington during the demobilization of the 91st Division. Until 1 July 1920, he was at the Army War College again. He returned to Europe with the American Forces in Germany, where he became Chief of Staff to Gen. Henry T. Allen. He stayed in Europe until March 1923, when he married Isabelle Gros. His next command was the Fourth Coast Artillery District at Fort McPherson, Georgia. On 15 November 1924, he commanded the Third Infantry Division. He retired on 19 October 1925. His decorations included both the Distinguished Service Medal and the Silver Star (United States) and the Croix de Guerre (France), and he was made Commander of the Legion of Honor and Commander of the Order of Leopold I (Belgium). In retirement he lived in Nice, France, and he died there at the age of seventy-two, on 19 February 1933. Photo courtesy of the National Archives.

William Voorhees Judson

William Voorhees Judson (O-204), son of Charles E. Judson and Abby Cady Voorhees Judson, was on born 16 February 1865 in Indianapolis, Indiana. His English ancestors had come to Massachusetts in the seventeenth century. He attended Harvard University for two years before entering USMA, from which graduated number three of forty-four in the class of 1888. Peyton C. March and Guy Henry Preston (both *q.v.*) were two of his classmates. He spent his graduation leave in Europe. In 1891, he graduated from the Engineering School of Application. On 21 April 1891, he married Alice Carneal of Lexington, Kentucky. They had one son, Clay Judson. He was for several years assistant engineer on Lake Erie and the Upper Mississippi River, as well as in Galveston, Texas. From 1899 to 1900, he was Chief Engineer and President of the Board of Public Works of Puerto Rico. Later, he did rivers and harbors work in Georgia, Alabama and Washington, D.C. In Washington, he instructed at the Engineer School, and was also an assistant to the Chief of Engineers (USA). During the Russian-Japanese War of 1904 to 1905, he was military observer with the Russian Army, which the Japanese captured at Mukden. After he returned from Russia, he had four years of duty on Lake Michigan, during which time he invented, patented, and gave to the United States the rights to a floating caisson. This was a great money-saver, and was used extensively in breakwater construction. From 1909 to 1913, he was Engineer Commissioner for Washington, D.C., where his services and accomplishments were of great value. During 1913 and 1914, he was Assistant Division Engineer of the Atlantic side of the Panama Canal, after which he served in both Chicago and Baltimore, just before the U.S. entry into World War I. After 6 April 1917, he returned to Russia as military aide to the Root Mission sent by President Wilson to encourage Kerensky to remain an active participant in the war. On 5 August 1917, he was made a brigadier general (NA). After Senator Root's return to the United States, he continued for several months as head of the Root Mission, and also as military attache in Petrograd, until Kerensky was overthrown by the Bolsheviks under Lenin. He received a number of Russian decorations, and the United States awarded him the Distinguished Service Medal for his services there. Back in the States, he was given command of the 38th Infantry Division (National Guard troops from

Indiana, Kentucky and West Virginia) at Camp Shelby, Mississippi. From September to December 1918, he commanded the port of embarkation in New York. When the war was over, he reverted to his permanent rank of colonel of engineers and served as district engineer in Chicago until he retired due to disabilities in 1922. Harvard gave him an honorary M.A. He wrote many articles for professional journals, and had a very large circle of friends. At the age of fifty-eight, he died in Winter Park, Florida, on 29 March 1923. His rank as a brigadier general was restored posthumously in June 1930. Photo courtesy of Special Collections, USMA Library.

Jefferson Randolph Kean, M.D.

Jefferson Randolph Kean, M.D. (0-115) was born in 1860 in Lynchburg, Virginia. He was a military surgeon whose M.D. came from the University of Virginia in 1883. He was commissioned assistant surgeon in 1884, and served with the Ninth Cavalry in the West, in Florida and, during the Spanish-American War, in Cuba. He remained in Cuba under the provisional military governments. From 1902 to 1906 and from 1909 to 1913, he served in the Surgeon General's Office, and was responsible for the organization of the Medical Reserve Corps. He also set up a stockpiling system for medical field supplies for emergency use. In 1916, while assigned to the American Red Cross, he organized and equipped thirty-two base hospitals. During World War I he served in France. On 26 June 1918, he was promoted to brigadier general (NA), and became Deputy Chief Surgeon of the AEF. He received the Distinguished Service Medal for duty as Chief of the Department of Military Relief of the American Red Cross, administered by the U.S. Ambulance Service for the French Army. A descendant of Thomas Jefferson, he was organizer and first president of the Monticello Association, and was also a member of the commission that created the Jefferson Memorial in Washington, D.C. He died in 1950, at the age of ninety in Washington, D.C. The Signal Corps photo, from the National Archives, shows him being decorated as an officer of the Legion of Honor by Marshall Petain in Tours, France.

Charles Keller (0-331), son of Isaac Keller and Fanny Keller of Germany, was born on 13 February 1868 in Rochester, New York, where his father was a merchant. He entered USMA and graduated number two of fifty-four in the class of 1890. Edgar Jadwin, Fred W. Sladen and James A. Ryan (all *q.v.*) were three of his classmates. He was commissioned in the Corps of Engineers. On 8 November 1897, he married Frances Rosenfield in Ottumwa, Iowa. They had two sons Ira Charles Keller and Charles Keller, Jr. After a number of preliminary assignments, he was stationed in Detroit in 1905 as district engineer in charge of Lake Michigan survey and the 11th Lighthouse District. There he developed a submerged wire sweep for both hydrographic surveys and for locating navigational hazards. He was technical advisor to a congressional board looking into generating electricity from the Niagara River. From 1910 to 1913, he was the district engineer in Rock Island, Illinois, working on better tugs and barges to improve carrying capacity. In 1916, he was made Assistant to the Chief of Engineers in Washington, where he organized the administration that became part of the War Industries Board, working to prevent power shortages. In 1918, he was the Deputy Chief Engineer of the AEF. He was on the Board of Rivers and Harbors Engineers, and in 1921, he was made the Engineer Commissioner for Washington, D.C. In 1922, when the Knickerbocker Theater collapsed due to a snow overload, he not only took charge of the rescue and cleanup, but put building regulations in effect to prevent such disasters in the future. In 1923, he retired as a colonel. In June 1930, his rank as a brigadier general was restored by act of Congress. In retirement, he was a public utilities engineer, both in the States and in Mexico. He received the Distinguished Service Medal for his services in World War I, and was made an Officer of the Legion of Honor (France). In 1940, he was recalled for active duty in World War II, and served as the district engineer in Chicago. There he supervised the construction of camps, airfields and other military projects costing approximately $300,000,000 and purchased war materials and engineer equipment costing approximately $2,000,000. He retired again in 1943, received a Legion of Merit for his World War II service and worked for the Standard Gas and Electric Company. At the age of eighty-one he died in California, on 16 September 1949. Photo courtesy of the National Archives.

Charles Keller

William Lacy Kenly (0-13397) was born in 1864 in Baltimore, Maryland. He entered USMA, where he was one of the oldest members of his class, and graduated number eleven of forty-nine in the class of 1889. William W Harts, E. E. Winslow, Charles Crawford, William G. Haan and William Lassiter (all *q.v.*) were five of his classmates. He was commissioned in the Fourth Artillery. He married a Miss Closson, his colonel's daughter, and they had two sons. Before the Spanish-American War, he had a tour of duty at the Artillery

William Lacy Kenley

School at Fort Monroe. In April 1898, he was in Tampa, Florida with his battery. In June 1898, he was with the Fifth Corps in Cuba, and took part in the actions in El Caney and Santiago. By September, he was back in the United States, and by May 1899, he was with his battery in Manila for the Insurrection. During 1900 and 1901, he was an aide to Gen. Arthur MacArthur, and he was promoted to captain at that time. He served under and was recommended for promotion by Gen. Henry Lawton. In 1907, in the Philippines, he was promoted to major. He was assigned to recruiting duty in New York, and in 1912, he became a lieutenant colonel, went to the School of Fire, and served on the Mexican border. In 1916, as a colonel, he took the field officers course in aviation and won his wings. In August 1917, when he was en route to France with the Seventh Field Artillery, he was promoted to brigadier general (NA). In France, he was made Chief of the Air Service (AEF), until 28 February 1918, when he was returned to Washington as Director of Military Aeronautics. This duty lasted until 10 March 1919, when he reverted from major general (NA) to that of colonel (USA), his permanent rank. He had various assignments, chiefly recruiting, and at his own request retired after thirty-four years of service. In addition to the Distinguished Service Medal he was made an officer of the Legion of Honor (France) and Companion of the Bath (Great Britain). He enjoyed good health until the day he died at the age of sixty-four, in Washington, D.C., on 10 January 1928. Picture courtesy of the Association of Graduates, USMA.

Chase Wilmot Kennedy (0-44), son of Milton and Josephine Hutchinson Kennedy, was born on 4 January 1859 in Portsmouth, Ohio. He entered USMA and graduated number eighteen of fifty-two in the class of 1883. George H. Cameron, Tryee Rhodes Rivers and Omar Bundy (all *q.v.*) were three of his classmates. He was commissioned in the Third Infantry and performed frontier duty from 1883 to 1895. On 13 November 1889, he married Elizabeth Lord Jewett. He served in the Sanitary Corps in Cuba, and went on to the Philippines during the Insurrection. He also served in Alaska, France and Panama. On 15 May

Chase Wilmot Kennedy

1917, he was promoted to brigadier general (NA). From 23 August to 28 November 1917, he was commanding general of the 78th Infantry Division. From 27 February to 23 December 1918, he commanded the 85th Infantry Division. Starting on 28 April 1919, he commanded the Panama Canal Department, and from 1 November 1921 to 30 May 1922, he commanded the Ninth Coast Artillery District and the Ninth Training Center. On 30 November 1922, he retired as a brigadier general. His two-star rank was restored by act of Congress in June 1930. In retirement his family lived in Washington, D.C., where he died at the age of seventy-seven, on 23 November 1936. Photo courtesy of the Association of Graduates, USMA.

Lyman Walter Vere Kennon

Lyman Walter Vere Kennon (no ASN assigned), son of Charles Henry Vere Kennon and Adelaide Hall Kennon, was born on 2 September 1858 in Providence, Rhode Island. He entered USMA and graduated number fifty of fifty-three in the class of 1881. Andrew Summers Rowan (deliverer of the message to Garcia) was one of his classmates. He was commissioned and sent to the First Infantry. From 1881 to 1886, he performed frontier duty. On 3 April 1883, he married Annie Beecher Rice. From 1886 to 1890, he was an aide to General Crook. In 1891, he wrote his only book, *The Manual of Guard Duty*. During the Spanish-American War, he was in both the infantry and the Sanitary Corps, and for this service he was cited posthumously. He was a major, U.S. Volunteer Infantry from 1898 to 1899, and a colonel, 34th U.S. Volunteer Infantry during the Philippine Insurrection. He did exploration and surveying for the intercontinental railway in Central America, and also constructed the new road to Baguio (the Philippine summer capitol), for which he was complimented by President Theodore Roosevelt. In 1910, he graduated from the Army War College, and on 5 August 1917, he was promoted to brigadier general (NA). He commanded the 86th Infantry Division at Camp Grant, near Rockford, Illinois, both from 26 November 1917 to 15 February 1918 and from 21 March to 18 April 1918. He retired as a colonel and died at the age of sixty, in New York City, on 9 September 1918. His rank of brigadier general was restored posthumously in 1930. Photo from the National Archives.

Francis Joseph Kernan (0-19), son of John A. Kernan and Elizabeth C. Kernan, was born on 19 October 1859 in Jacksonville, Florida. He entered West

Francis Joseph Kernan

Point and he graduated number eighteen of fifty-three in the class of 1881. Harry and Henry Hodges, Edwin St. John Greble and Joseph T. Dickman (all *q.v.*) were four of his classmates. He was commissioned in the 21st Infantry and performed frontier duty from 1881 to 1885 and from 1887 to 1888. From 1885 to 1887, he was Professor of Military Science and Tactics in Florida and Louisiana. He was an assistant professor at USMA from 1888 to 1891. In 1898, he received a Silver Star Commendation for his service during the Spanish-American War. On 18 March 1898, he married Ella M. McCaffrey. From 1900 to 1903, he was an aide to General Arthur MacArthur in the Philippines. From 1905 to 1909, he was on the General Staff in Washington, and then he returned to the Philippines. In 1914, he graduated from the Army War College. On 23 March 1917, he was made a brigadier general and commanded the Eighth Infantry Brigade in El Paso, Texas. From May to August 1917, he was acting assistant Chief of Staff, and he prepared the official instructions for General Pershing, which had to be approved by both Newton D. Baker (the Secretary of War), and President Wilson. From 25 August 1917 to 18 September 1917, he was commanding general of the 31st Infantry Division (AEF). In September 1917, he commanded Camp Wheeler in Macon, Georgia. From 30 November 1917 to 29 July 1918, he organized and commanded the Service of Supply in France, for which he received the Distinguished Service Medal. From 29 July to 11 November 1918, he was in Switzerland, a member of the American mission to negotiate for the treatment and exchange of prisoners of war and detained civilians. From November 1918 to April 1919, he was technical advisor to the American commission to negotiate peace. He was promoted to major general (USA) on 14 October 1919, and was sent to the Philippines as commanding general. On 1 December 1922, he retired. At the age of eighty-five, he died in Florida, on 4 February 1945. Signal Corps photo courtesy of the National Archives.

James Taggart Kerr (0-61),was born on 22 April 1859 in Martin's Ferry, Ohio. He entered USMA and graduated number twenty-eight of fifty-three in the class of 1881. Andrew Summers Rowan (deliverer of the message to Garcia was one of his classmates. He was commissioned in the infantry and assigned to frontier duty until 1888. He was in the Sioux Campaign (1890 to 1891), and was an honor graduate of the Infantry and Cavalry School at Fort Leavenworth, Kansas in 1897. In Cuba during the Spanish-American War, he received a Silver Star Commendation, and was transferred to the Sanitary Corps. Taking part in the

James Taggart Kerr

suppression of the Philippine Insurrection, he was again awarded a Silver Star Commendation. In 1914, he was retired due to physical disability, but was returned to duty for World War I and became a brigadier general (NA) on 2 October 1917. During World War I, he served in the Adjutant General's Office in Washington from 1917 to 1919. In 1920, he was restored to the active list as a brigadier general (USA),and was Assistant Adjutant General from 1920 to 1922. At the age of eighty-nine, he died in Washington, on 13 April 1949. Photo from the National Archives.

Daniel Warren Ketcham (0-13377), son of Seth Ketcham and Almira Benham Ketcham, was born on 1 May 1867 in Burns City, Indiana. He entered USMA and graduated number twenty-one of fifty-four in the class of 1890. He was commissioned in the Artillery. In 1894, he graduated from the artillery school and in 1897, he served at Fort Warren, Massachusetts. On 9 October of that year, he married Edith V. Smith. In 1899, he was in Boston, and from 1899 to 1901, he was in Honolulu. He was at Fort Hamilton, New York from 1902 to 1903, and at Fort Totten from 1903 to 1904, where he graduated from the School of Submarine Defense. After five years in the Presidio in San Francisco between 1904 and 1909, he returned to Massachusetts and remained there from 1911 to 1912. From 1912 to 1914, he was on the General Staff in Washington, and in 1915, he served at Fort DuPont, Delaware. During 1916 and 1917, he was at Fort Myer, Virginia as president of the Artillery Board, and in 1917, he was a member of the Ordnance Board. In late 1917 and early 1918, he was again on the General Staff in Washington. He arrived in France on 17 June 1918, and graduated in September of that year from the General Staff College in Langres. He then commanded the 34th Coast Artillery Brigade until 1 February 1919. Back in the States, he commanded Camp Taylor, Kentucky from March to May 1919, when he retired as a colonel. His rank as a brigadier general (retired list) was restored in June 1930. He died at age sixty-eight, in Indiana, on 19 July 1935. Photo courtesy of the National Archives.

Daniel Warren Ketcham

Charles Evans Kilbourne, Jr.

Charles Evans Kilbourne, Jr. (0-858), son of Mr. and Mrs. Charles E. Kilbourne, was born on 23 December 1872 at Fort Whipple (later named Fort Myer), Virginia. He graduated from Virginia Military Institute in 1894 and was commissioned a second lieutenant on 20 May 1898. He advanced steadily through the grades until reaching major general (USA) on 9 July 1935. During the Spanish-American War, he served in the campaign to capture Manila, and later served in the Philippine Insurrection. In 1900, he was part of the China Relief Expedition when the Boxers besieged the city of Peking. He married Elizabeth Gordon Eghurt on 9 June 1900. He was an honor graduate of the Artillery School in 1903. He served with the General Staff from 1911 to 1913, and again from 1915 to 1919. On 1 January 1918, he was in France, and served briefly on the British and French fronts. He returned to France in May 1918 with the 89th Division, and remained until 6 October 1918, when he was given command of the 34th Heavy Artillery Brigade. He later commanded the Third Infantry Brigade in France and Germany. He returned to the states in 1919, and spent about five years on the staff of the Army War College. During 1924 and 1925, he was the commandant of Boston Harbor, and from 1925 to 1928, he was executive assistant, Office of the Chief of Coast Artillery. He commanded the Second Infantry Brigade in 1928 and 1929, and then commanded the Coast Artillery District of Manila and Subic Bays, War Plans Division, General Staff, until 1932. From 1932 to 1934, he was commanding general, Sixth Corps Area and Second Army. In 1936, he retired. He was superintendent of Virginia Military Institute from 1937 to 1946. His decorations included the Medal of Honor (U.S., 1899), the Distinguished Service Cross (Thiacourt, 1918), the Distinguished Service Medal, and the Croix de Guerre (France), the Royal Order of Olaf (Norway) and the Legion of Honor (France). He belonged to the United Confederate Veterans and was a Republican and an Episcopalian. He wrote four books for boys about the army and a five-volume baby-animal library. He lived in Lexington, Virginia. At the age of ninety, he died on November 1963. Photo courtesy of the Casemate Museum, Fort Monroe, Virginia.

John William Kilbreth (0-1260), son of John Kilbreth and Mary Cuthbertson Kilbreth, was born on 18 February 1876 in New York City. After graduating from the Westminster School in 1894, he entered Harvard and graduated with an A.B. in 1898. He was commissioned a second lieutenant in the Fourth Artillery on 9 September 1898, and served in the Philippines during the Insurrection with Light Battery F, Fourth Artillery, from 1899 to 1901. He was

John William Kilbreth

promoted to first lieutenant, and in 1902, he went to the artillery school. In 1909, he was a distinguished graduate of the School of the Line. In April 1904, he was made a captain and was assigned to the Sixth Field Artillery. Next he served as an instructor at the School of Fire for Field Artillery, from February to August 1915 and from August 1917 to May 1918. From June to August 1918, he served as Chief of Operations, First Army Artillery (AEF), and from August to October he served as Chief of Staff, First Army Artillery. On 10 October 1918, he was promoted to brigadier general (NA), and was assigned as commanding general, 55th Field Artillery Brigade, from October to December 1918. From December 1918 to February 1919, he served at general headquarters (AEF), and in February 1919, he resumed command of the 55th Field Artillery Brigade. He was on the Overseers Visiting Committee of the Department of Military and Naval Science at Harvard University. In 1921, he received the Distinguished Service Medal, and on 15 December 1922, he retired as a colonel. On 15 December 1922, he married Mrs. J. Stevens Ullman, and they lived on Fifth Avenue in New York. On 21 June 1930, he was promoted to brigadier general (retired list). He was for many years a vestryman of St. Thomas Protestant Episcopal Church in New York, and after his second marriage, to Mrs. Gertrude O. Barclay, he lived at 791 Park Avenue in New York. At the age of eighty-two he died, on 24 July 1958, survived by his wife, two stepsons and a stepdaughter. He was buried in Spring Grove Cemetery in Cincinatti. Photo courtesy of the Cincinnati Public Library.

Campbell King (0-674), son of Alexander King and Mary Lee Evans King, was born on 30 August 1871 in Flat Rock, North Carolina. He attended Charleston College. His military career began when he enlisted as a private in July 1897. He soon became a corporal. On 9 July 1898, he was commissioned a second lieutenant, Infantry (USA), and he served in Cuba, the Philippines, Hawaii, China, on the Mexican border and in France. He was a distinguished graduate of the Infantry and Cavalry School in 1905, and graduated from the Army Staff College in 1906. On 19 December 1907, he married Harriet Laurens, and they had two children a son, Duncan, and a daughter, Barbara. In 1911, he graduated from the Army War College. On 27 June 1917, he was assigned to the First Infantry Division in France, and was their Chief of Staff from December 1917 until September 1918. On 1 October 1918, he was promoted to brigadier general (NA), and he served as Chief of Staff of the Seventh Army Corps from October 1918 to July 1919. He took part in many battles and campaigns in

Campbell King

France. In 1920, he received an honorary M.A. from Harvard, and also graduated from the General Staff College. In addition to the honorary degree from Harvard he received the Distinguished Service Medal and the Croix de Guerre with palm, he was also made an officer of the Legion of Honor (France) and Commander of the Order of the Crown (Italy). Along with Col. George B. Duncan, he was one of the first two American officers to receive the Croix de Guerre, given to him for his service at Verdun. On 23 July 1924, he was promoted to brigadier general (USA). He was Assistant Chief of Staff (G-1) from 29 May 1925 to 1 May 1929. From 4 May 1929, he was commandant of the Infantry School at Fort Benning, Georgia. He was promoted to major general (USA) on 1 May 1932. On 31 May 1933, he retired, and went to live near his birthplace in Flat Rock, North Carolina. Photo courtesy of the National Infantry Museum, Fort Benning, Georgia.

Edward Leonard King

Edward Leonard King (0-517), son of Francis Dane King and Ann Malloy King, was born on 5 December 1873 in Bridgewater, Massachusetts. He entered USMA and graduated number forty-nine of seventy-three in the class of 1896. Lucius Roy Holbrook, George Henry Shelton and Dennis Nolan (all *q.v.*) were three of his classmates. He was commissioned and assigned to the Ninth Cavalry. In 1898, he married Nancy Vose Sumner, daughter of one of the great old American dragoon and cavalry families. They had one daughter, Nancy Sumner King (Mrs. Charles L. Andrews). He served during the Spanish-American War, and was an aide to Gen. Henry Lawton during the Philippine Insurrection. In the Philippines, he won both the Distinguished Service Cross and a Silver Star Commendation. His brother was Capt. Charles King, a cavalry officer who was retired for a physical disability and became famous as a writer on the subjects of both West Point and the Indian-fighting army. He was a distinguished graduate of the Army School of the Line in 1913, and in 1914, he graduated from the Army Staff College. In 1917, he graduated from the Army War College. He was promoted to brigadier general (NA) on 2 June 1918, and was

Chief of Staff of the 28th Division, Pennsylvania National Guard (AEF). He later commanded the 65th Infantry Brigade, replacing Gen. Henry R. Hill (*q.v.*). On 4 December 1922, he was promoted to brigadier general (USA), and from 1 July 1928 to 30 June 1925, he was commandant of the Cavalry School at Fort Riley, Kansas. From 1925 to 1929, he was commandant of the general service schools at Fort Leavenworth, Kansas, after which he was assistant Chief of Staff on the War Department General Staff for four years. From 1932 until his retirement, he was commanding general, Fourth Corps Area. He belonged to the Congregational Church. His other decorations included the Distinguished Service Medal and the Croix de Guerre. He was also made an Officer of the Legion of Honor (France). At the age of sixty, he died, on 27 December 1933. Photo from *The Assembly*, Association of Graduates, USMA.

Albert Decatur Kniskern

Albert Decatur Kniskern (0-13385), son of Philip W. Niskern and Cornelia Louisa Goodenow, was born in Monee, Illinois. His surname was originally Niskern; he added the "K". He entered USMA and graduated number twenty-five of seventy-seven in the class of 1886, Charles T. Menoher, Mason M. Patrick , John J. Pershing (all *q.v.*), and Edward W. McCaskey were four of his classmates. On 1 July 1886, right after graduation, he married Stelle Wheeler in Hastings, Michigan. They had two sons Lewis T. Kniskern and Philip W. Kniskern. He was commissioned in the infantry and performed frontier duty until 1887, when he resigned and spent four years as a civilian. In 1891, he was reappointed, and by 1898, he was a major, U.S. Volunteers. During the Philippine Insurrection, he was a commissary, and from 1911 to 1913, he was the Chief Commissary of the Philippine Division. During World War I, he was commanding officer of the Chicago Quartermaster Supply Depot, for which he was awarded the Distinguished Service Medal. On 1 October 1918, he became a brigadier general (NA). He retired in 1919 as a colonel, but his rank as a brigadier general was restored by act of Congress in 1930. At the age of sixty-eight, he died in Chicago, on 19 November 1930. Photo courtesy of Special Collections, USMA Library.

Francis John Koester (0-206), son of G. F. Koester and Mary Heap Koester, was born on 2 June 1863 in Pennsylvania. He attended Allegheny College in Meadville, Pennsylvania, then entered USMA and graduated number fifteen of forty-four in the class of 1888. Peyton C. March and Guy Henry Preston (both *q.v.*) were two of his classmates. He married Mabel Snow. When commissioned, he was sent to the Tenth Cavalry at Fort Grant, in southeast Arizona. From 1888 to 1893, he performed frontier duty, first in Arizona, then in Montana. From 1893 to 1897, he was Professor of Military Science and Tactics at Allegheny College in Meadville, Pennsylvania. He was at Fort Ethan Allen, Vermont until the outbreak of the Spanish-American War, when he went to Cuba with the Third Cavalry and took part in the Battle of Santiago that July. General Joseph Wheeler specifically commended him, and he was recommended for a brevet promotion. He spent about a year each at Fort Ethan Allen and Fort Myer, Virginia. He had two tours of duty in the Philippines. In the second, he was in Pershing's campaign against the Moros. Back in Washington, D.C., he organized and commanded a bakers and cooks training school. While serving in this capacity, an American army was sent to Cuba, and he was Chief Commissary of the expedition. He added prestige to the Subsistence Department. In 1909, he graduated from the Army War College, and spent several months in the office of the Commissary General. He was then stationed at Schofield Barracks, Oahu and Fort Robinson, Nebraska, before serving in the Adjutant General's Office in Washington. In 1916, he was sent as post adjutant to Fort William McKinley in the Philippines, and from there he went to Camp Stotsenberg. In 1917, he was promoted to colonel and sent to Fort D. A. Russell, Wyoming to command the new 25th Cavalry. This Regiment became the 83d Field Artillery and went to Camp Fremont, California. On 1 October 1918, he was promoted to brigadier general (NA) and commanded the 24th Field Artillery Brigade at Camp (later Fort) Knox, Kentucky. The Armistice prevented it from being shipped to France. In May 1919, he reverted to the rank of colonel and commanded Vancouver Barracks, after which he was on recruiting duty in San Francisco until his retirement on 2 June 1927. At the age of sixty-nine, he died in San Francisco, on 23 September 1932. He was buried in Arlington. Photo from *The Assembly*, Association of Graduates, USMA.

Francis John Koester

Charles Rieseck Krauthoff (0-67) was born on 6 October 1863 in St. Louis, Missouri. He enlisted as a private, light Battery F, Second Field Artillery on 3 August 1884. He was commissioned a second lieutenant in the Fourteenth lnfantry on 26 April 1895, and graduated from the Infantry and Cavalry School at Fort Leavenworth in 1898. On 26 April 1898, he was promoted to first lieutenant, 14th Infantry, and rose through the grades until he became

Charles Rieseck Krauthoff

a brigadier general (NA) in the Quartermaster Corps on 1 October 1918. On 15 July 1919, he became assistant Quartermaster General (USA), and on 7 December 1922, he retired after many years service. His decorations included the Distinguished Service Medal and the Medal for Bravery (Montenegro), and he was made a Commander of the Order of the Crown (Belgium), Officer of the Legion of Honor (France), Officer of the Order of the Crown (Roumania), Officer of the Order of the White Eagle (Serbia) and Officer of the Order of St. Sava (Serbs, Croats and Slovenes). At the age of seventy-two, he died, on 24 February 1936. Photo courtesy of the National Archives, Washington.

Edward Albert Kreger (0-377), son of William Kreger and Johanna H. Kreger, was born on 31 May 1868, near Keota, Iowa. He received a B.S. from Iowa State College in 1890, and he studied law at the State University of Iowa, the Iowa College of Law and Drake University. In 1891, he married Laura Mae Roddis, and they had one daughter, Vera Mae. His military experience began in the lowa State College Cadet Corps. He was a high school principal from 1891 to 1893 and superintendent in Cherokee, Iowa from 1894 to 1896. In January 1897, he was admitted to the Iowa Bar, and he started his practice in Cherokee. From 1893 to 1898, he was a captain and major in the Iowa National Guard, and was then a captain in the 52d Iowa Volunteer lnfantry from April to October 1898. He was a first lieutenant and captain in the 39th U.S. Volunteer lnfantry from 1899 to 1901. On 2 February 1901, he was commissioned a second lieutenant (USA). He graduated from the Infantry and Cavalry School at Fort Leavenworth, Kansas in 1905 and from the Army Staff College in 1906. With the 39th U.S. Volunteers, he served in Luzon and in the Philippines, and he was then transferred to the 28th Infantry on Luzon and Mindanao. From 1906 to 1908, he was an instructor of law at the Army Staff College. From 1907 to 1909, he was in Cuba and he became Judge Advocate of the Department of the Colorado (River) from 1909 to 1911. From 1909 to 1911, he was an assistant in the Judge Advocate General's Office in Washington. He was admitted to the Bar

Edward Albert Kreger

of the U.S. Supreme Court in 1912. From 1914 to 1917, he was Professor of Law at USMA. From May 1917 to February 1918, he was Assistant Provost Marshal General (USA). He was acting Judge Advocate General (AEF) from March 1918 to March 1919. From March 1919 to October 1921, he was acting Judge Advocate General (USA) and was Assistant Judge Advocate General from 1921 to 1924. He was Judge Advocate, Third Corps Area from 1924 to 1925. From 1925 to 1927 he was legal adviser to the American Delegation, Plebiscitary Commission, Tacna-Arica Arbitration in South America. During 1927 and 1928, he was Judge Advocate, Second Corps Area, and from 1928 to 1931, he was Judge Advocate General (USA). He supervised the preparation of the Courts-Martial in 1920 and of The Military Laws of the United States in 1921, and was a contributor to the National Encyclopedia. He received the Distinguished Service Cross for his service in the Philippines and the Distinguished Service Medal for his service as acting Judge Advocate General (AEF). Many military, legal, civic and historical organizations attracted his attention and secured his support. In retirement, his family they lived in San Antonio, Texas, where he died just before his eighty-seventh birthday, on 24 May 1955. He was buried in the National Cemetery at Fort Sam Houston. Photo courtesy of the National Archives.

Joseph Ernst Kuhn

Joseph Ernst Kuhn (0-42), was born on 14 June 1864 in Leavenworth, Kansas. He entered USMA and graduated number one of thirty-nine in the class of 1885. Charles Henry Muir, Willard Holbrook and Robert Lee Bullard (all *q.v.*) were three of his classmates. He was commissioned in the Corps of Engineers. In 1888, he graduated from the U.S. Engineer School in Willet's Point, New York, and for the rest of 1888 and 1889, he was assistant engineer of rivers and harbors in Detroit. He was an instructor in civil engineering at USMA from 1889 to 1894. From 1894 to 1896, he was assistant engineer of rivers, harbors and fortifications in San Francisco. From 1896 to 1900, he was Assistant to the Chief of Engineers in Washington. Then he returned to West Point, this time as engineer of buildings and grounds, doing construction work until 1903. He was sent to the Philippines, then to Japan as an observer with the Japanese armies in 1904 and 1905 He was in China in 1906. From 1906 to 1909, he was engineer in charge of rivers and harbors in Norfolk, Virginia. He was Director of Military Engineering at the Army Staff College at Fort Leavenworth, Kansas from 1909 to 1912. He spent two years in Philadelphia as engineer in charge of rivers, harbors and fortifications, and in 1913 and 1914, he was commandant of the Engineer School and Depot in Washington, D.C. In 1915 and 1916, he was the American Military Attache in Berlin and an observer with the German Army. In 1917, he was president of the Army War College, and from 1917 to 1919, he commanded the 79th Infantry Division (AEF). After the war, he went to Camp Kearny, California, Schofield Barracks, Hawaii and finally to Vancouver, where he received a promotion to major general (USA). On 19 October 1917, he married to Helen Squire, and they had two sons, Joseph and Richard. He retired in 1925. In addition to the Distinguished Service Medal, he received the Croix de Guerre and was made an Officer of the Legion of Honor (France). He was chairman of the Red Cross in San Diego, California. At the age of seventy-one, he died in California, on 12 November 1935. Photo courtesy of *History of the 316th Infantry* by Col. Clifton Lisle.

Charles Willauer Kutz

Charles Willauer Kutz (0-372), son of Allen Kutz and Emily Briner Kutz, was born on 14 October 1870 in Reading, Pennsylvania. He entered USMA and graduated number two of fifty-one in the class of 1893., M. L. Walker, G .G. Heiner (both *q.v.*),and Herbert B. Crosby were three of his classmates. He was commissioned in the Corps of Engineers. On 25 June 1895, he married Elizabeth Randolph Keim. They had two daughters Mrs. W. G. Bingham and Mrs. L. T. Ross. He performed rivers, harbors and fortifications duty in Baltimore from 1896 to 1900, and performed the same duty in Portland, Maine from 1900 to 1901. From 1903 to 1906, he was assistant to the Chief of Engineers in Washington, D.C. In 1906, he graduated from the Engineering School of Application, and from 1906 to 1908, he was an instructor in engineering in West Point. He returned to fortifications and harbors duty, serving in Seattle until 1911. Next he served as Chief Engineer in the Philippines from 1911 to 1914, after which he spent three years as Engineer Commissioner in Washington, D.C. He commanded an engineer regiment with the AEF in France, and back in the states he commanded the Engineer Camp Humphreys in Virginia (later named Fort Belvoir). He was a brigadier general (NA) from 1917 to 1920. From Fort Humphreys, he returned to his old assignment as Engineer Commissioner in Washington, D.C. until 1921. From 1921 to 1928, he served as division engineer of the Central Division in Cincinnati, Ohio. He was a member of the Mississippi River Commission, and his final assignment was as department engineer of the Hawaiian Department. He retired as a colonel in 1929. His rank of brigadier general (retired list) was restored in June 1930. In retirement, his family lived in Washington, D.C., and he was still active as engineer commissioner. He was a member of the American Society of Civil Engineers and the Army and Navy Club. At the age of eighty he died, on 25 January 1951. Photo from the National Archives.

Eugene Frederick Ladd

Eugene Frederick Ladd (0-13295), son of George A. Ladd and Louise Ladd, was born on 19 September 1859 at Thetford, Vermont. He attended USMA and graduated number twelve of thirty-seven in the class of 1884. William L. Sibert (*q.v.*) and Isaac Newton Lewis were two of his classmates. He was commissioned in the Ninth Cavalry, and spent the next twelve years performing frontier duty. During this time, on 30 May 1888, he married Miss Norman, and they had one daughter, Katherine Louise. During the Spanish-American War, he was in Cuba from 1900 to 1901, then was sent to the Philippines, where he served in the Adjutant General's Department. He retired due to disabilities in 1915, but came back to duty for World War I and was promoted to brigadier general (NA) on 5 August 1917. He was awarded the Distinguished Service Medal for his performance of duty as an Adjutant General. He again retired as a colonel, and he lived in Cohasset, Massachusetts, where at the age of sixty-seven he died, on 23 April 1927. His rank of brigadier general was restored posthumously in June 1930. Photo courtesy of Special Collections, USMA Library.

William Campbell Langfitt (0-13440), son of Obadiah Langfitt and Virginia Tarr Langfitt, was born on 10 August 1860 in Wellsburo, Virginia. He entered USMA and graduated number two of fifty-two in the class of 1883. George Cameron and Tyree Rhodes Rivers (both *q.v.*) were two of his classmates. He was commissioned in the Corps of Engineers and was promptly sent to the Engineer School of Application in Willet's Point, New York, where he graduated in 1885. On 4 December of that year, he married Anne St. John Bemis, and they had one daughter, Dorothy. From 1886 to 1888, he was in the engineer office, Department of the Columbia (River), and from 1888 to 1893, he worked on rivers and harbors improvements in Galveston, Texas. From 1893 to 1895, he worked on improvements to the Ohio River and its tributaries, and from 1895 to1898, he was an instructor at the Engineer School. He was a major with the Second U.S. Volunteer Engineers in the Hawaiian Islands from 1898 to 1899, after which he spent six years as engineer of the 13th Lighthouse District. In

William Campbell Langfitt

1905 and 1906 and from 1907 to 1910, he was commander of the Engineer School and Depot in Washington, D.C. In the interval between, he served as Chief Engineer of the Army of Pacification in Cuba. From 1910 to 1914, he worked on rivers and harbors improvements and on the water supply in Washington, D.C. Right before U.S. entry into World War I, he worked on rivers and harbors improvements in Savannah, Georgia and was Chief Engineer of the Southern Department. From May until August 1917, he organized and commanded the 13th Engineers. In August, he joined the AEF as Chief of Staff. By October 1917, he was in charge of all American forces on duty with the British Army, and on 12 March 1918, he was made chief of utilities in charge of transportation, Department of Construction and Forestry, Department of Light Railways and Roads and Motor Transportation Department. This title actually meant he was Chief Engineer of the AEF. He was promoted to brigadier general (NA) on 5 August 1917, and to major general (NA) on 17 December 1917. For his performance of this duty he received the Distinguished Service Medal and he was made a companion of the Most Honorable Order of the Bath (Britain), a Commander of the Legion of Honor (France), and a commander of the Order of the Crown (Belgium). He returned to the States, and was district engineer of the Second New York and Puerto Rican Engineer Districts, as well as engineer of the Northeastern District of New York City. He retired in 1922 and lived in Geneva, New York. His rank of major general (retired list) was restored in June 1930. At the age of seventy-three, he died in Washington, D.C., on 20 April 1934. Photo courtesy of the National Archives.

William Lassiter (0-70), son of Mr. and Mrs. D. W. Lassiter, was born on 29 September 1867 in Petersburg, Virginia. He entered USMA and graduated number twenty-three of forty-nine in the class of 1889. William W. Harts, E. E. Winslow, C. A. F. Flagler and C. D. Rhodes (all *q.v.*) were four of his classmates. Lassiter was commissioned in the Fourth Artillery, and he graduated from the artillery school in 1894. He served with a battery in Santiago, Cuba in July 1898. From 1898 to 1913, he was an instructor in tactics at USMA. He was sent to Fort Riley, Kansas, where he commanded the Seventh Battery Field Artillery until 1903. After that, he served for five years on the board preparing the field artillery drill regulations, followed by two years in the office of the Inspector General. He was on the General Staff from 1911 to 1913, and was in the Vera Cruz Expedition in 1914. In 1916, he became the military attache at the American Embassy in London. He was made a brigadier general (NA) and was appointed commanding

William Lassiter

general, 51st Field Artillery Brigade in Boston, Massachusetts. He was Chief of Artillery, First Corps (AEF), for which he was awarded the Distinguished Service Medal. After that, he was Chief of Artillery, Second Army, and on 8 August 1918, he became a major general (NA). In France, he participated in the Aisne-Marne, St. Mihiel and Toul Sector battles, and in the occupation of the Coblenz Bridgehead. On 19 April 1919, he became Chief of Artillery, Third Army, then returned to the States and reverted to his permanent rank of colonel, General Staff. He commanded Camp (later Fort) Knox, Kentucky from September 1920 to September 1921, then became G-3 (operations and training), Assistant Chief of Staff. He commanded the Panama Division in 1923 and the Panama Department in 1924. He followed General Pershing as chief of the Tacna-Arica Plebiscite Commission. During 1927 to 1928, he commanded the Sixth Corps Area, headquartered in Chicago. After a brief tour as commander of the Philippine Department, he returned to the States to command the Eighth Corps Area. His final assignment was to command the Hawaiian Department in 1931, and he retired that year. On 5 October 1935, he married Jeanette Johnson. His decorations included the Distinguished Service Medal, and the Croix de Guerre, and he was made a Knight Commander of the Order of St. Michael and St. George (Britain) and a Commander of the Legion of Honor (France). In retirement, he lived in Santa Barbara, California. At the age of ninety he died, on 29 March 1959. Photo from the National Archives.

Howard Louis Laubach (0-422), son of Amandus Laubach, a Union veteran of the Civil War who later studied medicine and became an army doctor in the West, was born on 24 August 1870, the eighth generation of his paternal line born in this country. His ancestor, Count Christian LaBagh, arrived in America shortly after William Penn and settled in the Lehigh Valley of Pennsylvania. When he was six years old, his father resigned from the army and practiced in Fort Wayne, Indiana. Here the boy received his elementary education. He entered USMA and graduated number seventeen of fifty-one in the class of 1893. Lincoln C. Andrews (*q.v.*) and Herbert B. Crosby were two of his classmates. Kenzie Wallace Walker, later chief of finance, was his roommate for four years and was best man at his wedding. He was commissioned in the infantry and served during the Philippine Insurrection. In 1895, as a second lieutenant, he married Katherine Brinck Hague, daughter of the outstanding Texas lawyer and jurist, Judge J. P. Hague of El Paso. They had one child, a daughter, who married Col. Farragut F. Hall (USA). In his plebe year, he accidentally injured one lung during a pontoon bridge drill, which caused him to lose a year at USMA and later contributed to his death. Before World War I, he had two tours of duty on the General Staff, from 1911 to 1912 and from 1913 to 1915. He was promoted to brigadier general (NA) on 8 August 1918, and both organized and commanded the 14th Infantry Division. After the war, he reverted to his permanent, pre-war rank of colonel. He was made brigadier general (USA), on 1 April 1931. On 31 August 1934, he retired and lived in St. Petersburg, Florida. He wrote a number of short stories, and was an accomplished genealogist. At the age of seventy-nine, he died at Walter Reed Army Medical Center in Washington, D.C., on 19 May 1950. Photo from *The Assembly*, Association of Graduates, USMA.

Howard Louis Laubach

Laurin Leonard Lawson

Laurin Leonard Lawson (0-1258), son of Magne Lawson and Hannah Lawson, was born on 11 March 1876 in St. Peter, Minnesota. This was the only instance in the production of this work where I not only had to write St. Peter, for information, but got it! He attended public schools in LaCrosse, Wisconsin. During the Spanish-American War, he was a private in the First Washington Infantry from 1898 to 1899. He was commissioned a first lieutenant, 39th U.S. Volunteer Infantry, in 1899. Mustered out in 1901, he was promptly recommissioned a second lieutenant (USA), Artillery. He was made a first lieutenant by 1903, and was transferred to the Third Field Artillery in 1907. On 12 August 1907, he was made a captain, Fourth Field Artillery. Three times he served in the Philippines. He was in Vera Cruz, Mexico in 1914, and was also with the Punitive Expedition in 1916 and 1917. He was promoted to colonel (NA) on 6 February 1918, and on 11 May 1918, he became commandant of the Artillery School at Fort Sill, Oklahoma. On 1 October 1918, he was promoted to brigadier general (NA). He left Fort Sill on 18 December and took command of the 15th Field Artillery Brigade at Camp Stanley, Texas. He died 28 January 1938. Photo from the National Archives.

Henry Grant Learnard

Henry Grant Learnard (0-299), son of James E. Leonard and Ellen Packard Leonard, was born on 9 August 1867 in Wright City, Missouri. His parents were both originally from Tipton, Michigan. He entered USMA and graduated number thirty-two of fifty-four in the class of 1890. Edgar Jadwin, James Lindsay, Fred W. Sladen and Harry H. Bandholz (all *q.v.*) were four of his classmates. After being commissioned in the Infantry, he served with the Third Exploring Expedition in Alaska in 1899, and was in the Philippines from 1899 to 1901, except for a short tour with the China Relief Expedition. He got a Silver Star Commendation and later, a Purple Heart. On 7 November 1901, he married Florida Lyon, and they had two children, Henry and Catherine. He was made a brigadier general (NA) on 18 February 1918, and served in the Adjutant General's office from 1917 to 1920, for which he received the Distinguished Service Medal. In 1926, he was promoted to brigadier general (USA). He retired in 1931. At the age of sixty-nine, he died in Washington, D.C., on 7 March 1937. Photo courtesy of Special Collections, USMA Library.

Joseph Dugald Leitch

Joseph Dugald Leitch (0-281), son of Dugald Leitch and Sarah Furgeson Leitch, was born on 5 March 1864 in Montague, Michigan. He entered USMA and graduated number forty-four of forty-nine in the class of 1889. William G. Haan, E. E. Winslow, W. W. Harts and William Lassiter (all *q.v.*) were four of his classmates. He was commissioned in the infantry and on 1 October 1891, he married Margaret Crandal, daughter of Col. F. M. Crandal (USA), a Civil War veteran then still on duty. He performed frontier duty in the Southwest and far West until 1898, when he was in Santiago and San Juan Hill in Cuba. He had three separate tours of duty in the Philippines, and was being on the Vera Cruz Expedition in 1914, the year he graduated from the Army War College. From 1910 to 1913 and again from 1917 to 1918, he was with the General Staff in Washington. He was promoted to brigadier general (NA) on 6 February 1918, and to major general (NA) on 1 October of the same year. He commanded the 15th Infantry Brigade at Camp Fremont, California, and also the 8th and 13th Infantry Divisions. He was appointed inspector general and Chief of Staff of the American Expeditionary Force in Siberia from 1919 to 1920, for which he received the Distinguished Service Medal. He retired on 5 March 1928, and at the age of seventy-four, he died in San Francisco, California, on 26 October 1938. Photo from the National Archives.

Michael Joseph Lenihan (0-201), son of James Lehihan and Catherine Granger Lenihan, was born on 2 May 1865 in Hopkinton, Massachusetts. He entered USMA and graduated number fifty-seven of sixty-four in the class of 1887. Richmond P. Davis, Charles Henry Martin, P. D. Lochridge (all *q.v.*), and T. Q. Donaldson were four of his classmates, as was George Washington Patrick, great grandnephew of George Washington, who did not graduate and was killed in a railway accident in Mexico in 1891. Lenihan was commissioned in the infantry and performed frontier duty for two years. He graduated from the Infantry and Cavalry School at Fort Leavenworth, Kansas in 1891, and was Professor of Military Science and Tactics at Seaton Hall College in South Orange, New Jersey from 1893 to 1897. He was in Cuba from 1898 to 1899, and was then in the Philippines until 1902. From 1906 to 1910, he was on the General Staff, and from 1913 to 1916, he was in Hawaii. In 1917, he graduated from the Army War College. He was promoted to brigadier general (NA) on 5 August 1917, when he was made commander of the 83d Infantry Brigade (AEF). In November 1917, he was transferred to the 153rd Infantry Brigade, and he was stationed in France until April 1919. When he returned to the States, he was an army instructor at the Naval War College for four years, and then commanded the Third Infantry Division. On 2 May 1929, he retired. His decorations included the Distinguished Service Medal, Purple Heart with oak leaf cluster and the Croix de Guerre with three palms, and he was made a Commander of the Legion of Honor (France). In retirement, he lived at his birthplace, in Hopkinton, Massachusetts. At the age of ninety-three, he died in Philadelphia, Pennsylvania, on 13 August 1958. Photo from Special Collections, USMA Library.

Michael Joseph Lenihan

James Westcott Lester (ASN unknown), son of Charles S. Lester and Lucy Cooke Lester, was born on 8 September 1859 in Saratoga Springs, New York. He graduated from Union College in 1881 with an A.B. and went on to

James Westcott Lester

Columbia Law School. On 25 November 1884, he enlisted as a private in the 22d Separate Company, New York National Guard. On 13 June 1888, he married Bertha North Dowd, and they had four children James D. Lester, Charles W. Lester, Dudley G. Lester and Ralph W. Lester. During the Spanish-American War, he served as a major in the Second New York Volunteer Infantry from 9 May to 25 November 1898. He was made a brigadier general, New York National Guard, on 6 June 1911, and a brevet major general on 7 January 1913. As a brigadier, he was on the Mexican border from 18 June 1916 until 17 March 1917. He was back on duty 18 July the same year, serving during World War I. On 5 August 1917, he was made a brigadier general (NA) and commanded the 54th Infantry Brigade at Camp Wadsworth, South Carolina, but on 30 September 1917, he was honorably discharged due to physical disability. By 30 April 1919, he was reassigned to duty as a brigadier general, New York National Guard, and was appointed commander on 17 December 1921. In 1923, he resigned and returned to his law practice. His home was in Saratoga Springs, New York, where he died at the age seventy-three, on 13 November 1932. Photo courtesy of his grandson, Milford D. Lester of Saratoga Springs, New York.

Edward Mann Lewis (0-55), son of William Henry Lewis and Julia Snively Lewis, was born on 10 December 1863 in New Albany, Indiana. This was the location of the old Jefferson Quartermaster Depot, right across the Ohio River from Louisville, Kentucky. He entered USMA and graduated number seventy out of seventy-seven in the class of 1886. Mason M. Patrick, Charles T. Menoher, John J. Pershing (all *q.v.*),and Edward McCaskey were four of his classmates. He also attended the DePauw University in Greencastle, Indiana and the University of California. He performed frontier duty from 1886 to 1892, then became Professor of Military Science and Tactics at DePauw. During the Spanish-American War, he served as adjutant of the 20th Infantry, and also as regimental adjutant during the Philippine Insurrection from 1899 to 1901. He

Edward Mann Lewis

served in San Francisco, California following the 1906 earthquake and fire. He was Professor of Military Science and Tactics at the University of California from 1908 to 1912, and went with the Vera Cruz Expedition to Mexico in 1914 as commander of the Illinois National Guard. From there he went to the military headquarters in Boston. By 11 July 1916, he was commanding general, Thirteenth Provisional Division at Llano Grande, Texas. He was also commanding general 76th Infantry Brigade (NA) from August to November 1917. From 1 December 1917 to 5 May 1918, he commanded the American troops in Paris, and was then given command of the Third Brigade, Second Division (AEF). He commanded the 30th Infantry Division from 6 July 1918 to March 1919, when he was sent to the Chief of Staff section, General Headquarters, (AEF). He was president of the Infantry Board, then commanded Camp (later Fort) Gordon, Georgia and later, the District of Douglas, Arizona. Back in the United States, he commanded the Second and the Third Infantry Divisions, and from 1922 to 1924, was Commanding General, Eighth Corps Area. His last assignment was command of the Hawaiian Department from 1925 to 1927. On 10 December 1927, he retired. He married Hattie Russel Balding, and they had three children Henry B. Lewis, Mrs. Adelaide Palmer McMullen and Thomas E. Lewis. His decorations and honors were many. He received the Distinguished Service Medal and two Croix de Guerre (Belgium and France), and was made a Knight Commander of the Order of St. Michael and St. George (Great Britain), Commander of the Legion of Honor (France), Commander of the Order of Leopold (Belgium) and Grand Officer of Danilo (Montenegro). He was Phi Beta Kappa and a member of the Society of Santiago de Cuba, as well as of the Union League of San Francisco and the Faculty Club of the University of California. In retirement, he lived in Berkeley, California. At the age of eighty-five, he died on 27 July 1949. He was buried in the Presidio. Photo courtesy of the Casemate Museum, Fort Monroe, Virginia.

Hunter Liggett

Hunter Liggett (0-3) was born in 1857 in Reading, Pennsylvania. He entered USMA and graduated number forty-one in the class of 1879. Fredrick S. Foltz, William D. Beach and Fredrick V. Abbot (all *q.v.*) were three of his classmates. He was commissioned in the infantry and performed frontier duty from 1887 to 1891. He served in Cuba and as a major of U.S. Volunteers in the Philippines. After graduating from the Army War College in 1910, he became its director until 1912, and served as its president in 1913. That same year, he was promoted to brigadier general (USA), and was back in the Philippines from 1915 to 1917. As a major general, he commanded the 41st Infantry Division from 20 December 1917 to 18 January 1918. From 20 January 1918 to 12 October 1918, he was commanding general, First Corps, and then was commanding general, First U.S. Army, for which he received the Distinguished Service Medal. He and Robert Lee Bullard were the only United States lieutenant generals of World War I, promoted to this rank on 16 October 1918. He was president of the Infantry Association, and in 1921, he retired as a major general, but was advanced to lieutenant general (retired list) in June 1930. He wrote two books *Commanding an American Army*, published in 1925, and *American Expeditionary Force*, published in 1927. At the age of seventy-eight, he died in San Francisco, on 30 December 1935. Photo from the Pennsylvania National Guard.

James Robert Lindsay (0-13498) was born on 12 August 1865 in Culhoun, Illinois. He entered USMA and graduated number sixteen of sixty-four in the class of 1890. Edgar Jadwin, James A. Ryan and Fred W. Sladen (all *q.v.*) were three of his classmates. He was commissioned and sent to the 14th Infantry at Vancouver Barracks, Washington. In June 1897, he graduated from the Infantry and Cavalry School at Fort Leavenworth, Kansas, and then took part in the Santiago Campaign in Cuba, first as a regimental quartermaster and later as a brigade quartermaster. On 11 October 1899, he was promoted to captain of the 13th Infantry and joined them on 30 May 1900, in Dagupan in the Philippines. He served a total of five tours of duty in the Philippines. In 1914, he took part in the Vera Cruz Expedition, and during 1916 and 1917, he was with the American forces in Tiensin, China. During World War I, he was first in the Presidio of San Francisco from June 1917 to January 1918, and was then at Camp Fremont, California, until 1 October 1918. On that date he was promoted to brigadier general (NA) and was sent to Camp Cody, New Mexico, where he commanded the post and the 97th Infantry Division until January 1919. In October 1920, he retired after thirty-four years of service, but then returned to active duty. He performed recruiting duty in New York City, then became Professor of Military Science and Tactics at the Louisville (Kentucky) Male High School, where he remained until shortly before his death. At the age of seventy-four, he died in Louisville, on 26 April 1940. His widow, Mrs. Eva M. Lindsay, and his son, Maj. James R. Lindsay, Jr., survived him. Photo from *The Assembly*, Association of Graduates, USMA.

James Robert Lindsay

Julian Robert Lindsey

Julian Robert Lindsey (0-405), son of John W. Lindsey and Julia Lindsey, was born on 16 March 1871 in Irwinton, Georgia. He entered USMA graduated number thirty-two of sixty-two in the class of 1892. Charles P. Sumerall (*q.v.*) was one of his classmates. He was commissioned in the cavalry, and from 1896 to 1900, he served in the Tactics Department at USMA. From 1900 to 1903, he was an aide to Gen. Adna R. Chaffee on the China Expedition at the time of the Boxer Rebellion. He served in China, in the Philippines, in Cuba, in Mexico and in France. On 11 June 1904, he married Hannah Broster, who died on 29 March 1905 after the birth of their only son, Julian Broster Lindsey. From 1912 to 1916, he was again in the Tactics Department at USMA. After the Punitive Expedition into Mexico, he went to France, where he commanded the 164th Infantry Brigade of the 82d Infantry Division (AEF), for which he received the Distinguished Service Medal. In April 1918, he was promoted to brigadier general (NA). He was promoted to brigadier general (USA) on 1 January 1932. He commanded Fort Knox, Kentucky, after which he retired in 1934. He belonged to the Columbia Country Club in Washington, D.C. as well as the Army and Navy Club. In 1942, he was promoted to major general (retired list). At the age of seventy-seven, he died at Walter Reed Army Medical Center in Washington, on 27 June 1948. He was buried in West Point. Photo courtesy of the National Archives.

William T. Littebrant (no ASN) was born in California. He entered USMA and graduated number forty-one of forty-four in the class of 1888. Peyton C. March and Guy Henry Preston (both *q.v.*) were two of his classmates. He was commissioned in the 19th Infantry. Two months later, he transferred to the Tenth Infantry, and from 1888 to 1892, he performed frontier duty. After this, he was Professor of Military Science and Tactics at the Missouri Military Academy. In 1889, he transferred to the Tenth Cavalry, and on 26 August 1896, he was promoted to first lieutenant in the Seventh Cavalry. On 2 February 1901, he was made a captain with the 12th Cavalry. During the

William T. Littebrant

Spanish-American War, he was in Cuba, from 1898 to 1901. On 1 October 1918, he was made a brigadier general (NA) and commanded the 19th Field Artillery Brigade at Fort Sill, Oklahoma until 1 March 1919. He reverted to his permanent rank of colonel. At the age of fifty-four, he died at Camp McClellan, Alabama, on 2 July 1919. His rank as a brigadier general was restored posthumously by act of Congress in June 1930. Photo from the National Archives.

Isaac William Littell

Isaac William Littell (0-13124), son of Isaac William Littell and Elizabeth Ball Littell, was born on 5 December 1857 in Elizabeth, New Jersey. He attended Stevens Industrial Technical School for two years, then entered USMA and graduated number twenty-eight of fifty-two in the class of 1883. He was commissioned in the Tenth Infantry, and later changed to the Quartermaster Corps. From 1884 to 1890, he performed frontier duty. On 22 January 1885, he married Julia Barrat, daughter of Captain Gregory Barrett (USA), a Civil War veteran from Maryland. He was made a first lieutenant on 21 August 1888, and with his captaincy transferred to quartermaster in 1895. From 1900 to 1901, he was a major, quartermaster, U.S. Volunteers. On 26 October 1901, he was discharged from the U.S. Volunteers and was commissioned a major in the Quartermaster Corps (USA). He was in the Philippines during the Insurrection. In 1908, as a lieutenant colonel, he was Deputy Quartermaster General, and as of 13 March 1911, he was a colonel, acting Quartermaster General. From 1911 to 1914, he was chief quartermaster of the Philippine Division. He was promoted to Brigadier General (NA) on 5 August 1917, and was in charge of cantonment construction all over the country, for which he was given the Distinguished Service Medal. He belonged to the Delta Tau Delta fraternity and the Army and Navy Club. In 1919, he retired as a brigadier general. At the age of sixty-six, he died in Washington, D.C., on 1 May 1924. Photo courtesy of the National Archives.

P. D. Lochridge (0-13402) was born on 2 December 1863 near Bexar, Alabama. His name is given as P. D. in both the Register of Graduates and the Army List. On authority of a general officer classmate, he never had or used a given name and was known throughout life solely as "P. D." If he ever did have one it was one of the better kept secrets of the army. He attended the College of Mississippi for three years, then entered USMA and graduated number twenty-one of sixty-four in the class of 1887. George O. Squier and Ernest Hinds (both *q.v.*)

P. D. Lochridge

were two of his classmates. He was an ardent student with an unfailing, dry sense of humor. He was commissioned in the Second Cavalry and performed frontier duty from 1887 to 1888 and from 1890 to 1891. While at Fort Walla Walla, Washington with the Second Cavalry, he met and married Carlotta Rawolle, daughter of Capt. William Charles Rawolle, a Prussian-born cavalry veteran of the American Civil War. They were married on 20 February 1889, and they had one son, Rawolle Lochridge. Other than school details, he served in the West and Southwest until 1898. He was in the pursuit of Geronimo from Fort Huachuca, Arizona. In 1893, he was an honor graduate of the infantry and cavalry school at Fort Leavenworth, Kansas. He was regimental adjutant of the Third Cavalry at Fort Myer, Virginia for three years. He was in Cuba and in the Puerto Rican Campaign from 1899 to 1901, serving as regimental commissary. In 1902, he served at Yellowstone National Park, which was then garrisoned by the army. On 13 January 1915, he was detailed to the General Staff in Washington. He was promoted twice in the same day, to lieutenant colonel and to colonel, on 1 July 1916. On 17 December 1917, he was promoted to brigadier general (NA). Beginning in April 1918, he headed the War Plans Division of the General Staff. During 1918 and 1919, he served on the Supreme War Council, for which he received the Distinguished Service Medal. In 1919, he retired as a colonel due to disabilities. In 1930, his rank as a brigadier general was restored. At the age of seventy-one, he died in Washington, D.C., on 17 June 1935. Photo courtesy of the Annual Report, Association of Graduates, USMA.

☆

Albert James Logan

Albert James Logan (no ASN assigned), son of Mr. and Mrs. James Logan, was born on 7 July 1857 in Pittsburgh, Pennsylvania. He attended Pennsylvania Military College from 1874 to 1876. In 1882, he established his own bedding and manufacturing company. On November of the same year, he married Susan E. Murphy. He was chairman of the Pittsburgh City Planning Commission and a director of both the Pittsburgh and National Chambers of Commerce. His military career began when he enlisted in Company F, 18th Pennsylvania Infantry (the Duquesne Grays) in March 1876. In 1895, he was appointed Quartermaster General of Pennsylvania. with the rank of colonel and served in the Spanish-American War. By 1898, he was colonel of the 17th

Pennsylvania Infantry. In 1902, he became Commissary General of Pennsylvania and performed staff duty until 1909, when he took command of the 18th Pennsylvania Infantry. On 22 September 1912, he was promoted to brigadier general and took command of the Second Brigade, National Guard of Pennsylvania, a position which he held during the Mexican border troubles until the federalization of National Guard troops for World War I. He was promoted to brigadier general (NA) on 15 July 1917. He commanded the 56th Infantry Brigade from 15 July 1917 until 28 January 1918, when he was discharged due to physical disabilities. He was a Presbyterian and a member of the State Armory Board and the Military Order of the World War. At the age of seventy-seven he died, on 17 December 1934. Photo courtesy of the Pennsylvania National Guard.

Rufus Estes Longan (0-562), son of Patrick H. Longan and Angeline Donobue Longan, was born 7 January 1873 in Dresden, Missouri. His family had come to Missouri before 1810. He attended Otterville College in Otterville, Missouri, after which he taught for three terms. He won his appointment to USMA in a competitive examination, and graduated number thirty-seven in the class of 1897. Harley B. Fergusson and Frank R. McCoy (both *q.v.*) were two of his classmates. He was commissioned in the 11th Infantry. On 16 May 1898, he married Susan Magoffin Luckett of Sedalia, Missouri. Her father was a nephew of Beriah Magoffin, former governor of Kentucky, and she was a relative of Susan Shelly Magoffin, whose diary, *Down the Santa Fe Trail*, is still in print. From April to July 1906, he was on duty in San Francisco after the earthquake and fire. He tried to get a cooks and bakers school started, and he succeeded in beginning the project in the army. From 1910 to 1912, he was in the Tactics Department at USMA, and he received a very favorable comment from the superintendent. From 1913 to 1915, he was stationed in Hawaii, and then he reported to Fort Leavenworth as a student in the School of the Line, where he was a distinguished graduate and received a promotion to major. He went to Fort Lawton, Washington, and then was assigned to the new 32d Infantry in Hawaii, where he remained until July 1917. He returned to San Francisco as an instructor at the officers training camp until 14 December, when he reported as Chief of Staff of the port of embarkation in Hoboken, New Jersey and worked for Gen. David C. Shanks. Years later, General Shank said he was "one of the best all-around officers known to me—loyal, energetic, possessed of excellent initiative and fine common sense." On 1 October 1918, he was promoted to brigadier general (NA), and continued his same duties until 10 November. After a very short

Rufus Estes Longan

tour of duty in the Northwest, he arrived in France on 2 January 1919. Two months later he got the flu and nearly died; he was in the hospital and on sick leave until 17 June 1919. He returned to the States, and on 27 June 1919, he reverted to his permanent rank of major. He was sent back to his former station at the port of embarkation in Hoboken. He was ranked out of his old assignment, so had to settled for a position as Assistant Chief of Staff. After about a year, he went to the Command and General Staff School at Fort Leavenworth, Kansas, was rapidly promoted to colonel again, and went to the Army War College. He became executive officer to the Chief of Infantry until 31 July 1923, when he retired. He held the Distinguished Service Medal and the Navy Cross (signed by the acting secretary of the navy, Franklin D. Roosevelt). Neither he nor Mrs. Longan were in very good health. They lived in Washington, D.C., where he sold insurance for a while, then ran one of the Baltimore city hospitals. They left Baltimore in 1933, and moved to San Antonio, Texas. He went to see a friend who was a physician in St. Louis, Missouri in 1936, was suddenly stricken ill and died about two weeks later, on 3 September 1936. He was buried at Jefferson Barracks, Missouri. Photo from the Annual Report, Association of Graduates, USMA.

Herbert Mayhew Lord

Herbert Mayhew Lord (0-68), son of Sabin Lord and Abbie Swett Lord, was born on 6 December 1859 in Rockland, Maine. He graduated in 1884 from Colby College in Maine with an A.B., and he received an M.A. from the same school in 1889. On 9 September 1885, he married Annie Stewart Waldo. He did newspaper work, then served on the Ways and Means Committee of the House of Representatives in Washington, D.C. until 1908. On 17 May 1898, he was appointed an "additional" major, paymaster, in the Maine Volunteers, from which he was discharged on 7 May 1901. He was commissioned a captain, paymaster (USA) on 5 February 1901, and on 15 July 1919 he was promoted to brigadier general (USA). During the war, he was Army Liberty Loan Officer and assistant to Major General Goethals with the title of director of finance (October 1918). He became Chief of Finance (USA) on 1 July 1920, and received an honorary LL.D. from his Colby College that same year. He was awarded the Distinguished Service Medal "for exceptionally meritorious and conspicuous service as assistant to the Quartermaster General and as Director of Finance." He retired from the army on 30 June 1922, and the next day he was appointed civilian Director of the Bureau of the Budget, a post he held until 31

May 1929. During his brief retirement, he lived in Washington, D.C. At the age of seventy he died there, on 2 June 1930. Photo from the National Archives.

LeRoy Springs Lyon (ASN unknown), son of John Lyon and Margaret Springs Lyon, was born on 15 October 1866 in Petersburg, Virginia. He graduated from Richmond College with an A.B. in 1886. He entered USMA and graduated number seven of sixty-five in the class of 1891. He was commissioned in the Seventh Cavalry, and from 1898 to 1899, he was an aide to Gen. Royal T. Frank in Chickamauga Park, Georgia, Anniston, Alabama and at headquarters, Department of the Gulf. He graduated from the Coast Artillery School at Fort Monroe, Virginia also in 1898, and was with the Second Artillery in Cuba. In 1902, he married Harriet Amsden. In 1903, he graduated from the School of Submarine Defense at Fort Totten, New York. From 1903 to 1906, he was district artillery engineer at Fort Barrancas, Florida. He served against the Moros in the Philippines between 1906 and 1907. In 1916 and 1917, he served in the Canal Zone. After a short stay in El Paso in 1917, he was sent to Camp Kearny, California to command the 65th Field Artillery Brigade. He was promoted to brigadier general (NA) on 5 August 1917. On 12 April 1918, he was promoted to major general (NA) and commanded the 31st Infantry Division (the Dixie Division), both at Camp Wheeler, Georgia and in France with the AEF. In November and December 1918, he commanded the 90th Infantry Division. After the war, he reverted to his permanent rank of colonel of Field Artillery and commanded the Field Artillery Basic School at Camp Taylor, Kentucky. At the age of fifty-three, he died in Kentucky, on 23 February 1920. Photo courtesy of the National Archives.

LeRoy Springs Lyon

Theodore Charles Lyster, M.D. (0-13367), son of Col. William Lyster (USA) and Martha G. D. Lyster, was born on 10 July 1875 at Fort Larned, Kansas. He attended public schools in Buffalo, New York and graduated from Detroit High School in 1893. In 1897, he graduated from the University of Michigan with a Ph.D., and he received his M.D. in 1899. He enlisted as a private and a hospital steward, serving on the ships *Relief* and *Missouri*, as well as at the Reserve Divisional Hospital in Siboney, Cuba, until 12 September 1898. On 3 October 1900, he was commissioned a first lieutenant and assistant surgeon. He served at the Manhattan Ear and Eye Hospital in New York from 1900 to 1904, when he went to the Ancon Hospital, Canal Zone, as chief of the Ear,

Theodore Charles Lyster, M.D.

Eye, Nose and Throat Clinic. In 1911, he was made chief of eye service at the Philippine University Hospital in Manila. During the American Occupation of Vera Cruz in 1914, he was Chief Health Officer. In France with the AEF during World War I, he was Chief of Aviation and Professional Services in the Surgeon General's Office. He was promoted to brigadier general (NA) on 3 June 1918. In 1919, he retired as a colonel, but his rank of brigadier general was restored by act of Congress on 16 August 1930. He married the Lua Withenbury, and they had one son, Thomas Charles Lyster, Jr. After 1920, he had a private practice in the medical firm of Lyster and Jones. He was a member of the American College of Surgeons and various other medical societies. He received the Distinguished Service Medal. At the age of fifty-eight he died, on 5 August 1933. Photo courtesy of the Walter Reed Army Medical Center, Washington.

Douglas MacArthur

Douglas MacArthur (0-57), son of the youngest colonel in the Union Army, was born on 26 January 1880 at Little Rock Barracks, Arkansas. His appointment to USMA came from Wisconsin, his father's native state, and he graduated number one of ninety-three in the class of 1903. He was commissioned in the Corps of Engineers. As a member of the War Department General Staff, he participated in the Vera Cruz Expedition of 1914. On 29 June 1914, as a major, he was made press release officer. On the evening of 19 February 1917 President Wilson had given a stag dinner, and left orders that he was not to be disturbed. This particular night Major MacArthur happened to be the General Staff Officer of the day when a telegraph arrived announcing the sudden and very unexpected death of Gen. Funston. Major MacArthur had to break into the party, report the news personally to President Wilson, and that of course broke up the party. Pershing was then made commander in France, and through MacArthur's efforts a press section was sent as part of his staff. He went to France, and on 26 June 1918, he was promoted to brigadier general (NA). He was Chief of Staff of the 42d (Rainbow) Division, and as of November 1918, he was commanding general, 42d Division. In France, he managed to earn two Distinguished Service Crosses, seven Silver Stars and two Purple Hearts. When he returned to the States, he was superintendent of West Point from 12 June 1919 to 30 June 1922. At West Point, he was host to the Prince of Wales (later King Edward VIII). He was promoted to brigadier general (USA) in 1920, and to major general in 1925. He was commanding general of the Philippine Department in 1930. On 21 November 1930, the Secretary of War, Patrick J. Hurley, appointed him Chief of Staff. Rumor reached Hurley that President Hoover was upset by the appointment, so Hurley went to see him, stood at attention before his desk and stated that if the president did not like his appointment, he could find a new Secretary of War as well. The appointment stood. MacArthur brought all tactical units into the First, Second, Third and Fourth U.S. Armies, and remained Chief of Staff until 1 October 1935. He received another Distinguished Service Medal for his service. He became Field Marshal of the Philippine Army in 1936, and retired as a general in 1937. He returned to active duty in 1941, and from 1942 to 1945 was Commander in Chief of the U.S. forces in the Pacific. From April 1942 to September 1945, he was also Commander in the Southwest Pacific. He received the Medal of Honor on 25 March 1942. His first marriage broke up while he was Chief of Staff in Washington, and sometime later, he married Jean Faircloth of Murfreesboro, Tennessee. They had one son. He was ordered out of the Philippines by the president, and he escaped just before the fall of Corrigedor, went to Australia and started the long journey back. He promised to return, and did. On 30 June 1943, he started a broad offensive through the New Georgia and New Guinea Campaigns. On 18 December 1944, he was made a five-star general of the army, outranked only by General Marshall, the Chief of Staff in Washington. On 2 September 1945, he took the surrender of the Japanese aboard the USS *Missouri*, signing it in his capacity as Supreme Allied Commander. He became Commander in Chief of the Far East Command on 1 January 1947. He received the thanks of the U.S. House of Representatives and of the U.S. Senate. From 1945 to 1951, he was Military Governor of Japan, for which modern Japan should thank him. From 25 June 1950 until 11 April 1951, he was Commander in Chief, Far East Command, and Supreme Commander of the Allied powers in Japan. He was exempted from retirement due to age, but he and President Truman had a disagreement, and he was relieved from duty and came back to the States to receive a hero's welcome. He had great oratorical ability and the capacity to make prose sound like poetry. His family lived at the Waldorf Towers in New York City, and he was Chairman of the Board of Remington-Rand. He died at Walter Reed Army Medical Center in Washington on 5 April 1964. He lay in state in the rotunda of the capitol, and was buried in Norfolk, Virginia. Though a controversial man, he was a very great one. He was one of the finest general officers in the service. Photo from the MacArthur Memorial, Norfolk, Virginia.

John Fitz Madden (0-366), son of Jerome Madden and Margaret Evans Madden, was born on 30 March 1870 in Sacramento, California. His attended St. Matthews Hall in San Mateo. In 1891, he was commissioned in the infantry. He married, and had one son; then they divorced, and he didn't remarry. He graduated from the Infantry and Cavalry School at Fort Leavenworth in 1897.

John Fitz Madden

He was in Cuba during the Spanish-American War, then served in the Philippines during the Insurrection. In 1916, at the time of the Punitive Expedition, he was chief quartermaster. In France shortly thereafter, he was assistant quartermaster of the First Infantry Division, and later, was assistant to the chief quartermaster in Paris. On 1 October 1918, he was promoted to brigadier general (NA). On 15 April 1920, he received his promotion to colonel (USA). In 1921, he graduated from the Army War College, and in 1922, he graduated from the General Staff School at Fort Leavenworth, Kansas. In 1923, he graduated from the Naval War College in Newport, Road Island. On 6 March 1931, he was promoted brigadier general (USA). He retired on 31 March of that year and lived in East Orange, New Jersey. He was made an officer of the Legion of Honor (France). He was an Episcopalian, he belonged to the Army and Navy Clubs in Washington and Manila, as well as to the Lambs in New York and the West Point Army Mess. At the age of seventy-six, he died in East Orange, New Jersey, on 19 May 1946. The photo, courtesy of the National Archives, was taken on 5 September 1918 in Paris, at which time he was assistant to the chief quartermaster.

John Skinner Mallory (0-8648), son of Col. Charles R. Mallory and Martha Skinner Mallory, was born on 1 November 1857 near Hampton, Virginia. He was a descendant of Phillip Mallory, who came from England to Virginia in 1656, and his great grandfather, Col. Francis Mallory, was killed in action in Newport News, Virginia during the American Revolution. His grandfather, Charles Mallory, was lieutenant governor of Virginia during the War of 1812; his father was both a member of the 1861 Constitutional Convention of Virginia and an officer in the Confederate Army. For his early education, he attended private schools in Hampton and Norfolk. He entered USMA and graduated number fifty-six of sixty-seven in the class of 1879. William D. Beach, Fredrick S. Foltz and Hunter Liggett (all *q.v.*) were three of his classmates. He made friends easily, and was held in high esteem. He was commissioned in the 20th Infantry,

John Skinner Mallory

and he spent twenty years with this regiment before becoming a captain. From 1879 to 1883, he performed frontier duty in the far West. In 1886, he married Sarah Reed in Portland, Oregon. She was the daughter of Judge and Mrs. John H. Reed. They had three sons, Henry Reed Mallory, Conn Mallory and John Stevenson Mallory, a USMA graduate and field artillery officer. In the Sioux Campaign of 1890 to 1891, he was acting chief commissary for Gen. Nelson A. Miles. In 1893, he wrote the *Small Arms Firing Manual*, which became the official manual for the services. He served in the Philippines under both General Otis and Gen. Arthur MacArthur. During 1900 and 1901, he was military attaché in China, and from 1903 to 1906, was on the War Department General Staff. In 1912, after graduating from the Army War College was promoted to colonel and commanded the 29th Infantry, in part at Camp Gaillard in the Canal Zone. On 5 August 1917, he was promoted to brigadier general (NA) and commanded the 153rd Depot Brigade at Camp Dix, New Jersey. Later, he commanded the 78th Infantry Division. In early 1918, he was assigned command of the Seventh Brigade (Fourth Division), but foreign service was denied him because of a failed a physical examination. In March 1918, he was discharged as a brigadier from the national army, reverted to the rank of colonel and commanded Camp Lee, Virginia and later, Camp Upton, New York. On 30 December 1918, he was retired due to disabilities, and lived in Lexington, Virginia. For two years, he taught Spanish at Virginia Military Institute, and was active in the Robert E. Lee Memorial Episcopal Church. On 21 June 1930, his rank of brigadier general was restored. He received two Silver Star Commendations for actions in the Philippines. At the age of seventy-four, he died on 2 February 1932. He was loyal friend, a jovial companion and a man of varied attainments. Photo from *The Assembly,* Association of Graduates, USMA.

Paul Bernard Malone

Paul Bernard Malone (0-442), son of John Malone and Anna Malone, was born on 8 May 1872 in Middletown, New York. He entered USMA and graduated number seventeen of fifty-four in the class of 1894. Francis LeJau Parker and Hamilton Hawkins (both *q.v.*) were two of his classmates. He was commissioned in the 13th Infantry. On 12 June 1895, he married Gertrude E. Kerwin. During the Spanish-American War, he served in the Santiago Campaign and in the Sanitary Corps, for which he received a Silver Star Commendation. He was in the campaign against Emilio Aguinaldo in Luzon in the Philippines from 1899 to 1901. From 1901 to 1905, he taught chemistry at West Point, and in 1909, was an honor graduate from the Army School of the Line. In

1910, he graduated from the Staff College, and during 1911 and 1912 served on the General Staff. In 1916 and 1917, he commanded a district in Texas on the Mexican border, and after that served with The Citizens Military Training Camps. In France, he was with the operations section of the headquarters staff of the AEF. He commanded the 23d Infantry Regiment, was promoted to brigadier general (NA) on 1 October 1918 and commanded the Tenth Infantry Brigade, part of the Fifth Infantry Division, during the St. Mihiel and Argonne battles. He commanded the Third Infantry Brigade, part of the Second Infantry Division, becoming assistant commandant of the Infantry School at Fort Benning, Georgia. In late 1922 and early 1923, he was at the Field Artillery School at Fort Sill, Oklahoma, after which he commanded the Second Field Artillery Brigade of the Second Infantry Division. Following this, were four months commanding the 12th Infantry Brigade. During 1928 and 1929, he commanded the Sixth Corps Area. From 1929 to 1935, he commanded the Third Corps Area in Baltimore, Maryland. His last assignment was to command the Fourth Army and Ninth Corps Area in San Francisco, California. He retired in 1936, and was given many honors, degrees and decorations. Between 1905 and 1911, he wrote five books on West Point, and was later an editor, a radio commentator and a public speaker. His home was in San Francisco. At the age of eighty-eight, he died in Sarasota, Florida, on 16 October 1960. Photo courtesy of the Casemate Museum.

William Abram Mann (0-13117) was born on 31 July 1854 in Altoona, Pennsylvania. After attending public school, he entered USMA and graduated number twenty-five of forty-three in the class of 1875. Tasker H. Bliss (*q.v.*), Robert P. P. Wainwright (Johnathan M. Wainwright's father) and James G. Sturgis (killed at Little Big Horn) were three of his classmates. He was commissioned and performed frontier duty from 1875 to 1892. On 10 September 1884, he married Elsie Moir. He was in the Pine Ridge Indian Campaign of 1890 and 1891, and accompanied his regiment to Cuba, where he took part in El Caney and the Siege of Santiago. He was cited for gallantry and received a Silver Star Commendation. After brief duty in the States, he went to the Philippines, to San Blas, Janinay, Passi, Dumarao and Romblon. Later, he was Adjutant General and Inspector General of the Visayan Military District. He was promoted to major, assigned to the 14th Infantry and returned with it to the States to commanded Fort Porter and Niagara, New York. He returned to the Philippine Islands as assistant Chief of Staff, then went to the Army War College in 1904. By 1911, he was a colonel, and he performed two tours of duty on the

William Abram Mann

General Staff and with the Cuban Pacification Army. In 1915, he was promoted to brigadier general (USA) and commanded the School of Fire for Field Artillery. Shortly after the declaration of war on 6 April 1917, he was promoted to major general and commanded the 42d (Rainbow) Division. They sailed to France that October. On 19 December 1917, he was relieved by Gen. Charles T. Menoher. He was a very popular commander, and his relief from the division command was universally regretted. When he returned to the States, he commanded the Second Corps Area on Governor's Island, New York. After he retired he was associated with the Equitable Trust Company and moved to the "Highlands" in Washington, D.C., where at the age of eighty he died, on 8 October 1934. Photo courtesy of the Association of Graduates, USMA.

Peyton Conway March

Peyton Conway March (0-6), son of Professor Francis A. March, a philologist at Lafayette College, was born on 27 December 1864 in Easton, Pennsylvania. He graduated from Lafayette College in 1884, then entered USMA and graduated number ten of forty-four in the class of 1888. Robert L. Howze and Guy Henry Preston (both *q.v.*) were two of his classmates. He was commissioned in the artillery. On 4 July 1891, he married Josephine Smith Cunningham, and they had five children. He served during the Spanish-American War as captain of the Astor Battery in the Philippines, for which he received the Distinguished Service Cross. Later, he was a major in the 33d U.S. Volunteer Infantry, for which he received five Silver Star Commendations. He was an aide to Gen. Arthur MacArthur, and in 1904, he was military observer with the Japanese Army. On 18 November 1904, his wife died. On 25 August 1925, he married Cora V. McEntee of New York, in London. He obtained the surrender of Gen. Venancio Aguinalda's Chief of Staff, and was made military and later civil governor of Ilocos. In 1911, he was the commissary general of the Philippines. In 1916, he was a lieutenant colonel of field artillery, and in 1917, he was promoted to brigadier general. On 5 August 1917, he was promoted to major general. In 1918, he became Chief of Staff (USA). He was one of only three officers raised by President Wilson to four-star rank for World War I; the other two were Tasker H. Bliss and John J. Pershing (both *q.v.*). During World War I, he was put in charge of all U.S. artillery forces in France. He served as Chief of Staff until 1921, when Pershing returned to the States and succeeded him. He retired on 1 November 1921. He received honors and decorations from the United States and many foreign countries. In 1953, Congress passed a joint resolution of thanks for his service during World War I. Death came in

Washington, D.C., on 13 April 1955. He was one of the last bearded general officers on duty in the United States Army. Photo courtesy of the Association of Graduates, USMA.

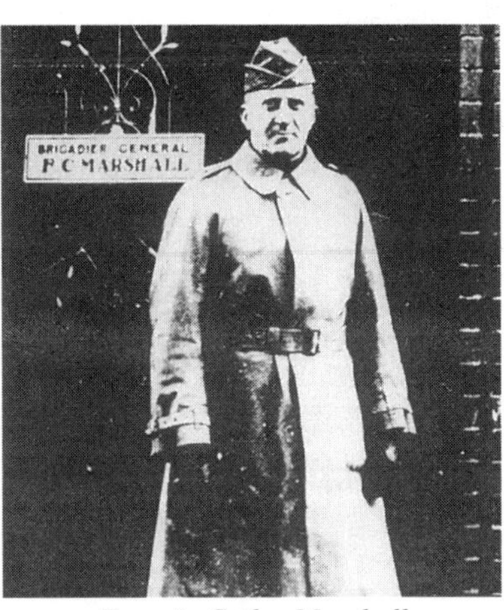

Francis Cutler Marshall

Francis Cutler Marshall (0-277), son of George A. Marshall and Miriam Cutler Marshall, was born on 26 March 1867 in Galena, Illinois. He entered USMA and graduated number nineteen of fifty-four in the cass of 1890. Edgar Jadwin (later the Chief of Engineers) was one of his classmates. He was commissioned in the Eighth Cavalry and served in the last of the Indian Wars from 1890 to 1891. On 5 September 1894, he married Sophie Page, daughter of Gen. John Henry Page, a Union veteran of the Civil War. He was in the China Relief Expedition of 1900 to 1901, for which he was cited posthumously. He taught tactics at USMA from 1904 to 1908, and served between the dates of his original commission and his promotion to brigadier general in the Eighth, Sixth, Second, Eleventh and Fifteenth Cavalry Regiments. On 17 December 1917, he was promoted to brigadier general (NA) and commanded the 165th Field Artillery Brigade, part of the 90th Infantry Division, until 20 October 1918. He was put in command of the Second Infantry Brigade, part of the First Infantry Division, until 28 May 1919, for which he received the Distinguished Service Medal. He was transferred to command the Eighth Infantry Brigade where he remained until 1 August 1919. He served in action at St. Mihiel and the Meuse-Argonne battle, and after the war, he was with the American Forces in Germany. His home was in Darlington, Wisconsin. His master's degrees were from both Wisconsin and Trinity Colleges. At the age of fifty-five, he was killed in an airplane crash near San Diego, on 7 December 1922. The wrecked plane and his remains were not discovered until the following year on 12 May; it was believed the plane was lost in a fog, crashed into the side of the Cuyamaca Mountains and burned. Marshall Field at Fort Riley, Kansas is named after him; he had been stationed there and loved his time there. Photo courtesy of Special Collections, USMA Library.

Richard Coke Marshall, Jr. (ASN unknown), son of Richard Marshall and Kate Wilson Coke Marshall, was born on 13 March 1879 in Portsmouth, Virginia. In 1898, he graduated from the Virginia Military Institute with a B.S. and was commissioned a captain, Fourth U.S. Volunteer Infantry on 29 June, to

Richard Coke Marshall, Jr.

serve in the Spanish-American War. On 8 June 1899, he was honorably mustered out of the U.S. Volunteers and returned to the Virginia Military Institute as Professor of Mathematics and Commandant of Cadets. He stayed there until 3 February 1902, when he accepted a regular army commission as second lieutenant of artillery. On 28 October 1903, he married Louise Baker. In 1904, he was an honor graduate of the Artillery School. He was made captain (USA) in 1908, and was promoted to brigadier general on 26 June 1918, after other national army promotions. He was the officer in charge of the Cantonment Division (later called the Construction Division) from 18 February 1918, and was responsible for all War Department construction in the continental United States and its territories. In 1918, this involved an $80,000,000 budget and 400,000 men. This service earned him a Distinguished Service Medal. In 1920, he resigned from the army to become general manager of the Association of General Contractors of America. He left in 1928 to become president of the Sumner Soillitt Company in Chicago, Illinois, where he lived in retirement. He was an Episcopalian, and he belonged to the Kappa Alpha Fraternity and the American Societies of Civil Engineering, Mechanical Engineering and Electrical Engineering. In Washington, he belonged to the Army and Navy Club and the Metropolitan; in Chicago, he belonged to the Union League of Engineers. At the age of eighty-two, he died on March 1961. Photo from the National Archives.

Charles Henry Martin (0-191), son of Judge Samuel H. Martin and Mary Hughes Martin, was born on 1 October 1863 in Carmi, Illinois. He studied at Ewing College in Illinois from 1881 to 1882. He entered USMA and graduated number nineteen of sixty-four in the class of 1887. Thomas Q. Donaldson, P. D. Lochridge and William Weigel (all *q.v.*) were three of his classmates, as was John Hanks Alexander, the second African-American to graduate from USMA. He was commissioned and sent to the 14th Infantry, and he performed frontier duty from 1887 to 1893. On 15 April 1897, he married Louise J. Hughes, and they had two sons and a daughter: Ellis, Samuel and Jane.

Charles Henry Martin

He served during the Philippine Insurrection with Gen. Wesley Merritt, and was in charge of street and sanitary arrangements in Manila. He took part in the China Relief Expedition, where he earned two Silver Star Commendations. From 1911 to 1913, he was on duty with the General Staff in Washington, D.C. From 1913 to 1915, he commanded the Third Oregon Infantry (Oregon National Guard), and from 1915 to 1917, he served on the Mexican border. He was chief instructor of the first Reserve Officers Training Camp in Leon Springs, Texas in 1917, and on 5 August of that year, he was promoted to brigadier general (NA). He commanded the 172nd Infantry Brigade at Camp Grant, Illinois. On 12 April 1918, he was promoted to major general (NA), and commanded the 86th Infantry Division from 1 May to 16 November of that year. He not only commanded three different divisions at the same time, but was also a corps commander. From 17 to 20 December 1918, he commanded the Sixth Corps, and from 30 December 1918 to June 1919, he commanded the 90th Infantry Division, for which he received the Distinguished Service Medal. He also commanded the Seventh Corps from April to 8 May 1919. He was commanding general, 92d Division from 19 November to 16 December 1918. From 19 September 1922 to 15 September 1924, he was Assistant Chief of Staff, G-1. He commanded the department and division on the Panama Canal from 1925 to 1927. On 1 October 1927, he retired. Later, he represented Oregon in the seventy-second and seventy-third congresses, and from 1935 to 1939, he was the governor of Oregon (a Democrat). At the age of eighty-two, he died in Portland, on 22 September 1946. Photo from the National Portrait Gallery, Washington.

Charles Irving Martin

Charles Irving Martin (0-101583), son of William Martin and Mary Martin, was born on 25 January 1871 in Ogle County, Illinois. He graduated from the Normal School at Fort Scott in 1892. On 28 November 1894, he married Lou Ida Ward, and they had one daughter, Mrs. Lillia Mae Markley. He was the clerk of the Bourbon County, Kansas district court from 1901 to 1905, and was admitted to the Kansas Bar, practicing in Fort Scott, Topeka and Wichita. He was admitted to the bar of the U.S. Supreme Court in 1923. He enlisted as a private in Company F, First Kansas Infantry on 26 August 1890, and was commissioned a second lieutenant in the same regiment on 6 April 1893. In August 1894, he was promoted to captain in the same unit. On 30 April 1898, he served as captain, 20th U.S. Volunteers, and on 22 July 1899, he was promoted to major, 20th Kansas Volunteer Infantry. He was in many engagements in the Philippines, and later was Inspector General of the Kansas National Guard as a brigadier, then Adjutant

General of Kansas. From 5 August 1917, he commanded the 17th Infantry Brigade of the 35th Division (AEF) as a brigadier general (NA). During May 1918, he was an observer with the British in France. He participated in the St. Mihiel offensive and was discharged from the National Army on 1 December 1918, but was promptly recommissioned a brigadier general, Kansas National Guard, commanding the 69th Infantry Brigade. From 1932 to 1935, he was a major general commanding the 35th (National Guard) Division of troops from Kansas, Nebraska and Missouri. In 1935, he retired from the military and became manager of the Veterans Administration facility in Wadsworth, Kansas. He was active in the Adjutant Generals Association, the Philippine and Spanish-American War Veterans Association, the American Legion and the Military Order of the World Wars, among others. In retirement, he lived in Cheyenne, Wyoming. At the age of fifty-nine, he died on 8 May 1930. He was buried in Wadsworth, Kansas. Photo courtesy of the Adjutant General's Office, Topeka, Kansas.

William Franklin Martin (0-152), son of Mr. and Mrs. Robert F. Martin, was born on 19 July 1863 in Ripley, Ohio. He entered USMA and graduated number thirty-seven of thirty-nine in the class of 1885. Joseph E. Kuhn, Charles Henry Muir, Willard Holbrook and Robert Lee Bullard (all *q.v.*) were four of his classmates. He was commissioned in the 25th Infantry and performed frontier duty from 1888 to 1891. On 20 July 1892, he married Josephine Edgerton. He was in Cuba during the Spanish-American War, spent four years in the Philippines and was in Cuba again from 1906 to 1908. He was on the General Staff before World War I, and on 5 August 1917, was promoted to brigadier general (NA). He commanded the Seventeenth Infantry Brigade at Camp Pike in Little Rock, Arkansas, then commanded the 87th Infantry Division from 22 November 1918 until it was inactivated in January 1919. He retired in 1927 as a colonel, but his rank of brigadier general was restored in June 1930. In retirement, he lived in Xenia, Ohio. At the age of seventy-eight, he died in Georgia, on 15 April 1942. Photo courtesy of Special Collections, USMA Library.

William Franklin Martin

Frank Gratin Mauldin (0-13449), son of Joab Mauldin and Deborah Reed Hollingsworth Mauldin, was born on 16 August 1864 in Pickens County,

Frank Gratin Mauldin

South Carolina. He entered USMA and graduated number twenty of fifty-four in the class of 1890. He was commissioned an additional second lieutenant in the Third Field Artillery, but was later transferred to the Coast Artillery. Columbian University (now George Washington University) granted him an LL.B. in 1893, and he was an instructor in law and history at USMA from 1896 to 1900, and also served under General Shafter in 1898 in Cuba. For four years, he commanded one of the army mine planters. From 1910 to 1913, he was with the Inspector General's Department. He commanded the Presidio of San Francisco, California, and also the Recruit Depot at Fort Slocum, New York. He was promoted to brigadier general (NA) on 5 August 1917, when he was commanding general, 59th Field Artillery Brigade at Camp Cody, near Deming, New Mexico. As of 18 September 1917, he was commanding general, 34th Infantry Division. In 1920, he retired as a colonel. His rank of brigadier general was restored in June 1930. At the age of seventy-five, he died in Florida, on 25 January 1940. Photo from Special Collections, USMA Library.

Ulysses Grant McAlexander

Ulysses Grant McAlexander (0-75), son of C. P. McAlexander and Margaret McAlexander, was born on 30 August 1864 in Dundas, Minnesota. He entered USMA and graduated as number fifty-three of sixty-four in the class of 1887. Richmond P. Davis, George O. Squier and Charles H. Martin (all *q.v.*)were three of his classmates, as were John Hanks Alexander and George Washington Patrick, great grand nephew of George Washington. He was commissioned and assigned to the 25th Infantry. From 1891 to 1895, he was Professor of Military Science and Tactics at Wesleyan University in Iowa. In Cuba during the Santiago Campaign, he was recommended for promotion for gallantry under fire. During 1898 and 1899, he was in charge of the office of the chief quartermaster, Department of the East. From 1900 to 1902, he was in the Philippines as an aide to Gen. John Francis Weston, a Civil War cavalryman who received a Medal of Honor for action in Cuba during the

Spanish-American War. By this time, he was in the General Staff Corps. He graduated from the War College in 1907. From 1907 to 1911 and from 1915 to 1916, he was Professor of Military Science and Tactics at Oregon Agricultural College. In 1916 and 1917, he was inspector and instructor of the Oregon National Guard. He was sent to France in June 1917 to command the 18th Infantry. From January to May 1918, he was inspector general of Base Number One. He commanded the 38th Infantry at the Second Battle of the Marne in July 1918. On 6 August 1918, he was promoted to brigadier general (NA) and commanded the 180th Infantry Brigade. These were Texas troops, and he commanded them until June 1919. During World War I, he participated in the Aisne, Champagne-Marne, Marne, Aisne-Marne, St. Mihiel and Meuse-Argonne battles. His regiment was instrumental in breaking the last great German offensive, and so was known as "the Rock of the Marne." He was wounded on both 16 and 23 July. A life-sized portrait of him was presented to the State of Texas by the Texas Brigade. He graduated from the General Staff College in 1920, and he commanded the Sixth Infantry Brigade (Third Division) in 1921. From June 1922 to July 1924, he served at Fort Douglas, Utah. There he was retired due to physical disability as a major general. Oregon State College granted him an LL.D. in 1930. His decorations included both the Distinguished Service Cross and the Distinguished Service Medal, the Croix de Guerre with palms (France) and the Croce di Guerra (Italy), and he was made an Officer of the Legion of Honor (France). He was elected honorary life president of "the Rock of the Marne" Post number 138, VFW, New York City and also of the Salt Lake Post, VFW, and he was a life member of the Society Santiago de Cuba. He wrote a history of the 13th Infantry in 1905, and he gave lectures on the second battle of the Marne and on leadership. On 20 August 1935 his wife died. His retirement home was in Portland, Oregon, where at the age of seventy-three, he died on 18 September 1936. Photo from the National Archives.

James William McAndrew

James William McAndrew (0-22) was born on 29 June 1862 in Hawley, Pennsylvania, on the Wayne/Pike county line. He entered USMA and graduated number twelve of forty-four in the class of 1888. Peyton C. March and Guy Henry Preston were two of his classmates. He was commissioned and sent to the 21st Infantry. He was in the Sioux Campaign of 1890 to 1891, at El Caney, Cuba on 1 July 1898 and at Santiago until its surrender on 16 July of that year. From 1899 to 1902, he was in the Philippines, and he was with his regiment in Alaska from 1905 to 1906. An honor graduate of the Army School of the

Line in 1910, he also graduated from the Army Staff College in 1911 and from the Army War College in 1913. During 1916 and 1917, he served in the General Staff Corps. On 5 August 1917, he was promoted to brigadier general (NA), and on 18 April 1918, he was promoted to major general (NA). From June 1917 to June 1919, he was Chief of Staff (AEF). He was brigadier general (USA) on 8 November 1918, and later, he was made commandant of the General Staff College in Washington. His decorations included the Distinguished Service Medal, KCMG (Great Britain) and the Croix de Guerre with two palms (France), and he was made an Officer of the Legion of Honor (France) and a Grand Officer of the Order of the Crown (Belgium), as well as a member of the Order of Santi Maurizio and E. Lazzaro (Italy). He was also given Montenegrin decorations and La Soliedariad (Panama). At the age of fifty-nine, he died on 30 April 1922. The photo, from the National Archives, was taken in France in 1918.

Henry Pinckney McCain

Henry Pinckney McCain (0-9), son of Mr. and Mrs. W. A. McCain, was born on 23 January 1861 in Carroll County, Mississippi. He entered USMA and graduated number twenty of thirty-nine in the class of 1885. Charles Henry Muir, Willard Holbrook, and Robert Lee Bullard (all *q.v.*) were three of his classmates. He was commissioned in the Third Infantry and performed frontier duty at Fort Shaw, Montana and Fort Snelling, Minnesota from 1885 to 1888. On 14 November 1888, he married Emiline DeMoss. From 1889 to 1891, he was Professor of Military Science and Tactics at Louisiana State University. During the Spanish-American War, he was acting assistant Adjutant General, both in Alaska and in several divisions in the Philippines. From 1899 to 1900, he was Chief Commissary and acting Judge Advocate of the Department of the Columbia (River). He transferred from the infantry to the General Staff Corps, and was Chief of Staff of the Department of Mindanao in the Philippines in March and April 1904. From 1904 to 1912, he was in the Adjutant General's Office in Washington, and from 1912 to 1914, he was Adjutant General of the Philippine Division. From 1914 to 1918, he was Adjutant General (USA), for which he received the Distinguished Service Medal. In August 1918, he took command of the 12th Infantry Division at Camp Devens, Massachusetts. He continued there until the division was demobilized on 31 January 1919. He was a temporary major general when he held the office of Adjutant General, and was promoted to major general (NA) on 27 August 1918. He was a major general (USA) when he retired on 22 July 1921, after forty years of service. In retirement, from 1927 to 1936, he served as governor of the Old Soldiers Home in Washington, D.C. At the age of eighty, he died in Washington, on 25 July 1941. Photo courtesy of Special Collections, USMA Library.

Walter Drew McCaw, M.D.

Walter Drew McCaw, M.D. (0-50), son of James Brown McCaw and Delia Patterson McCaw, was born on 10 February 1863 in Richmond, Virginia. He received his M.D. degree from the Medical College of Virginia in 1882. He also studied at Columbia until 1884, and he received his doctorate in science from there in 1932. He was commissioned an assistant surgeon (USA) in 1884, and was a captain assistant surgeon in 1889. During the Spanish-American War, he was a major in the Volunteer Service Brigade and a surgeon in June 1898, and he served in the Campaign of Santiago de Cuba. On 17 August 1899, he served as a major and surgeon with the 42d U.S. Volunteer Infantry. He was in the Philippines during the Insurrection from 1900 to 1901. During 1902 and 1903, he was in Washington teaching military hygiene and tropical medicine, and was also with the Army Medical School. He was promoted to lieutenant colonel on 1 January 1909, and to colonel, Medical Corps, on 9 May 1913. In 1914, he was Chief Surgeon, Division of the Philippines, and he commanded the division hospital in Manila in 1915. He became surgeon of the Southern Department in San Antonio, Texas in 1916, and was there on 19 February 1917, when General Funston died. He served in the Chief Surgeon's Office (AEF) from March to October 1918, when he himself became Chief Surgeon (AEF). He was commandant of the Army Medical Department Research and Graduate School from 1919 to 1923, and he served in the Departments of the Missouri (River), the Platte (River), East Texas and California. He was promoted to brigadier general (USA) on 5 March 1919. He retired on 10 February 1927 and lived in Woodstock, New York. His decorations included the Distinguished Service Medal and the Silver Star, and he was made Companion of the Bath (Great Britain), Commander of the Legion of Honor (France) and an Officer of the Order of St. Maurice Lazarus (Italy). He was a fellow of the American College of Surgeons, an associate fellow of the College of Physicians of Philadelphia and an honorary member of the Royal Society of Medicine and the Sons of the Cincinnati. At the age of seventy-six, he died on 7 July 1939. The photo, courtesy of the National Archives, was taken in Tours, France, on 10 April 1919, while he was being decorated with the Legion of Honor by Marshal Petain.

Manus MacCloskey

Manus MacCloskey (0-260), son of James E. MacCloskey and Catherine MacCloskey, was born on 24 April 1874 in Pittsburgh, Pennsylvania. He entered USMA and graduated number eight of fifty-nine in the class of 1898. Fox Conner, Malin Craig and Guy V. Henry, Jr. (all *q.v.*) were three of his classmates. He was commissioned and sent to the Fifth Artillery on 26 April 1898. He served in Santiago, Cuba from 10 to 19 August of that year. He commanded a platoon of light battery artillery at the military athletic tournament held at Madison Square Garden in New York City from 20 to 25 March 1899. He was in the Philippines and China from 1899 to 1901. He was wounded in action on 3 October 1899, but nonetheless participated in the march to Peking and the rescue of the legation there in August 1900. On 14 August 1901, he married Sara Monro, and they had two children: Monro and Sally. He was in the Philippines again in 1907, and was an honor graduate of the Army School of the Line in 1909. In 1910, he graduated from the Army Staff College. From 1911 to 1912, he commanded the West Point Battery at USMA, and in 1913, he commanded the First Battalion of the Third Field Artillery in Texas. During 1915, he was instructor of the National Guard Field Artillery at Tobyhanna, Pennsylvania. He commanded a regiment of National Guard Field Artillery from Virginia and New Hampshire from September 1916 to May 1917. He organized the 12th Field Artillery in June 1917 and took it to France in January 1918, commanding it in action in Verdun, Belleau Wood, Chateau Thierry and Soissons, where he was wounded on 19 July 1918. He was promoted to brigadier general (NA) on 8 August 1918, and commanded the 152nd Field Artillery Brigade in action on the Vesle, through the Argonne and to the end of the war. In Germany, he commanded the Second Field Artillery Brigade of the Second Infantry Division. When he returned to the States, he commanded Camp (now Fort) Knox, Kentucky. He was with the General Staff at Headquarters, Sixth Corps Area, Chicago, Illinois from January 1921 to 30 June 1924. From 1 July 1924 to 29 December 1925, he was Chief of Staff of the Sixth Corps (Organized Reserve). From 1926 to 1928, he was in Hawaii as commanding officer of the 11th Field Artillery. From January to April 1929, he was on Organized Reserve duty in New York City. He went back to Fort Sheridan in Chicago and served there from 1929 to 1931. He served at Fort Bragg, North Carolina from 1931 until 30 April 1938, when he retired. In 1933, he organized and administered the Civilian Conservation Corps in North Carolina. His last civilian job was as superintendent of the Cook Company Hospital in Chicago, from 1938 to 1947. His decorations included the Distinguished Service Medal, the Silver Star with oak leaf cluster, the Purple Heart with oak leaf cluster and the Croix de Guerre, and he was made an officer of the Legion of Honor (France) and a member of the Order of the

Crown (Italy). He was a member of the American College of Hospital Administrators and the Army and Navy Country Club in Washington, D.C. His retirement home was in Winnetka, Illinois. At the age of eighty-nine, he died, on 11 May 1963. Photo from the National Archives.

Nathaniel Fish McClure

Nathaniel Fish McClure (0-167), son of Ezra R. McClure and Nannie McClure, was born on 21 July 1865 in Crittendon, Kentucky. He entered USMA and graduated number twenty-three of sixty-four in the class of 1887. George Washington Patrick, great grandnephew of George Washington, and John H. Alexander, the second African-American to graduate from USMA, were two of his classmates. He was commissioned in the cavalry and performed frontier duty from 1887 to 1891. He married Mamie Chapin on 14 July 1890. He served in Puerto Rico from 1899 to 1900, then served in the Philippines from 1901 to 1903. In 1909, he was a distinguished graduate of the School of the Line, and in 1910, he graduated from the Army Staff College. From 1913 to 1916, he was an instructor at Army Service Schools. He went on the Mexican Punitive Expedition in the spring of 1916. He graduated from the Army War College in 1917, and was promoted to brigadier general (NA) on 17 December of that year. He commanded Base Camp Number One in San Nazaire, France until 1918, then commanded the 69th Infantry Brigade for two months and the 38th Division for five weeks, spending three months in combat with these two units. In late 1918 and early 1919, he was on duty in the office of the Chief of Staff in Washington. He was assistant commandant of the Disciplinary Barracks at Fort Leavenworth, Kansas from 1920 to 1922, and from 1923 to 1926, he was on duty with the Signal Corps. He retired as a colonel on 21 July 1929, but his rank of brigadier general was restored in June 1930. He belonged to the Military Order of the Carabao, the Association of Graduates, USMA, the U.S. Cavalry Association, the American Legion, the Veterans of Foreign Wars and the Military Order of the World Wars. He was a Democrat, and he belonged to a number of clubs. He wrote one book: *Class of 1887, United States Military Academy* (published in 1939). In retirement, he lived in Wardman Park in Washington, D.C., where he died at the age of seventy-six, on 26 June 1942. Photo from Special Collections, USMA Library.

Frank Ross McCoy

Frank Ross McCoy (0-560), son of General Thomas Franklin McCoy and Margaret Eleanor Ross McCoy, was born on 29 October 1874 in Lewistown, Pennsylvania. His family had come from Ireland to Pennsylvania in the first half of the eighteenth century. He attended Lewistown Academy, then entered USMA and graduated number thirty-four of sixty-seven in the class of 1897. He was commissioned in the Eighth Cavalry, then stationed at Fort Meade, South Dakota, but was later transferred to the Seventh Cavalry. He also served in the Sanitary Corps and on the General Staff. During the Philippine Insurrection, he was an aide to Leonard Wood from 1903 to 1906. After serving in the Moro Expedition from 1903 to 1906, he was military aide to President Theodore Roosevelt. In 1910, he served on the General Staff. During World War I, he served on the General Staff (AEF). He graduated from the Army War College, and on 16 August 1918, he was promoted to brigadier general (NA). He was commanding officer of the 165th Infantry Regiment, and he was commanding general of the 63d Infantry Brigade, for which he received the Distinguished Service Medal. In 1919, he was Chief of Staff of the American military mission in Armenia. He was promoted to brigadier general (USA) in 1922. In 1923, he was head of the American relief mission to Tokyo after the earthquake. On 26 January 1924, McCoy received his promotion to major general (USA), and in 1932 was part of the League of Nations inquiry into the Japanese seizure of Manchuria. On 31 October 1938, he retired from the army and made his home in Washington, D.C. From 1940 to 1942 he was president of the Association of Graduates, USMA, and from 1939 to 1945, he was president of the Foreign Policy Association. From 1946 to 1949, he was chairman of the Far Eastern Commission, and from 1951 to 1954, director of the Equitable Life Assurance. He received LL.D. degrees from Brown, Clark, Columbia, Princeton, Yale and Washington and Jefferson. At the age of seventy-nine, he died at Walter Reed Army Medical Center, on 4 June 1954. Photo courtesy of the Special Collections, USMA Library.

John Bacon McDonald (0-135) was born on 18 February 1859 in Athens, Alabama. He entered USMA and graduated number fifty-two of fifty-three in the class of 1881. Harry and Henry Hodges, Joseph T. Dickman and Andrew Summers Rowan (all *q.v.*) were four of his classmates. He was commissioned in the 25th Infantry, then transferred to the Tenth Cavalry. He married and had two sons and two daughters: Robert Dyer McDonald, Lt. John B. McDonald, Jr. (USN), Mrs. Gordon McPherson and Sue Alston McDonald. From 1881 to

John Bacon McDonald

1883, he performed frontier duty, and from 1888 to 1891, he was Professor of Military Science and Tactics at the Agricultural and Mechanical College in Auburn, Alabama. During 1897 and 1898, he was Professor of Military Science and Tactics at South Carolina Military Academy. From September to November 1898, he was mustering officer for the State of Alabama as a lieutenant colonel of Alabama volunteers. From 1900 to 1901, he served in the Philippines, and was wounded in Boronabong on 27 April 1901, after which he received a Silver Star. As a captain in the Third Cavalry, with twenty-one men on the firing line and one sergeant and six men left with the horses, he struck and defeated the insurgents with rifles and forty soldiers operating in thick brush, carrying bolos, and was severely wounded in the right lung. He was wounded by the first volley, and deserves credit for not permitting his men to know he was hurt until after the battle was over. His immediate commanding officer, in transmitting the report, remarked: "There is no braver officer in the service than Captain McDonald." He served for a number of years with the Inspector General's Department. On 17 December 1917, he was promoted to brigadier general (NA) and commanded the 181st Infantry Brigade, part of the 91st Infantry Division, in France and Belgium. When he returned to the States in 1919, he commanded the Presidio of San Francisco and the Disciplinary Barracks on Alcatraz Island in the San Francisco Bay. For his service in France, he received both the Distinguished Service Cross and the Distinguished Service Medal. In 1923, he was promoted to brigadier general (USA). On 8 February of that year, he retired. In addition to the decorations already mentioned, he was made Officer of the Legion of Honor and received the Croix de Guerre (France) as well as the Croix de Guerre (Belgium) and the War Cross (Italy). His wife died in 1925. At the age of sixty-seven, he died at Walter Reed Army Medical Center, on 15 March 1926. Photo courtesy of Special Collections, USMA Library.

Munroe McFarland (0-211), son of Mr. and Mrs. Cyrus D. McFarland, was born on 28 June 1867 in Baltimore, Maryland. His first American progenitor, Daniel McFarland, landed in Marblehead, Massachusetts in 1718. He entered USMA just before his seventeenth birthday and graduated number thirty-two of forty-four in the class of 1888. Peyton C. March and Guy Henry Preston (both *q.v.*) were two of his classmates. He was commissioned in the infantry and performed frontier duty from 1888 to 1893. During the Spanish-American War, he was a captain in the 18th Infantry, and he participated in the Battle of San Juan and the Siege of Santiago, then he was sent to Camp Wickioff, Long Island, New

York. He served in the Philippine Islands during the Insurrection. His wife was Frances Ogelvie of Buffalo, New York, and they had two daughters, Jean and Ruth. From 12 October 1908 to 1922 August 1910, he served in the Puerto Rican Regiment. In 1913, he was sent as military observer to Belgrade, Serbia during the Balkan Wars. On 15 May 1917, he was promoted to colonel, and on 17 December 1917, he was made brigadier general (NA) commanding general of the 162nd Infantry Brigade and later, the 81st Division (AEF). After the war, he was stationed at Camp Devens, Massachusetts, in charge of the discharge of officers. On 15 July 1919, he reverted to his permanent rank of colonel and commanded Jefferson Barracks near St. Louis, Missouri. He was commanding officer of the Intermediate Supply Depot in Chicago, Illinois, and from 15 August 1921 to 7 July 1922, he attended the Army War College in Washington. On 7 November 1922, he retired as a colonel and purchased a house in Hollywood. At the age of fifty-seven, he died in California, on 3 September 1924. He was a very conscientious officer. His rank of brigadier general was restored posthumously in June 1930. Photo from *The Assembly*, Association of Graduates, USMA.

Munroe McFarland

Edward Fenton McGlaghlin. Jr.

Edward Fenton McGlaghlin, Jr. (0-56), son of Edward Fenton McGlaghlin and Mary Lawrence McGlaghlin, was born on 9 June 1868 in Fond du Lac, Wisconsin. He entered USMA and graduated number twenty of forty-nine in the class of 1889. Charles Young, the third African-American to graduate from USMA, was one of his classmates. He was commissioned in the Third Artillery, and before he became a general officer, he also served in the Eighth and Tenth Field Artillery Regiments. On 26 November 1892, he married Louisa Harrison Chew, and they had three children: Fenton Harrison McGlaghlin, Helen O. McGlaghlin (Mrs. John E. Hatch) and Elizabeth McGlaghlin (Mrs. Joseph C. Odell). Both daughters married army officers. He attended the course in Submarine Mining at the Engineering School of Application in 1893. In 1896, he went to the Artillery School. During the Philippine Insurrection, he received special mention for gallantry in action at the Battle of Bud Dajo on Jolo, where he received a Silver Star Citation in 1906. From 1909 to 1911, he commanded the Recruit Depot at Fort McDowell, California. In 1912, he attended the School of Fire for Field Artillery, and from 1914 to 1916, he commanded that school. In 1916, he took the Field Officers Course in Army Service Schools, and in 1917, he graduated from the Army War College. On 5 August 1917, he was promoted to brigadier general (NA) and commanded the 165th Field Artillery Brigade, part of the 90th Division, from August to December 1917. From December 1917 to March 1918, he commanded the 57th Field Artillery Brigade, part of the 32d Infantry Division. From March to May 1918, he commanded the 66th Field Artillery Brigade and was Chief of Artillery, First Army Corps. During that period, on 12 April 1918, he was promoted to major general (NA). From May to November 1918, he was both commander of army artillery and Chief of Artillery (AEF), for which he received the Distinguished Service Medal. From 19 November 1918 to 30 September 1919, he commanded the First Infantry Division, part of the American forces in Germany. From 30 September 1919 to 30 June 1921, he commanded the Seventh Infantry Division. He was commandant of the Army War College from 1921 to 1923, and in 1923, he was promoted to major general (USA). He retired on 2 November 1923. In addition to the decorations already mentioned, he was made a Commander of the Legion of Honor and received the Croix de Guerre (France). In retirement, he lived in Washington, D.C., where at the age of seventy-eight, he died on 9 November 1946. Photo from the National Archives.

James Francis McIndoe (no ASN assigned), son of William McIndoe and Mary Stuart McIndoe, was born on 18 January 1868 in Lonaconing, southwest of Cumberland, Maryland. Both of his parents were born in Scotland. He spent two years at the Maryland Military and Naval Academy in Oxford, Maryland. While there, he commanded the cadet battalion. He entered USMA and graduated number four of sixty-five in the class of 1891. William J. Glasgow, John L. Hines and Odus C. Horney (all *q.v.*) were three of his classmates. He was commissioned in the Corps of Engineers and served for three years in the engineer battalion at the Engineer School in Willet's Point, New York. He made many friends in New York, among them Irena Cavanaugh, whom he married on 20 December 1893. They had three children: William (an army officer during World War I), Beatrice (wife of Capt. R. S. Burnell) and James. After engineer school, he was sent to serve with the Mississippi River

James Francis McIndoe

Commission in St. Louis. From there he went to Florence, Alabama, Chattanooga, Tennessee and Detroit, Michigan. He performed submarine mining and fortifications work at Fort Wadsworth and Sandy Hook, and later at Fort Totten, New York, where he commanded a battalion of engineers, which he took to Washington Barracks. He remained there until the end of 1904. From 1904 to 1908, he was in charge of rivers, harbors and fortifications work in New Orleans. He did the same work, adding to it the responsibility of lighthouses, in Portland, Oregon from 1908 to 1913. As a result of overwork and typhoid fever, he was in poor physical shape, and decided to take up golf. In 1917, he went from Portland to Manila to Leavenworth, then to the Mexican border. In July of that year, he organized and commanded the Second Engineer Regiment and took it to France with the Second Infantry Division. On 1 October 1918, he was promoted to brigadier general (NA). He became Chief Engineer, Forth Corps, and later, Director of Military Engineering and Supplies in Tours, France. At the age of fifty-one he became ill with pneumonia, and on 3 February 1919 he died. He was buried in France. He was posthumously awarded the Distinguished Service Medal. Photo courtesy of the Association of Graduates, USMA.

Augustine McIntyre, Jr.

Augustine McIntyre, Jr. (0-1118), son of 2nd Lt. Augustine McIntyre (Second Infantry) and Katherine Donahue McIntyre, was born on 19 July 1876 in Chattanooga, Tennessee. His father was murdered by moonshiners in Georgia on 14 February 1877 while on duty protecting civil officers. He entered USMA and graduated number fifty-two of fifty-four in the class of 1900. Robert E. Wood (*q.v.*)was one of his classmates. He was quite popular, and was always the one selected to harass the commandant or superintendent, so he earned the name "Villain." He also played baseball on the army team. He was commissioned in the cavalry, but soon transferred to artillery and served with the Sixth Artillery in Manila. He returned to the States in 1901 and was stationed on Alcatraz Island, and later, in the Presidio of San Francisco. On 10 May 1906, he married Jane Clemens Swigert, daughter of Col. and Mrs. Samuel Miller Swigert. He was a distinguished graduate of the Coast Artillery School in 1907, and in May of that year, he was permanently assigned to the field artillery. From 1907 to September 1911, he commanded B Battery, Third Field Artillery at Fort Sam Houston, Texas. He went to Fort Sill as a student officer and was retained after graduation as a senior instructor. He went on detached service in 1913 to study French artillery fire. In June 1914, he became a member of the machine gun board, and spent the following summer continuing his work in

Texas. From September 1914 to October 1915, he was back in Europe as an observer with the Austro-Hungarian Army. When he returned, he was assigned to the Fourth Field Artillery at Fort Myer, Virginia. He stayed there until March 1916, when he was sent to the First Field Artillery at Schofield Barracks, Territory of Hawaii. He was promoted to colonel (NA) and commanded the 326th Field Artillery at Camp Zachary Taylor in Kentucky. On 1 May 1918, he was promoted to brigadier general (NA) and commanded the 63d Field Artillery Brigade at Camp Shelby, Mississippi. They went overseas with the 38th Division, and he commanded this brigade until after the Armistice. He successively commanded the 63d, 154th, 4th and 1st Field Artillery Brigades. When he returned to the States in September 1919, he was in the great street parades in New York City and Washington. On 30 September 1919, he reverted to his permanent rank of major of field artillery and was sent to Fort Sill. In 1921, he went to the Army War College, and then spent four years in the office of the Chief of Field Artillery. For two years, he commanded the Sixth Field Artillery at Fort Hoyle, Maryland, then the 11th Field Artillery at Schofield Barracks, Hawaii. In March 1928, he went on General Staff Duty at headquarters of the Hawaiian Division as acting Chief of Staff and Assistant Chief of Staff, G-3, until April 1929. Reverting to the rank of colonel, he commanded the 13th Field Artillery at Fort Bragg, North Carolina. His terminal assignment was as commandant of the Field Artillery School at Fort Sill, Oklahoma. At the age of sixty-four, he was retired as a brigadier general, but he was recalled to active duty that same year as Professor of Military Science and Tactics at the University of Missouri. He received the Distinguished Service Medal at Fort Sill. The hardest blow of his life was his wife's death in San Antonio in 1952. At the age of seventy-eight, he died on 6 September 1954. He was outwardly reserved, engaging in manner and filled with the joy of living. Photo courtesy of *The Assembly*, Association of Graduates, USMA.

Frank McIntyre (0-7), son of Denis McIntyre and Mary G. McIntyre, was born on 6 January 1865 in Montgomery, Alabama. His father had come to the States from County Donegal, Ireland. After two years at the University of Alabama, he entered USMA and graduated number ten of seventy-seven in the class of 1886. Mason M. Patrick, Charles T. Menoher, John J. Pershing (all *q.v.*) and Edward W. McCaskey were four of his classmates. He was regarded as a mathematical prodigy. He was commissioned in the infantry and performed frontier duty during 1886 to 1887. After graduating from the Infantry and Cavalry School at Fort

Frank McIntyre

Leavenworth, Kansas, he returned to West Point and taught mathematics from 1890 to 1894. On 12 July 1892, he married Marie Dennett of San Antonio, Texas, and they had six children: James, Frank, Edward, Marie, Margaret and Nora. He was stationed with an infantry unit at Fort Wayne, Michigan. With the coming of the Spanish-American War, he was sent to Puerto Rico to command an infantry company, and he also served on the staff of Gen. Guy V. Henry, Sr. After being sent to the Philippines for the Insurrection, he returned to Washington, D.C. to serve on the General Staff. After two years, he began his long service with the Bureau of Insular Affairs, the army administrative section for American overseas possessions. He was promoted to major in 1907, and when he became assistant to Gen. C. W. Edwards (head of the bureau) in 1910, he was made a colonel. Two years later, in 1912, General Edwards was sent to command Fort D. A. Russell, Wyoming, so McIntyre was promoted to brigadier general and succeeded him as Chief of the Bureau of Insular Affairs. At the age of forty-seven, he was one of the youngest officers to be made a brigadier general in peacetime. During World War I, he took over Gen. Douglas MacArthur's censorship assignment when the general received orders for overseas duty. He was executive assistant to Peyton C. March, the Chief of Staff, and remained Deputy Chief of Staff until 1920. He retired as a major general in 1929, after fifteen years as Chief of the Bureau of Insular Affairs. In 1936, he returned to Montgomery, Alabama, where he managed several farms, raised Hereford cattle and owned a warehouse business. He received the Distinguished Service Medal, the War Cross (Czechoslovakia) and the Grand Cordon of the Striped Tiger (China). He was also made a Commander of the Legion of Honor (France) and a Knight Commander of the Order of the Bath (Great Britain). At the age of seventy-nine, he died in Miami Beach, Florida, on 16 February 1944. Photo courtesy of *The Assembly*, Association of Graduates, USMA.

George Willcox McIver

George Willcox McIver (0-113), son of Alexander McIver and Mary Willcox McIver, was born on 22 December 1858 in Carthage, North Carolina. He entered USMA and graduated number nineteen of thirty-seven in the class of 1882. Adelbert Cronkhite, Henry T. Allen (both *q.v.*) and Fredrick Gilmore Bonfils of the *Denver Post* were three of his classmates. He was commissioned in the Seventh Infantry and performed frontier duty from 1882 to 1891, during the last of the late Indian Wars. He was an instructor in West Point from 1891 to 1893. On 28 June 1893, he married Helen H. Smedberg. He was on duty in Cuba during the Spanish-American War, and also served in the Sanitary Corps, for which he received a Silver Star Commendation. During 1900 and 1901, he was stationed in Alaska, and from 1903 to 1904, he had his first tour of duty in the Philippines. By 1906, he was in San Francisco, California, helping the victims of the earthquake and fire. He was commandant of the School of Musketry from 1907 to 1911, and from 1912 to 1913, he was back in the Philippines. From 1915 to 1917, he was on duty with the Militia Bureau in Washington, D.C., Promotion to brigadier general (NA) came on 5 August 1917. He was assigned command of the 161st Infantry Brigade, part of the 81st Infantry Division (AEF). He received a Purple Heart. In 1922, he retired as a colonel of infantry. His rank of brigadier general was restored in June 1930. At the age of eighty-eight, he died in Washington, D.C., on 9 May 1947. Photo courtesy of the National Archives.

Charles Hedges McKinstry (0-13388) was born on 19 December 1866 in California. He entered USMA and graduated number two of forty-four in the class of 1888. Peyton C. March and Guy Henry Preston (both *q.v.*) were two of his classmates. He was commissioned in the Corps of Engineers, and from 1891 to 1893, he was an instructor in engineering in West Point. From 1898 to 1900, he was in charge of defensive works and harbors improvements in Key West, Florida. From 1901 to 1903, he was an instructor in civil engineering at the Engineer School in Willet's Point, New York, which included instruction in astronomy. From 1903 to 1906, he was in charge of fortifications, rivers and harbors work in southern California. He was Chief Engineer in the Philippine Islands Division from 1909 to 1911. On 5 August 1917, he was promoted to brigadier general (NA) and commanded the 158th Field Artillery Brigade. He was director of light railroads and roads (AEF). In 1919, he retired as a colonel. On 10 January 1920, his wife, Lillie Lawrence McKinstry, died in Miami, Florida. In June 1930, his rank of brigadier general was restored. At the age of ninety-four, he died in Santa Barbara, California, on 29 November 1961. Photo courtesy of Special Collections, USMA Library.

Charles Hedges McKinstry

John Eugene McMahon, Jr. (0-3541), son of Col. John E. McMahon (USA) and Esther Bryan McMahon, was born on 8 December 1860 in Buffalo,

John Eugene McMahon, Jr.

New York. After graduating from Fordham University in 1880 with an A.B. degree, he entered USMA and graduated number eleven of seventy-seven in the class of 1886. Mason Patrick, Charles T. Menoher and John J. Pershing (all *q.v.*) were three of his classmates. He was commissioned in the Fourth Artillery. On 12 May 1888, he married Caroline Bache and from 1890 to 1891 was an instructor in modern languages at USMA. From 1891 to 1895, he was an aide to Gen. A. D. McCook. During the Spanish-American War, he was the Adjutant General, Second Brigade, Provisional Division, from June to July 1898. He was in Puerto Rico in 1898 and 1899, and served during the Philippine Insurrection. On 17 December 1917, he was promoted to major general (NA). He commanded the Fifth Infantry Division (AEF) from 1 January to 18 October 1918. He was also commanding general, 41st Infantry Division (AEF) from 21 to 23 October 1918. He retired as a colonel due to disabilities in 1919, and at the age of fifty-nine, he died in New Jersey, on 28 January 1920. His rank of major general was restored posthumously in 1930. Photo courtesy of the National Archives.

William Vance McMaken

William Vance McMaken (no ASN assigned), son of Ezekiel Vance McMaken and Anna C. McMaken, was born on 11 February 1857 in New York City. His father was a native of Hamilton, Butler County, Ohio, and his mother was from West Winstead, Connecticut. His paternal grandfather was a veteran of the War of 1812, and his maternal ancestors served in the Continental Army during the American Revolution. When he was about seven, his family moved to Toledo, Ohio, where his father had been appointed postmaster by President Grant. He attended USMA with the class of 1878 for two years, but did not graduate. He worked in a mercantile business, then in real estate and insurance. On 31 October 1883, he married a former high school classmate, Georgie Dorr, daughter of the former mayor of Toledo. They had two daughters, Myra Dorr McMaken and Carrie Dorr McMaken. The interest in things military started when he was a small boy. He entered the Ohio National Guard and was the captain of an infantry company for nineteen years, then became colonel of the 16th Ohio Infantry, which at the time of the Spanish-American War was the Sixth Ohio Infantry. It was in the federal service for a year before it was mustered out in Augusta, Georgia, on 24 May 1899, after four months in Cuba. On 5 December 1899, he was promoted to a National Guard brigadier general and commanded the Ohio National Guard during a number of civil disturbances. On 5 August 1917, he was promoted to brigadier general (NA), and his old Sixth Ohio Infantry became the 147th Infantry Regiment. He commanded the 74th Infantry Brigade, part of the 37th Ohio Infantry Division, and served in Toledo and Montgomery, Alabama. As a result of the physical exams held in Washington during December 1917 and January 1918, he was discharged due to physical disability on 20 March 1918. Thereafter he lived in Toledo, and worked as an internal revenue collector and custodian of the Toledo federal building. His home was at 2215 Scottswood Avenue. At the age of sixty-five, he died of heart disease, on 13 January 1923. He was buried in Woodlawn Cemetery, Toledo. Photo courtesy of the National Archives.

George Henry McManus

George Henry McManus (0-327), son of Thomas McManus and Sarah R. McManus, was born on 23 December 1867 in Hudson, south of Waterloo, Iowa. He earned a degree from Iowa State Teachers College, then entered USMA and graduated number nine of fifty-one in the class of 1893. Herbert B. Crosby (later the Chief of Cavalry) was one of his classmates. He was commissioned in the artillery, and he stayed in the Coast Artillery when the Artillery Corps divided into field and Coast Artillery in 1907. On 7 January 1897, he married Gertrude Kessler, and they had four children: Sarah C. McManus (Mrs. H. W. McCurdy), George Henry McManus, Jr., Thomas Kessler McManus and Mary Alice McManus. He served in the China Relief Expedition and during the Philippine Insurrection, as well as in the Atlantic, the Pacific and the Philippines. During World War I, he was a troop movement officer at the port of embarkation in Hoboken, New Jersey. On 1 October 1918, he was promoted to brigadier general (NA). For his performance of this duty he received the Distinguished Service Medal and the Navy Cross. On 1 December 1931, he retired as a brigadier general (USA). At the age of eighty-six, he died in the Presidio of San Francisco, on 27 August 1954. The photo, courtesy of the Casemate Museum, shows him as the central figure.

Leslie James McNair

Leslie James McNair (0-1891), son of James McNair and Clars Manz McNair, was born on 25 May 1883 in Verndale, northwest of Little Falls, Minnesota. He entered USMA and graduated number eleven of one hundred twenty-four in the class of 1904. Pelham D. Glassford, Robert C. Richardson, Jr., Joseph Stilwell, Edmund L. Gruber, Innis Palmer Swift and Arthur H. Wilson were six of his classmates. He was commissioned in the Artillery Corps. On 15 June 1905, he married Clare Huster, and they had one son, Douglas C. McNair. He served in the Vera Cruz Expedition, and in 1916 and 1917, he served in the Mexican Punitive Expedition. From 1917 to 1919, he was with the AEF in France, during which time he was promoted to brigadier general (NA). For his performance of this duty he was awarded the Distinguished Service Medal and was made an Officer of the Legion of Honor (France). From 1919 to 1933, he was commandant of the Artillery School at Fort Sill, Oklahoma. He reverted to his permanent rank after the war, and did not get his status as a brigadier general restored until 1937. He was commandant of the Command and General Staff School from April 1939 until October 1940, in which year he was made a major general. In March 1942, he was promoted to lieutenant general and made Chief of the Army Ground Forces, which position he held until his death. He was wounded in action in North Africa in 1943, for which he received the Purple Heart. He was accidentally killed by our own Air Corps on 25 July 1944 while observing forward units. He was sixty-one years old. The former Washington Barracks, later named Fort Humphreys, was renamed in his honor. He was one of seventeen or eighteen U.S. army generals who served in both World War I and World War II. Photo from the National Archives.

William Sharp McNair (0-176), son of David McNair, and Lucinda Sharp McNair was born on 18 September 1868 in Tecumpseh, southwest of Ann Arbor, Michigan. His father was also born in Tecumpseh, and his mother was from Bucyrus, Ohio. He entered USMA and graduated number twenty-three of fifty-four in the class of 1890. He was commissioned in the Artillery Corps. On 26 December 1894, he married Louise Bestor Potts at Fort Barrancas, Florida, and they had four children: Mary Louise McNair (Mrs. Edward A. Sterling, Jr.), Dorothy McNair, William Douglas McNair (USMA, class of 1918) and Norma B. McNair. In 1896, he graduated from the Artillery School. He served in the China Relief Expedition, the Philippine Insurrection and the Moro Expedition of 1903, for which he received his first Silver Star Citation. In 1916 and 1917, he

William Sharp McNair

served as a brigadier general (NA) with the New York National Guard. In France, he commanded the artillery of the First Infantry Division, and he later commanded the 151st Field Artillery Brigade. He participated in the Meuse-Argonne and Sedan battles. He served as Chief of Artillery, First Army, and received the Distinguished Service Medal and another Silver Star. From 1920 to 1922, he was Chief of Staff of the Department of Panama. His rank of brigadier general was restored in 1930, and when he retired on 30 September 1932, he was a major general (USA). His only son, William Douglas McNair, was killed as an artillery observer in an air crash in Australia. In retirement, he lived in San Antonio, Texas. He was a Presbyterian. At the age of sixty-eight, he died on 6 April 1936. Photo courtesy of Special Collections, USMA Library.

Clarence Henry McNeil

Clarence Henry McNeil (0-3860) was born on 4 July 1873 in New York. He entered USMA and graduated number eleven of seventy-three in the class of 1896. Lucius R. Holbrook, Edward King and Dennis Nolan (all *q.v.*) were three of his classmates. He was commissioned in the artillery stationed at Fort Slocum, New York, and was transferred to Key West Barracks, Florida, to Forts Hamilton and Wadsworth, New York, back to Florida, to Washington Barracks, Washington D.C. and to Fort Hancock, New Jersey. He was an instructor in mathematics in West Point from 21 August 1899 to 6 January 1903, then served for two years as adjutant of the Field Artillery School at Fort Riley, Kansas. On 1 September 1905, he was sent to the School of Submarine Defense at Fort Totten, New York. After graduating, they retained him as an instructor until 23 April 1908. When the Artillery Corps split into field and Coast Artillery, he remained with the latter. On 10 December 1913, he was detailed to the Inspector General's Department, and from 1915 to 1918, he was with the Quartermasters Department. From 29 April to 11 June 1918, he commanded the 66th Coast Artillery Regiment. He served in the office of the Chief of Staff until 1 October 1918, when he was promoted to brigadier general (NA). He commanded the 37th Coast Artillery Brigade (AEF) from 21 October 1918 to 7

February 1919. From 4 March to 15 June 1919, he commanded thc South Atlantic Coast Artillery District, and from 15 May to 15 June, he was commanding general of the Southeastern Department as well. On 15 June 1919, he reverted to his permanent rank of lieutenant colonel of Coast Artillery. He was a student at the General Staff College from 15 August 1919 to 31 July 1920, when he graduated. During this time, on 25 June 1920, he was promoted to colonel of Coast Artillery. For a year and four months, he was executive assistant to the Chief of Coast Artillery, and he spent six months on the War Department General Staff, after which he was ordered home to await retirement. He retired after thirty years of service on 1 December 1922. On 21 June 1930, his rank of brigadier general was restored by act of Congress. At the age of seventy-four, he died in Berkeley, California, on 13 September 1947. Photo courtesy of the National Archives.

James Henry McRae

James Henry McRae (0-52), son of Daniel F. McRae and Marion McRae, was born on 24 December 1862 in Lumber City, west of Savannah, Georgia. He entered USMA and graduated number forty-eight of seventy-seven in the class of 1886. Mason Patrick, Charles T. Menoher and John J. Pershing (all *q.v.*) were three of his classmates. He was commissioned in the Third Infantry and performed frontier duty from 1886 to 1888. On 14 December 1887, he married Florence Stouch, daughter of Lt. Col. R. H. Stouch, a Civil War veteran originally from Pennsylvania. They had three children: Donald M. McRae, Dorothy McRae (Mrs. Lewis C. Beebe) and Mildred McRae (Mrs. Archibald M. Mixon). Both daughters married army officers. During the Spanish-American War, he was in the Battle of El Caney in Cuba, and he also served in the Sanitary Corps, for which he received his first Silver Star Commendation. During the Philippine Insurrection, he received his second Silver Star and was recommended for a brevet promotion. From 1905 to 1908, he served on the General Staff, and in 1911, he graduated from the Army War College. From 1913 to 1917, he served in the Adjutant General's Department, and on 5 August 1917, he was promoted to brigadier general (NA) and commanded the 158th Depot Brigade at Camp Sherman, Ohio. He also commanded the Ninth Infantry Brigade of the Fifth Infantry Division. On 12 April 1918, he was promoted to major general (NA) and commanded the 78th Infantry Division (AEF) until June 1919, when it was inactivated. For this service he received the Distinguished Service Medal. During 1921 and 1922, he was assistant chief, G-1 (personnel). From 1922 to 1923 and in 1924, he commanded the Philippine Division, and from 1924 to 1926, he served in the Philippine Department. On 24 February 1926, he remarried, to Helen Burgar Stouch, a former sister-in-law. He briefly commanded the Ninth Corps Area before his final assignment, command of the 11th Corps Area. He retired as a major general on 24 December 1927 and made his home in Berkeley, California. In addition to the decorations already mentioned, he was made a Companion of the Bath (Britain) and a Commander of the Legion of Honor (France). He also received the Croix de Guerre (France). At the age of eighty-six, he died on 1 May 1940. Photo from Special Collections, USMA Library.

Samuel McRoberts

Samuel McRoberts (no ASN assigned), son of Alexander Highlander McRoberts, a farmer, and Ellen Sisk McRoberts, was born on 20 December 1868 near Malta Bend, Missouri. His family had come from Scotland during the American Revolution. He attended Baker University, where he received an A.B. degree in 1891 and an M.A. in 1894. He graduated from the University of Michigan in 1893 and was admitted to the bar. He started his law practice in Chicago, Illinois. On 9 October 1895, he married Mary Agnes Caldwell of Wichita, Kansas. From 1895 to 1900, he was an attorney for Armour and Company (meatpackers). He transferred to their financial department, and in 1904, he was made treasurer of the company and manager of all Armour interests. The same year, his wife died. He resigned and went to New York. On 1 September 1906, he married Harriet Pearl Skinner of Creston, Iowa. He was vice president of the National City Bank in New York until 1917. In November 1917, he resigned and was commissioned a major of ordnance (NA). On 28 November of that year, he was promoted to colonel of ordnance and was made Chief of the Procurement Division. On 8 August 1918, he was promoted to brigadier general (NA) and sent to France, where he served until the end of the war. He was honorably discharged on 15 January 1919, but was recommissioned a brigadier general in the Officers Reserve Corps. The army's purpose in commissioning him and others was to infuse into the bureaucracy accomplished executives and production men. Because of his position, he was familiar with how much plants could produce and what production costs should be. In the AEF, he was responsible for acquiring and disposing of supplies as needed. His work in connection with demobilization was as important as his wartime duties. He resumed his career with the National City Bank, and was a director of, or an officer in, more companies than could be listed in several pages. He received the Distinguished Service Medal and the New York State Conspicuous Service Cross, and was made a Chevalier of the Legion of Honor. Baker University gave him an LL.D. in 1919. At the age of seventy-eight, he died in New York, on 8 September 1947. Photo courtesy of Oliver A. Knapp, Mt. Kisco, New York.

Robert Walter Mearns

Robert Walter Mearns (0-415), son of Andrew James Mearns, a farmer, and Martha Kennedy Mearns, was born on 16 July 1866 in Kemblesville, Pennsylvania. He attended the West Chester State Teachers College, then entered USMA and graduated number sixty-one of sixty-two in the class of 1892. Charles P. Sumerall, James A. Shipton, William Chamberlaine and Kirby Walker (all *q.v.*) were four of his classmates. He was commissioned in the 20th Infantry on duty at Fort Assiniboine, Montana, and later, at Fort Leavenworth, Kansas. In 1897, he graduated from the Infantry and Cavalry School at Fort Leavenworth. During the Spanish-American War, he was at El Caney and in the Santiago Campaign, and he received a Silver Star Commendation. In 1899, the 20th Infantry returned to the United States, then was sent to the Philippines. In 1905, he was on detached service with the Philippine scouts. In 1911, he returned to the States to rejoin the Twentieth Infantry. On 5 June 1913, he married Ethel Janet Brown. They had three sons: Robert, Fillmore and James. In 1914, while on the Mexican border, he was regimental adjutant of the 20th Infantry. After a brief tour of duty with the 12th Infantry, he was made head of reserve officers training at the University of Illinois. On 1 October 1918, he was promoted to brigadier general (NA). He commanded the 17th Infantry Division at Camp Beauregarde, Louisiana from November 1918 to February 1919, then reverted to his permanent rank of colonel and was assigned to recruiting duty in the Philadelphia area. In 1920, he performed the same duty in San Francisco, and later, he commanded the 47th Infantry at Camp (later Fort) Lewis, Washington. In December 1922, he retired as a colonel due to disabilities. He was a Presbyterian, and he belonged to many clubs and associations. He rode horses for recreation, and also enjoyed golfing and motoring. At the age of eighty-two, he died in Letterman General Hospital, San Francisco, on 23 May 1949. Photo courtesy of the National Archives.

Charles Thomas Menoher (0-34) was born on 20 March 1862 in Johnstown, Pennsylvania, where a flood occurred on 31 May 1889, drowning 2,300 people and causing $10,000,000 in damages. He entered USMA and graduated number sixteen of seventy-seven in the class of 1886. Mason M. Patrick,

John J. Pershing, Edward McCaskey and Peter Traub (all *q.v.*) were four of his classmates. He was commissioned in the First Artillery. He married Nannie Pearson, and they had four sons: Charles (who died young), Pearson (USMA, class of 1915, and later a brigadier general), Darrow and William. In 1894, he graduated from the Artillery School. During the Spanish-American War, he served with the First U.S. Volunteer Light Artillery in Chickamauga Park, Georgia, and in Havana. From 1899 to 1901, he was adjutant to the provost marshal general in Manila. He commanded the 28th Battery, Mountain Artillery, from 1901 to 1903. From 1903 to 1907, he served as provost marshal and assistant to the Chief of Staff of the Cuban Pacification Army. In 1907, he graduated from the Army War College. In 1916 and 1917, he commanded the Fifth Field Artillery. On 5 August 1917, he was promoted to brigadier general (NA). At the former French Cavalry School in Saumur, he commanded a School of Field Artillery Instruction until 14 December 1917. On 28 November 1917, he was made a major general (NA) and commanded the 42d Infantry Division for the remainder of the war. From 13 October 1918 to 17 December 1918, he commanded the Sixth Corps, and from 1919 to 1921, he was chief of the newly organized air service. He commanded the Hawaiian Division from 1922 to 1924, and the Hawaiian Department from 1924 to 1925. His last command was of the Ninth Corps Area. On 20 March 1926, he retired. He was awarded the Distinguished Service Medal and was decorated by the British, French and Italian governments. His retirement home was in Washington, D.C., where at the age of sixty-eight, he died, on 11 August 1930. Photo from the National Archives.

Charles Thomas Menoher

Wilder Stevens Metcalf (no ASN assigned), son of Isaac Metcalf and Antoinette Brigham Putnam Metcalf, was born on 10 September 1855 in Milo, Maine. He graduated from Oberlin College in 1878 with an A.B., and the same year he worked with Crozier and Shelton, cheese and butter manufacturers. He also married Mary Eliza Crozier of Wellington, Ohio. He stayed with the company until 1887, when he practiced law as a member of Russell and Metcalf, Attorneys. Following his Spanish-American War service, he practiced law by himself. The University of Kansas Law School gave him an LL.B. in 1897. He enlisted as a private in the Fifth Ohio Infantry, then became a second lieutenant. When he moved to Kansas, he again enlisted as a private, and stayed through the grades to brigadier general, KNG, retired. During 1898 and 1899, he was a major and colonel with the 20th Kansas Infantry and served in the Philippines, for

Wilder Stevens Metcalf

which he received a Congressional Medal. He was brevetted brigadier general by President McKinley. In 1900, he was a delegate-at-large in the Republican Convention in Philadelphia, Pennsylvania. The Secretary of War appointed him a member of the Militia Board for eight years. His wife died in 1914, and two years later he married Alice L. Bullene, on 8 January 1916. He was commissioned a colonel (NA) on 5 August 1917, and was promoted to brigadier general (NA) on 29 August 1917. He commanded the 77th Infantry Brigade at Camp Beauregarde, Louisiana, and was honorably discharged due to his age on 29 August 1917. He was president of the Douglas County Building and Loan Association, president of the Lawrence National Bank and chairman of the board of the Federal Home Loan Bank in Topeka, Kansas. For more than eight years, he was the United States pension agent in Topeka, and was commissioner of pensions in Washington, D.C. for four months, after which he resigned. For seventeen years, he was a member of the Lawrence, Kansas school board, and for four years he was a state senator. At the age of seventy-nine he died, on 1 February 1935. Photo from the National Archives.

Robert Edward Lee Michie

Robert Edward Lee Michie (no ASN assigned), son of Dr. J. Augustus Michie and Susan Jackson Michie, was born on 1 June 1864 in Bel Air, Albemarle County, Virginia. He entered USMA and graduated number twenty-six of thirty-nine in the class of 1885. Joseph E. Kuhn, Charles Henry Muir, Willard A. Holbrook and Robert Lee Bullard (all *q.v.*) were four of his classmates. He was commissioned in the Second Cavalry and performed frontier duty in Idaho, New Mexico, Arizona and Kansas. During that period, on 19 January 1887, he married Gray Beachy. During the Spanish-American War, he served as a major, U.S. Volunteers, from 1898 to 1899. From 1899 to 1900, he served in the Adjutant General's Department in Havana and in Pinar del Rio, Cuba. From 1900 to 1901, he was the Adjutant General, Department of the Missouri (River), and during 1903 and 1904, he was back in the Philippines. He was returned to Washington for duty with the General Staff, and was sent as observer to the

German Army Maneuvers of 1908. From 1904 to 1917, he again served with the General Staff. He was on duty on the Mexican border during 1912 and 1914. In 1917, he went with a special United States commission to Russia. On 5 August 1917, he was promoted to brigadier general (NA). He was assigned to command 53d Infantry Brigade at Camp Wadsworth, South Carolina, and took it to France with the AEF. There, at the age of fifty-four, he died on 4 June 1918. Photo courtesy Special Collections, USMA Library.

Edward Alexander Millar

Edward Alexander Millar (0-13433) was born on 25 June 1860 in Kentucky. He entered USMA and graduated number fourteen of thirty-seven in the class of 1882. Adelbert Cronkhite and Henry T. Allen (both *q.v.*) were two of his classmates. He was commissioned and assigned to the Third Artillery, and in 1886, he graduated from the Artillery School. From 1891 to 1896, he was an assistant instructor in engineering and artillery at the Artillery School at Fort Monroe, Virginia. During the Spanish-American War, he was an aide to Gen. Edward B. Williston (a Civil War veteran from Vermont), then served with troops during the Philippine Insurrection. He was on the Mexican border just before the United States entered World War I. He was promoted to brigadier general (NA) on 17 December 1917 and commanded the Sixth Field Artillery Brigade, part of the Sixth Infantry Division. In 1920, he retired as a colonel due to physical disabilities. In June 1930, his rank of brigadier general was restored. At the age of seventy-three, he died in Coronado, California, on 31 January 1934. Photo from the National Archives.

Samuel Warren Miller (0-103) was born on 10 February 1857 in Pennsylvania. He entered USMA and graduated number fifty-eight of sixty-seven in the class of 1879. He was commissioned in the Fifth Infantry and performed frontier duty from 1879 to 1889. He received a Silver Star Commendation for his services in the late Indian Wars, and from 1894 to 1898, he was Professor of Military Science and Tactics at Purdue University. During the Spanish-American War, he was in Tampa, Florida, and also served as chief mustering officer for Pennsylvania. He organized the 46th U.S. Volunteer Infantry and served in it as a major in the Philippines. He was inspector general of the First and Second Infantry Brigades in 1901. From 1906 to 1908, he was inspector general in the Philippines. From 1911 to 1914, he was commandant of the School of Musketry, and from 1913 to 1914, he visited foreign schools of musketry. On 5 August 1917, he was promoted to brigadier general (NA) and commanded Camp Custer, Michigan. From 25 November 1917 to 18 December 1917, he commanded the 85th Infantry Division. In 1921, he retired as a colonel, and in 1930, his rank of brigadier general was restored. At the age of eighty-three, he died in Washington, D.C., on 21 April 1940. Photo courtesy of the National Portrait Gallery, Washington, D.C.

WILLIAM L.MITCHELL

SAMUEL W.MILLER

William Lendrum Mitchell (0-63), grandson of Alexander Mitchell, an immigrant from Scotland who became a millionaire banker and railroad magnate, and son of Sen. John Lendrum Mitchell, was born on 29 December 1879, while his parents were temporarily residing in Nice, France. He was privately tutored and attended the Episcopal Academy in Racine, Wisconsin and Columbian Preparatory School (now George Washington University). At the age of eighteen, while still a junior in college, he enlisted as a private in the First Wisconsin Volunteer Infantry to serve in the Spanish-American War. Due to his father's influence, he was offered a commission as a second lieutenant in a volunteer signal company three weeks later. Both William Jennings Bryan and Gen. Adolphus Greely (then the Chief Signal Officer) furthered his career. He remained in the regular Signal Corps after the Spanish-American War, serving in Cuba, the Philippines and Alaska. In 1909, he graduated from the Army Staff College at Fort Leavenworth, Kansas, and in 1915, he was assigned to the Aviation Section, Signal Corps. He learned to fly on weekends in Newport News, Virginia during the winter of 1915 to 1916, and later he became an outstanding combat commander of air units during World War I. He was appointed assistant Chief of the Air Service in 1919 under Gen. Mason M. Patrick (*q.v.*). In 1925, he reverted to his rank of colonel and was stationed in San Antonio, Texas. He was the leading advocate of air power. His outspoken views led to a very spectacular court-martial in 1925 in Washington, D.C., in which he was convicted of insubordination and was suspended from rank and duty for five years. He resigned from the army on 1 February 1926 and wrote numerous articles on air power. At the age of fifty-six, he died in New York City, on 17 February 1936. In 1946, the chief of the new United States Air Force presented Mitchell's son with a medal in his father's honor, specifically authorized by Congress. There was a motion picture on the subject of his court-martial, starring Gary Cooper. He wrote three books: *Our Air Force* (published in 1921), *Winged Defense* (published in 1925) and *Skyways* (published in 1930), and may have written other works. *Mitchell, Pioneer of Air Power*, by Isaac Don Levine (published in 1941), *General Billy Mitchell, Champion of Air Defense*, by Roger Burlingame (published in 1952) and *My Brother Bill, the Life of Gen. Billy Mitchell*, by Ruth Mitchell (published in 1953) are books about his life. Photo from the National Archives.

George Davis Moore (0-306) was born in 1867 in Illinois. He entered USMA and graduated number forty-three of fifty-four in the class of 1890. Edgar Jadwin, James A. Ryan and Fred W. Sladen were three of his classmates. Originally commissioned in the 18th Infantry, he was promoted to first lieutenant and sent to the 23d Infantry. During the Spanish-American War, as of 22 May 1898, he served as a major, Fifth Missouri Infantry. On 9 November 1898, he was honorably mustered out of the volunteer service and was promoted to captain, 20th Infantry, on 15 December 1899. He served during the Philippine Insurrection, and went to France with the AEF. On 1 October 1918, he was promoted to brigadier general (NA), serving first as inspector general, Eleventh Corps, then as commanding general of the 169th Infantry Brigade. He retired in 1931 as a brigadier general, and lived in San Diego, California. At the age of eighty, he died on 12 December 1947. Photo from the National Archives.

George Davis Moore

John Frank Morrison (0-4), son of John Morrison and Hannah Lamont Morrison, was born on 20 December 1857 in Charlottesville, New York. He entered USMA and graduated number twenty-six of fifty-three in the class of 1881. Harry and Henry Hodges, Joseph T. Dickman and Andrew Summers Rowan (all *q.v.*) were four of his classmates. He was commissioned in the 20th Infantry and performed frontier duty from 1881 to 1887. On 16 August 1887, he

John Frank Morrison

married Kate McCleery. During the Spanish-American War, he served with the 20th Infantry in Cuba and also in the Sanitary Corps, for which he received a Silver Star Commendation. From 1899 to 1902, he was in the Philippines, serving during the Insurrection. In 1904, he was an observer with the Japanese Army. From 1906 to 1912, he was at the Command and General Staff School at Fort Leavenworth, Kansas, as senior instructor, and during that time, from April to August 1908, he was acting commandant as a major, the lowest ranking officer ever to hold that assignment. He served in Manila, and on 20 November 1915, he was promoted to brigadier general (USA) and commanded Camp Sevier, South Carolina. On 15 May 1917, he was promoted to major general (USA) and served in Europe from September to December. When he returned to the States, he was Director of Training (USA) until March 1918, when he was given command of the Eighth Infantry Division and then the 30th Infantry Division. He was commanding general of the Western Department from 1918 to 1919, for which he received the Distinguished Service Medal. He retired in 1921 as a major general. At the age of seventy-four, he died in Washington, D.C., on 22 October 1932. Photo from the National Archives.

Jay Johnson Morrow (0-363), was born on 20 February 1870 in Fairview, West Virginia. He entered USMA and graduated number five of sixty-five in the class of 1891. He was commissioned in the Corps of Engineers. In 1894, he graduated from the Engineering School of Application. On 15 October 1895, he married Harriet M. Butler. During 1895 and 1896, he was an instructor in military engineering at USMA, and had a second tour of this duty from 1898 to 1901. In 1901 and 1902, he was the military governor of the province of Zamboanga, and he remained in the Philippines until 1903. From 1907 to 1909, he was the Engineer Commissioner for Washington, D.C., and during 1916 and 1917, he was Maintenance Engineer and acting governor of the Panama Canal. He arrived in France in May 1918, and within a month, on 26 June 1918, he was promoted to brigadier general (NA). He served as Chief

Jay Johnson Morrow

Engineer of the First Army and as deputy Chief Engineer of the AEF. On 30 December 1918, he was assigned to command Camp Humphreys, Virginia. From the summer of 1919 until March 1921, he was again maintenance engineer of the Panama Canal. From March 1921 to October 1924, he was the Governor of the Panama Canal. During this period, in 1922, he retired from the army as a colonel. His rank of brigadier general was restored in June 1930. He was made an Officer of the Legion of Honor (France). His home was in Englewood, New Jersey, where at the age of sixty-seven, he died on 16 April 1937. The photo, courtesy of the National Archives, was taken on 24 February 1919, when he commanded Camp Humphreys, Virginia.

Benjamin Clarke Morse

Benjamin Clarke Morse (0-13477), son of Benjamin C. Morse, a prominent civil engineer who built the railroad tunnel through Tunnel Hill, Georgia, and Martha Blunt Morse, the daughter of a well known missionary to the Cherokee Indians, was born on 15 April 1859 in Macon, Missouri. While working at a bank in Marquette, Michigan, he was appointed to USMA, and he graduated number thirty-four of thirty-seven in the class of 1884. William L. Sibert (*q.v.*) and Isaac Newton Lewis, inventor of the Lewis machine gun, were two of his classmates. He was commissioned in the 23d Infantry. On 6 March 1890, he married Jessie Cable in Mackinac Island, Michigan. They had four children: John Cable Morse, Jessie Morse Raymond, Benjamin Clarke Morse III and Harriet Morse Keith. From 1890 to 1894, he was Professor of Military Science and Tactics at the Agricultural and Mechanical College of Texas (now Texas A and M). On his first Philippine tour in 1898, he was on duty in the Spanish arsenal, in charge of all the ordnance taken from the Spanish government. On his second Philippine tour, he was regimental quartermaster of the 17th Infantry, and also served as aide to Gen. William R. Shafter. During 1901 and 1902, he was assistant Adjutant General, then acting Adjutant General of the Department of California. During 1903 and 1904, he served in the Moro Campaign, and from 1906 to 1909, he served in the occupation of Cuba. When he left on 1 April 1909, the American flag was lowered and Cuba became an independent country. From 1910 to 1913, he was again a Professor of Military Science and Tactics, this time at the University of Illinois. In 1914, he was sent on the Vera Cruz Expedition. On 5 August 1917, he was promoted to brigadier general (NA). He was given command of the 169th Infantry Brigade at Camp Custer, Michigan on 25 April 1917. He was honorably discharged as a brigadier general on 1 April 1918, and served as colonel of 33d U.S. Infantry in the Canal Zone. In 1920, he retired as a colonel and lived in San Diego, California. His rank of brigadier general was restored in June 1930. At the age of seventy-four, he died in San Diego, on 26 April 1933. Photo courtesy of the Annual Report, Association of Graduates, USMA.

Charles Gould Morton

Charles Gould Morton (0-5), son of Allen Morton and Mary Colley Morton, was born on 15 January 1861 in Cumberland, Maine. He entered USMA and graduated number twenty of fifty-two in the class of 1883. George H. Cameron and Tyree Rodes Rivers (both *q.v.*) were two of his classmates. He was commissioned in the infantry and performed frontier duty from 1883 to 1888. On 15 October 1885, he married Ida Hastings, an army daughter. He was a Professor of Military Science and Tactics at the Florida Agricultural College from 1889 to 1890. This was followed by a long detail on recruiting duty in New York State and Maine, and also with troops in Fort Porter, New York, Fort Thomas, Kentucky and with the Maine National Guard. From May until October 1898, during the Spanish-American War, he was a lieutenant colonel with the First Maine Infantry. He did not get beyond New York State, as the war ended quickly. From 1900 to 1902, he was in the Philippines, and from 1902 to 1904, he attended the Army Staff College at Fort Leavenworth, Kansas. He returned to the Philippines, and in 1906, he became the Inspector General of the Philippine Division. As of September 1907, he was Inspector General of the Department of the Colorado (River) in the States. In 1912, he became Inspector General (USA). After 1913, he served on the Mexican border, and on 14 July 1916, he was promoted to brigadier general (USA) commanding the Tenth Infantry Division. On 15 May 1917, he was promoted to major general (NA) and placed in command of the 29th Infantry Division. This unit was composed of troops from both the North and South; the shoulder patch they wore was a circle of blue and grey. He trained the division at Camp McClellan, Alabama, and took it to France with the AEF. He commanded it from 25 August 1917 to 24 September 1917, from 6 December 1917 to 11 December 1917, from 26 December 1917 to 23 March 1918 and from 26 March 1918 to May 1919, when it was inactivated. For this service he received the Distinguished Service Medal. He then commanded the Hawaiian Department. In 1921, his wife died. He spent a few months in Washington, D.C., then commanded the Ninth Corps Area, headquartered in San Francisco. On 14 June 1922, he married a widow, Eleanor Moorhead Huff. At the age of seventy-two, he died in San Francisco, on 18 July 1933. Photo courtesy of the New Jersey Archives.

George Van Horn Moseley

George Van Horn Moseley (0-772), son of George Dallas Moseley and Alice Willett Moseley, was born on 28 September 1874 in Evanston, Illinois. He entered USMA and graduated number thirty-seven of seventy-two in the class of 1899. He was commissioned and sent to the Ninth Cavalry, and later served in the field artillery. On 20 July 1903, he married Alice E. Dodds, and they had two sons, George Van Horn Moseley, Jr. and Francis Loring Van Horn Moseley. He served during the Philippine Insurrection, and from 1903 to 1907, he was an aide to Gen. Jesse Matlock Lee. During this time, he was also commander of the Pulajane Expedition. He graduated from the Command and General Staff College in 1908, and from the Army War College in 1911. During World War I, he was Chief of Staff of the Seventh Infantry Division, and later G-4 (Service of Supply), General Headquarters (AEF). He was promoted to brigadier general (NA) on 26 June 1918, and served with the American forces in Germany. He was active in the opening of the Rhine River to all nations, for which he received the Distinguished Service Medal. In 1919, he was a member of the Harbord Commission to the Near East. In 1921, he was promoted to brigadier general (USA). In 1924, he and his wife were divorced. From 1927 to 1929 he was commanding general, First Cavalry Division, and in 1929, he was a mediator in the Mexican Revolution, which earned him another Distinguished Service Medal. On 23 June 1930, he married Florence DuBois, and they had one son, James W. Van Horn Moseley. From December 1931 to June 1933, he was Deputy Chief of Staff (USA). From 1930 to 1933, he was a member of the Joint Army-Navy Board. He commanded the Fifth Corps Area, then the Fourth Corps Area, and then the Third Army. In 1938, he retired. In addition to the decorations already mentioned, he received the Croix de Guerre with palm (France) and was made a Companion of the Order of the Bath (Britain), a Commander of the Legion of Honor, a Commander of the Order of the Crown (Belgium) and a Commander of the Order of the Crown (Italy). His retirement home was in Atlanta, where at the age of eighty-six, he died on 7 November 1960. Photo courtesy of *The Assembly*, Association of Graduates, USMA.

Andrew Moses (0-572), son of Norton Moses and Lucy Ann Lewis Moses, was born on 6 June 1874 in Burnet County, Texas. He attended the University of Texas, then entered USMA and graduated number fifty-six of sixty-seven in the class of 1897. He was commissioned in the infantry, transferred to field artillery, then transferred again to Coast Artillery. On 24 September 1897, he married Jessie Fisher, and they had one daughter, Kathleen (Mrs. Frank Denton Reed).

Andrew Moses

From 1901 to 1903, he served in the Cuban occupation. In 1906, he graduated from the School of Submarine Defense. From 1907 to 1911, he was Commandant of Cadets, and later, Professor of Military Science and Tactics at the Agricultural and Mechanical College of Texas (Texas A and M). He served with the National Guard and Organized Reserve in several locations. From November 1914 to August 1917, he was on the General Staff. He was promoted to brigadier general (NA) on 26 June 1918 and commanded the 156th Field Artillery Brigade, part of the 81st Infantry Division (AEF), for which he was awarded the Distinguished Service Medal. During 1919 and 1920, he was chairman of the Board for the Redelivery of Troop Transports. In 1921, he graduated from the Army War College. From 1921 to 1923 and from 1928 to 1929, he was Director of the Army War College. He commanded the coast and antiaircraft defenses of the Panama Canal during 1930 and 1931, and from October 1931 to October 1935, he was the Assistant Chief of Staff (USA). From 1936 to 1938, he commanded the Hawaiian Department, for which he received another Distinguished Service Medal, and he also commanded Schofield Barracks until he retired on 30 June 1938. He was a Mason, a Legionnaire and a member of the Military Order of the World Wars. In retirement, he lived in Washington, D.C., where at the age of seventy-two, he died on 22 December 1946. Photo courtesy of the National Portrait Gallery, Washington, D.C.

Charles Henry Muir

Charles Henry Muir (0-33) was born on 18 July 1860 on a farm in Erie, Michigan. He attended Ann Arbor High School, then taught for two terms. He entered USMA and graduated number eight of thirty-nine in the class of 1885. Willard Holbrook and Robert Lee Bullard (both *q.v.*) were two of his classmates. He was commissioned in the cavalry and performed frontier duty, including service in the Sioux Campaign, until 1892. He was an honor graduate of the Infantry and Cavalry School, and was number one on the Army Rifle Team of 1890. For four years, he served on the General Staff, and during the Spanish-American War, he was in the Santiago Campaign in Cuba and also in the

Philippines. He was recommended twice for the Medal of Honor and a brevet majority. During the Boxer Rebellion, he was sent to China as an observer. On 5 August 1917, he was promoted to brigadier general (NA), and on the following 28 November, he was promoted to major general (NA). He took command of the 28th Infantry Division (Pennsylvania National Guard) at Camp Hancock, Georgia, and took it to France. He commanded it in action and brought it back to the States in the spring of 1919. He received the Distinguished Service Cross, the Distinguished Service Medal, the Croix de Guerre, and was made a Knight Commander of the Order of St. Michael and St. George (Great Britain). In 1924, he retired, and at the age of seventy-three, he died in Baltimore, Maryland, on 8 December 1933. Photo courtesy of the Pennsylvania National Guard.

Edward Lyman Munson, M.D. (0-235), son of U.S. Judge Lyman E. Munson and Lucy A. Sanford Munson, was born on 27 December 1868 in New Haven, Connecticut. He graduated from Yale with an A.B. in 1890, an M.D. in 1892 and an A.M. in 1893. On 29 May 1893, he married Martha Schneeloch, and they had one daughter, Katherine. He was promoted to assistant surgeon (USN), captain, assistant surgeon (USA) on 12 May 1898, major on 11 July 1906, lieutenant colonel on 9 May 1915 and colonel on 15 May 1917. His last promotion was to brigadier general (NA) on 3 October 1917. He was a professor of hygiene at the Army Medical School in Washington, D.C., and later served on General Shafter's staff in Santiago, Cuba. From 1898 to 1899, 1901 to 1902 and 1915 to 1917, he was assistant to the surgeon general of the army. During 1903 and 1904, he was assistant to the Chief Surgeon of the Philippines, and from 1914 to 1915 and 1922 to 1924, he was adviser to the Philippine government in hygiene and sanitation. He was Professor of Military Hygiene at the Army Service Schools from 1908 to 1912, and assistant to the Surgeon General in charge of training of medical personnel from 1917 to 1918. He was chief of the morale branch of the General Staff in 1918, and in the same year, he was commanding general at Camp Greenleaf, Chickamauga Park, Georgia. He was in charge of the medical service during the U.S. Relief Mission to the earthquake area of Japan in 1923. In addition to the Munson Last Shoe (which became the standard shoe issued for the U.S. Army from right after WWI until after WWII), he was the inventor of several types of equipment adopted by the army. In 1932, he retired and served as Professor of Preventative Medicine at George Washington University and at the University of California. He retired as professor emeritus in 1939. He had a Distinguished Service Medal for his field train-

Edward Lyman Munson, M.D.

ing of officers and men in the Medical Corps, for organization of medical officer training camps and for the organization and administration of the morale branch of the General Staff. In addition, he was made a Companion of the Bath (Britain) and an Officer of the Order of the Red Cross (Japan). His memberships in clubs were many, and he wrote a number of books, including *Theory and Practice of Military Hygiene* (published in 1902), *A Study in Troop Leading and Sanitary Service in War* (published in 1910), *Sanitary Tactics* (published in 1911), a volume on hospitals in *The Photographic History of the Civil War* (published in 1911), *The Soldier's Foot and the Military Shoe* (published in 1912) and *The Management of Men* (published in 1921). From 1915 to 1918, he was editor of *The Military Surgeon*. In retirement he lived in New Haven, Connecticut. At the age of seventy-eight, he died on 7 July 1947. He was buried in Arlington. Photo from the National Archives.

Peter Murray

Peter Murray (0-300), son of Joshua Murray and Amanda Roark Murray, was born on 21 April 1867 on a ranch near present-day Visalia, California. His parents, both of notable Scots lineage, were of the highest type of American pioneer stock, of sturdy character and great courage. From South Carolina to Tennessee to Missouri, his ancestors followed the frontier west, and they arrived in California by covered wagon. He won his appointment to USMA in a competitive exam, and he graduated number forty of fifty-four in the class of 1890. He was the first appointee from his district to graduate. Edgar Jadwin, Fred W. Sladen and James A. Ryan (all *q.v.*) were three of his classmates. He was commissioned in the Fifth Infantry and sent to Fort Snelling, Minnesota, where he spent five years. During this period, he met Harriet Tingley Jewett in Youngstown, New York. She was the daughter of Gen. Horace Jewett, a Civil War veteran and Indian fighter. They were married on 16 November 1892, and they had two daughters: Frances J. Murray (wife of Samuel D. Sturgis, Jr., Corps of Engineers) and Janet E. Murray (Mrs. Charles D. Voorhies of Cape Cottage, Maine). He had a reputation for good judgment, thoroughness and being responsible. He served with the topographical mapping detail at Fort Yellowstone, Wyoming. During the Spanish-American War, he was adjutant of the 21st Infantry in Cuba, and he was present at San Juan Hill, where he earned a Silver Star Commendation. In 1899, he was promoted to captain and transferred to the 18th Infantry, where he spent the next ten years. In the Philippines, he was cited by Gen. Henry Lawton for gallantry under fire. When the 18th Infantry returned to the States, he was regimental quartermaster at both Fort D. A. Russel (now

Warren Air Force Base) and Fort Leavenworth, Kansas. In 1906, he was detailed to the staff of Major C. A. DeVol, depot quartermaster in San Francisco, during the earthquake and fire. In 1907, he was promoted to major and commanded a battalion of the 18th Infantry at Fort Slocum, New York. After 1911, he spent two years with the 11th Infantry at Fort Sam Houston, Texas. In 1912, he became treasurer of USMA in West Point, and displayed great managerial ability. On 17 December 1917, in France, he was promoted to brigadier general (NA) and commanded the Third Infantry Brigade, part of the Second Infantry Division. In May 1918, he was relieved due to physical disability after a brilliant performance as a brigade commander. Back in the States, he served for the remainder of the war in the War Plans Division of the General Staff, for which he received the Distinguished Service Medal. In 1921, he became the Chief of Staff of the Second Corps Area on Governor's Island, New York, where he served until 1 November 1924. He retired after thirty years of service. His wife became an invalid, and he cared for her in retirement. During this time, Lt. Gen. Robert Lee Bullard was very helpful to his family. His rank of brigadier general was restored in June 1930. At the age of seventy-three, he died in Cape Cottage, Maine, on 26 December 1940. Photo courtesy of *The Assembly*, Association of Graduates, USMA.

William Keith Naylor (0-635), son of William Alexander Naylor and Genevive Charlotte Naylor, was born on 24 November 1874 in Bloomington, Illinois. He graduated from Michigan Military Academy in 1894 and received an LL.B. from the University of Minnesota in 1898. He was admitted to the Minnesota Bar, and enlisted in the 14th Minnesota Volunteer Infantry on 8 May 1898. He was honorably discharged from the volunteer service on 24 July 1898, having been commissioned a second lieutenant (USA) on 9 July 1898. He served with the Ninth Infantry in the Philippines from 1898 to 1899 and in the China Relief Expedition in 1900, after which he spent about five years as an instructor in military history and strategy at various service schools. He was a distinguished graduate of the Infantry and Cavalry School at Fort Leavenworth, Kansas in 1904. On 27 December 1904, he married Margaret Wagner, daughter of Col. Arthur Lockwood Wagner (USA). They had three children: Margaret (Mrs. Dwight L. Adams), William K. Naylor, Jr. and Alexander Hay Naylor. He became a colonel (NA), and was promoted to brigadier general (NA) on 1 October 1918. He was Chief of Staff of the 33d Infantry Division that participated in the Somme Offensive, and he served in the Meuse-Argonne with the

William Keith Naylor

Third Corps as Chief of Staff. When he returned to the States, he was again promoted to instructor of strategy and military history at the service schools. He was the director of the staff school and director of the War Plans Division of the Army War College, as well as assistant Chief of Staff (USA) and Director of Military Intelligence (GS) from 1922 to 1924. He commanded the 15th Infantry in China from 1924 to 1926, and commanded the 13th Infantry in Boston Harbor in October 1926. On 27 May 1929, he was made Chief of Staff, Second Corps Area, on Governor's Island, New York. He was appointed Professor of Military Science and Tactics at the University of Illinois on 1 July 1933. He was promoted to brigadier general (USA) on 1 December 1933, and post commander, Fort Benjamin Harrison in Indianapolis, Indiana on 8 December 1933. He retired 30 November 1938. He received the Silver Star with oak leaf cluster for service in Tiensin, China in 1900 and the Meuse-Argonne in 1918. He also received the Distinguished Service Medal and the Croix de Guerre (France), and was made a commander of the Order of St. Michael and St. George (Britain), a Commander of the Order of the Crown (Italy), an Officer of the Legion of Honor (France) and a member of the Military Order of the Dragon (China). He was a Thirty-second-degree Mason and a Delta Chi, and he belonged to the Army and Navy Club in Washington. He also wrote several books: *The Principles of Strategy* (published in 1922), which was adopted as an official textbook by the Japanese government, *The Principles of War* (published in 1923) and *Marne Miracle* (published in 1924). At the age of sixty-seven, he died in Washington, D.C., on 3 August 1942. Photo from the National Archives.

Henry Clay Newcomer

Henry Clay Newcomer (0-125), son of David Newcomer and Mary Shelley Funk Newcomer, was born on 3 April 1861 in Upton, Pennsylvania, a town no longer on the map. He entered USMA and graduated number one of seventy-seven in the class of 1886. John J. Pershing (*q.v.*) was one of his classmates. He was commissioned in the Corps of Engineers. On 29 December 1886, he married Rebecca Kosier. From 1889 to 1892, he was assistant to Colonel Mendell in San Francisco, doing fortifications work. From 1892 to 1896, he was an assistant professor of engineering at USMA. From 1896 to 1900, he worked on improvements to the Mississippi River, and from 1898 to 1900, he served in the Little Rock, Arkansas, engineering district. He spent four years as assistant to the engineering commissioner for Washington, D.C., and from 1903 to 1904, he commanded Company E, Third Engineer Battalion at Washington Barracks. He was a member of the Board of Engineers for Rivers and Harbors.

From 1910 to 1914, he was Division Engineer for the Central Division (USA). His wife died on 31 March 1913. On 8 May 1915, he married Lily A. Foster. From 1916 to 1918, he was in the office of the Chief of Engineers (USA). From 6 August 1918 to 6 January 1919, he was Assistant Director of the Chemical Warfare Service. He was promoted to a brigadier general (NA) on 8 August 1918. From 1919 to 1920, he was department engineer, Hawaiian Department, and also commanded the Third Engineer Regiment. He retired in 1925 as a colonel. His rank of brigadier general was restored in June 1930. At the age of ninety-one, he died in Washington, D.C., on 3 December 1952. Photo courtesy of the National Portrait Gallery.

William Jones Nicholson (0-13411) was born on 16 January 1856 in Washington, D.C. He enlisted after Little Big Horn and was appointed second lieutenant in the Seventh Cavalry. He served with the regiment on the frontier against the Indians, and was ordnance officer of the regiment during the Spanish-American War. He was promoted to colonel in 1912, and he commanded the 11th Cavalry during the Mexican Punitive Expedition. On 5 August 1917, he was promoted to brigadier general (NA) and was commanding general of the 157th Infantry Brigade of the 79th Infantry Division in France, where had the distinction of capturing Montfaucon. He was commanding general of the 79th Infantry Division (AEF) from 26 November 1917 to 17 February 1918, from 22 May 1918 to 8 June 1918 and from June 1918 to 31 December 1918. At the age of seventy-five, he died in Washington, D.C, in 1931. The photo, from the National Archives, was taken at Camp Meade, Maryland, while he was commanding general of he 157th Infantry Brigade.

William Jones Nicholson

Robert Ernest Noble, M.D. (0-51), son of George Noble and Lucy Wadsworth Noble, was born on 5 November 1870 in Rome, Georgia. He graduated from Alabama Polytechnic Institute with an M.S. in 1891, and he received an M.D. from Columbia in 1899. He was appointed assistant surgeon (USA) on 29 June 1901, and he was the honor graduate from the U.S. Army Medical School that same year. From 1901 to 1903, he was in the Philippines. On 23 November 1905, he married Ella L. Lupton. From 1907 to 1914, he was with the Department of Sanitation, Isthmian Canal Commission, except for eight months between 1911 and 1912, when he was in charge of an antimosquito campaign in

Robert Ernest Noble, M.D.

Puerto Rico. During 1912 and 1913, he was sent to Ecuador to study yellow fever, after which he went to South Africa, working to discover the causes of pneumonia. From May to September 1914, he was on duty in Vera Cruz, Mexico, after which he served in the War Department from 1914 to 1918. On 9 May 1918, he was promoted to brigadier general (NA). He arrived in France on 25 October 1918. On 5 March 1919, he was promoted to brigadier general (USA), and also to assistant surgeon general (USA). He retired as a major general on 8 February 1925. He was a member of, and later director of, the Rockefeller Foundation. From May to December 1920, he was on the Yellow Fever Commission in the west coast of Africa. He was awarded the Distinguished Service Medal for operating the personnel division of the Surgeon General's Office and for expanding the number of medical doctors in the army from 1,500 to 30,000. He also received recognition while in charge of the hospital division of the Surgeon General's Office. He was made a commander of the Legion of Honor (France). In retirement, he lived in Anniston, Alabama, where at the age of eighty-five, he died on 18 September 1956. Photo courtesy of the National Archives.

Robert Houston Noble (0-144), son of Dr. and Mrs. William D. Noble, was born on 3 November 1961 in Federalsburg, Maryland. He entered USMA and graduated number thirty-two of thirty-seven in the class of 1884. He was commissioned a second lieutenant in the First Infantry on 15 June of that year. He served in the Geronimo Campaign of 1885 to 1886. On 15 June 1891, he was promoted to first lieutenant, 15th Infantry, and he promptly transferred back to the First Infantry. In 1892, he received an LL.B. from the University of Maryland and was admitted to the state bar. He was Professor of Military Science and Tactics at St. John's College in Annapolis, Maryland, where he was also a student. He was an aide to General Shafter from 1897 to 1899, and he served in the Santiago Campaign in Cuba and also in the Philippines. He was Adjutant General to Generals Grant, Hughes, Snyder and Baldwin, and Adjutant

Robert Houston Noble

General of the Department of Visayas in the Philippines from 1900 to 1902. He was an aide to Governors General Taft, Wright, Ide and Smith from 1902 to 1908. He was promoted to major, Ninth Infantry on 4 October 1907, and he had charge of militia affairs of the Western Department during 1913 and 1914. He commanded the 22d Infantry on the Mexican border from September 1914 to September 1916, and in the Mexican Punitive Expedition from November 1916 to February 1917. He was at Fort Bliss, Texas, then in Chickamauga Park, Georgia until 6 April 1918, when he went to France. He commanded the 30th Division from 12 to 14 June 1918, and also served with the 77th Infantry Division. He commanded the 158th Infantry Brigade, comprised of the 315th and 316th Infantry Regiments, which was a part of the 79th Division. When he returned to the States in April 1919, he was put in charge of National Guard affairs of the Western Department. On 14 May 1921, he married Ethel Sherwood. In 1922, he retired as a colonel. His rank of brigadier general was restored in 1930. At the age of seventy-seven, he died in California, on 27 October 1939. Photo from the National Archives.

Dennis Edward Nolan

Dennis Edward Nolan (0-83) was born on 22 April 1872 in Akron, northeast of Buffalo, New York. He entered USMA and graduated number fifty-one of seventy-three in the class of 1896. He was commissioned a second lieutenant and sent to the Third Infantry on 12 June 1896, and he was promoted to first lieutenant on 27 August of that year. He was promoted to major, U.S. Volunteer Cavalry on 10 August 1899, and to captain (USA) 30th Infantry on 6 July 1901. During the Spanish-American War, he served in the Sanitary Corps and received two Silver Star Commendations. On 21 August 1901, he married Julia Grant Sharp, and they had two children: Dennis E. Nolan, Jr. and Ellen Honora Nolan. He served in El Caney in Cuba from 1 July 1898. He was an aide to Gen. Chambers McKibbin in Santiago and Montauk Point, New York. From there he went to Camp Meade, Maryland, Camp McKenzie, Georgia and to the Philippines. From 1901 to 1903, he was an instructor in West Point. From 1903 to 1906, he was on General Staff duty. From 1906 to 1911 and from 1912 to 1913, he was in Alaska. He was on the General Staff again from 1915 to 1919. He was promoted to major,(USA) on 1 July 1916, to lieutenant colonel (NA) on 5 August 1917 and to colonel (NA) on the same day. He was promoted to brigadier general (NA) on 8 August 1918. He organized the Intelligence Section, general headquarters (AEF), and remained in charge of it until demobilization. He was commanding general, 55th Infantry Brigade (Pennsylvania National

Guard troops) from 29 September to 10 October 1918, during the Meuse-Argonne offensive. For this service he received the Distinguished Service Cross. He was promoted to brigadier general (USA) in 1920, and was Assistant Chief of Staff (USA), G-2 from September 1920 to September 1921. He was assistant Chief of Staff (USA), G-4 from 1 December 1923 to 31 September 1924. He was promoted to major general (USA) on 18 January 1925, and served as Deputy Chief of Staff (USA) from January 1925 until January 1927. During this period, he was a member of the Billy Mitchell court-martial. He was the chief army representative at the Geneva Arms Limitation Conference of 1926 and 1927. From 1927 to 1931, he was commanding general, Fifth Corps Area, and from 1931 to 1936, he was commanding general, Eleventh Corps Area. In 1936, he retired and lived in New York City. He was a Roman Catholic, and he belonged to the Army and Navy Club in Washington and the Chevy Chase Club. In addition to the decorations already mentioned, he received the Croix de Guerre with palm (France) and the Medal of Solidaridad (Panama), and he was made a Commander of the Bath (Britain), Commander of the Legion of Honor (France) and a Commander of the Crown (Italy and Belgium). He worked for the New York World's Fair from 1936 to 1940, and from 1938 to 1940, he was president of the Association of Graduates, USMA. At the age of eighty-three, he died in New York, on 24 February 1956. Photo from the Pennsylvania National Guard.

George Adolphus Nugent (0-591), son of Alfred E. Nugent and Elizabeth Pryer Nugent, was born on 26 December 1872 in Lansing, Michigan. His early years were spent in Fargo, North Dakota. He attended preparatory school in Highland Falls, New York, then entered USMA and graduated number thirteen of fifty-nine in the class of 1898. Fox Conner, Malin Craig, Robert C. Davis and Guy V. Henry, Jr. (all *q.v.*) were four of his classmates. He was the choir leader and is credited with the composition of two hymns. He was commissioned in the artillery and was stationed at Fort Trumbull, Connecticut, and then at Fort Terry, New York. He married Emma Bacon, and they had one daughter, Elizabeth (Mrs. Henry Blackiston). In the Philippines, he was assistant to the chief quartermaster. In 1907, he returned to the States and worked as quartermaster in the Presidio of San Francisco after the earthquake and fire. In 1909, he graduated with honors from the Coast Artillery School. In 1910, he completed the advanced course. From Fort Monroe, he entered the Army War College, and he joined the faculty in 1911. Staff assignments and faculty duty kept him busy until 1917, when he took command of the 342nd Field

George Adolphus Nugent

Artillery at Camp Funston, Kansas. On 8 August 1918, en route to France, he received his promotion to brigadier general (NA). He returned to the States to command the 23d Field Artillery Brigade and later, the 14th Field Artillery Brigade. He was assistant to the Chief of Coast Artillery, G-1 in Panama, and he served with the Inspector General's Office in Washington. In 1935, while he was Chief of Staff of the Second Corps Area on Governor's Island, his wife died. The following year, he married Mabelle M. Neale. On 31 December 1936, after more than thirty-eight years of service, he retired and lived in Old Lyme, Connecticut. At the age of eighty-five, he died in the Veteran's Hospital in Newington, Connecticut, on 5 January 1958. Photo from the Association of Graduates, USMA.

Louis Meredith Nuttman

Louis Meredith Nuttman (0-484), son of George and Louise Mentz Nuttman, was born on 28 January 1874 in Newark, New Jersey. He entered USMA and graduated number thirty-one of fifty-two in the class of 1895. Joseph Wheeler, Jr. (son of the Confederate cavalryman) and David Sheridan Stanley were two of his classmates. He was commissioned in the infantry and was in Cuba during the Spanish-American War, and also served in the Sanitary Corps, for which he received a Silver Star Commendation. During the Philippine Insurrection, he received two more Silver Stars, and on the China Relief Expedition, he received a fourth. He participated in the Moro Campaign in 1902, as well as in the Vera Cruz Expedition in 1914 and the Mexican Punitive Expedition in 1916 and 1917. On 1 October 1918, he was promoted to brigadier general (NA). He commanded both infantry regiments and brigades in France, for which he received the Distinguished Service Medal. In addition to the decorations already mentioned, he received the Croix de Guerre (France). In 1925, he was a colonel at headquarters of the Ninth Corps Area in the Presidio of San Francisco. In 1962, he married Agnes Parker, a native of Scotland who had been secretary to General Pershing during World War I. In 1932, he was promoted to brigadier general (USA), and in 1938, he retired. He was a nationally known contract bridge player, and after retiring he taught the game. He lived on Pacific Avenue in San Francisco, California, where at the age of 104 he died, on 4 November 1978. He is thought to have lived longer than any other USMA graduate. His wife not only survived him but lived until 15 July 1983. Photo courtesy of Special Collections, USMA Library.

Joseph Patrick O'Neil

Joseph Patrick O'Neil (0-140), son of Mr. and Mrs. Patrick O'Neill (sic), who had come from Ireland, was born on 27 December 1863 in Brooklyn, New York. His father, an infantry major, was killed in Fredricksburg, Virginia. He was raised at various army posts in the West, and was almost an Indian War veteran himself before he went to Notre Dame, from which he graduated in 1883 with a B.S. degree. The following year, he was commissioned in the 14th Infantry. In 1885, he made a reconnaissance of the Olympic Mountains in the far northwest, and he turned in a detailed report. As a result, one of those mountains was named after him. In 1887, he graduated from the Infantry and Cavalry School at Fort Leavenworth, Kansas, and during the 1890s he was stationed at Fort Custer, Montana to help restore order between the Crows and Cheyennes. On 15 January 1891, in Vancouver, Washington, he married Nina Maude Troup. During the Spanish-American War, he served in Cuba with the 25th Infantry, then had two tours in the Philippines and one in Alaska, ending in 1914. After graduating from the Army War College in 1915, he was sent to Plattsburg, New York, then to the Mexican border. Late in 1916, he was placed in command of the 21st Infantry in the Panama Pacific Exposition in San Diego. On 5 August 1917, he was promoted to brigadier general (NA) and commanded the 179th Infantry Brigade, part of the 90th Infantry Division. He took this brigade to France and commanded it very successfully in battle. He was under enemy fire for two and a half months. During November and December 1918, he commanded the 90th Infantry Division. He returned his brigade to the States in June 1919, and reverted to his permanent rank of colonel, commanding the Tenth Infantry in Michigan. He organized and commanded the first reserve officers training camp with students from nine states. In 1920, he was ordered to serve with the Pennsylvania National Guard, and in 1921, at his own request, he was returned to Oklahoma, where he had served during the war. He performed recruiting duty until he was retired due to age. He retired as a colonel, and his rank of brigadier general was restored in June 1930. In retirement, he lived in Portland, Oregon. He loved to hunt, ride horses, read and travel. He was a pleasant, happy person. Well past his seventy-fourth birthday, he died in Portland, on 27 July 1938. Photo courtesy of the National Archives.

Christopher T. O'Neill (no ASN assigned), son of Christopher O'Neill and Elizabeth O'Neill, was born on 24 June 1856 in Merthya, Tyevil, Wales, but was raised in Allentown, Pennsylvania. He graduated from the Allentown Business College and worked as a clerk and telegrapher for the Allentown Rolling Mills,

Christopher T. O'Neill

then as a bookkeeper for the Vulcan Dynamite Company. He was chief clerk at Hancock Chemical Company and Lehigh Valley Railroad Company, and then private secretary to Louis Soleiac of the Adelaide Silk Mills. In 1891, he was appointed superintendent of the state arsenal at Harrisburg until 1905, when he opened a sales office in New York for the Hanover Silk Company. He started an independent telephone company for Allentown and surrounding territory. On 16 August 1897, he enlisted in Company D, Fourth Pennsylvania Infantry, and stayed with the Pennsylvania National Guard for the remainder of his career. His was the first regiment in the state to be mustered into federal service for the Spanish-American War, and he became a colonel. He served with the regiment in Mt. Gretna, Pennsylvania, in Chickamauga Park, Georgia and on the Puerto Rican Expedition. He led his troops in the inaugural parade of President McKinley in 1901. They had forty days of duty in September and October 1900, during the Shenandoah and Panther Creek coal strikes. In 1902, they had thirty-eight days of duty at Mt. Carmel in Northumberland County. On 13 July 1916, he led a three-regiment infantry brigade to El Paso, Texas. On 19 February 1917, he arrived back in Allentown, but had only a brief stay at home. On 15 July 1917, he reported for duty for World War I. He commanded the 53d Depot Brigade of the 28th Infantry Division at Camp Hancock, outside Augusta, Georgia. When the brigade was broken up, he was transferred and commanded the Pioneer Brigade in Spartanburg, South Carolina. He was then transferred back to Camp Hancock, where on 23 March 1918, he was retired due to physical disability. After retirement, he served in Pennsylvania as keeper of the state arsenal. At the age of seventy-five, in his home at 37 South West Street in Allentown, Pennsylvania, he died as a result of pneumonia in March 1932. Photo courtesy of the Pennsylvania National Guard.

John Francis O'Ryan (0-135904), son of Francis O'Ryan and Anna Barry O'Ryan, was born on 21 August 1874 in New York City. He graduated from New York University in 1898 and was admitted to the New York Bar that same year. He enlisted as a private in Company G, Seventh New York Infantry in 1897. He married Janet Holmes in 1902. He was captain of the First Battery, New York National Guard in 1907, major of field artillery by 1911 and major general, New York National Guard in 1912. He graduated from the Army War College in 1914. In 1916, on the Mexican border, he commanded the New York Division. He was made a major general (NA) in 1917, and he commanded the 27th Infantry Division (AEF) in France and Belgium. For his service during

John Francis O'Ryan

World War I, he was awarded the Distinguished Service Medal and the Croix de Guerre with palms (Belgium and France), and he was made a Knight Commander of the Order of St. Michael and St. George (Great Britain), a Commander of the Legion of Honor (France), a Commander of the Order of Leopold (Belgium) and a Commander of the Order of St. Maurice and St. Lazarus (Italy). New York University gave him an honorary LL.D. in 1919. He was a partner in the legal firm of Loucks, O'Ryan and Cullen in New York City, and was state transit commissioner from 1921 to 1926. On 1 January 1934, he was appointed Police Commissioner of New York City, and in 1940, he was Chairman of the Economic Commission to Japan, Manchuria and Northern China. In 1941, he was state Director of Defense. He belonged to the Lawyer's Club in New York and the Metropolitan in Washington. His law office was in New York City, and he lived in Westchester County. He was active civically and politically throughout his life. At the age of eighty-six, he died in January 1961. Photo from the National Archives.

Francis LeJou Parker

Francis LeJou Parker (0-440), son of William H. Parker and Lucia G. Parker, was born on 24 June 1873 in Abbeville, South Carolina. He entered USMA and graduated number twelve of fifty-four in the class of 1894. He was commissioned in the Fifth Cavalry. From 1897 to 1998, he was an instructor in West Point, then was sent to serve in Cuba, Puerto Rico and the Philippines. He was an aide to Brig. Gens. Louis Henry Carpenter and George W. Davis, as well as to Gov. Gen. W. Cameron Forbes. In 1916, he was an observer with the Roumanian and Russian Armies, as well as being military attaché in Petrograd. He commanded the 312th Cavalry, and in France, the 119th Infantry. On 26 June 1918, he was promoted to brigadier general and took command of the 171st Infantry Brigade, then served with the Intelligence Section, General Headquarters (AEF). In 1920, he reverted to his permanent rank of colonel and commanded the First Cavalry Regiment, after which he was Chief of Staff of the Sixth Infantry Division. From 1921 to 1923, he was military attaché in Mexico

E. E. Booth, Will Rogers, and Major Hap Arnold

E. E. Booth and Will Rogers at Ft. Riley, Kansas

Dr.FRANCIS A.WINTER O-228

Leonard Wood, one of the outstanding American Officers of his century, an M.D. who also served as a line officer

City. From 1923 to 1926, he commanded the 12th Field Artillery. From 1926 to 1927, he served with the Inspector General's Department, and in 1927 and 1928, he was vice chairman of the National Board of Elections in Nicaragua. From January 1929 to August 1933, he was chief of the Bureau of Insular Affairs with the rank of brigadier general. From October 1933 to May 1934, he commanded the Second Field Artillery Brigade, and from 1934 to 1936, he commanded Fort Stotsenberg in the Philippines. His last command was of the First Cavalry Division at Fort Bliss, Texas. He retired in 1936 and lived in Charleston, South Carolina. At the age of ninety-two, he died on 16 May 1966. Photo from *The Assembly*, Association of Graduates, USMA.

Frank Parker

Frank Parker (0-451), son of Arthur Middleton Parker and Emma Parker, was born on 21 September 1872 in Georgetown County, South Carolina. He entered USMA and graduated number thirty of fifty-four in the class of 1894. Paul B. Malone, Hamilton S. Hawkins and George Estes, Jr. were three of his classmates. He was commissioned in the Fifth Cavalry, and stationed in Tampa, Florida with his regiment in 1898, then served in Puerto Rico until 1900, when he was returned to West Point as an instructor. In 1903, he was sent as a student to the French Cavalry School at Saumur. In 1904, he served as military attaché in Caracas, Venezuela. From 1905 to 1906, he was military attaché in Buenos Aires, Argentina, and from 1906 to 1908, he performed the same duty in Cuba. From 1909 to 1912, he was instructor and organizer of the Cuban Cavalry. In 1912, he attended the Ecole Superieure de Guerre in France. From 1913 to 1914, he was a member of the Cavalry Board. He returned to the Ecole Superieure in 1914. During 1916 and 1917, he was an observer with the French Army, and from April to December 1917, he was Chief of the American Military Mission at French headquarters. He commanded the 18th U.S. Infantry, and after his promotion to brigadier general (NA), he commanded the First Infantry Brigade of the First Infantry Division. From 18 October 1918 to 21 October 1918, he commanded the First Infantry Division, for which he received two Distinguished Service Medals and a recommendation by General Pershing for promotion to major general. He graduated from the Ecole Superieure de Guerre in 1920, and was an Assistant Professor there until 1921. He graduated from and was retained as an instructor at the Command and General Staff School, and he graduated from and was retained as an instructor at the Army War College in 1923. In 1924, he was promoted to brigadier general (USA). During 1924 and 1925, he commanded the Second Brigade, First Infantry Division, after which he was assistant Chief of Staff (USA) from 1927 to 1929. In 1929, he was promoted to major general (USA). Until 1932, he commanded the Sixth Corps Area, and during 1932 and 1933, he commanded the Second Army. From 1933 to 1935, he commanded the Philippine Department, and in February and March 1936, he commanded the First Infantry Division. From March to September 1936, he commanded the Third Army and the Eighth Corps Area. He retired on 30 September 1936. From 1942 to 1945, he directed the Illinois War Council. In addition to the decorations already mentioned, he received two Silver Star Citations, the Croix de Guerre with three palms (France) and the Grand Cross of the Order of the Crown (Italy). He was made a Commander of the Legion of Honor (France), a Commander of the Order of the Crown (Belgium), an Officer of the Order of Military Merit (Cuba), a commander of the Order of Polonia (Poland) and an Officer of the Order of Olaf, First Class (Norway). He married Katherine Hamilton Lahm, and they had two daughters: Katherine Lahm Parker and Ann Middleton Parker. In retirement, he lived at the Union League in Chicago, where he died at the age of seventy-four, on 13 March 1947. The photo, from the National Archives, shows him in France in 1918, conversing with Col. and Mrs. Theodore Roosevelt, Jr.

James Parker

James Parker (0-13114), son of the Honorable Cortlandt Parker and Elizabeth Stites Parker, was born on 20 February 1854 in Newark, New Jersey. He studied at Phillips Academy in Andover, Massachusetts and at Rutgers College in New Jersey. He entered USMA and graduated number thirty-one of forty-eight in the class of 1876. Eben Swift, Jr. and Hugh L. Scott (both *q.v.*) were two of his classmates. He was commissioned in the Fourth Cavalry. Rutgers awarded him a masters degree in 1878. In 1879, he married Charlotte M. Condit. From 1876 to 1888, he performed frontier duty, for which he received two Silver Star Commendations. He was on the Mexican border in Texas during 1878 and 1879. He served in the Ute Campaign in Colorado from 1879 to 1881 and in the Apache Campaign in Arizona from 1885 to 1886. From 1894 to 1898, he served in the Tactics Department at USMA. He was in Cuba from 1898 to 1899, then served in the Philippines, where he stayed until 1901. As a lieutenant colonel (USV), he received the Medal of Honor and two Silver Star Commendations. From 1901 to 1903, he was with the Adjutant General's Department in Washington, and during 1904 and 1905, he was Adjutant General, Northern Division (USA). In 1905 and 1906, he was commandant of the Cavalry School at Fort Riley, Kansas. From 1906 to 1909, he was with the Army of

Pacification in Cuba. He returned to the States and commanded the 11th Cavalry at Fort Oglethorpe, Georgia from 1909 to 1912. The same year, he was sent to Europe for four months with the Cavalry Reorganization Board, after which he commanded the First Cavalry Brigade in San Antonio, Texas. He was very busy with mobilization and training of troops in Texas during the 1916 and 1917 Mexican border troubles, and he commanded the 32d and 85th Infantry Divisions at different times between 1917 and 1918. During October and November 1917, he was an observer at the front in France, and he participated in a number of actions, for which he received the Distinguished Service Medal. He was retired due to age on 20 February 1918, and he lived in Newport, Rhode Island. He wrote two books: *The Mounted Rifleman* (published in 1916) and *The Old Army, Memories* (published in 1929). At the age of eighty, he died on 2 June 1934. Photo from the National Archives.

Mason Mathews Patrick (0-131), son of Dr. Alfred S. Patrick and Virginia Mathews Patrick, was born on 13 November 1863 in Lewisburg, West Virginia. He entered USMA and graduated number two of seventy-seven in the class of 1886. Charles Menoher, John J. Pershing, Julius A. Penn (all *q.v.*), and Edward W. McCaskey were four of his classmates. He graduated from the Engineer School of Application in 1889. In West Point, from 1892 to 1895, he was assistant instructor of practical military engineering, and during 1897 and 1898, he was in charge of the First and Second Districts, improving the Mississippi River. From 1898 to 1901, he was secretary of the Mississippi River Commission in St. Louis, Missouri. He married Grace W. Colley on 11 November 1902, and they had one son, Bream Colley Patrick. From 1901 to 1903, he was on duty in the office of the Chief of Engineers in Washington, after which he went back to West Point to serve as an instructor of engineering and to command the USMA Detachment of Engineers until 1906. He was Chief Engineer of the Army of Cuban Pacification from 1907 to 1909, then was assigned rivers and harbors duty in Norfolk, Virginia until 1912. During this period, he was also a member of the board for raising the USS *Maine*. From 1912 to 1916, he was in Detroit doing engineering work, improving the Great Lakes. In 1916 and 1917, he commanded the First Engineers and was also commandant of the Engineer School, Washington Barracks, Washington, D.C. From September 1917 to May 1918, he was Chief Engineer (AEF), Zone of Communications and Director of Forestry. He was Commander of the Service of Supply from 1 to 27 November 1917. He was promoted to major general (NA) on 26 June 1918. From May 1918 to June 1919, he

Mason Mathews Patrick

was Chief of the Air Service (AEF). In 1921, he was taught to fly, passed the flight tests and was rated as an airplane pilot. He wore his wings proudly. After the war, he became Chief Engineer of the Gulf Division, headquartered in New Orleans. He was assistant Chief Engineer from 1920 to 1921, and Commandant of the Engineer School at Camp Humphreys, Virginia. He was appointed first Chief of the Air Service of the entire United States in October 1921, and was reappointed in 1925. He retired after forty-one years of service on 13 December 1927, and was appointed Public Utilities Commissioner for Washington, D.C. and resigned from that position in 1933. He was awarded the Distinguished Service Medal and was made a Knight Commander, Order of the British Empire, a Commander of the Legion of Honor (France), an Officer of the Order of St. Maurice and St. Lazarus (Italy) and a Commander of the Crown (Belgium). At the age of seventy-eight, he died in Washington, D.C., on 29 January 1942. Photo courtesy of the National Archives.

William Sullivan Peirce

William Sullivan Peirce (0-69), son of Albert Gallatin Peirce and Julia Benjamin Peirce, was born on 16 May 1864 in Burlington, Vermont. He was a student at the University of Vermont from 1881 to 1884, and he received an honorary A.M. from there in 1908. He entered USMA and graduated number eight of forty-four in the class of 1888. Peyton C. March and Guy Henry Preston (both *q.v.*) were two of his classmates. He was commissioned in the First Artillery, but soon transferred to ordnance. He served as Assistant Ordnance Officer at Watervliet Arsenal, Sandy Hook Proving Ground, Rock Island Arsenal and the Springfield Armory. He was an inspector of ordnance at the Midvale and Bethlehem Steel Companies, and served as an assistant in the office of the Chief of Ordnance in Washington. On 19 April 1911, he married Harriet Roberts. From 1912 to 1918, he commanded Springfield Arsenal, for which he received the Distinguished Service Medal. On 18 February 1918, he was promoted to brigadier general (NA) and sent overseas with the AEF. He was an assistant to the Chief of Ordnance and a specialist in the manufacture of small arms. From 1920 to 1923, he was Assistant Chief of Ordnance. At the age of fifty-nine he died in Washington, D.C., on 10 July 1923, still on duty. Photo courtesy of the National Portrait Gallery, Washington.

Julius Augustus Penn, Jr. (0-184), son of Julius Augustus Penn and Mary Brock Penn, was born on 19 February 1865 in Mattoon, Illinois. He entered USMA and graduated number sixty-nine of seventy-seven in the class of 1886. Mason Patrick, Charles T. Menoher and John J. Pershing (all *q.v.*) were three of his classmates. He was commissioned in the 13th Infantry and performed frontier duty from 1886 to 1889. In 1891, he was valedictorian of his class at the Infantry and Cavalry School at Fort Leavenworth, Kansas. He was present at the Bannock Indian disturbance in 1895. In 1898, he went to Tampa, Florida, where he got typhoid fever. During 1898 and 1899, he was an instructor in the Tactics Department at USMA. He was sent to the Philippines as a major, U.S. Volunteers, to help suppress the insurrection, and for his performance of this duty he received a Silver Star Commendation. In June 1917, he commanded the 49th Infantry, and on 5 August 1917, he was promoted to brigadier general (NA) and served with the AEF. He commanded a brigade of the 38th Infantry Division, and later, answering strictly to General Headquarters (AEF), he was in charge of both war prisoners and general prisoners. He retired due to disabilities in 1924, and lived in Batavia, Ohio. At the age of sixty-nine, he died on 13 May 1934. Photo courtesy of the National Archives.

Julius Augustus Penn, Jr.

☆

Frederick Perkins

Frederick Perkins (0-13374) was born on 21 August 1857 in Maine. He entered USMA and graduated number forty-nine of fifty-two in the class of 1883. George H. Cameron and Tyree Rodes Rivers (both *q.v.*) were two of his classmates. He was commissioned in the Fifth Infantry and performed frontier duty from 1881 to 1891. From 1891 to 1894, he commanded the Provost Guard at the military prison at Fort Leavenworth, Kansas. During 1894 and 1895, he was adjutant of the prison, and during the Spanish-American War, he was sent to Cuba and also served in the Sanitary Corps. On 5 August 1917, he was promoted to brigadier general (NA) and commanded the 166th Infantry Brigade at Camp Sherman, Ohio. From 13 January to 23 March 1918, he commanded the 83d Infantry Division. In 1919, he retired as a colonel. In June 1930, his rank of brigadier general was restored by act of Congress. At the age of eighty-two, he died in California, on 27 April 1940. Photo from the National Archives.

John Joseph Pershing

John Joseph Pershing (0-1) was born on 13 September 1860 in the small town of Laclede, Missouri. His family's home is today a public exhibit. He entered USMA and graduated number thirty of seventy-seven in the class of 1886. He was commissioned in the cavalry and was sent to the far West. In 1891, he became Professor of Military Science and Tactics at the University of Nebraska in Lincoln, where he also taught mathematics. Two of his students were future writers Willa Cather and Dorothy Canfield (Fisher). He also studied law, and often considered quitting the army to go into practice with a promising young lawyer in Lincoln, Charles Gates Dawes. While a lieutenant, he also served as an aide to Gen. Nelson A. Miles. The nickname "Black Jack" was given to him by the cadets while he was serving as a tactical officer because of his outspoken advocacy of the use of African-American troops. He married Frances Helen Warren, daughter of Sen. Francis E. Warren, a Civil War veteran who received the Medal of Honor, and first governor of Wyoming as well as a U.S. senator from that state. During the Spanish-American War, he distinguished himself both in Cuba and in the Philippines. By 1905, he was military attaché in Japan and had a firsthand look at the Russo-Japanese War. In 1906, President Theodore Roosevelt promoted him to brigadier general over the heads of 862 senior officers. He remained in the Philippines until 1913. Because of the fire at the Presidio in California in 1915, he lost his wife and three daughters. Only his son Warren survived. When the Mexican bandit Pancho Villa raided Columbus, New Mexico, he commanded the Mexican Punitive Expedition, from 1916 to 1917. He commanded the AEF in France during World War I. He inspired great respect and carefully avoided politics. When he returned to the States after the war, he was promoted to General of the Armies, a rank unique to himself, and he continued to use the four-star insignia. From 1921 to 1924, he was Chief of Staff (USA). He was never placed on the retired list, but was relieved from duty and continued on full pay. As an aged widower, he lived in Walter Reed Army Medical Center in Washington, and frequently wintered in or near Tucson, Arizona. While there, he was often a guest at the Harold B. Thurber ranch north of Sonoita, where he met the great Minnesota doctors, Charlie and Will Mayo. At the age of eighty-seven, he died on 15 July 1948. He was buried with full military honors in Arlington National Cemetery. General George C. Marshall, in writing his obituary notice in *The Assembly*, said fifteen governments presented General Pershing with their highest honors. Twenty degrees were granted to him by universities. He was friendly, yet restrained, and ambitious, yet humble. Although serving in the army was his life's work, he was firm in his belief that the military must be subservient to the civil power of the government. He never usurped authority, but by the force of his personality extended his influence far beyond the scope of his functions. His death brought overwhelming evidence of the great respect and confidence in which he was held by the American people. Photo from the Pennsylvania National Guard.

Charles Leonard Phillips

Charles Leonard Phillips (0-13458) was born on 16 October 1856 in Illinois. He entered USMA and graduated number thirteen of fifty-three in the class of 1881. Henry and Harry Hodges and Andrew Summers Rowan (all *q.v.*) were three of his classmates. He was commissioned in the Fourth Artillery. During 1881 and 1882, he performed frontier duty. From 1885 to 1888, he was Professor of Military Science and Tactics at Maine State College, and he had the same assignment at Cornell College, Mt. Vernon, Iowa from 1892 to 1896. From 1896 to 1899, he was adjutant of Fort Monroe, Virginia and secretary of the Seacoast Artillery School. From 1905 to 1917, he commanded various Coast Artillery posts, among them Fort Dade and Key West Barracks in Florida and Fort McKinley in Maine. On 5 August 1917, he was promoted to brigadier general (NA) and commanded the 52d Field Artillery Brigade at Camp Wadsworth, Spartanburg, South Carolina. He commanded the 25th Infantry Division (New York National Guard troops) from 19 September 1917 to 6 December 1917, from 23 December 1917 to 29 December 1917 and from 22 February 1918 to 1 March 1918. He retired in 1920 as a colonel. His rank of brigadier general was restored by act of Congress in June 1930. At the age of eighty, he died in California, on 15 March 1937. The photo is courtesy of the Casemate Museum, Fort Monroe, Virginia.

Edward Hinkley Plummer (0-13123), son of Mr. and Mrs. William Walker Plummer, was born on 24 September 1855 in Esperanza, Elkridge, Maryland. He entered USMA and graduated number twenty of seventy-six in the class of 1877. Augustus Blockson (*q.v.*) was one of his classmates, as was Henry Ossian Flipper, the first African-American to graduate from USMA. He was commissioned in the Tenth Infantry and performed frontier duty from 1877 to 1898. It was during this period, on 13 October 1880, that he married Georgia Alice Moody. They had six children: Bessie M. Plummer, Edward H. Plummer, Harriet F. Plummer, Dwight R. Plummer, Thorington P. Plummer and Georgia M. Plummer. During the Spanish-American War, he organized and commanded the

35th U.S. Volunteer Infantry, which he commanded through its entire service. He also served in the Sanitary Corps, and was an aide to Gen. W. R. Shafter from 1898 to 1901. From July to August 1898, he was in charge of all land transportation, wagons and pack trains in Cuba. From 1904 to 1906, he commanded Fort Egbert in Eagle, Alaska, and from 1909 to 1910, he was stationed in Zamboanga in the Philippines. In 1911, he commanded the 28th Infantry in San Antonio, Texas, and from April to November 1914, he was provost marshal and acting mayor of Vera Cruz, Mexico. In 1915, he was at the Dallas State Fair, and served as a commander on the Mexican border. On 1 July 1916, he was promoted to brigadier general (USA). Between April and August 1917, he organized the Department of the Panama Canal and was its first commander. On 5 August 1917, he was promoted to major general (NA), then organized and commanded the 88th Infantry Division at Camp Dodge, Iowa. That November, he was sent to visit various battlefronts in France, and served with the British 46th Division, the French 62d Division and the U.S. First Infantry Division. From March to October 1918, he commanded Fort Sill, Oklahoma, and in October and November of that year, he commanded Camp Grant, Illinois. He retired as brigadier general on 30 November 1918, and he lived in Pacific Grove, California. There, at the age of seventy-one, he died, on 11 February 1927. His rank of major general was restored posthumously. Photo from the National Archives.

Edward Hinkley Plummer

☆

Benjamin Andrew Poore (0-160), son of Andrew Poore and Keziah Brooks Poore, was born on 22 June 1863 in Cantre, Alabama. He entered USMA and graduated number thirty-three of seventy-seven in the class of 1886. Mason M. Patrick, Charles T. Menoher and John J. Pershing (all *q.v.*) were three of his classmates. He was commissioned and sent to the 12th Infantry. On 22 June 1888, he married Miss Carleton, and they had three daughters: Katherine H. Poore, Priscilla C. Poore and Adelaide C. Poore. He was an instructor at USMA from 1893 to 1895, and was sent to Puerto Rico during the Spanish-American War, where

Benjamin Andrew Poore

he won his first Silver Star Commendation. From 1899 to 1902, he was in the Philippines serving as both regimental quartermaster and regimental adjutant, for which he received his second Silver Star. During 1909 and 1910, he was in Alaska, and from 1912 to 1916, he was on duty with the General Staff in Washington as Director of the Army War College. In 1916, he was in China and the Philippines. On 5 August 1917, he was promoted to brigadier general (NA). He commanded the 162nd Depot Brigade in Little Rock, Arkansas, then the Fourteenth Infantry Brigade in El Paso, Texas. From April 1918 to August 1919, he commanded the Seventh Infantry Brigade, part of the Fourth Infantry Division (AEF), for which he was awarded both the Distinguished Service Cross and the Distinguished Service Medal. From 14 to 27 August 1918 and from 22 to 31 October 1918, he commanded the Fourth Infantry Division and participated in the Aisne-Marne, St. Mihiel and Meuse-Argonne battles. After the Armistice, he served with the American forces in Germany until August 1919, when he was sent to command Fort D. A. Russel, Wyoming. In the following year, he commanded Vancouver Barracks and Camp (now Fort) Lewis, Washington. From October 1920 to November 1924, he commanded the First Infantry Regiment and the Fourth Infantry Brigade at Fort Sam Houston, Texas. From November 1924 to October 1925, he commanded the 12th Infantry Brigade and Fort Sheridan, Illinois. On 11 October 1925, he was promoted to major general (USA) and commanded the Seventh Corps Area in Omaha, Nebraska. On 22 June 1927, he retired. His wife died in 1929. On 22 October 1930, he married Flora B. Bullock. In addition to the decorations already mentioned, he received and the Croix de Guerre with palm (France) and the Croice de Guerre al Merito (Italy), and he was made an Officer of the Legion of Honor (France). He lived in Fitchburg, Massachusetts. At the age of seventy-seven, he died, on 27 August 1940. Photo courtesy of the National Portrait Gallery, Washington.

Guy Henry Preston (0-208) was born on 29 May 1864 in Massachusetts. He entered USMA and graduated number twenty-five of forty-four in the class of 1888. Peyton C. March (*q.v.*) was one of his classmates. He was commissioned in the First Cavalry Regiment and performed frontier duty from 1888 to 1891, serving in the Sioux Campaign, for which he received a Silver Star Commendation. He later served in the Second, Fourth, Eighth and Thirteenth Cavalry Regiments. During the Spanish-American War, he was in the Puerto Rican Expedition and served as major, 41st U.S. Volunteer Infantry. He also served during the Philippine Insurrection. His principle claim to fame is not men-

Guy Henry Preston

Horse with Brand

tioned at all in any of the standard references, so we illustrate it here. He invented the Preston Branding System for large animals that was adopted by the army, and copied by some states when their auto license plate numbers got too large. Each number identified two animals, one horse and one mule. The numbers started A000 to A999, then 00A0 to 99A9, then 000A to 999A followed by B000 to B999, etc. These brands were 2" high and 1 1/2" wide, on the near side of the neck only. Animals also had a US on the near shoulder, and both brands were applied the day of purchase. The letters G, I, O and Q were not used. Certain letters indicated which Remount Depot the animal had come from. The Quartermaster General maintained a Horse and Mule register and there was a record card (QM Form 417) for each animal. Preston once joked with Pershing that his (Preston's) brand was on every animal in the Army. And there were still many thousands of them in 1942. On 2 April 1918, he was made a brigadier general (NA) and commanded the Fourth Field Artillery Brigade at Camp Greene, North Carolina. He commanded the 160th Field Artillery Brigade, which he took from Camp Custer, Michigan to France at the end of July 1918. They served at the front in Brittany in October and November 1918. He served in the provost marshal's office in Treves, Germany, from March through June 1919. In July 1919, he reverted to his permanent rank of colonel. He commanded the First Cavalry in Douglas, Arizona during 1919 and 1920. His final command was of the General Intermediate Depot in San Francisco, California. He retired in 1930 and lived in Palo Alto, California, where at the age of eighty-eight, he died on 12 December 1952. The second photo, courtesy of *The Assembly*, Association of Graduates, USMA, shows Lieutenant Branson of the Seventh Cavalry on 28 March 1941 with his horse, which bears a Preston brand. The crownpiece of the halter (above the buckle) covers the first letter, but the others are visible. The photo is by the author.

Harrison Jackson Price (0-364), son of Albert Price and Sofia Bonner Price, was born on 3 April 1868 in Bellingham, West Virginia. In 1891, he graduated from Northern Ohio University with an A.B., and on 7 October of that year he was commissioned a second lieutenant in the 24th Infantry. He married Lucille Longuemare on 18 June 1895, and they had two daughters and a son: Helen, Lucille and Hardin. He was in Cuba from June to September 1898, and again from July to October 1899, then served three tours of duty in the Philippines. He was promoted to colonel (NA) on 5 August 1917, and he commanded the 325th Infantry of the 88th Division from October 1917 to October

1919. On 1 October 1918, he was promoted to brigadier general (NA) and commanded the 154th Infantry Brigade of the 77th Division from October 1918 to May 1919. He served in the Alsace-Lorraine sector and in the Meuse-Argonne offensive. After World War I, he reverted to his rank of colonel and served as Assistant Chief of Staff of the Second Corps Area on Governor's Island, New York. He was later in charge of National Guard affairs at the same station. From 1928 to 1932, he was Chief of Staff of the 80th (Organized Reserve) in Richmond, Virginia. He retired as a brigadier general on 30 April 1932. He continued to live in Richmond. At the age of seventy-seven, he died on 16 September 1945. Photo courtesy of the U.S. Army Military History Institute, Carlisle Barracks, Pennsylvania.

Harrison Jackson Price

William Gray Price, Jr. (ASN unknown), son of William Gland Price and Jane Campbell Price, was born on 23 March 1869 in Chester, Pennsylvania. He attended both public and private schools before entering Pennsylvania Military College. In civil life he was very successful in construction, building homes in the Philadelphia and Pittsburgh areas. He enlisted in Company B, Sixth Pennsylvania Infantry in 1886, and stayed with the Pennsylvania National Guard for the remainder of his life. He was transferred to the Third Pennsylvania Infantry, and he served as a lieutenant colonel during the Spanish-American War. On 23 April 1901, he was promoted to colonel, and he continued to command this regiment until he was promoted to brigadier general on 4 April 1910. He improved the efficiency not only of his regiment, but of the entire Pennsylvania National Guard. Although basically an infantry officer, he took command of and trained the 53d Field Artillery Brigade when it was formed at Camp Hancock, Georgia, commanded it in action in France, brought it home and discharged it. He was probably the only guard officer given such responsibility. His entire military career was spent in the 28th Division. While commanding the 53d Field Artillery Brigade, he served in the Marne, Vesle, Argonne and Leys-Scheldt operations. He was awarded the Distinguished Service Medal

William Gray Price, Jr.

and the Croix de Guerre (France and Belgium), and was made an Officer of the Legion of Honor (France). For his services he was thanked personally by both the King and Queen of Belgium. Major General Smedley Butler (USMC), another Chester County native, was a personal friend of his and was present on the stand at his retirement review. He had a wife, Sallie, four daughters, and three sons: J. P. E. Price, Col. Terrill Price and W. Aldrich Price. He also had many grandchildren and great grandchildren. His home was in Ridley Park near Philadelphia. At the age of ninety, he died at the Philadelphia Naval Hospital, on 25 February 1960. The photo, by the author, was taken in Mount Gretna in 1929 at division headquarters.

William Carroll Rafferty

William Carroll Rafferty (0-13405) was born on 11 April 1859 in Indiana. He entered USMA and graduated number four of fifty-two in the class of 1880. George W. Goethals, William S. Scott, (both *q.v.*), David J. Rumbough, and James Walker Benet (son of a Civil War veteran and brother of the poet Stephen Vincent Benet) were four of his classmates. He was commissioned in the First Artillery and graduated from the Artillery School in 1884. He was Professor of Military Science and Tactics at North Georgia Agricultural College from 1884 to 1887. He was promoted to first lieutenant in 1887. In 1894, he married Julia Kilpatrick, daughter of the well-known Civil War cavalry general, Judson Kilpatrick. From 1894 to 1897, he was a member of the Board of Regulation on Coast Artillery Fire. During 1897 to 1898, he was Professor of Military Science and Tactics at Seton Hall College in South Orange, New Jersey. He commanded the coastal defenses of Galveston, Texas in September 1900, when a devastating storm struck, taking the lives of six to eight thousand people. In 1908, he commanded the Coast Artillery District of Baltimore. He was promoted to brigadier general (NA) on 5 August 1917, when the States entered World War I, and he commanded the 54th Field Artillery Brigade, part of the 29th Division, in Anniston, Alabama and in France. Three times he was the commanding general of the 29th Division, composed of Maryland, Washington D.C. and Virginia troops. He retired as a colonel on 31 December 1919 and lived in Washington, D.C. At the age of eighty-two, he died there, on 22 May 1941. He was one of the last bearded American general officers during World War I. Photo courtesy of the New Jersey State Archives.

George Windle Read

George Windle Read (0-30), son of James C. Read and Elizabeth Windle Read, was born on 1 November 1860 in Indianola, a few miles south of Des Moines, Iowa. He entered USMA and graduated number forty of fifty-two in the class of 1883. George H. Cameron and Tyree Rodes Rivers (both *q.v.*) were two of his classmates. He was commissioned and sent to the 16th Infantry. He performed frontier duty from 1883 to 1889. On 2 September 1886, he married Burton Young, daughter of Gen. S. B. M. Young, and they had three children: Burton Y. Read, Margaret Elizabeth Read and George W. Read, Jr. He was Professor of Military Science and Tactics at the University of Iowa from 1889 to 1893. From 1893 to 1897, he served with troops in Texas, and from 1897 to 1899, he was an aide to Gen. James Franklin Wade. During the Spanish-American War, he served with the Evacuation Commission in Cuba from 1898 to 1899. From 1901 to 1902, he served in the Philippines. He was in California, Hawaii and on classified overseas duty from 1902 to 1904. From 1905 to 1909, he served on the General Staff, partly with the military government in Cuba and partly as president of the Claims Commission. In 1910, he was an umpire at the big maneuvers, held primarily for the National Guard, at Fort Riley, Kansas. From there back to the Philippines until 1912. From 1912 to 1914, he served on the Mexican border. From 1914 to 1917, he served in the Adjutant General's Department as adjutant of the Second Division and of the War Department back in Washington. He was promoted to brigadier general (NA) and commanded a brigade at Camp Upton on Long Island, New York, then returned to El Paso in command of a cavalry division. During World War I, he was commanding general, 30th Infantry Division and Eleventh Corps (AEF), for which he received the Distinguished Service Medal. He commanded the American port of embarkation in LeMans, France in 1919, and when he returned to the States, he commanded Camp Jackson, South Carolina. He commanded the Fifth Corps Area, then later the Philippine Department. On 19 November 1924, he retired. In addition to the decorations already mentioned, he received a Gold Medal from the Military Service Institution and a Croix de Guerre (France), and he was made a Knight Commander, Order of the Bath (Britain) and a Commander of the Legion of Honor (France). In retirement, he lived in Washington, and at age seventy-four, he died there, on 6 November 1934. Photo from the National Archives.

Robert Irwin Rees (0-991), son of Seth Rees and Eugenia Livermore Rees, was born on 9 November 1871 in Houghton, Michigan. He was the brother of Thomas H. Rees (*q.v.*), and they were one of four pairs of American

Robert Irwin Rees

general officer brothers in World War I. He graduated from the Michigan College of Mines in 1895 with both a B.S. and an E.M. degree, then went to Harvard for a year and spent another year at New York Law School. During the Spanish-American War, he was a corporal in Company B, Michigan Battalion of Engineers from May to October 1899. He was commissioned a second lieutenant, Third Infantry on 1 October 1899, and was promoted to first lieutenant on 9 April 1901. On 24 April 1904, he married Sara Isabel Gannett, and they had one son, Murray Gannett Rees, who also became a army officer. He was a distinguished graduate of the Army School of the Line in 1913, and he graduated from the Army Staff College in 1914. From June 1917 to December 1918, he was a member of the General Staff in Washington. His served there as chairman of the Committee on Education and Special Training, and was in charge of military and technical training of technicians and mechanics for the army. He also organized the Student Army Training Corps. On 1 October 1918, he was promoted to brigadier general (NA), and in December, he was sent to France, where he was on General Pershing's staff, in charge of all educational work in the AEF. In July 1919, he returned to the States and was assigned Chief of the Recreational Board, War Plans Division, General Staff. After retiring, he was Assistant Vice President of the American Telephone and Telegraph Company, in charge of the Department of Personnel and Public Relations. He was author of *Personnel Management*, published by the Alexander Hamilton Institute. His home was at 1 Fifth Avenue, New York City. He received the Distinguished Service Medal (France) and was made an Officer of the Legion of Honor. He enjoyed golfing and swimming. At the age of sixty-five, he died in Detroit, Michigan, on 23 November 1936. Photo courtesy of Michigan Technological University.

Thomas Henry Rees (0-155), son of Seth Rees and Eugenia Livermore Rees, was born on 18 October 1863 in Houghton, Michigan. He was the older brother of Robert Irwin Rees (*q.v.*) , and they were one of four pairs of American general officer brothers in World War I. He entered USMA and graduated number four of forty-four in the class of 1886. Mason M. Patrick, Charles T. Menoher, John J. Pershing and Edward W. McCaskey (all *q.v.*) were four of his classmates. He graduated from the Engineering School of Application in 1889. In 1890, he married Miss Happersett. At West Point, he served as an instructor in civil and military engineering from 1893 to 1898. He commanded an engineer battalion in the Santiago Campaign in Cuba, and he served in the Sanitary Corps as well. From 1898 to 1899, he commanded an engineer company in Willets

Thomas Henry Rees

Point, New York. From 1899 to 1901, he was in charge of rivers and harbors work in Florida. From 1902 to 1905, he was stationed at Fort Leavenworth, Kansas, first with the Department of Engineering at the Infantry and Cavalry School, then with the Army Staff College. He married a second time, to Blanche Baxter Jones, on 28 December 1907. From 1905 to 1908, he commanded the Third Engineer Battalion, then served at the Army War College until 1911. He was the department engineer in Chicago from 1908 to 1910, in charge of rivers and harbors work. He had the same assignment in San Francisco, California from 1911 to 1917, then was stationed in Manila and in Honolulu. On 17 December 1917, he was promoted to brigadier general (NA). He commanded the 152nd Field Artillery Brigade at Camp Upton, Long Island, New York, and took it to France with the AEF. He retired in 1922 as a colonel, due to disabilities. At the age of seventy-eight, he died in Washington, D.C., on 20 September 1942. His rank of brigadier general was restored in June 1930. Photo courtesy of Special Collections, USMA Library.

Frederick Emil Resche

Frederick Emil Resche (ASN unknown), son of Frederick J. Resche and Amalia Resche, was born on 1 April 1866 in Chemnitz, Saxony, Germany. At the age of twenty-one, on 1 June 1887, his family arrived in Minnesota. He joined the police force, then became the probation officer of St. Louis County, Minnesota, working out of the courthouse in Duluth. He enlisted as a private in the Minnesota National Guard, and soon commanded Company C, Third Minnesota Infantry. On 9 November 1889, he married Clara Simmen and they had one daughter, Elsbeth (Mrs. Joseph Carpenter). During the Spanish-American War, he commanded his infantry company, and immediately afterwards he was sent to put down the last Indian rebellion in America in Leech Lake, Minnesota. At the time of the Mexican Punitive Expedition, just before the U.S. entered World War I, he served briefly at Camp Cody, New Mexico. During World War I, he was promoted to brigadier general (NA) and commanded the 68th Infantry Brigade of the 34th Division. In civil life, he served as probation officer in Duluth for twenty-four years, and he retired in 1936. His family moved to Glendale, California, and in June 1946, several months before he died, he returned to Duluth and was honored at a dinner by twenty-two surviving members of his Spanish-American War infantry company. At the age of eighty, he died in Glendale, California, on 1 September 1946. Photo courtesy of the Minnesota Historical Society, St. Paul, Minnesota.

Charles Dudley Rhodes

Charles Dudley Rhodes (0-275), son of Maj. Dudley Woodbridge Rhodes and Marcia Parrish Rhodes, was born on 10 February 1865 in Delaware, Ohio. In 1885, he graduated with an A.B. from what is now George Washington University. He entered USMA and graduated number twenty-six of forty-nine in the class of 1889. William Lassiter, E. E. Winslow, William G. Haan and William W. Harts (all *q.v.*) were four of his classmates. He was commissioned in the Seventh Cavalry and performed frontier duty from 1889 to 1893, which included service in the Sioux Campaign. On 2 December 1890, he married Mary E. Counselman. From 1893 to 1895, he was Professor of Military Science and Tactics at Wesleyan University, Ohio. He was in the Santiago Campaign in Cuba as an aide to the Inspector General of the Army. He was also in the Sanitary Corps, and he earned a Silver Star commendation. He was Adjutant General of the Second Brigade, Second Division in 1898, and was recommended for a brevet majority. In 1900, as part of the China Relief Expedition, he commanded Troop C of the Sixth Cavalry, and was later Adjutant General of the First Brigade, then Adjutant General of the combined Anglo-American Expedition in China. Following this, he was almost continuously in the Philippines until 1912, distinguishing himself at every opportunity. For his service there, he received the Distinguished Service Cross. From 1914 to 1917, he commanded the Mounted Service School at Fort Riley, Kansas (later *the Cavalry* School). At the San Francisco Exposition in 1915, using troops from the Mounted Service School, he put on an exhibition which won a Silver Medal. In 1917, he commanded the 21st Cavalry Regiment, one of the cavalry regiments, numbered 16 through 25, which were formed for World War I and later became Field Artillery Regiments. The 21st Regiment became the 79th Field Artillery. He was promoted to brigadier general (NA) and commanded the 158th Field Artillery Brigade in three different battles in France. On 1 October 1918, he was promoted to major general (NA) and commanded the 42d Infantry Division and later, the 35th Infantry Division. During 1918 and 1919, he was chief of the American section of the Permanent Interallied Armistice Commission in

Belgium. In 1919, he commanded Base Section Number 4 in Bordeaux. In addition to the decorations already mentioned, he was made a Knight Commander of the Order of the Bath (Britain), an officer of the Legion of Honor (France) and a Commander of the Order of the Crown (Belgium). When he retired, he was a writer and lecturer. He belonged to many clubs and associations, and he wrote two books: *The Cavalry* (published in 1911) and *Robert E. Lee, the West Pointer* (published in 1932). At the age of ninety-two, he died in Washington, D.C., on 24 January 1948. The photo, from the National Archives, was taken with his graduating class from the General Staff College, Washington Barracks, D.C., in July 1920.

John Hogden Rice

John Hogden Rice (0-349), son of Virgil Rice and Aurelia R. Rice, was born on 6 January 1870 in St. Louis, Missouri. He entered USMA and graduated number eight of fifty-one in the class of 1893. Herbert Crosby was one of his classmates. He was commissioned in the Third Cavalry and stationed at Fort Sheridan, Illinois. He served during the serious strikes that occurred in the late summer and early fall of 1894. From 1895 to 1897, he was instructor of mathematics in West Point. On 21 November 1898, he was promoted to first lieutenant, ordnance. He was with troops in Florida during the Spanish-American War, and in Manila from 1901 to 1903. From 1906 to 1912, he was an assistant to the Chief of Ordnance in Washington, D.C. From 1912 to 1914, he commanded the arsenal in San Antonio, Texas and was Chief Ordnance Officer of the Southern Department. From 1915 to 1917, he served in the office of the Chief of Ordnance as Chief of the Carriage Division, (referring to gun carriages.) From 1917 to 1918, he was Chief of the Engineering Division of that same office, and during that time, he was promoted to brigadier general (NA), on 18 February 1918. In late June 1918, he arrived in France and was appointed Chief Ordnance Officer (AEF). He returned to the States in the late summer of 1919, and again served in the Office of the Chief of Ordnance, this time as Chief of Manufacture. On 1 July 1921, he retired as a colonel. He held various industrial positions until 1930. In June 1930, his rank of brigadier general was restored. His decorations included the Distinguished Service Medal, and he was made a Commander of the Legion of Honor (France). At the age of seventy, he died in New York, on 7 January 1940. Photo from the National Archives.

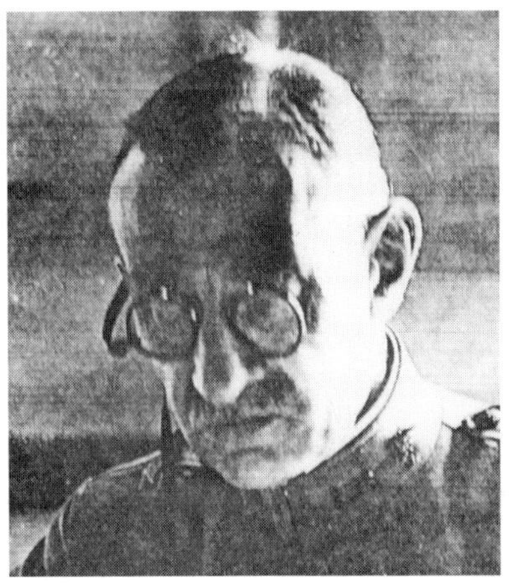
Charles Richard, M.D.

Charles Richard, M.D. (0-13347), son of Jacob Richard and Frederica Herbig Richard was born on 10 November 1854 in New York City. He graduated from the City College of New York with a B.S. degree, and from New York University in 1876 with an M.D. degree. From April 1876 to September 1877, he was an intern at the Charity Hospital in New York. He was assistant physician at Randall's Island Hospital from 1 October 1877 to 1 April 1878. On 8 November 1877, he married Laura R. Bailey, then spent two years lecturing on military and professional surgery in Colorado. On 3 June 1879, he was commissioned a first lieutenant, assistant surgeon (USA), and he was promoted to captain on 3 June 1884. He was commandant of the Army Medical Department Research and Graduate School in Washington from 1912 to 1915. He was promoted to brigadier general (NA) on 5 August 1917. During 1917 and 1918, he was Department Surgeon at Headquarters, Eastern Department, and Assistant to the Surgeon General of the Army in the War Department. He retired on 10 November 1918 and lived in New York City. At the age of eighty-five, he died on 19 April 1940. Photo courtesy of the National Archives.

Randolph Ayres Richards (ASN unknown), son of John F. Richards and Judith Ayres Richards, was born on 5 January 1863 in Milwaukee, Wisconsin. His father's family were of English and Dutch descent and had settled in America before the Revolution. His mother was of English descent, and one of her ancestors, Col. Charles Harrison, was a Virginia artilleryman on the staff of George Washington during the Revolution. His father ran a pharmacy and also practiced medicine. When he was three, his family moved from Milwaukee to Tomah in Monroe County. From 1882, he read law in the office of Col. George Graham, until 1887, when he passed the bar examination. On 19 October 1892, he married Eugenia A. Fox of Fergus Falls, Minnesota, and they had one child, Doris, who married Dr. John M. Scantelon of Sparta, Wisconsin. In January 1899, he moved his law practice to Sparta where, aside from his military time, he spent the remainder of his career. In 1913, he was

Randolph Ayres Richards

elected judge of Monroe County, and served as such with distinction until 1937. He was one of the organizers of Company K, Third Wisconsin Infantry, having been mustered in as a corporal with his company on 28 May 1884. In 1886, he was elected second lieutenant, and the following year he was promoted to captain. He commanded his company from 5 September 1887, until he was promoted to major in 1897 and was assigned to command the Third Battalion of the Third Wisconsin Infantry in the beginning of the Spanish-American War. The battalion served under Nelson A. Miles in the capture of Puerto Rico, and was mustered out in January 1899. He remained with the Wisconsin National Guard, and in July 1916, he was again mustered into Federal Service and was sent to the Mexican border. As a colonel, he commanded the regiment until 14 December 1916, when he resumed his duties as county judge. On 15 July 1917, he was mustered into federal service a third time, for World War I, and commanded the Third Wisconsin Infantry, part of the 32d Division. On 5 August 1917, he was promoted to brigadier general (NA) and reported to Camp MacArthur, Texas, where he commanded the 63d Infantry Brigade, part of the 32d Infantry Division. While stationed there, he served as judge advocate at a court-martial resulting from a serious race riot. He commanded the First Brigade, corps and army troops, after which he commanded the 192nd Infantry Brigade until December 1918, when he was discharged and resumed his duties as judge in Sparta. He was very active civically, and was one of the founders of the local post of the American Legion. He belonged to the Kiwanis, Masons and Knights of Pythias. He was editor in chief of a very comprehensive history of Monroe County. His commission in the National Guard Reserve was terminated due to age on 5 January 1927. At the age of eighty, he died in his home at 214 Cottage Street, Sparta, on 20 July 1943. He was buried in Woodlawn Cemetery. Photo courtesy of the Monroe County History Room.

Wilds Preston Richardson

Wilds Preston Richardson (0-13503), son of Oliver Preston Richardson and Hester Foster Wingo Richardson, was born on 20 March 1861 in Hunt County, northeast of Dallas, Texas. He entered USMA and graduated number twenty-two of thirty-seven in the class of 1884. DeRosey Cabell, William L. Sibert and Samuel D. Sturgis (all *q.v.*) were three of his classmates, as was Isaac Newton Lewis, inventor of the Lewis machine gun. He was commissioned and sent to the Eighth Infantry. He performed frontier duty from 1884 to 1889, mostly in western Nebraska, Arizona and California. In 1891 and 1892, he was an aide to Gen. A. V. Kautz in the Department of the Columbia (River).

From 1892 to 1897, he was an instructor in tactics at West Point, and in August 1897, he was ordered to serve in Alaska. Except for a few brief details, he remained there for twenty years. He was president of the Board of Road Commissioners, and his chief work was building Richardson Highway, 380 miles through the wilderness from Fairbanks to Valdez, where the oil spill of 1989 occurred. He was adjutant of the Department of Alaska, and was involved in the construction of Fort William H. Seward. On 5 August 1917, he was promoted to brigadier general (NA) and commanded the 78th Infantry Brigade at Camp Beauregarde, Louisiana. He also commanded the 80th Infantry Division from 28 December 1917 to 7 January 1918. From December 1918 to March 1919, he commanded the 55th Infantry Brigade, part of the 28th Division (the Keystone Division, Pennsylvania National Guard). His next assignment was as commander of American forces in Murmansk, northern Russia, where Norway, Finland and Russia meet. This was a difficult task, and for his performance of this duty he received the Distinguished Service Medal. When the war was over, he reverted to his permanent rank of colonel and retired on 31 October 1920. He made his home at the Army and Navy Club in Washington. He was a man of exceptional height and bulk with enormous hands and feet. While he was a strict disciplinarian, he was noted for his sympathy and generosity. He had great engineering skill, tremendous energy and an unflinching regard for his government's interests. It was said of him that he was one of the best loved men in the army. In April 1929, he became ill and went to Walter Reed Army Medical Center, and he died there at the age of sixty-eight, on 20 May 1929. In June 1930, his rank of brigadier general was restored posthumously. Photo courtesy of the Pennsylvania National Guard.

Tyree Rodes Rivers (0-137), son of William Rivers and Julia Flournoy Rivers, was born on 10 May 1862 in Mississippi. He was the brother of William C. Rivers (*q.v.*), and they were one of four pairs of American general officer brothers in World War I. He entered USMA and graduated number thirty-one of fifty-two in the class of 1883. He was commissioned in the Third Cavalry and performed frontier duty from 1883 to 1893. During this period, on 25 September 1894, he married Katherine Fenlon in Leavenworth, Kansas. From 1892 to 1893, he served in the Garza Campaign in Texas. He served in the Santiago Campaign in 1898, in part as an aide to Gen. S. B. M. Young. On 16 October 1898, he was promoted to captain and transferred to the Fourth Cavalry. From September 1898 to May 1899, he was with the Second Corps at Camp

Tyree Rodes Rivers

Meade in Gettysburg, Pennsylvania. From 1899 to 1901, he took part in operations against the insurgents in the Philippines. When he returned to the States, he was stationed at Fort Leavenworth, Kansas from 1901 to 1904, then served for a year in the Presidio in San Francisco, California. In October 1905, he was back in the Philippines for the campaign against the Moros, and on 5 March 1906, he was wounded in the storming of Mount Bud Dajo on Jolo Island. He was promoted to major in April 1907 and was transferred to the Ninth Cavalry, then transferred to the Fourth Cavalry on 26 April of the same year. He graduated from the Army War College in 1907. In June 1909, he was detailed to the Inspector General's Department and became Inspector General of the Department of Texas until he returned to the Philippines. He was promoted to lieutenant colonel and assigned to the 13th Cavalry, then returned to the States. On 1 July 1916, he was promoted to colonel. When the U.S. entered World War I, he was placed in command of the first Officers Training Camp at Fort Riley, Kansas. He was sent to Camp Sherman, Ohio, where he served during the terrible flu epidemic. On 1 October 1918, he was promoted to brigadier general (NA) and commanded Camp Sherman. He later commanded the 154th Depot Brigade at Camp Meade, Maryland. On 10 March 1919, he reverted to his permanent rank of colonel of cavalry. The following day, he was again detailed to the Inspector General's Department, and was stationed on Governor's Island, New York. Still on duty, he died there at the age of sixty-one, on 31 January 1923. Photo from the National Archives.

☆

William Cannon Rivers

William Cannon Rivers (0-168), son of William Rivers and Julia Flournoy Rivers, was born on 11 January 1866 in Pulaski, Tennessee. He was the brother of Tyree R. Rivers (*q.v.*), and they were one of four pairs of American general officer brothers in World War I. He entered USMA and graduated number twenty-four of sixty-four in the class of 1887. Richmond P. Davis, Charles Henry Martin and William Weigel (all *q.v.*) were three of his classmates. He was commissioned in the First Cavalry Regiment and performed frontier duty from 1887 to 1891, which included service in the last of the Indian Wars. He was assistant quartermaster at USMA from 1891 to 1893, and from 1895 to 1897, he was in charge of the White Mountain (Arizona) Apache Indians. On 19 October 1897, he married Mary Dancey Battle, and they had two sons: James B. Rivers and William F. Rivers. In 1898, he served on the General Staff. From 1906 to 1913, as a colonel, he served as Assistant Chief of the Philippine Constabulary. In 1914, he was promoted to brigadier general (temporary) and was chief of the Constabulary. He organized, trained and took to France the 76th Field Artillery Regiment (AEF), and commanded it in many battles. On 1 October 1918, he was promoted to brigadier general (NA) and commanded the Fifth Field Artillery Brigade, for which he received the Distinguished Service Medal. In 1927, he was promoted to major general (USA) and was appointed Inspector General of the Army, which post he held until his retirement on 11 January 1930. In addition to the decoration already mentioned, he received the Croix de Guerre (France). He belonged to the Sons of the Revolution, the American Hugenot Society, the Society of the Army of Santiago and the American Academy of Political and Social Sciences. In retirement, he lived in Warrington, North Carolina. At the age of seventy-seven, he died, on 10 July 1943. Photo courtesy of the National Archives.

Samuel Dickerson Rockenbach

Samuel Dickerson Rockenbach (0-397), son of Lieut. Frank J. Rockenbach (CSA) of the Army of Northern Virginia and Mrs. Frank J. Rockenbach, a descendant of colonial Virginia, was born on 27 January 1869 in Lynchburg, Virginia. He entered the Virginia Military Institute and graduated number three in the class of 1889 with a degree in civil engineering. Later, he commanded Kemper Military Institution and was a captain in the Missouri Militia. In 1901, after a competitive examination, he was commissioned in the Tenth Cavalry. He married Emma Baldwin, daughter of Brig. Gen. Theodore Anderson Baldwin, a Civil War veteran still on duty. In 1894, he attended the Troop Officers School at Fort Leavenworth, Kansas, then returned to the Virginia Military Institute as Commandant of Cadets and Professor of Mathematics. When he was asked to resign from the army to remain at the Virginia Military Institute, he refused and rejoined his regiment. During the campaign against the Cree Indians, he met and formed a permanent friendship with John J. Pershing (*q.v.*). During the Spanish-American War, he served in Cuba and Puerto Rico, and he rejoined his regiment in 1898 as adjutant and quartermaster. In 1904, he was sent to the Philippines and promoted to captain. He returned to the States in 1911. He traveled through Japan, Russia and Europe, studying the organization of various armies. He attended the Army War College, then was assigned to the 11th Cavalry and stationed in Colorado. From the outbreak of World War I, until 1915, he was an observer with the German Army, after which he was promoted to major, transferred to the Quartermaster Corps and assigned to General Pershing's staff. He prepared and organized Base Section Number One in France prior to the arrival of the first American troops in the spring of 1917. General Pershing chose him to head the newly organized Tank Corps because of his administrative talents, his ability to improvise and cooperate with the Allies and his experience with truck supply columns in the Mexican Punitive Expedition. He chose Maj. G. S. Patton, Jr. to train the men of twenty U.S. light tank battalions. He was the U.S. representative of the Inter-Allied Tank Committee, and was General Pershing's advisor. In August 1918, he was made Chief of the Tank Corps, First American Army. These tanks were used at St. Mihiel and in the Meuse-Argonne offensive, and won considerable praise from our allies. When he returned to the States in 1919, he reverted to his permanent rank of colonel, and he retained his position as Chief of the Tank Corps until June 1920, when tanks became part of the infantry. He transferred to the infantry and headed the tank school at Fort Meade, Maryland. He was promoted to brigadier general (USA) in June 1924. He commanded the military district of Washington from 1924 until July 1927, when he was transferred to the Second Cavalry Brigade. In 1928, he took command of the Second Artillery Brigade at Fort Sam Houston, Texas, where he remained until he retired in 1933. He had a home in Brownsville, Texas, and he stayed at the Chevy Chase Club when in Washington. At the age of eighty-three, he died at the club, on 16 May 1952. Photo courtesy of the Patton Museum of Cavalry and Armor, Fort Knox, Kentucky.

Harry Lovejoy Rogers (0-12), son of Capt. Joseph Sumner Rogers and Jeanette Wheeler Rogers, was born on 29 June 1867 in Washington, D.C. When he was ten years old his father resigned from the army and founded the Michigan Military Academy in Orchard Lake, Michigan. He graduated from his father's military academy in 1884, and was quartermaster and treasurer there from 1887 to 1897, when he became commandant of cadets. On 5 July 1892, he married Harriet Pray of Auburn, Maine, and they had two children: Helen F. Rogers (wife of Col. Rodney H. Smith, USA) and Lieut. Harry Rogers, Jr. With the coming of the Spanish-American War, he left the military academy to join the army. He was appointed major in the Pay Corps, but served mostly in the Quartermaster Corps. In 1916, he was quartermaster of the Southern Department, and was in charge of provisioning both General Funston's Expedition to Vera Cruz and General Pershing's Punitive Expedition to Mexico. He did this so well that on 5 August 1917, he was promoted to brigadier general (NA) and chief quartermaster of the AEF. On 26 February 1918, he was promoted to brigadier general (USA). In France, he built up an organization of 3,000 officers and 85,000 men that operated magnificently, with each function under a specific

Harry Lovejoy Rogers

officer who was in effect one of the quartermaster board of directors. To save as much shipping as possible and to prevent U-boat losses, he bought foreign food and supplies wherever practicable. This led to establishment of the General Purchasing Board headed by Gen. Charles Gates Dawes (*q.v.*). He established a garden service operated by rear-echelon, partially disabled soldiers. One of his many bakeries produced 400 tons of bread a day. In France, he built the largest ice-making plant under one roof in the world. He received the Distinguished Service Medal, the citation for which read: "He was able to meet each emergency in times fraught with untold difficulties, and by his energy and untiring zeal, he insured our troops of a constant supply of quartermaster stores, without which the ultimate success of our army could not have been attained." On 22 July 1918, he was made both major general (USA) and Quartermaster General, succeeding General Sharpe (*q.v.*). After World War I, he reorganized the Quartermaster Department. He was made a Commander of the Order of the Bath (Britain), a Commander of the Order of the Crown (Italy) and a Commander of the Order of Leopold (Belgium). On 27 August 1922, he retired due to disabilities and lived in Philadelphia. At the age of fifty-eight, he died there, on 12 December 1925. Building 8045 on B Avenue at Fort Lee, Virginia is named after him. Signal Corps photo from the National Archives.

William Henry Rose

William Henry Rose (no ASN assigned), son of George T. Rose and Emma Smith Rose, was born on 24 October 1881 in Safe Harbor, Lancaster County, Pennsylvania. After a year at Franklin and Marshall College in Lancaster, he entered USMA and graduated number nine of ninety-three in the class of 1903. Douglas MacArthur and Hugh S. Johnson (both *q.v.*) were two of his classmates. He was commissioned in the Corps of Engineers, and served his first tour of duty in the Philippines. On 20 September 1906, he married Marie Patton, the daughter of a judge in Pontiac, Illinois. They had one daughter, Mrs. Fred P. Reynolds of St. Croix, Virgin Islands, and two sons, William H. Rose, Jr. and George M. Rose, both of Arlington, Virginia. During 1906 and 1907, he served in the Cuban Pacification, and from 1912 to 1917, he was Chief Electrical Engineer of the Panama Canal. During 1917 and 1918, he was on duty in Washington as Director of Purchases for the Engineer Corps, for which service he received the Distinguished Service Medal. On 1 October 1918, he was promoted to brigadier general (NA). In 1919, he retired from the army and worked for Lockwood Green and Company, an engineering firm in Boston, Massachusetts. He was also an executive with Sears Roebuck and Company. His retirement home was in Bradenton, Florida. He was offered a chance to return to duty in uniform, but he served as civilian special assistant to the Chief of Engineers, in charge of bomber assembly plants in Dallas, Fort Worth, Tulsa and Kansas City, for which he received the Legion of Merit. He retired a second time and returned to Bradenton, Florida, where at the age of seventy-six, he died, on 5 October 1958. Both of his sons served as army officers during World War II. Photo courtesy of *The Assembly*, Association of Graduates, USMA.

Otho Bane Rosenbaum (0-455), son of Thomas M. Rosenbaum and Nannie Bane Rosenbaum, was born on 26 August 1871 in Marion, Virginia. He entered USMA and graduated number thirty-six of fifty-four in the class of 1894. Paul B. Malone and Hamilton S. Hawkins (both *q.v.*) were two of his classmates. He was commissioned in the infantry. On 26 August 1895, he married Katherine Marie Rawholle, and they had four children: Frederick B. Rosenbaum, Elizabeth C. Rosenbaum (Mrs. Ballard), Otho B. Rosenbaum, Jr. and William L. Rosenbaum. During the Spanish-American War, he served both in Cuba and in the Philippines, and he received the Distinguished Service Medal for gallantry in action in Santiago, Cuba. He was promoted to brigadier general (NA) on 26 June 1918. In 1922, he was an honor graduate of the Army School of the Line. In 1923, he graduated from the General Staff School, and in 1924, from the Army War College. He was a Lutheran, and he belonged to the Army and Navy Club in Washington as well as the Army and Navy Country Club. On 31 August 1935, he retired and lived in Washington, where at the age of ninety-one, he died on 21 December 1962. The photo, from the National Archives, was taken when he commanded the 315th Infantry at Camp Meade, Maryland.

Otho Bane Rosenbaum

John Wilson Ruckman (ASN unknown), son of Thomas Ruckman and Mary O'Brien Ruckman, was born on 10 October 1858 in Snyder, Illinois. He entered USMA and graduated number eleven of fifty-two in the class of 1883. William Shipp, who was killed at San Juan Hill in Cuba, and George Cameron (*q.v.*) were two of his classmates. He was commissioned and sent to the Fifth Artillery, and was soon transferred to the Coast Artillery, where he spent the remainder of his career. On 16 June 1887, he married May Hamilton, daughter of Col. John Hamilton (USA). He graduated from the Artillery School in 1892, then became the first editor of the journal of the U.S. Artillery from 1892 to

John Wilson Ruckman

1896. From 1899 to 1901, he served in Havana with the army of occupation, and from 1901 to 1904, he was an instructor at the School of Submarine Defense at Willett's Point, New York. He was sent to the Philippines, where from 1911 to 1912, he was the Inspector General. In 1915, he graduated from the Army War College, and in 1916, from the Naval War College. He commanded the Fifth Provisional Coast Artillery Regiment on the border in 1916. The same year, he was promoted to brigadier general (USA). He commanded the districts of El Paso and Laredo until July 1917. On 5 August 1917, he was promoted to major general and commanded the South Atlantic Coast Artillery District. He commanded the Southern Department until 1 May 1918, when he was sent to the Northeastern Department in Boston. He was a prolific writer on many technical subjects, and is credited with many inventions. At the age of sixty-two, he died in Massachusetts, on 7 June 1921. Photo courtesy of the National Archives.

Colden L'Hommedieu Ruggles (0-220), son of Gen. George D. Ruggles (USA) and Alma L' Hommedieu Ruggles, was born on 18 March 1869 in Omaha, Nebraska. He entered USMA and graduated number five of fifty-four in the class of 1890. Edgar Jadwin and James R. Lindsay (both *q.v.*) were two of his classmates. He was commissioned in the artillery and later transferred to ordnance. He married Mary Appleton Miller, daughter of Brig. Gen. Marcus P. Miller (USA), and they had one daughter, Colden (Mrs. E. L. Florance). Until 1900, he served on Governor's Island, New York, Fort Monroe, Virginia, Sandy Hook Proving Ground, and in the Frankfort Arsenal in Philadelphia. From 1900 to 1903, he was Inspector of Ordnance. In 1903, he received an E. E. degree from Lehigh University. He was inspector of the Bethlehem Steel Company, and from 1903 to 1908, he served at the Watertown, Massachusetts arsenal. From 1908 to 1911, he was Professor of Ordnance and Gunnery in West Point, New York. From 1911 to 1913, he commanded the Benicia, California arsenal, northeast of San Francisco, and was also ordnance

Colden L'Hommedieu Ruggles

officer for the Western Department. From 1913 to 1915, he was in command of the Manila Ordnance Depot and was ordnance officer for the Philippine Department. From 1915 to 1917, he commanded the Sandy Hook Proving Ground. In 1918, he built the Aberdeen Proving Ground, near Baltimore, Maryland. On 8 August 1918, he was promoted to brigadier general (NA) and received the Distinguished Service Medal for his work in Aberdeen. In 1918, he was both Chief of the Inspection Division of Ordnance and on duty with the AEF. From 1919 to 1921, he was Chief of the Technical Staff of the Ordnance Department. From August 1921 to June 1922, he was a student at the Army War College. From 1923 to 1930, he served as brigadier general (USA), assistant to the Chief of Ordnance. He was U.S. delegate to an international conference on the international arms trade in Geneva in 1925. In 1930, he retired. At the age of sixty-four, he died in South Carolina, on 2 April 1933. The photo, from the National Archives, was taken after a forty-mile hike in March 1911 in the Philippines.

☆

Edgar Russel

Edgar Russel (0-185), son of Richard Russel and Elizabeth Williams Russel, was born on 20 February 1862 in Pleasant Hill, just southwest of Kansas City, Missouri. He entered USMA and graduated number eleven of sixty-four in the class of 1887. George Owen Squier, Chief Signal Officer and the first Ph.D. in the army, was one of his classmates. He was commissioned and sent to the Third Artillery. On 18 April 1893, he married Florence Kimball. From 1893 to 1898, he was both an instructor in chemistry and assistant professor of chemistry, mineralogy and geology at USMA. During the Spanish-American War, he commanded a signal company in the Philippines, and he became the Chief Signal Officer for Southern Luzon. He received two Silver Star Commendations for his service during the Philippine Insurrection. Both Gen. Henry Lawton and Gen. Arthur MacArthur recommended him for brevet promotion for "exceptionally skillful and meritorious services." From 1903 to 1905, he helped to construct the Washington-to-Alaska cable. He was assistant to the Chief Signal Officer again from 1906 to 1908, and from 1908 to 1912, he commanded the Army Signal School at Fort Leavenworth, Kansas. From 1912 to 1915, he was again in the office of the Chief Signal Officer, and in 1916, he became the Chief Signal Officer of Hawaii. He held the same assignment in the Southern Department during 1916 and 1917, then became the Chief Signal Officer (AEF). For this he received the Distinguished Service Medal. He was promoted to brigadier general (NA) on 2 October 1917. He reverted to his rank of colonel (USA) on 15 August

1919, then was reappointed brigadier general (USA) on 11 October 1921. As of 3 September 1919, he was Chief Signal Officer, Eastern Department. He retired as a major general due to disabilities on 6 December 1922. In addition to the decorations already mentioned, he was made a Companion of the Bath (Britain) and a Commander of the Legion of Honor (France). At the age of sixty-three, he died in New York City, on 26 April 1925. Photo courtesy of Special Collections, USMA Library.

James Augustine Ryan (0-13370), son of James Ryan and Hanna Doran Ryan, was born on 22 October 1867 in Danbury, Connecticut. He won his appointment to USMA in a competitive examination, and graduated number twenty-eight of fifty-four in the class of 1890. He was commissioned in the Tenth Cavalry at Fort Apache, Arizona. He took part in the skirmishes with the Apache Kid and other renegades of Geronimo's band. While serving at Fort Assiniboine, Montana, he rounded up a large number of Cree Indians and turned them over to the Royal Canadian Mounted Police to be returned to their reservations. He served with the only other African-American cavalry regiment (the Ninth) at Fort Robinson, Nebraska, then volunteered for duty in the Alaskan Relief Expedition, which he commanded. On 1 May 1898, he received special orders from the Secretary of War via telegraph to rejoin his regiment in Tampa, Florida with the army's largest pack train. He commanded Troop A, Ninth Cavalry, during the Santiago Campaign, was appointed regimental quartermaster and returned with his unit to Fort Grant, Arizona. He was on recruiting duty in Denver, Colorado, then became an aide to Gen. Henry C. Merriam until August 1900, when he rejoined his regiment on its way to Peking, China. Peking was captured by the time they got to Nagasaki, Japan, so he spent the next four years in the Philippines. At the close of the pacification of Cuba, he returned with his troop to Fort Sheridan, Chicago, Illinois. He was appointed professor of modern languages in West Point, and he stayed there, with one interruption, until the Mexican Punitive Expedition. In July 1914, he was sent on a mission to Berlin with the Assistant Secretary of War, and was in charge of the U.S. Commission in Berlin to repatriate stranded American citizens. On the Mexican Punitive Expedition he served with the 13th Cavalry, and he was General Pershing's Chief of Intelligence. On 17 December 1917, he was promoted to brigadier general (NA) and commanded the First Cavalry Brigade, 15th Cavalry Division. He retired as a colonel in 1919. His rank of brigadier general was restored in June 1930. He was a Roman Catholic, and he belonged to the

James Augustine Ryan

Army and Navy Club in Washington and the Catholic Club in New York City. He was very active in retirement, involved in business, finance, public health and diplomacy. His home was in Chicago, Illinois. At the age of eighty-eight, he died in St. Petersburg, Florida, on 4 January 1956. Photo courtesy of *The Assembly*, Association of Graduates, USMA.

George Coolidge Saffarans

George Coolidge Saffarans (0-13398) was born on 20 July 1869 in Memphis, Tennessee. He entered USMA and graduated number forty-one of sixty-five in the class of 1891. William J. Glasgow, John L. Hines, Andrew Hero, Jr. and Odus C. Horney (all *q.v.*) were four of his classmates. He was commissioned in the infantry. During the Spanish-American War, he served as a major of Kentucky Volunteer Infantry, and he also served during the Cuban occupation from 1899 to 1900. He was in the Philippines, and in 1916 and 1917, he served with General Pershing's Mexican Punitive Expedition. In France, he became the Provost Marshal of the District of Paris from 3 January to 3 May 1918, for which he was awarded the Distinguished Service Medal. On 26 June 1918, he was promoted to brigadier general (NA). In 1919, he retired as a colonel due to disabilities. He lived in retirement in Paducah, Kentucky. At the age of fifty-six, he died in Georgia, on 7 February 1926. His rank of brigadier general was restored posthumously in June 1930. Photo courtesy of the Association of Graduates, USMA.

William Hampden Sage (0-43) was born on 6 April 1859 in New York. He entered USMA and graduated number twenty-one of thirty-seven in the class of 1882 as a classmate of Adelbert Cronkhite, Henry T. Allen (both *q.v.*) and Fredrick G. Bonfils of the *Denver Post*. He was commissioned and sent to the Fifth Infantry. He performed frontier duty from 1882 to 1890. During 1892 and 1893, he was Professor of Military Science and Tactics at the Central University of Kentucky. From 1894 to 1898, he performed garrison duty in Texas, and during the Spanish-American War, he served as an aide to Brig. Gen. Samuel Ovenshine. He was adjutant of the First and Second Brigades of the First Division, and received the Medal of Honor for action on the Zapote River in the Philippines on 13 June 1889. He performed civil government duties in the Philippines until 1903. From 1906 to 1907, he was on duty at the Army War College, then became Adjutant General of the Department of the Columbia

(River). In 1916 and 1917, he was on the Mexican border, and from September 1917 to March 1918, he commanded Camp Shelby, Mississippi. He was sent to France, then was promoted to major general (NA) on 5 August 1917 and served as commanding general, 38th Division from 25 August to 19 September 1917 and from 12 December 1917 to 15 March 1918. During 1919 and 1920, he was with the American forces in Germany. At the age of sixty-three, he died in Omaha, Nebraska, on 4 June 1922. He was cited posthumously for his services in the Philippines. His obituary in the Annual Report of the Association of Graduates in 1923 mentions a son, Bill, but makes no mention of his wife. The photo, from the National Archives, was taken at Camp (later Fort) Gordon, Georgia.

William Hampden Sage

Charles McKinley Saltzman (0-249) was born on 18 October 1871 in Pandora, Iowa. He entered USMA and graduated number twenty-nine of seventy-three in the class of 1896, he was a classmate of Lucius R. Holbrook (*q.v.*), Edward L. King, Dennis Nolan and Stephen O. Fuqua who did not graduate but later became the Chief of Infantry. Saltzman was commissioned in the Fifth Cavalry, and was an aide to Maj. Gen. Henry Clay Merriam. He transferred to the Signal Corps and was an honor graduate of the Signal School in 1906. On 9 May 1899, he married Mary Peyton Eskridge, and they had one son, Charles Eskridge Saltzman. During the Spanish-American War, he served in Las Guasimas, San Juan Hill and Santiago, as well as in the Philippine Insurrection and the Moro Campaign. He was Chief Signal Officer of the Eastern Department from 1913 to 1915, and he held the same position for U.S. troops in the Canal Zone in 1915 and 1916. On 1 September 1915, he became executive officer in the office of the Chief Signal Officer in Washington. On 15 May 1917, he was promoted to colonel, and he was promoted to brigadier general (NA) on 24 July 1917. He graduated from the Army War College in 1921, and was U.S. delegate to the International Radio Conference in London in 1922. On 9 January 1924, he served as Chief Signal Officer (USA) and was U.S. delegate to the International Telegraph Conference in Paris in 1925. In 1927, he represented the U.S. at the International Radio Telegraph Conference in Washington. On 8 January 1928, he retired from the army. In 1929, he was appointed to the Federal Radio Commission, and was chairman from 1930 to 1932. He was vice president of the U.S. Shipping Board Merchant Fleet Corporation in 1933. He had two citations for gallantry during the Spanish-American War and received the Distinguished Service Medal and a Silver Star Commendation for service in World War I. He lived in Silver Springs, Maryland. At the age of seventy-one

Charles McKinley Saltzman

he died, on 25 November 1942. His son also served as Chief Signal Officer, and they were the only such father-and-son pair commanding a branch of the United States Army. The photo, from General Gibbs's son, taken at Gibbs's swearing-in ceremony on 9 January 1928, shows six consecutive Chief Signal Officers of the army, from left to right: Adolphus W. Greely, James Allen, George P. Scriven, George O. Squier, Charles M. Saltzman and George S. Gibbs.

William Roderick Sample (0-209), son of Rev. and Mrs. William A. Sample, was born on 29 June 1866 in Memphis, Tennessee. He entered USMA and graduated number twenty-nine of forty-four in the class of 1888. Peyton C. March and Guy Henry Preston (both *q.v.*) were two of his classmates. He was commissioned in the 14th Infantry and performed frontier duty from 1888 to 1891. In 1891, he married Bettie M. C. Saunders of Birmingham, Alabama. From 1893 to 1895, he served with the Arkansas National Guard. During the Spanish-American War, he served as captain of volunteers until 7 April 1899, participated in the Battle of San Juan Hill and was recommended for a brevet promotion. From 1899 to 1902, he was in the Philippines, and from 1904 to 1906, he served in Alaska. At the time of the Mexican Punitive Expedition, he commanded a base camp of the expedition in Columbus, New Mexico. In 1917, he commanded the officers training camp at Madison Barracks, New York, until 17 December 1917, when he was promoted to brigadier general (NA). In France with the AEF, he commanded the advance section of the Service of Supply, for which he received the Distinguished Service Medal. In 1930, he retired as a brigadier general and lived at Fort Smith, Arkansas. At the age of ninety, he died in Atlanta, Georgia, on 12 September 1956. Photo from the National Archives.

William Roderick Sample

Farrand Sayre

Farrand Sayre (0-141), son of Emilius Kitchell Sayre and Elizabeth Pierson Sayre, was born on 17 June 1861 in Lewis County, Missouri, on the west side of the Mississippi. He entered USMA and graduated number twenty-one of thirty-seven in the class of 1884. William L. Sibert (*q.v.*) and Isaac Newton Lewis (inventor of the Lewis machine gun) were two of his classmates. He was commissioned in the cavalry and performed frontier duty from 1884 to 1889. During this period, on 10 May 1888, he married Kate Hamlin Phelps, and they had one daughter, Elizabeth (Mrs. Robert H. Kilbourne). During the Spanish-American War, he served with the Eighth Cavalry in Cuba. At Fort Sill, Oklahoma, he was in charge of Apache prisoners from 1900 to 1904. He graduated from the Infantry and Cavalry School at Fort Leavenworth, Kansas in 1905, and was an honor graduate of the Army Staff College in 1906. From 1906 to 1913, he was an instructor at the Army Service Schools. In 1917, he commanded the Brownsville district of the U.S.-Mexican border. He was promoted to brigadier general (NA) on 1 October 1918. During 1918 and 1919, he commanded the First Cavalry Brigade. He remained in command of the Brownsville district until 1920. From 1920 to 1925, he commanded a district of the Panama Canal Zone. In 1925, he retired as a colonel. In June 1930, his rank of brigadier general was restored. He received an A.M. degree from Johns-Hopkins in 1936, and a Ph.D. from the same institution two years later. He wrote *Map Maneuvers*, *Diogenes of Sinope* and *The Greek Cynics*. In retirement, he lived in Baltimore. At the age of ninety he died, on 17 April 1952. Photo from the National Archives.

Samuel John Bayard Schindel (no ASN assigned), son of Capt. Jeremiah Peter Schindel and Martha Bayard Schindel, was born on 3 June 1871 in Camden, New Jersey. He entered USMA and graduated number five of fifty-one in the class of 1893. Herbert B. Crosby (later Chief of Cavalry) was one of his classmates. He was commissioned in the Third Artillery and within two years, he transferred to the Sixteenth Infantry, then served in the Sixth Infantry and the Third Infantry. From 1895 to 1898, he served with troops at Fort Thomas, Kentucky, in the Santiago Campaign and the Battle of San Juan Hill. He also served in the Sanitary Corps, for which he was cited posthumously. From 1899 to 1902, he was in the Philippines. On 11 November 1903, he married Isa Urquhart Glenn. During 1905 and 1906, he was again in the Philippines, and in 1907, he served as observer at the Swiss Army Maneuvers. In 1908, he graduated from the Army War College. He was in the Moro Expedition of 1911, and was on duty with the General Staff from 1912 to 1918. On 8 August 1918, he was promoted to brigadier general (NA) and put in command of the 21st Infantry Brigade at Camp (later Fort) Meade, Maryland. He served there until March 1919, when he returned to General Staff duty. His last assignment was at Fort Leavenworth, Kansas. His home was in Allentown, Pennsylvania. At the age of forty-nine, he died in Washington, D.C., on 11 March 1921. His rank of brigadier general was restored in June 1930. Photo from Special Collections, USMA Library.

Samuel John Bayard Schindel

Hugh Lenox Scott

Hugh Lenox Scott (0-12989), son of Rev. William McKendry Scott and Mary Elizabeth Hodges Scott, was born on 22 September 1853 in Danville, Kentucky. He was a great-great grandson of Benjamin Franklin. His father died when he was about seven or eight, and his mother took him to Princeton, New Jersey, where he was raised. He went to school in Lawrenceville and to college in Princeton before entering USMA. He was suspended for one year for hazing, but latter graduated number thirty-six of forty-eight in the Class of 1876. He was commissioned in the Ninth Cavalry and transferred almost immediately to the Seventh Calvary. He performed frontier duty from 1876 to 1894. He was greatly interested in American Indians, and became an expert in sign language. At this time, Troop L in any regiment was the Indian troop, and he commanded Troop L of the Seventh Cavalry, made up of Kiowas, Comanches and Apaches soldiers, not Indian scouts. In 1892, Troop L of the Seventh Cavalry, the last of these Indian troops, was disbanded. He had a knack for bringing dissident elements together, and so was placed in charge of investigating the "Ghost Dance" disturbances of 1890 and 1891. From 1894 to 1897, he was in charge of the Apache prisoners at Fort Sill, Oklahoma. During the Spanish-American War, he served as a major of U.S. Volunteers, Adjutant General of the Department of Cuba, and acting Governor General until 1902. From 1903 to

1906, he served in the Philippines as Military Governor of Sulu, and earned two Silver Star Commendations. On 23 March 1913, he was promoted to brigadier general (USA). From 2 April 1914 to 17 November 1917, he was Assistant Chief of Staff of the army. On 16 November 1914, he followed Gen. William W. Wotherspoon as Chief of Staff. He was succeeded by Gen. Tasker H. Bliss on 22 September 1917. For which he received the Distinguished Service Medal. In 1915, he settled disputes in Naco, Cochise County, Arizona and with the Paiutes in Bluff, Utah. On 30 April 1915, he was promoted to major general (USA), and in August, he was sent to the Mexican border, where he succeeded in recovering property of foreigners that had been "confiscated" by Pancho Villa. In 1917, he was a member of the U.S. Commission to Russia, and from 2 January to 16 March 1918, he was Commanding General, 78th Infantry Division. He was the third oldest American general to serve during World War I (all three of whom were born in 1853). He retired in 1917, but continued on active duty until 1919. During 1922 and 1923 he was a member of the New Jersey Highway Commission. He unveiled the bust of Benjamin Franklin at Franklin's induction to the Hall of Fame for Great Americans. He is credited with having averted war with Mexico on several occasions. At the age of eighty, he died at Walter Reed Army Medical Center in Washington, on 30 April 1934. Photo from the Association of Graduates, USMA.

William Sherley Scott (0-13127), son of Col. Thomas M. Scott and Elizabeth Sherley Scott, was born on 12 January 1856 in McKinney, north of Dallas, Texas. He entered USMA and graduated number twenty-six of fifty-two in the Class of 1880. George W. Goethals (*q.v.*) was one of his classmates. He was commissioned and sent to the 1st Cavalry and performed frontier duty from 1880 to 1885. In 1887, he graduated from the Infantry and Cavalry School at Fort Leavenworth, Kansas. On 30 November of that year, he married Nellie Z. Hastings. In 1889 to 1890, he was Professor of Military Science and Tactics at the Texas Agricultural College, and from 1890 to 1891 he participated in the last of the late Indian Wars in the Sioux Campaign. From 1890 to 1894, he was secretary of the Infantry and Cavalry School, and from 1894 to 1898 was adjutant of the First Cavalry Regiment. During the Spanish-American War, from 1898 to 1899, he served as a Lieutenant Colonel of U.S. Volunteers and as Assistant Adjutant General of the Seventh Army Corps in Cuba. He was also Assistant Adjutant General of the Philippine Division from 1902 to 1903. From 1903 to 1906, he was assistant chief of the Philippine Constabulary with the rank of

William Sherley Scott

brigadier general. He was Adjutant General of the Department of Texas from 1910 to 1913, and from 1913 to 1916 , he had the triple assignment of being in charge of militia affairs, Southern Department, serving as adjutant, First Cavalry Brigade and serving as Chief of Staff, 15th National Guard Division. He was in Leon Springs, Texas, from May to August 1917, in command of the first officers training camp there. He was promoted to brigadier general (NA) on 5 August 1917, and from August to September, he commanded the 59th Infantry Brigade. He was commanding general, 30th Infantry Division, from 19 September to 14 October 1917, and from December 1917 to 10 August 1918, he commanded Base Section Number 2 in Bordeaux, France. From 19 August to 21 October, he commanded the 41st Infantry Division (AEF). He commanded the 153rd Depot Brigade at Camp Dix, New Jersey, and from December 1918 to 26 October 1919, he commanded Fort Oglethorpe, Georgia, and the demobilization center there. His last command was of Fort Sam Houston, Texas. He retired as a brigadier general in January 1920, and worked as a vice president of the Sam Houston State Bank and Trust Company. From 1923 to 1941, he was president of the National Bank of San Antonio, Texas. His decorations included medals for service in the Indian Wars, the Spanish-American War, the Cuban Occupation, the Puerto Rican Campaign, on the Mexican border and in World War I. He was made an officer of the Legion of Honor (France). His retirement home was in San Antonio, Texas, where at the age of eighty-four, he died on 31 August 1941. Photo from the National Archives.

George Percival Scriven (0-13109), son of Charles Henry Scriven and Elizabeth Schuff Scriven, was born on 21 February 1854 in Philadelphia, Pennsylvania. He studied at the University of Chicago, and spent two years at the Rensselaer Polytechnic Institute in Troy, New York, before entering USMA. He graduated number five of forty-three in the Class of 1878. James Franklin Bell was one of his classmates. He was commissioned in the Eighth Infantry, but soon transferred to the artillery and then to the Signal Corps. From 1880 to 1884, he was an assistant professor at USMA. On 7 February 1891, he married Bertha Bragg, daughter of Gen. Edward Stuyvesant Bragg of Wisconsin. In 1894, he was appointed military attaché in Mexico City, and in the same year served as military attaché in Rome, which post he held until 1897. In 1896, he was present at the coronation of the Tsar of Russia. During 1897, he briefly served with the Turkish Army. In 1898, during the Spanish-American War, he served in Cuba and was Chief Signal Officer, Department of the Gulf. In 1898, he was sent to the Philippines as Chief Signal Officer for Gen. Wesley Merritt. From August to November 1900, he was Chief Signal Officer of the China Relief Expedition, for which he was twice cited. In 1904, he was on duty at the St. Louis Exposition, and from 1904 to 1909, he was Chief Signal Officer, Department of the East. From 1909 to 1911, he was again in the Philippines, and from 1911 to 1913 he was assistant to the Chief Signal Officer in Washington. On 5 May 1913, he was promoted to brigadier general (USA) and appointed

Chief Signal Officer. He retired on 3 February 1917 after forty-two years of service, and asked for active duty in the event of war. His wife died in 1914, and on 6 October 1915, he married Elizabeth McQuade. On 17 September 1917, at the behest of President Wilson, he was returned to duty and sent to Rome as observer with the Italian armies. In July and August 1918, he was on duty at the Army War College. He received many decorations, and wrote a number of articles and books including: *The Nicaracuan Canal and Its Military Aspects*; *Transmission of Military Information* and *The Story of the Hudson's Bay Company*. In retirement, he lived in Washington, D.C., and at the age of eighty-six, he died in North Carolina, on 7 March 1940. The photo, taken at Gibbs' swearing-in ceremony on 9 January 1928, and donated for this purpose by Gen. Gibbs' son, shows six consecutive Chief Signal Officers of the army, from left to right: Adolphus W. Greely, James Allen, George P. Scriven, George O. Squier, Charles M. Saltzman and George S. Gibbs.

George Percival Scriven

David Cary Shanks, Jr. (0-28), son of David C. Shanks and Sarah Boone Shanks, was born on 6 April 1861 in Salem, Virginia. He was a student at Roankoe College in Salem from 1874 to 1878. He entered USMA and graduated number thirty-three of thirty-seven in the class of 1884. William L. Sibert (*q.v.*) and Isaac Newton Lewis, inventor of the Lewis machine gun, were two of his classmates. He was commissioned in the 18th Infantry. From 1888 to 1894, he performed frontier duty, during which time, on 5 October 1893, he married Nancy Chapman. They had two daughters: Katherine (Mrs. William Malloy, USN) and Sarah (Mrs. Stephen J. Chamberlain, USA). From 1894 to 1898, he was Professor of Military Science and Tactics at the Virginia Polytechnic Institute. During the Spanish-American War, he served as a major of Virginia volunteers. From 1899 to 1901 he served during the Philippine

David Cary Shanks, Jr.

Insurrection, and from 1903 to 190, he was governor of the province of Cavite. During World War I, he was commander of the Port of Hoboken, New Jersey. He was promoted to major general on 5 August 1917. From September 1918 to 30 November 1918, he commanded the 16th Infantry Division at Camp Kearny, California, for which he was awarded the Distinguished Service Medal. Like the 16th through 24th Cavalry Regiments, this was a short-lived training unit that never saw service in the field. He also received the Navy Distinguished Service Medal. In 1925, he retired and wrote a book on management of the American soldier. In retirement, he lived in Washington, D.C., where at the age of seventy-nine, he died on 10 April 1940. Photo from the National Archives.

Henry Granville Sharpe

Henry Granville Sharpe (0-12994), son of Gen. George Henry Sharpe and Caroline Hasbrouck Sharpe, was born on 30 April 1858 in Kingston, New York. He entered USMA and graduated number forty-six of fifty-two in the class of 1880. He was commissioned in the Fourth Infantry. George W. Goethals, William S. Scott and James Walker Benet (all *q.v.*) were three of his classmates. On 1 June 1882, he resigned from the army, and on 12 September 1883, he was reappointed as a captain, Commissary of Subsistence. He was Post Commissary, USMA from 1884 to 1889. The remainder of his career was spent in the Commissary and Quartermaster Departments. On 2 June 1887, he married Kate H. Morgan. In 1897, he was the Army Commissary for the relief of flood victims in Cairo, Illinois and Memphis, Tennessee. During the Spanish-American War, from April to July 1898 he was Chief Commissary at Camp George H. Thomas in Chickamauga Park, Georgia, and he served as commissary of the Army Corps from July to October 1898, as well as in the Department of Puerto Rico from October to December. At that time the Quartermaster Corps did not include all the functions it does now, and procurement of food was a commissary function. From 1902 to 1904, he was Chief Commissary, Division of the Philippines. On 12 October 1905, he was promoted to brigadier general and was Chief Commissary of the United States Army, which post he held until 1916. In 1912, he was shifted to the Quartermaster Corps, but his duty assignment remained the same. On 16 September 1916, he was promoted to major general and became Quartermaster General of the army. On 12 July 1918, he was made a major general, and he commanded the Southeastern Department until 28 May 1919. From June to September 1919, he served in France. He wrote several books, all on quartermaster duties: *The Art of Subsisting Armies in War, The Art of Supplying Armies* *in the Field as Exemplified During the Civil War* for which he received a Gold Medal, *The Provisioning of the Modern Army in the Field*, and *The Quartermaster Corps in the Year 1917, in the World War*. He was the first World War One Quartermaster General. On 1 May 1920, he retired. At the age of eighty-nine, he died in Rhode Island, on 13 July 1947. Building 11528 at Fort Lee, Virginia, is named after him. Photo courtesy of the National Archives.

Fredrick Benjamin Shaw (0-498), son of Charles D. Shaw and Margaret Dickson Shaw, was born on 24 June 1869 in Burlington, New Jersey. On 9 November 1892, he enlisted in the 21st Infantry, where he served until he was commissioned in the Fifth Infantry on 23 March 1896. On 22 August 1898, he was promoted to first lieutenant and served in Cuba, Puerto Rico and the Philippines. On 15 April 1901, he was promoted to captain On 8 July 1908, he married Mary B. Davis and they had two girls and three boys: Marian (wife of Gen. H. L. Peckham), Barbara (wife of Col. F. M. Hinshaw), Fredrick, Robert and Daniel. General Shaw also served on the Mexican border just before the United States entered World War I and with the AEF in France. From 27 November 1917 to 11 March 1918, he was Chief of Staff of the 87th Infantry Division. On 1 October 1918, he was promoted to brigadier general (NA) then reverted to his permanent rank of colonel after the war. He wrote two books, one a genealogical work on the Shaw family, the other a history of the Second Infantry Regiment. The 1932 army list shows him as a colonel, instructor to the Kentucky National Guard, stationed in Louisville. He retired in the mid-1930s and lived in Arlington, Virginia. Photo from the National Archives, Washington.

Fredrick Benjamin Shaw

George Henry Shelton (0-14504) was born in 1871 in Seymour, Connecticut. He entered USMA and graduated number thirty-six of seventy-three in the class of 1896. Fox Conner, A. A. Fries, Malin Craig, Robert C. Davis and Guy V. Henry, Jr. (all *q.v.*) were five of his classmates. He was commissioned in the 11th Infantry. He was promoted to first lieutenant on 18 September 1898, and by 4 May 1901, he was a captain in the 25th Infantry. On 1 January 1902, he transferred to the 11th Infantry, and he served during the Philippine Insurrection.

George Henry Shelton

From 1908 to 1912, he was with the Bureau of Insular Affairs. On 26 June 1918, he was promoted to brigadier general (NA) and served as Chief of Staff, 26th Infantry Division (New England National Guard troops) during World War I for which he was given the Distinguished Service Medal (posthumously). He died as a colonel, on 2 November 1920. His rank of brigadier general was restored by act of Congress in June 1930. Photo from Special Collections, USMA Library.

John Henry Sherburne, Jr. (ASN unknown), son of John Henry Sherburne and Elizabeth Nye Sherburne, was born on 29 January 1877 in Boston, Massachusetts. He graduated from Harvard in 1899 with an A.B., and he received an LL.B. from Harvard in 1901. That same year; he married Mary Patterson Harris, and they had four children: John, Alice, Elizabeth and Sidney. In 1901, he was admitted to the bar in Massachusetts and he started his law practice with Sherburne, Powers and Needham. From 1916 to 1917, on the Mexican border troubles, he served as a colonel of Massachusetts Field Artillery. In 1918, he went to France with the AEF, and on 26 June 1918, he was promoted to brigadier general (NA). After the war, he served as a brigadier general, Officers Reserve Corps. From 1919 to 1920 he was Food Administrator of Massachusetts. He was a delegate to the Republican national conventions of 1920, 1921,1922, 1923, 1924 and 1928. In 1924, he was Chairman of the Commission on the Revision of the Massachusetts Highway Laws, and from 1926 to 1931, he was Chairman of the Board of Howard University in Washington. From 1930 to 1940, he was president of the Massachusetts Safety Council. On 3 September 1931, he married Helen Kemp. From 1 July 1942 to 12 April 1943, he was Adjutant General of Massachusetts as a brigadier general. His decorations included the Silver Star and Purple Heart. France made him a Commander of the Legion of Honor and a Commander of the Etoile Noir. He was made an honorary citizen of Chateau Thierry and Bellau, France. His home and his law offices were in Boston, Massachusetts.

John Henry Sherburne, Jr.

At the age of eighty-two, he died on 25 July 1959. He was buried in Cambridge, Massachusetts. Photo from the Military Records of Massachusetts, Natick.

James Ancil Shipton

James Ancil Shipton (0-13419), was born on 10 March 1867 in Ironton, Ohio. His early boyhood was spent on a farm. After high school, he taught school for three years and was principal of a five-room high school. He entered USMA and graduated number fifteen of sixty-two in the class of 1892. Charles P. Sumerall (*q.v.*) was one of his classmates. He was commissioned and sent to the Fourth Artillery. He loved to travel, and spent his graduation leave in Europe with a classmate, Henry Whitney (*q.v.*). In Germany he became a favorite of Gen. Claus Hurst. As a result of a private riding match between them, the German Army sent a detail to West Point to study the horsemanship training of American cadets. He attended the Artillery School, but before finishing was sent to Brazil as military attaché. He traveled extensively and sent in many reports and monographs. At this time the Spanish-American War broke out, and despite many applications he did not receive orders for active service. He took leave, went to Washington, presented his case, and was appointed a major of the U.S. Volunteer Infantry. He was ordered to the Philippines in November 1899, and served through the Insurrection until July 1901. His service, both with troops and as a provisional governor, was distinguished. He was wounded, contracted enteric fever and sent back to the States. He was assigned to the 52d Coast Artillery Company at Governor's Island, New York. On 17 December 1902, he married Georgia Lincoln of Little Rock, Arkansas. After graduating from the School for Submarine Defense at Fort Totten, New York in 1906, he was sent to study at the General Electric plants in Schenectady, Pittsfield and Lynn. From June 1907 to December 1909, he was in command of the Torpedo Depot at Fort Totten, New York designing and testing the Army's submarine defenses. In October 1911, he was sent to Argentina as military attaché. While there, he traveled extensively through Argentina, Peru, Bolivia and Chile, reporting on production and consumption of coal for the Panama Canal Commission. During this tour, ex-president Theodore Roosevelt visited South America. They met, and he became Roosevelt's unofficial aide and longtime friend. Roosevelt wrote a very complimentary "thank you" about him to the War Department, and mentioned him in his book *The River of Doubt*. In 1914, he returned to Fort Terry, New York, and that fall he was sent to the Army War College, where he was retained as an instructor. In July 1917, he was sent to France to organize an antiaircraft function of the artillery for the AEF. He was promoted to brigadier general (NA) on 5 August 1917, on which occasion General Pershing gave him the stars he had worn while commanding the Mexican Punitive Expedition. He became Chief of Antiaircraft Artillery (AEF), and on 1 July 1918, he requested relief from this post and was given command of the 55th Field Artillery Brigade. During the St. Mihiel offensive, he commanded the 89th Infantry Division Artillery, and during the Argonne offensive, he commanded the 37th Infantry Division. From December 1918 to June 1919, he commanded the Service of Supply troops in Nancy, France, and during June and July he visited both the American forces in Germany and all of the battle fronts. After thirty-one years of service he retired, on 20 February 1920, and reverted to his permanent rank of colonel of Coast Artillery. He spoke French, Spanish, Portuguese and German fluently. He belonged to many fraternal organizations. In retirement he lived in Little Rock, Arkansas. He went into business there, and was a valued and respected citizen. At the age of fifty-nine, he died there, on 15 February 1926. His rank of brigadier general was restored posthumously. Photo from the National Archives.

Walter Cowan Short (0-399) was born on 2 April 1870 in Columbus, Ohio. He attended the Michigan Military Academy and won his original commission in a competitive examination. His first service was at Fort Ringgold, 103 miles upriver from Brownsville, Texas, in a troop of the Third Cavalry commanded by Capt. John G. Bourke. He participated in operations incident to the Garza uprising on the Mexican border. In the spring of 1892, he was transferred to the Sixth Cavalry at Fort Niobrara, Nebraska, during the "Rustler War" in Wyoming. He commanded the Indian troop of the Sixth Cavalry (traditionally Troop L of any regiment). He was also in Chicago during the railroad strikes of 1894. After this, the Sixth Cavalry was transferred to Fort Myer, Virginia, until the Spanish-American War. He went to Cuba with his regiment and was twice wounded; the second time was at San Juan Hill, where he was given first aid and saved by then-lieutenant John J. Pershing. In May 1899, he returned to Cuba, rejoined his regiment and was promoted to major of volunteers in the 35th US Volunteer Infantry in the Philippines. After the Insurrection, he returned to the States, was mustered out of the volunteers, and on 23 February 1901, was promoted to captain (USA) and was assigned to the 13th Cavalry at Fort Keough, Montana. In 1901, he married Hortense DuBois, daughter of Mr. and Mrs. Oren DuBois of DuBois, Clearfield County, Pennsylvania. They had one daughter, who married Lieut. Verne D. Mudge of Fort Bliss, Texas. With the establishment of the Cavalry School at

Walter Cowan Short

Fort Riley, Kansas in 1902, he was appointed First senior instructor He remained there until 1907, working closely with Col. George H. Cameron (*q.v.*) to establish the School for Horseshoers. In 1907, he was sent to the French Cavalry School at Saumur as a student for the purpose of studying methods of teaching. He graduated from Saumur and returned to Fort Riley, Kansas as Assistant commandant of the Cavalry School. He had charge of the American delegation of riders to the Olympic Games in Amsterdam, and he attended several of the Olympic equestrian events over the years. He remained at the Cavalry School until 1911, when he was ordered to the First Cavalry, then stationed at the Presidio in San Francisco, California. For sometime during this duty, he was commander of the troops at Yosemite National Park. In 1913, he was transferred to the Fourth Cavalry at Schofield Barracks, Hawaii. On 24 December 1915, he was promoted to major and assigned to the 16th Cavalry at Fort Ringgold, Texas, during the Mexican border troubles. In May 1917, he was promoted to lieutenant colonel of cavalry (USA), and on 5 August 1917 he was promoted to colonel of infantry (NA). He organized and trained the 337th Infantry, part of the 82d Infantry Division. From April to September 1918, he organized and trained the 315th Cavalry, and one squadron of the 312th Cavalry. He also organized the 71st and 72d Field Artillery Regiments from the 312th and 315th Cavalry Regiments. From September to October 1918, he commanded the Eighth Infantry Regiment; then, he was promoted to brigadier general (NA) and commanded the 32d Infantry Brigade of the 16th Infantry Division. In 1919, reverting to his permanent rank of Lieutenant Colonel of cavalry, he was ordered to Fort Leavenworth, Kansas as a student. He graduated in 1920 and commanded the 16th Cavalry and Fort Sam Houston, Texas. That October, he was sent to the Inspector General's Department, serving two years in San Francisco and two years in Honolulu. He was promoted to brigadier general (USA), on 4 October 1927, and was assigned to the Advance Air Corps school in Langley Field, the Infantry School at Fort Benning, Georgia and the Cavalry School at Fort Riley. On 8 September 1928, he took command of the 2nd Cavalry Brigade at Fort Bliss, Texas. He commanded the First Cavalry Division from 1930 to 1932, and again in 1934. He retired 30 April 1934 and lived in San Diego, California. Horses and horsemanship were his principal matters of interest. At the age of eighty-one, he died in the Naval Hospital in San Diego, on 5 March 1952. Photo is courtesy of the First Cavalry Division Museum, Fort Hood, Texas.

William Luther Sibert (0-12993), son of William J. Sibert and Marietta Ward Sibert, was born on 12 October 1860 in Gadsden, Alabama. He attended the University of Alabama from 1878 to 1880. He entered USMA and graduated number seven of thirty-seven in the class of 1884. DeRosey Cabell (*q.v.*) and Isaac Newton Lewis (inventor of the Lewis machine gun) were two of his classmates. He was commissioned in the Corps of Engineers, and graduated from the Engineer School of Application in 1887. In September of that year, he married Mary Margaret Cummings, and they had five boys and a girl: William O. Sibert,

William Luther Sibert

Franklin C. Sibert, Harold W. Sibert, Edwin L. Sibert, Martin D. Sibert and Mary Elizabeth Sibert. From 1887 to 1892, he did rivers work in Kentucky. From 1892 to 1894, he worked on the Great Lakes Ship Canal, and from 1894 to 1898, he performed rivers and harbors duty in Arkansas. During 1898 and 1899, he was an instructor in engineering at the Engineer School. In 1899 and 1900, he was Chief Engineer of the Seventh Army Corps and simultaneously managed a railroad in the Philippines. From 1900 to 1907, he was back in the States doing rivers and harbors duty on the Ohio River. He served on the Isthmian Canal Commission from 1907 to 1914, and he did such a remarkable job that he was promoted to brigadier general, (USA) and received the thanks of Congress. In the summer of 1914, he worked on flood prevention in China. On 15 May 1917, he was promoted to Major general, (USA) and commanded the First Infantry Division (AEF), in France. For the first five months of 1918, he commanded the Southeastern Department, in the United States. He organized and commanded the Chemical Warfare Service,(USA) from May 1918 to February 1920, for which he received the Distinguished Service Medal. He was Chairman of a Board of Engineers and Geologists appointed by President Hoover in July 1928 to study the feasibility of building what later became the Hoover Dam on the Colorado River. In addition to the decoration already mentioned, was made an Officer of the Legion of Honor (France). At the age of seventy-five, he died in Bowling Green, Kentucky, on 16 October 1935. The photo, from the National Archives, was taken in Gondrecourt, France, when he commanded the First Infantry Division.

Edward Sigerfoos (no ASN assigned) was born in Potsdam, Ohio. On 1 August 1891 he was appointed a second lieutenant, Fifth Infantry, from civil life. On 26 April 1898, he was promoted to first lieutenant and served during the Spanish-American War. He was promoted to captain of infantry on 2 February 1901. In France during World War I, he organized and commanded the Army School of the Line in Langres, for which he received the Distinguished Service Medal. He was placed in command of the 56th Infantry Brigade of the 28th Infantry Division (Pennsylvania troops), and was killed in

Edward Sigerfoos

action while the news of his promotion to brigadier general was on its way to him, on 7 October 1918. He undoubtedly had the briefest career as a general officer of anyone in the Army since Elon Farnsworth during the Civil War. His residence was Arcanum, Ohio. Photo courtesy of the Pennsylvania National Guard.

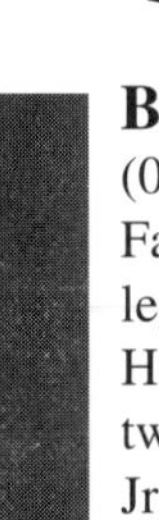

Benjamin Taylor Simmons

Benjamin Taylor Simmons (0-488), was born on 27 August 1871 in Fairfield, North Carolina. He attended college for two years before entering USMA. He graduated number forty-three of fifty-two in the class of 1895. Joseph Wheeler, Jr. and Louis M. Nuttman (both *q.v.*) were two of his classmates. He was commissioned in the infantry and spent most of his time with the Fourth and 16th Infantry Regiments. In the United States, he served at Fort Douglas, Utah, Fort Sherman, Idaho, Fort Leavenworth, Kansas, Fort Crook, Nebraska, Fort Thomas, Kentucky, Fort Spokane, Washington, Eagle Pass, Texas and in Washington, D.C. During the Spanish-American War, he served at San Juan Hill and the Siege of Santiago, for which he received a Silver Star Commendation. In the spring of 1899, he was sent to the Philippines, received another Silver Star Commendation and served in numerous engagements. During World War I he served at headquarters, Southern Department at Fort Sam Houston, Texas. Later, he organized and commanded the 344th Infantry Regiment at Camp Grant, Illinois, then served with the War Department General Staff. On 1 October 1918, he was promoted to brigadier general (NA) and commanded both the 19th Infantry Division and the163rd Depot Brigade at Camp Dodge, Iowa. Long after the war, in 1923, he received a telegram from the officers of the 344th: "Forty five former officers of the 344th Infantry Regiment greet you. At tonight's dinner, as a mark of respect for you and out of admiration for your leadership of the 344th, we stand at attention for the period of one minute!" His training of the Tenth Division was marked by the same efficiency and strong leadership. After the war, he reverted to his rank of colonel, and on 3 July 1932, he was retired due to disabilities. He lived quietly with his wife and son in Washington, D.C. and frequently returned to Fairfield, North Carolina. At the age of sixty-one, he died in Washington, D.C., on 17 April 1933. Photo from *The Assembly*, Association of Graduates, USMA.

George Sherwin Simonds

George Sherwin Simonds (0-764), son of William O. Simonds and Ellen Sherwin Simonds, was born on 12 March 1874 in Cresco, Iowa. He entered USMA and graduated number twenty-six of seventy-two in the class of 1899. He was commissioned in the 22d Infantry. Leon B. Kromer (later Chief of Cavalry) was one of his classmates. After serving with his regiment in the Philippines, he commanded gunboats: the *Oeste* in 1899, the *Florida* in 1900 and the *Laguna de Bay* from 1900 to 1901. For the first half of 1901, he was with the China Relief Expedition, and after serving with troops in Nebraska and Oklahoma, he taught at USMA from 1904 to 1908. He served for two years in Alaska, five years on the Mexican border and two more years teaching tactics in West Point. He arrived in France in June 1917, and was adjutant of the 26th (Yankee) Division. He was Chief of Staff of the Second Corps, for which he received the Distinguished Service Medal. He commanded the American Embarkation Center in LeMans, and participated in four major battles. From 1919 to 1924 he was at the Army War College, first as a student, then as an instructor, and also as assistant commandant. In the fall of 1924, he commanded the Tank School at Fort Meade, Maryland, before going to the Canal Zone, where he commanded an infantry brigade. From 1927 to 1931, he was Assistant Chief of Staff, War Plans Division in the War Department. During 1931and 1932 he was on duty at the Geneva Disarmament Conference, and from 1932 to 1935, was commandant of the Army War College. He was promoted to brigadier general (USA) in 1924. He served on the War Department General Staff from 1927 to 1931. In 1933, he was again promoted to major general (USA) and served as Deputy Chief of Staff (USA) from September 1935 to September 1938. He commanded the Fourth Army and the Ninth Corps Area until 24 May 1938, when he was succeeded by Gen. Albert J. Bowley (*q.v.*). In addition to the decoration already mentioned, he was made a Companion of the Bath (Britain), an Officer of the Order of the Crown (Italy), and an Officer of the Legion of Honor (France). He retired in 1938. At the age of sixty-four, he died in San Francisco, California, on 1 November 1938. Photo from the National Archives.

Fred Winchester Sladen (0-78), son of Maj. Joseph Alton Sladen of England and Martha Winchester Sladen, was born on 24 November 1867 in Lowell, Massachusetts. He attended public schools in Omaha before entering USMA. He graduated number twenty-seven of fifty-four in the class of 1890. He was commissioned in the 14th Infantry. During the late Indian Wars, he performed frontier duty. Durning the Spanish-American War, he was an aide to Gen.

Fred Winchester Sladen

Elwell S. Otis from 1897 to 1900. From 1900 to 1904, he was in the Tactics Department in West Point, and from 1904 to 1906, he served at Vancouver Barracks in Washington, again with the 14th Infantry. His service included relief duty in San Francisco, California after the earthquake and fire. On 8 October 1903, he married Elizabeth Lefferts of New York City, and they had two children: Elizabeth Morris Sladen and Fred W. Sladen, Jr. In 1907, he was detailed to the General Staff, and on 7 April 1908, he became Secretary of the General Staff. From 1911 to 1914, he was Commandant of Cadets at USMA. He went with the 15th Infantry to Tiensin, China. From 1914 to 1916,and during 1916 and 1917, he served on the Mexican border with the 21st Infantry. During 1917, he organized and commanded the Citizens Military Training Camps in San Francisco, California, the forerunner of the Citizens Military Training Camps of the 1920s and 1930s. During 1917 and 1918, he was in the office of the Chief of Staff in Washington. He was promoted to brigadier general (NA) on 17 December 1917, and he commanded the Fifth Infantry Brigade, part of the Third Infantry Division (AEF). He was in all of the major battles involving American troops, for which he received both the Distinguished Service Cross and the Distinguished Service Medal. He did not return to the States with the Third Brigade, but remained as commander of the First Brigade of the American Forces in Germany until his eventual return to the States in 1921. After commanding Fort Sheridan, Chicago, he became Superintendent of USMA until 1926, when he served as commander of the Philippine Department in Manila. In 1928, he was sent, to Baltimore to command the Third Corps Area. He retired in 1931. At the age of seventy-seven, he died in New London, New Hampshire, on 10 July 1945. The photo, from the National Archives, was taken while he was with the Third Division in France.

William Renwick Smedberg, Jr. (0-421), son of a regular army colonel was born on 3 January 1871, in San Francisco, California. He entered USMA and graduated number sixteen of fifty-one in the class of 1893. Lincoln C. Andrews (*q.v.*) and Herbert B. Crosby were two of his classmates. He was interested in baseball, football and social events. He was commissioned in the cavalry, then returned to West Point, first as a tactical officer, then as a teacher of modern languages. During the Philippine Insurrection, he served as an aide to Gen. S. B. M. Young, and participated in eight engagements there, as well as in Las Guasimas and San Juan in Cuba, where he won his first Silver Star Commendation. He served under Gen. Hugh L. Scott, and was an aide to Gen.

Leonard Wood. After the Spanish-American War he specialized in machine-gun warfare, and was commended by General Funston. In 1917, he was senior instructor at the Officers Training Camp at Madison Barracks. In September 1917, he activated the 305th Infantry Regiment at Camp Upton, Long Island, New York and trained its 3,600 personnel. This unit reached Calais, France on 30 April 1918, and trained for a time with the British and then with the French. Between 11 August and 14 September 1918, the 305th Infantry participated in the Vesle defensive, the advance to the Aisne and the Argonne Forest. For this service he was cited for bravery in divisional orders, and on 14 October 1918, he was promoted to brigadier general (NA). He commanded the 305th Infantry for fourteen months, which was known as "Smedberg's Regiment." He commanded the 153rd Infantry Brigade, then the 63d Infantry Brigade, which was a part of the army of occupation, the American Forces in Germany. He received the oak leaf cluster (second award) for his Silver Star, and was a graduate of both the Command and General Staff School and the Army War College. He was Inspector General of the Ninth Corps Area and served with the War Department General Staff as G-1. He commanded the Eighth Cavalry, then the Second Cavalry Brigade. From 1932 until his retirement on 31 January 1935, he was Chief of the Administrative Division of the National Guard Bureau. At the age of seventy-one, he died in Walter Reed Army Medical Center, on 9 October 1942. Photo courtesy of the National Archives.

William Renwick Smedberg, Jr.

☆

Abiel Leonard Smith (0-13112), son of Dr. Joseph D. Smith of Fauquier County, Virginia and Martha Leonard Smith, was born on 14 July 1857 in Fayette, Howard County, Missouri. As a boy, he lived in St. Joseph, Missouri. He entered USMA and graduated number forty of forty-three in the class of 1878. J. Franklin Bell (*q.v.*) and John F.R. Landis were two of his classmates. He was commissioned in the 19th Infantry and performed frontier duty from 1878 to 1888. He served in the Apache campaign in 1886, was brevetted captain for bravery, and was a member of the troop that captured

Abiel Leonard Smith

Geronimo. He was military aide to President Cleveland during Cleveland's first administration. On 19 June 1890, he married Florence Compton, daughter of Brig. Gen. Charles Compton, and they had four children: Abiel L. Smith, Jr., Dorothy Smith, Charles Compton Smith and Margaret Smith. His wife died in 1904. He transferred from infantry to cavalry to commissary. During the Spanish-American War, he was a lieutenant colonel of United States Volunteers. After the Russo-Japanese War, he traveled incognito on a government mission through Manchuria to ascertain what the Japanese were doing there, and reported that they had made strong inroads into the country. On 22 December 1916, he was promoted to brigadier general, served in the Quartermaster Corps, (USA), and was stationed in the office of the Secretary of War in Washington. He retired on 3 January 1918. In retirement he lived in Carmel, Putnam County, New York. At the age of eighty-eight, he died at the home of his daughter, Mrs. Mason C. Shoup, in New York City, on 24 April 1946. He had nine grandchildren and a great grandson when he died. Photo from Archives, Association of Graduates, USMA.

Harry Alexander Smith (0-335), son of Mr. and Mrs. Henry T. Smith, was born on 18 June 1866 in Atchison, Kansas. He entered USMA and graduated number thirty-nine of sixty-five in the class of 1891. Odus C. Homey, Andrew Hero, Jr., William J. Glasgow and John L. Hines (all *q.v.*) were four of his classmates. He was commissioned in the First Infantry and served with them in California until 1896, during which time, on 27 October 1892, he married Harriet Newcomb. They had two boys: Newcomb Smith and William A. Smith. From 1896 to 1898 he served with the Kansas National Guard. During the Spanish-American War he was a major of Kansas Volunteers, serving in Cuba and the Philippines. From 1902 to 1912, he was Senior Instructor in Law at the Army Service Schools, and from 1912 to 1914, he was an instructor in military art. He went to Vera Cruz with General Funston in 1914, and when he returned to the States, he was adjutant of the Fifth Infantry Brigade in Galveston, Texas. From April 1916 to August 1917, he served in China. He was on duty with the General Staff in Washington in the fall of 1917. By 26 November 1917, he was in France, serving as an Assistant commandant of the Army Service Schools in Langres, France, for which he received the Distinguished Service Medal. In May 1918, he served as Commandant, and continued as such until Armistice Day, when he was placed in charge of civil affairs of the American Forces in Germany. In July 1919 he returned to the United States and served as Assistant comman-

Harry Alexander Smith

dant of the Army War College in Washington. In October 1922 , he was promoted to brigadier general, USA, and commanded the 16th Infantry Brigade. From 1923 to 1925 he was commandant of the Command and General Staff School at Fort Leavenworth, Kansas. On 1 July 1925 he became Assistant Chief of Staff (G-3) of the army. In 1926 he was promoted to major general, USA, and was sent as a U.S. representative to the coronation of the Shah of Persia. On 1 June 1927 he received his last command as commanding general, Seventh Corps Area, headquartered in Omaha, Nebraska. He was a Presbyterian, and lived in Atchison, Kansas (his birthplace). In addition to the decoration already mentioned, he was made a Companion of the Bath (England), the Legion of Honor (France) Order of the Crown of Oak (Luxembourg) and Commander of the Order of La Solidaridad (Panama). Still on duty, at the age of sixty-two, he died in Omaha, Nebraska, on 26 May 1929. Photo from the National Archives was taken in November 1927.

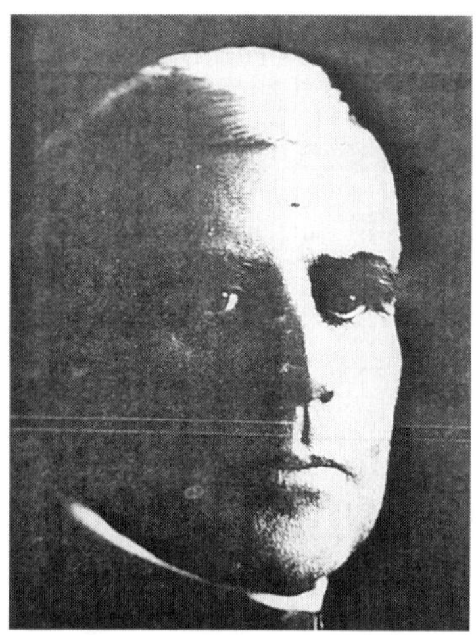

Mathew Charles Smith

Mathew Charles Smith (0-428), son of Mr. and Mrs. Mathew Thomas Smith, both natives of Ireland, was born on 25 March 1868 in Camden, Wilcox County, Alabama. His father served in the Confederate Army during the Civil War. He attended a private preparatory school in Bethlehem, Pennsylvania, then studied engineering at Lehigh University for two years, also in Pennsylvania. He entered USMA and graduated number thirty of fifty-one in the class of 1893. Herbert B. Crosby (later Chief of Cavalry) was one of his classmates. He was commissioned and assigned to the Second Cavalry at Fort Huachuca, Arizona, and later served at Fort Wingate, New Mexico. From 1897 to 1901, he taught in West Point, and during the same period, he served in the Spanish-American War. In 1901, he served with the 14th Cavalry in Leavenworth, Kansas as regimental adjutant. From 1903 to 1905, he was on Mindanao Island in the Philippines, then returned to the Presidio of Monterey. He served in San Francisco, California during the earthquake and fire and was transferred to the Presidio there. Later, he commanded cavalry posts in Walla Walla, Washington and at Boise Barracks, Idaho. On 6 November 1907, he married Celeste Y. Pickering, daughter of an army officer. They had two boys and two girls: Mauree C. Smith, James P. Smith, Catherine Y. Smith and Mathew C. Smith, Jr. From 1909 to 1911, he was stationed at Fort Stotsenberg, Luzon, in the Philippines, after which he was sent again to Leavenworth to attend both the Army School of the Line and the Army Staff College. From 1913 to 1916, he served on the Mexican border, and during 1916 and 1917, he served again in the

Philippines. Late in 1917, he was sent to Camp Travis, Texas, where he organized and trained American troops as engineer battalions. Early in 1918, he commanded the 129th Infantry, a National Guard unit, after which he organized and commanded the 309th Cavalry. This cavalry was soon broken into two field artillery regiments, one of which he commanded. On 10 October 1918, he was promoted to brigadier general (NA) and commanded the 95th Infantry Division organized at Camp Sherman, Ohio. From 1919 to 1924, he served on the War Department General Staff. He served at Fort Thomas, Kentucky as Chief of Staff, Fifth Corps, and later, in Cincinnati with the 83d Infantry Division, an Organized Reserve unit. In 1928, he was ordered to the Canal Zone, where he commanded the Panama-Pacific General Depot. His final assignment was with the Organized Reserve in Portland, Oregon. On 25 March 1932, he retired due to age. Two weeks short of his seventy-third birthday, he died in Los Angeles, California, on 11 March 1941. Photo courtesy of the National Archives.

William Ruthven Smith

William Ruthven Smith (0-71), son of Robert McPhail Smith and Litita Trimble Smith ,was born on 2 April 1868 in Nashville, Tennessee. He studied at Vanderbilt University for two years before entering USMA. He graduated number ten of sixty-two in the class of 1892. He was commissioned in the First Artillery. For eleven years he was an instructor and assistant professor at USMA. He taught chemistry from 1895 to 1898, ordnance and gunnery from 1898 to 1901 and mathematics from 1903 to 1907. On 4 December 1901, he married Mary Prince Davis, daughter of Gen. George B. Davis (USA). They had two children: Katherine Alexander Smith and William R. Smith, Jr. On 5 August 1917, he was promoted to brigadier general (NA). He was assistant to the Chief of Coast Artillery for four years and was director of the Department of Electricity and Mine Defense at Fort Monroe, Virginia for four years. During World War I, he was placed in charge of building and putting into operation the first antisubmarine net. From 18 September 1917 to 5 December 1917, he commanded the 37th Infantry Division (AEF). On 26 June 1918, he was promoted to major general (NA), and on 13 July, he was placed in command of the 36th Infantry Division, which command he held until its inactivation in 1919. For this service he received the Distinguished Service Medal. He was promoted to brigadier general (USA) in 1920, and was commandant of the Seacoast Branch of the Coast Artillery School during 1923 and 1924. In 1924, he was promoted to major general (USA), and from 26 February 1928 to 30 April 1932, he served as Superintendent at USMA. He retired on 30 April 1932 and became

Superintendent of the Suwanee Military Academy in Tennessee. In addition to the decoration already mentioned, he received the Croix de Guerre and was made a Commander of the Legion of Honor (France). At the age of seventy-three, he died in West Point, New York, on 15 July 1941. Photo courtesy of *The Assembly*, Association of Graduates, USMA.

William Josiah Snow

William Josiah Snow (0-25), son of William Dunham Snow and Mary Newell Snow, was born on 16 December 1868 in Brooklyn, New York. He entered USMA and graduated number twenty-four of fifty-four in the class of 1890. Edgar Jadwin, Fred W. Sladen and James A. Ryan (all *q.v.*) were three of his classmates. He was commissioned in the First Artillery. On 19 April 1892, he married Isabel Locke, and they had one son, William A. Snow. Until the Spanish-American War, he served at Forts Hamilton, Slocum and Monroe. In 1898, he graduated from the Artillery School, after which he was regimental quartermaster of the Seventh Field Artillery, serving in Cuba and the Philippines. He organized and commanded the 20th Battery, Field Artillery, at Fort Riley, Kansas and Fort Robinson, Nebraska. During 1906 and 1907, he was secretary of the School of Application for Cavalry and Field Artillery. In 1908, he graduated from the Army War College. From 1910 to 1914, he served in the War Department. He founded the Field Artillery Association and started the *Field Artillery Journal*, of which he was editor during those four years. In 1915, he served in Hawaii and the Philippines, and in 1917, he served as a colonel on the Mexican border. That same year, he reorganized the School of Fire at Fort Sill, Oklahoma. From 27 July to 26 September 1917, he was commandant of the Field Artillery School, and also in 1917, he was promoted to brigadier general (NA) and commanded the 156th Field Artillery Brigade at Camp Jackson, South Carolina. On 26 June 1918, he was promoted to major general (NA), and on 10 February 1918, he became the first Chief of Field Artillery (USA). He retired on 19 December 1927. He was awarded the Distinguished Service Medal, and he was made a Companion of the Bath (Britain) and a Commander of the Legion of Honor (France). He lived in Washington, D.C., and maintained a summer home in Blue Ridge Summitt, Pennsylvania. At the age of seventy-eight, he died in Washington, on 27 February 1947. Photo courtesy of the Field Artillery Museum, Fort Sill, Oklahoma.

Oliver Lyman Spaulding

Oliver Lyman Spaulding (0-703), son of Oliver L. Spaulding and Mary Cecelia Swegles Spaulding, was born on 25 June 1875 in St. Johns, Michigan. In 1895, he graduated from the University of Michigan with an A.B. Degree, and he received an LL.B. from the same school the following year. He was commissioned a second lieutenant, artillery (USA) in 1898, and served in northwestern Alaska from 1898 to 1899. In 1900, he was on the China Relief Expedition, and in 1901, he served in the Philippine Insurrection. On 29 December 1902, he married Alice Chandler, and they had one son, Edward C. Spaulding. He graduated from the Artillery School at Fort Monroe, Virginia in 1903 and from the Army Staff College at Fort Leavenworth, Kansas in 1905. He remained at Fort Leavenworth as an instructor until 1910. In 1911, he graduated from the Army War College. From 1913 to 1915, he served on the Mexican border. From 1915 to 1917, he served in the Philippines again, and he was Assistant Commandant at the Artillery School at Fort Sill, Oklahoma from 1917 to 1918. He was promoted to brigadier general (NA) on 26 June 1918. With the AEF during 1918 and 1919, he served in France, Luxembourg and Germany. He was on the General Staff (AEF) in 1919 as chief of the historical section, then taught until 1924 at the Army War College in Washington. From 1926 to 1929, he was stationed in Hawaii, then served as Professor of Military Science and Tactics at Harvard until 1935, when he returned to the Army War College to teach until 1939. He received a master's degree from Harvard in 1932, and in 1938, the University of Michigan granted him an LL.D. He retired in 1939 with forty-one years of service as a brigadier general, and became a lecturer in military history at Lowell Institute in Boston, Massachusetts and at George Washington University in Washington, D.C. In 1941, he was recalled to active duty and taught again at the Army War College. His was one of the longer records of service in this century, and he was one of a small number of general officers to serve in both world wars. For his service he received the Distinguished Service Medal and was made an officer of the Legion of Merit. He was also made a Commander of the Order of the Black Star (France). He belonged to three different fraternities, including Phi Beta Kappa. He was an Episcopalian and a Mason, and he belonged to several major clubs. His literary works include *Notes on Field Artillery* (Fourth Edition published in 1918), *Warfare* (published in 1925), *The United States Army in War and Peace* (published in 1937), *Pen and Sword in Greece and Rome* (published in 1937), *The Second Division AEF in France 1917-19* and *Ahriman, A Study in Aerial Bombardment* (published in 1939). In retirement, he lived in Washington, D.C., where at the age of seventy-one, he died on 27 March 1947. The photo, from the National Archives, was taken when he was head of the Historical Section in Chaumont (GHQ AEF) in France.

John Charles Speaks

John Charles Speaks (ASN unknown), son of Charles W. Speaks and Sarah Hesser Speaks, was born on 11 February 1859 in Canal Winchester, Ohio. In 1889, he married Edna Lawyer, and they had four children: Charles, Stanford, John, and Margaret. He enlisted in the Ohio National Guard as a private, and by the time of the Spanish-American War, he was a major, Fourth Ohio Volunteer Infantry, serving in the Puerto Rican Campaign. At the time of the 1916 Mexican border trouble, following the Pancho Villa raid, he was in command of the Second Brigade, Ohio National Guard. During World War I, until March 1918, he commanded the 73d Infantry Brigade of the 37th Division. He served for over forty years with the National Guard. In civilian life, he was in the lumber business. From 1907 to 1918, he was the fish, game and conservation officer for the State of Ohio. After World War I, he was a congressman from the 12th Ohio District, from 1921 to 1931. He was a Republican and was a member of the Masons, Shrine, Knights Templar, Knights of Pythias and Rotary. His permanent home was in Columbus, Ohio, at 1378 Neil Avenue. At the age of eighty-six, he died, on 6 November 1945. He was buried in the Union Cemetery in Canal Winchester, Ohio. The photo, from the Library of Congress, Washington, D.C., was taken when he was a congressman.

Marcellus Garner Spinks

Marcellus Garner Spinks (0-594), son of Dr. E. E. Spinks and Valeria Garner Spinks, was born on 25 June 1874 in Meridian, Mississippi. After attending Mississippi Agricultural and Mechanical College in Starkville, he entered USMA and graduated number twenty of fifty-nine in the class of 1898. Fox Conner, Malin Craig, Robert C. Davis, A. A. Fries and Guy V. Henry, Jr. (all *q.v.*) were five of his classmates. He was commissioned in the artillery corps, and when it split in 1907 into Coast and Field Artillery, he stayed with the Coast Artillery. He was stationed at Forts Columbus and Hamilton, both in New York. He attended the Coast Artillery School at Fort Monroe, Virginia until 1901. At Forts McHenry and Howard, in Maryland, he served with the quartermaster and the commissary until November 1903. On Christmas day of 1903, he married Carolyn Lucelia Clabaugh of Baltimore, and they had one son, Albert Garner Spinks, who graduated from Princeton in 1931 and later went into the Coast Artillery. He was sent to California, to Manila, and then to the headquarters of the Cuban Pacification Army in November 1907. From 1907 to 1912, he commanded Coast Artillery companies and instructed the reserve in New York and Maine. From 1913 to 1915, he served as assistant to the chief, Division of Militia Affairs, in Washington. He served as an Inspector General with the 90th Infantry Division at Camp Travis, Fort Sam Houston, Texas, where he was very well regarded by Gen. Henry T. Allen (*q.v.*), the division commander. He served under Gen. George H. Cameron in the Fourth Infantry Division, and on 23 March 1918, he left for France to report to headquarters, Service of Supply. At headquarters (AEF), he served as Assistant Inspector General. On 1 October 1918, he was promoted to brigadier general (NA) and was sent to attend the Army War College. It was reported in 1918 that he was "an officer of fine physique, pleasing address, tact, common sense, good judgment and force, a superior officer in every way." When he completed his course at the Army War College, he was relieved of the detail to the Inspector General's Department and became Chief of Staff of the Coast Artillery Training Center at Fort Monroe. After that, he had two different staff assignments at corps headquarters in Boston, Massachusetts, then became commanding officer, 62d Coast Artillery Regiment, Fort Totten, New York. He was Chief of Staff of the Panama Canal Division until November 1930. From 1930 to 1934, he was again in the office of the Inspector Generals, this time as acting Inspector General. In September 1934, he became Inspector General of the Second Corps Area, headquartered on Governor's Island, New York. In June 1938, he was retired due to physical disability incurred in the line of duty. His service during World War I won him the Distinguished Service Medal, and he was made an Officer of the Legion of Honor (France), a Commander of the Order of the Crown (Belgium) and a Commander of the Order of the Crown (Italy). He was known as Bill to his friends, and his most outstanding characteristic was his tenacity, which, combined with a remarkable sense of honesty, was the cornerstone of his personality. He retired to Hampton, Virginia, where at the age of sixty-nine, he died on 28 November 1943. Photo courtesy of *The Assembly*, Association of Graduates, USMA.

George Owen Squier (0-8), son of Almon Justice Squier and Emily Gardner Squier, was born on 21 March 1865 in Dryden, Michigan. His mother died when he was seven, so he was taken to his grandfather's farm in the same state. By competitive examination he won an appointment to USMA, and graduated number seven of sixty-four in the class of 1887. William Weigel, P. D. Lochridge (both *q.v.*), Charles Henry Martin, Thomas Q. Donaldson, and John Hanks Alexander (the second Negro to graduate from USMA) were five of his classmates. He was commissioned in the Third Artillery and was sent to Fort McHenry, Baltimore. He applied for and was granted postgraduate study at

George Owen Squier

Johns-Hopkins and was likely the first Ph.D. in the army. He studied under some of the finest minds of his generation. He helped to start the artillery journal, started an electrical engineering laboratory at Fort Monroe and was army representative at the Columbian Exposition in 1893. He was a military scientist and inventor. He measured the muzzle velocity of artillery shells and was the pioneer in the application of radio and remote control by radio. He laid the first interisland submarine cables in the Philippines, and he established the Signal School at Fort Leavenworth, Kansas. In 1905, one of his staff was a young lieutenant named William Mitchell (*q.v.*). He had great interest in and taught military ballooning and aviation at Fort Leavenworth. He was Assistant commandant of the Signal School from 1905 to 1911. In 1907, he became Assistant Chief Signal Officer, and it was he who drew the first military aircraft specifications, conducted acceptance trials of the Wright Flyer at Fort Myer, Virginia and recommended a national aeronautical research laboratory. He served for two years in London as military attaché and formed friendships with Lee DeForest and Lord Kitchener. Through Kitchener, he was invited to watch the first military use of aircraft. He was called back to the States, and nine months later, on 14 February 1917, he became the Chief Signal Officer with the rank of brigadier general (USA). He was promoted to major general (NA) on 6 October 1917. As Chief Signal Officer, he followed Gen. George P. Scriven and was succeeded by Gen. Charles M. Saltzman on 31 December 1923. At the age of sixty-nine, he died in Washington, on 24 March 1934. In the photo, courtesy of General Gibbs's son, six Chief Signal Officers are standing in chronological sequence—Adolphus W. Greely, James Allen, George P. Scriven, George O. Squier, Charles M. Saltzman and George S. Gibbs. The photo was taken at Gibbs's swearing-in ceremony on 9 January 1928.

Sanford Bailey Stanbery (no ASN assigned) was born on 21 December 1871 in Millersburg, Ohio. His great-uncle had been attorney general of the United States. When he was young, his family moved to Toledo, Ohio. For several years he was a teacher in a Lucas County rural school. He later worked in a lumberyard and learned the business well. He moved to Cincinnati and became a lumber broker. At the age of twenty-one, he enlisted in the Ohio National Guard. He advanced rapidly, and during the Spanish-American War, he went to Cuba as a major. He stayed with the Army of Pacification in Havana for a year, and when he returned to Toledo, he was promoted to colonel and commanded the regiment. In 1902, he organized the S. B. Stanbery Lumber Company in

Sanford Bailey Stanbery

Cincinnati and resigned his command and commission. He married a woman named Jenny, and they had four sons: Sanford M. Stanbery, Carroll Stanbery, John Stanbery and Lloyd Stanbery. After his first wife's death, in 1904, he married Mamie Litton. When the United States entered World War I, he was too old for officer training school, so for a second time he enlisted as a private, in the Ohio Infantry. After one month of enlisted service, he was promoted to colonel (NA) and commanded the 145th Infantry. General Charles S. Farnsworth recommended him for promotion to brigadier general (NA), which took effect on 1 October 1918. He was a successful commander in battle. While in France, he had a reunion with two of his sons, Sanford and Carroll. From 30 October 1918 to 10 April 1919, he commanded the 155th Infantry Brigade, for which he was awarded the Distinguished Service Medal. It was unusual for a guard colonel to be made a brigadier, and also unusual to be promoted from private to colonel in one month. After the war, he returned to Cincinnati and resumed business as a lumber broker, and later became a Trustee of the Southern Railroad. His home was on Corbly and Sutton Avenues in Mt. Washington, near Cincinnati, Ohio. At the age of sixty, he died on 14 December 1931. Photo courtesy of the Cincinnati Public Library.

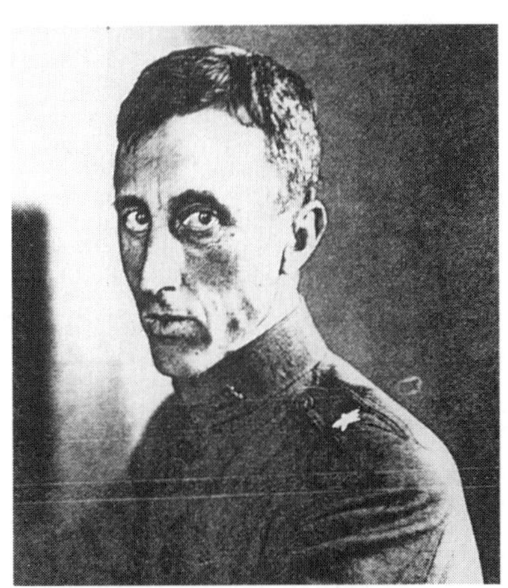

Alfred Andrews Starbird

Alfred Andrews Starbird (0-662), son of Winfield Scott Starbird, who served as an enlisted man in the Seventh Maine Battery during the Civil War, and Emeline Hardy Roberts Starbird, was born on 15 July 1875 in Paris, Maine. He graduated with a B.S. degree from the University of Maine in 1898, and on 13 May of that year, he enlisted as a sergeant in the First Maine Infantry for the Spanish-American War. On 9 July 1898, he was commissioned a second lieutenant, artillery (USA), and later served in the Philippines, the States, and in Europe. He received the Distinguished Service Medal as well as many campaign medals. On 20 July 1911, he married Ethel Dodd, and they had three children: Alfred, Catherine and Ethel Allen. He was a colonel of field artillery, he served during the war in the office of the Inspector General in the War Department. He graduated from the General Staff College at Washington Barracks in 1920. In retirement, he lived in Burlington, Vermont. He was a fellow of the Institute of American Genealogy, a thirty-second-degree Mason and a Republican. At the age of eighty-six, he died on 26 December 1956. One of his sons, Alfred Dodd Starbird, was fifth in the class of 1933 at USMA, commissioned in the engineers and retired in 1972 as a lieutenant general. One of his grandsons, Edward Alfred Starbird, graduated from USMA in 1962 and retired in 1992 as a colonel of engineers in Tacoma, Washington. A grandson, Charles Dodd Starbird graduated from USMA in 1990 and served in the Corps of Engineers. The photo, from the National Archives, was taken while he was serving in the Inspector General's Office.

Robert Eugene Steiner

Robert Eugene Steiner (ASN unknown), son of Mr. and Mrs. Joseph Steiner, was born on 9 May 1862 near Greenville, Alabama. In 1880, he graduated from the University of Alabama with an A.B. degree, and he received his master's degree the following year. In 1919, he was awarded an LL.D., and he received an LL.B. from Harvard in 1884. On 16 December 1814, he married May Flowers, and they had five children: Robert E. Steiner, Jr., Kate Steiner, Helen Steiner, John J. F. Steiner and May Steiner. He practiced law in Greenville until 1892, and subsequently practiced in Montgomery, primarily in the field of railroad law. In 1886, he was elected a member of the Alabama House of Representatives, and in 1892, he was elected to the Alabama Senate. In 1895, he was city attorney for Montgomery, and he was a delegate to the Democratic national convention in St. Louis, Missouri in 1904. In his military career, he started as a captain of the Greenville Guards, and he was a major in the Second Alabama Infantry (National Guard). In 1916, he raised a regiment of cavalry and became a colonel, commanding the regiment on the Mexican border. On 19 March 1917, he was promoted to brigadier general, Alabama National Guard, and on 5 August 1917, he was promoted to brigadier general (NA). He commanded the 62d Infantry Brigade, part of the 31st Infantry Division, which he took to France. He returned to Alabama in command of the 31st Infantry Division, and in 1919, he was recommissioned a brigadier general, Alabama National Guard. His residence and office were in Montgomery, where he died at he age of ninety-three, on 26 September 1955. Photo courtesy of Robert E. Steiner, III, Esq.

John Edmondson Stephens

John Edmondson Stephens (no ASN assigned), son of James Richard J. Stephens and Elizabeth Edmondson Stephens, was born on 8 November 1874 near Brentwood, just outside of Nashville, Tennessee. The Battle of Nashville was to the north, within sight of his home, and that of Franklin took place only a few miles to the south. His father was a veteran of four years in the Confederate Army. He first attended the Battleground Academy in Franklin, then attended Vanderbilt University in Nashville for two years. He entered USMA and graduated number nine of fifty-nine in the class of 1898. Fox Conner, Malin Craig, Robert C. Davis and Guy V. Henry, Jr. (all *q.v.*) were four of his classmates. He was commissioned in the Seventh Field Artillery, requested immediate leave and returned to Vanderbilt to receive his degree. He served in the Sixth, Fifth and Third Field Artillery Regiments. From 1900 to 1904, he was an instructor in mathematics in West Point. During this period, on 24 April 1901, he married Anita de Garmendia, daughter of Sr. Carlos de Garmendia y Cordova, and they had three children: Corinne de Garmendia Stephens (Mrs. Fredrick Peebles), John Edmondson Stephens, Jr. (USN) and James Richard Stephens, II. For a short time in 1917, he served in the Inspector General's Department. From October 1917 to June 1918, he was on the War Department General Staff, primarily in the War Plans Division. He was an honor graduate of the Artillery School at Fort Monroe and a distinguished graduate of the School of the Line and Army Staff College at Fort Leavenworth, Kansas. On 26 June 1918, he was promoted to brigadier general (NA) and went to France in command of the 61st Field Artillery Brigade, which he commanded until his he died of bronchial pneumonia at the age of forty-four, on 5 January 1919. Photo courtesy of the Annual Report, Association of Graduates, USMA.

Merch Bradt Stewart (0-515), son of James Robinson Stewart and Grace Bushong Stewart, was born on 24 June 1875 in Mitchel Station, Virginia. One of his ancestors had come from Edinburgh via Londonderry, Ireland, in the early eighteenth century. He attended the Glenn Falls Academy, then entered USMA and graduated number forty-seven of seventy-three in the class of 1896. Lucius Roy Holbrook, Edward L. King and Dennis E. Nolan (all *q.v.*) were three of his classmates. He was commissioned in the infantry and served in the Santiago Campaign during the Spanish-American War, for which he earned his first Distinguished Service Medal. On 16 February 1898, he married Nan Wheelihan of Necedah, Wisconsin, and they had one son, Peter Stewart. He also served in the Sanitary Corps, for which he received a Silver Star Commendation.

He served in the Philippines and during the Cuban Occupation. From 1904 to 1907, he served in the Tactics Department at USMA. During World War I, he was Chief of Staff of the 76th Infantry Division. He was promoted to brigadier general (NA) on 26 June 1918 and commanded the 175th Infantry Brigade, part of the 88th Division, for which he received a second Distinguished Service Medal. After World War I, he was stationed in West Point as Commandant of Cadets. From 1926 to 1927, he was Superintendent of the academy. In 1925, he was promoted to brigadier general (USA). In 1927, he retired due to disabilities as a major general. He served on three very influential boards: the Infantry Equipment Board, the Infantry Drill Regulations Board and the Panama Land Defense Board. He also wrote a number of articles, pamphlets and books, among them the *Handbook for Infantry NCOs*; *The Nth Foot in War*; *Military Character, Habit, Deportment, Courtesy and Discipline*; *Self Helps for the Citizen Soldier*; *Military Training for Boys* and *Our Flag and its Message*. In addition to the decorations already mentioned, he was made an Officer of the Legion of Honor (France) and received the Croix de Guerre. At the age of fifty-nine, he died in St. Augustine, Florida, on 3 July 1934. Photo from the USMA Library.

Merch Bradt Stewart

Fredrick W. Stilwell

Fredrick W. Stilwell (no ASN assigned), son of Capt. Richard Stilwell, a Civil War veteran and one of the founding fathers of Scranton, Pennsylvania, and Margaret Snyder Stilwell, a descendant of Gen. Peter Kichlein, commander of troops in the Battle of Long Island during the American Revolution, was born on 14 June 1865 in Scranton, Pennsylvania. During the Spanish-American War, he was a major with the 13th Pennsylvania Infantry, serving in Mt. Gretna, Pennsylvania, at Camp Meade, Maryland, at Camp Alger, Virginia and at Camp McKinstry, Georgia. He entered federal service for World War I on 5 August 1917 and was commissioned a brigadier general (NA) on 29 August 1917. His principal stations were in Philadelphia and at Camp Hancock, outside of Augusta, Georgia. He commanded the 55th Infantry Brigade and was the senior brigadier general in the 28th Division, which he commanded several times. In civil life he was a banker. He was a declared physically unfit for further duty by the general officers physical examinations in the winter of 1917 and 1918, and on 30 January 1918, he resigned and returned to Scranton, where he was treasurer of, and lived in, the local YMCA. He never married, and was last heard from at the age of seventy-nine when he disappeared from Scranton. Anyone who has further knowledge of him, please communicate with the author. Photo courtesy of the Pennsylvania National Guard.

This is NOT F.S.Strong
See inside back cover

Frederick Smith Strong (0-13125), son of Mr. and Mrs. Samuel F. Strong, was born on 12 November 1855 in Paw Paw, southwest of Kalamazoo, Michigan. He entered USMA and graduated number eleven of fifty-two in the class of 1880. George W. Goethals, David J. Rumbough and James W. Benet (all *q.v.*) were three of his classmates. He was commissioned in the Fourth Artillery. On 3 October 1883, he married Alice Marion Johnson, and they had one son, Frederick Smith Strong, Jr. From 1884 to 1888, he was Professor of Military Science and Tactics at Michigan Military Academy. He performed frontier duty from 1890 to 1891, which included service in the Sioux Campaign. From 1892 to 1895, he served again at Michigan Military Academy. During the Spanish-American War, he was a major of United States Volunteers, and from 1902 to 1904, he was Superintendent of Michigan Military Academy. From 1911 to 1913, he was commandant of the Seacoast Branch of the Artillery School. He was promoted to brigadier general (USA) on 4 May 1915, and on 5 August 1917, he was promoted to major general (NA). He commanded the 40th Infantry Division until 20 April 1919, which included service in the AEF. On 17 August 1919, he retired as a brigadier general and lived in San Diego, California, where at the age of seventy-nine, he died on 9 March 1935. The photo, from the National Archives shows him wearing a campaign hat while on reviewing stand at Camp Kearny, California on 30 August 1918.

Samuel Davis Sturgis, Jr. (0-47), son of Samuel Davis Sturgis and Jerusha Hilcox Sturgis, was born on 1 August 1861 in St. Louis, Missouri. After attending Washington University in St. Louis, he entered USMA and graduated number thirteen of thirty-seven in the class of 1884. William L. Sibert and DeRosey Cabell (both *q.v.*) were two of his classmates, as was Isaac Newton Lewis, inventor and manufacturer of the Lewis machine gun. He was commis-

Samuel Davis Sturgis, Jr.

sioned in the First Artillery, and from 1891 to 1896, he was an aide to Gen. Wesley Merritt. On 29 July 1896, he married Bertha Bement, and they had three children: Samuel Davis Sturgis, III, Elizabeth T. Sturgis (Mrs. Hugh A. Murrill) and Robert Bement Sturgis. He was Assistant Adjutant General of the Department of the Pacific and the Eighth Corps in 1898, and he participated in the Campaign against Manila. From January to May 1899, he was Adjutant General, Department of Pinar del Rio, then served as Assistant Adjutant General of the Philippine Division from 1899 to 1901. From 1907 to 1911, he was on the General Staff, and from 1911 to 1913, he was with the Third Field Artillery at Fort Sam Houston, Texas. From 1913 to 1916, he was colonel of the First Field Artillery in Hawaii. In July 1916, he organized the Seventh Field Artillery in San Antonio, Texas. On 1 July 1917, he was promoted to brigadier general (NA). He commanded Camp Funston, then just east of Fort Riley, Kansas, now on the Fort Riley Reservation. In August 1917, he was promoted to major general (NA) and given command of the 87th Division at Camp Pike, Little Rock, Arkansas. He arrived in France on 11 September 1918 and was with the First and 42d Divisions during the Meuse-Argonne offensive. From November 1918 to 12 April 1919, he commanded the 80th Infantry Division. When he returned to the States, he commanded several installations in rapid succession: Camp Gordon, Atlanta, Camp Pike, Arkansas and Camp Sherman, Ohio. From 1921 to 1924, he commanded the Panama Canal Department. His last command, from 1924 until his retirement on 1 August 1925, was of the Third Corps Area, headquartered in Baltimore. At the age of seventy-one, he died in Washington, on 7 March 1933. The photo, from the National Archives, was taken while he was commanding the 87th Division.

Henry Delp Styer (0-13371), son of William Barrett Styer and Katherine Delp Styer, was born on 21 September 1862 in Sellersville, between Philadelphia and Allentown, Pennsylvania. He attended Franklin Marshall College in Lancaster from 1877 to 1879. He taught country school for a year, then entered USMA and graduated number twenty-nine of thirty-seven in the class of 1884. William L. Sibert, DeRosey Cabell and Edwin Burr Babbitt (all *q.v.*) were three of his classmates. He was commissioned in the infantry and performed frontier duty from 1884 to 1892. On 3 June 1891, he married Bessie Wilks in Salt Lake City, Utah, and they had three children: Wilhelm Delp Styer, Charles Wilks Styer and Katherine Elizabeth Styer (Mrs. Adrian M. Hurst). During the Spanish-American War, he spent three years in the Philippines, and he received special mention for his capture of Vicente Prado, a notorious guerrilla leader. He had two separate tours as Professor of Military Science and Tactics at the Utah Agricultural College, from 1892 to 1896 and from 1903 to 1906. He returned to the Philippines until 1909, when he was given command of Fort Niagara, New York. After graduating from the Army War College, he was made Senior Instructor and Inspector of the New Jersey National Guard. In 1918, he was promoted to brigadier general (NA) and commanded the 181st Infantry Brigade at Camp (now Fort) Lewis, Washington. In August 1918, he commanded the AEF in Siberia. In April 1919, he retired as a colonel, his permanent rank. He was recalled to active duty, then retired again in 1922. After extensive travel, he homesteaded forty acres near Winterhaven, Florida. In 1932, he moved to Coronado, California, where he died at the age of eighty-one, on 11 May 1944. The photo, from the National Archives shows him at Camp Lewis, Washington.

Henry Delp Styer

Charles Pelot Summerall

Charles Pelot Summerall (0-21), son of Elhanan Bryant Summerall and Margaret Pelot Summerall, was born on 4 March 1867 in Lake City, Florida. He graduated from Porter Military Academy in Charleston, South Carolina, then entered USMA and graduated number twenty of sixty-two in the class of 1892. George Blakely and James Ancil Shipton (both *q.v.*) were two of his classmates. He was commissioned in the infantry, and the following year, he transferred to the artillery. During the Spanish-American War, he was an aide to Gen. William M. Graham, commander of the Second Corps, and then was an aide to Gen. Alexander C. M. Pennington, commanding the Department of the Gulf. From 1899 to 1901, he was in the Philippines, where he earned his first Silver Star Commendation. He served in the China Relief Expedition of 1900 to 1901, for which he received two more Silver Star Commendations. On 14 August 1901, he married Laura Mordecai, and they had one son, Charles P. Summerall, Jr., who in 1932 was a first lieutenant in the 16th Field Artillery. He was sent to Alaska to locate and organize Fort William H. Seward. From 1905 to 1911, he was in the Tactics Department at West Point, and from 1912 to 1917, he served in the Militia Bureau, and later, in the National Guard. He was a member of the United States Military Mission to England and France from May to July 1917. He was promoted to brigadier general (NA) in 1917 and commanded the 67th Field Artillery Brigade, and later, the First Field Artillery Brigade. He was promoted to major general (NA) on 26 June 1918 and commanded the First Infantry Division from 11 July to 15 October 1918. On 12 October 1918, he was given command of the Fifth Corps, until 5 March 1919. From 2 to 11 May 1919, he commanded the Forth Corps. For his performance of duty in the divisional and corps commands, he received both the Distinguished Service Cross and the Distinguished Service Medal. During July and August 1919, he was a member of the Interallied Commission in Fiume, Italy, and he was on duty with the American Commission to negotiate peace until 31 August 1919. He was Chief of Staff (USA) from 21 November 1926 until 20 November 1930, for which service he was given his four star rank. In 1931, he retired and became president of the Citadel in Charleston, South Carolina, which, along with the Virginia Military Institute, has furnished a great number of fine regular officers. After the war, he collected many honorary degrees including an LL.D. from Hobart College in 1921, one from Williams College in 1927, one from the College of Charleston in 1935, one from Brown University in 1936, a Doctor of Military Science degree from Pennsylvania Military College in 1921 and another from the Citadel in 1954. He was a great battle leader and received a number of battle, campaign and merit medals . He was very easy to spot in a group, as he always wore a white collar insert under his blouse collar, and his overseas cap had an unusually high peak, fore and aft, not usual to an American uniform. After retiring from the Citadel, he lived in Aiken, South Carolina. At the age of eighty-nine, he died in Washington, on 14 May 1955. Photo courtesy of *The Assembly,* Association of Graduates, USMA.

Archibald Henry Sunderland (0-1102) was born on 2 September 1876 on a farm near Delavan, Illinois. He attended the University of Illinois, then entered USMA and graduated number twenty-four of fifty-four in the class of 1900. Augustine McIntyre and Robert E. Wood (both *q.v.*) were two of his classmates. He was commissioned in the artillery and sent to the Columbus Barracks, then served in Manila beginning January 1901. He served with a mountain battery in Pershing's campaign against the Moros. In 1903, he returned to the States and served in the field artillery at Fort Riley, Kansas, after which he taught

Archibald Henry Sunderland

mathematics in West Point for four years. He was intensely interested in both math and the academy. He eventually transferred to the Coast Artillery. In 1910, he married Rosaline Morton Brand in Worchester, Massachusetts, and they went as a newly married couple to Fort Ward, Bainbridge Island, Washington. They had a daughter, Jane (wife of Lt. Col. Harold Broudy, USA) and a son, Morton, (called John Henry) (USN). In 1911, they were moved to Fort Monroe, Virginia, which was the first of many tours there. In 1914, he was part of an expedition to rescue American tourists stranded in Europe. He remained in Holland as military attaché and worked with the Belgian Relief Group. During World War I, he was sent to France as Director of the Heavy Artillery School in Mailly, France. When he returned to the States, he became the first commander of Fort Eustis, Virginia. He went from major (RA) to lieutenant colonel (NA) to brigadier general (NA) on 1 October 1918, then back to major (RA), all within nine months. He ran the Coast Artillery Training School from 1918 to 1919, for which he received the Distinguished Service Medal. On his second tour in Manila, from 1922 to 1924, he served in the Japanese Earthquake Relief Expedition. From 1925 to 1929, he served at Forts Eustis and Monroe, then had charge of the harbor defenses of Puget Sound. From 1930 to 1932, he was on the staff of the Hawaiian Department, and served as Chief of Staff. He returned to Fort Monroe in 1932, then served as president of the Coast Artillery Board until 1936, when he became Chief of Coast Artillery as a major general. In 1940, he was retired due to age. He lived in Hampton, Virginia. In December 1960, his wife died. At the age of eighty-six, he died in Annapolis, Maryland, on 31 October 1963. He was a beloved gentleman, an excellent officer and a kind father. Photo courtesy of *The Assembly*, Association of Graduates, USMA.

Eldridge LeRoy Sweetser

Eldridge LeRoy Sweetser (ASN unknown), son of Eldridge L. Sweetser and Hannah Simson Sweetser, was born on 25 September 1869 in Medford, Massachusetts. He attended public school in Everett, graduated from the Chauncey Hall School for Boys in Boston and in 1897, graduated from the Boston University Law School. He enlisted in the Massachusetts Militia in Malden on 20 June 1898. He was a first sergeant at the age of twenty-seven and served in Company L, Fifth Massachusetts Infantry. He was mustered into federal service on 1 July 1898 and was commissioned a second lieutenant on 20 October 1898. On 31 October 1899, he married Maude E. Pettinghill of Everett, and they had one son, Howard R. Sweetser. During the Mexican Punitive Expedition, he served on the Mexican border. He returned to Boston with his unit on 7

November 1916. He stayed there until they were mustered out on 24 November, commanding the Second Brigade of Massachusetts troops. From 17 March to 24 July 1917, he was the Adjutant General of Massachusetts. On 25 July 1917, he was promoted to brigadier general (NA) and served with the 27th Division during World War I. As a civilian, he was a banker and a judge. At the age of eighty-one, he died at his home in Everett, on 26 January 1951. Photo from the National Archives.

Eben Swift, Jr. (0-13115), son of Dr. Ebenezer Swift (USA) and Sarah Capers Swift, was born on 11 May 1854 at Fort Chadbourne, Texas. He attended Racine College in Wisconsin, Washington University in St. Louis, Missouri and Dickinson College in Carlisle, Pennsylvania, then entered USMA and graduated number twenty-nine of forty-eight in the class of 1876. James Parker and Hugh L. Scott (both *q.v.*) were two of his classmates. He was commissioned in the 14th Infantry, then transferred and was assigned to the Fifth Cavalry the following month. He performed frontier duty from 1876 to 1893. From 1887 to 1897, he was an aide to Gen. Wesley Merritt. During this time, in May 1880, he married Suzanna Palmer, and they had five children: Eben Swift, III, Innis Palmer Swift (last commanding general of a horse cavalry division, USA), Wesley Merritt Swift, Clara Swift (Mrs. Humphrey) and Katherine Swift (Mrs. McKinney). During the late Indian Wars, he served against the Sioux, Cheyennes, Bannocks and Utes. He served in Cuba, Puerto Rico and in the Philippines against the Moros. During the Spanish-American War, he was colonel of the Fourth Illinois Volunteer Infantry, from 1898 to 1899. He graduated from the Army War College in 1907 and taught at the Infantry and Cavalry School, as well as serving as commandant of the command and General Staff school at Fort Leavenworth, Kansas from August to October 1916. On 30 September 1916, he was promoted to brigadier general (USA). He was Chief of Staff of the Western Department, and later commanded the Second Cavalry Brigade in Mexico from 1916 to 1917. He commanded the cavalry division at Fort Bliss, Texas, and in 1917, he both commanded Camp Gordon Augusta, Georgia and organized and commanded the 82d Infantry Division. He was with the AEF in France until February 1918, then commanded the United States Forces in Italy and at the same time was chief of the American Military Mission to Italy. He retired as a brigadier general in the summer of 1918, and his two-star rank was restored in June 1930. At the age of eighty-three, he died in

Eben Swift, Jr.

Washington, D.C., on 25 April 1938. Photo from the Annual Report, Association of Graduates, USMA.

Harry Taylor

Harry Taylor (0-65), son of John Franklin Taylor and Lydia Taylor, was born on 26 June 1862 in Tilton, New Hampshire. He entered USMA and graduated number six of thirty-seven in the class of 1884. William L. Sibert, DeRosey Cabell and Samuel D. Sturgis (all *q.v.*) were three of his classmates. He was commissioned in the Corps of Engineers and served in Washington and Oregon, performing rivers and harbors duty on the Columbia River. He graduated from the Engineer School of Application in 1887, and from 1891 to 1896, he worked on the defenses of Puget Sound. On 30 October 1901, he married Adele Austin Yates. During 1903 and 1904, he was Engineer Officer for the Department of Luzon in the Philippines. He commanded the Third Engineer Battalion and was involved in the construction of fortifications. From 1906 to 1991, he was in charge of defenses on the Long Island Sound, and from 1911 to 1916, he was assistant to the Chief of Engineers (USA). In 1916 and 1917, he was on Governor's Island, New York, in charge of all of the military engineering in the state. During 1917 and 1918, he was Chief Engineer of the AEF in France. On 5 August 1917, he was promoted to brigadier general (NA), and in September, he was made assistant to the Chief of Engineers (USA). He built utilities and facilities for the Service of Supply, which earned him a Distinguished Service Medal. From 1924 until his retirement in 1926, he was the Chief of Engineers as a major general. In addition to the decoration already mentioned, he was made a Commander of the Legion of Honor (France). In retirement, he lived in Washington, D.C., where at the age of sixty-seven, he died on 27 January 1930. Photo courtesy of the National Archives.

William Sidney Thayer, M.D. (ASN unknown), son of James B. Thayer and Sophia Ripley Thayer, was born on 23 June 1862 in Milton, Massachusetts. His brother, Ezra R. Thayer, was dean of Harvard Law School from 1910 to 1915. He graduated from Harvard with an A.B. in 1885 and from Harvard Medical School in 1889. He was Phi Beta Kappa and did postgraduate study in Berlin and Vienna. His contributions to military medicine were notable indeed and he managed quite a reputation before returning. He also served on the staff of Johns-Hopkins Hospital and University in Baltimore under Dr. William

Osler. In 1901, he married Susan C. Read of Charleston, South Carolina. He was a visiting physician at Johns-Hopkins Hospital, and later became both Professor of Medicine and Physician in Chief there. He served two terms as a member of the Board of Overseers of Harvard University, and he was a member of the Board of Trustees of the Carnegie Institute in Washington. From June 1917 to January 1918, he was Deputy Commander of the Red Cross Mission to Russia as a major. His wife died while he was there. He joined the Medical Corps in 1918 as a major, and on 1 October 1918, he was promoted to brigadier general (ORC). He was Chief Consultant for the Medical Services of the AEF. Thayer General Hospital in Nashville was named after him. He made numerous contributions to the study of the circulatory system, and he investigated leukemia, typhoid and malaria. He was awarded the Red Cross of Russia in 1918 and the Distinguished Service Medal, and he was made a Commander of the Legion of Honor (France). He wrote and lectured on the subject of malaria. His home was in Baltimore, Maryland, where at the age of sixty-eight, he died on 10 December 1932. He had a unique personality; he was simple, courteous, just and tolerant, and was a man of integrity. Photo courtesy of Johns-Hopkins.

William Sidney Thayer, M.D.

John Taliaferro Thompson

John Taliaferro Thompson (0-13227), son of Mr. and Mrs. James Thompson, was born on 30 December 1860 in Newport, Kentucky. His mother was related to the Monroe, Madison, Harrison and Taylor families of Virginia. He attended Indiana University for two years, then entered USMA, and graduated number eleven of thirty-seven in the class of 1882. Henry T. Allen and Adelbert Cronkhite (both *q.v.*) were two of his classmates. On 27 July 1882, he married Juliet Estelle Hagans, daughter of Judge Marcellus B. Hagans of Cincinnati, Ohio, and they had one son, Marcellus Hagans Thompson, who worked with his father both in the development of the Tommy Gun (Thompson Machine Gun) and in the arms business. He was commissioned in the Second Artillery, and two years later took the torpedo course in the Engineer School in Willet's Point (now Fort Totten), New York. In 1890, he graduated from the Artillery School. From 1896 to 1898, he was senior instructor in ordnance and gunnery at USMA. During the Spanish-American War, he was a lieutenant colonel of volunteers, Chief Ordnance Officer, Forth Army Corps and commanded a depot in Tampa, Florida. He served for many years at both the Springfield and Rock Island arsenals, and was assistant to the Chief of Ordnance in Washington, sometimes serving as acting Chief of Ordnance. In 1914, he retired as a colonel to take an executive position with the Remington Arms Company. In Eddystone, Pennsylvania, he designed and built the largest small arms plant in the world to make rifles for the Russians and the British. During World War I, he returned to duty with ordnance, and on 5 August 1917, he was promoted to brigadier general (NA). He was personally responsible for the M-1917 version of the M-1903 Springfield rifle, and produced more rifles at less cost than any of the Allies. He held over twenty patents, mostly for small arms. He and his son developed the Thompson submachine gun, which was adopted by the United States Army. At the age of seventy-nine, he died in Great Neck, Long Island, New York, on 21 June 1940. He was modest, friendly, pleasant and humorous. Photo courtesy of Special Collections, USMA Library.

Henry Davis Todd, Jr. (0-88), son of Henry Davis Todd, a naval officer and mathematician, and Flora Johnson Todd, was born on 29 August 1866 in Claverick, near Hudson, New York. He attended private schools and St. John's College in Annapolis, Maryland, then graduated in 1886 from the University of Pennsylvania with a B.S. He entered USMA and graduated number seven of fifty-four in the class of 1890. Fred W. Sladen, Edgar Jadwin and James A. Ryan (all *q.v.*) were three of his classmates. He was commissioned in the artillery and served at Washington Barracks in Key West, Florida and at Fort McPherson, Georgia. From 1894 to 1898, he was an instructor in ordnance and gunnery in West Point. During this period, he married Emma N. Green, and they had three children: Henry P. Todd, Harriet S. Todd (Mrs. William Cooper Foote) and Harrison Tyler Todd. During the Spanish-American War, he was on recruiting duty, then served in Battery K, Seventh Artillery both in Florida and at Fort Schuyler, New York. From 1900 to 1901, he was a student at the Artillery School at Fort Monroe, Virginia. After a year of troop duty, he went to the School of Submarine Defense at Fort Totten, New York, from which he graduated in 1903. From 1903 to 1908, he was adjutant of the Naragansett Bay Artillery District, stationed in Rhode Island. From 1905 to 1907, he was artillery engineer for the Boston Artillery District. In 1908, he graduated from the Army War College, then

Henry Davis Todd, Jr.

served for four years with the General Staff as secretary of the Army War College and in the G-2 section in Manila. He worked on the coastal defenses of the New England coast until 1915, when he returned to Fort Monroe, where he was editor and manager of the Coast Artillery Journal. On 5 August 1917, he was promoted to brigadier general (NA), then served on the Machine Gun Board, which recommended the adoption of the Browning water-cooled machine gun. From 19 September to 7 December 1917, he commanded the 33d Infantry Division as a brigadier general. He organized and trained the 58th Field Artillery Brigade at Camp Logan, Texas, and in May 1918, he took this unit to France. For his service in France, he was awarded the Distinguished Service Medal, three Silver Star Commendations and a Purple Heart. He commanded the divisional artillery of the First Infantry Division, which included his own 58th Field Artillery Brigade, the 76th Field Artillery Regiment and a battalion of the Forty-fourth Coast Artillery, likely the most artillery in the field under one commander. After the Armistice, they were billeted in Luxembourg, and in May 1919, he returned the 58th Field Artillery Brigade to Camp Grant, Illinois, where they were demobilized. In 1920, he graduated again from the Army War College. He was sent to the Naval War College in Newport, Rhode Island, but this order was canceled due to his promotion to brigadier general (USA) and his assignment to command the 31st Coast Artillery Brigade at Camp Lewis, Washington. From 1921 to 1923, he was in the Philippines, and when he returned to the States, he commanded the Ninth Coast Artillery District in San Francisco, California. From 1926 to 1929, he was on Oahu, Hawaii. In 1927, during this time, he was promoted to major general (USA). During 1929 and 1930, he was commandant of the Seacoast Branch of the Artillery School at Fort Monroe, Virginia. From this post, he retired. In 1920, the University of Pennsylvania granted him a master's degree. At the age of ninety-seven, he died in Washington, D.C., on 22 January 1964. Photo courtesy of *The Assembly*, Association of Graduates, USMA.

Orval Pool Townshend

Orval Pool Townshend (0-862), son of Richard W. Townshend, a United States Congressman from Illinois, and Augusta Pool Townshend, was born in 1872 on the family property in Pool Hill, McLeansboro, Illinois. He attended the New York Military Academy, then entered the service as captain of Company B, Ninth Illinois Infantry. He married Florence Robinson, and they had a daughter, who married and lived in Texas. At the close of the Spanish-American War, he was sent to Puerto Rico to command British West Indian troops. In 1916, he was promoted to lieutenant colonel, and in 1918, he commanded the Puerto Rican military. On 1 October 1918, he was promoted to brigadier general (NA), at the age of forty-six. He was called an adopted son of Puerto Rico by act of the Puerto Rican legislature. Seventy-two municipalities on the island recorded their resolutions of thanks to him. During World War I, he commanded the 66th Infantry in Panama. This was the same 66th Light Infantry (tanks) that was at Fort Meade in the early 1930s. From 1920 to 1924, he was instructor of the Maryland National Guard, and from 1924 to 1926, he was assistant to the Chief, Bureau of Insular Affairs, in the War Department, in charge of civil affairs of the Philippines and Puerto Rico. In 1928, at the age of fifty-six, he retired and lived in Shawneetown, Illinois. He was a Mason, and was very active in local civil affairs. At the age of sixty-two, he died very peacefully at home, on 12 May 1934. He was buried in Westwood Cemetery in Shawneetown. Photo courtesy of the National Archives.

Clarence Page Townsley

Clarence Page Townsley (0-13122), son of Elias Page Townsley and Louisa Thompson Townsley, was born on 25 September 1855 in DeKalb, New York. He graduated from New York State Normal School in Potsdam in 1872, then entered USMA and graduated number fourteen of fifty-three in the class of 1881. Henry and Harry Hodges, Joseph T. Dickman and Andrew S. Rowan (all *q.v.*) were four of his classmates. He was commissioned in the Fourth Artillery. He graduated from the artillery school at Fort Monroe in 1884, then from the Torpedo School in Willet's Point, New York in 1885. On 7 January 1891, he married Marian Howland, and they had two girls and a boy: Helen Howland Townsley, Marian Page Townsley and Clarence P. Townsley, Jr. He was an professor at USMA from 1885 to 1888. During the Spanish-American War, he served as a major of volunteers and as Chief Ordnance Officer of Volunteers. He served on the staff of the Chief of Artillery, and was Chief Ordnance Officer in Havana. From 1909, he was commandant of the Coast Artillery School at Fort Monroe, Virginia, until 1911, when he was sent to command the Second Provisional Coast Artillery Regiment in Texas. From 1912 to 1916, he was superintendent of USMA. During this period, in 1913, he received a doctorate in science from Union College. On 1 July 1916, he was promoted to brigadier general (USA), and he was promoted to major general (NA) on 5 August 1917. From 13 October 1917, he commanded the 30th Infantry Division. On 29 November 1918, he retired as a brigadier general and lived in Washington, D.C. At the age of seventy-one, he died on 28 December 1926. The photo, from the National Archives, was taken at Camp Sevier, Greensville, South Carolina.

Peter Edward Traub

Peter Edward Traub (0-159) was born on 15 October 1864 in New York City. He entered USMA and graduated number thirty-one of seventy-seven in the class of 1886. John J. Pershing, Mason M. Patrick, Charles T. Menoher and Edward McCaskey(all *q.v.*) were four of his classmates. He was commissioned in the First Cavalry and performed frontier duty from 1886 to 1891, serving against the Crow and Sioux Indians. He was an instructor and assistant professor in the Foreign Languages Department at USMA from 1892 to 1898. During the Spanish-American War, he served with his unit, Troop G of the First Cavalry, in Las Guasimas, Cuba, at the Battle of San Juan and at the siege of Santiago. He was recommended for promotions to captain and major. He also served in the Sanitary Corps, for which he received a Silver Star Commendation. In Puerto Rico in 1899, he was an aide to Gen. Guy V. Henry. During 1900 and 1901, he was Adjutant General of the Department of Luzon in the Philippines. From 1902 to 1904, he again headed the Foreign Languages Department at USMA. From 1904 to 1907, he was in the Army Staff College, but spent most of his time on confidential missions to foreign countries. He was a member of the mission that was invited by Kaiser Wilhelm II to witness the German Army Maneuvers in Breslau in 1906. From 1907 to 1911, he was Associate Professor of Modern Languages at USMA. From 1914 to 1917, he campaigned against the Moros in the Philippines. He was promoted to brigadier general (NA) on 5 August 1917 and to major general (NA) on 15 June 1918. As a brigadier general, he commanded the 26th Infantry Division from 12 to 22 October 1917, from 31 October to 11 November 1917 and from 25 November to 1 December 1917. As a major general, he commanded the 35th Infantry Division from 2 to 25 November 1918 and from 7 to 27 December 1918. He also commanded the 41st Infantry Division from 28 December 1918 until its inactivation at Camp Pike, Arkansas in June 1919. After the war, he reverted to his rank of colonel. On 19 April 1928, he was promoted to brigadier general (USA), and on 15 October of that same year, he retired as a brigadier general and lived in Augusta, Georgia. In 1930, his two-star rank was restored. In addition to the decorations already mentioned and two Purple Hearts, he was made a Commander of the Legion of Honor (France) and received the Croix de Guerre with palm. At the age of ninety-one, he died in Manchester, New Hampshire, on 27 September 1956. Photo from Special Collections, USMA Library.

Charles Gould Treat (0-41), son of Joseph Bradford Treat and Priscilla Jane Gould Treat, was born on 30 December 1859 in Orono, Maine. He entered

USMA and graduated number thirteen of thirty-seven in the class of 1882. Adelbert Cronkhite and Henry T. Allen (both *q.v.*) were two of his classmates. He was commissioned in the Fifth Artillery. He married Margaret Louise Cornell, and they had two daughters: one married Brig. Gen. A. V. Arnold, and the other became Mrs. A. B. Butler of Tulsa, Oklahoma. In 1894, he served as an aide to Gen. O. O. Howard. During the Spanish-American War, he was a major of volunteers, after which he was a captain in the Seventh Artillery. During 1900 and 1901, he was Senior Instructor in Artillery in West Point, and from 1901 to 1905, he served as Commandant of Cadets. In 1911, he graduated from the Army War College. On 18 October 1916, he was promoted to brigadier general (USA). On 5 August 1917, he was promoted to major general (NA). He commanded Camp Sheridan in Montgomery, Alabama, and from there he was sent to the Western Department in San Francisco, California. He was chief of the American Military Mission to Italy from June 1918 to May 1919, for which he received the Distinguished Service Medal. He also commanded Base Section Number Eight, and the AEF in Italy. After the war, he was sent to Camp Sherman, Ohio, then to the Philippines in 1920. That same year, his wife died. Later, he married Edith Pennington. On 27 April 1922, he retired as a brigadier general. He was an earnest student; he graduated from the Engineer School and the Army War College, and he also studied the British forces in France and submitted a valuable report with recommendations. He was the father of polo in the army, and through his efforts the War Department began to value polo horsemanship. He was active in maintaining the foxhounds at Fort Riley, Kansas. He represented the War Department in the eighth Olympics in Paris in 1924. He was an enthusiastic golfer, noted for carrying only three clubs and for putting with one hand. His two-star rank was restored in 1930. At the age of eighty-one, he died in Washington, D.C., on 11 October 1941. No man had more or better friends; his cheerful and kindly character opened many doors to him. His tact and sincerity were a great asset to the army in its delicate contacts with the armies of Europe. Photo from *The Assembly*, Association of Graduates, USMA.

Charles Gould Treat

Guy Eastman Tripp (ASN unknown), son of Alonzo R. Tripp, a lawyer, and Abbie Yeaton Tripp, was born on 22 April 1865 in Wells, Maine. He attended Berwick Academy for two years and graduated in 1882. In 1883, at the age of eighteen, he worked for the Eastern Railway and rose rapidly to a position of authority. On 25 August 1887, he married Elaine O'Connell of Salem, Massachusetts, and they had three daughters: Mary A. Tripp (Mrs. Clifford

Guy Eastman Tripp

Hemphill of New York), Olive A. Tripp (Mrs. Nelson B. Gatch of Greenwich, Connecticut) and Adah Tripp (Mrs. Fischer of Trenton, New Jersey). In 1890, he worked with Thompson-Houston Electric Company, electrifying a railroad near Boston, Massachusetts. He was a storekeeper, then a traveling auditor. In 1897, he went to work for Stone and Webster, construction engineers and operators of public utilities. He became vice president, and he made an analytical study of the entire field of public utilities. He was traveling auditor, an accountant and an investigator. In January 1912, he became Chairman of the Board of Westinghouse Electric and Manufacturing Company, and he maintained that position through his wartime military service, until he died. At the request of the Ordnance Department, he was commissioned a major of ordnance and served as Chief of the Production Division. Eight months later, on 8 August 1918, he was promoted to brigadier general (NA) and served as assistant to the Chief of Ordnance. After the Armistice, President Wilson personally awarded him the Distinguished Service Medal "for particularly meritorious service." In November 1918, he returned to civil life, but continued to cooperate with the War Department. In 1924, he was awarded an LL.B. by Bates College in Lewistown, Maine, and that same year, he published *Superpower as an Aid to Progress*. In 1923 and 1924, he traveled around the world, particularly as part of the international development of Westinghouse. In Japan, he was made an Officer of the Order of the Sacred Treasure, Second Class, which was the highest award they could give to a private citizen. In 1926, he published another book, *Electric Development as an Aide to Agriculture*. He was a director of twenty-five companies, including RCA, American Sugar Refining Company and Chase National Bank. He had an operation in New York City at the age of sixty-two for intestinal complications and died shortly thereafter, on 14 June 1927. There was a full-page picture of him and an article on page thirty-six of *American Magazine*, November 1919. Photo courtesy of Westinghouse Electric.

Alexander MacKinzie Tuthill (0-257735), son of William H. Tuthill and Christina MacKinzie Tuthill, was born on 22 September 1871 in South Lebanon, Sullivan County, New York. When he was young, his family moved to Los Angeles, California. He graduated from the medical school of the University of Southern California in 1895. In 1896, he married May E. Heimann of Los Angeles, they had two daughters, Dorothy (Mrs. Lange of Indianapolis) and Christine (Mrs. Warbasse). He practiced in Los Angeles until 1896, when he went to Morenci, Arizona as an assistant surgeon for the Detroit Copper

Alexander MacKinzie Tuthill

Company, where he worked until 1916. He was a private in the California National Guard, and when he went to Morenci, he organized Troop A, Arizona Guard Cavalry, and was captain. In August 1910, Arizona dropped the cavalry troop and organized the First Arizona Infantry with Tuthill as colonel. He commanded this regiment in Naco, Arizona on the Mexican border in 1916 and 1917. On 5 August 1917, he was promoted to brigadier general (NA) and was given command of the 79th Infantry Brigade, 40th Division (AEF). From August 1918 to March 1919, he was overseas. He was one of the few National Guard Line brigadiers who continued to command his unit throughout the war. He was Adjutant General of Arizona for many years, and commanded the 45th Division after Gen. Roy Hoffman (*q.v.*) retired. The Arizona National Guard permanent training camp in Flagstaff, Fort Tuthill, is named after him. He practiced medicine until 1952, when he was relieved of his National Guard duties, was promoted to lieutenant general and was made State Director of Selective Service. At about this time, Mrs. Tuthill died after a long illness. At the age of eighty-six, he died on 25 May 1958, still State Director of Selective Service. Photo courtesy of the Arizona National Guard.

Lawrence Davis Tyson

Lawrence Davis Tyson (no ASN assigned), son of Richard Tyson and Margaret Louise Turnage Tyson, was born on 4 July 1861 in Greenville, North Carolina. He received an LL.B. from the University of Tennessee, then entered USMA and graduated number fifty-one of fifty-two in the class of 1883. George H. Cameron and Tyree Rodes Rivers (both *q.v.*) were two of his classmates. He was commissioned and sent to the Ninth Infantry. Several years later, on 10 February 1886, he married Bettie Humes McGhee. He was promoted to first lieutenant on 15 October 1889, and he was Professor of Military Science and Tactics at the University of Tennessee from 1891 to 1895. That same year, he was admitted to the bar of Tennessee. He resigned from the regular army on 15 April 1896 and became president of the Poplar Creek Coal and Iron Company, president of the East Tennessee Coal and Iron Company, president of the Coal Creek Mining and Manufacturing Company and president of and publisher for the Knoxville Sentinel Company. On 20 May 1898, President McKinley appointed him colonel of the Sixth United States Volunteer Infantry. He served in Puerto Rico during the Spanish-American War, and was mustered out on 15 March 1899. He was promptly promoted to brigadier general and Inspector General on the staff of the governor of Tennessee. He was a member of the Tennessee House of Representatives and Speaker of the House. In 1908, he was a delegate-at-large to the Democratic national convention. He was a candidate for the Senate in 1913, and later won the election for the 1925-to-1931 term. He was promoted to brigadier general (NA) on 5 August 1917 and was appointed commanding general of the 59th Infantry Brigade, which he commanded with the British in Ypres and Lys Canal in the Somme sector. He broke through the Hindenburg line in Bellincourt and Nauroy, for which he received the Distinguished Service Medal. He was discharged on 15 April 1919. He was an Episcopalian, and he lived in Knoxville. At the age of sixty-eight, he died in Pennsylvania, on 24 August 1929. Photo from the National Archives.

LaRoy Sunderland Upton

LaRoy Sunderland Upton (0-334), son of Capt. John B. Upton (USA) and Julia Sherman Upton, was born on 8 October 1869 in Decatur, Michigan. He entered USMA and graduated number thirty-eight of sixty-five in the class of 1891. John L. Hines (*q.v.*) was one of his classmates. He was commissioned in the infantry and served at various posts in New York until 1898, when he rejoined his regiment in Montauk Point, Long Island, New York. From 1899 to 1902, he was the customs collector in Tunas de Zaza and Manzanilla, Cuba. On 4 September 1902, he married Agnes Millar. He spent the next six years in the Philippines. He was Provost Marshal in New York during 1911 and 1912, and from 1912 to 1913, he was on duty at the Panama Canal. After graduating from the Army School of the Line at Fort Leavenworth, Kansas, he returned to Panama, then was sent north to the Mexican border, to Eagle Pass, Texas. From 26 June 1917 to 14 May 1919, he served with the AEF in France as commanding officer of the Ninth Infantry, and after his promotion to brigadier general (NA) on 8 August 1918, as commander of the 57th Infantry Brigade. For this service he received the Distinguished Service Cross and the Distinguished Service Medal, the Croix de Guerre with three palms (France), the War Cross for Merit (Italy) and La Soledaridad (Panama), and he was made a Companion of the Order of St. Michael and St. George (Britain) and an Officer of the Legion of Honor (France). He was promoted to brigadier general (USA) in 1923. At the age of fifty-six, he died in Hawaii, on 1 March 1927. Photo courtesy of the New Jersey State Archives.

Cornelius Vanderbilt III

Cornelius Vanderbilt III (ASN unknown), son of Cornelius Vanderbilt II and Alice Claypoole Gwynne Vanderbilt, was born in 1873 in New York City. He was the grandson of William Henry Vanderbilt and the great grandson of Commodore Vanderbilt (1794 to 1877), founder of the family fortune. He graduated from Yale with an A.B. in 1895, and he received a Ph.D. and an M.E. from Yale in 1898. He married Grace Wilson, daughter of the financier Richard T. Wilson, and they had two children, Cornelius IV and Grace. He designed a practical locomotive tender, i.e. a coal car, and was involved with the Illinois Central Railroad, for which Abraham Lincoln had once been attorney. In 1917, he was a colonel commanding the 102nd Engineers (New York National Guard). He was promoted to brigadier general (NA) on 8 July 1918. After World War I, he served as a brigadier general (ORC). He lived at 650 Fifth Avenue in New York City, and he maintained offices at 32 Nassau Street. At the age of sixty-eight, he died in New York City, on 2 March 1942. The photo, courtesy of the National Archives, was taken when he was stationed at Camp (now Fort) Lewis, Washington.

Robert Campbell Van Vliet (0-13340) was born on 22 August 1857 in Kansas. He entered USMA with the class of 1879, but only studied there from July to December 1875. He was commissioned in the Tenth Infantry in December 1876 and performed frontier duty. By 3 March 1911, he was colonel of the 25th Infantry. On 30 August 1913, he was given command of the Fourth Infantry. During 1916 and 1917, he served on the Mexican border. On 5 August 1917, he was promoted to brigadier general (NA) and commanded the 173rd Infantry Brigade at Camp Pike, Arkansas. He received both the Silver Star and the

Robert Campbell Van Vliet

Purple Heart. On 8 June 1918, he retired as a colonel. In June 1930, his rank of brigadier general was restored. In 1932, he lived in Shrewsbury, New Jersey. At the age of eighty-six, he died in Florida, on 27 October 1943. The photo, from the National Archives, was taken when he was a captain during the Spanish-American War.

Cecil Crawley Vaughan, Jr.

Cecil Crawley Vaughan, Jr. (ASN unknown) was born on 8 July 1868 in Southampton County, Virginia. His forebears had served honorably in the American Revolution, the War of 1812 and the Civil War. He attended both public and private schools before going to Randolph Macon, from which he graduated in 1886. His father founded a bank in Franklin, which he managed after his father's death. In 1888, he married Katherine Keith of Athens, Tennessee, and they had three daughters and a son. In 1892, he joined the Fourth Virginia Volunteer Infantry as an enlisted man, and in four years, he was promoted to first lieutenant, Company One, Fourth Virginia Infantry. He served during the Spanish-American War, but did not go to Cuba. Several of his commissions were signed by Claude A. Swanson, then governor of Virginia, but later Franklin Delano Roosevelt's Secretary of the Navy. By 1900, he was a colonel, 71st Virginia Volunteer Infantry, and by 1907, he was promoted to brigadier general commanding the First Brigade, Virginia Volunteers. He was promoted to brigadier general (NA) on 22 August 1917, and he commanded the Virginia brigade that later became part of the 29th Division. He also commanded the 54th Depot Brigade. He failed the physical examination required by General Pershing in 1917 and 1918, and so was honorably discharged from the National Army. Back in Virginia, he was promoted to major general and was retained by the Virginia National Guard. He was a pioneer for good roads in Virginia and was interested in automobiles. From 1921 until his death, he was a member of the Virginia State Senate. He was a Methodist and an Odd Fellow, and was encouraged to run for governor of Virginia, but showed no interest in it. At the age of sixty, he died on 21 March 1929. Photo courtesy of his grandson, Mr. C. A. Cutchins III, of Norfolk, Virginia.

Charles Edward Vollrath (no ASN assigned), son of Charles Vollrath and Eva E. Hocker Vollrath, was born on 28 June 1858 in Bucyrus, Ohio. He learned

Charles Edward Vollrath

the cabinetmaker's trade before graduating from Bucyrus High School, then went on to attend Wittenberg College in Springfield, Ohio. He graduated from Princeton in 1883 with an A.B. degree and received an A.M. in 1886. On 30 April 1884, he enlisted as a private, Company A of the Eighth Ohio Infantry. By 28 June 1884, he was promoted to sergeant major. In 1885, he was admitted to the Ohio Bar, and he practiced in Bucyrus. By 30 June 1886, he was captain of Company A. On 27 June 1888, he married Millie Wise, and they had six children: Jeanne, Edna, Charles, Victor, Carol and Edward. During the Spanish-American War, he served as a major in the Eighth Ohio Infantry in Santiago. As a colonel in 1899, he commanded "McKinley's own," men from Crawford and Stark Counties, Ohio, and they went to Cuba. He was the first man from Ohio to set foot on Cuban soil, and he was present at the surrender of Santiago. The Bucyrus Chamber of Commerce presented him with a horse named Bucyrus, which he rode as a colonel commanding the Eighth Ohio Infantry on the Mexican border in 1916. He returned to active duty for World War I on 15 July 1917. On 5 August 1917, he was promoted to brigadier general (NA) and commanded the 66th Depot Brigade, the 66th Artillery Brigade and the 41st Infantry Division. He commanded the 82d Infantry Brigade (AEF). He was the only Ohio National Guard officer to serve with the rank of brigadier general throughout the war. He was made a commander of the Order of the Black Star (France), a rather unusual decoration. On 1 March 1919, he was honorably discharged from the National Army and resumed his law practice in Bucyrus. He was a Republican, and he belonged to the English Lutheran Church. At the age of seventy-two, he died, on 21 January 1931. He was buried with full military honors in Oakwood Cemetery in Bucyrus two days later. Photo courtesy of William H. Vollrath, and information from his granddaughter, Mrs. Edna V. Carmean of Bucyrus, Ohio.

Lutz Wahl (0-340) was born on 2 November 1869 in Milwaukee, Wisconsin. He entered USMA and graduated number forty-three of sixty-five in the class of 1891. John L. Hines (*q.v.*) was one of his classmates. He was commissioned in the infantry and later transferred to the Adjutant General's Department. He served during the Philippine Insurrection and later, with the War Department General Staff. In 1916, he graduated from the Army War College. On 12 April 1918, he was promoted to brigadier general (NA), which

Lutz Wahl

position he held until 31 October 1919. During this time, he commanded the 14th Infantry Brigade, for which he received the Distinguished Service Medal. From 24 to 28 October 1918, he commanded the Seventh Infantry Division. In 1921, he graduated from the General Staff College, and from 2 July 1927 to 30 December 1928, he was Adjutant General of the Army. At the age of fifty-nine, he died in Washington. The photo, from the National Archives, shows him being sworn in as Adjutant General.

Charles Carroll Walcutt, Jr. (0-157), son of Charles C. Walcutt, who served in the Ohio Volunteers during the Civil War and became a lieutenant colonel in the Tenth Cavalry, and Phoebe Neil Walcutt, from Belfast, Ireland, was born on 20 June 1861 in Columbus, Ohio. He was appointed to USMA by President Hayes and graduated number twenty-seven of seventy-seven in the class of 1886. Mason M. Patrick, Charles T. Menoher, John J. Pershing and Edward W. McCaskey (all *q.v.*) were four of his classmates. He was commissioned and sent to the Eighth Cavalry, and he performed frontier duty from 1886 to 1891. On 26 August 1891, he married Julia Cretton at Fort Sheridan, Illinois. In 1893, he graduated from the Infantry and Cavalry School, and he also served in the Third, Second and Fifth Cavalry Regiments. During the Spanish-American War, he was a captain, acting quartermaster of volunteers. From 1899 to 1901, he was a major in the 44th United States Volunteer Infantry during the Philippine Insurrection. He was on the staffs of General Anderson and General Lawton and was assistant to the depot quartermaster in Manila. In 1901 and 1902, he was on duty in Washington, and in 1902, he became constructing quartermaster at Whipple Barracks, just north of Prescott, Arizona. In 1912, he served in Washington in the Bureau of Insular Affairs, first as assistant chief, then as acting chief and lastly, as chief. On 26 June 1918, he was promoted to brigadier general (NA). He retired in 1926 as a colonel, but his rank of brigadier general was restored in 1930. In 1932, he lived in the Seneca Hotel in Columbus, Ohio. At the age of eighty-five, he died at Fort Hayes, Ohio, on 17 December 1946. Photo courtesy of Special Collections, USMA Library.

Charles Carroll Walcutt, Jr.

Meriwether Lewis Walker

Meriwether Lewis Walker (0-419), son of Thomas Lindsay Walker, M.D. and Catherine Dabney Walker, was born on 30 September 1869 in Lynchburg, Virginia. He entered USMA and graduated number three of fifty-one in the class of 1893. Lincoln C. Andrews (*q.v.*) and Herbert Ball Crosby were two of his classmates. He graduated from the Engineer School in 1896. On 28 September 1904, he married Edith Carey, daughter of Gen. Asa Bacon Carey, and they had one daughter, Carey Dabney Walker (Mrs. R. B. Luckey). From 1912 to 1914, he was Director of the Army Field Engineering School, and from 1914 to 1916, he taught military engineering in West Point. He was the Chief Engineer on General Pershing's Mexican Punitive Expedition in 1916 and 1917, then went to France as Chief Engineer for the 41st Infantry Division (AEF). From January to July 1918, he was principal assistant to the Chief Engineer of the AEF, and during this period, on 26 June, he was promoted to brigadier general (NA). From August 1918 to August 1919, he headed the motor transport of the AEF, for which he received the Distinguished Service Medal. During 1919 and early 1920, he was an instructor at the Army War College, and from 15 August 1920 to 1 July 1921, he was commandant of the Engineer School at Fort Humphreys, Virginia. From 1924 to 1928, he was governor of the Canal Zone, and during that time, on 1 July 1927, he was promoted to brigadier general (USA). From October 1928 to August 1933, he commanded the 18th Infantry Brigade in Boston, Massachusetts. On 30 September 1933, he retired and lived in Martha's Vineyard, Massachusetts. In addition to the decoration already mentioned, he was made an Officer of the Legion of Honor (France). At the age of seventy-seven, he died on 29 July 1947. In the photo, from the National Archives, he's wearing pince-nez glasses with black rubber frames.

Robert Douglas Walsh (0-13381) was born on 14 October 1860 in Alleghany, California. He entered USMA and graduated number thirty-seven of fifty-two in the class of 1883. George H. Cameron and Tyree Rodes Rivers (both *q.v.*) were two of his classmates. He was commissioned in the 22d Infantry, but soon transferred to the cavalry. He performed frontier duty until 1891, which included service in the Apache Indian Wars. This earned him a brevet to first lieutenant. He served at Fort Walla Walla, Washington, Boise Barracks and Vancouver Barracks, then served in the Philippines as a lieutenant colonel, United States Volunteers from 1899 to 1902. When he returned to the States, he went to Fort Leavenworth, Kansas and graduated from the Army War College in

1912. In 1916, he commanded the Eighth Cavalry. On 5 August 1917, he was promoted to brigadier general (NA) and commanded the 178th Infantry Brigade at Camp Beauregarde, Louisiana. From 1 December 1917 to 29 July 1919, he commanded Base Number One in St. Nazaire, France. He was Deputy Director General of Transportation, commanded Base Number Two in Bordeaux and lastly, was commanding general, 164th Infantry Brigade until 31 May 1919. On 30 June 1919, he retired as a colonel with forty-one years of service. He was awarded the Distinguished Service Medal and was made a Commander of the Legion of Honor (France). At the age of sixty-seven, he died in Washington, D.C., on 15 August 1928. His rank of brigadier general was restored posthumously in June 1930. Photo courtesy of the National Archives.

Robert Douglas Walsh

Frank Bingley Watson

Frank Bingley Watson (0-491), son of Charles Clark Watson and Mary Wheeler Watson, was born on 9 February 1870 in Sharp's, Virginia. He was a printer in Salem, New Jersey for five years, then entered USMA and graduated number forty-nine of fifty-two in the class of 1895. Joseph Wheeler, Jr. (son of the Confederate cavalry general who was brought back to duty in the United States Army at the time of the Spanish-American War) and Louis M. Nuttman (*q.v.*) were two of his classmates. He was commissioned in the 19th Infantry and served in the States until 1898. On 1 November 1898, he married Sara M. W. Dunn, and they had one son, Numa Augustin Watson. In 1898 and 1899, he was in Puerto Rico, then served in the Philippines until 1902. From 1904 to 1906, he served in Alaska, and he was back in the Philippines from 1909 to 1910. In 1910, he served as quartermaster captain, assistant to the constructing quartermaster and commanded the army service detachment in West Point. In 1915, he went with the 26th Infantry to the Mexican border. In 1917, he served briefly with the 153rd Depot Brigade at Camp Dix, New Jersey, then went to Camp McClellan, Alabama, where he commanded the 115th Infantry Regiment, part of the 29th (Blue and Gray) Division. In 1918, he was on the War Department

General Staff. On 8 August 1918, he was promoted to brigadier general (NA). In 1918 and 1919, he commanded the 13th Infantry Division and also the 26th Infantry Brigade in American Lake, Washington. He commanded United States troops in the Butte, Montana strikes in 1919, then commanded the Presidio of San Francisco. He returned to West Point as constructing quartermaster and commander of the army service detachment until late 1920. In 1921, he commanded the 52d Infantry Regiment at Camp Grant, Illinois, as well as serving as the Chief of Staff, Sixth Infantry Division. He later commanded the Second Infantry at Fort Sheridan, Chicago, Illinois. From 1927 to 1931, he was senior instructor of the Maryland National Guard, and then he commanded the 35th Infantry at Schofield Banks, Hawaii. On 23 February 1934, he retired as brigadier general. His wife died on 10 May 1952. He was active with the Association of Graduates, the Army Athletic Association, the Infantry Association, the American Legion and the Sojourner, and he lived in Bridgeton, New Jersey. At the age of eighty-five, he died in Munich, Germany, on 24 July 1955. The photo, from the National Archives, was taken when he was at the Presidio in San Francisco.

Erasmus Morgan Weaver, Jr.

Erasmus Morgan Weaver, Jr. (no ASN assigned), son of Erasmus M. Weaver and Fanny Mary Bangs Weaver, was born on 23 May 1854 in Lafayette, Indiana. He entered USMA and graduated number fourteen of forty-three in the class of 1875. Tasker H. Bliss (*q.v.*) and Robert P. Page Wainwright were two of his classmates. He was commissioned in the artillery and later transferred to Coast Artillery. He was Professor of Military Science and Tactics at Western Reserve University in Ohio from 1877 to 1880. From 1883 to 1886, he was Professor of Military Science and Tactics at South Carolina Military Academy in Charleston. In 1888, he was an honor graduate of the Artillery School. He taught electricity and chemistry at USMA from 1888 to 1891 as an assistant professor. During 1895 and 1896, he studied electricity and physics at MIT in Cambridge, Massachusetts. During the Spanish-American War, he was a captain, First United States Artillery, then a lieutenant colonel of the Fifth Massachusetts Infantry. In 1900, he reverted to major of artillery. From 1908 to 1910, he was on the War Department General Staff as the Chief of Militia Affairs in the Office of the Secretary of War. In March 1911, he was promoted to brigadier general, Chief of Coast Artillery. On 6 July 1916, he was promoted to major general (USA). During 1917 and 1918, he was on the War Council in the War Department. On 23 May 1918, he was retired due to age. He wrote one book, *Notes on Military*

Explosives (published in 1906). At the age of sixty-six, he died in Washington, on 13 November 1920. Photo from the National Archives.

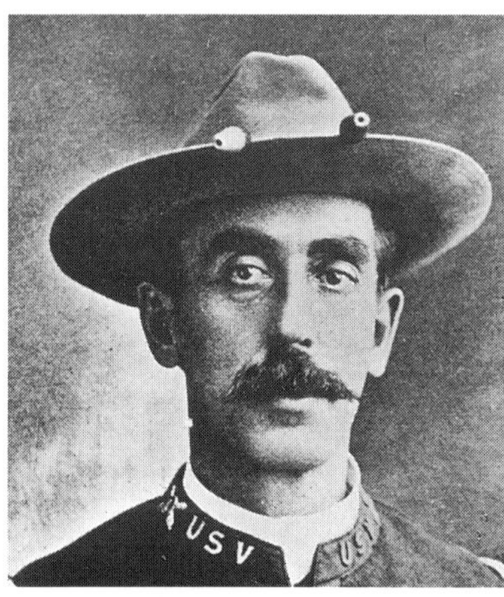

Edgar A. Wedgwood

Edgar A. Wedgwood (no ASN assigned), son of Andrew J. Wedgwood and Theresa A. Gould Wedgwood, was born on 2 May 1856 in Lowell, Massachusetts. He was educated as a violinist and was very fond of music, but nonetheless went into the practice of law. His family moved to Grand Island, Nebraska (on the Platte), where he became sheriff at a young age and was known as "The Kid Sheriff of Nebraska." He was admitted to the bar in 1883. On 1 June 1886, he married Annie M. Shelton, a survivor of the fire in Chicago. They had three children: Fredrick T. Wedgwood, Bruce A. Wedgwood (a Signal Corps major during World War I) and Edgara Wedgwood (Mrs. R. C. Dugdale of Salt Lake). He stayed in Grand Island until 1890, then moved to Provo, Utah, where he continued to practice law. He was very serious about religion, and became a senior deacon of the Baptist Church. During the Spanish-American War, he enlisted as private in the Utah National Guard and was elected first lieutenant on the same day. He got another 100 volunteers and became captain of Battery A. He served in twenty-three battles in the Philippines, and he was wounded in the pursuit of Emilio Aguinaldo. In 1907, the governor of Utah made him the State Adjutant General, a post he held for ten years. He was a very high-ranking attorney and a member of the National Militia Board. After the United States entered World War I, he became one of the only two civilians appointed to the rank of brigadier general (NA). He commanded the 82d Infantry Brigade and was the first commanding general of Camp Greene, North Carolina. Due to rapidly failing health, he was relieved from active duty in 1918, shortly before his unit left for France. His chief recreations were yachting, rowing, music, chemistry and drawing. At the age of sixty-three, he died on 31 January 1920. Photo courtesy of the Adjutant General of Utah.

William Weigel (0-193) was born on 25 August 1863 in New Brunswick, New Jersey. He entered USMA and graduated number twenty-seven of sixty-four in the class of 1887. Richmond P. Davis, George O. Squier and P. D. Lochridge (all *q.v.*) were three of his classmates. He was commissioned in the infantry. From 1894 to 1898, he was on duty at USMA. During the Spanish-American War, he served as a captain of volunteers in Cuba. In Samar in the Philippines, after Company C of the 19th Infantry had been massacred, he held out against the insurgents for sixteen days with forty-eight men. By the time the United States entered World War I, he was colonel of the First Infantry. On 5 August 1917, he was promoted to brigadier general (NA) and assigned to the 28th Division (Pennsylvania National Guard). He served with that division during the Battle of the Marne and the fighting along the Vesle. On 28 August 1918, he was promoted to major general and placed in command of the 88th Division, for which he earned the Distinguished Service Medal and was cited by Marshal Petain of France. He was also awarded the Croix de Guerre with two palms and was made a Commander of the Legion of Honor. From 1925 to 1927, he commanded the Philippine Department and Division. He retired in 1927. At the age of seventy-two, he died in New York City, on 4 March 1936. Photo courtesy of the 28th Division.

William Weigel

Briant Harris Wells

Briant Harris Wells (0-463), son of Heber Wells, the first Mayor of Salt Lake City and the brother of the first governor of Utah, was born in 1871 in Salt Lake City, Utah. He entered USMA and graduated number forty-eight of fifty-four in the class of 1894. Paul B. Malone, Hamilton Hawkins and George H. Estes, Jr. were three of his classmates. He was commissioned in the infantry and sent to Fort Omaha, Nebraska. In 1895, he returned to Salt Lake City and married Mary Jane Jennings. They had three children: Briant Harris Wells, Jr., Tom Wells and Jane Wells (Mrs. Fredrick Townsend of Scarsdale, New York). During the Spanish-American War, he went to Cuba with the Second Infantry. He served at San Juan Hill, where he received a Spanish bullet, the Purple Heart, the Silver Star and an instant promotion. He also served in the Sanitary Corps. He rode horses a great deal and was a seasoned hiker. In the Philippines, he was first a company commander, then a regimental commissary, then quartermaster. He was a talented administrator and executive. When he returned to the States, he joined the 29th Infantry, which was just being formed, and was stationed at Fort Douglas, Utah, a beautiful post just uphill on the eastern edge of Salt Lake City. It was he who selected the Indiantown Gap Military Reservation site in Eastern Pennsylvania as well as the Pine Camp site in Northern New York State. He served on the Mexican border from 1916 to 1917, then on the War Department General Staff. He and another colonel were having dinner with Douglas MacArthur when word came through of MacArthur's promotion to colonel, and the two of them pinned the eagles on MacArthur, then drank a toast to his success. He was sent to France to serve with the Supreme War Council under Tasker H. Bliss (*q.v.*) and was the American Liaison to Marshal Foch. General Bliss later allowed him to perform troop duty so he would be promoted. He was Chief of Staff to Generals Bundy, Muir and Sumerall in the Sixth and Fourth Corps. When he returned to the States, he served on the War Department General Staff as Chief of the War Plans Division. General Pershing rated him number two of the forty-three brigadier generals he knew personally. He received the Distinguished Service Medal for command of the Infantry School and the First Infantry Division. In 1930, he went to Hawaii, his last command. In 1935, he retired there and became vice president of the Hawaiian Sugar Planters Association. He worked to fight racism against Asians in Hawaii and on the West Coast. At the age of seventy-seven, he died in Long Beach, California, on 10 June 1949. He was known to classmates as "Z.B." He was capable, sincere man and a fine officer, and he was respected and well regarded. Photo from *The Assembly*, Association of Graduates, USMA.

William Ernest Welsh (0-459) was born in 1870 in Hanover, south York County, Pennsylvania. He entered USMA and graduated number forty-four of fifty-four in the class of 1894. Paul B. Malone, Hamilton S. Hawkins and George H. Estes, Jr. (all *q.v.*) were three of his classmates. He was commissioned in the infantry. He served in the Bannock War in 1895. During the Spanish-American War, he won a Silver Star Commendation. He also served in the Philippines during the Insurrection. During World War I, in France, he commanded the 346th Infantry Regiment, part of the 87th Infantry Division. On 1 October 1918, he was promoted to brigadier general (NA) and was the inspector general of the infantry training section of GHQ, for which he received the Distinguished Service Medal. At the age of sixty, he died in Washington, D.C., on 19 June 1932. Photo courtesy of the National Archives.

William Ernest Welsh

William Irving Westervelt

William Irving Westervelt (0-1093), son of George William Westervelt of South Carolina and Ida deRyee Westervelt of Alabama, was born on 11 September 1876 in Corpus Christi, Texas. He entered USMA and graduated number sixteen of fifty-four in the class of 1900. Augustine McIntyre and Robert E. Wood (both *q.v.*) were two of his classmates. He was commissioned in the Artillery Corps, and when that arm split in 1907, he served with the field artillery, then eventually transferred to ordnance. He served during the Philippine Insurrection, and later, he was an instructor at the Pennsylvania State Military College. On 12 April 1918, he was promoted to brigadier general (NA) and served as assistant to the Chief of Field Artillery (AEF), for which he received the Distinguished Service Medal. On 26 December 1918, he married Dorothy Jocelyn in Evreux, France, and they had three children: Peter Jocelyn Westervelt, Dirch deRyee Westervelt and Jane Edgell Westervelt. In 1919, he was president of the Caliber Board. He retired in 1928 as a lieutenant colonel. His rank of brigadier general was restored by act of Congress in June 1930. From 1928 to 1940, he worked with Sears Roebuck and Company. He was also a director of Ross and Company and a director and officer of Office Manufacturing Industries, Inc. He retired in 1932. In retirement, he lived in Winnetka, Illinois. At the age of eighty-three, he died in Brattleboro, Vermont, on 1 March 1960. He lived at 83 Summit Street, Burlington, Vermont. Photo courtesy of Special Collections, USMA Library.

Charles Brewster Wheeler (0-13386), son of Christopher Wheeler and Mary Safford Wheeler, was born on 3 May 1865 in Matteson, Illinois. He entered USMA and graduated number four of sixty-four in the class of 1887. William Weigel, P. D. Lochridge, Charles Henry Martin(all *q.v.*) and Thomas Q. Donaldson were four of his classmates. He was commissioned in the Fifth Artillery, then, as a first lieutenant, he transferred to the ordnance in 1890. On 3 April 1893, he married Zella Lentilhon. He served in the office of the Chief of Ordnance from 1896 to 1906, and during 1906 and 1907, he was Chief

Charles Brewster Wheeler

Ordnance Officer of the Philippine Division and commanded the Manila Ordnance Depot. From 1908 to 1917, he commanded the Watertown, New York arsenal. On 4 March 1917, he was called back to the office of the Chief of Ordnance. On 5 August 1917, he was promoted to brigadier general (NA). On 19 December 1917, he served as acting Chief of Ordnance, for which he was given the Distinguished Service Medal. In April 1918, he became Chief Ordnance Officer (AEF). On 3 September 1919, he retired and was vice-president of Eaton, Crane, Pike and Company of Pittsfield, Massachusetts. In addition to the decoration already mentioned, he was made a Companion of the Order of the Bath (Britain) and a Commander of the Legion of Honor (France). His rank of brigadier general was restored in 1930. In retirement, he lived in Massachusetts. At the age of eighty, he died in Wayland, Massachusetts, on 11 April 1946. Photo from the National Archives.

Henry Howard Whitney

Henry Howard Whitney (0-13460), son of Rev. Walter Whitney and Eliza Kegerris Whitney, was born on 25 December 1866 in Glen Hope, Pennsylvania. After graduating with honors in 1884 from Dickinson Seminary in Williamsport, Pennsylvania, he entered USMA and graduated number eleven of sixty-two in the class of 1892. Charles P. Sumerall, James A. Shipton, William Chamberlaine (all *q.v.*) and Kirby Walker were four of his classmates. He was commissioned in the Fourth Artillery. On 25 February 1897, he married Ellen Wadsworth Closson, and they had two children: Julie E. Whitney, who died when she was very young, and Henry Wadsworth Whitney. During the Spanish-American War, he was a captain, Assistant Adjutant General of Volunteers from 12 May 1898 to 12 May 1899. He also served as military attaché in Buenos Aires. In May 1898, under orders from the Secretary of War, he visited Cuba incognito, and he also made a military reconnaissance of Puerto Rico disguised as an English sailor, for which he received the Distinguished Service Cross. The information he gathered was the basis of the military campaign in Puerto Rico under Gen. Nelson A. Miles. He was an aide to General. Miles from 1900 to 1903, accompanying the general on his trip around the world. In 1907, he graduated from the School of Submarine Defense at Willet's Point, New York. From 1911 to 1914, he was in the Philippines, and on 13 January 1914, he became Adjutant of the Western Department in San Francisco, California. In 1916, he commanded the Coast Artillery at Fort Winfield Scott in San Francisco. In June 1916, he was transferred back to the Adjutant General's Department and sent to El Paso, Texas. In

April 1917, he was again adjutant of the Western Department. On 5 August 1917, he was promoted to brigadier general (NA). He commanded the 63d Field Artillery Brigade at Camp Shelby, Mississippi. In France, he was a member of the General Staff (AEF), and he was Chief of Staff of the District of Paris in 1918 and 1919. On 30 June 1920, he retired as a colonel after thirty-two years of service. On 21 June 1930, he was promoted to brigadier general (USA). He lived in Long Beach, California. His decorations included the Distinguished Service Cross and the Distinguished Service Medal, and he was made an Officer of the Legion of Honor (France), a Commander de la Couronne de Roumanie avec Glaives (Roumania) and a Commander de Danilo 1 (Montenegro). He belonged to many prestigious clubs and associations. At the age of eighty-two, he died in New Jersey, on 2 April 1949. The photo, from the National Archives, was taken in Paris.

Pegram Whitworth (0-464), son of William T. Whitworth and Laura Pegram Whitworth, was born on 5 August 1871 in Mansfield, Louisiana. From 1886 to 1889, he attended Thatcher Military Institute. He entered USMA and graduated number fifty-three of fifty-four in the class of 1894. He was commissioned in the infantry. He served in the Philippine Insurrection from 1899 to 1900 as an aide to Gen. Arthur MacArthur, for which he received two Silver Star Citations. On 18 April 1899, he married Emiline Cole Smith, and they had one son, Pegram Whitworth, Jr. He served two tours of duty in the Philippines, from 1901 to 1902 and from 1906 to 1908. From 1909 to 1912, he served the constructing quartermaster in Galveston, Texas, and from 1912 to 1916, he served in the Canal Zone. During this time, in 1915, he graduated from the Army School of the Line. In 1917, he was an instructor and battalion commander of the first officers training camp at the Presidio in San Francisco, California. In 1917, he was colonel of the 362nd Infantry. On 8 August 1918, he was made brigadier general (NA) and commanded the 71st Infantry Brigade (AEF) until July 1919, for which he was cited by Marshal Petain of France. From 1924 to 1929, he was Professor of Military Science and Tactics at the University of Alabama. In 1932, he was colonel of the Sixth Infantry at Jefferson Barracks, St. Louis, Missouri. From late 1932 to 1933, he was Chief of Staff of the Second Infantry Division. In 1933, he was promoted to brigadier general (USA) and commanded the Sixth Infantry Brigade at Fort Douglas, Utah. He was also in charge of thirty companies of the Civilian Conservation Corps (CCC). He retired in 1935 and lived in

Pegram Whitworth

Los Angeles, California, where at the age of eighty-seven, he died on 9 May 1959. Photo courtesy of Dr. Jerry Oldshue, University of Alabama Library.

Wilber Elliott Wilder

Wilber Elliott Wilder (0-13490), son of Elliott S. Wilder and Sylvia Gilkey Wilder, was born on 16 August 1856 in Michigan. He entered USMA and graduated number thirty-two of seventy-six in the class of 1877. Augustus P. Blocksom, William M. Black and Thomas Henry Barry (all *q.v.*) were three of his classmates. He was commissioned in the Fourth Cavalry and performed frontier duty until 1895. In 1884, he married Violet Blair Martin, and they had five children: Throop M. Wilder, Wilber E. Wilder, Sylvia Wilder, Cornelia M. Wilder and Violet B. Wilder. From 1895 to 1898, he was adjutant of USMA, New York, and from March to June 1899, he commanded Fort Yellowstone, Wyoming. He received the Medal of Honor and was brevetted captain for actions in Horse Shoe Canyon, New Mexico in 1882. During the Spanish-American War, in 1898, he was a colonel of New York volunteers. He went to the Philippines as a lieutenant colonel commanding the Macabebe Scouts, and in 1900, he was Superintendent of Police in Manila. He stayed in the Philippines until 1909. From 1916 to 1917, he was on the Mexican Punitive Expedition. On 5 August 1917, he was promoted to brigadier general (NA) and commanded the 168th Infantry Brigade. He retired as a colonel in 1920. By a special act of Congress, his rank of brigadier general was restored in 1927. He belonged to several army and navy clubs, and to the University Club in New York City. From 11 March 1949 until 30 January 1952, he was the oldest living graduate of USMA. At the age of ninety-five, he died on Governor's Island, New York. Photo from the National Archives.

Harry Eugene Wilkins (0-13399), son of James Eugene Wilkins and Phoebe Clarisa Gilbert Wilkins, was born on 22 April 1861 in Geneseo, Illinois. He entered USMA and graduated number fourteen of sixty-four in the class of 1887. P. D. Lochridge, Charles H. Martin, William Weigel , George O. Squier (all *q.v.*) and Thomas Q. Donaldson were five of his classmates. He was commissioned in the infantry and also served as a commissary and a quartermaster. From 1887 to 1889, he performed frontier duty. On 26 October 1890, he married Annie C. Kohlhauff, and they had one daughter, Margaret. His wife died on 7 October 1903 and was buried in Arlington National Cemetery. He married Ida S. Sanders,

Harry Eugene Wilkins

who died on 1 June 1920 and on 27 September 1921, he married Jean Palmer. In 1898, he was an aide to Gen. Alfred Elliott Bates and then served during the Philippine Insurrection. He became Chief Commissary during the Cuban Pacification, and when General Funston led the Vera Cruz Expedition in 1914, he was chief commissary. In 1917, he went to France as assistant to the Chief Quartermaster (AEF). On 1 October 1918, he was promoted to brigadier general (NA) and was in charge of the General Quartermaster Depot of New York. He was also Zone Supply Officer. Later, he had a similar assignment in Chicago. For his performance of duty in New York, he received the Distinguished Service Medal. In 1919, he retired as a colonel and lived in Des Moines, Iowa, where he was associated with the Wilkins Brothers department store. In June 1930, his rank of brigadier general was restored by act of Congress. He was treasurer of the Des Moines Morris Plan Bank, as well as being one of the managing officers. He belonged to many organizations. His home was at 1645 Pennsylvania Avenue, Des Moines, Iowa. In February 1940, he was involved in an accident and suffered a broken hip. This resulted in his death at the age of eighty, on 15 August 1941. He was called "Harry" by his friends, and he was extremely well regarded, respected and loved. Photo from *The Assembly*, Association of Graduates, USMA.

☆

Clarence Charles Williams

Clarence Charles Williams (0-14) was born on 8 November 1869 in Nacoochee, Georgia. He was appointed to USMA from Georgia, and graduated number four of fifty-four in the class of 1894. Paul B. Malone, Hamilton S. Hawkins and George Estes, Jr. (all *q.v.*) were three of his classmates. He was commissioned in the artillery, and he later transferred to ordnance. During the Spanish-American War, he commanded the Astor Battery, for which he received a Silver Star Commendation. From 1906 to 1908, he was Inspector of Ordnance at the Bethlehem Steel Company in South Bethlehem, Pennsylvania. From December 1907 to January 1912, he was a member of the Joint Army and Navy Board to formulate specifications for gun forgings. For the first six months of

1912, he was sent to Sheffield, England to inspect ordnance materiel being obtained from the Hadfield Steel Foundry. When he returned to the States, he was assistant to the commanding officer at the Watertown, New York arsenal. From 26 November 1914 to 14 May 1915, he was an observer with the German Army. On 6 April 1915, he was promoted to lieutenant colonel. From 14 May 1915 to 27 June 1916, he was again a member of the Joint Army and Navy Board. Between October 1915 and 27 June 1916, he was a member of the Board of Engineers, the Board for Testing Rifled Cannon and the Joint Army and Navy Board on Smokeless Powder. During the mobilization of the National Guard on the Mexican border, from 27 June 1916 to 28 February 1917, he was the Department Ordnance Officer of the Southern Department. From 28 February to 19 May 1917, he was assistant to the Chief of Ordnance as well as a member of the Machine Gun Board. From 26 May 1917 to April 1918, he was Chief Ordnance Officer (AEF). In France, on 5 August 1917, he was promoted to brigadier general (NA) and received the Distinguished Service Medal for his service as Chief Ordnance Officer. From 30 April to 16 July 1918, he was acting Chief of Ordnance in Washington. On 16 July 1918, he was promoted to major general and served as the Chief of Ordnance, which post he held until 1 April 1930. In 1919, he was made an Officer of the Legion of Honor (France). He retired in 1930 and lived in South Hampton, Massachusetts. He was recalled to active duty for World War II, for which received the Legion of Merit. At the age of eighty-three, he died in Woodstock, Virginia, on 13 June 1958. Photo courtesy of the Association of Graduates, USMA.

Herbert Owen Williams (0-347), son of John Dickson Williams and Elizabeth Marion Williams, was born on 5 August 1866 in Fulton, just east of Tupelo, Mississippi. He entered USMA and graduated number fifty-six of sixty-five in the class of 1891. Odus C. Horney, Andrew Hero, Jr., William J. Glasgow and John L. Hines (all *q.v.*) were four of his classmates. He was commissioned in the infantry. In 1897, he graduated from the Infantry and Cavalry School at Fort Leavenworth, Kansas. In 1898, during the Spanish-American War, he served as a lieutenant colonel of Mississippi Volunteers. He served in the Philippines during the Insurrection, then was an instructor in law at the Infantry and Cavalry School from 1903 to 1907. In 1912, he graduated from the Army War College. On 1 October 1918, he was promoted to brigadier general (NA) and served with the office of the Inspector General until 1919, for which he received the Distinguished Service Medal. On 22 November 1919, he married Gertrude I.

Herbert Owen Williams

Edwards. From 1919 to 1922, he was Chief of Staff of the Pacific Department, and from 1922 to 1926, he was executive officer in the Office of the Inspector General. In 1926, he was promoted to brigadier general (USA). He retired in 1930 and lived in California. At the age of seventy, he died on 13 August 1936. Photo courtesy of the National Portrait Gallery.

Roger deCoverly Williams

Roger deCoverly Williams (no ASN assigned), son of Benjamin Franklin Williams and Mary Gates Mathie Williams, was born on 29 August 1856 in Bourbon County, Kentucky. He was a descendant of Roger Williams, the founder of Rhode Island, and several officers of the American Revolution. He had the personal distinction of being the youngest person ever matriculated at Kentucky University at that time, and he served for two years with the Pension Bureau and Internal Revenue Service of the federal government. He chose his middle name, taken from the eighteenth-century British work *The Spectator*, in which Sir Roger deCoverly was one of the characters. The far West intrigued him, and he was one of a pioneer party of fourteen who went into the Black Hills of South Dakota and occupied a stockade just south of present Rapid City. During the Sioux Campaign of 1876, he was war correspondent for the *San Franciso Chronicle* and the *Denver Tribune*, attached to General Crook's command. He managed to travel all over the far West, through Deadwood and Leadville, Colorado, British Columbia, Arizona and New Mexico. He knew Buffalo Bill Cody, Wild Bill Hickock and Calamity Jane as well as many other interesting characters, including Theodore Roosevelt. He returned to Kentucky in 1879 and established the Kentucky Copper Works and Iron Foundry, of which he was the president and owner. For thirty years, he was a member of the Kentucky National Guard. In November 1887, he married Minnie Lyle Sayre, and they had two children: Mary Sayre Williams (Mrs. Lucas B. Combs) and Roger Williams, Jr. (who became an army officer). He was very active civically and socially, and he enjoyed hunting and mounted sports. In 1898, at the behest of Theodore Roosevelt, he organized a troop of cavalry for the Rough Riders, but the war ended before they saw active service. From 1916 to 1917, he served on the Mexican border, commanding the district from Fort Hancock (downriver from El Paso) to Las Cruces, New Mexico. During World War I, he commanded the 76th Infantry Brigade, and in France with the AEF, he was on duty at headquarters, First Army. Among his written works were *Horse and Hound* (published in 1905), *Old Times in the Black Hill* (published in 1906), *Wolf Hunting and Coursing*, (published in 1908), *Deer Hunting in the West Indies* (published in 1909) and *The Fox Hound* (published in 1914). At the age of sixty-eight, he died in his home in Lexington, on 12 December 1925. Photo courtesy of Mrs. Sidney Sayre Combs.

William Wilson and staff

William Wilson (no ASN assigned), son of James Wilson and Anna Whitney Wilson, was born on 16 June 1855 in Seneca, New York. He graduated from Hobart College in Geneva, New York with an A.B. On 29 November 1878, he married Mary E. Hipple, and they had one son, James Whitney Wilson. After graduation, he went into the nursery business in Geneva. In 1880, he enlisted as a private in the 34th Separate Company (New York National Guard). On 28 February 1882, he was commissioned a first lieutenant. In 1889, he switched from the nursery business to hardware. From 1899 to 1900, he was on the military staff of Gov. Theodore Roosevelt. He was a member of the Militia Council of New York during 1912 and 1913 and was a member of the State Armory Commissioners from 1914 to 1919. On 10 June 1914, he was promoted to brigadier general and commanded the Fourth Brigade (New York National Guard). His hardware store burned down in 1916. He commanded the Third Brigade (New York National Guard) on the Mexican border from June to December 1916. On 5 September 1917, he was made brigadier general (NA). He commanded the National Guards of the Eastern Division from August to October 1917. From 1 November 1917 to 3 January 1918, he commanded the 78th Infantry Brigade at Camp Beauregarde, Louisiana. From January to November 1918, he commanded the Second Provisional Brigade at Camp Wadsworth, South Carolina. He was commanding general for the Provisional Detachment for corps and army troops from November 1918 to March 1919, while serving as commanding general of Camp Wadsworth. On 18 July 1919, he was honorably discharged. On 21 June 1928, was promoted to brigadier general (USA). He was a Presbyterian. In retirement, he lived in Nobleton, Florida. At the age of eighty-one, he died on 6 January 1937. The photo, from National Archives, shows him, center front, with his staff.

Edwin Baruch Winans

Edwin Baruch Winans (0-351), son of Edwin B. Winans, former governor of Michigan, and Elizabeth Galloway Winans, was born on 31 October 1869 in Hamburg, Michigan. He entered USMA and graduated number nineteen of sixty-five in the class of 1891. Odus C. Horney, Andrew Hero, Jr., William J. Glasgow and John L. Hines (all *q.v.*) were four of his classmates. He was commissioned in the Fifth Cavalry. On 1 June 1892, he married Edith M. Auman, daughter of Gen. William Auman (USA), and they had two daughters: Katherine A. Winans (wife of Russell L. Maxwell, USA) and Elizabeth G. Winans (wife of W. R. Grove, Jr., USA). He served in the Fifth, Fourth and Seventh Cavalry Regiments, and from 1891 to 1897, he served in the Indian Territory (now Oklahoma) and Texas. During 1897 and 1898, he was Professor of Military Science and Tactics at the Michigan Military Academy, founded and operated by the father of Gen. Harry Rogers (*q.v.*). During the Spanish-American War, he was a major of the Michigan Volunteer Infantry, and he also served in the Sanitary Corps. He was sent to the Philippines in 1899. He was on the China Relief Expedition in 1900 as well as the Mexican Punitive Expedition of 1916 and 1917, where he earned a Silver Star Commendation. On 26 June 1918, he was promoted to brigadier general (NA) and commanded the 64th Infantry Brigade (AEF), for which he received the Distinguished Service Medal. He served with the American forces in Germany. On 8 February 1920, his wife died. On 23 February 1920, he was promoted to colonel of cavalry (USA), and also to brigadier general. In 1927, he was promoted to major general (USA). He served as superintendent of USMA from 23 October 1927 to 25 February 1928. He commanded the Hawaiian Division, then the Eighth Corps Area, headquartered at Fort Sam Houston, San Antonio, Texas. On 31 October 1933, he retired as a major general and lived in Vienna, Virginia, just outside of Washington, D.C. On 5 September 1943, he married Esther Walker. In addition to the decorations already mentioned, he received the Croix de Guerre with two palms and was made an Officer of the Legion of Honor (France). At the age of seventy-eight, he died in Walter Reed Army Medical Center in Washington, D.C., on 31 December 1947. Photo from the First Cavalry Division Museum, Fort Hood, Texas.

George Albert Wingate (ASN unknown) was born on 24 February 1871 in Brooklyn, New York. He enlisted as a private in Company D, 23d New York Infantry on 18 March 1889 and rose through noncommissioned ranks to first sergeant and sergeant major before being commissioned in 1895. From 1 January 1899 to 31 December 1900, he was an aide to the governor of New York, Theodore Roosevelt. His New York National Guard service lasted until 24 February 1935, when he was placed on the retired list. From 30 June 1916 to 13 March 1919, he was in federal service for World War I with the 27th (New York) Infantry Division and commanded the 105th Field Artillery Regiment and later, the 52d Field Artillery Brigade from 16 July 1917 to 15 September 1917, from 19 September 1917 to 5 December 1917, from 2 May 1918 to 6 January 1919 and from 9 January 1919 to 31 March 1919, when they were demobilized. He was promoted to brigadier general (NA) on 12 April 1918. His field artillery brigade supported both the 33d and 79th Divisions in addition to his own 27th Division during the Meuse-Argonne and St. Mihiel offensives. After discharge from federal service on 31 March 1919, he continued serving with the New York National Guard until he was retired due to age. His home was at 61 Jefferson Avenue, Brooklyn, where at the age of eighty-four, he died on 2 April 1955. Photo courtesy of the National Archives.

George Albert Wingate

Frank Long Winn

Frank Long Winn (0-164), son of William Winn and Carrie Hord Winn, was born on 4 October 1864 in Winchester, Kentucky. For two years he attended Center College in Danville, Kentucky. He entered USMA and graduated number fifty-two of seventy-seven in the class of 1886. Mason M. Patrick, Charles T. Menoher, John J. Pershing and Edward McCaskey (all *q.v.*) were four of his classmates. He was commissioned in the First Infantry and performed frontier duty from 1886 to 1889. On 5 November 1890, he married Dora Boardman, and they had one daughter, Dora Winn (Mrs. Lovell Langstroth). Immediately after his marriage, he served in the Sioux Campaign of 1890. His wife died in 1891. From 1893 to 1897, he was Professor of Military Science and Tactics at the University of California. In 1898, during the Spanish-American War, he was in Cuba, and as a result of his performance in El Caney, he was recommended for a brevet captaincy. From 1899 to 1901, he served in the Philippine Insurrection and was recommended for a brevet majority. He received a Silver Star Commendation in Cuba and another in the Philippines. From 1904 to 1909, he was an aide to Lt. Gen. Arthur MacArthur. On 15 October 1910, he married Katherine McCord. From 1916 to 1917, he was on the Mexican Punitive Expedition. He was promoted to brigadier general (NA) on 5 August 1917. He commanded the 177th Infantry Brigade at Camp Funston (now Fort Riley), Kansas from 5 September 1917 to May 1918. He commanded the 89th Division as a brigadier general from 26 November 1917 to 24 December 1917, from 29 December 1917 to 12 April 1918 and from 1 June 1918 to 6 September 1918. On 1 October 1918, he was promoted to major general (NA) and again commanded the 89th Division, from 12 November 1918 to May 1919, when it was inactivated. For this service he received the Distinguished Service Medal. He also received the Croix de Guerre with two palms and was made a Commander of the Legion of Honor (France). In 1920, he became Inspector General of the Eleventh Corps Area, and in May 1921, he served as Chief of Staff. In 1922, he commanded the Fourth Coast Artillery District at Fort McPherson, Georgia. On 5 December 1922, he retired due to disabilities. His retirement home was in Los Gatos, California. At the age of seventy-six, he died in the Palo Alto Hospital in California, on 24 February 1941. Photo courtesy of the National Archives.

John Sheridan Winn (0-205) was born on 26 November 1863 in Kentucky. He entered USMA and graduated number nine of forty-four in the class of 1888. Peyton C. March and Guy Henry Preston (both *q.v.*) were two of his classmates. He was commissioned in the Second Cavalry and performed frontier duty from 1888 to 1892. From 1892 to 1896, he was an instructor in mathematics in West Point, New York. He also served in the Ninth and Fourth Cavalry Regiments. He was with the Second Cavalry in Tampa, Florida in 1898, in Cuba until 1902 and on duty in the Philippines from 1906 to 1907. On 17 December 1917, he was promoted to brigadier general (NA) and was Inspector of the Southern Department. He commanded several infantry brigades in the AEF, for which he received the Silver Star. In 1922, he retired as a colonel, his permanent rank, and lived in Berkeley, California. At the age of seventy-six, he died, on 24 January 1940. Photo courtesy of the National Archives.

John Sheridan Winn

Eben Eveleth Winslow

Eben Eveleth Winslow (0-215) was born on 13 May 1866 in Washington, D.C. He entered USMA and graduated number forty-one of forty-nine in the class of 1889. William W. Harts, Charles Crawford, William G. Haan, William Lassiter and Charles Young (the third African-American to graduate from the academy and the first to retire as a colonel), were five of his classmates. He was commissioned in the Corps of Engineers and performed rivers, harbors and fortifications duty in the area of Mobile, Alabama until 1896. He was sent to USMA as an instructor until 1898. In July of that year, he served in the Battle of San Juan in Cuba, then was sent to Memphis, Tennessee, where he worked on improvements to the Mississippi River until 1902. He spent a year in Wilmington, North Carolina, then four years in Norfolk, Virginia. During 1906 and 1907, he was commandant of the Engineer School at Washington Barracks, then served in the office of the Chief of Engineers. From 1914 to 1918, he was assistant to the Chief of Engineers, during which period, on 5 August 1917, he was promoted to brigadier general (NA). For his performance of this duty he received the Distinguished Service Medal. In 1922, he was retired as a colonel due to disabilities. At the age of sixty-two, he died in his home in Raleigh, North Carolina, on 28 June 1928. He was survived by his widow, a daughter, Mary, and a son, Lieut. W. R. Winslow. His rank of brigadier general was restored posthumously by act of Congress in July 1930. Photo courtesy of Special Collections, USMA Library.

Francis Anderson Winter, M.D. (0-228), son of William Drew Winter and Sarah Sterling Winter, was born on 30 June 1876 in St. Francisville, a few miles upstream from Baton Rouge, Louisiana. His family had come from England to Maine in the mid-eighteenth century, and he was a descendant of John and Priscilla Alden. His early education was at a Jesuit school in Louisiana, then at a military academy in Warrenton, Virginia. He received his M.D. from Washington University in 1889, interned in St. Louis and began a practice there with another doctor. He entered the army in 1892 and

Francis Anderson Winter, M.D.

was commissioned an assistant surgeon with the rank of first lieutenant. He served in the West until 1897, when he was sent to USMA. On 27 October 1897, he married Mary D. Smith of Warrenton, Virginia, and they had one daughter, Mary Stuart Winter (Mrs. Edmund G. Chamberlain). He was a medical officer with the cavalry in Cuba during the Spanish-American War, and in 1899, he was sent to the Philippines as a medical officer with the 12th Infantry. He returned to the States in 1901. He served in Arizona, and in 1905, he was sent back to the Philippines for two years. He was stationed at Fort Myer, Virginia and was an instructor at the Army Medical School in Washington. In 1909, he became an assistant to the Surgeon General of the army. In 1912, he was promoted to lieutenant colonel, and from 1913 to 1916, he commanded the Army and Navy General Hospital in Hot Springs, Arkansas. He returned to Manila until 1917, when he was brought back to the States for World War I. He was sent to France as a colonel, Chief Surgeon of the Service of Supply. He received the Distinguished Service Medal for his performance as Chief Surgeon of the Lines of Communications (AEF). On 1 May 1918, he was promoted to brigadier general (NA) and became Chief Surgeon of Base Section Number Three in England, where he increased the facility for American troops from 400 to 12,000 beds. In 1918 and 1919, he was commandant of the Army Medical Department research and graduate school in Washington, after which he served as Chief Surgeon of the Southern Department. In 1922, he retired as a colonel and operated a hospital in Bethlehem, Pennsylvania. His rank of brigadier general was restored in 1930. He was socially active and fond of reading and study. At the age of sixty-three, he died in Washington, on 11 January 1931. Photo courtesy of the Walter Reed Army Institute of Research, Washington, D.C.

Edmund Wittenmyer

Edmund Wittenmyer (0-200) was born on 25 April 1862 in Buford, Ohio. He entered USMA and graduated number fifty-five of sixty-four in the class of 1887. P. D. Lochridge, Charles Henry Martin, William Weigel (all *q.v.*) and Thomas Q. Donaldson were four of his classmates. He was commissioned and sent to the Ninth Infantry, and he later served with the Fifteenth, Tenth, Fifth, Sixth and Twenty-seventh Infantry Regiments. He was on duty at the World's Fair in Chicago in 1893. He served in Cuba in 1898 and 1899 and in the Philippines in 1900. In 1900, he also served as adjutant of the Second Brigade of the China Relief Expedition, and from 1906 to 1910, he served in the Pacification of Cuba. In 1914, he was military attaché in Cuba. On 5 August 1917, he was promoted to brigadier general (NA) and commanded the 153rd Infantry Brigade at Camp Upton, Long Island, New York. On 1 October 1918, he was promoted to major general (NA), and from 28 October 1918, he commanded the Seventh Infantry Division until its inactivation on 22 September 1921. For this service he received the Distinguished Service Medal. He reverted to his rank of colonel and was promoted to brigadier general (USA) in 1922. In 1923, he retired and lived in Peebles, Colorado. His rank of major general was restored in 1930. At the age of seventy-five, he died in Washington D.C., on 3 July 1937. Photo from the National Archives.

Paul Alexander Wolf (0-305) was born on 23 December 1868 in Kewanee, Illinois. He entered USMA and graduated number forty-one of fifty-four in the class of 1890. Edgar Jadwin, James A. Ryan and Fred W. Sladen (all *q.v.*) were three of his classmates. He was commissioned in the infantry and served in the last of the late Indian Wars as well as in Cuba during the Spanish-American War. He also served during the Philippine Insurrection and the Vera Cruz Expedition in 1914, and General Funston made him military governor of Vera Cruz. He was a distinguished marksman, and was one of the best rifle shots in the army. On 17 December 1917, he was promoted to brigadier general (NA) and commanded the 66th Infantry Brigade, part of the 33d Infantry Division (AEF), for which he received the Distinguished Service Medal. At the close of the AEF rifle, pistol and musketry competition in LeMans, France in 1919, he tried out for the American team. He was likely the only general officer to try out for a rifle team. After the war, he commanded the Ninth Infantry at Fort Sam Houston, Texas, and coached his own regimental rifle team. In addition to the decoration already mentioned, he received the Croix de Guerre and was made an Officer of the Legion of Honor (France) and a Companion of the Bath (Britain). When he was a lieutenant, the rule was that any officer who complained about the mess automatically became the new mess officer. He endured this assignment for several months and could get no one to complain about the meals. One morning at breakfast another lieutenant came in, and when he brought him his coffee the lieutenant mumbled, "Cold coffee, eggs overdone, toast burnt." He was all ears, listening intently for more complaint, but the officer smiled sweetly and said, "But that's the way I like my breakfast." He retired due to disability in 1932. He was promoted to major general (retired list) in 1942. He was one of the greater sportsmen in the service; he played tennis, golfed, fished and enjoyed bowling, football and baseball. His favorite recreations were hunting and fishing. He embodied the diplomat as well as the commander, and always prided himself on

Paul Alexander Wolf

having a happy garrison. At the age of eighty-five, he died in San Antonio, Texas, on 12 January 1954. Photo from *The Assembly*, Association of Graduates, USMA.

Leonard Wood

Leonard Wood (0-2), son of Charles Jewett Wood and Caroline Hagar Wood, was born on 9 October 1860 in Winchester, New Hampshire. His ancestors for eight generations had lived in New England following their arrival on the *Mayflower*. His education began at a private academy and Harvard Medical School, from which he graduated in 1884 with an M.D. He began his army service as a contract surgeon in 1885, and he served in the Apache Campaigns with Capt. Henry Lawton, for which he belatedly received a Medal of Honor in 1898. By then he had transferred to the line and was colonel of the First United States Volunteer Cavalry, better known as the Rough Riders. His good friend Theodore Roosevelt was lieutenant colonel, and succeeded to regimental command when Wood got his star. On 18 November 1890, he married Louise Condit-Smith, a ward of Justice Field of the Supreme Court. The entire United States Supreme Court was present as witnesses at their wedding. They had two sons: Osborne C. Wood and Leonard Wood, Jr. He was promoted to brigadier general, then to major general for his actions in Las Guasimas and at San Juan Hill. He had a superb record as military governor of Cuba, and was promoted to major general (USA) on 8 August 1903. He was appointed governor of the Moro Province in the Philippines and commanded the Philippine Department from 1906 to 1908. He served as Chief of Staff (USA) from 1910 to 1914 and was the principal leader of the preparedness movement before the United States entered World War I. President Wilson kept him from serving in the AEF, perhaps because he was a friend of Theodore Roosevelt. In 1920, he was a serious contender for the Republican nomination for the presidency. On 5 October 1921, he retired after thirty years of service. In 1921, he headed the Wood-Forbes Mission to the Philippines, then remained as governor until 1927. He was a man with a powerful physique, driving energy, adamant convictions and a strong character. As the result of an operation, he died at the age of sixty-six in Boston, Massachusetts, on 7 August 1927. There is a two-volume biography of him by Herman Hagedorn. Fort Leonard Wood, Missouri is named after him. Photo courtesy of Col. Ezekiel Ortiz, New Mexico National Guard, Santa Fe, New Mexico.

Robert Elkington Wood (0-3847), son of Robert Whitney Wood and Lillie Collins Wood, was born on 13 June 1879 in Kansas City, Missouri. He entered USMA and graduated number thirteen of fifty-four in the class of 1900. Augustine McIntyre (*q.v.*) was one of his classmates. He was commissioned and sent to the Third Cavalry. He served in the Philippines during the Insurrection until 1902. From 1903 to 1905, he was on the Isthmian Canal Commission. In 1905, he became chief quartermaster and a Director of the Panama Railroad Company, and he was involved in the construction of the Panama Canal. On 30 April 1908, he married Mary Butler Hardwick, and they had five children: Anne H. Wood, Frances E. Wood, Sarah S. Wood, Robert W. Wood and Mary Stoval Wood. In 1915, he retired as a major and was assistant to the president of General Asphalt Company. He went back to duty for World War I as a lieutenant colonel. He was promoted to brigadier general (NA) on 15 April 1918. During 1918 and 1919, he was acting Quartermaster General (USA), for which he received the Distinguished Service Medal. From 1919 to 1924, he was vice president of Montgomery Ward Company in Chicago, Illinois. From 1924 to 1928, he was vice president of Sears Roebuck and Company, and in 1928, he was made president. He was elected to the Merchants Mart Hall of Fame. In the mid-1930s, he had an argument with President Franklin D. Roosevelt, which earned him the sympathy and support of people who might otherwise never have known his name. From 1939 to 1954, he was the chairman of the board of Sears, Roebuck and Company. From 1942 to 1945, he was a consultant for the Army Air Force, for which he received the Legion of Merit. After 1954, he was the chairman of the Sears Finance Committee. In addition to the decoration already mentioned, he received the Philippine Island Insurrection Medal and the Panama Canal Medal, and he was made a companion of the Order of St. Michael and St. George (Britain) and an officer of the Legion of Honor (France). At the age of ninety, he died on 6 November 1969. Photo courtesy of the USMA Archives.

Robert Elkington Wood

William Thomas Wood (0-13251), son of Preston Wood and Jane Wood, was born on 19 June 1854 in Irving, Illinois. He entered USMA and graduated number forty-two of seventy-six in the class of 1877. Augustus P. Blocksom, Thomas Henry Barry (both *q.v.*) and William Murray Black, were three of his classmates. He was commissioned and sent to the Fourth Infantry. On 27 September 1877, he married Janet T. Sanford, and they had one daughter, Janet (Mrs. H. C. Pillsbury, USA). He was Professor of Military Science and Tactics at the Illinois Industrial University from 1880 to 1883 and performed

William Thomas Wood

frontier duty until 1890. He served at Fort Clark and Fort Bliss, Texas before becoming Chief Ordnance Officer of the Department of the Pacific in 1898. From March to November 1899, he was collector of customs at Cebu in the Philippines. He was the treasurer of the Philippine Archipelago and the Island of Guam from 1899 to 1900. For his service during the Spanish-American War, he received two Silver Star Commendations and a Purple Heart, and he was cited in War Department orders for gallantry in action near Manila. After the Philippine Insurrection, he served in the Inspector General's Department until 1910, when he took command of the 19th Infantry and Camp Jossman in the Philippines. From 1911 to 1913, he commanded the recruit depot at Jefferson Barracks, St. Louis, Missouri, which was the training center for the dragoons before the American Civil War. In 1913, he retired as a colonel due to disabilities. On 16 May 1917, he was returned to active duty and served in Washington in the office of the Inspector General. On 18 February 1918, he was promoted to brigadier general (NA). Except for a short inspection tour of Europe from May to July 1919, he remained in the Office of the Inspector General until 1920. He received the Distinguished Service Medal (presented by General Pershing) for his service as Senior Assistant to the Inspector General of the army. He retired as a colonel again, and his rank of brigadier general was restored in 1930. At the age of eighty-nine, he died in the Walter Reed Army Medical Center in Washington, on 18 December 1943. Photo from the USMA Archives.

John Edwin Woodward

John Edwin Woodward (0-411) was born on 24 May 1870 in Poultney, Vermont. He entered USMA and graduated number fifty-one of sixty-two in the class of 1892. Charles P. Sumerall, James A. Shipton and William R. Smith (all *q.v.*) were three of his classmates. He was commissioned in the infantry and later transferred to the Adjutant General's Department. He served during the Philippine Insurrection and the Moro Expedition of 1903. From 1912 to 1914, he was an aide to Gen. Thomas H. Barry (*q.v.*). During World War I, he commanded the 113th Infantry Regiment. On 8 August

1918, while commanding Camp Upton, New York, he was promoted to brigadier general (NA). He commanded the 152nd Depot Brigade until 4 September 1918, after which he commanded the 24th Infantry Brigade. Beginning in February 1919, he commanded the 151st Depot Brigade. His principal stations were Washington, D.C., Governor's Island, New York, Camp Upton, New York, Douglas, Arizona, Camp McClellan, Alabama and Fort Leavenworth, Kansas. From 1929 to 1934, he served as Adjutant General of the Second Corps Area, headquartered on Governor's Island. In 1934, he retired as a brigadier general (USA) due to disabilities. He lived in Mendon, Vermont and was the senior officer of the Adjutant General's Department. At the age of seventy-four, he died on 4 August 1944. He was survived by his widow and two daughters, Mrs. Norma Leslie Woodward and Lieut. (junior grade) Nancy C. Woodward, and three sons, John J. Woodward of Washington, D.C., Cdr. E. C. Woodward (USN) and 1st Lieut. T. P. Woodward (USA). He had eight grandchildren. Photo from Special Collections, USMA Library.

William Mason Wright

William Mason Wright (0-32), son of Edward Wright and Dora Wright, was born on 24 September 1863 in Newark, New Jersey. He entered USMA with the class of 1886, stayed for two years, then was commissioned in the Second Infantry on 19 January 1885, the year before the rest of his class graduated. Mason M. Patrick, Charles T. Menoher, John J. Pershing and Edward W. McCaskey (all *q.v.*) were four of his classmates. In 1891, he graduated from the Infantry and Cavalry School at Fort Leavenworth, Kansas. In June of that year, he married Marjorie Jerauld and they had three children: William, Jerauld and Marjorie. After the Santiago Campaign in Cuba, he served in the Philippines. From 1 August 1907 to 6 April 1908, he was secretary of the General Staff, and he served with General Funston in Vera Cruz in 1914. He was promoted to brigadier general (NA) on 15 May 1917. On 5 August 1917, he was promoted to major general (NA) and commanded first the 35th Infantry Division with the British, then the 89th Infantry Division. He commanded the 35th Infantry Division from 25 August 1917 to 18 September 1917 and again from 10 December 1917 to 15 June 1918. He commanded the Third Corps from 17 June 1918 to 14 July 1918, the Fifth Corps from 12 July 1918 to 21 August 1918, the Seventh Corps from 19 August 1918 to 6 September 1918 and the First Corps from 13 November 1918 to 25 March 1919, the date of its inactivation. He served as Assistant Chief of Staff (USA) G-4 (supply) until July 1921, when he was given command of the Ninth Corps Area, headquartered in San Francisco,

California. His final assignment was as commander of the Hawaiian Department, where he served until September 1922. On 31 December 1922, he retired as a lieutenant general (USA). In addition to the decoration already mentioned, he received the Croix de Guerre with palm and was made a Commander of the Legion of Honor (France), a Knight Commander of the Order of St. Michael and St. George (Britain), a Grand Officer of the Order of Leopold (Belgium) and an Officer of the Order of the Rising Sun (Japan). He was promoted to lieutenant general after the war. At the age of seventy-nine, he died in Washington, D.C., on 16 August 1943. The photo, from the National Archives, was taken at Camp Doniphan, Fort Sill.

Richard Whitehead Young (no ASN assigned), son of Joseph Angel Young and Margaret Whitehead Young, was born on 19 April 1858 in Salt Lake City, Utah. From 1874 to 1877, he studied at the University of Utah. He entered USMA and graduated number fifteen of thirty-seven in the class of 1882. Adelbert Cronkhite and Henry T. Allen (both *q.v.*) were two of his classmates, as was Fredrick Gilmore Bonfils of the Denver Post. He was commissioned and sent to the Fifth Artillery. On 5 September 1882, he married Minerva Richards. He studied at Columbia University, from which he received an LL.B. in 1884. He was then admitted to the New York State Bar. He was a captain and acting Judge Advocate General on the staff of Gen. Winfield Scott from 1884 to 1886. In 1889, he resigned from the army and practiced law in Salt Lake City. During 1890 and 1891, he was the Latter Day Saint member of the Salt Lake City Council. In 1895, he entered the Utah National Guard and was promoted to brigadier general. During the Spanish-American War and the Philippine Insurrection, he commanded a battery of light artillery from Utah as a major, and for his service in the Philippines he received the Medal of Honor. He was Associate Justice of the Supreme Court of the Philippines from 1899 to 1901. In 1917, he was colonel of the First Utah Artillery and later, of the 145th Field Artillery. On 12 April 1918, he was promoted to brigadier general (NA). He wrote one book, *Mobs and the Military* (published in 1888). His home was in Salt Lake City, where at the age of sixty-one, he died on 27 December 1919. Photo courtesy of the National Archives.

Richard Whitehead Young

Charles Xavier Zimmerman, son of Carl Zimmerman and Theresa Zimmerman, was born on 18 January 1865 in Cleveland, Ohio. He enlisted in the

Charles Xavier Zimmerman

Fifth Ohio Infantry on 8 May 1884. He married Anna Hill, who died in mid-December 1897. During the Spanish-American War, he commanded Company F, Fifth Ohio Infantry. On 5 June 1900, he married Ethel Vogt. He served in the Ohio National Guard, and was promoted to brigadier general (NA) on 5 August 1917. He was commanding general of the 73d Infantry Brigade, part of the 37th Infantry Division, from 19 November 1917 to 17 January 1918, from 22 January 1918 to 18 February 1918, from 23 February 1918 to 15 March 1918, from 17 March 1918 to 22 April 1918, from 28 April 1918 to 6 June 1918 and from 9 June 1918 to 8 October 1918. On 5 February 1919, he was discharged. He served at Camp Sheridan, Alabama, Camp Lee, Virginia and Camp Beauregarde, Louisiana. With the AEF in France, he served during the Meuse-Argonne offensive in the defensive sector. After World War I, he moved to New York City, where at the age of sixty-one, he died of cancer, on 13 November 1926. He was buried in Knollwood Cemetery, Mayfield Heights, Ohio. Photo from the National Archives.

The biographies of the following three officers are not strictly within the scope of this book as they were not generals who served during World War I, but they are often mentioned in the other biographies and are too interesting to pass up!

John Lincoln Clem (0-12983), son of Roman Clem and Mary Weber Clem, was born on 13 August 1851 in Newark, Ohio. He ran away and attempted to enlist in both the Third Ohio Infantry and the 22d Michigan Volunteer Infantry, but was rejected by both for his youth and height-he was less than five feet tall. The 22d Michigan Infantry accepted him as a drummer on 1 May 1862 and provided him with a cut-down uniform and a cut-down musket. When things were going badly at Shiloh and most of the men were energetically running the wrong way, he kept on drumming and advancing, nearly alone.

John Lincoln Clem

General Grant appeared by his side, and the combination of the two inspired many of the men to turn and face the Confederates. Thus he earned his nickname, "the Drummer Boy of Shiloh." In Chickamauga, he was isolated from his unit and was pursued by a Confederate colonel, who burst into scornful laughter at the sight of him. He responded with a point-blank shot from his musket. Over half of the men in his regiment were killed, and the remainder, including Johnny, were taken prisoner. After sixty-three days, he escaped. General W. S. Rosencrans made him a sergeant and put him on duty at his headquarters. He was proud of his cap, which had three holes from Rebel bullets from Chickamauga. In addition to the two battles already mentioned, he was present in Perryville, Stone River, Resaca, Kennesaw Mountain, Atlanta and Nashville. After the war, he returned to Ohio to finish his schooling. He attempted to enter USMA but he failed the entrance exam. President Grant personally coached him for his next exam, which he also failed. President Grant then appointed him second lieutenant in the 24th Infantry on 18 December 1871. He graduated from the Artillery School at Fort Monroe in 1875. On 24 May of that year, he married Anita Rosetta French, daughter of W. H. French. His wife died in 1899. On 3 September 1903, he married Bessie Sullivan of San Antonio, Texas, and they had two children: John L. Clem, Jr. and Anna E. Clem. From 1903 to 1906, he was quartermaster of the Philippine Division, and from 1906 to 1911, he was quartermaster of the Department of Texas. From 1911 to 1915, he was quartermaster of the Department of the (Great) Lakes, headquartered in Chicago, Illinois. On 13 August 1916, he was promoted to brigadier general (USA), and on 29 August 1916, he was promoted to major general (USA). He was the last Civil War veteran on active duty, and the ranking general in the army for length of service. He was a Republican and a Catholic. His retirement home was in San Antonio. At the age of eighty-five, he died on 13 May 1937. Photo courtesy of the National Archives.

Fredrick Funston

Fredrick Funston (no ASN assigned), son of United States Congressman Edward Hogue Funston (also known as "Foghorn Funston"), was born on 9 November 1865 in New Carlisle, Ohio. He attended the University of Kansas. He was a commissioner for the Department of Agriculture during the Exploration of Alaska in 1893 and 1894 as well as during the exploration of Death Valley. He was also a newspaper reporter, a Santa Fe railroad conductor and a coffee planter in Central America. He was married and had two sons (one of whom died very young) and two daughters. In 1896, he volunteered in the Cuban Army under Maximo Gomez and Calixto Garcia. Within eighteen months, he was in eighteen engagements and four battles and had nineteen horses killed under him, one of which landed on his hip and gave him a permanent limp. He became sick and was captured by the Spanish and sentenced to death, but eventually, he was liberated. He returned to Kansas in 1898 and lectured across the state about Cuba, which brought him to the attention of the governor, John W. Leedy. When the United States declared war with Spain, Kansas was asked to raise three regiments of volunteers, and Leedy gave him command of the Twentieth Kansas Regiment. The regiment was ordered to San Francisco, California, but he was sent to Tampa, Florida to be questioned by Gen. W. R. Shafter, who would lead the troops in Cuba. He was only thirty-two, a militia colonel, and was not even in uniform when he reported to Shafter. It was a very chilly reception, the first of many. He was snubbed by General Miles as well. When he returned to San Francisco, he drove himself and his men hard. They arrived in Manila on 30 November 1898 and were assigned to the Second Division under Gen. Arthur MacArthur who, having been the youngest colonel in the Union Army, had no objections to the young militia colonel. In the spring of 1899, a drive was started north, up the railroad to the Lingayen Gulf, and his name was mentioned often. He was not only a young militia colonel, but he was tiny, less than five-foot-five and just over 100 pounds. When asked how long he could hold his position, his reply was, "Until my regiment is mustered out." He was promoted to brigadier general of volunteers at the age of thirty-three and won the Congressional Medal of Honor. Early in September 1899, his regiment returned to the States, but by December he was back in the Philippines commanding a district in northern Luzon. The insurgents steadily dwindled over the next fourteen months, leaving a hardened group commanded by Emilio Aguinaldo, a self-proclaimed dictator. Relying on their hatred of Aguinaldo's Tagalogs, he conceived the idea of using Macabebe scouts to capture him at his own headquarters. General MacArthur told him he was under orders to return to the States for discharge, but he got an extension for special duty. The general told him of the hazards, and said he did not expect to see him alive again. Exactly two weeks later, Funston called on General MacArthur, who was still in his dressing gown, and reported that Aguinaldo was under guard in a nearby room. MacArthur was jubilant, and recommended to the War Department that Funston be retained in the volunteers until he could be appointed brigadier general in the regular army. President McKinley did just that, with much protest from the regular army. However, as they got to know him better, many regular officers supported him, among them Thomas H. Barry (*q.v.*). He continually tried to improve the enlisted pay and rations. At the time of the San Francisco earthquake and fire, he was acting division commander in the temporary absence of General Greely. There was no time to ask Washington for help; he took command and did well in preventing looting, stopping the spread of fire and getting water, food and shelter to people. He was praised nationwide, even by the very newspapers that had criticized him. He did not declare martial law, but got things done using tact and persuasion. In 1910, he was commandant of the Army Service Schools. By 1913, he was back in the Philippines and in April 1914, he commanded the Vera Cruz Expedition, relieving the navy there. On 17 November 1914, he was promoted to major general (USA). He was the overall commander at the time of the Mexican Punitive Expedition. He pioneered the pattern of high-level military command, and so was chosen to command the American forces in France. When the United States troops were returning from Mexico, he left his headquarters to inspect and watch the Eleventh cavalry pass in review. The regimental adjutant was Lt. Joe Viner, son-in-law of Col. Henry T. Allen (*q.v.*). General Pershing accompanied him as adjutant. Lieutenant Viner took the reports of the squadron commanders, reported to the regimental commander and then joined the staff to await the arrival of the reviewing party. The lieutenant's horse was a handsome white animal, recently purchased from a local rancher. Army policy prohibited stallions in military units, so his new mount had been immediately gelded. Viner and the new regimental vet performed the operation and missed one testicle, which of course left the animal a stud. Of this fact no one was the wiser, until the review. It seems the General's mount was not only a mare, but was in heat, and the predictable occurred. As Funston and Pershing rode out to the place of honor for the review, Viner's mount gave a loud whinny, charged and mounted Funston's mare with the general still in the saddle. The little general fought successfully to retain his seat, but there was considerable damage to his dignity and composure. Several minutes elapsed before aides could separate the wildly pawing and plunging pair. The regimental formation dissolved into a formless mass as riders abandoned reins to hold their sides in helpless laughter. Order was eventually restored, but the review was ragged-looking indeed. Pershing's near apoplexy dissolved into cold fury. An abashed Lieutenant Viner stood before him that night to receive a merciless dressing down. He was dismissed with the words, "I never want to see you again, lieutenant." Pershing later confessed to Allen that he had nearly drawn his saber and chased Viner off the parade ground, and that it was only the fact that he was Allen's son-in-law that had prevented his court-martial. The strain of Funston's work eventually wore him down. On 19 February 1917, after a marvelous dinner at the St. Anthony Hotel in San Antonio, Texas, he made the remark, "Isn't the music beautiful!" He peacefully closed his eyes and died at the age of fifty-one. He was buried in San Francisco. Photo courtesy of the National Archives.

Andrew Summers Rowan (0-13817), son of John M. Rowan and Virginia Wirt Summers Rowan, was born on 23 April 1857 in Gap Mills, Virginia. He entered USMA and graduated number forty-two of fifty-three in the class of 1881. Harry Foote Hodges, Henry Clay Hodges, Joseph T. Dickman and Edwin St. John Greble (all *q.v.*) were four of his classmates. He was commissioned in the 15th Infantry and performed frontier duty from 1881 to 1889. He was stationed in Pembina, North Dakota. From 1893 to 1898, he served in the Adjutant General's Office. Just before the outbreak of the Spanish-American War, he was on duty with military intelligence in the War Department. He served under Col. Arthur Wagner, the chief. On 8 April 1898, after the sinking of the United States battleship *Maine* in Havana Harbor on 15 February, President McKinley sent for Colonel Wagner and asked whether he knew any man who could deliver a message to Col. Calixto Garcia, the leader of the Cuban revolutionists. Wagner replied that he had a young lieutenant in his office who could do it. President McKinley told him to proceed. Colonel Wagner returned to his office and took Rowan out to lunch at the Army and Navy Club. They were barely seated when he asked Rowan when the next ship would sail for Jamaica. Wagner had a reputation as an inveterate joker, and though Rowan suspected this was a joke, he excused himself for a few minutes, came back and reported, "The *Adirondak* sails at noon tomorrow for Jamaica." He was told to go and was given the president's instructions. He arrived in Jamaica on 20 April, war was declared 21 April and the following day, he was directed to join Garcia as quickly as possible. It was 100 miles across open sea to Cuba, and the Spanish patrol boats were numerous. The journey through Cuba was even more risky than the sea crossing. He had many close calls and narrowly escaped assassination, but he did reach Garcia and delivered his message. For this service he received the Distinguished Service Cross and was eulogized by Elbert Hubbard in one of the more famous and widely circulated essays of this century, "The Message to Garcia." He became a celebrated American hero. During the Spanish-American War, he was a lieutenant of volunteers. He served nineteen years in the Tenth Infantry. On 1 December 1909, he retired as a major after thirty years of service. He lived with his wife at 1036 Vallejo Street, San Francisco, California. At the age of eighty-five, he died on 10 January 1943. Photo from *The Assembly*, Association of Graduates, USMA.

Andrew Summers Rowan

A Message To Garcia

by Elbert Hubbard

In all this Cuban business there is one man who stands out on the horizon of my memory like Mars at perihelion.

When war broke out between Spain and the United States, it was very necessary to communicate quickly with the leader of the insurgents. Garcia was somewhere in the mountain fastnesses of Cuba—no one knew where. No mail or telegraph Message could reach him. The President must secure his cooperation—and quickly.

What to do?

Someone said to the President, "there is a fellow by the name of Rowan who will find Garcia for you, if anybody can."

Rowan was sent for and given a letter to be delivered to Garcia. How "the fellow by the name of Rowan took the letter, strapped it over his heart, in four days landed by night off the Coast of Cuba from an open boat, disappeared in the jungle, and in three weeks came out on the other side of the island, having traversed a hostile country on foot and delivered his message to Garcia are things I have no special desire now to tell in detail.

The point I wish to make is this: McKinley gave Rowan a letter to be delivered to Garcia: Rowan took the letter and did not ask, "Where is he?"

By the Eternal! there is a man whose form should be cast in deathless bronze and the statue placed in every college in the land. It is not book-learning young men need, nor instruction about this and that, but a stiffening of the vertebrae which will cause them to be loyal to a trust, to act promptly, concentrate all their energies: do the thing—"Carry a Message to Garcia."

General Garcia is dead now, but there are other Garcias. No man who has endeavored to carry out an enterprise but has been well nigh appalled at times by the imbecility of the average man—the inability or unwillingness to concentrate on a thing and do it. Slipshod assistance, foolish inattention, dowdy indifference, and half-hearted work seem the rule—and no man succeeds unless, by hook or crook, or threat, he forces and bribes other men to assist him; or mayhap, God in his goodness performs a miracle and sends him an Angel of Light for an Assistant. You, reader, put this matter to a test. You are sitting now in your office: six clerks are within call. Summon any one and make this request: "Please look in the encyclopedia and make a brief memorandum on the life of Corregio."

Will the clerk quietly say, "Yes, sir," and go do the task?

On your life, he will not. He will look at you out of a fishy eye and ask one or more of the following questions:

Who was he?

Which encyclopedia?

Was I hired for that?

Don't you mean Bismark?

What's the matter with Charlie doing it?

Is he dead?

Is there any hurry?

Shan't I bring you the book and let you look it up yourself?

What do you want to know for?

And I will lay you ten to one that after you have answered the questions, and explained how to find the information, and why you want it, the clerk will go off and get one of the other clerks to help him try to find Garcia and then come back and tell you there is no such man. Of course I may lose my bet, but according to the law of averages, I will not. Now if you are wise, you will not bother to explain to your "assistant" that Corregio is indexed under the Cs, not the Ks, but you will smile sweetly and say "Never mind" and go look it up yourself.

And this incapacity for independent action, this moral stupidity, this infirmity of the will, this unwillingness cheerfully to catch hold and lift—these are things that put pure socialism so far in the future. If men will not act for themselves, what will they do when the benefit of their efforts is for all? A first mate with a knotted club seems necessary; and the dread of "getting the bounce" Saturday night holds many a worker to his place. Advertise for a stenographer, and nine out of ten who apply can neither spell nor punctuate—and do not think it necessary to. Can such a one write a letter to Garcia?

"You see the bookkeeper," said the foreman to me in a large factory,

"Yes, what about him?"

"Well, he's a fine accountant, but if I'd send him uptown on an errand, he might accomplish the errand all right and, on the other hand, might stop at four saloons on the way, and when he got to Main Street, would forget what he had been sent for."

Can such a man carry a message to Garcia?

We have recently been hearing-much maudlin sympathy expressed for the "downtrodden denizens of the sweatshop" and the "homeless wanderer in search of honest work" and with it all often go many hard words for the men in power.

Nothing is said about the employer who grows old before his time in a vain attempt to get frowzy ne'er-do-wells to do intelligent work; and his long patient striving with "help" that does nothing but loaf when his back is turned. In every store and factory there is a constant weeding out process going on. The employer is constantly sending away "help" that have shown their incapacity to further the interests of the business and others are being taken on. No matter how good times are, this sorting continues; only, if times are hard and work is scarce, the sorting is done finer—but out and forever out, the incompetent and the unworthy go. It is the survival of the fittest. Self interest prompts every employer to keep the best—those who can carry a message to Garcia.

I know one man of really brilliant parts who has not the ability to manage a business of his own, and yet who is absolutely worthless to anyone else, because he carries with him constantly the insane suspicion that his employer is opressing or intending to opress him. He cannot give orders, and he will not receive them. Should a message be given him to take to Garcia, his answer would probably be, "Take it yourself."

Tonight this man walks the streets looking for work, the wind whistling through his threadbare coat. No one who knows him dares employ him, for he is a regular firebrand of discontent. He is impervious to reason, and the only thing that can impress him is the toe of a thick soled number nine boot.

Of course I know that no one so morally deformed is no less to be pitied than a physical cripple; but in our pitying, let us drop a tear or two for the men who are striving to carry on a great enterprise, and whose working hours are not limited by the whistle; and whose hair is fast turning white through the struggle to hold in line dowdy indifference, slipshod imbecility, and heartless ingratitude which, but for their enterprise, would be both hungry and homeless.

Have I put the matter too strongly? Possibly I have; but when all the world has gone a-slumming, I wish to speak a word of sympathy for the man who succeeds—the man who, against great odds, has directed the efforts of others and, having succeeded, finds there's nothing in it—nothing but bare board and clothes.

I have carried a dinner pail and worked for a day's wages, and I have also been an employer of labor, and I know there is something to be said on both sides. There is no excellence, per se, in poverty. Rags are no recommendation, and all employers are not rapacious and high-handed, any more than all men are virtuous.

My heart goes out to the man who does his work when the "Boss" is away as well as when he is at home. And the man who, when given a letter to Garcia, quietly takes the missive, without asking any idiotic questions and with no lurking intention of chucking it into the nearest sewer, or of doing aught else but deliver it, never gets laid off or has to go on strike for higher wages. Civilization is one long, anxious search for just such individuals. Anything such a man asks shall be granted; his kind is so rare that no employer can afford to let him go. He is wanted in every city, town and village—in every office, shop, store and factory. The world cries out for such; he is needed and needed badly—the man who can "Carry a Message To Garcia."

Appendix A
Interesting Data on these Generals

General Officer Brothers

Lucas and Willard Holbrook
Robert I. and Thomas Rees
Charles S. and George Blakely
William C. and Tyree R. Rivers

Commissioned Directly From Civil Life

William W. Atterbury
Charles Gates Dawes
Samuel McRoberts
Guy E. Tripp

U.S. Medical Officer Generals

W. H. Arthur
H.P. Birmingham
A. E. Bradley
J. M. T. Finney
W. C. Gorgas
J. D. Glennan
M. W. Ireland
J. R. Kean
T. C. Lyster
W. F. McCaw
E. L. Munson
R. E. Noble
Charles Richard
W. S. Thayer
F. A. Winter
A. M. Tuthill*
Leonard Wood*

* served as line officers

First Doctor of Philosophy in the Army

George O. Squier, Chief Signal Officer

Where They Came From

They were born in 39 states and the District of Columbia plus six foreign countries. New York, Pennsylvania, Ohio, Illinois, and Missouri furnished most of them, in that order. The foreign countries were England, Wales, France, and Germany.

General Officers in Both WWI and WWII

George R. Allin
R. W. Briggs
William Edward Cole
William D. O'Connor
Malin Craig
Edward H. DeArmond
B. P. Disque
R. M. Danford
John N. Hodges
Charles Keller
Douglas MacArthur
August McIntyre
Leslie J. McNair
J. H. Sherburne, Jr.
Oliver L. Spaulding
C. C. Williams

Appendix B
Higher Education (Honorary Degrees Not Included):

Institution	Name
Alabama Agricultural and Mechanical College	Robert Lee Bullard
Alabama Polytechnic Institute	Robert Ernest Noble, M.D.
Alleghany College (Pennsylvania)	Francis J. Koester
Allentown Business College	Christopher T. O'Neill
Bates College (Maine)	Mark L. Hersey
Bellevue Hospital Medical College	William C. Gorgas
Boston University Law School	E. L. Sweetzer
Center College (Kentucky)	Thomas Cruse
	Frank L. Winn
Charleston College	Campbell King
Cincinnati Law School	Charles G. Dawes
City College of New York	Charles Richard, M.D.
	T. H. Barry
Claverack College (New York)	R. M. Blatchford
Colby College (Maine)	Herbert M. Lord
	George W. Goethals
College of Mississippi	P. D. Lochridge
Columbia University	A. D. Andrews
	E. T. Donnelly
	William E. Harvey
	Andrew Hero, Jr.
	Walter Drew McCaw, M.D.
	Robert Ernest Noble, M.D.
Columbia Law School	James W. Lester
Columbian University (later called George Washington University)	James D. Glennan, M.D.
Cornell	Lincoln C. Andrews
Detroit College of Medicine	Merritte W. Ireland
Dickinson College (Carlisle)	Eben Swift
	Henry H. Whitney
East Florida Seminary	A. H. Blanding
Eastern State Normal School (Maine)	E. E. Hatch
Ewing College (Illinois)	Charles Henry Martin
Fordham University	John E. McMahon, Jr.
Fort Scott Normal School (Kansas)	Charles Irving Martin
Franklin and Marshall College	W. M. Black
	Robert C. Davis
	William H. Rose
	Henry D. Styer
Geneseo State Normal School	John L. Chamberlin

George Washington University	James D. Glennan, M.D.
	William L. Mitchell
	Charles D. Rhodes
Georgetown College (Kentucky)	Henry T. Allen
Georgetown University	Malin Craig
Griswold College (Iowa)	Clement A. F. Flagler
Harvard	Marlborough Churchill
	William V. Judson
	John W. Kilbreth
	Robert I. Rees
	John Henry Sherburne
	Robert E. Steiner
	William S. Thayer, M.D.
Harvard Medical School	John M. T. Finney, M.D.
	William S. Thayer, M.D.
	Leonard Wood, M.D.
Hobart College	William Wilson
Hubbard College (Texas)	Robert L. Howze
Indiana University	John T. Thompson
Iowa State College	Hubert T. Allen
	Edward A. Kreger
Iowa State Teachers College	George H. McManus
Iowa State University	J. D. Barrette
Jefferson Medical College	A. E. Bradley, M.D.
Johns-Hopkins University	George O. Squier, Ph.D.
Kansas State Agricultural College	W. P. Burnham
	James G. Harbord
Kansas State Normal School	Roy Hoffman
Knox College (Illinois)	Harry C. Hale
Lafayette College (Pennsylvania)	Edgar Jadwin
	Peyton C. March
Lehigh University	Mathew C. Smith
Marietta College (Ohio)	Charles G. Dawes
Michigan College of Mines	Robert I. Rees
Mississippi Agricultural and MechanicalCollege	Marcellus G. Spinks
Mount Union College	Evan M. Johnson, Jr.
New York Military Academy	Orval P. Townshend
New York State Normal School	C. P. Townsley
New York University Law School	A. D. Andrews
	E. T. Donnelly
	John Francis O'Ryan
	Robert I. Rees
Northern Ohio University	Harrison J. Price
Northwestern University	George H. Cameron
Norwich University	F. T. Austin
Notre Dame	Joseph P. O'Neil

Oberlin College	Wilder S. Metcalf
Otterville College (Missouri)	Rufus E. Longan
Pennsylvania Military College	William G. Price, Jr.
Pierce Business College (Pennsylvania)	Charles W. Barber
Princeton University	Richard Coulter
	William W. Harts
	Hugh L. Scott
	Charles E. Vollrath
Racine College (Wisconsin)	Eben Swift
Randolph-Macon	Cecil C. Vaughan, Jr.
Rensellaer Polytechnic Institute (New York)	
	R. M. Blatchford
	George P. Scriven
Richmond College (Virginia)	LeRoy S. Lyon
Rutgers College	Joseph C. Castner
	James Parker
Scarrett College (Missouri)	Harvey C. Clark
St. John's College	Henry Davis Todd, Jr.
Stevens Industrial Technical School	Isaac W. Littell
Thatcher Military Institute	Pegram Whitworth
Tulane University	Andrew Hero, Jr.
University of Alabama	Frank McIntyre
	William L. Sibert
	Robert E. Steiner
University of Chicago	George P. Scriven
University of Delaware	Herbert Deakyne
University of Georgia	George H. Estes, Jr.
	Walter A. Harris
University of Heidelberg (Germany)	John Biddle
University of Illinois	A. H. Sunderland
University of Iowa	George S. Gibbs
University of Kansas	Fredrick Funston
University of Maine	A. A. Starbird
University of Maryland	William H. Arthur, M.D.
University of Michigan	John Biddle
	Henry P. Birmingham, M.D.
	Henry J. Hatch
	Theodore C. Lyster, M.D.
	Samuel McRoberts
	Oliver L. Spaulding
University of Minnesota	A. W. Bjornstad
	William K. Naylor
University of Missouri	Enoch H. Crowder
University of Nashville	John E. Stephens
University of Pennsylvania	Raymond W. Briggs

University of the South	William C. Gorgas, M.D.
	Henry Jervey, Jr.
University of South Carolina	Johnson Hagood
University of Southern California Medical School	Alexander M. Tuthill, M.D.
University of Tennessee	Percy O. Bishop
University of Texas	Andrew Moses
University of Utah	Richard W. Young
University of Vermont	C. J. Bailey
	William Henry Burt
	William S. Pierce
University of Virginia	Jefferson R. Kean, M.D.
University of West Virginia	Gordon G. Heiner
University of Wisconsin	F. E. Bamford
	Charles R. Boardman
	Peter W. Davison
Vanderbilt University	Lytle Brown
	John W. Heard
	William R. Smith
Virginia Agricultural and Mechanical College	George H. Jamerson
Virginia Medical College	Walter Drew McCaw, M.D.
Virginia Military Institute	William B. Cochran
	Charles E. Kilbourne, Jr.
	R. C. Marshall
	Samuel D. Rockenbach
Washington University (Missouri)	Edward Burr
	William H. Johnston, Jr.
	Samuel D. Sturgis, Jr.
	Eben Swift
Washington University Medical School	Francis A. Winter, M.D.
West Chester State Normal School (Pennsylvania)	Robert A. Brown
	Robert W. Mearns
Williston Seminary (Massachusetts)	R. M. Blatchford
Wittenberg College	Charles E. Vollrath
Wyoming Seminary (Pennsylvania)	Charles B. Drake
	Joseph A. Gaston
Yale	W. W. Atterbury
	Preston Brown
	Sherwood A. Cheney
	Edward L. Munson, M.D
	Cornelius Vanderbilt

Bibliography of Published Sources

Benwell, Harry A. *History of The Yankee Division (26th)*. Boston: Cornwell &Co., 1919

Cullum, George Washington. *Biographical Register of Graduates of the United States Military Academy*, 3rd Edition. Boston: Houghton Mifflin, 1891

Cutchins, John A. *History of the 29th Division, Blue & Gray*. Philadelphia, Pennsylvania, 1921.

French, *History of Westchester County, New York*. Lewis Historical Publishing Company, 1925.

George, Albert E. and Edward H. Cooper. *Pictorial History of the 27th Division,* USA.Boston: Ball Publishing co., 1920.

Hagood, Johnson, *Services of Supply*. Boston: Houghton-Mifflin, 1927.

Heitman, Francis B. *Historical Register and Dictionary of the United States Army, GPO Washington, D.C.* 1903. Urbana: University of Illinois Press, 1965, facsimile reprint.

Hurley, Alfred F. *Billy Mitchell, Crusader for Air Power.* Bloomington, Indiana and London: Indiana University Press, 1964.

Landrum, Charles H. *Michigan In the (1st) World War, Military and Naval Honors of Michigan Men and Women*. Lansing, Michigan: Michigan Historical Commission,1925.

Murphy, Elmer A. *Thirtieth Division in the (1st) World War*. Lepanto, Arkansas: Old Hickory Publishing Company, 1920.

Ohio Adjutant General's Department. *Official Register of Ohio Soldiers, Sailors, and Marines in the World War, 1917-1918*. Columbus, Ohio: F.H. Heere Printing Co.,1926.

Strobridge, Col. William. *Golden Gate to Golden Horn*. San Francisco: San Mateo Historical Association

Twichell, Col. Heath. *Allen: The Biography of an Army Officer*. New Brunswick, New Jersey: Rutgers University Press, 1974.

Wilhard, Roger Day. *History of Lower Tidewater Virginia*. New York: Lewis Historical Publishing Co. Vol. 3, 1959.

U.S. Army, War Department. *Army List & Directory*. Washington, D.C. GPO, 1922.

Anonymous, *American Decorations: A List of Awards of the Congressional Medal, The Distinguished Service Cross and the Distinguished Service Medal*. Washington, D.C.: GPO, 1927.

Anonymous, *Annual Report* of *the Association of Graduates*, USMA, pre 1940.

Anonymous, *Army Almanac*. Washington, D. C.: GPO, 1950.

Anonymous, *Assembly, The*; Association of Graduates, USMA from 1940 on.

Anonymous, *Cavalry Journal*. Baltimore, MD: U.S. Cavalry Association, late 19th and 1st half of 20th Century

Anonymous, *Genealogical and Biographical Annals of Northumberland County, Pennsylvania*. Chicago: J. L. Floyd & C., 1921.

Anonymous, *History of the 33rd Division (Illinois)*. Chicago: States Publishing Society,1921.

Anonymous, *Pennsylvania in the (1st) World War, An Illustrated History of the 28th Division* USA. Chicago: States Publishing Society, 1921.

Anonymous, *Rasp, The*. Fort Riley Kansas, 1913-1927.

Anonymous, *Register of Graduates USMA, 1965*. West Point, New York: Association of Graduates, USMA 1965.
Anonymous, *Roster of Commissioned Officers, Virginia Volunteers*. Richmond, Virginia: Adjutant Generals of Virginia, 1921.
Anonymous, *26th Division Summary of Operations in the (1st) World War*. Washington, D.C.: GPO, 1944.
Anonymous, *Who Was Who in the American Military*. Chicago: Marquis' Who's Who,1975.
Association of Graduates, USMA (pre-1940) *Annual Report*
Association of Graduates, USMA (post-1940), *The Assembly*
Association of Graduates, USMA *Register of Graduates*, 1965.

Newspapers

Arizona Republic, Phoenix, Arizona
Bureau County (Ohio) Republican
El Paso Times (Texas)
Evening Tribune, San Diego, California
Herald, St. Peter, Minnesota
Herald Leader, Lexington, Kentucky
Milwaukee (Wisconsin) Sentinel
New York Times
San Antonio (Texas) Light
San Diego (California) Union
San Francisco (California) Examiner
St. Petersburg (Florida) Times

Appendix C

Pentland Press, Inc. wishes to clarify the following:

The following photographs:

pp. 147: The top photograph shows Gen. Farrand Sayre commanding Brownsville District of the Mexican Border.

pp. 271: Top right photograph is William Lendrum Mitchell. Lower left photograph is Samuel Warren Miller.

pp. 291: Top photograph is Francis Anderson Winter, M.D.

pp. 351: The person pictured is erroneously identified as Frederick Smith Strong.

James Theodore Dean was born 12 May 1865. (pp. 105)

James Guthrie Harbord's ASN is (0-18). (pp. 159)

Peter Charles Harris was born in Kingston, Georgia. (pp. 161)

Roy Hoffman was honorably discharged from the National Army in March 1919. (pp. 184)

John Alexander Johnston performed frontier duty from 1879 to 1882. (pp. 205)

Edward Albert Kreger graduated from the Infantry and Cavalry School at Leavenworth, Kansas. (pp. 219)

Herbert Mayhew Lord retired from the army on 30 June 1922. (pp. 235)

Clarence Henry McNeil was a student at General Staff College from 15 August 1919 to 31 July 1920. (pp. 265)

Guy Henry Preston. The second photo is by the author. (p. 301)

Thomas Henry Rees's rank of brigadier general was restored in June 1930, prior to his death. (p. 306)

William Luther Sibert was born on 12 October 1860 in Gadsden, Alabama. (p. 333)

Edward Sigerfoos was born in Potsdam, Ohio. (p. 334)

Cecil Crawley Vaughan, Jr. was promoted to first lieutenant, Company I, Fourth Virginia Infantry. (p. 368)

ERRATA

PAGE 351..F.S.STRONG. IN AN EFFORT TO ENHANCE & ENLARGE THE PIC OF GEN STRONG, THE PRINTER CROPPED THE PICTURE AND IN SPITE OF THE *TEXT* AND *SUBJECT* OF THE BOOK, NEATLY ELIMINATED STRONG ENTIRELY AND PUBLISHED THE COMPLETELY INAPROPOS PICTURE OF THE CIVILIAN. HE LEAVES YOU WITH A FINE SLICE OF THE GENERAL'S LEFT SLEEVE. HERE IS A COPY *OF A COPY* OF THE ORIGINAL.